WRITING AND COMMUNITY ENGAGEMENT

WRITING AND COMMUNITY ENGAGEMENT

A Critical Sourcebook

EDITED BY

Thomas Deans
University of Connecticut

Barbara Roswell
Goucher College

Adrian J. Wurr
University of Idaho

BEDFORD / ST. MARTIN'S   Boston   •   New York

For Bedford/St. Martin's

Executive Editor: Leasa Burton
Developmental Editor: Sarah Macomber
Senior Production Supervisor: Dennis J. Conroy
Marketing Manager: Molly Parke
Text Design: Anna Palchik
Project Management: DeMasi Design and Publishing Service
Cover Design: Donna L. Dennison
Composition: Jeff Miller Book Design
Printing and Binding: RR Donnelley & Sons Company

President: Joan E. Feinberg
Editorial Director: Denise B. Wydra
Editor in Chief: Karen S. Henry
Director of Marketing: Karen R. Soeltz
Director of Editing, Design, and Production: Marcia Cohen
Assistant Director of Editing, Design, and Production: Elise S. Kaiser
Manager, Publishing Services: Emily Berleth

Library of Congress Control Number: 2010921022

Manufactured in the United States of America.

4 3 2 1 0 9
f e d c b a

For information, write: Bedford / St. Martin's, 75 Arlington Street, Boston, MA 02116   (617-399-4000)

ISBN-10: 0-312-56223-3
ISBN-13: 978-0-312-56223-6

ACKNOWLEDGMENTS
Acknowledgments and copyrights appear at the back of the book on pages 528–29, which constitute an extension of the copyright page.

It is a violation of the law to reproduce these selections by any means whatsoever without the written permission of the copyright holder.

CONTENTS

INTRODUCTION

Teaching and Writing Across Communities: Developing Partnerships, Publics, and Programs

Many think of composition studies as animated by the question, How should we teach writing? Yet embedded within that question is the more fundamental one of what it means to teach college writing. Composition has circled back to that core issue of purpose at key moments in its history: in the 1970s, for example, when open admissions and questions of access challenged the field; in the 1980s when critical theory and liberatory pedagogies took hold; and in the 1990s when digital technologies began to accelerate at a furious pace. Provoked in part by the kinds of community-based pedagogies featured in this book, the field is once again asking, What does it mean to teach college writing?

The essays and excerpts in this collection respond to that question with expanded understandings of literacy, powerful theories of rhetoric, incisive analyses of the activity of writing, cautionary tales, experience-tested teaching practices, and inspiring program models. They present many manifestations of community engagement, variously linked to first-year composition, advanced rhetoric, creative writing, technical communication, writing centers, community publishing, advocacy projects, and neighborhood literacy networks. Collectively the authors are asking—not for the first time, but differently and more generously than in the past—how we can prepare students for both the traditional academic curriculum and the responsibilities of civic life. Collectively, they are asking—not for the first time, but differently and more critically than in the past—which ethical and ideological principles should guide our practices as writing teachers. Collectively, they are asking—not for the first time, but differently and more assertively than in the past—how we might live out those principles pragmatically in our choices of what and how to teach.

This work has piqued the curiosity of writing teachers, writing program administrators, writing center directors, and graduate students, many of whom are asking, What is all the fuss about? It has drawn keen interest among those on the brink of trying something new, who say, Someday I want to teach that kind of community-engaged course. Even for those with little interest in service-learning, the articles and excerpts gathered here expand the

1

scholarly conversation about the purposes of teaching, learning, and writing in—and beyond—the university. Rhetorics of engagement are emerging to complement and extend the rhetorics of critique that have long held sway in composition studies. Such rhetorics of engagement emphasize both personal and political agency; they welcome and grapple with difference; they hinge on collaborative inquiry and action. These approaches often cross customary divisions within English studies and forge alliances with diverse others, seizing the power of poetry, publication, performance, community organizing, or multimedia to take writing public and, in the process, transform public discourse.

When we speak of writing and community engagement we are tapping into the long intellectual traditions of rhetoric and ethics. In his contribution to this volume James Dubinsky enumerates those links, recalling how Greek and Roman rhetoricians imagined the relationship between persuasion and the public good and how students, when they write for community agencies, reanimate both the instrumental and civic dimensions of classical rhetoric. Several of the scholars in this collection frame their work in the rhetorical tradition because rhetoric, in both its classical and contemporary manifestations, has always been about both education and application, both theory and practice, both the teaching of language and persuasion in school and the uses of language and persuasion in the public sphere.

For most teachers, however, sea changes in American higher education provide a more immediate context for community writing. Although we can trace myriad antecedents for university outreach to communities, ranging from the land grant movement of the 1860s to the civil rights movement of the 1960s, most relevant to the current work of college writing teachers is the national push toward student volunteer service that emerged in the 1980s and the enthusiasm for academic service-learning that followed.

The 1990s were heady times for service-learning not only because faculty were experimenting with new courses but also because service-learning research emerged as its own distinct field, complete with journals, conferences, and professional organizations.

Ernest Boyer invited a reconsideration of scholarship, calling for the integration of research, service, and teaching and advocating a scholarship of application through which academics would partner with communities to address significant societal issues. Campus Compact, founded in 1985, emerged as a truly national network, and the American Association for Higher Education made community engagement a marquee priority, launching an entire book series to promote discipline-based academic service-learning. We saw the founding of AmeriCorps and the Corporation for National and Community Service. The *Wingspread Principles for Good Practice for Combining Service and Learning* (Honnet and Poulsen) codified best practices for the service-learning centers that seemed to pop up like daisies at colleges and universities across the United States. Large empirical studies of service-learning trumpeted encouraging findings, including those demonstrating that students report greater personal and intellectual engagement in service-learning courses, achieve cognitive gains such as mastering course content and analyzing problems as embedded in complex systems, and register personal development keyed to enhanced self-efficacy, appreciation of diversity, and participation in civic life. Books such as Jane Kendall's *Combining Service and Learning: A Resource Book for Community and Public Service*, Barbara Jacoby's *Service-Learning in Higher Education: Concepts and Practices*, and Janet Eyler and Dwight Giles's *Where's the Learning in Service-Learning?* synthesized that research and argued for its wider application. The *Michigan Journal of Community Service Learning*, an interdisciplinary journal with a social science emphasis, in concert with annual research conferences, helped to establish service-learning research as a distinct field of inquiry.

Building on the momentum of its "social turn," composition studies saw a similar burst of activity in the 1990s as more and more teachers of first-year composition, technical communication, and advanced rhetoric experimented at the intersections of writing pedagogy and community action. Tom Deans's "English Studies and Public Service," included in this volume, traces how those teachers channeled the field's enthusiasm for critical pedagogy, cultural studies, identity politics, and critical theory toward grounded community engagement. Some, including Cheryl Duffy, Bruce Herzberg, Brock Haussamen, Angelique Davi, Michelle Dunlap, and Ann Green, all featured in this collection, sought to motivate their students by putting outreach experiences at community sites—tutoring youth, staffing homeless shelters, exchanging perspectives with nursing home residents—into conversation with the kinds of readings on social justice and public policy that typically populate composition readers. Some were eager to highlight practical applications by having students experience the challenges, complexities, and rewards of writing for local organizations and audiences beyond the classroom. Nora Bacon's "The Trouble with Transfer," Tom Deans's "Shifting Locations," and Jim Dubinsky's "Service-Learning as a Path to Virtue," included here, describe courses in which students produced agency newsletters, conducted research, and wrote grant applications and public relations materials for nonprofits. Other community-engaged teachers, represented in this volume by David Coogan, Glynda Hull, Michael James, Lorraine Higgins, Elenore Long, and Linda Flower, explored strategies to jump-start dialogue on local problems, convening diverse constituencies to participate in public discourse. These curricular innovations were soon translated into papers at the Conference on College Composition and Communication (CCCC) and articles for the field's academic journals. *Reflections* transformed from newsletter to peer-reviewed journal, providing a forum for scholars in the burgeoning field.

Out of all of this activity, the 1997 book *Writing the Community: Concepts and Models for Service-Learning in Composition* delivered a synthesis and agenda. In their introduction to that important collection, Linda Adler-Kassner, Robert Crooks, and Ann Watters declared the arrival of service-learning in composition as a "microrevolution" and outlined its potential to remedy institutional fragmentation. They adopted an underdog posture and were especially concerned with naming the logistical obstacles to service-learning's growth, as well as with gesturing toward what might result if academic institutions were to reimagine teaching, research, and service as more deeply integrated. Some of the articles and excerpts in this collection carry on in that spirit.

But there are real differences between where we were in 1997 and where we are now, and more of our selections highlight those differences. Most significantly, the field has realized that its agenda should be less about clearing a path for service-learning's advancement in the academy than about the *relationships* between universities and local communities—in all their promise and in all their contradictions—that form the nexus of this work. The field is asking not just, What do good courses and placements look like? but also, What kinds of relationships should we be developing? and What ways of writing, knowing, teaching, public dialogue, and social change do those relationships make possible? Rethinking such relationships and their consequences is at the heart of rethinking what it means to teach writing, and we can see these more recent priorities in the terms that have moved to the foreground—community literacy, inquiry, network, community arts, public writing, writing beyond the curriculum, street—as use of the word *service-learning* has receded.

We can also see progress in the field's ongoing inquiry into reciprocity not so much as a problem to be solved as a process to be theorized. These deepening explorations of reciprocity, each highlighting the local and the particular, have themselves taken diverse forms. Some scholars have argued for the explanatory power of activity theory to unpack the multiple and often subtle dimensions of any community-based writing project for faculty and students alike (see Deans, "Shifting Locations"). In "Alinsky's Reveille" (included here), Eli Goldblatt adapts Saul Alinsky's principles of community organizing to develop a new, more deeply collaborative model for neighborhood literacy projects in which community partners establish priorities and academics facilitate access to resources. Steve Zimmer, Paula Mathieu ("Students in the Streets," in this volume), and others challenge the implicit assumption of community deficits and university leadership embedded in earlier codifications of best practices, advocating instead that university participants assume the more modest role of "ally" and aspire to more flexible and tactical, rather than strategic, orientations toward collaboration. Numerous contributors to this volume reflect on the reciprocal processes by which teachers, students, courses, departments, and even institutions are transformed thanks to the knowledge constructed in collaborations with community participants.

The field's emphasis on rhetoric and inquiry rather than on particular courses or institutional dilemmas was presaged in Linda Flower and her colleagues' work at the Community Literacy Center. Her initial focus on rhetoric, community problem solving, and intercultural inquiry, now more fully developed into a comprehensive rhetorical model for personal and public inquiry (included here), inspired many of the scholars in this volume and has proved to be particularly durable even as she has continued to develop the approach, most recently weaving in theories of the public sphere.

In 1997 these theories of the public sphere were not on the radar of service-learning's early adopters, even though Susan Wells's seminal article on that topic, "Rogue Cops and Health Care: What Do We Want from Public Writing?" (reprinted here), was published in 1996. Nor were community-oriented composition teachers familiar with the often sophisticated client-based projects that their colleagues in professional communication were conducting with local nonprofits. By bringing together works that shaped the first wave of scholarship on community writing in composition with those from various subfields in English (technical communication, literacy studies, writing centers, composition theory, rhetoric, linguistics, writing across the curriculum), as well as with key voices from outside of English studies, this volume seeks not only to highlight the "best of" the research tradition but to redress a pattern of parallel play that has too long characterized the field of writing and community engagement. Few people read across the full spectrum of the scholarship, too often recapitulating the field's evolution through their own development and ignoring lessons already learned. Therefore we draw from the cross-disciplinary *Michigan Journal of Community Service Learning* as well as from books within English studies; we reprint as many articles from *College English* and *College Composition and Communication* as we do from the *Community Literacy Journal* and *Reflections*, two journals devoted to community-engaged work. The result is a collection that revisits perennial concerns such as reciprocity, diversity, learning outcomes, and best teaching practices but also extends to emerging developments in community literacy.

WHAT TEACHERS OF COMMUNITY WRITING NEED TO KNOW

One key insight proffered by nearly every community-engaged scholar is that each university/community partnership is shaped by local opportunities and limitations, local people and priorities. At the same time, the last two decades of scholarship on writing and community engagement affirm central themes time and again. We want newcomers to be attuned to what the cumulative research tradition tells us rather than to muddle through by trial and error. The six sections of this collection offer an introduction to that tradition.

The first two sections are foundational, albeit in different ways. "Writing in Communities" has the most general title because it takes up the most general issues. If writing instructors are to open their typically controlled, teacher-centered, and text-driven classrooms to the press of local community life, they should be aware of how literacy is figured differently across various contexts. We know from several decades of literacy research that writing is a deeply context-dependent activity, that literacy learning happens both inside and outside schools, and that literacy learning is a social and ideological process rather than simply a textual transaction. All those findings encourage community-academic partnerships even as they alert teachers who experiment with them that they should not hold fast to one static definition of writing—whether academic, workplace, personal, or "real-world"—or assume that writing comprises a readily transferrable set of formal skills. Deborah Brandt, Ann Gere, Diana George, Glynda Hull, and Michael James offer historical and contemporary perspectives to transcend the simple binary of "classroom" and "community" as they take us into what Gere terms the "extracurriculum," exploring how reading, writing, and rhetoric work in civic groups, families, schools, community centers, and the streets. Several short pieces first published in *Hospitality*, the free newspaper of the Open Door Community in Atlanta, and in the *Journal of Ordinary Thought*, a quarterly publication that draws from writing workshops in Chicago's low-income neighborhoods, illustrate the commitments and varieties of self-sponsored writing among ordinary people and demonstrate some of the many ways that writing is used—and is useful—in everyday life.

"The Terms of Service-Learning" turns to the intersection of communities with classroom pedagogy and includes what many would consider foundational texts. The excerpt from Tom Deans's *Writing Partnerships* introduces the key terms *writing about the community*, *writing for the community*, and *writing with the community*, a taxonomy that has shaped much of the discourse in the field. Bruce Herzberg cautions that, unless structured deliberately, service-learning can unintentionally reinforce the very inequalities it may seek to redress, a lesson Keith Morton reminds us is not unique to English studies. These essays are representative of a significant body of literature (see Ball and Goodburn; Boyle-Baise; Butin; Franklin; Taylor) that teases out the assumptions embedded in such key terms as *community* and *service*. These texts can well be used by both teachers and undergraduates hoping to be critical and intentional about community work. Together, the sources in Part Two trace the field's varied intellectual genealogies, with influences as diverse as communitarian politics, Marxist social theory, John Dewey's democratic pragmatism, religious traditions, government programs, grassroots activism, noblesse oblige, and the "can do" American ethos. They highlight the contested nature of the terms and priorities for community writing, a phenomenon that may frustrate those seeking a stable definition or a formula for teaching, but that also fuels the field's intellectual vitality.

The contributors to Part Three, "Rhetoric, Civic Writing, and the Public Sphere," marshal theories of rhetoric, politics, and the public sphere to explain their strategies for undertaking ambitious community writing projects. Rejecting as the archetype of public writing the hypothetical "letter to the editor" (Ervin), each explores the ways in which publics can be understood as constructed and local. Susan Wells and David Coogan step back to apply theories of the public sphere and materialist rhetoric to their respective teaching experiences. In the article by Lorraine Higgins, Elenore Long, and Linda Flower we find innovative strategies for rhetorical invention and community action, strategies born from the experience of the Community Literacy Center (CLC) in Pittsburgh but applicable to many other contexts. Excerpts from community publications on street violence and on learning disabilities illustrate some of the methods that varied constituencies—youth, parents, teachers, college students, police officers, businesspeople, social workers, academics, religious leaders—employ collaboratively as they engage in problem solving and inquiry. We encourage readers to consult the CLC and Carnegie Mellon Community Think Tank online archives or Flower's book *Community Literacy and the Rhetoric of Public Engagement* to gain a more complete understanding of the context for the selections highlighted in this anthology.

Although issues of representation, reciprocity, privilege, and difference are considered throughout this collection, the articles in the fourth section, "The Ethics of Engagement," specifically address key ethical dilemmas. College faculty are trained to think in terms of their own subject matter and their own learning objectives, and even though teachers enter into community-based pedagogies with good intentions, community perspectives are often eclipsed. The selections in Part Four challenge teachers to interrogate not just their students' but their own roles as community actors, introducing such models as the public intellectual (Ellen Cushman) and the knowledge activist (Eli Goldblatt). These articles make visible the "lost subjects" of the service learning story (Tracy Carrick, Margaret Himley, and Tobi Jacobi), recount the sometimes painfully ironic unintended consequences of institutionalized approaches to service-learning (Paula Mathieu), and highlight the perspectives of community organization participants. Together, these articles articulate a second, more nimble and responsive generation of best practices, focused less on institutional expertise and community "needs" and more committed to welcoming diversity, enhancing community assets, and developing community leadership.

Over the past ten years, the field has thought more and more in terms of partnerships, relationships, and coalitions that extend beyond any single course, which is why the title to Part Five features "Writing Programs" rather than "Writing Courses." Scholars in this section are asking how we might shake ourselves free from the normative sense of college writing programs and writing centers as delivery systems for college composition and academic literacy. Couldn't they become networks that sustain various kinds of literacy and writing as Michelle Comstock, Michele Simmons, and Jeffrey Grabill suggest? For more than thirty years, writing across the curriculum (WAC) has given us a running start on this project by emphasizing the ways that writing can bridge disciplinary communities. Steve Parks, Eli Goldblatt, and Michelle Hall Kells take WAC to the next logical step by sketching what writing across academic and nonacademic communities can look like, while Tiffany Rousculp offers an expansive and inviting conception of writing centers. Excerpts from *Espejos y Ventanas/Mirrors and Windows* and *Soul Talk: Urban Youth Poetry*, anthologies distributed by the community publishing venture born of Parks and Goldblatt's efforts, offer a glimpse into the fruits of these innovations. Individually and collectively, these scholars remind us that cultivating community connections is not about heaping more work on already burdened writing programs but about rethinking and reenergizing those programs to draw on, and prepare students to participate in, a fuller universe of discourse and knowledge.

Even as the field thinks more and more in terms of programs, relationships, and networks, we know that most community-based pedagogies start with a course—with an individual teacher trying out a new way of teaching writing. The articles in Part Six, "Pedagogies in Action," exemplify best practices in a variety of settings: basic writing, first-year composition in two- and four-year schools, advanced composition, professional writing, prison-university workshops. This final section may provide a compelling entry point for readers eager to familiarize themselves with a range and variety of pedagogical approaches. Each critically reflects on a particular course or set of courses, exploring the complex linkages and calibrations among pedagogic goals, types of projects, community priorities, and specific assignments. These articles simultaneously investigate key questions for the field as a whole, including the impact of service-learning on the quality of student writing (Adrian Wurr), the challenges students and faculty encounter when moving between academic and nonacademic practices (Nora Bacon), and the value of theories of racial identity formation to understand the interplay of race, class, and gender in community-engaged classrooms (Angelique Davi, Michelle Dunlap, and Ann Green). In dialogue with Lori Pompa's and Tobi Jacobi's scholarship on literacy projects in correctional settings, several short pieces created in a workshop at the Maryland Correctional Institution for Women provide a sampling of the ways that writers experiment with generic conventions to reflect on and transform experience.

AGENDAS FOR FURTHER RESEARCH ON COMMUNITY WRITING: PROCESS, PRODUCTS, AND PARTICIPANTS

The variety and quality of the selections in this volume affirm both the crackling energy and increasing theoretical sophistication of community writing initiatives during the past two decades. Practitioner-scholars have been generous in sharing their innovations, establishing a dynamic interplay among community action, reflection, and theory building. Much energy has, appropriately, been devoted to charting and navigating a new terrain and challenging oneself and others both to articulate and enact the ethical commitments integral to the work; community-engaged scholars are not a complacent bunch. A recent review of the literature we conducted with Nora Bacon and James Dubinsky (Bacon et al.) revealed that most of the published studies on community writing take the form of critical reflections on practice. Few studies, however, draw on empirical research methods such as ethnography or discourse analysis, and few take up assessment even though assessment has long been a concern of the larger service-learning research community (Bringle, Phillips, and Hudson; Furco; Gelmon et al.). In all, we know a good deal about what exemplary community partnerships look like and how to theorize about them in sophisticated ways but relatively little about the effects of literacy collaborations on university students or community participants. Even less is known about the writing itself.

Given the rapid growth of community-engaged pedagogies and the demands they put on teachers, perhaps it is not a surprise that more is not known about the impact of writing about, for, and with communities. We hope, though, that the wealth of experience shared in this collection will inspire readers to begin to build more intentionally on what is known, and to deepen and sharpen inquiry into the consequences of particular pedagogical and project choices. No doubt we will see an acceleration of writing for social justice in digital spaces, as Hull and James suggest, and as the example of the Cherokee Nation multimedia project on which Cushman's students collaborated illustrates. No doubt we will see more work like Wurr's done at the intersections of service-learning and second language writing as the demographics of both universities and the United States change. And no doubt many other innovative practices will emerge in response to academic trends and the press of community life. While the articles and excerpts in this volume effectively prepare teachers to design projects that respond creatively and critically to such challenges, researchers working at the intersection of composition and community action still need to adopt a more robust range of methods.

A research agenda that aims to be more expansive than applying theory to practice might begin with an inventory of community-engaged pedagogies: What kinds of university-community partnerships are most common and successful? What roles do teachers and community partners play in crafting assignments, determining genres, advising writers? What texts are read in these courses and to what ends? What do instructors typically de-emphasize or relinquish to support community collaborations? What is the longevity of these partnerships and how are they supported and sustained? Building on the critical analyses of exemplary projects that tend to be the focus of most current scholarship, the gathering of this data would put us on the road toward understanding how community writing is developing as a system.

Such research would extend to the print, digital, and multimodal texts that emerge from university-community partnerships, and especially to the production and circulation of those texts. What kinds of documents are most often produced? How are they put to use? This focus on writing and writing processes would return us to questions that have been the core of composition research since the process movement of the 1970s but that need to be reconsidered in the community writing contexts: How are invention, response, revision, and identity enacted in these new kinds of partnerships?

Especially difficult to determine are the effects of participation in community-engaged courses on students' writing proficiency. For example, while Kendrick and Suarez found that service-learning did not have a positive impact on student writing quality, Astin et al., Feldman et al., and Wurr found that it did. How one defines "good writing" and the methods of analysis used to assess this may account for these differences: Kendrick and Suarez used holistic portfolio assessment and semester grades; Astin et al. used self-reports; Feldman et al. and Wurr triangulated primary trait scores with other measures such as holistic essay scores and surveys. Because public writing and community literacy initiatives aspire to a wide range of purposes, this question of writing proficiency is as challenging as it is critical.

Even less well understood is the impact of university-community collaborations on the community members who participate. Like our students, whose journals reflect on critical incidents, point to cross-cultural insights, celebrate "aha" moments, and treasure expressions of mutuality, engaged scholars critically reflect on practice using many of the same strategies. Rarely, however, do we invite community participants to reflect on or document their learning or transformation. Rarely do we use our finely tuned disciplinary tools to systematically analyze the writing community members produce over time. Even a mature program like the Pittsburgh Community Literacy Center is hard-pressed to evaluate the longer-term effects of participation in intercultural inquiry projects. And just as term papers piled outside a professor's door at semester's end beg questions about the efficacy of teacher response, the all-too-common stories of reports never delivered and proposals never implemented (including those recounted by Mathieu in this volume) challenge us to ask in much more systematic ways about the value of university writing initiatives—both the processes and the products—for the individuals and organizations with whom we partner.

The public turn in composition, spreading quickly throughout the profession, has been cultivated by a visionary and dedicated group of scholar-practitioners who have devised ways both to "walk the walk" and provide mutual support for the growing number of teachers interested in community literacy. As exemplars of Boyer's fully engaged scholars, they have melded research, service, and teaching to nurture the CCCC Special Interest Group on Service-Learning and Community Literacy, served as editorial board members of *Reflections* and the *Community Literacy Journal*, and developed the theories that guide much of our work. The Community Literacy Conference hosted by Temple University in the spring of 2008 offered us a forum to discuss with others the question of a community writing "canon"; this book reflects not just the choices of the three editors, but the wisdom of a coalition of experienced scholars. We are especially grateful to those among these pioneering groups who served as reviewers of this volume: Nora Bacon, University of Nebraska, Omaha; Eli Goldblatt, Temple University; Brooke Hessler, Oklahoma City University; Tobi Jacobi, Colorado State University; Amy Taggart, North Dakota State University; Steve Parks, Syracuse University; Tiffany Rousculp, Salt Lake City Community College; Diane Chin, University of Illinois at Chicago; James Dubinsky, Virginia Polytechnic Institute; Mary French, University of Texas at Arlington; and two anonymous reviewers. These thoughtful readers challenged us to more fully integrate the different strands in the work of the past decade and helped to construct the "big tent" under which we are gathered. We extend special thanks to Nora Bacon and Jim Dubinsky; the review of the literature that we developed with them, with the encouragement of Kathi Yancey and the support of an NCTE Research Grant, served as the basis for this collection. We also appreciate the generosity of Ellen Cushman, Diana George, Linda Flower, and Steve Parks for contributing examples of the exciting writing that is being created in diverse communities. We have been fortunate, indeed, to have worked with Leasa Burton and Sarah Macomber of Bedford/St. Martin's on this project. We are deeply grateful for their deft guidance and for their insightful and enthusiastic support not just of this collection, but of the hopeful vision of literacy it heralds.

WORKS CITED

Adler-Kassner, Linda, Robert Crooks, and Ann Watters, eds. *Writing the Community: Concepts and Models for Service-Learning in Composition.* Washington, DC: American Association for Higher Education and NCTE, 1997. Print.

Astin, Alexander W., Lori J. Vogelgesang, Elaine K. Ikeda, and Jennifer A. Yee. *How Service-Learning Affects Students.* Los Angeles: UCLA Higher Education Research Institute, 2000. Print.

Bacon, Nora, Thomas Deans, James Dubinsky, Barbara Roswell, and Adrian Wurr. *Community-based and Service-Learning Writing Initiatives: A Survey of Scholarship and Agenda for Research.* Unpublished CCCC research report prepared for the National Council of Teachers of English, 2005. Print.

Ball, Kevin, and Amy M. Goodburn. "Composition Studies and Service Learning: Appealing to Communities?" *Composition Studies* 28.1 (2000): 79–94. Print.

Boyer, Ernest L. "The Scholarship of Engagement." *The Journal of Public Service and Outreach* 1.1 (1996): 11–20. Print.

Doyle-Baise, Marilynne. "Learning Service: Reading Service as Text." *Reflections* 6.1 (2007): 67–86. Print.

Bringle, Robert G., Mindy A. Phillips, and Michael Hudson. *The Measure of Service Learning: Research Scales to Assess Student Experiences.* Washington, DC: American Psychological Association, 2004. Print.

Butin, Dan W. *Service-Learning in Higher Education: Critical Issues and Directions.* New York: Palgrave Macmillan, 2005. Print.

Chappell, Virginia. "Good Intentions Aren't Enough: Preparing Students to Learn through Service." *Reflections* 4.2 (2005): 31–53. Print.

Comstock, Michelle R. "Writing Programs as Distributed Networks: A Materialist Approach to University-Community Digital Media Literacy." *Community Literacy Journal* 1.1 (Fall 2006): 44–66. Print.

Ervin, Elizabeth. "Encouraging Civic Participation among First-Year Writing Students; or, Why Composition Class Should Be More Like a Bowling Team." *Rhetoric Review* 15 (1997): 382–98. Print.

Eyler, Janet, and Dwight Giles. *Where's the Learning in Service-Learning?* San Francisco: Jossey-Bass, 1999. Print.

Feldman, Ann M., et al. "The Impact of Partnership-Centered, Community-Based Learning on First-Year Students' Academic Research Papers." *Michigan Journal of Community Service Learning* 13.1 (2006): 16–29. Print.

Flower, Linda. *Community Literacy and the Rhetoric of Public Engagement.* Carbondale: Southern Illinois UP, 2008. Print.

Franklin, Betty Smith. "Reading and Writing the World: Charity, Civic Engagement, and Social Action." *Reflections* 1.2 (2000): 24–29. Print.

Furco, Andrew. *Self-Assessment Rubric for the Institutionalization of Service-Learning in Higher Education.* Providence, RI: Campus Compact at Brown University, 2002. Web. 14 Nov. 2009. <http://www.servicelearning.org/filemanager/download/Furco_rubric.pdf>.

Gelmon, Sherril B., Andrew Furco, Barbara Holland, and Robert Bringle. "Beyond Anecdote: Further Challenges in Bringing Rigor to Service-Learning Research." Paper presented at the 5th Annual International Conference on Service-Learning Research, East Lansing, MI, November 2005. Print.

Grabill, Jeffrey T. "Technical Writing, Service Learning, and a Rearticulation of Research, Teaching, and Service." *Innovative Approaches to Teaching Technical Communication.* Eds. Tracy Bridgeford, Karla Saari Kitalong and Dickie Selfe. Logan, UT: Utah State University Press, 2004. 81–92. Print.

Honnet, Ellen Porter, and Susan J. Poulsen. *Wingspread Special Report: Principles of Good Practice for Combining Service and Learning.* Racine, WI: Johnson Foundation, 1989. Print.

Jacoby, Barbara, ed. *Service-Learning in Higher Education: Concepts and Practices.* San Francisco: Jossey-Bass, 1996. Print.

Kendall, Jane C., et al. *Combining Service and Learning: A Resource Book for Community and Public Service.* Raleigh, NC: National Society for Internships and Experiential Education, 1990. Print.

Kendrick, Richard, and John Suarez. "Service-Learning Outcomes in English Composition Courses: An Application of the Campus Compact Assessment Protocol." *Reflections* 3.1 (2003): 36–54. Print.

Simmons, W. Michele, and Jeffrey T. Grabill. "Toward a Civic Rhetoric for Technologically and Scientifically Complex Places: Invention, Performance, and Participation." *College Composition and Communication* 58.3 (2007): 419–48. Print.

Taggart, Amy Rupiper and H. Brooke Hessler. "Stasis and the Reflective Practitioner." *Reflections* 5.1 (Spring 2006): 153–72. Print.

Taylor, Joby. "Metaphors We Serve By: Investigating the Conceptual Metaphors Framing National and Community Service and Service-Learning." *Michigan Journal of Community Service Learning* 9:1 (Fall 2002): 45–57. Print.

Wurr, Adrian J. "Service-Learning and Student Writing: An Investigation of Effects." *Service-Learning through a Multidisciplinary Lens: Advances in Service-Learning Research.* Eds. Andrew Furco and Shelley Billig. Vol. 2. Berkeley, CA: Information Age, 2002. 103–21. Print.

Zimmer, Steve. "The Art of Knowing Your Place: White Service Learning Leaders and Urban Community Organizations." *Reflections* 6.1 (2007): 7–26. Print.

PART ONE

Writing in Communities

1   *Sponsors of Literacy*

DEBORAH BRANDT

In his sweeping history of adult learning in the United States, Joseph Kett describes the intellectual atmosphere available to young apprentices who worked in the small, decentralized print shops of antebellum America. Because printers also were the solicitors and editors of what they published, their workshops served as lively incubators for literacy and political discourse. By the mid-nineteenth century, however, this learning space was disrupted when the invention of the steam press reorganized the economy of the print industry. Steam presses were so expensive that they required capital outlays beyond the means of many printers. As a result, print jobs were outsourced, the processes of editing and printing were split, and, in tight competition, print apprentices became low-paid mechanics with no more access to the multi-skilled environment of the craftshop (Kett 67–70). While this shift in working conditions may be evidence of the deskilling of workers induced by the Industrial Revolution (Nicholas and Nicholas), it also offers a site for reflecting upon the dynamic sources of literacy and literacy learning. The reading and writing skills of print apprentices in this period were the achievements not simply of teachers and learners nor of the discourse practices of the printer community. Rather, these skills existed fragilely, contingently within an economic moment. The pre-steam press economy enabled some of the most basic aspects of the apprentices' literacy, especially their access to material production and the public meaning or worth of their skills. Paradoxically, even as the steam-powered penny press made print more accessible (by making publishing more profitable), it brought an end to a particular form of literacy sponsorship and a drop in literate potential.

The apprentices' experience invites rumination upon literacy learning and teaching today. Literacy looms as one of the great engines of profit and competitive advantage in the 20th century: a lubricant for consumer desire; a means for integrating corporate markets; a foundation for the deployment of weapons and other technology; a raw material in the mass production of

From *College Composition and Communication* 49.2 (1998): 165–85.

information. As ordinary citizens have been compelled into these economies, their reading and writing skills have grown sharply more central to the everyday trade of information and goods as well as to the pursuit of education, employment, civil rights, status. At the same time, people's literate skills have grown vulnerable to unprecedented turbulence in their economic value, as conditions, forms, and standards of literacy achievement seem to shift with almost every new generation of learners. How are we to understand the vicissitudes of individual literacy development in relationship to the large-scale economic forces that set the routes and determine the wordly worth of that literacy?

The field of writing studies has had much to say about individual literacy development. Especially in the last quarter of the 20th century, we have theorized, researched, critiqued, debated, and sometimes even managed to enhance the literate potentials of ordinary citizens as they have tried to cope with life as they find it. Less easily and certainly less steadily have we been able to relate what we see, study, and do to these larger contexts of profit making and competition. This even as we recognize that the most pressing issues we deal with—tightening associations between literate skill and social viability, the breakneck pace of change in communications technology, persistent inequities in access and reward—all relate to structural conditions in literacy's bigger picture. When economic forces are addressed in our work, they appear primarily as generalities: contexts, determinants, motivators, barriers, touchstones. But rarely are they systematically related to the local conditions and embodied moments of literacy learning that occupy so many of us on a daily basis.[1]

This essay does not presume to overcome the analytical failure completely. But it does offer a conceptual approach that begins to connect literacy as an individual development to literacy as an economic development, at least as the two have played out over the last ninety years or so. The approach is through what I call sponsors of literacy. Sponsors, as I have come to think of them, are any agents, local or distant, concrete or abstract, who enable, support, teach, model, as well as recruit, regulate, suppress, or withhold literacy—and gain advantage by it in some way. Just as the ages of radio and television accustom us to having programs *brought* to us by various commercial sponsors, it is useful to think about who or what underwrites occasions of literacy learning and use. Although the interests of the sponsor and the sponsored do not have to converge (and, in fact, may conflict) sponsors nevertheless set the terms for access to literacy and wield powerful incentives for compliance and loyalty. Sponsors are a tangible reminder that literacy learning throughout history has always required permission, sanction, assistance, coercion, or, at minimum, contact with existing trade routes. Sponsors are delivery systems for the economies of literacy, the means by which these forces present themselves to—and through—individual learners. They also represent the causes into which people's literacy usually gets recruited.[2]

For the last five years I have been tracing sponsors of literacy across the 20th century as they appear in the accounts of ordinary Americans recalling how they learned to write and read. The investigation is grounded in more than 100 in-depth interviews that I collected from a diverse group of people born roughly between 1900 and 1980. In the interviews, people explored in great detail their memories of learning to read and write across their lifetimes, focusing especially on the people, institutions, materials, and motivations involved in the process. The more I worked with these accounts, the more I came to realize that they were filled with references to sponsors, both explicit and latent, who appeared in formative roles at the scenes of literacy learning. Patterns of sponsorship became an illuminating site through which to track the different cultural attitudes people developed toward writing vs. reading as well as the ideological congestion faced by late-century literacy learners as their sponsors proliferated and diversified (see my essays on "Remembering Reading" and "Accumulating Literacy"). In this essay I set out a case for why the concept of sponsorship is so richly suggestive for exploring economies of literacy and their effects. Then, through use of extended case examples, I demonstrate the practical application of this approach for interpreting current conditions of literacy teaching and learning, including persistent stratification of opportunity and escalating standards for literacy achievement. A final section addresses implications for the teaching of writing.

Sponsorship

Intuitively, *sponsors* seemed a fitting term for the figures who turned up most typically in people's memories of literacy learning: older relatives, teachers, priests, supervisors, military officers, editors, influential authors. Sponsors, as we ordinarily think of them, are powerful figures who bankroll events or smooth the way for initiates. Usually richer, more knowledgeable, and more entrenched than the sponsored, sponsors nevertheless enter a reciprocal relationship with those they underwrite. They lend their resources or credibility to the sponsored but also stand to gain benefits from their success, whether by direct repayment or, indirectly, by credit of association. *Sponsors* also proved an appealing term in my analysis because of all the commercial references that appeared in these 20th-century accounts — the magazines, peddled encyclopedias, essay contests, radio and television programs, toys, fan clubs, writing tools, and so on, from which so much experience with literacy was derived. As the 20th century turned the abilities to read and write into widely exploitable resources, commercial sponsorship abounded.

In whatever form, sponsors deliver the ideological freight that must be borne for access to what they have. Of course, the sponsored can be oblivious to or innovative with this ideological burden. Like Little Leaguers who wear the logo of a local insurance agency on their uniforms, not out of a concern for enhancing the agency's image but as a means for getting to play ball, people throughout history have acquired literacy pragmatically under the banner of others' causes. In the days before free, public schooling in England, Protestant Sunday Schools warily offered basic reading instruction to working-class families as part of evangelical duty. To the horror of many in the church sponsorship, these families insistently, sometimes riotously demanded of their Sunday Schools more instruction, including in writing and math, because it provided means for upward mobility.[3] Through the sponsorship of Baptist and Methodist ministries, African Americans in slavery taught each other to understand the Bible in subversively liberatory ways. Under a conservative regime, they developed forms of critical literacy that sustained religious, educational, and political movements both before and after emancipation (Cornelius). Most of the time, however, literacy takes its shape from the interests of its sponsors. And, as we will see below, obligations toward one's sponsors run deep, affecting what, why, and how people write and read.

The concept of sponsors helps to explain, then, a range of human relationships and ideological pressures that turn up at the scenes of literacy learning—from benign sharing between adults and youths, to euphemized coercions in schools and workplaces, to the most notorious impositions and deprivations by church or state. It also is a concept useful for tracking literacy's materiel: the things that accompany writing and reading and the ways they are manufactured and distributed. Sponsorship as a sociological term is even more broadly suggestive for thinking about economies of literacy development. Studies of patronage in Europe and *compradrazgo* in the Americas show how patron-client relationships in the past grew up around the need to manage scarce resources and promote political stability (Bourne; Lynch; Horstman and Kurtz). Pragmatic, instrumental, ambivalent, patron-client relationships integrated otherwise antagonistic social classes into relationships of mutual, albeit unequal dependencies. Loaning land, money, protection, and other favors allowed the politically powerful to extend their influence and justify their exploitation of clients. Clients traded their labor and deference for access to opportunities for themselves or their children and for leverage needed to improve their social standing. Especially under conquest in Latin America, *compradrazgo* reintegrated native societies badly fragmented by the diseases and other disruptions that followed foreign invasions. At the same time, this system was susceptible to its own stresses, especially when patrons became clients themselves of still more centralized or distant overlords, with all the shifts in loyalty and perspective that entailed (Horstman and Kurtz 13–14).

In raising this association with formal systems of patronage, I do not wish to overlook the very different economic, political, and educational systems within which U.S. literacy has developed. But where we find the sponsoring of literacy, it will be useful to look for its function within larger political and economic arenas. Literacy, like land, is a valued commodity in this economy, a key resource in gaining profit and edge. This value helps to explain, of course, the lengths people will go to secure literacy for themselves or their children. But it also explains why the powerful work so persistently to conscript and ration the powers of literacy. The competition to harness literacy, to manage, measure, teach, and exploit it, has intensified throughout the century. It is vital to pay attention to this development because it largely sets the terms for individuals' encounters with literacy. This competition shapes the incentives

and barriers (including uneven distributions of opportunity) that greet literacy learners in any particular time and place. It is this competition that has
made access to the right kinds of literacy sponsors so crucial for political and
economic well-being. And it also has spurred the rapid, complex changes that
now make the pursuit of literacy feel so turbulent and precarious for so many.

In the next three sections, I trace the dynamics of literacy sponsorship
through the life experiences of several individuals, showing how their opportunities for literacy learning emerge out of the jockeying and skirmishing for
economic and political advantage going on among sponsors of literacy. Along
the way, the analysis addresses three key issues: (1) how, despite ostensible
democracy in educational chances, stratification of opportunity continues to
organize access and reward in literacy learning; (2) how sponsors contribute
to what is called "the literacy crisis," that is, the perceived gap between rising
standards for achievement and people's ability to meet them; and (3) how encounters with literacy sponsors, especially as they are configured at the end of
the 20th century, can be sites for the innovative rerouting of resources into
projects of self-development and social change.

SPONSORSHIP AND ACCESS

A focus on sponsorship can force a more explicit and substantive link between
literacy learning and systems of opportunity and access. A statistical correlation between high literacy achievement and high socioeconomic, majority-
race status routinely shows up in results of national tests of reading and
writing performance.[4] These findings capture yet, in their shorthand way,
obscure the unequal conditions of literacy sponsorship that lie behind differential outcomes in academic performance. Throughout their lives, affluent
people from high-caste racial groups have multiple and redundant contacts
with powerful literacy sponsors as a routine part of their economic and
political privileges. Poor people and those from low-caste racial groups have
less consistent, less politically secured access to literacy sponsors—especially
to the ones that can grease their way to academic and economic success. Differences in their performances are often attributed to family background
(namely education and income of parents) or to particular norms and values
operating within different ethnic groups or social classes. But in either case,
much more is usually at work.

As a study in contrasts in sponsorship patterns and access to literacy, consider the parallel experiences of Raymond Branch and Dora Lopez, both of
whom were born in 1969 and, as young children, moved with their parents to
the same, mid-sized university town in the midwest.[5] Both were still residing
in this town at the time of our interviews in 1995. Raymond Branch, a European American, had been born in southern California, the son of a professor
father and a real estate executive mother. He recalled that his first grade classroom in 1975 was hooked up to a mainframe computer at Stanford University
and that, as a youngster, he enjoyed fooling around with computer programming in the company of "real users" at his father's science lab. This process

was not interrupted much when, in the late 1970s, his family moved to the midwest. Raymond received his first personal computer as a Christmas present from his parents when he was twelve years old, and a modem the year after that. In the 1980s, computer hardware and software stores began popping up within a bicycle-ride's distance from where he lived. The stores were serving the university community and, increasingly, the high-tech industries that were becoming established in that vicinity. As an adolescent, Raymond spent his summers roaming these stores, sampling new computer games, making contact with founders of some of the first electronic bulletin boards in the nation, and continuing, through reading and other informal means, to develop his programming techniques. At the time of our interview he had graduated from the local university and was a successful freelance writer of software and software documentation, with clients in both the private sector and the university community.

Dora Lopez, a Mexican American, was born in the same year as Raymond Branch, 1969, in a Texas border town, where her grandparents, who worked as farm laborers, lived most of the year. When Dora was still a baby her family moved to the same midwest university town as had the family of Raymond Branch. Her father pursued an accounting degree at a local technical college and found work as a shipping and receiving clerk at the university. Her mother, who also attended technical college briefly, worked part-time in a bookstore. In the early 1970s, when the Lopez family made its move to the midwest, the Mexican-American population in the university town was barely one percent. Dora recalled that the family had to drive seventy miles to a big city to find not only suitable groceries but also Spanish-language newspapers and magazines that carried information of concern and interest to them. (Only when reception was good could they catch Spanish-language radio programs coming from Chicago, 150 miles away.) During her adolescence, Dora Lopez undertook to teach herself how to read and write in Spanish, something, she said, that neither her brother nor her U.S.-born cousins knew how to do. Sometimes, with the help of her mother's employee discount at the bookstore, she sought out novels by South American and Mexican writers, and she practiced her written Spanish by corresponding with relatives in Colombia. She was exposed to computers for the first time at the age of thirteen when she worked as a teacher's aide in a federally-funded summer school program for the children of migrant workers. The computers were being used to help the children to be brought up to grade level in their reading and writing skills. When Dora was admitted to the same university that Raymond Branch attended, her father bought her a used word processing machine that a student had advertised for sale on a bulletin board in the building where Mr. Lopez worked. At the time of our interview, Dora Lopez had transferred from the university to a technical college. She was working for a cleaning company, where she performed extra duties as a translator, communicating on her supervisor's behalf with the largely Latina cleaning staff. "I write in Spanish for him, what he needs to be translated, like job duties, what he expects them to do, and I write lists for him in English and Spanish," she explained.

In Raymond Branch's account of his early literacy learning we are able to see behind the scenes of his majority-race membership, male gender, and high-end socioeconomic family profile. There lies a thick and, to him, relatively accessible economy of institutional and commercial supports that cultivated and subsidized his acquisition of a powerful form of literacy. One might be tempted to say that Raymond Branch was born at the right time and lived in the right place—except that the experience of Dora Lopez troubles that thought. For Raymond Branch, a university town in the 1970s and 1980s provided an information-rich, resource-rich learning environment in which to pursue his literacy development, but for Dora Lopez, a female member of a culturally unsubsidized ethnic minority, the same town at the same time was information- and resource-poor. Interestingly, both young people were pursuing projects of self-initiated learning, Raymond Branch in computer programming and Dora Lopez in biliteracy. But she had to reach much further afield for the material and communicative systems needed to support her learning. Also, while Raymond Branch, as the son of an academic, was sponsored by some of the most powerful agents of the university (its laboratories, newest technologies, and most educated personnel), Dora Lopez was being sponsored by what her parents could pull from the peripheral service systems of the university (the mail room, the bookstore, the second-hand technology market). In these accounts we also can see how the development and eventual economic worth of Raymond Branch's literacy skills were underwritten by late-century transformations in communication technology that created a boomtown need for programmers and software writers. Dora Lopez's biliterate skills developed and paid off much further down the economic-reward ladder, in government-sponsored youth programs and commercial enterprises, that, in the 1990s, were absorbing surplus migrant workers into a low-wage, urban service economy.[6] Tracking patterns of literacy sponsorship, then, gets beyond SES shorthand to expose more fully how unequal literacy chances relate to systems of unequal subsidy and reward for literacy. These are the systems that deliver large-scale economic, historical, and political conditions to the scenes of small-scale literacy use and development.

This analysis of sponsorship forces us to consider not merely how one social group's literacy practices may differ from another's, but how everybody's literacy practices are operating in differential economies, which supply different access routes, different degrees of sponsoring power, and different scales of monetary worth to the practices in use. In fact, the interviews I conducted are filled with examples of how economic and political forces, some of them originating in quite distant corporate and government policies, affect people's day-to-day ability to seek out and practice literacy. As a telephone company employee, Janelle Hampton enjoyed a brief period in the early 1980s as a fraud investigator, pursuing inquiries and writing up reports of her efforts. But when the breakup of the telephone utility reorganized its workforce, the fraud division was moved two states away and she was returned to less interesting work as a data processor. When, as a seven-year-old in the mid-1970s, Yi Vong made his way with his family from Laos to rural Wisconsin as part of the first resettlement group of Hmong refugees after the Vietnam War, his school district—which had no ESL programming—placed him in a school for the blind and deaf, where he learned English on audio and visual language machines. When a meager retirement pension forced Peter Hardaway and his wife out of their house and into a trailer, the couple stopped receiving newspapers and magazines in order to avoid cluttering up the small space they had to share. An analysis of sponsorship systems of literacy would help educators everywhere to think through the effects that economic and political changes in their regions are having on various people's ability to write and read, their chances to sustain that ability, and their capacities to pass it along to others. Recession, relocation, immigration, technological change, government retreat all can—and do—condition the course by which literate potential develops.

SPONSORSHIP AND THE RISE IN LITERACY STANDARDS

As I have been attempting to argue, literacy as a resource becomes available to ordinary people largely through the mediations of more powerful sponsors. These sponsors are engaged in ceaseless processes of positioning and repositioning, seizing and relinquishing control over meanings and materials of literacy as part of their participation in economic and political competition. In the give and take of these struggles, forms of literacy and literacy learning take shape. This section examines more closely how forms of literacy are created out of competitions between institutions. It especially considers how this process relates to the rapid rise in literacy standards since World War II. Resnick and Resnick lay out the process by which the demand for literacy achievement has been escalating, from basic, largely rote competence to more complex analytical and interpretive skills. More and more people are now being expected to accomplish more and more things with reading and writing. As print and its spinoffs have entered virtually every sphere of life, people have grown increasingly dependent on their literacy skills for earning a living and exercising and protecting their civil rights. This section uses one extended case example to trace the role of institutional sponsorship in raising the literacy stakes. It also considers how one man used available forms of sponsorship to cope with this escalation in literacy demands.

The focus is on Dwayne Lowery, whose transition in the early 1970s from line worker in an automobile manufacturing plant to field representative for a major public employees union exemplified the major transition of the post-World War II economy—from a thing-making, thing-swapping society to an information-making, service-swapping society. In the process, Dwayne Lowery had to learn to read and write in ways that he had never done before. How his experiences with writing developed and how they were sponsored—and distressed—by institutional struggle will unfold in the following narrative.

A man of Eastern European ancestry, Dwayne Lowery was born in 1938 and raised in a semi-rural area in the upper midwest, the third of five children of a rubber worker father and a homemaker mother. Lowery recalled how, in his childhood home, his father's feisty union publications and left-leaning newspapers and radio shows helped to create a political climate in his household. "I was sixteen years old before I knew that god-damn Republicans was two words," he said. Despite this influence, Lowery said he shunned politics and newspaper reading as a young person, except to read the sports page. A diffident student, he graduated near the bottom of his class from a small high school in 1956 and, after a stint in the Army, went to work on the assembly line of a major automobile manufacturer. In the late 1960s, bored with the repetition of spraying primer paint on the right door checks of 57 cars an hour, Lowery traded in his night shift at the auto plant for a day job reading water meters in a municipal utility department. It was at that time, Lowery recalled, that he rediscovered newspapers, reading them in the early morning in his department's break room. He said:

> At the time I guess I got a little more interested in the state of things within the state. I started to get a little political at that time and got a little more information about local people. So I would buy [a metropolitan paper] and I would read that paper in the morning. It was a pretty conservative paper but I got some information.

At about the same time Lowery became active in a rapidly growing public employees union, and, in the early 1970s, he applied for and received a union-sponsored grant that allowed him to take off four months of work and travel to Washington, D.C. for training in union activity. Here is his extended account of that experience:

> When I got to school, then there was a lot of reading. I often felt bad. If I had read more [as a high-school student) it wouldn't have been so tough. But they pumped a lot of stuff at us to read. We lived in a hotel and we had to some extent homework we had to do and reading we had to do and not make written reports but make some presentation on our part of it. What they were trying to teach us, I believe, was regulations, systems, laws. In case anything in court came up along the way, we would know that. We did a lot of work on organizing, you know, learning how to negotiate contracts, contractual language, how to write it. Gross National Product, how that affected the Consumer Price Index. It was pretty much a crash course. It was pretty much crammed in. And I'm not sure we were all that well prepared when we got done, but it was interesting.

After a hands-on experience organizing sanitation workers in the west, Lowery returned home and was offered a full-time job as a field staff representative for the union, handling worker grievances and contract negotiations for a large, active local near his state capital. His initial writing and rhetorical activities corresponded with the heady days of the early 1970s when the union was growing in strength and influence, reflecting in part the exponential expansion in information workers and service providers within all branches of government. With practice, Lowery said he became "good at talking," "good at presenting the union side," "good at slicing chunks off the employer's case." Lowery observed that, in those years, the elected officials with whom he was negotiating often lacked the sophistication of their Washington-trained union counterparts. "They were part-time people," he said. "And they didn't know how to calculate. We got things in contracts that didn't cost them much at the time but were going to cost them a ton down the road." In time, though, even small municipal and county governments responded to the public employees' growing power by hiring specialized attorneys to represent them in grievance and contract negotiations. "Pretty soon." Lowery observed, "ninety percent of the people I was dealing with across the table were attorneys."

This move brought dramatic changes in the writing practices of union reps, and, in Lowery's estimation, a simultaneous waning of the power of workers and the power of his own literacy. "It used to be we got our way through muscle or through political connections," he said. "Now we had to get it through legalistic stuff. It was no longer just sit down and talk about it. Can we make a deal?" Instead, all activity became rendered in writing: the exhibit, the brief, the transcript, the letter, the appeal. Because briefs took longer to write, the wheels of justice took longer to turn. Delays in grievance hearings became routine, as lawyers and union reps alike asked hearing judges for extensions on their briefs. Things went, in Lowery's words, "from quick, competent justice to expensive and long-term justice.

In the meantime, Lowery began spending up to 70 hours a week at work. sweating over the writing of briefs, which are typically fifteen- to thirty-page documents laying out precedents, arguments, and evidence for a grievant's case. These documents were being forced by the new political economy in which Lowery's union was operating. He explained:

> When employers were represented by an attorney, you were going to have a written brief because the attorney needs to get paid. Well, what do you think if you were a union grievant and the attorney says, well, I'm going to write a brief and Dwayne Lowery says, well, I'm not going to. Does the worker somehow feel that their representation is less now?

To keep up with the new demands, Lowery occasionally traveled to major cities for two- or three-day union-sponsored workshops on arbitration, new legislation, and communication skills. He also took short courses at a historic School for Workers at a nearby university. His writing instruction consisted mainly of reading the briefs of other field reps, especially those done by the college graduates who increasingly were being assigned to his district from union headquarters. Lowery said he kept a file drawer filled with other people's briefs from which he would borrow formats and phrasings. At the time of our interview in 1995, Dwayne Lowery had just taken an early and somewhat bitter retirement from the union, replaced by a recent graduate from a master's degree program in Industrial Relations. As a retiree, he was engaged in local Democratic party politics and was getting informal lessons in word processing at home from his wife.

Over a 20-year period, Lowery's adult writing took its character from a particular juncture in labor relations, when even small units of government began wielding (and, as a consequence, began spreading) a "legalistic" form of literacy in order to restore political dominance over public workers. This struggle for dominance shaped the kinds of literacy skills required of Lowery, the kinds of genres he learned and used, and the kinds of literate identity he developed. Lowery's rank-and-file experience and his talent for representing that experience around a bargaining table became increasingly peripheral to his ability to prepare documents that could compete in kind with those written by his formally-educated, professional adversaries. Face-to-face meetings became occasions mostly for a ritualistic exchange of texts, as arbitrators generally deferred decisions, reaching them in private, after solitary deliberation over complex sets of documents. What Dwayne Lowery was up against as a working adult in the second half of the 20th century was more than just living through a rising standard in literacy expectations or a generalized growth in professionalization, specialization, or documentary power—although certainly all of those things are, generically, true. Rather, these developments should be seen more specifically, as outcomes of ongoing transformations in the history of literacy as it has been wielded as part of economic and political conflict. These transformations become the arenas in which new standards of literacy develop. And for Dwayne Lowery—as well as many like him over the last 25 years—these are the arenas in which the worth of existing literate skills become degraded. A consummate debater and deal maker, Lowery saw his value to the union bureaucracy subside, as power shifted to younger, university-trained staffers whose literacy credentials better matched the specialized forms of escalating pressure coming from the other side.

In the broadest sense, the sponsorship of Dwayne Lowery's literacy experiences lies deep within the historical conditions of industrial relations in the 20th century and, more particularly, within the changing nature of work and labor struggle over the last several decades. Edward Stevens Jr. has observed the rise in this century of an "advanced contractarian society" (25) by which formal relationships of all kinds have come to rely on "a jungle of rules and regulations" (139). For labor, these conditions only intensified in the 1960s and 1970s when a flurry of federal and state civil rights legislation curtailed the previously unregulated hiring and firing power of management. These developments made the appeal to law as central as collective bargaining for extending employee rights (Heckscher 9). I mention this broader picture, first, because it relates to the forms of employer backlash that Lowery began experiencing by the early 1980s and, more important, because a history of unionism serves as a guide for a closer look at the sponsors of Lowery's literacy.

These resources begin with the influence of his father, whose membership in the United Rubber Workers during the ideologically potent 1930s and 1940s, grounded Lowery in class-conscious progressivism and its favorite literate form: the newspaper. On top of that, though, was a pragmatic philosophy of worker education that developed in the U.S. after the Depression as an anti-communist antidote to left-wing intellectual influences in unions. Lowery's parent union, in fact, had been a central force in refocusing worker education away from an earlier emphasis on broad critical study and toward discrete techniques for organizing and bargaining. Workers began to be trained in the discrete bodies of knowledge, written formats, and idioms associated with those strategies. Characteristic of this legacy, Lowery's crash course at the Washington-based training center in the early 1970s emphasized technical information, problem solving, and union-building skills and methods. The transformation in worker education from critical, humanistic study to problem-solving skills was also lived out at the school for workers where Lowery took short courses in the 1980s. Once a place where factory workers came to write and read about economics, sociology, and labor history, the school is now part of a university extension service offering workshops — often requested by management — on such topics as work restructuring, new technology, health and safety regulations, and joint labor-management cooperation.[7] Finally, in this inventory of Dwayne Lowery's literacy sponsors, we must add the latest incarnations shaping union practices: the attorneys and college-educated co-workers who carried into Lowery's workplace forms of legal discourse and "essayist literacy."[8]

What should we notice about this pattern of sponsorship? First, we can see from yet another angle how the course of an ordinary person's literacy learning — its occasions, materials, applications, potentials — follows the transformations going on within sponsoring institutions as those institutions fight for economic and ideological position. As a result of wins, losses, or compromises, institutions undergo change, affecting the kinds of literacy they promulgate and the status that such literacy has in the larger society. So where, how, why, and what Lowery practiced as a writer — and what he didn't practice — took shape as part of the post-industrial jockeying going on over the last thirty years by labor, government, and industry. Yet there is more to be seen in this inventory of literacy sponsors. It exposes the deeply textured history that lies within the literacy practices of institutions and within any individual's literacy experiences. Accumulated layers of sponsoring influences — in families, workplaces, schools, memory — carry forms of literacy that have been shaped out of ideological and economic struggles of the past. This history, on the one hand, is a sustaining resource in the quest for literacy. It enables an older generation to pass its literacy resources onto another. Lowery's exposure to his father's newspaper-reading and supper-table political talk kindled his adult passion for news, debate, and for language that rendered relief and justice. This history also helps to create infrastructures of opportunity. Lowery found crucial supports for extending his adult literacy in the educational networks that unions established during the first half of the 20th century as they were consolidating into national powers. On the other hand, this layered history of sponsorship is also deeply conservative and can be maladaptive because it teaches forms of literacy that oftentimes are in the process of being overtaken by new political realities and by ascendent forms of literacy. The decision to focus worker education on practical strategies of recruiting and bargaining — devised in the thick of Cold War patriotism and galloping expansion in union membership — became, by the Reagan years, a fertile ground for new forms of management aggression and co-optation.

It is actually this lag or gap in sponsoring forms that we call the rising standard of literacy. The pace of change and the place of literacy in economic competition have both intensified enormously in the last half of the 20th century. It is as if the history of literacy is in fast forward. Where once the same sponsoring arrangements could maintain value across a generation or more, forms of literacy and their sponsors can now rise and recede many times within a single life span. Dwayne Lowery experienced profound changes in forms of union-based literacy not only between his father's time and his but between the time he joined the union and the time he left it, twenty-odd years later. This phenomenon is what makes today's literacy feel so advanced and, at the same time, so destabilized.

Sponsorship and Appropriation in Literacy Learning

We have seen how literacy sponsors affect literacy learning in two powerful ways. They help to organize and administer stratified systems of opportunity and access, and they raise the literacy stakes in struggles for competitive advantage. Sponsors enable and hinder literacy activity, often forcing the formation of new literacy requirements while decertifying older ones. A somewhat different dynamic of literacy sponsorship is treated here. It pertains to the potential of the sponsored to divert sponsors' resources toward ulterior projects, often projects of self-interest or self-development. Earlier I mentioned how Sunday School parishioners in England and African Americans in slavery appropriated church-sponsored literacy for economic and psychic survival. "Misappropriation" is always possible at the scene of literacy transmission, a reason for the tight ideological control that usually surrounds reading and writing instruction. The accounts that appear below are meant to shed light on the dynamics of appropriation, including the role of sponsoring agents in that process. They are also meant to suggest that diversionary tactics in literacy learning may be invited now by the sheer proliferation of literacy activity in contemporary life. The uses and networks of literacy crisscross through many domains, exposing people to multiple, often amalgamated sources of sponsoring powers, secular, religious, bureaucratic, commercial, technological. In other words, what is so destabilized about contemporary literacy today also makes it so available and potentially innovative, ripe for picking, one might say, for people suitably positioned. The rising level of schooling in the general population is also an inviting factor in this process. Almost everyone now has some sort of contact, for instance, with college educated people, whose movements through workplaces, justice systems, social service organizations, houses of worship, local government, extended families, or circles of friends spread dominant forms of literacy (whether wanted or not, helpful or not) into public and private spheres. Another condition favorable for appropriation is the deep hybridity of literacy practices extant in many settings. As we saw in Dwayne Lowery's case, workplaces, schools, families bring together multiple strands of the history of literacy in complex and influential forms. We need models of literacy that more astutely account for these kinds of multiple contacts, both in and out of school and across a lifetime. Such models could begin to grasp the significance of re-appropriation, which, for a number of reasons, is becoming a key requirement for literacy learning at the end of the 20th century.

The following discussion will consider two brief cases of literacy diversion. Both involve women working in subordinate positions as secretaries, in print-rich settings where better educated male supervisors were teaching them to read and write in certain ways to perform their clerical duties. However, as we will see shortly, strong loyalties outside the workplace prompted these two secretaries to lift these literate resources for use in other spheres. For one, Carol White, it was on behalf of her work as a Jehovah's Witness. For the other, Sarah Steele, it was on behalf of upward mobility for her lower middle-class family.

Before turning to their narratives, though, it will be wise to pay some attention to the economic moment in which they occur. Clerical work was the largest and fastest growing occupation for women in the 20th century. Like so much employment for women, it offered a mix of gender-defined constraints as well as avenues for economic independence and mobility. As a new information economy created an acute need for typists, stenographers, bookkeepers, and other office workers, white, American-born women and, later, immigrant and minority women saw reason to pursue high school and business-college educations. Unlike male clerks of the 19th century, female secretaries in this century had little chance for advancement. However, office work represented a step up from the farm or the factory for women of the working class and served as a respectable occupation from which educated, middle-class women could await or avoid marriage (Anderson; Strom). In a study of clerical work through the first half of the 20th century, Christine Anderson estimated that secretaries might encounter up to 97 different genres in the course of doing dictation or transcription. They routinely had contact with an array of professionals, including lawyers, auditors, tax examiners, and other government overseers (52–53). By 1930, 30 percent of women office workers used machines other than typewriters (Anderson 76) and, in contemporary offices, clerical workers have often been the first employees to learn to operate CRTs and personal computers and to teach others how to use them. Overall, the daily duties of 20th-century secretaries could serve handily as an index to the rise of complex administrative and accounting procedures, standardization of information, expanding communication, and developments in technological systems.

With that background, consider the experiences of Carol White and Sarah Steele. An Oneida, Carol White was born into a poor, single-parent household in 1940. She graduated from high school in 1960 and, between five maternity leaves and a divorce, worked continuously in a series of clerical positions in both the private and public sectors. One of her first secretarial jobs was with an urban firm that produced and disseminated Catholic missionary films. The vice-president with whom she worked most closely also spent much of his time producing a magazine for a national civic organization that he headed.

She discussed how typing letters and magazine articles and occasionally proofreading for this man taught her rhetorical strategies in which she was keenly interested. She described the scene of transfer this way:

> [My boss] didn't just write to write. He wrote in a way to make his letters appealing. I would have to write what he was writing in this magazine too. I was completely enthralled. He would write about the people who were in this [organization] and the different works they were undertaking and people that died and people who were sick and about their personalities. And he wrote little anecdotes. Once in a while I made some suggestions too. He was a man who would listen to you.

The appealing and persuasive power of the anecdote became especially important to Carol White when she began doing door-to-door missionary work for the Jehovah's Witnesses, a pan-racial, millennialist religious faith. She now uses colorful anecdotes to prepare demonstrations that she performs with other women at weekly service meetings at their Kingdom Hall. These demonstrations, done in front of the congregation, take the form of skits designed to explore daily problems through Bible principles. Further, at the time of our interview, Carol White was working as a municipal revenue clerk and had recently enrolled in an on-the-job training seminar called Persuasive Communication, a two-day class offered free to public employees. Her motivation for taking the course stemmed from her desire to improve her evangelical work. She said she wanted to continue to develop speaking and writing skills that would be "appealing," "motivating," and "encouraging" to people she hoped to convert.

Sarah Steele, a woman of Welsh and German descent, was born in 1920 into a large, working-class family in a coal mining community in eastern Pennsylvania. In 1940, she graduated from a two-year commercial college. Married soon after, she worked as a secretary in a glass factory until becoming pregnant with the first of four children. In the 1960s, in part to help pay for her children's college educations, she returned to the labor force as a receptionist and bookkeeper in a law firm, where she stayed until her retirement in the late 1970s.

Sarah Steele described how, after joining the law firm, she began to model her household management on principles of budgeting that she was picking up from one of the attorneys with whom she worked most closely. "I learned cash flow from Mr. B____," she said. "I would get all the bills and put a tape in the adding machine and he and I would sit down together to be sure there was going to be money ahead." She said that she began to replicate that process at home with household bills. "Before that," she observed, "I would just cook beans when I had to instead of meat." Sarah Steele also said she encountered the genre of the credit report during routine reading and typing on the job. She figured out what constituted a top rating, making sure her husband followed these steps in preparation for their financing a new car. She also remembered typing up documents connected to civil suits being brought against local businesses, teaching her, she said, which firms never to hire for home repairs. "It just changes the way you think," she observed about the reading and writing she did on her job. "You're not a pushover after you learn how business operates."

The dynamics of sponsorship alive in these narratives expose important elements of literacy appropriation, at least as it is practiced at the end of the 20th century. In a pattern now familiar from the earlier sections, we see how opportunities for literacy learning—this time for diversions of resources— open up in the clash between long-standing, residual forms of sponsorship and the new: between the lingering presence of literacy's conservative history and its pressure for change. So, here, two women—one Native American and both working-class—filch contemporary literacy resources (public relations techniques and accounting practices) from more educated, higher-status men. The women are emboldened in these acts by ulterior identities beyond the workplace: Carol White with faith and Sarah Steele with family. These affilia- tions hark back to the first sponsoring arrangements through which American women were gradually allowed to acquire literacy and education. Duties as- sociated with religious faith and child rearing helped literacy to become, in Gloria Main's words, "a permissible feminine activity" (579). Interestingly, these roles, deeply sanctioned within the history of women's literacy—and operating beneath the newer permissible feminine activity of clerical work— become grounds for covert, innovative appropriation even as they reinforce traditional female identities.

Just as multiple identities contribute to the ideologically hybrid character of these literacy formations, so do institutional and material conditions. Carol White's account speaks to such hybridity. The missionary film company with the civic club vice president is a residual site for two of literacy's oldest campaigns—Christian conversion and civic participation—enhanced here by 20th-century advances in film and public relations techniques. This ideo- logical reservoir proved a pleasing instructional site for Carol White, whose interests in literacy, throughout her life, have been primarily spiritual. So lit- eracy appropriation draws upon, perhaps even depends upon, conservative forces in the history of literacy sponsorship that are always hovering at the scene of acts of learning. This history serves as both a sanctioning force and a reserve of ideological and material support.

At the same time, however, we see in these accounts how individual acts of appropriation can divert and subvert the course of literacy's history, how changes in individual literacy experiences relate to larger scale transforma- tions. Carol White's redirection of personnel management techniques to the cause of the Jehovah's Witnesses is an almost ironic transformation in this regard. Once a principal sponsor in the initial spread of mass literacy, evange- lism is here rejuvenated through late-literate corporate sciences of secular per- suasion, fund-raising, and bureaucratic management that Carol White finds circulating in her contemporary workplaces. By the same token, through Sarah Steele, accounting practices associated with corporations are, in a sense, tracked into the house, rationalizing and standardizing even domestic prac- tices. (Even though Sarah Steele did not own an adding machine, she penciled her budget figures onto adding-machine tape that she kept for that purpose.) Sarah Steele's act of appropriation in some sense explains how dominant forms of literacy migrate and penetrate into private spheres, including private consciousness. At the same time, though, she accomplishes a subversive diversion of literate power. Her efforts to move her family up in the middle class involved not merely contributing a second income but also, from her desk as a bookkeeper, reading her way into an understanding of middle-class economic power.

Teaching and the Dynamics of Sponsorship

It hardly seems necessary to point out to the readers of *CCC* that we haul a lot of freight for the opportunity to teach writing. Neither rich nor powerful enough to sponsor literacy on our own terms, we serve instead as conflicted brokers between literacy's buyers and sellers. At our most worthy, perhaps, we show the sellers how to beware and try to make sure these exchanges will be a little fairer, maybe, potentially, a little more mutually rewarding. This essay has offered a few working case studies that link patterns of sponsorship to processes of stratification, competition, and reappropriation. How much these dynamics can be generalized to classrooms is an ongoing empirical question.

I am sure that sponsors play even more influential roles at the scenes of literacy learning and use than this essay has explored. I have focused on some of the most tangible aspects—material supply, explicit teaching, institutional aegis. But the ideological pressure of sponsors affects many private aspects of writing processes as well as public aspects of finished texts. Where one's sponsors are multiple or even at odds, they can make writing maddening. Where they are absent, they make writing unlikely. Many of the cultural formations we associate with writing development—community practices, disciplinary traditions, technological potentials—can be appreciated as make-do responses to the economics of literacy, past and present. The history of literacy is a catalogue of obligatory relations. That this catalogue is so deeply conservative and, at the same time, so ruthlessly demanding of change is what fills contemporary literacy learning and teaching with their most paradoxical choices and outcomes.[9]

In bringing attention to economies of literacy learning I am not advocating that we prepare students more efficiently for the job markets they must enter. What I have tried to suggest is that as we assist and study individuals in pursuit of literacy, we also recognize how literacy is in pursuit of them. When this process stirs ambivalence, on their part or on ours, we need to be understanding.

Acknowledgments: This research was sponsored by the NCTE Research Foundation and the Center on English Learning and Achievement. The Center is supported by the U.S. Department of Education's Office of Educational Research and Improvement, whose views do not necessarily coincide with the author's. A version of this essay was given as a lecture in the Department of English, University of Louisville, in April 1997. Thanks to Anna Syvertsen and Julie Nelson for their help with archival research. Thanks too to colleagues who lent an ear along the way: Nelson Graff, Jonna Gjevre, Anne Gere, Kurt Spellmeyer, Tom Fox, and Bob Gundlach.

NOTES

1. Three of the keenest and most eloquent observers of economic impacts on writing teaching and learning have been Lester Faigley, Susan Miller, and Kurt Spellmeyer.

2. My debt to the writings of Pierre Bourdieu will be evident throughout this essay. Here and throughout I invoke his expansive notion of "economy," which is not restricted to literal and ostensible systems of money making but to the many spheres where people labor, invest, and exploit energies—their own and others'—to maximize advantage. See Bourdieu and Wacquant, especially 117–20 and Bourdieu, Chapter 7.

3. Thomas Laqueur (124) provides a vivid account of a street demonstration in Bolton, England, in 1834 by a "pro-writing" faction of Sunday School students and their teachers. This faction demanded that writing instruction continue to be provided on Sundays, something that opponents of secular instruction on the Sabbath were trying to reverse.

4. See, for instance, National Assessments of Educational Progress in reading and writing (Applebee et al.; and "Looking").

5. All names used in this essay are pseudonyms.

6. I am not suggesting that literacy that does not "pay off" in terms of prestige or monetary reward is less valuable. Dora Lopez's ability to read and write in Spanish was a source of great strength and pride, especially when she was able to teach it to her young child. The resource of Spanish literacy carried much of what Bourdieu calls cultural capital in her social and family circles. But I want to point out here how people who labor equally to acquire literacy do so under systems of unequal subsidy and unequal reward.

7. For useful accounts of this period in union history, see Heckscher; Nelson.

8. Marcia Farr associates "essayist literacy" with written genres esteemed in the academy and noted for their explicitness, exactness, reliance on reasons and evidence, and impersonal voice.

9. Lawrence Cremin makes similar points about education in general in his essay "The Cacophony of Teaching." He suggests that complex economic and social changes since World War II, including the popularization of schooling and the penetration of mass media, have created "a far greater range and diversity of languages, competencies, values, personalities, and approaches to the world and to its educational opportunities" than at one time existed. The diversity most of interest to him (and me) resides not so much in the range of different ethnic groups there are in society but in the different cultural formulas by which people assemble their educational—or, I would say, literate—experience.

WORKS CITED

Anderson, Mary Christine. "Gender, Class, and Culture: Women Secretarial and Clerical Workers in the United States, 1925–1955." Diss. Ohio State U, 1986.

Applebee, Arthur N., Judith A. Langer, and Ida V. S. Mullis. *The Writing Report Card: Writing Achievement in American Schools*. Princeton: ETS, 1986.

Bourdieu, Pierre. *The Logic of Practice*. Trans. Richard Nice. Cambridge: Polity, 1990.

Bourdieu, Pierre and Loic J. D. Wacquant. *An Invitation to Reflexive Sociology*. Chicago: Chicago UP, 1992.

Bourne, J. M. *Patronage and Society in Nineteenth-Century England*. London: Edward Arnold, 1986.

Brandt, Deborah. "Remembering Reading, Remembering Writing." *CCC* 45 (1994): 459–79.

———. "Accumulating Literacy: Writing and Learning to Write in the 20th Century." *College English* 57 (1995): 649–68.

Cornelius, Janet Duitsman. *'When I Can Ready My Title Clear': Literacy, Slavery, and Religion in the Antebellum South*. Columbia: U of South Carolina, 1991.

Cremin, Lawrence. "The Cacophony of Teaching." *Popular Education and Its Discontents*. New York: Harper, 1990.

Faigley, Lester. "Veterans' Stories on the Porch." *History, Reflection and Narrative: The Professionalization of Composition, 1963–1983*. Eds. Beth Boehm, Debra Journet, and Mary Rosner. Norwood: Ablex, 1999.

Farr, Marcia. "Essayist Literacy and Other Verbal Performances." *Written Communication* 8 (1993): 4–38.

Heckscher, Charles C. *The New Unionism: Employee Involvement in the Changing Corporation.* New York: Basic, 1988.

Horstman, Connie and Donald V. Kurtz. *Compadrazgo in Post-Conquest Middle America.* Milwaukee: Milwaukee-UW Center for Latin America, 1978.

Kett, Joseph F. *The Pursuit of Knowledge Under Difficulties: From Self Improvement to Adult Education in America 1750–1990.* Stanford: Stanford UP, 1994.

Laqueur, Thomas. *Religion and Respectability: Sunday Schools and Working Class Culture 1780–1850.* New Haven: Yale UP, 1976.

Looking at How Well Our Students Read: The 1992 National Assessment of Educational Progress in Reading. Washington: U.S. Dept. of Education, Office of Educational Research and Improvement, Educational Resources Information Center, 1992.

Lynch, Joseph H. *Godparents and Kinship in Early Medieval Europe.* Princeton: Princeton UP, 1986.

Main, Gloria L. "An Inquiry Into When and Why Women Learned to Write in Colonial New England." *Journal of Social History* 24 (1991): 579–89.

Miller, Susan. *Textual Carnivals: The Politics of Composition.* Carbondale: Southern Illinois UP, 1991.

Nelson, Daniel. *American Rubber Workers & Organized Labor, 1900–1941.* Princeton: Princeton UP, 1988.

Nicholas, Stephen J. and Jacqueline M. Nicholas. "Male Literacy, 'Deskilling,' and the Industrial Revolution." *Journal of Interdisciplinary History* 23 (1992): 1–18.

Resnick, Daniel P., and Lauren B. Resnick. "The Nature of Literacy: A Historical Explanation." *Harvard Educational Review* 47 (1977): 370–85.

Spellmeyer, Kurt. "After Theory: From Textuality to Attunement with the World." *College English* 58 (1996): 893–913.

Stevens, Jr., Edward. *Literacy, Law, and Social Order.* DeKalb: Northern Illinois UP, 1987.

Strom, Sharon Hartman. *Beyond the Typewriter: Gender, Class, and the Origins of Modern American Office Work, 1900–1930.* Urbana: U of Illinois P, 1992.

2 *Kitchen Tables and Rented Rooms:*
The Extracurriculum of Composition

ANNE RUGGLES GERE

Two prisoners in contingent cells communicate by blows struck on the wall. The wall separates them, but it also permits them to communicate.

–SIMONE WEIL

In a rented room on Leavenworth Street in the Tenderloin District of San Francisco a group of women gathers on Friday afternoons from two to five to provide one another advice and feedback on their writing. The Tenderloin District, identified by many as a home for drug dealers, welfare recipients, criminals, and mental health patients, also provides a home for several writing groups including the Tenderloin Women's Writing Workshop. Carol Heller, who has studied this group, notes that although these women have little formal education, they take their writing seriously; they offer one another encouragement as well as criticism and suggest revisions. As Carolyn, a member of the group, put it, "We can disagree with each other's views, but the point of this workshop is to do the work" (Heller, *Multiple Functions* 225).[1]

In Lansing, Iowa, a small farming community, a dozen writers gather around Richard and Dorothy Sandry's kitchen table. They meet on Monday evenings during the lull between fall harvest and spring planting and spend two hours reading and responding to one another's writing. In their prose they look at the experience of farming, old equipment, the process of milking cows, and country schools. Frequently writers talk about their plans before they begin writing, gathering suggestions and ideas for shaping their material. These writing workshops are part of what Robert Wolf, the workshop facilitator, calls the Rural Renovation Proposal, which aims to revitalize both the economy and democracy of small towns by building community and consensus among individuals who can then address local problems.

From *College Composition and Communication* 45.1 (1994): 75–92.

Participants in groups like the Tenderloin Women's Writing Workshop and the Lansing, Iowa, Writers Workshop represent a tiny portion of the enormous number of individuals who meet in living rooms, nursing homes, community centers, churches, shelters for the homeless, around kitchen tables, and in rented rooms to write down their worlds. These writers bear testimony to the fact that writing development occurs outside formal education. As Simone Weil reminds us, walls can be a means of communication as well as a barrier, and I propose that we listen to the signals that come through the walls of our classrooms from the world outside.

Hobbled by poverty, histories of alcoholism and drug addiction, along with the indignities of aging, the women in the Tenderloin Women's Writing Workshop take strength from finding that their experience is worth expressing. As one member of the Women's Writing Workshop says, "You write down your world and then you read it to other people and they affirm you for it" (Heller, *Writers* 6). Anita Ardell, a recovering cancer patient, expresses a similar view, "I had never before written. They've encouraged me incredibly. . . . You are given the freedom to try. You feel brave here. You feel brave at the women writers group" (Heller, *Multiple Functions* 174). Participants in the Lansing, Iowa, Writers' Workshop also find that writing enhances their self-esteem. Bob Leppert, a farmer with little formal education, says, "I never felt like I had anything that anyone was interested in hearing" (Wagner, "Alamakee Farmers"). Eighty-three-year-old Clara Leppert, the oldest member of the Lansing Workshop, echoes this feeling, "We didn't think we could write. . . ." (Wagner, "Writers in Overalls"). Despite their inexperience, workshop participants gain confidence and begin to think of themselves as writers.

In addition to increasing positive feelings, workshops outside classroom walls discipline participants to hone their craft as writers. Mary TallMountain, a member of the Tenderloin Women's Writing Workshop and a published author, explains, "They're my readers. I write down everything they say and at some point in time, when it's quiet and spiritually proper, when my mind and whole system are attuned to the writing, I go through it" (Heller, *Multiple Functions* 83). Maria Rand, another member of the workshop, affirms this: "Some of the women are hesitant because nobody ever asked them their opinions about anything. But unless you read your work and get reactions from different groups of people, you're not a writer. You're just dilettanting around. You gotta get rejected and get applause. You gotta get both sides. I'll always be in writing groups. That's where I get my energy from" (Heller, *Multiple Functions* 91–92). The Lansing, Iowa, group also helps members develop their writing skills. A local reporter explains, "They offer positive criticism of one another's work. They read books and essays by established writers and pick the work apart, talking about the elements that make it effective" (Wagner, "Alamakee Farmers").

Opportunities for performance provide a major incentive for writers to develop their skills. The Tenderloin Reflection and Education Center, which sponsors the Women's Writing Workshop, holds regular public readings where workshoppers present their work to a live audience. Despite the anxieties they feel at reading their writing aloud to strangers, individual members and the group as a whole enjoy the opportunity to display their work. As Heller notes, these readings strengthen the relationship between the storyteller and those who hear the story, along with the larger community as a whole (Heller, *Multiple Functions* 130). The Center also helps maintain a local newsletter, *Tender Leaves*, to which workshop participants contribute regularly, and the Tenderloin's Exit Theater has produced plays written by Workshop participants. When he began working with the Lansing group, Robert Wolf explained that "public readings with discussions afterwards" would be the heart of the project (*Voices* 2). Publication also features prominently in this group's work. Several members of the workshop contributed to *Voices from the Land*, a book that has attracted national attention. Bill Welsh, one of these contributors, observes, "I never dreamed of this. I don't feel like any kind of a big shot. I still wear my overalls" (Wagner, "Writers in Overalls").

Reaching out into the community with prose performances develops in participants the perception that writing can effect changes in their lives. The stated purpose of the Lansing, Iowa, Writers' Workshop—to build community in order to solve local problems—is enacted by individual members (Wolf, *Newsletter*). Greg Welsh, a member of the Workshop, employed writing to deal with the time when his family's cattle herd was accidentally poisoned by a contaminated bale of hay. Greg explains, "Writing about it was one way for me to understand how I felt. It was a way for me to reconcile some differences I had with members of my family" (Wagner, "Alamakee Farmers"). In addition to changing the quality of personal relationships, workshop participants often use writing to alter the material conditions of their lives. A piece by one of the Tenderloin women writers led to a fund-raising event for a publication called *Homeless Link* along with increased activism on behalf of homeless people, and a Black History study group developed because of another participant's play, "Ain't I Right Too?" (Heller, *Multiple Functions* 216). The public readings of the Lansing group have led individuals to consider organic alternatives to chemical farming (Wagner, "Alamakee Farmers").

Positive feelings about oneself and one's writing, motivation to revise and improve composition skills, opportunities for publication of various sorts, the belief that writing can make a difference in individual and community life—these accomplishments of workshops outside classroom walls mirror the goals most of us composition teachers espouse for our students. Workshops outside classroom walls frequently, however, succeed with those individuals deemed unsuccessful by their composition instructors. Few of the participants in the Tenderloin Women's Writing Workshop or the Lansing, Iowa, Writers' Workshop had much formal education, and many had negative experiences with schooling. They did not think of themselves as writers because teachers had taught them they could not write. Yet these individuals wrote effectively in workshops, published their writing, and gained personal and community recognition for their work. Although it remains largely invisible and inaudible to us, writing development occurs regularly and successfully outside classroom walls.

One explanation for our relative unfamiliarity with groups such as those in Lansing and the Tenderloin lies in the way we tell our history. Like representatives of most emerging fields, we in composition studies have sought to establish our right to a place in the academy by recounting our past, and this historiography has focused inside classroom walls. One version of composition's history has concentrated on American instructional practices of the nineteenth and twentieth centuries. Albert Kitzhaber's study of rhetoric in nineteenth century American colleges helped establish this tradition. Drawing upon nineteenth century textbooks, Kitzhaber describes the theory and practice of composition in higher education during the latter part of the nineteenth century. Historians such as Donald Stewart, Robert Connors, and James Berlin, even though they adopt differing stances toward their materials, emulate Kitzhaber's model in looking to composition texts, course descriptions, statements of instructions, and other institutional artifacts as sources for information about composition theory and practice. A related historical narrative constructs for composition a genealogy that extends back to Classical Rhetoric. Scholars such as James Murphy, Edward P. J. Corbett, and Winifred Bryan Homer have aided this construction by delineating the composition-rhetoric connections. Robert Connors, Lisa Ede, and Andrea Lunsford extol the benefits of this union, asserting that until recently "rhetorical scholars in speech communication emphasized theoretical and historical studies, while those in composition focused on pedagogy," but the wedding of rhetoric and composition has provided the former with an "outlet for application" and relieved the latter of its "historical and theoretical vacuum" (12–13). In addition, they claim, this merger has helped "to make composition and its necessary theoretical background in rhetoric acceptable to departments of English" (13).

While we might debate how acceptable composition has become in English departments, the terms in which composition's history has been represented arouse little dissent: In concentrating upon establishing our position within the academy, we have neglected to recount the history of composition in other contexts; we have neglected composition's extracurriculum. I borrow this term "extracurriculum" from Frederick Rudolph, who uses it to describe the literary clubs, the fraternity system, and the organized athletics instigated by undergraduates during the nineteenth century. Rudolph argues that this extracurriculum served to make undergraduates "a remarkably important element in the power structure of the American college" (*American College* 136). Arthur Applebee also uses the term "extracurricular," but for him it describes one of three traditions—the ethical, the classical, and the extracurriculum—from which English studies emerged. Applebee defines the extracurriculum as the nonacademic tradition that contributed to the development of English studies. Like Rudolph, he employs the term extracurriculum to describe eighteenth and nineteenth century college literary clubs and recounts how these groups discussed vernacular literature not judged worthy of academic study. As Applebee explains, college literary clubs also sponsored libraries, speakers, and magazines, providing a context where students could "polish their skills in English composition" (12). Applebee's extracurriculum does not include fraternities or athletic groups but it confirms Rudolph's point that the extracurriculum lent undergraduates power in American colleges because the curriculum was adapted to their interests. Gerald Graff emulates Applebee's description of extracurricular literary clubs, noting their contribution to the development of English studies.

Significantly, Rudolph, Applebee, and Graff all describe the extracurriculum as a white male enterprise. Literary societies at women's colleges and women's literary groups on co-ed campuses receive no more attention than do those of African Americans. In addition, each of these narratives positions the extracurriculum as a way-station on the route toward a fully professionalized academic department, thereby implying that the extracurriculum withered away after helping to institutionalize English studies. There is no suggestion that the extracurriculum continues to exist or perform cultural work. This erasure of the extra-professional takes on particular irony in Graff's work as his discourse advances the very professionalism he decries. As Jonathan Freedman puts it, "The effacement or replacement of the non-academic perspective by a thoroughly academicized one that professionalism accomplished is recapitulated in the narrative form in which the story of professionalism is told."

In contrast, my version of the extracurriculum includes the present as well as the past; it extends beyond the academy to encompass the multiple contexts in which persons seek to improve their own writing; it includes more diversity in gender, race, and class among writers; and it avoids, as much as possible, a reenactment of professionalization in its narrative. In looking at the relationship between composition studies and the "outside/other" represented by the extracurriculum, my project shares much with Susan Miller's *Textual Carnivals*, a text which also discusses the extracurriculum. This excellent book has informed my thinking, and I share Miller's interest in considering the relationship between nonacademic writing and composition instruction; although Miller gives more attention to the political forces surrounding composition's institutional location, and I am more interested in the cultural work undertaken by various groups of writers, our projects converge.

My methodology for looking at composition's extracurriculum owes much to recent accounts of literacy practices outside formal education. Investigations of community literacy practices by Shirley Brice Heath, of workplace literacy by Glynda Hull, of multiple discourse communities by Patricia Bizzell, and of "unofficial literacy" by Ruth Hubbard all provide angles of vision for looking at composition's extracurriculum. They suggest the need to uncouple composition and schooling, to consider the situatedness of composition practices, to focus on the experiences of writers not always visible to us inside the walls of the academy. Drawing on this tradition, my account focuses explicitly on self-sponsored pedagogically oriented writing activities outside the academy. In defining the extracurriculum this way, I deliberately exclude from my story the writing instruction carried out in workplaces, extension courses, and workshops for which participants pay large fees. The extracurriculum I examine is constructed by desire, by the aspirations and imaginations of its participants. It posits writing as an action undertaken by motivated individuals who frequently see it as having social and economic consequences, including transformations in personal relationships and farming practices.

Just as accounts of literacy practices outside the walls of the academy uncouple literacy and schooling, so my account of the extracurriculum of composition separates pedagogy from the traditional pedagogue. Composition's extracurriculum acknowledges a wide range of teachers, including texts published for aspiring writers. From the Colonial Period to the present, publications designed for persons who seek to improve their writing have contributed to composition's extracurriculum. One of the most popular, George Fisher's *The American Instructor: Or, Young Man's Best Companion* was first published in Philadelphia in 1748, and issued in 17 editions between 1748 and 1833. Aimed at the emerging entrepreneurs of the period, Fisher's book emphasized the importance of composition for business and asserted: "To write a good fair, free and commendable hand, is equally necessary in most if not all the affairs of life and occurrences of business" (A2). Fisher goes on to offer sentences to copy, models of letters for various occasions as well as instructions for making a quill pen, holding the pen in the hand, positioning the light, and making red and black ink. He also includes directions for keeping ink from freezing or molding: "In hard frosty Weather, Ink will be apt to freeze; which if once it doth, it will be good for nothing; for it takes away all its Blackness and Beauty. To prevent which (if you have not the Convenience of keeping it warm, or from the Cold) put a few Drops of Brandy, or other Spirits, into it, and it will not freeze. And to hinder its Moulding, put a little Salt therein" (43). This form of composition's extracurriculum continued after the Revolutionary War with publications such as *The Complete Letter Writer* (1793), *The Farmer and Mechanic's Pocket Assistant* (1818), and *The Art of Epistolary Composition* (1826).[2]

Not only did publications like these offer an alternative to the academy's instruction in composition, they frequently criticized the way composition was taught in schools. *A Help to Young Writers*, a self-help guide published in 1836, found fault with the "vapid subjects" assigned by teachers and with the tendency of schools to teach composition as though it bore no relationship to good conversation. This self-help guide went on to assert that "composition is nothing more than conversation put on paper" and demonstrated this by advising writers in question and answer form (Heath 34).

As magazines developed during the nineteenth century, composition's extracurriculum flourished in their pages as well. As Nicole Tonkovich Hoffman has shown, Sarah Hale, editor of *Godey's Ladies Magazine* from 1828–1878, offered considerable advice to writers. Like the authors of self-help books, Hale includes material on the technology of writing. Instructions for cutting a pen-point and models of handwriting appear in the pages of *Godey's*. Hale also gives attention to the processes of writing. An 1838 column, for example, recommends what Hale calls "mental composition" for developing more active reading. According to Hale, mental composition "can be pursued at any time and place without the requisite paraphernalia of written composition. . . . it greatly conduces to the development of the judgment, to make frequent pauses, and trace out the inference, and the particular bearing and tendency of detached portions of it; and upon its completion to consider the general scope, its moral tone, the correctness of the sentiments advanced and the character of the style" (191). Hale goes on to recommend writing in response to reading, not note taking but "the keeping of a common-place book, to sketch down one's views, opinions, and sentiments, upon every subject or topic, which may have interested the mind in the perusal of a work" (191).

Godey's was not the only magazine to include advice for individuals interested in developing their composition skills, but it was the most influential women's magazine until the last two decades of the nineteenth century when it was supplanted by the more consumer-oriented *The Ladies Home Journal*. Although less didactic than *Godey's*, *The Ladies Home Journal* continued composition's extracurriculum. Editor Edward Bok's column in an 1890 issue of the *Ladies Home Journal*, for example, included admonitions to aspiring authors such as, "Whenever possible use the typewriter. If you have not a machine yourself, send your manuscript to some typewriting establishment and let it be copied. The expense is trifling, but the value to a manuscript can hardly be overestimated. . . . Avoid corrections, erasures and interlineations. Don't do on paper what you ought to do mentally. Again—and on this point I cannot be too emphatic—do not roll your manuscript. If there is one thing more than any other which irritates a busy, practical editor, it is a rolled manuscript" (12). An 1894 column by J. MacDonald Oxley includes directives for a "Mutual Research Club" whose essential feature is the preparation of papers on given subjects and the rule is that each member should have a paper ready for every meeting." Oxley continues, "The modus operandi is as follows: A subject having been selected, and a night of meeting decided upon, the members proceed to prepare their papers. These, at least ten days before the meeting, are sent in to the secretary who binds them together, adding several blank pages at the back. They are then circulated among the members, who pass them on from one to the other, having first entered any note or comment that may suggest itself on the blank pages provided for the purpose. Then at the night of the meeting each member reads his or her paper, and the reading concluded, a general discussion takes place" (16).

Although we can never know precisely how these publications of composition's extracurriculum were used, their number, multiple editions, and wide circulation document that they WERE used. We can speculate that at least some of them played a role in the many self-help groups that also constituted composition's extracurriculum. The egalitarian view of knowledge that characterized European settlers who arrived on this continent led them to organize for self improvement. Cotton Mather started a self-help group in Boston during the colonial period and in 1728, Ben Franklin joined with several friends to form a mutual improvement group that required each member to "once in three months produce and read an essay of his own writing on any subject he pleased" (Goodman 98). As the new republic took shape, many young men formed self-improvement groups. In Boston in 1833, for example, more than 1500 young men belonged to groups that gave composition a central place in their activities. Individuals wrote reports on local issues and these reports were read and discussed at meetings. The Lyceum, founded in 1826, had 3000 clubs in 15 states by 1836, and fostered self-improvement through writing, as did the Chautauqua Literary and Scientific Circle (CLSC), founded in 1878. This 1904 letter from a CLSC member in Syracuse, New York, demonstrates the extracurriculum of composition in action:

> The members are expected to write two papers upon subjects assigned to them by the president who selects carefully such as pertain strictly upon the year's study. This part of the program is thoroughly enjoyed as a special effort is put forth by each member to put only such thoughts upon paper which may prove helpful. An able critic from whose valuable assistance much benefit has been derived is usually in attendance unless professional duties demand her absence. (CLSC, 1904 Record Book)

Many self-help groups included a critic among the officers. Usually elected on the basis of skill in identifying errors, this critic assumed special responsibility for noting faults of syntax and diction in papers read before the group. The critic's commentary, combined with the general club discussion, provided members significant guidance for improving their prose. The Bay View Circles, an offshoot of Chautauqua, also followed an annual course of study which included writing papers on topics under discussion. In 1897, the *Bay View Magazine*, which published the curriculum for the Circles, included this reminder: "Work has a two-fold purpose: The first is to share with the circle the results of research; the other is the benefit the member receives in knowledge and in discipline of writing." It also offered this advice: "In preparing papers, never be content to give dry and detailed facts, but invest the subject with your own individuality" (7).

Spurned by many of these groups, middle class African Americans formed self-help associations of their own early in the nineteenth century. Typical of these, the New York Garrison Society, founded in 1834, concentrated its discussions on education and liberty and devoted its meetings to "singing, praying and the reading of original compositions" (Porter 568). Other African American expressions of composition's extracurriculum included the Philadelphia Association for Moral and Mental Improvement of the People of Color, The Young Men's Literary and Moral Reform Society of Pittsburgh and Vicinity, the New York African Clarkson Society, the Washington Convention Society, the Young Men's Lyceum and Debating Society of Detroit, and the Boston Philomathean Society. Many of these groups included both men and women, but African American women led the way in organizing single-sex forms of composition's extracurriculum by establishing ladies literary societies in Philadelphia, Washington, D.C., New York, Boston, Buffalo, and Rochester before 1836. William Lloyd Garrison, editor of *The Liberator*, addressed the Female and Literary Society of Philadelphia in 1832. When members of this society entered the meeting room, they placed their anonymous weekly compositions in a box from which they were later retrieved and criticized. Garrison was so impressed with the writing produced by The Female and Literary Society that he subsequently published several selections in *The Liberator*, thus instituting a tradition of African American clubwomen publishing their work.

Faced with the double challenge posed by their race and gender, African American clubwomen embraced writing's capacity to effect social and economic change, to enact their motto, "lifting as we climb." The Women's Era Club, founded in Boston by Josephine St. Pierre Ruffin in the latter part of the nineteenth century, issued a newspaper *The Woman's Era* in which clubwomen published their writing, and African American women appeared frequently in the pages of *The Liberator* as well as *The Guardian*, *The Conservator*, and *Voice of the Negro*. Prior to the Civil War, African Americans living in the south created another kind of extracurriculum in the form of secret schools. These schools—comprised of one person who could read and write and a group of individuals who wanted to learn—would meet during the night or on Sundays when slaves had a bit of free time. The mandate for graduates of these secret schools was to teach others. Kept secret because the punishment for trying to learn to read and write was severe beating or even death, these schools enabled a number of graduates to write their own passes to freedom. As Thomas Holt puts it, "Just as blacks maintained an invisible church, separate from the one that whites provided for them, they also maintained secret schools. These schools could be found in every major southern city and in countless rural communities and plantations. Their teachers were often barely literate themselves, but they passed on what little they knew to others in what one may call a chain letter of instruction" (94).

White women also contributed to composition's extracurriculum. Between 1839 and 1844, Margaret Fuller offered well-educated women subscription memberships to conversations designed to provide women an opportunity to reproduce their learning as men did, and although talk was the dominant mode, Fuller required participants to write. She explained: "At the next meeting I read these [writings] aloud and canvassed their adequacy without mentioning the names of the writers" (Hoffman 299). Clearly Fuller saw writing as a means of fostering thinking and she encouraged women to write as part of their self-education. For example, she advised one woman this way:

> I should think writing would be very good for you. A journal of your thoughts and analyses of your thoughts would teach you how to generalize and give firmness to your conclusions. Do not write down merely your impressions that things are beautiful or the reverse, but what they are and why they are. (Hoffman 302)

White women's clubs wielded considerable cultural force during the period between 1880 and 1920, and most clubs required members to write papers. The Saturday Morning Club of Boston, for example, stipulated in its bylaws: "Papers shall be read to the president (or to someone designated by her) at least a week before the discussion date" (Rudolf, SMC Yearbook). Since newer members wrote a higher percentage of the papers, this system of supervision guaranteed that less experienced writers received more direct instruction in this form of the extracurriculum. Elizabeth Moore et al.'s *English Composition for College Women* (1914) demonstrates the ubiquitous nature of club papers during this period by including a chapter on the club paper. In addition to sample papers and suggestions for topics, the chapter includes this description: "A club paper may be considered a popular exposition of some subject of general utility or interest" (67).

The extracurriculum of composition reached across class lines. One account of a working class women's club appears in Lucy Larcom's *A New England Girlhood*. Larcom, who worked in the textile mills of Lowell, Massachusetts, describes "The Improvement Circle" in which she and her co-workers met "for writing and discussion" (174). Papers read in the Improvement Circle were often published in "The Lowell Offering," a journal edited by a young woman who worked in the mills. Other forms of composition's extracurriculum appeared in the clubs organized in Settlements—such as Jane Addams' Hull House in Chicago, the Philadelphia Guild of Working Women, founded in 1893, and the Women's Educational and Industrial Union, founded in 1877. In these and other such associations, working class women wrote about their worlds and helped one another become better writers.

This brief account documents some of the publications and groups that sustained the extracurriculum of composition in the past. Current publications such as William Zinsser's *Writing Well: An Informal Guide to Writing* and magazines such as *The Writer's Market* have taken the place of *The Young Man's Companion* and columns in *Godey's Ladies Magazine,* but today's writers continue to separate pedagogy from the classroom pedagogue and seek advice from texts in the extracurriculum. The Garrison Society's "singing, praying, and reading of original compositions" and Margaret Fuller's conversational advice to women writers may be silenced, but groups such as the Tenderloin Women Writer's Workshop and the Lansing, Iowa, Writer's Workshop have taken up their task of bringing together individuals of varying classes, genders, and races who meet to read and respond to one another's writing. These ongoing and vital manifestations of the extracurriculum challenge us to take a wider view of composition. In suggesting a more inclusive perspective, I am not advocating that composition studies work to appropriate the extracurriculum or tear down classroom walls. Rather, I propose that we avoid an uncritical narrative of professionalization and acknowledge the extracurriculum as a legitimate and autonomous cultural formation that undertakes its own projects. Such an inclusive perspective can lead us to tap and listen to messages through the walls, to consider how we can learn from and contribute to composition's extracurriculum in our classes.

That word *class* suggests possibilities, since it designates at once a political/economic social group and the site where we in composition studies enact much of our working lives. Normal usage separates social class from academic class, but a look at the origins of the word suggests a close relationship between the two. The Latin word *Classis* referred to the most prosperous

Roman citizens, the ones who paid the highest taxes. In the second century Aulus Gellius used the name of these wealthy citizens to designate the best writers. As Richard Terdiman says, "This subterranean valorization of *economic power masquerading as quality* has stuck to 'class' ever since" (226). If we look at the relationships between economic power and attributions of quality in our writing classes, we cannot avoid noting that those with least economic power, often people of color, are most likely to be designated as "basic writers." Significantly, writing centers, which lie outside classes yet remain intimately related to them, offer rich opportunities for communicating with worlds outside the academy. Students often bring extracurricular texts such as self-sponsored poems, resumes, and personal letters to these liminal sites. By stepping outside our classes in both economic and academic terms, we can contribute to and learn from the extracurriculum as we reconsider relationships between economic power and attributions of quality in the writing of our student bodies.

The term *student body* suggests potential for creating another bond through the walls separating the classroom and the extracurriculum. Schooling implies a disciplining of the student's body. Nineteenth century images of classrooms with the instructor standing on a raised dais over students seated in desks bolted to the floor, of teachers caning students' bodies, and of students standing to recite have given way to the more familiar images of instructors seated near students, of moveable desks arranged in a semi-circle, and of students' fingers poised over a keyboard. But schooling in general and composition in particular still inscribes itself on students' bodies. The relaxed physical environment of the extracurriculum suggests that we rethink the relationship between physical and mental discipline. Why, for example, has the move toward whole language pedagogies among our colleagues in elementary schools been accompanied by the introduction of cushions, beanbag chairs, and carpets in classrooms? How do we see the correlation between whole language—a pedagogy that unites reading and writing while affirming students' inherent language abilities—and a blurring of domestic and academic scenes? This blurring suggests new ways of looking at the relation of public and private life, even of eliding distinctions between the two. It also recalls the material conditions of writing. While few of us are concerned with providing our students recipes for making red ink or instructing them in ways to prevent it from molding or freezing, we do confront such complex material questions as how to provide equality of access to computers for word processing. Reconsidering the relations between domestic and classroom economies may help us develop creative responses to the material constraints of writing. Thinking along these lines we would do well to recall Kenneth Burke's image of intellectual history as a parlor where participants enter and leave the ongoing conversation. This domestic/academic image resonates with feminist explorations of the trajectories of public and private.

In urging that we look again at the relationship between domestic and academic scenes, I am emphatically not suggesting that we move away from professionalism in our field. We know too well the history of the Harvard

Reports issued at the turn of the century. These reports, which had an enormously negative impact on composition studies, demonstrate what can happen when questions about composition are answered by non-professionals: The most superficial aspects of writing receive the greatest attention, and the more complicated and important questions remain unasked and unanswered. We who teach composition, and particularly we who claim membership in CCCC, have, in recent years, given considerable energy to professionalism. We have asserted that writing instructors have or require specialized training and that they deserve the respectability born of educated knowledge. I applaud these efforts, particularly where they have served to improve the working conditions of writing teachers. But I'd like to suggest that we scrutinize the culture of professionalism. For instance, professionalism incorporates both material and ideological functions. Its economic function creates a link between education and the marketplace by insisting, for example, that composition teachers ought to be paid adequately because they possess special training. Embracing this economic function implicates us in an ideology that justifies inequality of status and closure of access. Composition's extracurriculum can remind us of the need for increased access in writing instruction. In response we can strengthen our vigilance against reductive forms of assessment and against instructional practices and curricular plans that make writing a barrier to be overcome rather than an activity to be engaged in. We can also learn to value the amateur. The culture of professionalism, with its emphasis on specialization, abhors amateurism, but composition's extracurriculum shows the importance of learning from amateurs. After all, as the Latin root *amatus* reminds us, members of the Tenderloin Women's Writing Workshop or the Lansing, Iowa, Writers Workshop write for *love*.

An unswerving concentration on professionalism can also blind us to the power relations in our classrooms. One of the clearest messages of the extracurriculum concerns *power*. As Frederick Rudolph noted, the extracurriculum of the nineteenth century vested students with power in curriculum decisions. We see that power acknowledged (and usurped) today as student film societies become departments of and courses in film studies. In a related way composition studies can draw upon and contribute to circulations of power in its extracurriculum. Our incorporation of the workshop practices that originated in student literary societies exemplifies one way. Another is suggested by a sketch Mary TallMountain read at the Tenderloin Women Writers Workshop. This sketch portrays a fellow Indian who loses his identity and ultimately his life in San Francisco:

> I watched that man for six months in the line at St. Anthony's shelter. I watched him and watched him and watched him. I could see beyond the dirt and all the things holding him back. He was a brave man to me. I felt he had come to the end of his way. The next thing he knew he was riding through the prairies on his horse. And the filthy street changed into the long grass in a strangely familiar valley and Bilijohn was riding. Riding. He didn't hear the high keening screech of brakes, didn't see the lithe swerve of the shining town car. He heard only a distant call: Bily! Bily

John! and his own answering holler. Yeah, I'm coming as fast as I can!
He didn't feel the massy jolt as the sharp hood scooped him skyward,
his eyes still measuring the weeping clouds. The half-empty, gray-green
bottle arced into the gutter and tumbled down the torrent of flotsam, the
Thunderbird belching out of it. Indian Bilijohn galloped on through the
long amber grass, heels pummeling the bright flanks. (Heller, "Writers"
77–78)

Mary TallMountain demonstrates the power of representing one's own community, in insisting on Bilijohn's dignity and humanity against mainstream
accounts of poverty and alcoholism among Native Americans, she exemplifies the point made by a good deal of fashionable critical discourse: the importance of considering who will represent whom in what terms and in what
language. Like medical doctors who learn from nutritionists, shamans, and
artists, without compromising their professional status, we can benefit from
examining how the extracurriculum confers authority for representation and
how we might extend that authority in our classes. Our students would benefit if we learned to see them as individuals who seek to write, not be written
about, who seek to publish, not be published about, who seek to theorize, not
be theorized about. Ultimately, however, we in composition studies would
benefit from this shift because, as Susan Miller reminds us, "placing those
who teach composition in the role of hired mother/maid has a great deal to
do with the presexual, preeconomic, prepolitical subjectivity imposed on
composition *students*" (192). By helping to change the subjectivities of our students, we open the possibility of enhancing our own (professional) positions.

The fact that sketches like Mary TallMountain's are read regularly at the
Tenderloin Women's Writing Workshop speaks to the issue of *performance* in
the extracurriculum. Here, as Maria Rand says, "You gotta get rejected and
get applause." Clubs that mandated oral readings of papers, the office of the
critic who commented on syntax and diction in self-help groups, the presumption of the editor of *The Ladies Home Journal* that writers would be sending their manuscripts, rolled or not, to busy editors—all of these items from
the history of composition's extracurriculum show the direct relationship
between writing and performance. Like the British working class balladeer of
the mid-nineteenth century who exchanged original compositions for a pint
of ale, writers in the extracurriculum demonstrate how writing effects changes,
both tangible and intangible. Thinking of writing as performance reminds us
that it occupies an uncertain space between the concrete and the symbolic.
This might prompt us to reconsider performance in our own teaching and
research. As Porter Perrin shows, college composition before 1750 in this
country centered on the declamation, a pedagogical practice which required
students to read aloud to an audience compositions they had previously written. Pedagogies of performance like these reinforce writing's liminal status
between materiality and idea and demonstrate it as "a centered space from
which we do not exit in the same form" (Benston 435).

The transformative quality of writing's performance speaks to the cultural work it accomplishes. Within classroom walls, composition frequently

serves a gatekeeping function by providing an initiation rite that determines whether newcomers can master the practices and perspectives of academic discourse. Those who do not succeed in composition classes rarely last long in higher education. For a significant number of those who survive this initiation, alienation results. These are students who succeed in composition by distancing themselves from persons and experiences important in their everyday lives. Composition thus accomplishes the cultural work of producing autonomous individuals willing to adopt the language and perspectives of others. Composition's extracurriculum frequently serves the opposite function by strengthening ties with the community. In his study of the development of schooled literacy among the British working class of the 19th century, David Vincent observes that, "Composition was eventually admitted to the official curriculum in 1871, but as a means of exploiting the Penny Post, not of imitating penny dreadfuls" (218). Penny dreadfuls, episodic narratives that rely strongly on the songs and melodramatic tales common among working-class people, were held in low regard by school instructors who saw composition as a means of copying the sentences of others. Yet, as Vincent shows, working-class children educated in these schools were as likely to use their skills to write penny dreadfuls as letters for the penny post. Similarly, when our own students enter the extracurriculum, they frequently write their own versions of penny dreadfuls. That is, the form and content of what they write reflects their connections with their own communities. For women of the nineteenth century the genre of club paper represented one such connection, and the extracurricular selections that students bring to our writing centers manifest another. When persons in groups such as the Tenderloin Women's Writing Workshop and the Lansing, Iowa, Writers' Workshop write about people they know, about the homeless, about farming, composition's extracurriculum accomplishes the cultural work of affirming and strengthening their connections with their own communities.

These communities outside our classroom walls have, if books on the best-seller list in recent years provide any indication, demonstrated considerable dissatisfaction with much of what transpires in higher education. While one reasonable response is to counter with books telling the story from our side of the classroom wall, we run the risk of talking past those on the other side, of constructing walls as divisions rather than means of communicating. A more productive alternative involves considering our own roles as agents within the culture that encompasses the communities on both sides of the classroom wall.

This consideration implies rethinking the narratives we construct about composition studies. Instead of a historiography based exclusively on textbooks used in schools and colleges, on the careers and works of prominent teachers and scholars, on the curricular decisions made by universities and on texts produced by students, we can consider the various sites in which the extracurriculum has been enacted, the local circumstances that supported its development, the material artifacts employed by its practitioners, and the cultural work it accomplished. This expanded historical account will attend to the New York Garrison Club along with Porter Perrin's discussion of the teaching of rhetoric in the American college before 1750. It will recognize that a group of unschooled young men who met on Friday evenings to share and respond to one another's writing contributes to the story of composition as surely as does an examination of textbooks written by Fred Newton Scott. It will look to *Godey's Magazine* as well as Hugh Blair's *Lectures on Rhetoric and Belle Lettres* for information on how writers of another age learned their craft.

While history offers a source of inspiration for the future, its vision cannot be realized without cultural work in the present. As we consider our own roles of social agency we can insist more firmly on the democracy of writing and the need to enact pedagogies that permit connections and communication with the communities outside classroom walls. This does not mean appropriating the extracurriculum but merely assigning it a more prominent status in our discourses. Whether or not we rise to this challenge, composition's extracurriculum will persist and our students can join it as soon as they step outside our classroom walls and enter what Tillie Olson calls "all the life that happens outside of us, beyond us." We may discipline their bodies with school desks and hand positions for keyboarding, but they write outside and beyond us in an extracurriculum of their own making. They may gather in rented rooms in the Tenderloin, around kitchen tables in Lansing, Iowa, or in a myriad of other places to write their worlds. The question remains whether we will use classroom walls as instruments of separation or communication.

Acknowledgments: An earlier version of this article was presented at the 1992 Penn State Rhetoric Conference, and many conference participants helped me think toward revisions. In particular, Stephen Mailloux, Deborah Minter, Jack Selzer, and Nancy Shapiro offered very useful comments. Members of my writing group—Arnetha Ball, Deborah Keller-Cohen, Rosina Lippi-Green, Pamela Moss, and Annemarie Palincsar—urged me through multiple revisions, and Karen Burke-Lefevre provided a very timely and generous reading when I needed it most. I thank them all.

NOTES

1. I am grateful to Carol Heller for sharing with me her extensive work with and ideas about the Tenderloin Women's Writing Workshop.
2. I wish to thank Deborah Keller-Cohen for introducing me to these early American texts.

WORKS CITED

Applebee, Arthur. *Tradition and Reform in the Teaching of English.* Urbana: NCTE, 1974.
Bentson, Kimberly W. "Being There: Performance as Mise-en-Scène, Abscene, Obscene and Other Scene." *PMLA* 107 (1992): 434–449.
Bok, Edward. "Editor's Column." *Ladies Home Journal* 7 (1890): 12.
Chautauqua Literary and Scientific Circle Record Book, CLSC Clubhouse, Chautauqua, New York, 1904 (unpaged).
"Column." *Bay View Magazine* 5.2 (1897): 6.
Connors, Robert, Lisa Ede, and Andrea Lunsford. *Essays on Classical Rhetoric and Modern Discourse.* Carbondale: Southern Illinois UP, 1984.
Fisher, George. *The American Instructor: Or, Young Man's Best Companion.* Philadelphia: Franklin and Hall, 1748.

Freedman, Jonathan. "Beyond the Usual Suspects: Theorizing the Middlebrow." Unpublished paper, U of Michigan, 1993.

Goodman, Nathan, Ed. *A Benjamin Franklin Reader*. New York: Crowell, 1945.

Graff, Gerald. *Professing Literature: An Institutional History*. Chicago: U of Chicago P, 1987.

Hale, Sarah Josepha. "Editor's Column." *Godey's Ladies Magazine* 16 (1838): 191.

Heath, Shirley Brice. "Toward an Ethnohistory of Writing in American Education." *Writing: The Nature, Development and Teaching of Written Communication*. Ed. Marcia Farr Whiteman. Hillsdale, NJ: Lawrence Erlbaum, 1981.

Heller, Carol Elizabeth. "Writers of the Tenderloin." Unpublished essay. U of California, Berkeley, 1987.

———. "The Multiple Functions of the Tenderloin Women's Writing Workshop: Community in the Making." Diss. U of California, Berkeley, 1992.

———. *Until We Are All Strong Together: Women Writers in the Tenderloin*. New York: Teacher College Press, 1997.

Hoffman, Nicole Tonkovich. "Scribbling, Writing, Author(iz)ing Nineteenth Century Women Writers." Diss. U of Utah, 1990.

Holt, Thomas. " 'Knowledge Is Power': The Black Struggle for Literacy." *The Right to Literacy*. Eds. Andrea A. Lunsford, Helene Moglen, and James Slevin. New York, MLA, 1990. 91–102.

Hubbard, Ruth. Notes from the Underground: Unofficial Literacy in One Sixth Grade." *Anthropology and Education Quarterly* 20 (1989): 291–307.

Kitzhaber, Albert Raymond. "Rhetoric in American Colleges, 1850–1900." Diss. U of Washington, 1953.

Larcom, Lucy. *A New England Girlhood*. Boston: Houghton, 1889.

Miller, Susan. *Textual Carnivals: The Politics of Composition*. Carbondale: Southern Illinois UP, 1991.

Moore, Elizabeth, Dora Gilbert Tompkins, and Mildred MacLean. *English Composition for College Women*. New York: Macmillan, 1914.

Oxley, J. MacDonald. "Column." *Ladies Home Journal* 9 (1894): 16.

Perrin, Porter Gale. "The Teaching of Rhetoric in the American Colleges before 1750." Diss. U of Chicago, 1936.

Porter, Dorothy B. "The Organized Educational Activities of Negro Literary Societies, 1828–1846." *The Journal of Negro Education* 5 (1936): 555–576.

Rudolph, Frederick. *American College and University: A History*. New York: Vintage, 1962.

———. Saturday Morning Club Yearbook, 1898, Schlesinger Library, Cambridge, MA.

Terdiman, Richard. "Is There Class in This Class?" *The New Historicism*. Ed. H. Aram Veeser. New York: Routledge, 1989.

Vincent, David. *Literacy and Popular Culture: England 1750–1914*. Cambridge: Cambridge UP, 1989.

Wagner, Jay P. "Alamakee Farmers Cultivate Writing Habits." *Des Moines Register* 12 March 1991.

———. "Writers in Overalls." *The Washington Post*. 2 January 1993.

Wolf, Robert. *Free River Press Newsletter* 1. (January, 1993): 1.

———, ed. *Voices from the Land*. Lansing, Iowa: Free River Press, 1992.

3

The Word on the Street: Public Discourse in a Culture of Disconnect

DIANA GEORGE

In 1993 Anne Gere identified what she called the "extracurriculum" of composition, the self-sponsored writing among ordinary people who "meet in living rooms, nursing homes, community centers, churches, shelters for the homeless, around kitchen tables, and in rented rooms to write down their worlds" (p. 35 in this volume). In that CCCC address, Gere proposed that "we listen to the signals that come through the walls of our classrooms from the world outside" (p. 35)—in effect suggesting that composition had yet to understand how writing is used and is useful in everyday life. Gere's talk has certainly been a touchstone for literacy scholars for nearly a decade now, and, yet, until recently we've seen little classroom material that actually takes very seriously that extracurriculum of composition.[1]

Of course, it is not new to speak of writing in terms of local or political motivation. In one of what she calls her "historical and polemical" essays on composition in the university, Sharon Crowley asks us to recall the lessons of ancient rhetoric, "whose proponents were unabashedly interested in influencing the course of cultural and political events. Teachers of ancient rhetorics," writes Crowley, "assumed that people compose only when they are moved by some civic exigency. Unlike the composing principles taught in current-traditional pedagogy (and in some versions of process pedagogy) . . . the composing principles taught in ancient rhetorical theories were fully situated in public occasions that required intervention or at any rate stimulated a composer's desire to intervene" (263).

We have often, in teaching writing, reminded students that what they write and how they present it has much to do with the reason for writing, the moment in time, the audience they have in mind, the material circumstances surrounding the writing, and more. And yet, we have only begun to investigate how the circumstance—what John Trimbur identifies as the "call to write"—works itself out beyond the walls of our classrooms. Though it is true that popular literacy studies are becoming more and more crucial to the

From *Reflections* 2.2 (2002): 5–18.

work we do in composition, I would argue that this field of study has much yet to learn about how writing/how composing functions in response to civic exigency. Such knowledge might actually lead us to accomplish the one thing we have argued for years our composition and communication classrooms ought to do: prepare students to be active participants in a democracy.

If anyone has been moved by civic exigency to a "call to write," certainly the women and men I describe below have. In what follows, I want to examine that "call"—that motivation—and set the writing that follows from it in the larger context of how communication does function for active participants in the politics of a nation.

When I began this work over two years ago, my thought was to locate the places in everyday life where anything like what we might call local activism is going on. I wanted to be able to explain the role writing/composing plays in the work of nonprofit and independent groups—local coalitions for the homeless, women's shelters, Catholic Worker houses, soup kitchens, environmental groups, local land trust groups, and others that are common throughout the country.

In organizing and in carrying out the activities of the organization, these individuals must rely on some means of communication—usually a newsletter, a small newspaper, brochures, signs, banners, posters, public service announcements, and, more recently, web sites—to get the word out, raise funds, and build memberships or foster coalitions. Such groups are filled with "active participants" in this democracy. Many of them do not think of themselves as writers but found themselves at a moment when writing was needed if the organization was to survive.

I started in a very limited way: For several months I read the newsletters and newspapers that came to my house published by about a dozen or so of these groups from across the country—*Guadalupe*, the newsletter for Casa Maria, a Catholic Worker house in Tucson as well as newsletters and newspapers from Catholic Worker houses in Houston, San Antonio, New York, Milwaukee, Worcester, and Minneapolis; *Freedomways*, *New Hope House* newsletter, *Gatherings*, and other prison ministry newsletters in the south; publications like *Hospitality* and *Sojourners* which are papers and magazines written for and about street people and soup kitchens in Atlanta, Washington, D.C., and rural Georgia. From my own community, I examined *Off the Beaten Path*, a newsletter from the Barbara Kettle Gundlach Shelter Home for Abused Women; the newsletter of the Copper Country Peace Alliance; newsletters from local environmental and land trust groups, and more.

Like David Barton and Mary Hamilton who in *Local Literacies* write of their attempts to uncover and document "everyday literacies which are often unrecognized in dominant discourses about literacy" (5), my aim has been to uncover the literacy practices of marginalized groups—the small voices that, now and then, lead to big action. To do that, I had to locate the people who actually produce these publications and learn what their call/their motivation has been, what constraints they face, how their publication is produced and circulated, to and on behalf of whom they are writing, how they locate their audience, and how they see themselves or their organization fitting into the larger landscape of social or civic action, and—most important for this paper—how (or, indeed, *if*) they identify themselves as writers.

Mine is a large project that is ongoing, but I propose here to tell the story of one community and one newsletter which led me to the stories of four communities and the people who work in and write for them.

> My interview with **Ed Weir** and his story of the beginnings of *New Hope House*, a hospitality house in rural Georgia for families of prisoners on death row, led me to interview—
>
> **Murphy Davis** who with her husband Ed Loring began the *Open Door Community* in Atlanta and its paper *Hospitality*. And, those interviews and the history of *The Open Door* led me to—
>
> **Hannah Loring-Davis**, then a student at Guilford College in North Carolina, who helped found the independent student paper *The Student Activist* and to—
>
> **Joe Roos**, a co-founder with Jim Wallis of the Sojourner Community in Washington, D.C., and *Sojourner Magazine*. These all led me back inevitably to—
>
> The life of **Dorothy Day** and the beginnings of the Catholic Worker Movement and especially the newspaper *The Catholic Worker* which led to—
>
> The origins of *The Nation Magazine* and the influence, on Day, of papers like *The Masses* and *The Daily Worker*—all of which might very well seem a far remove from the writing classroom or even from literacy studies, in general, but I don't believe so.

Begging the reader's patience, then, I begin.

IT ALL CONNECTS

In that little trail of people and papers and organizations, it must be clear that one of the first things I discovered was something very simple: These cheaply produced, often unprofessional looking papers and newsletters defy what some have called the Culture of Disconnect. They do not exist in a vacuum. They reject the fragmentation many of us experience as or at least suspect is characteristic of life in the 21st century. Moreover, they actually do effect change, on the local level and beyond, in the lives of the people they work with and for.

I won't, however, rest too long here in what might be taken for foolish optimism. In her discussion of writing and the public sphere, Susan Wells reminds us that the relations of students and teachers to the public are marked by what she calls a "simultaneous sense of exclusion and attraction." There is a suggestion in these words that many students and their teachers want to engage but don't believe there really is a way to enter such a large and faceless debate, if, indeed, there even is a debate at all. That alienation is especially true in the world of large news and publishing conglomerates, of CNN and NBC and MSNBC; of Time/Warner and AOL and Disney and *US Magazine* and ABC[2] and more. That doesn't leave most of us much of a voice, does it?

Perhaps the answer to this question lies in how we identify our audience and what we expect from our part of the conversation. Wells writes, "I have never known a writer, student or teacher, who wanted a smaller audience, or a narrower readership; I have never known a writer who felt unproblematically at home in the discursive forms of broad political or social address" (332–333). I would say that perhaps Wells has hit on just the problem with the way we too often approach political or social address.

In the work I describe below, I have, in fact, known writers who wanted a smaller audience, a narrower readership. And, I encounter these writers all of the time in the small, activist publications I carry with me for this work. Here, for example, is how Dorothy Day describes the moments of the first issue of *The Catholic Worker*:

> I had sent my copy to the printer—news accounts of the exploitation of Negroes in the South, and the plight of the sharecroppers; child labor in our own neighborhood; some recent evictions; a local strike over wages and hours; pleas for better home relief, and so on—and we were waiting for proofs.
>
> When they came we cut them out and started making a dummy, pasting them up on the eight pages of a tabloid the size of *The Nation*, writing headlines, and experimenting with different kinds of type. Peter looked over what I had written as it came back from the printer. I could see that, far from being happy about it, he was becoming more and more disturbed. One day, while looking over some fresh proofs, he shook his head. His expression was one of great sadness. "It's everyone's paper," he said. I was pleased. I thought that was what we both wanted. "And everyone's paper is no one's paper," he added with a sigh. (Loaves 17)

Peter Maurin believed that a newspaper could bring about what he called "clarification of thought"—the first step in moving others to action. "Men," he told her—this was 1933—"must think before they can act. They must study" (Day, *Loaves* 7). He was calling for a paper that could and would be radical. A newspaper that is for everyone is a newspaper that speaks to no one and, thus, moves no one to action. What Maurin was after was a public voice speaking to those who would listen and be moved to act. This is very different from the faceless, nameless public we too often set up in our classrooms.

Like *The Catholic Worker*, none of the newsletters and newspapers that constitute my study can be called "everyone's" paper. They speak to special interest groups on unpopular topics and take radical positions. To be quite honest, they ask their readers to do the impossible:

End the death penalty.

Feed, clothe, and house ALL the poor.

Stop abuse.

End violence.

End poverty.

In other words, they are groups calling for not just radical but outrageous action. Outrageous action isn't a subject for broad audience appeal.

As Barton and Hamilton remind us, literacy practices "are shaped by social rules which regulate the use and distribution of texts, prescribing who may produce them and have access to them" (7). That, of course, is especially true for publications that circulate as newsletters and newspapers. We know what such publications look like and from looks alone can immediately identify one as mainstream or not. Many of the publications I examined are printed primarily on the most inexpensive paper available and sport somewhat amateurish graphics though the arguments presented within are often quite complicated and—for any mainstream publication—quite long. *Hospitality*, for example, often follows the example of *The Catholic Worker* and features articles running three, even four tabloid-sized pages long suggesting that the writers do expect their readers to want more, not less, information.

More to the point, though the publications I am talking about represent alternative, even radical voices, they are also produced in the very ordinary context of the newsletter, the small tabloid or newspaper, the political speech, the sermon, the witness, the broad sheet, and the public appeal. Notice, for example, that when Dorothy Day describes laying out the first issue of *The Catholic Worker*, she started making a dummy, pasting it up on "a tabloid the size of *The Nation*" (17).

Identifying with a publication like *The Nation* is not accidental. First of all, Day's own background was with small, alternative, leftist newspapers. Her brother worked for the dime-novel sized labor paper, *The Day Book*, a publication that introduced her to Eugene Debs and the IWW and to both national and international labor politics. Day's own first job was with the Socialist paper *The Call*. In her autobiography, *The Long Loneliness*, Day writes of absorbing a radicalism from *The Day Book* and from the words of Jack London, Upton Sinclair, and other socialist writers she encountered through these small papers and magazines (41).

Her model, *The Nation*, was a magazine begun in 1865 at a time when the press was being pulled by serious factions emerging from the Civil War and Reconstruction. In their prospectus, the founders wrote that one main object of this new magazine was to be "the discussion of the topics of the day, and, above all, of legal, economical, and constitutional questions, with greater accuracy and moderation than are now to be found in the daily press" (Vanden Heuvel 1). At least one stated motivation for its founding, then, was to set the record straight.

Setting the record straight is, in fact, what all of the people I interviewed identified as one primary motivator as they set themselves to the task of creating a paper. Ed Weir of New Hope House and Murphy Davis of The Open Door both see their publications as offering an alternative view—setting the record straight. Murphy, in particular, pointed to the recent Time/Warner-AOL acquisition to say that there was little out there that was not coming from essentially the same source—the same people own most of the mainstream press. There is very little chance out there, she said, for alternative voices.

MOTIVATION—THE CALL

Ed

Ed and Mary Ruth Weir run New Hope House, a hospitality house for families of prisoners on Georgia's death row. They are exceptionally quiet people who get by on almost nothing. New Hope House—and the Weirs' livelihood—is supported by non-tax-deductible contributions. In other words, they must depend on folks who are more interested in the work of New Hope House than in finding a good place for a tax deduction. Ed and Mary Ruth attend trials, sit with the families of the accused, help file appeals if it is necessary, visit death row prisoners, and get the word out that there is opposition in Georgia to the death penalty.

Their newsletter, published from Possum Trot Road, is as unassuming as a newsletter can get, and just looking at it readers might not imagine that it has much of an effect on many people at all. Yet this little publication is crucial in creating a network of support for the anti-death penalty movement in Georgia.

In rural Georgia, you don't find many people who are outspokenly against the death penalty in a way, at least, that might move them to take action, form a community, spend time demonstrating, that sort of thing. So, the newsletter, according to Ed, helps unite a network of friends who watch the courts for death penalty trials, let Ed and Mary Ruth know what's going on, get in touch with families of the accused, visit prisoners, and support New Hope House.

According to Ed, the newsletter had to be written for the most basic of reasons:

To raise money for New Hope House.

To "keep the subject in the minds of the people."

To maintain the network of people (especially Georgians) working against the death penalty.

To inform supporters on current events relating to death penalty trials and legislation.

The newsletter often cannot, however, do what Ed initially wanted it to do: It can't tell the stories of the prisoners and their families because drawing too much attention to one prisoner is likely to put that prisoner at risk—even likely to move up an execution date. So, he has to write *about* them, not name them, but give his readers enough to understand the case.[3]

It's a pretty tricky rhetorical situation, especially for someone who claims he never saw himself, really, as a writer and can't remember ever taking a writing class—that at Vanderbilt he majored in "getting out."

And, yet, writing was a part of what, even as a child, Ed recognized as something adults did. His grandfather wrote a column for the local paper in Douglas, Georgia, where Ed grew up, and even as he claimed not to be a writer at all, he told the story of how he and a friend stumbled onto an old printing press and started making up a neighborhood paper—with neighbor

FIGURE 3–1   New Hope House Newsletter from Possum Trot Road, by Ed Weir

SUPPORT FOR PEOPLE

ON GEORGIA'S DEATH ROW,

THEIR FAMILY AND FRIENDS

May 1998

THE SHORT STORY OF A VICTIM'S FAMILY

Marianna, the mother of Joe, is sitting between her sisters and one brother-in-law on one side and a friend Beth on the other side. They are on the front row directly behind Joe and his two lawyers sitting at the defense table. Marianna's church friends are sitting on the row behind. Ed and John Cole-Vodicka sit on the next row. The whispers from the baliffs tell us the jury has decided a punishment of either the death sentence or life without parole. Marianna is a short, sturdy woman but not overweight. She wears skirts to the ankles that slightly spread out rather than cling tightly. Her hair is cut short. Marianna's face is nice to see. Except that she looks worn and weary. Over the past eight days she has often left the courtroom to sob. She has probably cried many times over the past four years since Joe was arrested. Beth is a contrast in appearance - tall, slender, longish blond hair, in a sports jacket, and loose fitting long pants.

As we wait for the judge to begin, Beth is smiling and talking in Marianna's ear. Beth turns and mouths some words to Ed which he doesn't understand. The two get up and meet in the aisle. Beth asks "This is a good sign that the jury has taken only an hour?" "Usually it is not." Ed has heard very little in the trial to think that Joe will not get the death penalty.

It is easier for 12 people to all agree to execute a person who just 24 hours ago they decided had committed murder than it is to spare one's life without any possibility of parole.

The judge begins by instructing everyone not to display any signs of emotion when the verdict is read. How absurd! Not to cry out when a mother is told that her child will be strapped in a chair with electrodes attached to head and legs and then thousands of volts will be pounded into the body to kill. Even absurd to think victims' families who have been yearning for a justice of death wouldn't sob if the jury decided life without parole.

The judge reads the jury verdict form: "We the jury sentence the defendant Joe Smith to DEATH." The judge, in a rare display of voice inflection, maybe emotion, maybe only for show, raises his voice and blurts out the word DEATH.

(Source: Ed Weir/New Hope House)

news and recipes and jokes and stories. The two rode around town on their bikes distributing their paper to the neighbors.

Ed's story reminded me of my brothers and sisters and I who played "school" with boxes for desks, "mass" with pressed white bread for the communion host, and "store" with empty cans and boxes from the kitchen—games we created to mimic adults. Ed was becoming his grandfather as he wrote and printed the daily news, and so when it came time to write a newsletter of his own—one with much more social and political significance than the one of childhood games—he already knew where to begin.

Murphy Davis

Ed Weir knows Murphy Davis because New Hope House began out of The Open Door's prison ministry program. Murphy had been a death penalty opponent for many years even before the creation of the Open Door Community. *Hospitality*—the newsletter from The Open Door—covers prison issues as well as the politics of homelessness. Members of The Open Door participate in vigils before executions, go to trials, visit prisoners and their families, and serve on the Board of New Hope House. They are part of the network kept alive partially through Ed Weir's little newsletter.

Murphy is an ordained Presbyterian minister who says she must have taken the required writing courses in college though she doesn't remember them. She took sermon writing, of course, but dismissed it as a writing course—though much of the quality of a well-wrought sermon does come through in her writing. She writes for and helps to edit *Hospitality*, a newspaper that started as a newsletter. The newsletter, like New Hope House's newsletter, was started because it had to be:

To raise money.

To recruit volunteers.

To notify the community.

When Murphy told of changing from a newsletter format to a small newspaper, she had in mind "something like *The Catholic Worker*." The influence extends beyond Dorothy Day, however. Murphy and her husband Ed Loring had also been reading a radical Christian paper called *The Post-American* founded by Joe Roos and Jim Wais. The *Post-American*, it turns out, was the precursor to *Sojourners* magazine and the Sojourners Community in Washington, D.C.

Joe Roos and Jim Wallis

Joe Roos, a co-founder with Jim Wallis of the Sojourners Community, knows Murphy Davis and Ed Loring. He remembers their daughter Hannah Loring-Davis as a toddler, now the co-founder of her own independent paper at Guilford College. He also knows Ed Weir and the work of New Hope House.

In a history of *Sojourners*, co-founder Jim Wallis describes the exigency which moved him, with Joe Roos and others, to begin a paper:

We knew there had to be other people who were feeling the same things we were. . . . I have sometimes likened the publication of the *Post-American* to the raising of a flagpole. Many people on the ground, at the grass roots, were longing for an alternative to the narrow versions of Christian faith they were experiencing in their churches, but they didn't know one another. (15)

In changing the paper *Post-American* to the magazine *Sojourners*, Wallis and Roos were actually making a commitment to community and not simply to getting the word out to like-minded people. Wallis describes it this way:

> The relationship between the members of our little group was the foun-
> dation for the publication of the magazine. . . . The magazine gave a
> focus to our relationship, a task around which we gathered, and the ex-
> citement of new ideas soon became the catalyst for thoughts about a
> community. (94)

And, this actually returns us to Dorothy Day and Peter Maurin and *The Catholic Worker*.

Jim Wallis says that "the number of people touched by Dorothy Day is beyond counting. This evangelical boy from the Midwest was one" (162). Peter
Gathje's history of the Open Door Community says something of the same for
Murphy Davis and Ed Loring: In their attempts to find direction for their own
work with the homeless, they traveled to Mary House in New York. On the
train home, Ed read Day's autobiography *The Long Loneliness*. Gathje writes
that "as he and Murphy shared their reading . . . they began to see what this
call of hospitality would require of them" (28).

It is no accident, then, that Murphy had "something like *The Catholic
Worker*" in mind when she created *Hospitality*, and it is no accident that Jim
Wallis experienced real pride when someone told him that Sojourners Com-
munity was like "a Protestant *Catholic Worker*" (163).

CONCLUSION

I began my observations by saying that I learned something very simple: that
these little newsletters and cheaply printed papers (*The Catholic Worker* still
sells for one cent) defy the Culture of Disconnect. They might look unimpor-
tant, but they apparently do extremely important work both within and outside the organizations that produce them. They connect people and ideas and
they do have an effect on the ways people live their lives. That connection is,
in fact, the primary motivation of these writers.

Perhaps the problem with teaching public discourse is not so much that,
as Wells notices, our advice to students is too abstract/the audience we imagine too faceless—though that is certainly a problem. Perhaps the real problem
is that too many believe that small changes/small movements don't really
mean much. They don't really change much.

And, yet, if I look at an organization like Sojourners or Catholic Worker
Houses or New Hope House, it is very clear to me that one of the few ways
most of us even have access to alternative views is through these networks
of small newsletters and newspapers that reach out to like-minded readers.
Certainly, the only way the American public is likely to know that there is
poverty in this country—unless they are experiencing it themselves—is
through the people working with the impoverished.

More to the point, it is when we open our classrooms to communication
of all sorts—not just to E. B. White (though he wrote beautifully) or to academic cultural critique (though much of it is timely and of great interest) and,
especially, not just to *Time, Newsweek*, and *US News and World Report*—that we
begin to understand the role communication plays in the lives of active
participants in this democracy.

FIGURE 3–2   *The Student Activist*, Edited by Second Generation Activist
Hannah Loring-Davis

The
Student Activist

Issue No. 5   Feb. 28, 2000

INSIDE

Millicent Brown discusses African American History and Activism

UNAM Student Movement: Getting the Truth Out

The Student Activist is a colaborative effort of Guilford College students. It is our goal to highlight and address issues important to social justice - specifically those that have been overlooked and underrepresented in mainstream America. We strive to further both indivual and group determination at Guilford and in the wider community.

Editorial Board:
Simon Kress: 316-3889
Hannah Loring-Davis: 316-3882
Johnnie Parker: 316-3272
Scott Pryor: 316-3869
Chris Roose: 316-3879
Amy Roose: 316-3873
Devender Sellars: 316-3863
Leonora Tisdale: 316-3134
studentactivist @mail.com
The Student Activist is solely responsible for its content.

Justice for Daryl Howerton Forces Racial Justice to Forefront

by Matthew Spencer

Justice for the already deceased Daryl Howerton means working to educate ourselves and others in order to obtain justice in the present, especially to end the police brutality whose victims are poor and overwhelmingly African-American, Latino, and other people of color. On September 8, 1994, Daryl Howerton, a 19-year old black male, was the subject of a call to 911. He had been seen cutting up meat and feeding it to guard dogs behind a tire store in Greensboro. Daryl was asked to leave. When he did not a tire store employee called 911. The employee told the dispatcher that, "a man is eating with the dogs, he needs help, and someone should come and take him to the hospital."

An ambulance was not sent. Instead, the police were notified of a "suspicious person" by the dispatcher, and a squad car manned by Charles Fletcher and trainee Jose Blanco was sent out. Meanwhile, Daryl had removed all of his clothing except for a toboggan and sunglasses. When the police arrived on the scene he was standing naked in front of a barbershop holding a steak knife in his hand. Disregarding Greensboro Police Department procedure to try and defuse a potentially dangerous situation, the two officers immediately engaged the situation by yelling, "Stop!" and "Drop the knife!" The next procedure that was disregarded cost Daryl his life and wounded two bystanders.

Greensboro Police Department procedure requires officers to clear the area of bystanders before the use of deadly force. This was not done, and within 42 seconds of arriving on the scene, Daryl had been shot six times, including once in the back. Trainee Blanco fired the first shot. Eyewitnesses say that Daryl was face down on the ground when the last two shots entered his body. Daryl was dead within an hour.

Daryl's mother, Brenda Howerton, filed a wrongful death suit against the two officers. However, on October 27, 1998, both officers were acquitted of using excessive force or violating Daryl's civil rights. Irregularities permeated the courtroom proceedings, but one of the most startling was the autopsy report. It would have shown that Daryl had to be on the ground when the last shots were fired into his body. The autopsy report was not allowed.

Nine eyewitnesses, including Daryl's friend Jamie Moore, testified that Daryl never tried to stab anyone. The police officers testified that they never felt threatened by Daryl, but began shooting because he tried to stab Jamie. Under Ms. Howerton's leadership, the Justice for Daryl Howerton Committee asked during this time why nine members of the black community were not seen as credible eye-witnesses, but the testimony of the two white officers who were themselves on trial, was accepted by the court.

Forums at North Carolina A&T State University and Guilford College during the winter of 1998 raised much discussion on the underlying racism which encourages and allows such brazen and violent behavior by law enforcement. These forums, led by the Justice for Daryl Howerton Committee, brought much discussion to the racism that is sorely apparent in Daryl's murder. They also shed light on the differences in the treatment of the black community versus the white community by the police and military. Examining these relationships from a historical and present day perspective, A&T State University students discovered undercover police officers at a forum on their largely black campus on October 20, 1998. When complaints were filed, they were told that the officers were sent because the forum was, "dangerous, explosive and a possible uprising might take place." There were no officers present at the predominantly white Guilford College when the same forum was

Please see **Howerton,** *page 7*

Please see **Howerton,** *page 7*

(Source: The Student Activist, ed. Hannah Loring-Davis)

Hannah Loring-Davis knows this. As a Guilford College student, she joined with students from Guilford and other surrounding colleges to establish a student paper, *The Student Activist*, that would actually publish stories on national and international politics, stories not written from the point of view of whatever administration is currently in power. Like Ed Weir, she was following the adults in her life who had already shown her what it could mean to write something that matters to other people, something that would unite those around her who did not recognize themselves in the stories of most mainstream college newspapers. More than that, because she grew up watching her parents write for and read alternative press papers, she knew where to begin. Perhaps in the end, it is finding out where to begin that is left out in most of our talk of public writing. And, it is in reading the extraordinary words of ordinary men and women writing for local, little known causes, that we might just discover where to begin.

NOTES

1. John Trimbur's *The Call to Write* is a notable exception to that rule. In it, Trimbur takes the notion that writing is situated and social—that we write in response to a need, an event, a moment—and uses it (from Lloyd Bitzer's treatment of exigency) to create a composition text that looks a good deal different from what we have come to expect in such books. That theme, that we write in response to a "call," determines the very nature of both the instruction and the assignments throughout.

2. ABC recently announced that, in addition to its partnership with Disney Corporation, it now has an ongoing relationship with *Us Magazine*, confirming for many the connection between television news and *Entertainment Weekly*.

3. This has been especially true since the Fall of 2001 when Georgia resumed executions after a three-year court battle over whether or not the electric chair constituted cruel and unusual punishment. By the time the courts had decided it did, the Georgia Department of Corrections had equipped its death chamber with equipment for lethal injection. Between October and December of 2001, four prisoners were executed using lethal injection, and the rate of executions is likely to rise in 2002.

WORKS CITED

Barton, David and Mary Hamilton. *Local Literacies: Reading and Writing in One Community*. London: Routledge, 1998.

Crowley, Sharon. *Composition in the University: Historical and Polemical Essays*. Pittsburgh: Pittsburgh UP, 1998.

Davis, Murphy. *The Open Door Community*. Interviews with the author.

Day, Dorothy. *Loaves and Fishes*. 1963. Maryknoll, NY: Orbis Books.

Day, Dorothy. *The Long Loneliness*. 1952. San Francisco: Harper and Row, 1997.

Gathje, Peter. *Christ Comes in the Stranger's Guise: A History of the Open Door Community*. Atlanta: Peter Gathje, 1991.

Gere, Anne. "Kitchen Tables and Rented Rooms: The Extracurriculum of Composition." 1993. Address. Rpt. in *College Composition and Communication* 45.1 (1994): 75–92.

Loring-Davis, Hannah. *The Student Activist*. On-line interview with the author.

Roos, Joe. On-line and personal interviews with the author.

Vanden Heuvel, Katrina ed. *The Nation 1865–1990: Selections from the Independent Magazine of Politics and Culture*. New York: Thunder's Mouth Press, 1990.

Wallis, Jim. *Revive Us Again: A Sojourner's Story*. Nashville: Abington Press, 1983.

Weir, Ed. New Hope House. Interview.

Wells, Susan. "Rogue Cops and Health Care: What Do We Want from Public Writing?" *CCC* 47.3 (October 1996): 325–341.

4

The Death Penalty: Deterrent or Legalized Murder?

ELLIS ROBERTS

This article is an example of the community-based journalism that Diana George discusses in "The Word on the Street: Public Discourse in a Culture of Disconnect" (p. 50 in this volume). It was originally published in Hospitality, *the newspaper of the Open Door Community, an Atlanta residential community rooted in commitments to social justice and Christian spirituality. In this piece Roberts, a high school senior, draws on his experiences working with the anti–death penalty movement.*

FIGURE 4–1   Roberts's Article as It Appeared in *Hospitality*

From *Hospitality* 28.4 (2009): 1, 9.

The death penalty is an issue that is very easy to ignore. It is easy for people to set themselves apart from the institution that executes people. Most people choose to ignore the issue almost completely, treating it as a world apart from their own.

For many people, it is difficult to grapple with or even acknowledge social injustice. It is difficult to think that, while we live our lives comfortably, there are people in our state prisons waiting to be executed. So instead of trying to care, most of us simply choose to push it out of our minds. And it is this very ignorance that fuels the system. As long as no one is willing to at least give the death penalty serious thought, the system will proceed with executions unchecked. By ignoring the issue, we are in fact blindly endorsing the system that executes people.

I became acquainted with the anti–death penalty movement within the past year, due to some very admirable people in Atlanta who have spent much of their lives fighting against it. Eduard Loring and his wife, Murphy Davis of the Southern Prison Ministry, the co-founders of the Open Door Community, have been great influences on me. Attorney Doug Ramseur, a Georgia Capital Defender who dedicates his life to defending death row inmates, is also a very good role model in this cause. These people have been pivotal in energizing me into openly opposing the death penalty.

My introduction to the death penalty was the case of Curtis Osborne. Curtis Osborne was convicted of murdering Lisa Seabourne and Arthur Jones to avoid paying a debt to Arthur Jones. Attorney Johnny Mostiler was assigned to Osborne's defense. Mostiler intentionally botched Osborne's defense because of his racism. One of Mostiler's white clients reported that Mostiler told him that he would not adequately defend Osborne because he believed that "that little ni––er deserves the chair." On top of this, Mostiler did not tell Osborne that if he had pleaded guilty, he could have had his sentence reduced to life. In the absence of a guilty plea, Osborne was convicted and sentenced to death.

Aside from the racism in the case, it was determined that Osborne had many psychological problems that may have led him to commit murder. He was known to have a major depressive disorder and had suffered childhood abuse. He was also known to be on crack cocaine. All these factors, psychologists suggested, contributed to a paranoia that made it easy for him to lose control. But despite all these circumstances, Curtis Osborne was executed by the state of Georgia on June 4, 2008.

A HUNGER TO EXECUTE

My second experience with the death penalty came with the case of Jack Alderman. Jack Alderman was convicted of murdering his wife, based solely on the testimony of John Brown, who claimed to be Alderman's accomplice in the killing. Alderman was sentenced to death and spent 34 years on death row before being executed on September 16, 2008. Before the killing, he had no criminal record and was said by many to be a very peaceful person. In prison, he was described by other inmates as peaceful and a role model for others. If he committed murder, it was not in accordance with his past actions and personality. He rotted away on death row for more than three decades as the State Board of Pardons and Paroles consistently denied his appeals and requests for clemency.

My third experience, which is probably the most publicized Georgia death penalty case, has been with Troy Davis. He was convicted of killing Savannah police officer Mark MacPhail and was sentenced to death in 1991, based on the testimony of nine witnesses. Since then, seven of the nine witnesses have recanted their original stories, many citing police coercion, and one of the two remaining witnesses has been implicated by other witnesses as being the actual killer. No murder weapon or DNA evidence has ever been found linking Troy Davis to the killing. But despite Davis's overwhelmingly strong case for innocence, prosecutors and the Board of Pardons and Paroles have refused to acknowledge the new circumstances, insisting that his execution go forward as planned. It was astonishing, and uplifting, when a federal court finally granted an appeal for Troy Davis on December 9, 2008. At this writing, we are waiting for a decision from the 11th U.S. Circuit Court of Appeals to see whether Troy will be executed or live to have his case more carefully scrutinized by the courts.

These three cases shine a lot of light on the injustices of the death penalty. Prosecutors are hungry to execute—so hungry, in fact, that they don't seem to care about evidence or innocence or fairness at trial. In an issue as serious as a death penalty case, prosecutors should at least be required to view and consider all the evidence and circumstances. But they don't always do this, and as a result, many mistakes have been made. Racism was ignored in Curtis Osborne's case. Also, according to the Death Penalty Information Center, 130 death row inmates have been exonerated in the United States since 1973, mostly due to new evidence, presented after their convictions, that proved their innocence. All these men and women had to waste away in prison waiting to be executed for crimes they did not commit.

Despite the frequent mistakes, prosecutors who lead juries to make wrongful convictions are rarely held accountable for their actions. How can a system that involves killing people be allowed to exist if it makes mistakes so often? The institution of the death penalty is a grave danger to the public if it is going to target innocent people and not be better regulated.

LOST OPPORTUNITY

Aside from legal injustices, these cases point to the moral injustice of the death penalty. Executions take place out of the belief that the only solution to violent crime is to exterminate the perpetrators. But this fails to acknowledge that people have the capacity to change. A man or woman who murders and goes to prison may not be the same person thirty years later.

Curtis Osborne, for example, did commit a serious crime, but he did it out of passion. It is very possible that time in prison could give somebody like him the opportunity to repent of the crime and undergo a change. Jack Alderman, despite the serious nature of the crime he was convicted of, always projected peace and love to all he met during his incarceration. But the death penalty does not give inmates the chance to change. It assumes that people who murder once will be murderers for the rest of their lives. By killing such people, society loses the opportunity of reforming them and giving them the chance to become functional members of society.

The institution of the death penalty is skewed in every possible way. In its hunger to kill as many people as possible, the system has shown a systematic disregard for extenuating circumstances, innocence and fairness at trial. It also fails to consider the good nature of many of those it sentences to death, never allowing or giving them any incentive to change for the better.

But despite the injustice, people continue to accept the system, refusing to acknowledge its wrongdoings. It is of the utmost importance, if the death penalty is ever to be reined in or abolished, that people stop turning a blind eye to it and acknowledge it at face value. The system is less willing to kill people with the whole world looking over its shoulder.

5   *Finding a Home for Rick*

HEATHER BARGERON

Like "The Death Penalty: Deterrent or Legalized Murder?" (p. 61 in this volume) this article was originally published in Hospitality *and provides another example of the kind of engaged writing that Diana George affirms in "The Word on the Street: Public Discourse in a Culture of Disconnect" (p. 50). Heather Bargeron, a volunteer at the Open Door Community in Atlanta, reflects on her frustrations with trying to help a homeless person negotiate social service systems and argues for reform. Like students who explore the nexus between "service" and "learning," Bargeron calls attention to the many ways that direct experience supplements and corrects both common civic assumptions and academic perspectives on homelessness. A full archive of past* Hospitality *issues can be found through the Web site of the Open Door Community (http://opendoorcommunity.org/).*

FIGURE 5–1   Bargeron's Article as It Appeared in *Hospitality*

From *Hospitality* 22.10 (2003): 4.

I t had been a typically slow Friday morning on house duty. The community has recently categorized the Friday a.m. house duty rotation as "house sitting" because the Open Door is closed for services to the homeless on Fridays, and ostensibly the only real requirements of the person on house duty are to answer the phone, receive donations, and make sure that the house doesn't burn down. But just because our door is closed doesn't mean that the suffering of the poor and homeless ceases, and this particular morning that reality would hit me harder than usual.

At about 11:30 a.m. there was a knock at the front door that changed the course of that Friday dramatically. When I opened the door, I was met by a man who said, with a thick foreign accent, "I have brought a man here to stay." My first thought was that some guest had arrived whom I had forgotten about or who was not on the weekly schedule. To some extent, that was true.

I followed the man out the door to his vehicle, which I quickly realized was a taxi. He opened the back door and helped a man who was clearly disabled out of the car. The man had a walker, but he struggled to stand or walk even with this apparatus. I stood watching in silence as the two men discussed the fare for the cab ride. The driver told the other man that it would only be $20, but the man insisted on giving him $30.

The driver left, and I asked the man his name and what I could do for him. He told me his name was Rick, and he had stayed in a hotel the night before somewhere in the suburbs of Atlanta. He had visited a Catholic church, and they had told him he could come to the Open Door for housing. He had just arrived in town the day before from Maryland where, as he explained, he had become too much of a burden on his children, who had families of their own. So he came to Atlanta seeking a new life. He had $450 on him. He was willing to work and to pay rent.

A wave of familiar rage swept over me. This was not the first time that a person in need of shelter had been referred to the Open Door by someone who either did not know or did not care that the Open Door is not a shelter. But this was the first time that I had encountered a person who clearly did not have the physical ability to walk or even take the bus to seek shelter elsewhere. It was clear that I would have to do the legwork for him. I was angry at the person at the Catholic church who had referred him to the Open Door. And (by way of confession) I was angry at this man standing in front of me because I had no idea how to help.

I explained with futility that the Open Door is not a shelter, and I apologized for the fact that he was given incorrect information. This was all irrelevant, of course. Rick still needed housing. So I asked him to wait for a bit while I went inside to make some phone calls. Surely someone in this city would take him in.

I didn't know where to start. I could send him down the road to the Clermont or the Ponce Hotel, but he would only be able to stay a week or two on $450. Plus he would need to pay for food, and when he couldn't make ends meet, he would be back on the street. The only two shelters in Atlanta that I know of where one can enter without a formal referral are the Atlanta Union Mission and the Task Force for the Homeless' Pine Street Shelter. I have visited both of those facilities and, given the living conditions, I would not recommend them to any person, much less a person with a disability.

Tonnie King suggested that I call the Clifton Presbyterian Church shelter, the shelter out of which the Open Door was born. They have been helpful in the past by taking people in for a short term without too much red tape. They told me that they were already one over their bed capacity for that night. I was frustrated, but I empathized with the constant pressure to "just serve one more."

Surely someone *else* would take Rick in.

I called the Salvation Army shelter. They were full. I tried to call the Task Force's hotline just to see if they had any suggestions, but I was put on hold for so long that I finally got aggravated and hung up. I called Welcome House, a place that offers low-rent apartments to people with disabilities. The woman there told me that they may have a space for him, but he would have to go through an application process, and it might be a week or more before he would even know if he were approved or not. What was he supposed to do in the meantime? She suggested that I call the Midtown Assistance Center.

Surely *they* would have a space for Rick. They didn't, but they did give me the name and direct number of a woman at Crossroads Ministry who might be able to work something out for a disabled person. After an hour of "no," I was so grateful just to have a person's name. The woman at Crossroads was very sympathetic and helpful. She knew the owner of a boarding house for people with disabilities. She told me that she would have him call me within the next five minutes. He called and explained that he had a room available for $350 per month including three meals a day. He asked me a few questions about Rick's condition, and then he agreed to pick Rick up in the next hour. I was ecstatic, and I brought Rick into our living room to wait. After three hours (during which I agonized over whether or not this guy was really going to show or if I would start this whole process all over again), he arrived and Rick left, attempting to pay me for my trouble on his way out the door.

I learned more that day about the housing crisis in Atlanta than I have in the past 18 months of living at the Open Door—because this time *I* was making the phone calls, getting turned away, waiting on hold for hours, and being asked for a referral or application that would be processed weeks from now. It is quite literally enough to drive a person to drink. And I'm sure that my phone calls were more well-received than those of any homeless person—not because people working in all of the various shelters and homeless ministries around the city do not want to help, but because they are simply overwhelmed by the need for housing as I was on this Friday afternoon. Yes, homeless people need rehab programs. Yes, they need job assistance programs. Yes, they need temporary shelters. But on Friday Rick needed a home, and he's not the only one.

6 *Don't You Know Everybody Got Issues?*

SANDRA GILDERSLEEVE FREEMAN

This piece first appeared in the Journal of Ordinary Thought *(JOT), a quarterly periodical published by the Neighborhood Writing Alliance, which creates opportunities for adults in Chicago to write, publish, and perform works about their lives. Founded in 1991, JOT provides a forum for people to reflect on their personal histories and everyday experiences in writing. It describes itself as founded on the propositions that "every person is a philosopher," that expressing one's thoughts fosters creativity and change, and that taking control of life requires people to think about the world and communicate their thoughts to others. Freeman's prose reflection on place and parenting appeared in the winter 2009 issue.*

FIGURE 6–1 Freeman's Piece as It Appeared in the *Journal of Ordinary Thought*, Winter 2009

From *Journal of Ordinary Thought* (Winter 2009): 9.

I know you got issues, man, but don't you know everybody got issues? You come complaining about the job as if you think I got it made in a fourteen-room house with a demanding 2-year-old who already knows she is a queen. You think it's been easy for me to have to leave my job, a place of work I felt was challenging, because of medical reasons and be a stay-at-home mom? It's a position for which I feel my family doesn't even appreciate me, most of the time. I slave tirelessly each and every day, picking up everybody's items everywhere, all over the entire house. I cook fresh, healthy meals each and every day. I wash dishes at least three times a day. I make up beds. I try to balance the bankbook from a tightly fixed income. I shop for food, clothes, the household items. It's not just shopping, but shopping so that everybody is satisfied. Do you think this is easy? Do you think this house was made into a home overnight?

Don't you know I realize the neighborhood is becoming more dangerous, especially for our bright, beautiful, well-mannered son, and I'm stressed with fear for him? Don't you know I cry an abundant river every time he leaves this house because I'm scared he won't be coming back again? Because it might just be his luck to be caught up in a gang crossfire, or he might really get beaten to death because he chooses not to be a part of teenage violence in the hood? Oh, what am I to do? A mother who is medically, mentally, sometimes spiritually, and often economically depressed? Yeah, I got issues and I know you got issues! Man, don't you know everybody got issues? I'm just saying, Honey, can't you come home sometimes and say that you love me?

7   *Grandma Dearest*

CHI-AN CHANG

Like "Don't You Know Everybody Got Issues?" (p. 68 in this volume) this piece was originally published in the Journal of Ordinary Thought *(JOT) and also takes up family matters, albeit in a different genre and from a different perspective. Those interested in reading more from JOT or learning more about the Neighborhood Writing Alliance workshops can consult the JOT Web site (http://www.jot.org/).*

GRANDMA DEAREST

Chi-an Chang

Scrapping the darkness of your back
the ripples of life etched like waves
line after line after line
indecipherable mystery of your youth.

You lie there like a child, soft, warm but waning,
weary of the sun yet refusing to let down
that façade of power you so wish to keep
that strength, that dignity, that

which is still yours if you just believe.
Grandma dearest lies sloshed in sweat
drenched by age and dulled by days
taciturn to tell the truth of her ways.

If I had not asked, would you have asked
for the love of your grandchild?
Scrapping away the sunstroke off your back
memories of chocolate sweetness arrive:

In Shi-men-ting you took us to escape
from lovers' quarrels and life's struggles.
In that tiny flat for two, you squashed in
love for four, tending to our needs.

I moaned when my head ached
and you would scrape,
with porcelain spoon and tiger balm,
down my shoulder and neck,

stroking away the pain.
Grandma dearest, please
believe you are not weak
when your body is on the wane.

FIGURE 7–1   Chang's Piece as It Appeared in the *Journal of Ordinary Thought*, Spring 2009.

From *Journal of Ordinary Thought* (Spring 2009): 21.

Scrapping the darkness of your back
the ripples of life etched like waves
line after line after line
indecipherable mystery of your youth.

You lie there like a child, soft, warm but waning,
weary of the sun yet refusing to let down
that façade of power you so wish to keep
that strength, that dignity, that

which is still yours if you just believe.
Grandma dearest lies sloshed in sweat
drenched by age and dulled by days
taciturn to tell the truth of her ways.

If I had not asked, would you have asked
for the love of your grandchild?
Scrapping away the sunstroke off your back
memories of chocolate sweetness arrive:

In Shi-men-ting you took us to escape
from lovers' quarrels and life's struggles.
In that tiny flat for two, you squashed in
love for four, tending to our needs.

I moaned when my head ached
and you would scrape,
with porcelain spoon and tiger balm,
down my shoulder and neck,

stroking away the pain.
Grandma dearest, please
believe you are not weak
when your body is on the wane.

8 Geographies of Hope: A Study of Urban Landscapes, Digital Media, and Children's Representations of Place

GLYNDA A. HULL
MICHAEL ANGELO JAMES

Traveling from the University of California, Berkeley, to the adjacent community of West Oakland, one cannot help but observe a changing landscape—from leafy green to grey concrete, from relative affluence to an urban poverty that is stark. Several years ago, we founded a community technology center in the heart of this urban neighborhood that is just a local bus ride from the university campus, yet light years distant in terms of its residents' educational and economic prospects and social futures. Our university–community partnership called Digital Underground Storytelling for Youth (DUSTY)[1] brings University of California undergraduate and graduate students together with youth from the West Oakland community. There they work, play, and create using digital multimodal, multimedia literacies to cross geographic, racial, cultural, socioeconomic, and semiotic divides. In this chapter, we reflect on our work from the vantage point of five years of collaboration to develop and sustain DUSTY, make it responsive to community partners and participants, document its activities, and assess its role. In particular, taking inspiration from recent scholarship in the field of cultural geography (e.g., Harvey, 2000; Mitchell, 2002; Soja, 1996), we attempt here to think spatially as well as historically and socially about West Oakland as an urban neighborhood, and about the role that a community/university collaborative like DUSTY can play in reconstituting images of place and self. We begin by describing the policy and academic backdrops for DUSTY.

PERSPECTIVES ON SPACES FOR LEARNING AND LITERACY AFTER SCHOOL

Over the last 10 years, there has been a renaissance of after-school programs in the United States, designed to fill the gap between school turning out and parents returning home, motivated by reports that designate after-school hours as at-risk time (cf. Halpern, 2002, 2003). Federal support for such pro-

From *Blurring Boundaries: Developing Writers, Researchers and Teachers: A Tribute to William L. Smith*. Ed. Peggy O'Neill. Cresskill, NJ: Hampton Press, 2007. 225–89.

grams has recently been reduced or withdrawn, yet the need for after-school programs outstrips their availability, and they remain noticeable players in today's educational arena (cf. National Institute on Out-of-School Time, 2003). The programs are not, however, without their detractors, because controversial evaluations have recently demonstrated the difference that after-school programs do not seem to make in children's safety and academic achievement (cf. Kane, 2004). From our experience, a key ideological struggle around after-school programs today is determining their nature—whether they will be extensions of the school day, designed only or primarily to continue or assist with academic work, or whether they will focus on something different or something additional: cultural enrichment, arts education, youth development, or other activities that are not as constrained by the enormous current pressures on schools to improve tests scores or to march lock-step to a mandated textbook or curriculum standards (cf. Hull & Schultz, 2002). The broad question, then, is what kind of space—materially, socially, and in terms of available symbolic resources—might we imagine for learning and relationships after-school?

Over 15 years ago, Cole (1996) began to create after-school programs that were alternative spaces for learning, rather than replications of the school day. This work paralleled the increased interest in after-school programs mentioned earlier, but Cole's work was distinctive in being driven by an interest in exploring the implications of cultural-historical activity theory for reconceptualizing learning. Such explorations, Cole and his colleagues found, could take place more effectively out of school than in formal classrooms, because constraints on curricula and participant structures in the former were fewer. Thus was born a set of after-school programs and a national and international consortium of collaborators who shared Cole's theoretical assumptions.

Simply put, Cole and colleagues conceptualized after-school programs as "activity systems" that blurred boundaries between work and play, that provided a structure for participation allowing movement between expert and novice roles, and that took advantage of widely available computer technologies, such as e-mail and electronic games. Cole's conceptualization also linked the university and the community, bringing graduate students and undergraduates to the after-school program, and working collaboratively with community partners such as Boys' and Girls' clubs to establish the program. Called the 5th Dimension initially, this work later inspired a set of after-school programs affiliated with each of the eight University of California campuses (cf. Gutiérrez, Baquedano-Lopez, & Tejeda, 1999; Underwood, Welsh, Gauvain, & Duffy, 2000). This later project, UCLinks, was a direct response to the dismantling of affirmative action within the University of California in 1996. The hope was that well-designed, theoretically motivated after-school programs, such as UCLinks and the 5th Dimension, could increase the chances that children from low-income communities and beleaguered schools, especially youth of color, would aspire to and be able to attend a college or university, thereby sustaining or even increasing diversity on campuses such as UC Berkeley.

DUSTY began as a UCLinks site; it thereby shares some of the important features of Cole's and his colleagues' conceptualization, in particular the linkage between university students and youth from the community; the commitment to establish a collaboration that draws on the strengths and resources of both community and university partners; and an interest in fashioning a space for learning that contrasts what is offered during the school day. In our work at DUSTY, we have viewed the linkage between the university and the local community as reciprocal border crossing and space creation—as a movement back and forth across social, geographic, economic, cultural, and semiotic divides and the creation through this movement of a new space for learning, one that turns the periphery into the center. We have been attentive to the way in which such a traversal of borders has implications for how we conceptualize DUSTY and its role in the community. As the opening to this chapter suggests, the differences in physical space and material resources that characterize the University and the West Oakland community, noticeable at every entry and exit, have pushed us to be aware of this larger community context and the ways in which that context both influences and is modestly influenced by our community technology center and after-school programs.

As a university–community collaborative that organizes undergraduate students to work, play, and create with children and youth at a community center, DUSTY (and UCLinks) is also part of a movement in higher education called *service learning* (cf. Furco & Billig, 2002). Prompted by recent federal legislation, but rooted in long-held conceptions of experiential learning such as Dewey's (1938), service learning courses aim to position students to serve their local community, as well as reflect on these experiences in the context of an academic course on a college campus. Thus, in the spirit of Dewey, such courses ideally connect the learning that students do in a formal classroom with participation and responsibility in the larger society. One especially vigorous and intellectually alive branch of service learning has developed within composition studies; teachers of writing in universities and colleges now regularly send their students to community-based organizations to assist with or perform writing activities or literacy-related tutoring (cf. Deans, 2000). As is demonstrated in this chapter, DUSTY also has as its centerpiece certain writing and literacy-related activities—in particular, multimedia, multimodal composing; our undergraduates both learn these new kinds of composing themselves and support children and youth from the community in their use of new and old literacies. Another way that service learning scholarship within composition studies resonates with our work at DUSTY is its critical consciousness about what constitutes an ethical relationship between the university and the community. Early on important concerns were expressed about the nature of service, particularly the unhappy possibility that university students could approach their community work with a kind of missionary zeal that reduced community members to objects for salvation (cf. Boyle-Baise, 2002; Herzberg, 1994; Himley, 2004; Welsh, 2002). Frank and helpful explorations of sustainability have also been a prominent thread, as faculty confront their university's disinterest in service and engage in the balancing act that allows them to link their teaching and research with service to the community (Cushman, 1999, 2002).

To be sure, most of the scholarship on service learning in composition studies has tended to focus on the university end of the collaboration. Although this should not be surprising, the effect has often been, from our point of view, to relegate the communities served to the shadows, places where adults and youth are sometimes characterized as needy and different or leading marginal lives. Flower (2002) describes typical inquiry patterns of service learning this way: "The research on service-learning is indeed preoccupied with *our* expertise; with developing pedagogical agendas, interrogating our middle-class ideologies, producing satisfying academic dichotomies and incisive critiques" (p. 184). Thus, the geography of service learning often becomes one of reconnaissance: forays to scout out a possibly unfriendly territory with the intent of returning to cover. For this reason, we have found especially compelling the service learning scholarship that is grounded in the community—projects involved in the creation and sustenance of community programs over time—and that explores the tensions and challenges of traversing and recharting community and university borders. We draw inspiration particularly from Flower and her colleagues (Flower, 2002, 2003; Long, Peck, & Baskins, 2002; Peck, Flower, & Higgins, 1995), who have worked within the settlement house tradition in Pittsburgh, Pennsylvania, to carry out long-term collaborations that blend university intellectual traditions with community interests and resources under the label of *intercultural inquiry*. Such inquiry, as Flower and her colleagues have persuasively documented, involves challenges to the habits of mind of those in the academy as it simultaneously supports literate action among community members. One of the central metaphors that they use in their work has an important spatial dimension—the dinner table, around which participants draw their chairs both literally and symbolically, to converse and engage in joint problem solving and the important process that Flower terms the *negotiation of meaning*.

Certainly a central theme of Flower, Peck, Long, and Baskins' joint work has been to enable participants to discover and enact their agency as individuals and community members, people operating within constraints of course, but actors increasingly aware of their ability to have an effect, especially through the deployment of strategic uses of language and literacy. The primary theoretical underpinning of DUSTY has likewise centered on identity formation, and especially the role of language and other semiotic systems in this process. We have written in detail about this framework elsewhere (Hull & Katz, in press), but in brief we have described how all semiotic systems—language, writing, images, music, dance—give us a means to embody and enact a sense of self in relation to others. In the words of Urciuoli (1995), "The creation of meaning is above all embedded in human relationships: people enact their selves to each other in words, movements, and other modes of actions" (p. 189). Thus, at DUSTY we have aimed to position participants to tell their important stories about self and community, and to use those moments of narrative reconstruction to reflect on past events, present activities, and future goals. Our curriculum encourages participants to construct stories that position themselves as agents, as young people and adults able to articulate and act on their own "wishes, desires, beliefs, and expectancies" (Bruner, 1994, p. 41) and as local and global community members able to remake their worlds (Freire, 1970). Further, we have provided a powerful mediational means for their storytelling (cf. Cole, 1996; Vygotsky, 1934/1986, 1978). At this particular historical moment, which is characterized by a pictorial turn (Mitchell, 1994; cf. Kress, 2003), we believe such means include the technical skills and social practices that constitute the version of multimedia composing that we refer to as *digital storytelling* (cf. Lambert, 2002). The variety of representational activities that occur at DUSTY—be they spoken word performances, written narratives, photo collections, storyboards, musical compositions, animations, or digital stories—we conceptualize as identity texts to call attention to the primacy given at DUSTY to fostering and enacting agentive and socially responsible identities through the use of a range of semiotic systems (Leander, 2002; cf. Leoni & Cohen, 2004).

In this chapter, we extend our theoretical lens to include ideas about space, place, and landscape drawn from the field of cultural geography and related disciplines. Recently, interest has grown within literacy studies around such ideas (see especially Leander, 2002; Leander & Sheehy, 2004), with researchers such as Moje (2004) investigating how youth enact different identities according to the different spaces they occupy, as they marshal the available resources, textual and material, that are associated with those spaces. Understanding how *space*, *place*, and *landscape* (terms we illustrate later) intersect with senses of self, community, and agency is especially pivotal in our work and, we believe, relevant to service learning programs and other educational efforts that cross borders literally and symbolically. Soja (2004), a well-known critical geographer, has written persuasively about the spatial turn that is spreading fast among the human sciences. He argues that, whereas the historical and the social have long been accepted as important analytic dimensions, the spatial has been neglected. Yet he notes that, increasingly, we are coming to understand how the social, historical, and spatial are interwoven and in fact inseparable. Paraphrasing Henri Lefebvre (on whose influential work he and many other critical geographers built), Soja observes that, "all social relations remain abstractions until they are concretized in space" (p. xiv). It is noteworthy that Soja and other theorists are fierce about not wanting to promote an orthodoxy in terms of how to conceptualize spatiality. Instead, they urge that we hold open "our critical geographical imagination" (Soja, 2004, p. 2) and resist rigid relations among terms such as *space*, *place*, and *landscape* (Mitchell, 2002). In this chapter, we accept Soja's and Mitchell's invitation as we attempt to use recent theorizing on spatiality to gain a fresh vantage point on our community technology center, our activities there, and our university–community collaboration.

Thus, in this chapter, we use the terms *space*, *place*, and *landscape* to animate our analysis of community relations and multimedia representational activities. In so doing, we follow Mitchell's (2002) helpful presentation of these terms as a "dialectical triad" (p. x). "If a place is a specific location," he writes, "a space is a 'practiced place,' a site activated by movements, actions, narratives, and signs, and a landscape is that site encountered as image or 'sight'" (2002, p. x).[2] To illustrate, our community technology center, located in a renovated Victorian that used to be a convent, across the street from a church and an elementary school, in the heart of the West Oakland neighborhood known as the "lower bottoms," is a place. Our collective use of that place—through our curriculum and our social relationships, our pedagogy and our participants, and our vision of border crossing and multimedia making—turns that place into a lived space. When our participants describe and represent the community center, which they know as DUSTY, in their multimedia stories, written accounts, oral narratives, and in relation to themselves, it becomes a landscape. We especially like Mitchell's point that there is no hierarchy or chronological ordering to these terms. Although spatial activities can transform a place, a place can also, of course, afford or constrain activities in a social space. A landscape might have agency, predisposing viewers to conceptualize a place or engage in certain kinds of activities in a lived space.

In the sections that follow, we examine data collected through ethnographic methods over a period of four years, using some of the perspectives provided by critical geography, including Mitchell's distinctions among space, place, and landscape. Our data include photographs and other visual representations, as well as field notes, interviews, and long-term participant observation. Throughout we ask: How is the construction of identities, both individual and collective, influenced by and enacted through spatiality? Toward the end of this chapter, we consider how what we have learned might be of use to community-based and university educators and researchers in the after-school movement and in service learning efforts, especially in relation to the multimodal version of literacy that we call *digital stories*. To offer a counterpoint to the service learning literature that emphasizes university participants' experiences, we foreground here the experiences and points of view of community participants.

THE WEST OAKLAND COMMUNITY: AN ACTIVIST PAST AND AN UNCERTAIN FUTURE[3]

Once a mixed-use area of residences and industry, West Oakland, California, where DUSTY is located, slipped into economic decline with the end of World War II, when shipbuilding and defense-related industries were dramatically reduced (cf. Noguera, 1996). As its economic base declined, its European ethnic residents were replaced by African Americans migrating from the South and, more recently, by low-income Chicano/Latino and Asian/Pacific Islander families. Currently, West Oakland consists of some 7,000 households representing approximately 20,000 people. Seventy-four percent of residents are African American, 14 percent are Chicano/Latino, 10 percent are Asian/Pacific Islanders, 2 percent are White, and 1 percent are American Indians or Other. This section of the city has been designated as a Federal Enhanced Enterprise Community and is characterized by all of the symptoms of intense urban poverty and the educational inequities that accompany it. The neighborhood's income level and jobless rates, in fact, make its residents some of the most disadvantaged in the San Francisco Bay Area and, indeed, the nation. Educational statistics for West Oakland are similarly poor, with many students scoring far below state and national averages. Low academic performance is a disturbing and long-term trend. At the public elementary school located across the street from DUSTY, recent scores from the California Standards Test showed that 67 percent of fifth graders did not score in the proficient range in English Language Arts, and 68 percent did not score in the proficient range for math. At a Catholic middle school, also across the street from DUSTY, approximately 80 percent of students performed below grade level. The main public high school in West Oakland recently had an Academic Performance Index of 437, which places it in the state's lowest decile.[4]

Today in West Oakland, there are few signs remaining of the community's rich history, which included a bustling economy mid-century when the city's dry docks, railroad system, and factories attracted immigrants from throughout the world and African Americans from the South. Its activist culture during the 1960s played a pivotal role in the civil rights movement and the establishment of the union of Sleeping Car Porters and the Black Panther Party (Ginwright, 2004; cf. Rhomberg, 2004). Yet recovering and preserving that rich history, revitalizing the community, and empowering residents educationally and economically are the aims of many private citizens, local businesses, schools, and nonprofit agencies. Our DUSTY center for digital media and literacy, located in the heart of the community, is one small contribution to that effort. . . .

Youth and Out-of-School Space and Time: Envisioning DUSTY

After-school programs in the United States date from the late 1800s, when the need for child labor decreased, compulsory schooling began to be the norm, and youth thereby found themselves with time on their hands during out-of-school hours. Worried that youth would get into trouble during this newly unsupervised time, educators and reformers developed playground programs that eventually expanded to include indoor activities, too, the antecedents of today's after-school programs (Halpern, 2002). Like the youth of a century ago, who took to the streets when given leisure from work and school, youth in Oakland and many urban centers are now often at loose ends, at once disengaged from school, lacking opportunities for work, and forced to do without social spaces and activities that could meaningfully fill their out-of-school hours. To illustrate, over the last few years in Oakland, a battle of sorts has erupted between urban youth on the one hand, and the police force and some residents, on the other. Young people in effect took to and claimed the streets, usually during late evening hours, by holding sideshows, or car-centered street rallies. At sideshows drivers blocked traffic, spun their cars in circles, doing donuts, while other youth gathered, looked on, and played music. Sometimes these gatherings attracted upward of 400 youth, and they quickly evoked concerns about safety, noise, and mischief.[5]

We do not find it surprising that youth invent sideshows and engage in other transgressive activities to spatially, bodily, and symbolically display their agency, and we think that an analysis of such activity has something important to teach us about marginalized youth. Designing and controlling space is an important means of constructing youth culture; as Massey (1998) notes, "From being able to have a room of one's own (at least in richer families) to hanging out on particular corners, to clubs where only your own age group goes, the construction of spatiality can be an important element in building a social identity" (p. 128). Valentine, Skelton, and Chambers (1998) point out that, "the space of the street is often the only autonomous space that young people are able to carve out for themselves" (p. 7). One way, then, to understand sideshows and the community's response to them is to view them as young people's attempts to create spaces for themselves and, at the same time, adults' age-old attempts, not without reason, to control youth's spaces and behaviors.

We began DUSTY to provide a safe space physically and socially for children and youth during the after-school and evening hours and during summertime. As we illustrate in the next section, our programmatic work has centered on designing and offering programs for children and youth on creating digital stories, or multimedia, multimodal narratives, and digital music.[6] That is, we hoped to draw youth off the streets and into DUSTY through the appeal of media, music, and popular culture (Hull, 2003; Morrell, 2004) as we simultaneously pushed school-based definitions of *literacy* to include the visual and the performative (cf. Hull, 2003; Hull & Zacher, 2004). In addition, this focus would take us part of the distance in closing for the West Oakland community what is popularly called the *digital divide*. Although debate continues about the extent and nature of this divide that separates people who have access to empowering uses of cutting-edge information technologies from those who don't (cf. Compaine, 2001; Fairlie, 2003; Warschauer, 2004), there is no doubt that youth from communities like West Oakland routinely lack such opportunities. Thus, as a living space for learning, we wanted DUSTY to provide youth with equitable access to cutting edge technologies for communication and creative expression. As discussed earlier, through positioning youth to tell stories about self, family, and community through multiple media and modalities, we intended to help them develop senses of self as powerful, capable, and successful communicators. By bringing university students to the West Oakland community, and children to the university, and by continually widening the vistas of university students and children through literal and symbolic movement across communities, we hoped to enable the youth to take steps toward and develop sensibilities for shaping their futures.[7]

CHILDREN'S VISTAS AND VOICES

It was a rainy day in March, and most of the children who had been attending our middle school DUSTY program had already gone home. A UC Berkeley undergraduate mentor stood outside the building with Stephen, one of the middle schoolers; the day darkened as they waited and waited longer still for Stephen's ride home to appear. Stella, the undergraduate, was worried about the 12-year-old. They had worked together on homework and a digital music program. But that day he had seemed withdrawn and had finally mentioned to Stella, speaking quietly and tearfully, that his dad had just passed away. It was later, after Stella and Stephen had stood on the curb together, watching evening settle onto the neighborhood as youth loudly congregated on the street corner and cars zoomed past with their spinners and 20-inch rims, that the young boy solemnly asked: "Do you really think kids in this neighborhood will go to college?"

The question was a poignant moment for Stella, who had been talking to the children about going to college, as was the DUSTY custom. Stephen in particular had been interested in this topic and was perhaps also inspired by a recent field trip to campus.[8] There had been other outings away from West Oakland as well, including a concert by Alicia Keys, the rhythm and blues super star, at a venue on the other side of the city, complete with an autograph signing afterward especially for DUSTY youth. Given all of this in conjunction with his dad's death, perhaps it is not surprising that Stephen might have been thinking about going places, maybe leaving the neighborhood, and hopefully attending college. Perhaps he visualized contrasts in landscape and especially sensed the constraints that one's locale could bring to bear on his and others' social futures.

There is a big scholarship on spatiality as it relates to the study of children. One tradition builds on Piaget's (1971) interest in how reasoning about the environment develops over time, including children's orientation in space and their mapping abilities (cf. Erickson, 1977; Matthews & Limb, 1999). Within geography there have been studies dating from the early 1970s on the social inequalities that result from the "built environment" (Aitken, 2001), such as unjust geographical allocations of educational resources like play spaces (Bunge & Bordessa, 1975). More recent work in geography is characterized by Aitken (2001) as "about the practices of young people, their communities, and the places and institutions that shape (and are shaped by) their lives" (p. 20). "Places are important for young people," he continued, "because these contexts play a large part in constructing and constraining dreams and practices" (p. 20).

We too have been interested in charting how place, space, and landscape, as associated with the community of West Oakland, play a role in "constructing and constraining dreams and practices" of area youth. But equally as important, throughout interventions at DUSTY, we have been committed to positioning youth, by providing access to potentially powerful representational tools and practices, to speak back to spatial constraints. Mitchell (2002) notes that, "landscape exerts a subtle power over people, eliciting a broad range of emotions and meanings that may be difficult to specify" (p. vii). Hearing Mitchell, we are well warned concerning the subtleties that accompany the articulation of identities in relation to place and landscape. Nonetheless, in the following section, we hope to demonstrate in an initial way some of the ideas and concerns that youth in our programs have expressed about their locales, as well as to suggest how our youth have seemed to enact identities in relation to space, place, and landscape through multimodalities and multimedia.

In our archives, approximately 200 digital stories have been created thus far by youth, children, and adults at DUSTY. Two- to 5-minute movies, the stories usually begin with a written script that is eventually accompanied by images, photographs, artwork, or snippets of video; a musical soundtrack; and the narrator's voice reading or performing the script. The still visuals are stitched together with an editing program through faces, dissolves, checkerboards or a myriad other transitions, thus allowing the illusion of movement. As a rough first cut at analyzing these stories, we developed a catalog of their major genres and purpose:

> Genres: Autobiographical Narratives; Poems/Raps; Social Critique/Public Service Announcements; Reenactments or Extensions of Stories, Cartoons, and Movies; Animations; Reports; Biographies and Interviews
>
> Purposes: Offer a Tribute to Family Member(s), Friend(s); Recount/Interpret a Pivotal Moment/Key Event; Represent Place, Space, Community; Preserve History; Create Art/Artifact; Play/Fantasize; Heal/Grieve/Reflect; Reach/Inform/Influence Wider Audience

Of course, many authors had multiple purposes, and sometimes the digital stories blurred genres, as befits their dynamic and evolving nature; these categories yet provide a broad if unrefined sense of forms and uses. Our archives revealed a number of digital stories by children, youth, and adults whose centerpiece was the representation of place, space, and community, and in what follows we examine one of these in detail. At this stage in our work, we do not make any claims about the relative frequency or stability of the categories. This is our first pass at developing an analytic system for understanding youth's representation of place, and self in relation to place, through multimedia/multimodality.[9]

STORIES OF IDENTIFICATION AND DISTANCING

As we reviewed the stories in our archives, we realized that, from the inception of the DUSTY program, children and youth had created a remarkable number of stories that located themselves in relation to their neighborhoods. To suggest the flavor and range of these compositions, here are some examples. One 13-year-old boy, interested in paying homage to his posse, constructed a story that pictured each of his many friends and named them one by one, but he also carefully demarcated their neighborhood, taking photographs of street signs and domiciles and distinguishing West Oakland from East Oakland. He announced his home turf as the best section of the city in which to live, far superior to other neighborhoods. A younger boy wrote a story about a trip to Alaska, contrasting its weather and other features with those of Oakland. Most interesting to us, however, was his inclusion in the

Oakland portion of a photo of the local children's hospital, announcing that this was the place where he had been born. He was quite taken aback and not at all persuaded when his mother, on viewing his digital story for the first time, told him that he had not been born at that particular hospital after all. A 9-year-old girl who had recently moved from another city contrasted her new home with her old one, and expressed considerable longing for a quieter, more pastoral space to live than West Oakland. This was, in fact, a theme that surfaced in other stories: the noise of the city and its lack of aesthetically appealing space. Another little girl developed her entire story around the pleasures of visiting a particular place, her auntie's house, where special privileges abounded.

Children choose to write about particular topics for many reasons, including the promptings of their teachers, the examples provided through previous students' work, their own interests and predilections, and the conventions that have developed and are typically promulgated in schools and other educational settings around what constitutes an appropriate storyline. Although we accept all of these possibilities as possible and likely contributors and influences, what we wish to explore here is the importance for many children of locating themselves in a particular space—"this is my house, I'm a person from West Oakland, I was born here"—and also of professing or sometimes examining their relationship with a landscape and a locale— "I'm from East Oakland, and it is a cool place; I don't like my neighborhood because it's so noisy where I live." As Duncan and Duncan (2004) note, "people continually attempt to stabilize and establish secure identities and, more often than not, anchor them in place" (p. 30).

Identification with a particular place is surely a usual part of children's development, but we believe that this process takes on a special salience in neighborhoods like West Oakland, which are segregated economically, socially, and ethnically, and where many children and youth regularly experience their immediate environs as unsafe places, and where almost continuously they encounter representations of their communities as violent, unhealthy, and undesirable. The other part of our argument is that multimedia and multimodality constitute especially fitting vehicles for children and youth to represent their lives spatially. Digital stories are relentlessly visual; no matter what words and music fill the air, the stories proceed and direct composers' and viewers' attention through images and video. Because place and landscape can be readily captured through images, a digital story can provide an exceptional canvass for the exploration of the spatial. Finally, and this point is the most suggestive of all those we hope to make, we believe that forms of composing, such as digital storytelling, have the potential to afford children and youth the representational means to see themselves in relation to places, spaces, and landscapes in new ways.

We turn next to what strikes many viewers as an exceptionally powerful digital story about place, space, and landscape by a young author. Created by Jamal,[10] a 9-year-old boy who lived in East Oakland but attended DUSTY's summer program, the digital story is a minute and a half long and contains

17 images, each linked to the other by a lively visual transition such as "opening doors" or "cartwheels" that blend one picture into the next. Entitled "My Neighborhood," it is narrated by Jamal, while the jazz of Miles Davis—a cut from "Sketches of Spain"—sounds an exceptionally plaintive backdrop. The story is based on a well-known writing assignment about the senses: "Compose a poem in first person that reveals what you hear, see, feel, smell, and taste." In preparation for writing, the children participated in several preparatory activities, including a walk about the neighborhood adjacent to DUSTY, where they took note of what was salient to them.

Here is the final version of the text of Jamal's poem:

I hear the sirens of an ambulance speeding by.
I hear the sound of a car skidding.
I hear kids laughing at the boy who fell down.

I see kids running down the street to the ice cream truck.
I see a brotha selling drugs on the street.
I see Asians walking up the street.

I feel the strong warm breeze against my face.
I feel the rough wall of my house.
I feel my shirt sticking to my back.

I smell the nasty aroma of urine.
I smell chicken from inside my house.

I smell BBQ sauce.
I taste the cinnamony, sugary churro.
I taste the soft chocolate milk in my mouth
I taste the dry air on my tongue.

I hear a car speeding by.
I know that this neighborhood is bad.

These lines, although wonderfully evocative, make up but the skeleton of Jamal's digital story; next we attempt to give a sense of its body, its visual components. To be sure, it is exceedingly difficult to describe multimodality through the vehicle of a book chapter, and in any case it is analytically challenging to capture what is powerful about successful multimodal pieces. Their blending of words, images, voice, music, and motion creates meaning and an experience of meaning-making that differs from and exceeds what is possible through single or fewer modalities.[11] To begin to suggest what is distinctive about Jamal's digital multimodal composition, over and above the linguistic text of his poem, next we juxtapose the lines of the poem with a brief description of the image or images with which they are paired.[12]

a. I hear the sound of a car skidding (*three Internet images: ambulance, car, skid marks on pavement*)

b. I hear kids laughing at the boy who fell down (*Internet image of a group of children in a circle, laughing and looking down*)

c. I see kids running down the street to the ice cream truck (*Internet image of an ice cream truck*)

d. I see a brotha selling drugs on the street (*Internet image of a dark-skinned man taking money from a White man with one hand and passing him something with the other*)

e. I see Asians walking up the street (*Internet image of a smiling family posed for the camera, father holding one daughter, mother's hand on a second daughter's shoulder*)

f. I feel the strong warm breeze against my face (*photograph of Jamal's smiling face, cut out and superimposed on an Internet image of a beach scene with palm trees*)

g. I feel the rough wall of my house (*same smiling photograph of Jamal, this one whole, his hand touching a wall behind him*)

h. I feel my shirt sticking to my back (*photograph of Jamal from behind, on his porch at night, leaning over the railing and looking downward, as if at a street below*)

i. I smell the nasty aroma of urine (*Internet image of a bag of urine such as might be collected in a hospital*)

j. I smell chicken from inside my house (*Internet image of a whole baked chicken, angle taken from above*)

k. I smell BBQ sauce (*Internet image of a bottle of "Dr. Dan's BBQ Sauce"*)

l. I taste the cinnamony, sugary churro (*upclose Internet image of fried pastry sticks*)

m. I taste the soft chocolate milk in my mouth (*Internet image of a pint and a quart of chocolate milk*)

n. I taste the dry air on my tongue (*same photo as for the previous line*)

o. I hear a car speeding by (*Internet image of a "muscle" car, the same as the first image*)

p. I know that this neighborhood is bad (*photograph of dilapidated houses juxtaposed to skyscrapers on Oakland's skyline*)

Bracketing the story was a black title screen with white writing and a list of rolling credits. The movie ended with the screen going black in splotches, as if paint were spattering onto the surface. The rolling credits screen, also white on black background, thanked the audience for watching the movie, and in a funny subversion of the usual conventions for watching movies, advised that no applause was necessary and warned viewers not to come again! Jamal signed his movie with a fictional production company, "Mad Dog Productions," named after a cartoon character from the TV show "Kim Possible," and he listed an imaginary Web site for it.

As we illustrate, the overall mood of Jamal's movie was serious. An ode on place with images that powerfully contextualized the words that Jamal spoke, and a jazz soundtrack that strongly evoked a melancholy mood, juxtaposing musical sophistication and world-weariness with a child's innocent voice, "My Neighborhood" could be seen as a young author's reflection on place in relation to himself. There are pleasant sensations described and positive images offered to be sure: the smell of chicken cooking in the house, children running to the ice cream truck, the soft feel of chocolate milk in one's mouth. It is also the case that adult viewers can see the child behind his wise piece, and this indeed adds to this digital story's charm. For example, there is a child's aesthetic at work in selecting energetic transitions between images, his fondness for the "bells and whistles" that are easily produced via editing programs these days. In addition, in age-appropriate fashion, Jamal matched his images to his words literally; that is, his words indexed images instead of functioning more symbolically, to use Peirce's (1955) typology. Nonetheless, we would argue that it is also impossible to view Jamal's movie without recognizing a young mind in thoughtful dialogue about space, place, and landscape, or to escape the impression that important identity work is represented in this story.

To briefly present what we think Jamal's story signifies about spatiality in relation to identity, we draw on our analysis of an interview with his DUSTY instructor about Jamal, his composition process, and the other children and their work in the program; a retrospective interview with Jamal, in which he watched, commented on, and answered questions about "My Neighborhood" with his instructor; conversations with his parents; and artifacts associated with Jamal's work (including a detailed lesson plan for the poetry/senses unit and additional poems, journal entries, and one other digital story that Jamal created during a previous DUSTY summer session).

Our first point is that, in writing his poem and selecting his images, Jamal drew actively on his sense of what was salient about his neighborhood in terms of both material places and lived spaces. This might be surmised by an analysis of the story, but was confirmed through our interviews and other data. He clearly recognized that in his neighborhood could be found danger, violence, poverty, and crime, and he thought these features important to represent. For example, in commenting on his choice of a skidding car and the ambulance pictured at the opening of his story (Line a), Jamal volunteered that "almost every day I hear an ambulance." These ambulances, he said, always seemed to be going in the same direction, to the same place, to pick up people who had been fighting, been in car accidents, or overdosed. Sometimes, he mentioned, he saw people smoking dope in his neighborhood when he went outside to ride his bike with one of his family members, and once he thought he saw a drug deal taking place down the hill from his house as he stood on his porch (consequently, Line d and the Internet image of a "brotha" selling drugs).

Perhaps the most startling negative sense of place came with the line, "The nasty aroma of urine," and the accompanying Internet image of a large bag of the same. Jamal giggled a little when asked how he had found that image ("I typed in *urine*") and then went on to explain more solemnly how, twice, he had smelled urine when he walked in an alleyway near his house — experiences that seemed to have made a strong impression on him given the detail he recalled about these and related discoveries. An unmistakable dimension, then, of Jamal's story is his negative contextualization of neighborhood. Lest there be any doubt about this, he chose to end his poem with what his DUSTY instructor had explained could be a sixth sense, a statement about what one knows: (Line p) "I know that this neighborhood is bad." When queried regarding this claim about his community, Jamal stated twice, with emphasis, "Some parts of it *is* bad," and mentioned the littered streets and the presence of drugs. He also identified the exact location of the photo that he had paired with this last line, a picture of dilapidated old houses in West Oakland juxtaposed to the downtown city's modern skyline. When asked what part of the city this Internet photo represented, he replied, "West Oakland and that's downtown Oakland behind it." When asked if he was sure, he replied with no hesitation, "I'm sure because I've been there before, and I've seen these buildings and these houses." In other parts of his interview, Jamal additionally revealed his knowledge of local geography, distinguishing West and East Oakland, areas within the same city that nonetheless possessed separate identities, fostering a sometimes virulent territoriality. He clarified that, although some of his images depicted West Oakland, where DUSTY is located, he intended for his poem to represent the neighborhood where he lived, East Oakland. However, he found both areas similar in containing neighborhoods that had parts that he deemed "bad."

While Jamal characterized his neighborhood and other parts of the city, he also revealed his understandings of how place intersects with racial and ethnic identity. Place and space, as many cultural geographers now note, can make a difference in terms of "how racial and ethnic identities have come to be understood, expressed, and experienced" (Berry & Henderson, 2002, p. 6). As an African-American child, and as revealed in his digital poem, Jamal had developed his own racially sensitive geography, a map, if you will, on which were charted roles, situations, and activities as they were influenced by race and ethnicity. About the famous urine photo, for example, Jamal explained that it was a "Black man" who had been urinating in the alleyway, although he confessed to not having seen him. He explained, however, that he had once seen a Black man sleeping there and that "most of them [presumably people in general or Black people in particular who sleep outside] don't have homes." Jamal was also aware of more conventional housing patterns that were racially influenced and that impacted relationships. Line e of his poem, "I see Asians walking up the street," was matched with a picture of a smiling Asian family, parents and children. In commenting on this part of his poem, Jamal observed that, although his neighborhood was mixed, "down the street from me, most people on the block is Asian." When asked whether he was friends with the Asian kids, Jamal said, no, because he had not met them yet. His three African-American friends in the neighborhood, he explained, all lived very near him, either across the street or down an alleyway.[13] This made their friendships geographically possible and desirable in an urban environment.[14]

As mentioned earlier, Jamal's digital poem contained a number of positive associations related to neighborhood—for example, a smiling Asian family walking on the street, the ice cream truck seen in the distance, the taste of Mexican pastry, and the smell of a chicken roasting inside the house. These simple, often sensory pleasures, juxtaposed to the harsher world of the neigh-borhood already detailed, perhaps serve to increase rather than decrease the somber feel of Jamal's poem, especially when combined with the mood set by Miles Davis' jazz. A devotee of jazz—he had many favorites, but mentioned by name John Coltrane and Miles Davis ("He is my most favorite")—Jamal selected the background music by listening to all of the cuts on the album and choosing the one he felt was most suitable. "I like the way it goes with my movie," he explained simply. However, one sequence of lines and images seemed to signal a separation from the dangers and sadness of the street and the neighborhood—Lines f through h, which are based on two photos that Jamal's mom took of him at home. In Line f, he depicts the feeling of a warm breeze on his face by transplanting his smiling image to a backdrop of palm trees and ocean.[15] In Line g, we again see Jamal's face from the previous screen, but this time it is in context as he stands in front of a wall at his house, touching its rough surface with one hand. His mom took the third image from behind him to suggest the feel of his shirt sticking to his back as he stood on his porch at night, looking out and down as if to the street below. Jamal mentioned several times that he could see things from his porch, like drug deals or ambulances. This series of images, offered in the middle of his poem, suggested to us Jamal's protected positionality in relation to his neighbor-hood; that is, he could choose to observe and contemplate in safety what was happening on the streets, staying connected but also remaining apart—a ter-rific geographic metaphor for growing up safely and healthfully in an urban environment.

After watching his digital poem and discussing his claim and illustra-tions that his neighborhood was a bad place, but a bad place that also con-tained good things, Jamal's instructor asked him whether he would like to live elsewhere:

> If you could live anywhere, where would you live? Have you seen other neighborhoods you'd rather live in than yours?
>
> No! (*as if shocked*)
>
> Really? But I thought you said your neighborhood's bad!
>
> It is! (*as if bewildered*)
>
> But you still want to live there?
>
> Right. (*as if convinced*)

The son of two caring parents who protected him and encouraged him to study; a boy who described himself as smart, looked toward college, and imagined a career in technology (he told his instructor that he planned to be the DUSTY "technologist" when he grew up); an independent thinker and doer who could, if he needed, go against the grain (he refused to join a popular program where kids could make digital beats and rhymes because he preferred jazz to hip-hop), Jamal's ability to create an accomplished digi-tal poem and to think productively about surrounding place, space, and landscape had many deep roots. In addition, we believe that his considerable abilities were enabled by his journey each day to DUSTY, crossing from his East Oakland neighborhood to West Oakland; by the material space and resources that DUSTY offered around multimodal technologies; and by the lived space that his instructors and mentors enacted, through assignments, field trips, activities, and relationships, in service of enabling youth to create and learn.

In summary, we would argue that Jamal's place-based identity in relation to Oakland neighborhoods had dimensions of both identification and distancing, and these were depicted in his multimodal digital poem with an impact that would be difficult to duplicate in a conventional linguistic text. In making his digital poem, Jamal created a landscape of West Oakland, his own complex representation of his neighborhoods, a multidimensional depiction that contrasts in its complexity the flatter, more stereotypical portraits found on neighborhood billboards. It is this representational power that is precisely what DUSTY hopes to offer its participants—the space, material and symbolic resources, relationships, and curricular direction that are needed to examine oneself in relation to present and imagined social worlds. Concluding his essay on place, space, and landscape, Mitchell (2002) wondered, "Do we make places, or do they make us?", and he acknowledged "the shifting valences of this question" (p. xii). By creating a space that positions children, youth, and adults to construct representations of landscape and place in relation to themselves, we hope to foreground and foster human agentive potential.[16]

Conclusion: Constructing Hopeful Spaces

We believe that service learning and after-school programs represent opportunities to help construct hopeful learning spaces for children and youth in our most neglected communities. We therefore urge a shift in the attention by those academics who are involved in this kind of work—from a focus primarily or solely on university perspectives and needs to a joint focus on sustained, long-term participation in local communities. Doing so will involve finding ways to move beyond depictions of local neighborhoods that only romanticize or demonize, toward understandings that build on historical, social, and spatial analyses—somewhat in the way Jamal does in his digital poem. On the basis of our work at DUSTY and that of others elsewhere, we further believe that a strong case can be made for crafting after-school spaces that do more than replicate the school day. In the tradition of Cole (1996), we see much to be gained from experimenting with the "in-between-ness" of school time and nonschool time. As one of the children at DUSTY explained, a child who struggled deeply with the literacy requirements of schooling as well as with establishing friendships, DUSTY for him stood for something in the middle, "between school and fun," to use the words he used in his digital story. This child, especially through his relationships with undergraduate mentors, began to sort through some of his social and academic difficulties in the hybrid space of an after-school program (cf. Roche-Smith, 2004). We believe that the same has been true for many children, especially through the creation of identity texts like those that constitute the DUSTY version of digital storytelling.

A primary assumption underpinning DUSTY is the power of being able to represent—to depict one's own social reality in relation to another's, and to do so using the most current and potent mediational means. At this moment, that powerful means is multimedia and multimodality. For perhaps the first time in history, ordinary individuals can potentially wield some of the communicational wizardry that used to be reserved for mass media and the elite—assuming, that is, that access is provided to material tools and supportive social practices. Regularly through DUSTY we show kids' and adults' stories on the big screen of a local theater or other public space, and we invite their friends and relatives and the wider community to view these multimodal creations and have a conversation about what they represent. At one such event, a young girl's story about the noise and litter in West Oakland attracted the interest of a city councilwoman for the neighborhood who hoped to improve it aesthetically. Youth also exchange stories with children in other locales and other countries, conducting swaps of digital media, including original beats and rhymes. Thereby we redraw the boundaries of place again, extending our sense of community to include an interconnectedness with others far removed in physical distance. Being able to communicate compellingly with words, images, sound, and movement, and being able to produce artifacts that can traverse geographical, social, and semiotic boundaries bring us close to a new definition of *literacy* (cf. Hull, 2003).

Examining children's compelling digital stories, and reflecting on the possibilities of traversing boundaries, we are apt to forget the extreme challenges that accompany attempts to sustain community and university partnerships. There is a danger, then, through chapters such as this, of creating a fictionalized, idealized landscape of after school. Thus, we look forward to examining the uphill battles that characterize our kind of work—for example, the almost constant worry regarding sustainability, the evolving relationships with local nonprofits that can prove surprisingly combative (perhaps because of an increased competition for a smaller and smaller pool of funding), the continual need to be accountable to the local community in ways that one does not always foresee or sometimes agree with, and a range of tensions inspired by the different realities of those who come from the university and those who live in the West Oakland community.

Geographer David Harvey (2000), writing as the last century closed and reflecting on the world's vast inequalities and our failures in the United States to create the kind of just society for which many yearn, nonetheless concludes, as we do, with optimism: "I believe that in this moment in our history we have something of great import to accomplish by exercising an optimism of the intellect in order to open up ways of thinking that have for too long remained foreclosed" (p. 17). He sets about theorizing the decline and revitalization of inner cities, using Baltimore as an example, and calls for a utopian imagining that would afford the design of a more equitable future. He sharply critiques the degradation of urban landscapes, and just as passionately offers a vision for what cities might become if we train ourselves to think outside existing structures and norms. The parallels between the declining inner city of Baltimore, as described by Harvey, and similar sections of Oakland, California, where we live and work, are striking, and we take heart from his encouragement to imagine alternatives. To be sure, after-school programs and service learning programs are about as marginal as organizations can be in relation to the institutions of school and university—hardly spaces from which to mount a challenge to inequalities and injustices. But we believe, and we hope we have suggested in this chapter, that it is both crucial and enlivening to choose marginality (cf. hooks, 1990) and then to create lived spaces where hopeful projects and good work are freshly imagined and kept alive. We think of DUSTY, in this way at this moment, as providing the chance to construct a space that draws on the local neighborhood, its schools, and the university community, but also transcends them, recharting our geography as we traverse it, if you will, making possible some things that are impossible in either setting alone.

NOTES

1. We gratefully acknowledge the support of the following funders: the U.S. Department of Education's Community Technology Centers program; the University of California's UCLinks Program; the Community Technology Foundation of California; the City of Oakland's Fund for Children and Youth; and the Robert F. Bowne Foundation. We appreciate as well the support of our university and community partners: the Graduate School of Education, University of California, Berkeley; the Prescott-Joseph Center for Community Enhancement; Allen Temple Baptist Church; Cole Middle School; and the Castlemont Community of Small Schools. We salute the DUSTY staff, instructors, undergraduates, and participants who make our work together seem more like play. We thank Verda Delp, Tiffany Hooker, Mark Jury, Mira-Lisa Katz, Nora Kenney, Stacy Marple, Mark Nelson, Laura Nicodemus, Mike Rose, and Jessica Zacher for their insightful comments on and assistance with this chapter. Nora Kenney was the DUSTY instructor who taught Jamal, the child who is our case study in this chapter. We thank her for her insights about him as well as for her skill in interviewing him. She was assisted by Amanda Esteva, who worked with Jamal on the digital poem featured here, as did Pauline Pearson Hathorn. We thank them all for their excellent work with Jamal and the other DUSTY students. Finally and especially, we thank Jamal—for his creativity, his generosity of spirit, a wisdom that went beyond his years, and his willingness to share his work with us and a larger audience.

2. In offering these understandings of space, place, and landscape, Mitchell helpfully combined insights from LeFebvre (1974) on perceived, conceived, and lived space, and de Certeau (1984), who juxtaposed place with space, which he conceptualized as "a practiced place" (p. 117).

3. For a more detailed account of Oakland's history, we recommend Rhomberg (2004).

4. These data on schools and test scores came from the California State Department's Web site, except for the statistics on the Catholic school, which was personal communication with the school's principal.

5. See www.indybay.org/print.php?id=1566613 for a photograph taken at a sideshow and a brief description of these gatherings. After a young person was killed in a car accident associated with one of the Oakland sideshows, the state mobilized, and a bill was passed outlawing and penalizing the gatherings.

6. Our discussion in this chapter is primarily about digital storytelling and its intersection with the enactment of identities in relation to spatiality. For an account of the deep connection between music-making and identity, see Hudak (1999).

7. Although we do not describe the curriculum and pedagogy that underpin DUSTY in this chapter, a detailed account is provided in Roche-Smith (2004).

8. Our undergraduate mentors write field notes about their observations and interactions at DUSTY. Here are Stella's field notes about Stephen's many questions regarding college:

> Stephen said he wanted to be an author, a lawyer, or the president. I asked him why he came to the tutoring sessions and he said he wanted to because it helped him with his

work. He is very motivated to learn and he said he loved learning and really wanted to go to college. He then started asking me all these questions about college like how do you get in, where do you live, how do you pay for it. I told him some people get scholarships and a lot of people take out loans. I explained to him what loans were. He listened very intently and nodded after everything I said. He said he might want to go to law school and he mentioned Harvard. He was like, "That's a really good school isn't it?" I replied, "One of the best!" He asked how to get into law school and I told him how he needed to go to college first and get good grades and then take the LSATs, and then write a personal statement. He was so interested and asked me so many questions.

9. To our knowledge, this is the first such study of this topic, either within literacy studies or cultural geography.

10. Jamal is a self-selected pseudonym; the names of other children and undergraduate participants have also been changed. To further protect Jamal's privacy, we have not made his digital poem available. However, to see examples of the kinds of stories children and adults at DUSTY create, please visit this Web site: www.oaklanddusty.org.

11. Some of our recent research has focused on devising a framework for analyzing multimodal digital stories (cf. Hull & Nelson, 2005).

12. Jamal's digital story did not include the first line from his poem about hearing the sirens of ambulances. When he viewed his story and discussed it with us, he noted that this was a mistake and said he would like for that line to be included or for the picture of an ambulance to be deleted.

13. However, Jamal was not able to represent his friends as African Americans pictorially in his digital story because he could not find the images he wanted of African-American children on the Internet. Line b, "I hear kids laughing at the boy who fell down," is therefore illustrated with an Internet photo of White children laughing and gazing downward. However, Jamal reported that this part of his poem was based on his own experience of falling off his bike because of the cracks in the pavement, and his friends, who were African American, laughing at him. He had wanted these children to look like his real friends. The difficulty of finding images of African Americans through image searches on the Internet is a frequent complaint at our community technology center.

14. We have documented many instances in which small local neighborhoods are divided geographically in ways that constrain participation in activities and the creation of relationships. For example, some parents would not allow their children to walk a small number of blocks to DUSTY, even during daylight hours, because they would thereby have to traverse borders associated with youth gangs. To give another instance, once when we sponsored a music event at another community center, an event that brought participants from the university and various neighborhood enclaves together, the man who controlled drug sales on that block stopped by to announce that this was his street, to inspect the event, and then give his blessing to the gathering.

15. When we viewed his movie with Jamal, he objected to the screen on which he had cut out his face and superimposed it on a beach scene, because he said his face did not look "real" in scale against the backdrop.

16. In this chapter, we analyzed only one kind of spatially sensitive digital story—one whose most salient dimensions were identification and distancing. Additional categories not presented here include imaginary landscapes, territoriality, interconnectedness, and diasporas, and we hope to study and write about these in our subsequent work.

REFERENCES

Aitken, S. C. (2001). *Geographies of young people: The morally contested spaces of identity.* London & New York: Routledge.

Berry, K. A., & Henderson, M. (2002). Introduction: Envisioning the nexus between geography and ethnic and racial identity. In K. A. Berry & M. Henderson (Eds.), *Geographic identities of ethnic America: Race, space, and place* (pp. 1–14). Reno: University of Nevada Press.

Boyle-Baise, M. (2002). *Multicultural service learning: Educating teachers in diverse communities.* New York: Teachers College Press.

Bruner, J. (1994). The remembered self. In U. Neisser & R. Fivush (Eds.), *The remembering self: Construction and agency in self narrative* (pp. 41–54). Cambridge: Cambridge University Press.

Bunge, W. W., & Bordessa, R. (1975). *The Canadian alternative: Survival, expeditions and urban change.* Geographical Monographs, No. 2. Toronto: York University.

Cole, M. (1996). *Cultural psychology: A once and future discipline.* Cambridge, MA: Harvard University Press.

Compaine, B. M. (Ed.). (2001). *The digital divide: Facing a crisis or creating a myth?* Cambridge, MA: MIT Press.

Cushman, E. (1999). The public intellectual, service learning, and activist research. *College English, 61*(3), 328–336.

Cushman, E. (2002). Sustainable service learning programs. *College Composition and Communication, 54*(1), 40–65.

Deans, T. (2000). *Writing partnerships: Service-learning in composition.* Urbana, IL: National Council of Teachers of English.

de Certeau, M. (1984). *The practice of everyday life.* Berkeley: University of California Press.

Dewey, J. (1938). *Experience and education.* New York: Macmillan.

Duncan, J. S., & Duncan, N. G. (2004). *Landscapes of privilege: The politics of the aesthetic in an American suburb.* New York: Routledge.

Erickson, E. H. (1977). *Toys and reasons.* New York: Norton.

Fairlie, R. W. (2003, November). *Is there a digital divide? Ethnic and racial differences in access to technology and possible explanations.* Final report to the University of California, Latino Policy Institute and California Policy Research Center.

Flower, L. (2002). Intercultural inquiry and the transformation of service. *College English, 65*(2), 181–201.

Flower, L. (2003). Talking across difference: Intercultural rhetoric and the search for situated knowledge. *College Composition and Communication, 55*(1), 38–68.

Freire, P. (1970). *Pedagogy of the oppressed.* New York: Continuum.

Furco, A., & Billig, S. H. (Eds.). (2002). *Service-learning: The essence of the pedagogy.* Greenwich, CT: Information Age Publishing.

Ginwright, S. A. (2004). *Black in school: Afrocentric reform, urban youth, and the promise of hip-hop culture.* New York: Teachers College Press.

Gutiérrez, K., Baquedano-Lopez, P., & Tejeda, C. (1999). Rethinking diversity: Hybridity and hybrid language practices in the third space. *Mind, Culture, & Activity: An International Journal, 6*(4), 286–303.

Halpern, R. (2002). A different kind of child development institution: The history of after-school programs for low-income children. *Teachers College Record, 104*(2), 178–211.

Halpern, R. (2003). *Making play work: The promise of after-school programs for low-income children.* New York: Teachers College.

Harvey, D. (2000). *Spaces of hope.* Berkeley: University of California Press.

Herzberg, B. (1994). Community service and critical thinking. *College Composition and Communication, 45*(3), 307–319.

Himley, M. (2004). Facing (up to) "the stranger" in community service learning. *College Composition and Communication, 55*(3), 416–438.

hooks, b. (1990). *Yearning.* Boston: South End Press.

Hudak, G. (1999). The "sound" identity: Music-making and schooling. In C. McCarthy, G. Hudak, S. Miklaucic, & P. Saukko (Eds.), *Sound identities: Popular music and the cultural politics of education* (pp. 447–474). New York: Peter Lang.

Hull, G. A. (2003). Youth culture and digital media: New literacies for new times. *Research in the Teaching of English 38*(2), 229–233.

Hull, G. A., & Katz, M.-L. (2006). Crafting an agentive self: Case studies on digital storytelling. *Research in the Teaching of English, 41*(1).

Hull, G. A., & Nelson, M. (2005). Locating the semiotic power of multimodality. *Written Communication, 22*(2), 224–262.

Hull, G., & Schultz, K. (Eds.). (2002). *School's out! Bridging out-of-school literacies with classroom practice.* New York: Teachers College Press.

Hull, G., & Zacher, J. (2004, Winter/Spring). What is after-school worth? Developing literacies and identities out-of-school. *Voices in Urban Education, 3,* 36–44.

Kane, T. J. (2004). *The impact of after-school programs: Interpreting the results of four recent evaluations.* William T. Grant Foundation Working Paper.

Kress, G. (2003). *Literacy in the new media age.* London: Routledge.

Lambert, J. (2002). *Digital storytelling: Capturing lives, creating community.* Berkeley: Digital Diner Press.

Leander, K. M. (2002). Locating Latanya: The situated production of identity artifacts in classroom interaction. *Research in the Teaching of English, 37,* 198–250.

Leander, K. M., & Sheehy, M. (Eds.). (2004). *Spatializing literacy research and practice.* New York: Peter Lang.

Lefebvre, H. (1974). *The production of space* (D. Nicholson-Smith, Trans.). Malden, MA: Blackwell.

Leoni, L., & Cohen, S. (2004, September 18). *Identity texts: Bringing students' culture to the fore of literacy.* Paper presented at the International Conference on Cultural Diversity and Language Education, University of Hawaii at Manoa.

Long, E., Peck, W. C., & Baskins, J. A. (2002). "Struggle": A literate practice supporting life-project planning. In G. Hull & K. Schultz (Eds.), *School's out! Bridging out-of-school literacies with classroom practice* (pp. 131–161). New York: Teachers College Press.

Massey, D. (1998). The spatial construction of youth cultures. In T. Skelton & G. Valentine (Eds.), *Cool places: Geographies of youth cultures* (pp. 121–129). London: Routledge.

Matthews, H., & Limb, M. (1999). Defining an agenda for the geography of children: Review and prospect. *Progress in Human Geography, 23*(1), 61–90.

Mitchell, W. J. T. (1994). *Picture theory: Essays on verbal and visual representation.* Chicago: University of Chicago Press.

Mitchell, W. J. T. (2002). Space, place, and landscape. In W. J. T. Mitchell (Ed.), *Landscape and power* (2nd ed., pp. vii–xii). Chicago: University of Chicago Press.

Moje, E. B. (2004). Powerful spaces: Tracing the out-of-school literacy spaces of Latino/a youth. In K. M. Leander & M. Sheehy (Eds.), *Spatializing literacy research and practice* (pp. 15–38). New York: Peter Lang.

Morrell, E. (2004). *Linking literacy and popular culture.* Norwood, MA: Christopher-Gordon Publishers.

National Institute on Out-of-School Time. (2003). *Making the case: A fact sheet on children and youth in out-of-school-time.* Wellesley, MA: Center for Research on Women, Wellesley College.

Noguera, P. (1996). Confronting the urban in urban school reform. *The Urban Review, 28*(1), 1–19.

Peck, W. C., Flower, L., & Higgins, L. (1995). Community literacy. *College Composition and Communication, 46,* 199–222.

Peirce, C. S. (1955). Logic as semiotic: The theory of signs. In J. Buchler (Ed.), *Philosophical writings of Peirce* (pp. 98–119). New York: Dover.

Piaget, J. (1971). *Structuralism.* New York: Basic Books.

Rhomberg, C. (2004). *No there there: Race, class, and political community in Oakland.* Berkeley: University of California Press.

Roche-Smith, J. (2004). *Crossing frontiers and discovering paths: Young adolescents in a digital storytelling program.* Unpublished doctoral dissertation, University of California, Berkeley.

Soja, E. W. (2004). Preface. In K. M. Leander & M. Sheehy (Eds.), *Spatializing literacy research and practice* (pp. ix–xv). New York: Peter Lang.

Soja, E. W. (1996). *Thirdspace: Journey to Los Angeles and other real- and imagined-places.* Malden, MA: Blackwell.

Underwood, C., Welsh, M., Gauvain, M., & Duffy, S. (2000). Learning at the edges: Challenges to the sustainability of service-learning in higher education. *Journal of Language and Learning Across the Disciplines, 4*(3), 7–26.

Urciuoli, B. (1995). The indexical structure of visibility. In B. Farnell (Ed.), *Human action signs in cultural context: The visible and the invisible in movement and dance* (pp. 189–215). Metuchen, NJ, & London: Scarecrow.

Valentine, G., Skelton, T., & Chambers, D. (1998). Cool places: An introduction to youth cultures. In T. Skelton & G. Valentine (Eds.), *Cool places: Geographies of youth cultures* (pp. 1–32). London: Routledge.

Vygotsky, L. (1934/1986). *Thought and language.* Cambridge, MA: Cambridge University Press.

Vygotsky, L. (1978). *Mind in society: The development of higher psychological processes.* Cambridge, MA: Harvard University Press.

Warschauer, M. (2004). *Technology and social inclusion: Rethinking the digital divide.* Cambridge, MA: MIT Press.

Welch, N. (2002). "And now that I know them": Composing mutuality in a service learning course. *College Composition and Communication, 54*(2), 243–263.

PART TWO

The Terms of Service-Learning

9   *English Studies and Public Service*

THOMAS DEANS

The pairing of college writing instruction with community action marks a relatively new (and growing) movement in rhetoric and composition. Increasingly, novice college writers are working in teams to compose research reports, newsletter articles, and manuals for local nonprofit agencies; tutoring children and bringing that experience back to the classroom as a text to be analyzed alongside other texts; and collaborating with urban youth to craft documents in intercultural, hybrid rhetorics. As one who sees promise in such community-based pedagogies, I have entered the fray, integrating community outreach into my teaching as well as developing university–community partnerships hinging on writing instruction. In this study I step back from the range of existing service-learning courses and projects in order to explore how the movement relates—in theory and in practice—to composition studies. My approach balances discussions of composition theory, critical pedagogy, and rhetoric with three case studies of particular service-learning initiatives.

The Commission on National and Community Service defines service-learning as a method of teaching that: (a) provides educational experiences under which students learn and develop through active participation in thoughtfully organized service experiences that meet community needs and that are coordinated in collaboration with school and community; (b) is integrated into the students' academic curriculum or provides structured time for a student to think, talk, or write about what the student did and saw during the service; (c) provides a student with opportunities to use newly acquired skills and knowledge in real-life situations in their own communities; and (d) enhances what is taught in school by extending student learning beyond the classroom and into the community, thus helping students to develop a sense of caring for others (*National Community Service Trust Act of 1993*). Thus, service-learning is not volunteerism or community service; nor is it simply an academic internship or field placement. While service-learning

From *Writing Partnerships: Service-Learning in Composition*. Urbana, IL: National Council of Teachers of English, 2000. 1–24.

may draw on these practices, it is at heart a pedagogy of action and reflection, one that centers on a dialectic between community outreach and academic inquiry. I use the terms *service-learning, community-based learning,* and *community writing* to refer to programs covered under this definition and, more generally, to initiatives that move the context for writing instruction beyond the bounds of the traditional college classroom in the interest of actively and concretely addressing community needs.

Reports of service-learning from the field are largely encouraging. Practitioners have opened new contexts for teaching and learning that simultaneously address disciplinary learning goals and pressing community needs. Teachers and students speak of reenergized classrooms and a boost in motivation. Moreover, pedagogical values now universally lauded in composition—active learning, student-centered learning, cooperative learning, lifelong learning, cross-cultural understanding, critical thinking, authentic evaluation—are built into the very blood and bone of most community-based academic projects. Until recently, much of the evidence in support of service-learning has been anecdotal—teaching narratives of renewed student engagement, improved writing competency, and expanded social awareness and ethical development. Because part of this study is about trusting experience, we should not dismiss out of hand the teaching lore in support of service-learning. But there is also a growing body of empirical research that analyzes how community-based pedagogies relate to particular learning and development outcomes, and much of that research, like the teaching narratives, points to promising possibilities for service-learning.

For example, in a comprehensive study of college-level service-learning, Janet Eyler, Dwight E. Giles Jr., and John Braxton gathered data from fifteen hundred students at twenty colleges and universities in an attempt to answer some key questions about the value added to student learning by combining community service and academic study. The study measured students' self-assessments of citizenship skills (including listening and verbal skills, leadership skills, and capacity for tolerance), confidence that they can and should make a difference in their communities, community-related values, and perceptions of social problems and social justice. As might be expected, the data revealed that students who opt for a service-learning component in a course differ significantly from those who opt out. Students who selected the service-learning option scored higher on virtually every outcome measured (10).

More important, the study finds that participation in service-learning has a discernible effect on student learning. The authors conclude that service-learning programs appear to have an impact on students' attitudes, values, and skills, as well as on the way they think about social issues, even over the relatively brief period of a semester (13). However, the authors qualify that conclusion: "While the effect is significant, it is small; few interventions of a semester's length have a dramatic impact on outcomes. What is impressive is the consistent pattern of impact across a large number of different outcomes; service-learning is a consistent predictor and often the only significant or best predictor beyond the pre-test measure of the variable" (13). As might be expected, positive interaction with faculty, one of the other factors measured in the study, also contributed independently to many outcomes; still, according to the researchers, "these interactions did not wash out the effect of service on students" (11). Furthermore, service-learning was "the only significant or best predictor" of two student outcomes that are of particular interest to composition teachers: the capacity of students *to see problems as systemic*, and the ability *to see things from multiple perspectives*. The study suggests that service-learning makes a unique impact on college students with respect to these two factors, improving student outcomes with greater predictability than even the level of faculty–student interaction.[1] In turn, if one assumes that an important goal of composition courses is to encourage critical consciousness, then one needs to attend to service-learning, insofar as it is a pedagogy that helps students see problems as systemic and helps them acknowledge multiple perspectives.

In a different study, using data collected from 3,450 students (2,309 service participants and 1,141 nonparticipants) attending forty-two institutions, the Higher Education Research Institute at the University of California at Los Angeles analyzed the impact of community outreach work on students. After accounting for the influence of the characteristics that predispose students to engage in community service (not service-learning, but community service more generally), researchers discovered significant positive correlations between service and student outcomes in all three areas they measured: civic responsibility, academic attainment, and life skills (Sax and Astin). For example, with respect to civic responsibility, undergraduates who engaged in service were more likely than nonparticipants to strengthen their commitment to promoting racial understanding, to participating in community action programs, and to influencing social values. With respect to academic development, those who engaged in service saw their grades rise slightly, were nearly 50 percent more likely to spend at least one hour a week interacting with faculty, and spent more time studying than did nonparticipants. With respect to life skills, service participants showed greater positive change in all outcomes analyzed, with the largest differences occurring in understanding of community problems, knowledge and acceptance of various races and cultures, and interpersonal skills. Moreover, a separate longitudinal study of more than twelve thousand students over a nine-year period confirmed long-term benefits, particularly greater commitments to racial understanding and to civic involvement in the years after college.[2]

While these results of the UCLA studies pertain to community service in general, researchers found additional benefits for students in course-based service-learning. Students who have participated in academic service-learning report a deeper commitment to their communities, better preparation for careers, improved conflict management, and greater understanding of community problems.[3] Likewise, a cluster of other empirical studies of service-learning suggests discernible learning and development outcomes (see Osborne, Hammerich, and Hensley; Mabry; Reeb, Katsuyama, Sammon, and Yoder; Miller; Markus, Howard, and King; Kendrick).

The results of such research are important because they confirm and sharpen the anecdotal support for service-learning, even as they temper the sometimes overenthusiastic claims made in its name. Still, quantitative studies never tell the whole story; they often overlook significant contextual concerns and they always have limitations (the research discussed above, for example, is based almost exclusively on self-reported data). Moreover, and of particular note for my focus on college composition, these studies tell us precious little about situated student writing or rhetorical competency. Because of this oversight, composition researchers themselves need to take up the charge and investigate community writing projects in context, as I do in the three case studies of community–university partnerships that form the core of this book.

While I focus on English studies, and more specifically on college writing instruction, we should note that service-learning is afoot across the disciplines. In the sciences, social sciences, arts, humanities, and preprofessional disciplines, one can find active, even if relatively small, pockets of community-based learning at a range of colleges and universities. Some early adopters of service-learning are working in isolation; some are connecting with others on their campuses; some are networking within their disciplinary and professional organizations; and some are collaborating across disciplines and campuses through national organizations that promote service-learning. Those opting for community-based pedagogies are a diverse lot who hail from a range of institutions and who practice varied approaches to teaching and social action, but they all share a commitment to improving the quality of undergraduate education by combining classroom learning with community outreach. They believe that they have discovered an innovation that encourages curricular synergies and student learning in ways that traditional pedagogies often do not.

Such claims might sound familiar, since in years past we have experienced cross-disciplinary swells of enthusiasm for such movements as writing across the curriculum and instructional technology. These movements are akin to service-learning not simply because they are cross-disciplinary and focus on improving pedagogy, but also because, when done well, all encourage active, rigorous, and reflective learning. These approaches invite students to assume agency in their own education and to draw on that education when venturing beyond campus. Moreover, just as composition specialists have played leading roles in cross-curricular movements such as writing across the curriculum, it is important that they assert themselves as leaders in the service-learning movement. Not only do most service-learning projects—no matter the discipline—involve significant writing components, but also they advance teaching values—student-centered learning, collaborative inquiry, critical reflection—that compositionists have long championed.

There is, of course, a salient irony in inviting writing teachers to embrace the term "service," which has been a problematic word for composition studies for so long (see Crowley; Mahala and Swilky). However, service-learning practitioners do not associate service with *sub*service or with academic housekeeping. Instead, they redirect the meaning of the word toward its more vital associations with democracy, outreach, and social action. Furthermore, far from the composition field's experience of "service" dragging it into institutional limbo, the affirming sense of civic service in service-learning might even have the potential, as suggested recently by Ellen Cushman, to play a significant role in the ongoing efforts of English studies to characterize its teacher-scholars as "public intellectuals" ("Public").

WHY NOW?

Some forms of what is now being called service-learning have been practiced for decades under other banners—experiential learning, fieldwork, literacy outreach, action research, and certain kinds of critical pedagogy. However, as the number of courses and programs continues to grow, as formal service-learning administrative units are added to colleges and universities, and as a corpus of scholarly work on service-learning begins to take shape, one can discern something genuinely new under way in the current movement. With respect to composition, the editors of a recent collection of essays on service-learning and composition have gone so far as to name it a "micro-revolution"—small enough to go unnoticed by large segments of the profession but significant enough to prompt a rethinking of how we conceive of the teaching of writing and, more specifically, its connection to social action (Adler-Kassner, Crooks, and Watters).

All this raises the question, *Why now?* And, in particular, *Why now for rhetoric and composition?* Most service-learning practitioners who experiment with community-based pedagogies do so because they see them as a way to improve their teaching, to motivate students, to advance disciplinary learning, to facilitate student agency, or to enact values they hold dear, such as expanding public consciousness of social injustice or connecting cognitive learning to grounded social action. Yet some have tagged service-learning an educational fad, the latest in a long line of pedagogical quick fixes that will recede once the next big thing comes along. Still others have dismissed service-learning outright on the assumption that it represents a dressed-up version of paternalistic charity or noblesse oblige that will inevitably reproduce the injustices it purports to address.

Such dismissals of service-learning tend not only to prejudge the movement before examining its actual practices and outcomes but also to ignore the seismic shifts now under way in higher education. Such shifts are highlighted by some of our most perceptive observers of university life—people like Ernest Boyer, Clark Kerr, and Derek Bok. All suggest that we have entered a critical period in which colleges and universities need to reimagine not only how they go about teaching and doing research but also how they relate both to their host communities and to society more generally. Bok, former president of Harvard, questions whether "our universities are doing all that they can and should to help America surmount the obstacles that threaten to sap our economic strength and blight the lives of millions of our people" (6).

Boyer, a longtime observer of higher education, urges colleges and universities to "respond to the challenges that confront our schools, and our cities" ("Creating" 48). Kerr, once president of the University of California system, predicts that "better integration of education with work and public service is clearly forthcoming" (223). In concert with such institutional changes, higher education in the United States is also in the process of reimagining the very definition and purpose of liberal learning, with many voices arguing the need for a Deweyan pragmatist orientation that avoids the extremes of both "ivory tower" and utilitarian conceptions of education in favor of an integrative perspective that puts liberal education in service to democracy (see Orrill). The service-learning movement does not pretend to have the only fitting response to such sweeping concerns, but it does claim, and rightly so, to take them seriously and to respond at the level of teaching and learning.

Major theoretical shifts in the disciplines have also set the stage for service-learning—changes that make this movement more than simply an innovative teaching approach. In particular, the disciplinary discourse of rhetoric and composition, as it has unfolded over the past decade, posits a sound theoretical footing for community-oriented pedagogies. As a discipline, rhetoric and composition has adopted the broadly defined "social perspective" on writing. The discipline prefers to see itself as having evolved from studies of the lone writer to more contextual understandings of composing; from a narrow, functional definition of literacy, focused on correctness, to a broader definition; from an exclusive focus on academic discourse to the study of both school and nonacademic contexts for writing; from presuming white middle-class culture as normative to analyzing and inviting cultural difference; and from gatekeeping at the university to facilitating the advancement of all students.

Many scholars have suggested that in order for compositionists to align our practice with theoretical stances more social in orientation, we should adopt a critical pedagogy or cultural studies approach. I find such advocacy for having students read and analyze culture and ideology extremely promising; students should indeed learn habits of cultural critique and critical reading (which we usually ask them to express in academic essays). Yet I also recognize the theoretical and pedagogical corollary that students should learn to *write* themselves into the world through producing rhetorical documents that intervene materially in contexts beyond the academy. Just as some feminist scholars contend that critiques of patriarchal structures need to push beyond the language and genres dictated by the dominant culture, so too is there a need for writing teachers who imagine composition as a site for social justice work to push beyond the traditional genres dictated by the academy. In other words, we must persist in more coherently and more creatively matching our writing strategies to the claims we make for our reading strategies.

Most service-learning writing teachers, like composition instructors who are committed to critical literacy or cultural studies approaches, underscore the imperative to *read* the complex social forces that constitute one's cultural context—what Freire calls "reading the word and the world" (Freire and Macedo). But service-learning instructors also ask students to *write* purpose-driven documents for audiences beyond the classroom. Thus, in addition to inviting abstract critical *interpretation* of cultural phenomena, service-learning initiatives demand the logical corollary, that is, grounded, active *intervention* in the very cultural context we inhabit.

If the general inclination of members of the discipline is to theorize about writing as a social act, then service-learning is one means by which to under-score and extend this commitment. Take, for example, some of the most widely held theoretical stances in composition studies and how service-learning af-firms and potentially extends each one:

- While the social turn in composition has resulted in widening the audience for student writing from the lone teacher to peer groups, service-learning does the same and takes *the next logical step of widening the audience for student writing to include those beyond the classroom.*

- While the social turn in composition encourages teachers and students to see their writing not as skills and drills but as participation in a disciplinary discourse community, service-learning writing takes *the next logical step of asking students and teachers to situate their work in both disciplinary and wider non-academic communities.*

- While the social turn in composition has led researchers to study sites of writ-ing and literacy beyond the academy, community-based writing takes *the next logical step of asking students themselves to write within nonacademic discourse communities.*

- While the social turn in composition underscores the need to encourage mul-ticultural awareness and understanding in our classrooms, community-based writing takes *the next logical step of asking students to cross cultural and class boundaries by collaborating with community partners who often inhabit subject posi-tions different from those of the students.*

- While the social turn in composition (particularly as it takes the form of critical pedagogy) speaks to the ethical, democratizing, and consciousness-raising potential of the writing classroom, many forms of service-learning confirm such critical intellectual habits and go *the next logical step of marrying them with pragmatic civic action.*

Therefore service-learning—and, within that broad umbrella, what oth-ers alternately call community service writing, community-based learning, literate social action, activist research, or academic outreach—can be viewed as the fruition of some of the most important contemporary theoretical claims of rhetoric and composition studies. Given such theoretical footings—in ad-dition to the promising cognitive and motivational outcomes suggested by the first wave of programs—it is no wonder that interest in service-learning is on the ascent at institutions ranging from community colleges to liberal arts colleges to research universities.

Furthermore, if we take the long view, in the history of Greek and Roman rhetoric we find compelling warrants for service-learning. Aristotle's *Rhetoric* was intended, after all, not to help students succeed in school settings but rather to equip rhetors to intervene in the public sphere. Isocrates, Cicero, Quintilian, and a host of others speak of the need to connect rhetorical practice to civic responsibility, which is, certainly, a central concern of contemporary service-learning theory and practice. Likewise, in the sweep of U.S. history—from Thomas Jefferson and Benjamin Franklin to Jane Addams and John Dewey—one finds examples of experiential learning combined with democratic aspirations that support a service-learning approach to teaching and learning.

EMERGING CONVERSATIONS ABOUT SERVICE-LEARNING

Throughout the history of U.S. higher education, service to the community—be it the local, national, or global community—has been integral to the missions of a wide range of colleges and universities, whether motivated by an ethic of public service, a mandate to extend research to the general public, or a commitment to particular religious beliefs. The current service-learning movement builds on this past and on several strands of educational history that emphasize the integration of higher learning with grounded social action, especially the extension programs spawned by the land grant movement of the 1860s, the progressive education reforms of the first half of the twentieth century, and the civil rights and activist movements of the 1960s (Stanton, Giles, and Cruz).

Likewise, English studies has a long-standing tradition of concern for social justice. Much of our theory is propelled by commitments to democracy, equality, critical literacy, and multiculturalism. Moreover, much of our classroom practice is motivated by a commitment to prepare all students for reflective and critical participation in their personal, cultural, working, and civic lives. Yet as English teachers, we focus nearly all our energies on the textual realm and limit our teaching of reading and writing to the classroom space, trusting that the critical and imaginative habits of mind we encourage in the classroom will carry over into the world beyond. I believe that many such habits *do* carry over; but I also recognize the need for connecting the work of English studies directly to action in local communities. Just as critical theory and cultural studies have demanded that we widen our reading beyond the traditional literary canon, service-learning demands that we widen the sites for writing and learning beyond campus gates. Some disciplines that have long-standing traditions of integrating fieldwork with academic study, such as education or anthropology, find this move quite natural. However, for teachers of composition and for others in the humanities, moving beyond the bounds of campus may feel unfamiliar, even risky.

Recent enthusiasm for service-learning across the disciplines and at all levels of schooling should hearten us, as should the first wave of community-based college writing courses. Across the country, service-learning is being heralded as a promising pedagogical approach by scores of school and community partners. It also finds allies in university administrators, foundations, local community leaders, government agencies, professional associations, and the general public. Thus, those new to service-learning can benefit from growing networks of service-learning educators and learn from their collective experiences—the successes as well as the failures.

Community-based learning is new to nearly all quarters of English studies, except for some small pockets of technical writing and journalism. And even though the past ten years have seen a surge in rhetoric and composition scholarship focused on sites of writing beyond the classroom, our teaching practices, for the most part, lag behind this research trend, particularly with respect to writing in nonprofit and community settings. However, important experiments in service-learning, as well as research into the theoretical dimensions of this pedagogy, are now under way—and with increasing range and vigor. Some teachers are dipping a toe in the water, adding a small or optional service-learning component to an existing composition course. Some are wading in waist deep by more fully integrating community writing into new and existing courses. Some are diving in headfirst, setting up comprehensive programs, collaborating with other administrative units on campus, and cultivating long-term relationships with community partners.

Service-learning is also working its way into the professional forums and disciplinary discourses of English. At the 1997 Conference on College Composition and Communication (CCCC), thirty-three papers headlined service-learning; two workshops advised participants on how to start a program; two special interest groups convened; and one keynote speaker lauded service-learning as a particularly apt response to major institutional changes in higher education. The 1998 CCCC featured many service-learning papers and added a symposium and a number of local community site visits during the conference. The 1999 CCCC continued this upswing in interest with a range of diverse papers, workshops, and presentations on service-learning.

Networks formed by and for teachers and scholars in rhetoric and composition have emerged and continue to develop—for example, the CCCC Service-Learning and Community Literacy Special Interest Group. National organizations working to support service-learning now include such groups as Campus Compact, the American Association for Higher Education, the National Society for Experiential Education, the National Information Center for Service Learning, the American Association of Community Colleges, and the National Council of Teachers of English. The Invisible College, a cross-disciplinary faculty association focused specifically on service-learning in the disciplines, is now active. Furthermore, service-learning is supported by various administrative units at particular universities, such as Edward Ginsberg Center for Service and Learning at the University of Michigan, the Feinstein Institute for Public Service at Providence College, the Bentley College Service-Learning Project, and the Haas Center for Public Service at Stanford University, among others.

Scholarly publication, perhaps the most powerful legitimizing force in the academy, is also making a place for service-learning. Publications offering broad overviews and bibliographies of service-learning are now available (e.g., Barber and Battistoni; Delve, Mintz, and Stewart; Jacoby; Julier; Kendall and Associates; Kraft and Swadener; Leder and McGuinness; Lempert; Lisman; Parsons and Lisman; Rhoads; Rhoads and Howard; Schine; Waterman; Zlotkowski). The first peer-reviewed journal devoted to service-learning, *The Michigan Journal of Community Service Learning*, was launched in 1995. In rhetoric and composition, the first collection of essays explicitly connecting service-learning and composition studies, *Writing the Community: Concepts and Models for Service-Learning in Composition*, was published in 1997. Articles are starting to surface in *College Composition and Communication*, *College English*, *Composition Studies*, and *The Writing Instructor*. More and more composition graduate students are writing dissertations that center on service-learning. Without doubt, further research and reflection on community writing is in the pipeline. Community-based learning in composition may still be a largely experimental and marginal activity, but it seems to have secured at least a beachhead in the disciplinary discourse. . . .

GUIDING PURPOSES

While service-learning practices are gaining steam, and some particular programs are well-researched, the movement as a whole remains largely unstudied. Among the available research on courses and projects, there is little sense of how one initiative relates to others or to the broader landscape of composition studies, rhetoric, and critical theory. Therefore, this study adopts a comparative and contextualizing approach, even as it examines three particular service-learning projects in action. It is guided by five purposes:

- To examine the theoretical assumptions of a diverse range of university/community partnerships that hinge on college-level writing instruction and rhetoric.

- To sort those community writing practices into coherent categories, so as to understand more clearly their literacy aims, ideological assumptions, and curricular goals.

- To relate the aims, assumptions, and practices of service-learning writing initiatives to current scholarly discourses in composition studies, rhetorical theory, and critical theory—and in particular to the writings of John Dewey and Paulo Freire.

- To balance deliberations on theory with discussions of lived experience by presenting empirical case studies of three exemplary service-learning writing projects.

- To assert that service-learning writing initiatives deserve a place in the college English curriculum, and to suggest how teachers and administrators might thoughtfully design and support such courses and programs.

As a first step in analyzing service-learning, I propose a taxonomy for this relatively new but already quite diverse movement in writing pedagogy and research. Yet even as I do this, I examine root theoretical and curricular concerns in English studies. I take my cue, in part, from James Britton's early work. Describing the contributions of Britton and Albert Kitzhaber to the Dartmouth Conference of 1966, Joseph Harris sees them as speaking out of two fundamentally different theoretical frames—Kitzhaber wanting to define the field of English, and Britton questioning the assumptions and aims of the field. Harris remarks: "While Kitzhaber looked to theory for a map of the subject to be studied, for a set of principles that would organize what we need to know about how texts are composed and interpreted, Britton took a more rhetorical or performative view of it as a means to an end, a form of reflection on action whose aim is to change teaching in direct and immediate ways" (142).

I do some mapping by dividing community writing programs into three categories: writing *for* the community; writing *about* the community; and writing *with* the community. However, I also critically examine my categories, putting each in dialogue with scholarship in composition and critical theory. Ultimately, my findings function, in Harris's words, as "a form of reflection on action whose aim is to change teaching in direct and immediate ways."

SORTING COURSES AND PROGRAMS: THREE PARADIGMS FOR COMMUNITY WRITING

A dizzying range of courses and programs march under the banner of service-learning. Just as approaches to teaching composition vary widely, so too do the ways that teachers combine writing instruction and community action through service-learning. The variety of initiatives currently under way is at once encouraging and overwhelming. Some courses look like standard composition courses with a service-learning add-on (whether required or optional). Some are (or resemble) technical writing courses or internship programs with a nonprofit rather than a corporate focus. Some foreground critical pedagogy and cultural critique. Some center on intercultural inquiry or problem solving. Some devote nearly all of their energies to personal narratives of and reflections on student outreach experiences. Some gather a mixed bag of service-learning strategies into one course. Some are comprehensive literacy projects or cross-disciplinary efforts rather than revamped composition courses. Given this range—and in order to discuss community writing with any degree of clarity—we must first sort through the variety of courses and programs.

One method of sorting composition initiatives that has surfaced in service-learning research is a division between "writing *about* service" and "writing *as* service" (Bacon). Making such a division is helpful. But to my mind, the most fruitful way to sort service-learning initiatives is to discern their distinct literacy goals and then group courses according to their assumptions and aims. In other words, one needs to ask, "What is this service-learning course supposed to *do*?" As Laura Julier suggests, a thoughtful investigation of service-learning in composition throws us back upon a basic question of purpose with which all teachers of writing must wrestle, what Erika Lindemann has called a "prior question."

The taxonomy I propose emerges from putting questions of purpose to a range of service-learning courses and programs. From "What is this service-learning course supposed to *do*?" follow other more specific questions, such as: Which literacy outcomes does each service-learning initiative privilege? What kind(s) of texts does each initiative generate? How does each define "social action"? What are the ideological assumptions embedded in each course or curriculum? How are relationships arranged among student, teacher, and community partner? Which audiences are being addressed? How is student writing assessed?

Putting such questions to current service-learning initiatives leaves us with three distinct groupings of community writing programs: those that write *for* the community; those that write *about* the community; and those that write *with* the community. Figure 9–1 illustrates these differences. Note that the chart is intended as a hypothesis, a schema that outlines how different types of service-learning initiatives foreground discernibly different literacies and learning outcomes. The three categories are, of course, simplifications that will betray the lived complexities of actual programs—that is, all the lines I've drawn will leak. Much like James Britton's creation of the "poetic," "expressive," and "transactional" categories to describe the range of student writing, the taxonomy is intended as a heuristic for unpacking the aims and assumptions of a diverse range of literacy practices. . . .

In short, writing-*for*-the-community courses are those through which college students collaborate with understaffed nonprofit agencies to provide workplace documents (grant research, newsletter articles, news releases, manuals, brochures) for the given agency. The student or team of students enters into a client relationship with the nonprofit, and the writing that the student or team generates constitutes both a service for the nonprofit client and a medium for student learning in a "real-world" rhetorical situation. This approach to community writing changes the traditional composition classroom in three major ways: it adds workplace and public genres to traditional essay genres; it shifts the exigency and motivation for writing from meeting teacher and grading expectations to meeting the standards articulated by the community partner; and it changes the teacher–student relationship because the classroom instructor is no longer the sole authority in creating or assessing assignments. Writing-*for* courses, with their instrumental bent, value workplace literacies and thus differ significantly from most courses that abide in the writing-*about*-the-community paradigm.

In writing-*about*-the-community courses, students engage in traditional community service (often tutoring youth or working at a homeless shelter) and then draw on that lived experience in their writing of essays. Gaining lived experience through working with people in need can open new perspectives for students, particularly as they write about complex social issues. Here the emphasis is generally on personal reflection, social analysis, and/or cultural critique. How these are weighted depends on the instructor. Even though the source materials (including the student outreach experiences) and the topic choices (which often emerge from those outreach experiences) for

FIGURE 5–1   Three Paradigms for Community Writing

	Writing for the Community	Writing about the Community	Writing with the Community
Primary Site for Learning	Nonprofit agency	Classroom	Community center
Privileged Literacies	Academic and workplace literacies	Academic and critical literacies	Academic, community, and hybrid literacies
Most Highly Valued Discourse	Workplace discourse	Academic discourse	Hybrid discourses
Primary Learning Relationship	Student–agency contact (instructor as facilitator)	Student–instructor (service as facilitator)	Student–community member (instructor as facilitator)
Institutional Relationship	Instructor–agency contact person	Instructor–community site contact	Instructor/department–community center
Goals	(1) Students learn nonacademic writing practices and reflect on differences between academic and workplace rhetorics. (2) Students reflect on service experience to attain critical awareness of community needs. (3) Students provide needed writing products for agencies.	(1) Students serve at schools or community sites and reflect on their experiences. (2) Students develop critical consciousness and habits of intellectual inquiry and societal critique. (3) Students write journals and compose academic-style essays on community issues and/or pressing social concerns.	(1) Students, faculty, and community use writing as part of a social action effort to collaboratively identify and address local problems. (2) Students and community members negotiate cultural differences and forge shared discourses. (3) University and community share inquiry and research.
Assessment	Can the students move ably between academic and workplace discourses? Have students critically reflected on the writing and service processes? Did students produce documents that will be of real use to the agencies?	Have students provided adequate service to the community site? How sophisticated a critique of social concerns can students demonstrate in academic discussion and writing? Has student academic writing improved?	Have local and academic community members engaged in collaborative writing or research? Can students reflect critically on issues such as cultural difference? Has the local problem been effectively solved, addressed, or researched?

student writing differ from those of most composition classrooms, students express their reflection, analysis, or critique in familiar academic discourses (the journal, the reflective essay, the research paper), and are evaluated according to largely traditional methods of academic assessment. Thus, writing-*about* courses tend to advance academic and critical literacy goals.

Writing-*with*-the-community initiatives take a different approach, often adopting a grassroots sensibility. These programs elude easy categorization but generally follow a pattern in which university faculty and students collaborate directly with community members (rather than through established nonprofit or governmental agencies) to research and address pressing local problems. Writing-*with* initiatives take many forms, including activist research, literacy work, proposal writing, and collaborative problem solving. They tend to value many different literacies (academic, community, and even hybrid literacies) and often devote significant attention to intercultural communication. . . .

With the chart of service-learning categories I do not mean to imply that programs do not cross fences. In fact, they do. For example, at Michigan State University, first-year writing is usually taught within a curriculum focusing on U.S. civic history. Since 1994, the writing program has been introducing service-learning in some sections, including projects through which students work with nonprofit agencies, writing *for* agency needs (newsletters, brochures, research, and so on). Yet they also read, discuss, and write *about* service, ethics, democracy, and social action in U.S. history and culture.[4] . . . [C]ourses I teach are often similarly divided (in terms of the class time, amount of student writing, and methods of assessment) between reading and writing *about* the community and producing needed written documents *for* nonprofit agencies. Still, I maintain that the writing-*about*-the-community and writing-*for*-the-community strands of such courses, while complementary, value distinctly different literacies, engage distinctly different learning processes, require distinctly different rhetorical practices, and result in distinctly different kinds of texts.

I do not argue that any one of the three paradigms is morally superior or inherently more ethical than the others. Each is built on its own assumptions, evinces its own internal logic, and works toward different goals. Any one of the paradigms might work best within a particular local community or college context. Understanding the fitness, the *kairos*, of a particular approach to its particular context is the most pressing imperative. Thus, rather than attempt to construct a hierarchy that argues for a "best" kind of service-learning, I prefer to analyze the key differences among programs, as well as the implications of those differences. As Keith Morton points out, some service-learning theorists and practitioners measure their efforts using a "continuum" which places charity as the lowest form and advocacy as the highest form of service. Articulating an alternative to such hierarchical thinking and ranking, Morton argues instead that "there exist a series of related but distinct community service paradigms, each containing a world view, a problem statement and an agenda for change" ("Irony" 24). Morton's three community service paradigms are charity, project, and social change, and his method for sorting them seems to me both generous-minded and analytically sound. He emphasizes that we should feel free to evaluate the *quality* of particular initiatives as they aspire to the goals of particular paradigms (their "thinness" or "thickness"). However, to judge but one paradigm truly worthy would unnecessarily limit the diversity of approaches right from the start and, in turn, create the misleading impression that only one kind of service—advocacy—really matters.

I borrow Morton's method, but not his particular categories, in proposing three paradigms for service-learning in rhetoric and composition. Writing *for* the community, writing *about* the community, and writing *with* the community constitute three related but distinct paradigms, and each, done well, has its own integrity (and its own limitations) based on its own assumptions and goals. A particular course fitting any one of the paradigms could be conducted either coherently or haphazardly, thoughtfully or uncritically. Much depends on the foresight, planning, and follow-through of the particular instructor. Thus, every service-learning course and teacher should heed the ancient Greek dictum: know thyself. This demands that service-learning teachers interrogate the assumptions and aims embedded in their own practices and proceed in the light of critical self-awareness.

THE ETHICS OF SERVICE: QUESTIONS OF POWER, REPRESENTATION, AND RECIPROCITY

Before moving on to articulate a theoretical foundation for service-learning and discuss case studies, it is vital that we step back and consider key ethical concerns attendant to any form of community outreach. Many teachers are wary, and rightly so, of the dangers of community service, and in particular the habit of casting individuals and communities in the uneven roles of "server" and "served." Take, for example, John McKnight's searing indictment of how professionalized service systems tend to define need. McKnight alerts not only professional servers (like social or health care workers) but also service-learning practitioners to the potentially counterproductive and disabling consequences of their efforts.

> Professionalized definitions of need produce a logical and necessary set of remedial assumptions, each with its own intrinsically disabling effects.
>
> The first of these assumptions is the mirror image of the individualized definition of need. As *you* are the problem, the assumption is that *I*, the professionalized server, *am the answer. You* are not the answer. *Your peers* are not the answer. *The political, social and economic environment* is not the answer. Nor is it possible that there is no answer. *I*, the professional, am the answer. The central assumption is that service is a unilateral process. *I*, the professional, produce. You, the client, consume. . . .

> We will have reached the apogee of the modernized service society
> when the professionals can say to the citizen:
> We are the solution to your problem.
> We know what problem you have.
> You can't understand the problem or the solution.
> Only we can decide whether the solution has dealt with your problem.
> ("Disabling" 239–41; see also McKnight, *Careless*)

McKnight's critique of deficit model approaches to professionalized service resonates with similar arguments in composition studies against deficit models of basic writing. His skepticism about the role of the server raises important issues that need to be on the minds of service-learning teachers and students. Community-based learning faces the complex ethical issues inherent in the service professions (including social work, medicine, and teaching), the ethical quandaries attendant upon research conducted by ethnographers and anthropologists, and the questions of power that accompany collaboration across disparities of wealth and privilege. Among the most formidable challenges for service-learning are broaching such ethical matters with critical rigor, designing programs for mutuality with community constituencies, and problematizing the "do-gooder" mentality entrenched in our culture and our students (see Rhoads). Abiding ethical questions for service-learning include:

- How can service-learning avoid the precarious server/served relationship critiqued by McKnight? Who is serving whom, and why?

- When is service-learning in danger of lapsing into habits of paternalistic charity or noblesse oblige?

- When and how do service-learning pedagogies reproduce rather than disrupt dominant ideologies?

- How do service-learning advocates fruitfully confront the differences in power, class, race, ethnicity, identity, and culture that often separate universities and their members from local communities and their members? When are these issues avoided, and at what cost?

- How do the often problematic histories of universities intervening in surrounding communities relate to current practices?

- How does service-learning structure a reciprocal and dialectical relationship between "serving" and "learning"? In other words, how does one avoid "using" community constituencies for the benefit of student education and at the same time maintain academic rigor?

- When are community partners really benefiting from service-learning? And when are they not?

- What happens when students enter local communities for only brief encounters, usually a semester or shorter, despite the preferences of many community partners for long-term commitments?

- How should instructors deal with unmotivated or resistant students? Also, how should they deal with well-intentioned but relatively immature or underskilled students?

Simply posing these questions is almost enough to send one running from service-learning. But while such inquiries are demanding, they are not defeating. Some (but not all) of the issues have been anticipated and addressed in the several iterations of the "Principles of Good Practice" in the service-learning literature (Honnet and Poulsen; Lisman 127–47; Mintz and Hesser). Certainly, we must continually raise these key ethical questions in our research on service-learning. Even more important, we have a responsibility to bring them squarely into the classroom and to our community partners for reflection and dialogue—which, fortunately, is something that many service-learning teachers already do.

Lorie J. Goodman recommends sustained inquiry into the ethical dimensions of service and furthermore reminds us that service-learning advocates should reexamine their most commonplace terms, including *community* and *service*. As Goodman explains, *community* has become a contested term in composition studies. Scholars have questioned how certain uses of community (which often assumes an emphasis on consensus) can function to gloss over important matters of difference and squelch dissent. The same process characterizes service-learning programs which fail to account for the voices and perspectives of community members, which can be steamrolled in the rush to meet student and academic demands. Use of the word *service* evokes not only the specter of unequal server–served relations (recall McKnight above) but also a gendered history in which women, both within and outside the academy, have been enculturated to submerge their selves in service to others (see JoAnn Campbell).

Ethical questions persist for service-learning, and they need to be addressed in a critical but hopeful spirit. One could fill a semester (and more) with theoretical and philosophical deliberations on the ethical concerns and dilemmas attendant to community outreach. However, a service-learning pedagogy demands not only contemplation but also action. Devoting all of one's teaching energies to abstract reflection forecloses any opportunity for grounded action and can ultimately lead to intellectual detachment, fatalism, or paralysis. In contrast, service-learning strives for an equitable balance between serving and learning, an equitable dialectic between pragmatic action and critical reflection, and an equitable consideration of university and community perspectives. Perfect balance, perfect dialectic, perfect consideration will ever be elusive. Thus, service-learning courses always entail risk. (But doesn't everything worthwhile?) Shying from that risk by insisting on perfection or some form of ideological purity is bound not only to sabotage student agency but also to trap both teachers and students in a loop of abstract deliberation, ever avoiding the test of experience.

Fruitful inquiry into the abiding ethical complexities of service is central to responsible service-learning courses and to what Robert Rhoads terms "critical community service" (204). Open dialogue on key social justice issues, exacting self-awareness, and reciprocal relationships with community partners need to be fundamental components of community-based pedagogies.

This hopeful but critical stance—demanding an active, engaged ethics—is evident in the pragmatist philosophy of John Dewey and the liberatory pedagogy of Paulo Freire. Their work provides context and depth to current discussions on the relationship of community writing practices to composition studies. They also offer service-learning practitioners compelling theoretical foundations that support experiential learning, community involvement, and a dialectic of critical reflection and grounded action.

NOTES

1. For a more complete discussion of the results of this study, see Eyler and Giles's *Where's the Learning in Service-Learning?*
2. One further notable finding from the UCLA study: students who participate in service as undergraduates are more likely to donate money as alumni (a fact that may pique the interest of college administrators).
3. These findings are summarized in Sax and Astin. The studies on which the article is based can be found in Sax, Astin, and Astin, and, for the longitudinal study, in Astin, Sax, and Avalos.
4. For a more detailed overview of this program, see Cooper and Julier, *Writing in the Public Interest.*

WORKS CITED

Adler-Kassner, Linda, Robert Crooks, and Ann Watters, eds. *Writing the Community: Concepts and Models for Service-Learning in Composition.* Washington, DC: American Association for Higher Education and NCTE, 1997.

Astin, Alexander W., Linda J. Sax, and Juan Avalos. "Long-Term Effects of Volunteerism During the Undergraduate Years." *The Review of Higher Education* 22.2 (1999): 187–202.

Bacon, Nora. "Community Service and Writing Instruction." *National Society for Experiential Education Quarterly* 14 (Spring 1994): 14–27.

Barber, Benjamin R., and Richard M. Battistoni, eds. *Education for Democracy: Citizenship, Community, Service: A Sourcebook for Students and Teachers.* Dubuque: Kendall, 1993.

Bok, Derek Curtis. *Universities and the Future of America.* Durham: Duke UP, 1990.

Boyer, Ernest. "Creating the New American College." *Chronicle of Higher Education* 9 March 1994: 48.

Britton, James N. *Language and Learning.* London: Allen Lane, 1970.

Campbell, JoAnn. "'A Real Vexation': Student Writing in Mount Holyoke's Culture of Service, 1837–1865." *College English* 59 (1997): 767–88.

Cooper, David D., and Laura Julier, eds. *Writing in the Public Interest: Service-Learning in the Writing Classroom. A Curriculum Development and Resource Guide.* East Lansing: The Writing Center at Michigan State University, 1995.

Crowley Sharon. "Composition's Ethic of Service, the Universal Requirement, and the Discourse of Student Need." *JAC: A Journal of Composition Theory* 15.2 (1995): 227–39.

Cushman, Ellen. "The Public Intellectual, Service Learning, and Activist Research." *College English* 63 (1999): 328–36.

Delve, Cecelia I., Suzanne D. Mintz, and Greig M. Stewart, eds. *Community Service as Values Education.* San Francisco: Jossey, 1990.

Eyler, Janet, and Dwight E. Giles, Jr. *Where's the Learning in Service-Learning?* San Francisco: Jossey, 1999.

Eyler, Janet, Dwight E. Giles, Jr., and John Braxton. "The Impact of Service-Learning on College Students." *Michigan Journal of Community Service Learning* 4 (Fall 1997): 5–15.

Freire, Paulo, and Donaldo P. Macedo. *Literacy: Reading the Word and the World.* New York: Bergin, 1987.

Goodman, Lorie J. "Just Serving/Just Writing: Writing the Community." *Composition Studies* 26.1 (1998): 59–71.

Harris, Joseph. "The Rhetoric of Theory." *Writing Theory and Critical Theory.* Ed. John Clifford and John Schilb. New York: MLA, 1994: 141–47.

Honnet, Ellen Porter, and Susan J. Poulsen, eds. *Wingspread Special Report: Principles of Good Practice for Combining Service and Learning.* Racine, WI: Johnson Foundation, 1989.

Jacoby, Barbara, ed. *Service-Learning in Higher Education: Concepts and Practices.* San Francisco: Jossey, 1996.

Julier, Laura. "Community Service Pedagogy." *A Guide to Composition Pedagogies.* Ed. Gary Tate, Amy Rupiper, and Kurt Schick. Oxford: Oxford UP, 2000.

Kendall, Jane C. *Combining Service and Learning: A Resource Book for Community and Public Service.* 3 Vols. Raleigh: National Society for Internships and Experiential Education, 1990.

Kendrick, Richard J., Jr. "Outcomes of Service-Learning in an Introduction to Sociology Course." *Michigan Journal of Community Service Learning* 3 (Fall 1996): 72–81.

Kerr, Clark. *Higher Education Cannot Escape History: Issues for the Twenty-First Century.* Albany: State U of New York P, 1994.

Kraft, Richard J., and Marc Swadener, eds. *Building Community: Service Learning in the Academic Disciplines.* Denver: Colorado Campus Compact, 1994.

Leder, Drew, and Ilona McGuinness. "Making the Paradigm Shift: Service Learning in Higher Education." *Metropolitan Universities: An International Forum* 7 (1996): 47–56.

Lempert, David H. *Escape from the Ivory Tower: Student Adventures in Democratic Experiential Education.* San Francisco: Jossey, 1996.

Lisman, C. David. *Toward a Civil Society: Civic Literacy and Service Learning.* Westport, CT: Bergin, 1998.

Mabry, J. Beth. "Pedagogical Variations in Service-Learning and Student Outcomes: How Time, Contact, and Reflection Matter." *Michigan Journal of Community Service Learning* 5 (Fall 1998): 32–47.

Mahala, Daniel, and Jody Swilky. "Remapping the Geography of Service in English." *College English* 59 (1997): 625–46.

Markus, Gregory B., J. Howard, and D. King. "Integrating Community Service and Classroom Instruction Enhances Learning: Results from an Experiment." *Educational Evaluation and Policy Analysis* 15 (1993): 410–19.

McKnight, John. *The Careless Society: Community and Its Counterfeits.* New York: Basic, 1995.

———. "Professionalized Service and Disabling Help." *Disabling Professions.* Ed. Ivan Illich. New York: M. Boyers, 1977. 69–91. Rpt. in *Service-Learning Reader: Reflections and Perspectives on Service.* Ed. Gail Albert. Raleigh: National Society for Experiential Education, 1994. 233–42.

Miller, Jerry. "The Impact of Service-Learning Experiences on Students' Sense of Power." *Michigan Journal of Community Service Learning* 4 (Fall 1997): 16–21.

Mintz, Suzanne D., and Gary W. Hesser. "Principles of Good Practice in Service-Learning." *Service-Learning in Higher Education: Concepts and Practices.* Ed. Barbara Jacoby. San Francisco: Jossey, 1996. 26–51.

Morton, Keith. "Issues Related to Integrating Service-Learning into the Curriculum." *Service-Learning in Higher Education: Concepts and Practices.* Ed. Barbara Jacoby. San Francisco: Jossey: 1996. 276–96.

———. "The Irony of Service: Charity, Project and Social Change in Service-Learning." *Michigan Journal of Community Service Learning* 2 (fall 1995): 19–32.

National Community Service Trust Act of 1993. Pub. L. 103–83. 21 Sept. 1993. Stat. 107. 785–923.

Orrill, Robert, ed. *Education and Democracy: Re-Imagining Liberal Learning in America.* New York: College Entrance Examination Board, 1997.

Osborne, Randall E., Sharon Hammerich, and Chanin Hensley. "Student Effects of Service-Learning: Tracking Change Across a Semester." *Michigan Journal of Community Service Learning* 5 (Fall 1998): 5–13.

Parsons, Michael H., and C. David Lisman, eds. *Promoting Community Renewal through Civic Literacy and Service-Learning.* San Francisco: Jossey, 1996.

Reeb, Roger N., Ronald M. Katsuyama, Julie A. Sammon, and David S. Yoder. "The Community Service Self-Efficacy Scale: Evidence of Reliability, Construct Validity, and Pragmatic Utility." *Michigan Journal of Community Service Learning* 5 (Fall 1998): 48–57.

Rhoads, Robert A. *Community Service and Higher Learning: Explorations of the Caring Self.* Albany: State U of New York P, 1997.

Rhoads, Robert A., and Jeffrey P. F. Howard, eds. *Academic Service Learning: A Pedagogy of Action and Reflection.* New Directions for Teaching and Learning 73. San Francisco: Jossey, 1998.

Sax, Linda J., and Alexander W. Astin. "The Benefits of Service: Evidence from Undergraduates." *Educational Record* 78.3/4 (1997): 25–32.

Sax, Linda J., Alexander W. Astin, and Helen S. Astin. "What Were LSAHE Impacts on Student Volunteers?" *Evaluation of Learn and Serve America, Higher Education: First Year Report.* Ed. Maryann Jacobi Gray. Santa Monica: RAND Corp, 1996.

Schine, Joan G., ed. *Service Learning: The Ninety-Sixth Yearbook of the National Society for the Study of Education.* Chicago: U of Chicago P (distributor), 1997.

Stanton, Timothy K., Dwight E. Giles, Jr., and Nadinne I. Cruz. *Service-Learning: A Movement's Pioneers Reflect on Its Origins, Practice, and Future.* San Francisco: Jossey, 1999.

Waterman, Alan S., ed. *Service-Learning: Applications from the Research.* Hillsdale, NJ: Erlbaum, 1997.

Zlotkowski, Edward. *Successful Service-Learning Programs: New Models of Excellence in Higher Education.* Bolton, MA: Anker, 1998.

10 The Irony of Service: Charity, Project, and Social Change in Service-Learning

KEITH MORTON

. . . an ironic situation occurs when the consequences of an act are diametrically opposed to its intentions, and the fundamental cause of the disparity lies in the actor himself and his original purposes.

–REINHOLD NIEBUHR (in Gene Wise, *American Historical Explanations*)

A significant body of research on the impacts of community service on college student development and academic learning has begun to emerge during the past five years. While it is clearly neither conclusive nor complete— longitudinal studies on the relationship between or among service-learning and mastery of content, career choice, voting behavior, charitable giving, and activity in civic and voluntary associations are noticeably absent—the evidence suggests that community service linked to academic study is an effective teaching tool (Boss, 1994; Cohen & Kinsey, 1994; Markus, Howard, & King, 1993).

As valuable and reasonably consistent as the emerging data is, it does not shed much light on the nature and meaning of the community service that is performed. A common language for discussing service is only slowly emerging in service-learning organizations, and it is an abbreviated and blunt language at present. Questions are being raised about how one assesses community impact, beyond the rudiments of volunteer hours and being invited back. In addition, it is increasingly common to come across, at conferences and meetings (e.g., of the Campus Outreach Opportunity League, the National Society for Experiential Education and Campus Compact), language that describes a continuum of activity ranging from service to advocacy.

Dwight Giles and Janet Eyler (1994a) of Vanderbilt University, among others, have launched an ambitious and necessary three-year research project that attempts to isolate the duration and intensity of service as variables in

From *Michigan Journal of Community Service Learning* 2 (1995): 19–32.

student development and learning. Drawing on a theory of experiential education grounded in the philosophy of John Dewey (1994b), they outline a research agenda of nine fundamental questions. The first two of these questions are the subject of this paper: "Is there a continuum of service-learning experiences?" and "Do different service-learning experiences have different impacts because of individual characteristics?" (pp. 92–93).

Answers to these questions are important because they suggest that service experiences may be optimally structured to enhance learning. In the pages that follow, I describe my reflections on these questions, review a cross-section of related theoretical literature, and report on our approach to creating a new public and community service major at Providence College. Among other considerations in creating the major has been the problem of how to structure service opportunities. As a partial response to this problem I have begun to systematically interview students, faculty, administrators, and community partners about the nature and meaning of their work. The preliminary evidence, I will suggest, does not support the hypothesis of a continuum from charity to justice. Rather, the evidence seems to suggest a series of three related but distinct paradigms of service. Drawing on our experience at Providence College, I will explore the implications of choosing between the continuum and the paradigm models of service.

The questions raised by Giles and Eyler are deceptively simple. Implicit in the first question is a logically powerful idea: that there exists in fact a continuum of typological forms of service that flow into one another. Implicit in the second question is the suggestion that participating in different forms of service will lead to different learning outcomes. It may be, as Marshall McLuhan argued in a different context, that the medium is the message.

Most commonly, a service continuum is presented as running from charity to advocacy, from the personal to the political, from individual acts of caring that transcend time and space to collective action on mutual concerns that are grounded in particular places and histories. Charity emerges on this continuum as giving of the self, expecting nothing in return, and with no expectation that any lasting impact will be made. Generally, from this perspective, it is better to suspend expectations. The risk inherent in charity is the risk of caring for another human being.

Advocacy, at the other extreme, is change oriented, and implies an agenda—speaking to others with a powerful voice. Acts of service are steps in a larger strategy to bring about change, quite often assessed as the redistribution of resources or social capital. The risks of advocacy are political. In this compelling description, one moves from charity to advocacy motivated by a growing care and passion for the people served, and by an increasingly complex analysis of the situation that created the need for service in the first place. Advocacy need not replace charity, but advocacy is seen as a more mature expression of compassion. Charity, if it continues, serves as a "home base," a sort of refueling stop for the tedious work of advocacy. The concept of a continuum, then, compels us to act as if "progress" consists of moving students "farther along," that is, out of charity and toward advocacy.

I know that the idea of a continuum has informed my own work. Attempting to move students along some continuum such as this, I have asked the perpetual question, "Why?" and have expected that a combination of curiosity and compassion would lead some students to make commitments to help change the circumstances that introduced problems into the lives of people they came to care about.

For my theoretical grounding, I have borrowed liberally from Elisabeth Griffith's (1984) biography of Elizabeth Cady Stanton, and from Lawrence Goodwyn's (1978) analysis of the Populist movement. Griffith describes Stanton, who is best known for her advocacy of women's suffrage, as moving through a cycle of "anguish, anger, analysis and action" (p. 103). Service, I have thought, is a strategy for simultaneously meeting an immediate need and provoking anguish, anger, and analysis. This approach is buttressed by Goodwyn's observation that the Populist movement was organized, in large part, by agricultural lecturers whose "very duties . . . exposed [them] to the grim realities of agricultural poverty with a directness that drove home the manifest need to do something." (p. 45). The overwhelming poverty they encountered prompted them to search for solutions; and at a critical juncture, political organizing seemed the best option. What has seemed important to me in Stanton's biography and the unfolding of the Populist movement is that people were educated into advocacy, prompted by their compassion, their anguish (from the Norse for "public grief"), and their profound need to change the problem they encountered. The educational cycle moved from personal concern, to education and problem identification, to a cycle of action and reflection (Morton, 1989).

I have seen this process in action, for example, with a group of students I joined on an Alternative Spring Break trip to Brownsville, Texas, in 1988. Home repairs, visits to Casa Oscar Romero, a Central American refugee center, and other limited, arguably charitable experiences led two of the eight students into longer term political action on U.S./Central American issues, led one to return to Brownsville as an elementary school teacher, prompted a fourth to go to Nicaragua for one year, and reinforced the commitment of a fifth to work in an inner-city school in her hometown.

I do not wish to suggest that Eyler and Giles are arguing that a continuum of service exists; or that where you enter on that continuum shapes and limits learning. Their point is to advocate for inquiry into these questions. I am arguing, however, that assumptions about progress are a powerful element in how many practitioners view, structure, and assess their service-learning courses and programs. I want to argue, as well, that the ideas of a continuum and progress from charity to advocacy do not square with how people do service or why they do it. Rather than a continuum, I want to suggest that three relatively distinct paradigms of service exist, what I will call charity, project development, and social change (a term I prefer to advocacy for reasons I will outline below). Each paradigm is based upon distinctive worldviews, ways of identifying and addressing problems, and long-term visions of individual and community transformation. Further, it seems to me that each paradigm contains a range from "thin" to "thick," that is from expressions which lack integrity or depth to those which have integrity and depth. Educationally, this means that, rather than moving students along a continuum, we are doing two things simultaneously: challenging and supporting students to enter more deeply into the paradigm in which they work; and intentionally exposing students to creative dissonance among the three forms.

CONTINUUM

The case for a continuum of service generally focuses on the limitations inherent in "less-mature" forms of service, and suggests that progress or growth is achieved by responding to those limitations. Several bodies of literature exist to support the concept of a continuum, ranging from the professional literature of participatory action research (Elden, 1993), to the work of Ivan Illich (1968) and John McKnight (1989), to the social science literatures on community development, social change, and community organizing (Lackey, 1987). The arguments put forward in this collective literature can be summarized as a typology that places charity, project, and social change models of service as the beginning, middle, and end points on a continuum of service, with a side debate over whether or not social change is, in fact, a form of service. I have imagined the continuum not as a flat line, but as a series of ranges bounded by investment in relationship building and commitment to understanding and addressing the root causes of problems (see Figure 10–1).

FIGURE 10–1   Critical Elements in Three Paradigms of Service

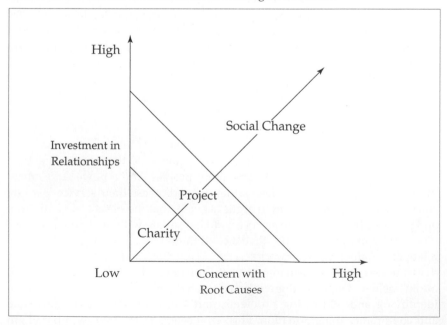

Charity

When considered as part of a continuum, charity is often viewed as the provision of direct service where control of the service (resources and decisions affecting their distribution) remains with the provider. The service is generally limited in time and makes limited claims about impact on the people involved. It is described in the *Guidelines for Development* of the Christian Conference of Asia (1980) as temporary, confined to particular, affected people and auxiliary to the ongoing life of the people. Planning and delivery of services are limited and fragmentary, the decision making process is closed, and little, if any, attempt is made to understand or effect the structural causes of the problem. The only appropriate time for charity, argue the authors of the *Guidelines*, is intervention in a natural or human-created catastrophe such as an earthquake, famine, or war. John McKnight in "Why Servanthood Is Bad" (1989) and Ivan Illich in "To Hell with Good Intentions" (1968) provide two oft-cited critiques, arguing that charity focuses on naming the deficits of those served, rather than their strengths, and creates a long-term dependency of those served on those with the resources. "Never," I was instructed by a community organizer in Bangladesh, "do something for someone that they could possibly do for themselves. This is our iron rule" (Shaha, 1990). From this perspective, charity seems weak, destructive, and—despite the best of intentions—as likely to make a situation worse as to remedy it.

Project

Project models, in their turn, focus on defining problems and their solutions and implementing well-conceived plans for achieving those solutions. Houses are built for those who might not otherwise own a home; tutoring is made available to those who need it; sports leagues are designed to occupy and train youth. The organizing principle of program approaches to service lies in the development of partnerships of organizations that collectively have access to the resources necessary to "make something happen." A community center, a mayor's office, a high school, a department at a college, and a corporation might cooperate, for example, to create a job readiness program for high school seniors. The impacts can be positive, relatively long term, and, to some extent, systemic. The criticisms of this approach center on three things: unintended consequences, the role of experts, and the relationship between planning and action.

"Unintended consequences" is a phrase used to suggest that an otherwise successful program may generate outcomes that exacerbate the original problem or lead to new problems. In criticizing a service-learning mentoring program her son belonged to, for example, a mother pointed out to a staff member whom I supervised that having one of her three children served created an inequality between this child and her two siblings, leading to regular conflict. "We're a family," she concluded, "and we need a program that works with us as a family" (Johnstad, 1991).

From a critical perspective, the experts necessary to design and manage a program magnify inequalities of power, and make the served dependent on the expert. This is a particularly dangerous trap for colleges and universities which are generally regarded as repositories of expertise, and employ research tools that non-experts cannot master. How can you teach someone to fish (to modify the common proverb) if you and they don't believe they can master the technology? A related concern, which spills over into the realm of planning and action, is problem definition: experts define problems differently than the people living them, primarily by applying analytical tools—theories—to the latter's situation. As helpful as these tools may be, they illuminate only a part of a given reality, and the danger lies in mistaking this part for the whole.

Finally, project approaches to service generally adopt some form of management by objectives, usually at the request of funders: define the problem, outline a solution, name the activities you will carry out and an ideal time line, and state the measurement criteria you will use to evaluate your performance. Given this construction, completed before funds are made available to begin work (not to mention the pressures of one-to-three year limits of funding), most programs then focus on working to their measurement criteria. Putting aside questions regarding quality of outcome, this scenario makes it extremely difficult to create a reflective environment that may lead to redefining the problem, the activities, or the measurement objectives. In short, there is no inherent process requiring that the organization learn from its practice until after its work is concluded. *Face of the Twin Cities*, a planning document of the United Way of Minneapolis (1991), describes the frustration of agencies locked into this way of providing community services: "More service agencies are responding to social, economic, and health problems as character deficits in the individuals experiencing the problems, as opposed to consequences of social system issues. By blaming the victim, the root causes of problems are ignored" (p. 27). As startling an admission as this may seem for an organization such as the United Way, it has had little noticeable effect on how they raise or distribute funds. Agencies are responding in this way, it goes almost without saying, because this is what funders—including the United Way—most often reward.

Social Change

I prefer the term social change to advocacy because "advocacy" is a term with professional connotations, and an "advocate" is often a person with greater strength and expertise protecting the rights of weaker or less knowledgeable people; that is, the term, as important as it is, does little to clarify the meaning of service. Social change or "transformation" models typically focus on process: building relationships among or within stakeholder groups, and creating a learning environment that continually peels away the layers of the onion called "root causes." Practice—education or action—emerges over time out of the relationships or most current understanding of root causes.

Hedley Dimock, for example, in his booklet *Intervention and Collaborative Change* (1981), discusses two assumptions he has come to about changing social systems: "1. The social system (group, community, or organization) is the focus of change . . . 2. Those people affected by the change should be involved in making that change" (pp. 10–11). These assumptions are based on Dimock's understanding of and extrapolation from small group process, and on the weaknesses of other, non-collaborative "interventions." Gerald Taylor (1989), an organizer with the Industrial Areas Foundation (the inheritor of Saul Alinsky's legacy of community organizing), states the point even more forcefully: "participation without power is a fraud . . . that creates cynics." In fact, most social change or social transformation models of service focus directly and indirectly on politically empowering the powerless. To quote the *Guidelines for Development* again, a person working from a perspective of transformation "sees the problems of the poor and oppressed, not as basically functional, but as rooted in and perpetuated by the structural organization of society—as a process whereby they are excluded from economic gain and political power by strategies which preserve the concentration of privilege in society . . . [transformation] demands analysis at both the micro and macro levels. It sees power as the real issue, works for the people's power and joins them in their struggle" (p. 26). In short, social change or transformation models are theoretically about empowerment of the systematically disenfranchised. This emphasis answers the limitations of charity and project approaches to service by helping people to do for themselves in "the world as it is, not as we wish it to be."

Social change is a difficult model to critique because, in its idealized form, it is an end point on the "good" side of a continuum. That is, social change is the gold standard for evaluating service, and any critique runs the danger of being self-referential or tautological. Nevertheless, social change models may be evaluated by the depth and integrity of relationships among the people who come together for the purpose of bringing about positive change, and by their commitment to an educational cycle that brings them ever closer to a clear understanding of the root causes of problems and effective strategies for addressing them.

ALTERNATIVES TO A CONTINUUM OF SERVICE

Some theorists, notably Harry Boyte, dispute the existence of a continuum, positing instead distinct modes of public interaction. In building the case for a renewed "citizen politics," for example, Boyte and his colleagues at the University of Minnesota (Breuer, 1992; Project Public Life, 1991) identify four common modes of political problem solving: institutional politics, advocacy politics, community politics, and helping politics (1992, p. 13). While Boyte's focus is primarily on how people define and act in "public," his approach is helpful for thinking about the nature of service. Citizen politics, based upon a "realistic belief in change, and balancing power and achievement" is good, as it builds the capacity of people to do for themselves; the other forms, in

Boyte's view, are significantly flawed. Helping politics are flawed because power remains solely in the hands of the servants; advocacy because it is reactionary and places the tools for solving community problems everywhere but with the protesters; institutional politics because they depend on experts and lack citizen involvement; and community politics because it is limited in scale and is time intensive. Furthermore, helping politics are personal and private, apolitical, and ultimately have little "public" meaning (for a parallel perspective see McKnight, 1995). Boyte's approach effectively focuses attention on the power relationships between servant and served and on whether or not the work has public or civic meaning.

As useful as it is, Boyte's perspective has limited ability to describe service, because its greatest strength—an application of a strongly democratic conception of political organization—does not have a way of recognizing service as anything other than a weak form of charity. Rather than functioning as a heuristic device for understanding what people do as service in terms of what it means to them, grids such as this are tools developed for critical assessment and, like the continuum, are based upon a clear hierarchy of value.

Given the similarities in language and values between continuum and grid models of service, it would be easy to view the grid as a parallel alternative to a continuum. Unlike a continuum, a grid suggests the possibility of describing "domains" of action in two dimensions with a limited set of characteristics. That is, a grid begins to move away from the idea of linear progression and suggest the theoretical possibility that people adopt distinctive ways of doing service.

PARADIGMS OF SERVICE

While the continuum and the grid serve as powerful analytical tools, and touch on issues at the heart of service, they do not seem to reflect accurately what it is that people actually do in their community service work. I assume that people engage in service-learning because it makes sense to them: that they have a roughly coherent (if sometimes unarticulated) intellectual, emotional, and psychological motivation for choosing to engage in service linked to learning. I am persuaded, as well, as Steve Schultz (1993) has argued, that our program models express our assumptions.

My observations suggest that there exist a series of related but distinct community service paradigms that I will refer to as charity, project, and transformation. Each paradigm, I will argue, contains a worldview, a problem statement, and an agenda for change. Each paradigm has "thin" versions that are disempowering and hollow, and "thick" versions that are sustaining and potentially revolutionary. These paradigms do not "flow" into one another, and the rare move from one to another is experienced initially as dissonance and then as epiphany: the new paradigm makes meaning of the self in the world more persuasively than did the previous paradigm.

The descriptive language for these paradigms does not differ radically from the language employed in the discussion of the continuum or the grid perspectives on service. But, it adds to that language the positive dimensions of charity and project as well as social change approaches to service, and attempts to work empirically from practice toward a theoretical framework for describing what it is that people do as service.

I began to question my own assumptions about a "continuum" of service as I listened to college students and community partners describe their motivations for and experiences of service. Teaching a course titled "Introduction to Service in Democratic Society" in the Fall of 1994, I was struck by the students' ability to simultaneously understand the criticisms of charity, take seriously the concept of institutionalized injustice, and still insist that the proper measures for evaluating their service performance were affective and personal. One person in this class of mostly first-year students said, for example, that the real measure of her impact at a local community center was that the "children remember my name and hug me when I get there." I was also challenged by conversations with religiously based colleagues—Catholic, Protestant, and Jewish, on and off campus—to explore more carefully the meaning of charity. I was reminded that "tsedakah," the Hebrew word for charity, is based on the idea of anger at injustice provoking one to remedy that injustice (Neusner, 1988; Tunick, 1994). I was reminded, too, that responding to injustice is not optional, but an obligation, a part of what it means to keep the faith. A review of the Catholic Catechism (1994)—prompted by my joining the faculty of a Catholic college—found this language: "Without the help of grace, men would not know how 'to discern the often narrow path between the cowardice which gives in to evil, and the violence which under the illusion of fighting evil only makes it worse.' This is the path of charity, that is, of the love of God and neighbor . . . it respects others and their rights. It requires the practice of justice . . . [and] inspires a life of self-giving" (p. 462). A Quaker and a Congregationalist reminded me separately of the revolutionary implications of their belief "that there is that of God in every person." Charity, in their terms, began with the radical act of recognizing the worth of every person.

I also found it important to acknowledge and reflect on the fact that I came to teaching via seven years of work with the Minneapolis YMCA. Conversations with colleagues there reminded me of the life-long commitments made by some of them to simply run things "the right way, for the right reasons, the way they should be done." These people were committed not to what they see as "abstractions" of charity or social justice, but to creating organizations that "make it happen," that educate youth, build homes, strengthen families, and otherwise challenge us to live up to the "ideals of our society." Prompted by these conversations and ideas, I began to wonder what I would find out if I elected to take charity and project types of service as seriously as I did social change types of service.

In order to more systematically approach what these people had to say, I conducted in-depth interviews with four community informants and Providence College's Vice President for Academic Administration. The community informants were selected because they were active with the Feinstein

Institute, represented significantly different types of service (community organizer, director of a homeless shelter, director of a youth corps, and executive director of a community center), and seemed to me to do their work effectively. The vice president was interviewed because he is a Dominican priest and directs the academic and faculty side of the campus. He is also a Church historian by training and has given significant thought to the relationship between "liberal education" and the "Catholic mission" of Providence College. In addition, I supervised three undergraduate students who conducted patterned exit interviews with 14 students who had participated as teaching assistants in the pilot year of the Feinstein Institute. Finally, as part of our course evaluations in six service-learning courses offered in the Spring of 1995, we asked students to respond to a crude survey that attempted to describe the relationship between motives for and acts of service (see Table 10–1).

Charity as a Paradigm

Charity, as the descriptions above suggest, has many potential and some inherent weaknesses. Certainly, in common usage, it is a term that has come to mean the well-off doing service to the poor if and when they feel like it, and then only on their terms. History suggests that this is not an accidental corruption of the original meaning of "charity." In our survey, however, of eight possible responses to the question, "Why do you volunteer?," nearly 25 percent of the students—20 of 82 respondents—chose as their main reason, "I want to help someone less fortunate than myself." In addition, nearly 50 percent of the respondents felt that, "Right now I make the biggest impact on the world" by "providing direct service to another person." Charity is a positive term for these students: a recognition of their obligation to help, and an expression of their recognition that our society affords them very few opportunities to make a contribution.

The director of the homeless shelter—in the process of transitioning out of his role after 12 years of work—described the tension he felt between the dual needs of caring for the individual persons he encountered, and working systemically to eliminate the structural causes of poverty. He began "25 years ago [feeling] that giving food and shelter was a concrete and unequivocal act of meaning and community building." This direct service, he said, "still acts as an anchor, personally and spiritually." He noted that the shelter he has worked at "comes out of the Catholic Worker movement, with its philosophy of connecting direct service with the long-term: giving the poor what they have a right to have—it's theirs. It's based on unconditional giving: don't change [the poor]; change the powers that marginalize them. This is the meaning of the 'Sermon on the Mount.'" The problem, he pointed out, is that "it is easy to help someone one time, but how often can you do this? How often can you witness someone's deterioration and still stay with it?" He summarized how he was trying to resolve the tension between his "spiritual anchor" and his desire to make change: "Now, I'm trying to wean myself in practice from results. I'm sick of results. You can't be attached to the fruits of

TABLE 10–1 Motives Informing Community Service

	N	%
1. Why do you volunteer?		
It makes me feel good about myself	6	7.3
It provides an opportunity for me to be exposed to and learn from other cultures	17	20.7
I want to give back to the community	16	19.5
I want to help someone less fortunate than myself	20	24.4
I want to change society	9	11.0
I want to gain experience in my chosen career field (or, explore possible careers)	7	8.5
It is central to my spiritual commitments	3	3.7
Other	4	4.9
TOTAL	82	100%
2. Right now I feel I make the biggest impact on the world (choose only one):		
Providing direct service to another person	40	49.4
Helping to set up and support community service organizations that are addressing immediate community needs	18	22.2
Advocating for social change	17	21.0
Other	6	7.4
TOTAL	81	100%
3. Over the course of my life, I feel I will make the biggest impact by (choose only one):		
Providing direct service to another person	24	30.8
Helping to set up and support community service organizations that are addressing immediate community needs	31	39.7
Advocating for social change	20	25.6
Other	3	3.9
TOTAL	78	100%
4. I feel that current community needs would be eliminated if everyone (choose only one):		
Provided direct service to another person	27	32.5
Helped to set up and support community service organizations that are addressing immediate community needs	31	37.4
Advocated for social change	20	24.1
Other	5	6.0
TOTAL	83	100%

Note: For question 1, response options consisted of an 8-point scale ranging from "being most important" (1) to "being least important" (8). For this question, "N" represents the number of respondents who indicated "most important."

your work. Until now, I have been very attached. It's my attachment to results that is wearing me out. I'm working to let go of this—broadening my cosmology, context, perception. I'm learning what Dan Berrigan means when he says, 'hope is not in time.'"

From a different perspective, Thomas McGonigle, a Dominican priest and vice president at Providence College, began by noting that the Dominicans are an order of "preachers, undergirded by study, reflection, and prayer." Central to Dominican study is the idea of "witness," linked to the Greek for "martyr." Based on the Acts of the Apostles, the Dominicans understand witness as an invitation to come and participate in community. At this moment of invitation, one faces a choice that "has the potential to be transformative of the individual and the community. . . . What is heard, seen, handled—is that to which we bear witness." After establishing the communal nature of witness and transformation, he goes on to suggest that, "the essential nature of service is witness . . . involving oneself in activities benefiting others and, if necessary, laying down one's life; challenging structures that are not life-giving. Service always means an encounter with powers out there: confronting conditions that make service necessary in the first place. We are responding to the word of God, and have no choice but to do what we are called to do. The prophetic stance teaches that 'if it is of God, it will succeed.'" And finally, restating the centrality of community, he concludes that, "in the religious life, individuals are called within community. It is the community which has a mission. The spirit comes to individuals in the context of a whole community. As the modern world emerges and individuals are divorced from community, you get individuals trying to do good things." While not directly stated, the suggestion is that charity has devolved, in many instances, to "individuals trying to do good things." Charity, in these terms, has been stripped of much of its initial meaning, become privatized, and so has lost much of its power to transform individual or community. Scattered as we are, the sustaining community is not large or powerful enough to bring about change.

Clearly, in experiences of the students, the shelter director, and the vice president, charity means something more than what John Dewey (1908) defined as "a superior class achieving merit by doing things gratuitously for an inferior class" (p. 334). What is suggested here is an understanding of charity that offers a coherent worldview, and begins with an individual grounded in community. Both the director of the homeless shelter and the vice president for academic administration, via significantly different routes, have come to the understanding of Berrigan's assertion that "hope is out of time." From this perspective, charity is spiritually based service, outside of time and space, that bears witness to the worth of other persons. For persons operating primarily out of this understanding of service, charity may be an act of faith or, more radically and more simply, an ideal way of being in the world. Responding to the statement on the survey, "I feel that current community needs would be eliminated if everyone . . . ," nearly 33 percent of students chose "provided direct service to another person." In the long term, sustaining this spiritual commitment is seen as the only way to create a just world.

Project as a Paradigm

In that same survey, nearly 50 percent of students responded that they felt they made the biggest impact through direct service. When given the same choices about where they would make the greatest impact over the course of their lives, 40 percent of the students—including many who for now chose direct service—answered, "helping to set up and support community organizations that are addressing immediate community needs." In short, 40 percent of the students expected that their futures included involvement in organizations meeting direct needs.

The directors of the youth service corps and the community center whom I interviewed had functional definitions of community and service. Community, said the youth service director, "is geographic, a neighborhood. The neighborhood is the smallest meaningful unit in much of our society. . . . I have a very physical, geographic picture in my head . . . a neighborhood is the smallest geographic unit that provides people with the basics needed to function: learn, work, play, create." Similarly, service is "getting something done, beginning with asking, what is the most essential part of the community to work with." After describing a personal history of growing up in a politically active family and doing "advocacy" types of service all through high school and into early college, he notes that, " I came to realize that [advocacy] was all about getting rid of some bad thing—the driving emotion was anger. . . . [I started wondering] what happens after we get rid of these, and are looking for constructive alternatives. . . . What is satisfying is creating something. This is slower, not an adrenaline rush, but it's more effective." He concludes, "We need to stop reinventing the wheel, stop creating new organizations, and consolidate our existing resources, have them work to their greatest capacity."

The director of the community center follows a similar line of thought, adding to it concerns about understanding the boundaries between staff and volunteer roles, and about external forces that he believes will lead to the failure of a significant number of small community organizations in the next five years. The bottom line in his organization is "learning to plan and deliver to our mission as an organization." This involves careful planning, and ongoing training for staff and volunteer leaders. He is concerned with program development, especially programs that will help make youth and recent immigrants employable, and programs that will help create more jobs in the community. Echoing the youth corps director, he observes that "this means working smarter with what we have, and working harder to link together the institutions in the neighborhood that are willing to support these efforts."

From the perspectives of the youth corps and community center directors, the essential problems are how to create greater opportunity for participation with limited resources, and how to efficiently focus existing resources so that they have maximum impact. There is little sense that the institutions of society are inherently flawed. Rather, the problem is that not everyone can participate equally. They approach problem solving as a management issue, but do not necessarily work in a linear fashion. They expect that programs developed to resolve particular issues will create or lead to new issues: a community garden built as part of a job skills program, for example, may be vandalized and focus attention on how to respond to vandalism. Tutoring children may lead to English as a Second Language instruction and then into a support system for families that have recently immigrated. The logic of the project approach assumes that no solutions are ultimate, and that thoughtful, reasoned approaches leading to measurable action—doing something—is the appropriate response to community needs. Organization and expertise are highly valued. Ethical leadership, surviving over time, and listening to and encouraging the participation of those served are as important to both directors as setting and meeting objectives, competing for resources, and "building the organization."

Social Change as a Paradigm

In the survey, 11 percent of the students gave as their reason for volunteering, "I want to change society." Nearly 21 percent answered that "right now I feel that I make the biggest impact on the world by . . . advocating for social change." Twenty-six percent responded that, over the long haul, they would make their biggest impact "by advocating for social change."

The community organizer, whose personal history includes a long stint as a Protestant minister, begins by describing the religious and spiritual grounding of his work. He describes growing up in a close-knit family, with "a strong sense of gratitude, that I owed back—not to my family so much, but to the larger world somehow." He describes a sometimes painful process of learning over his life where and how to make a difference in people's lives. Returning several times to his spiritually based understanding of service, and noting that "Politics in the larger [electoral] sense is not so relevant to the community's needs," he says that "in the 1970s I decided to make my sphere of influence a geographic neighborhood. . . . Now I'm an organizer. Neighborhoods are important. They particularize the general. Democracy has to work some*place* (his emphasis). Caring has to work in the particular." Reflecting on his own work, he notes the visible and invisible boundaries of the largely immigrant neighborhood in which he works, and concludes that the "organizing core should be streets and blocks, rather than service groups [neighborhood agencies and institutions]." Sighing that this type of organizing is too slow to be do-able, he observes, "We need to learn how we need each other." He describes his respect for one of the South East Asian groups "that is a model for us: we need to strengthen our own [as they are doing] before we reach out; and we need to reach out in strength, not weakness."

While his motivation is spiritual, he is uncomfortable with the word "service." "Doing service, you have to protect against paternalism, which is the root of a lot of problems . . . giving requires a certain amount of ego, and can be self-serving, lessening those served. They become objects fulfilling your need to serve."

This organizer's work is a compromise between his sense of how he believes the world should be and the world as it is; a compromise between the impossibly high standards he set for himself as a young man and his ability to make an impact where he is able. He is profoundly aware of the world as it is, joking, "Never be so heavenly minded that you're no earthly good." In closing, he describes how he has learned to always return to "my own sense of integrity and learning to live with that . . . even though it's ultimately impossible . . . you're always caught between your responsibilities and your limits."

While personal integrity may seem a surprising emphasis for a community organizer, it is in my experience an issue that comes up regularly. It is the perspective of a veteran union organizer I recently met who has gone back to seminary after a 15-year hiatus, and it is captured in the words of Ernesto Cortes (Rogers, 1994), an organizer for the Industrial Areas Foundation. "Organizing," says Cortes, "is a fancy word for relationship building. No organizer ever organizes a community. . . . If I want to organize you, I don't sell you an idea. What I do, if I'm smart, is try to find out what's in your interest. What are your dreams?" And again, "That's why we organize people around their values—not just the issues. The issues fade and they lose interest. But what they really care about remains—family, dignity, justice, and hope. And we need power to protect what we value" (pp. 17, 31). Change, from this perspective, comes about when otherwise ordinary people find ways to bring their values, their actions, and their world into closer alignment with each other.

DISCUSSION

In describing charity, project, and social change as paradigms of service, I have tried to present them in ways that suggest what I see as their internal logic, using terms inherent to the form. I have tried to suggest, briefly, what each paradigm of service might look or "feel" like when it is done with integrity, that is, with consistency between its ideals and its practice. Each of the paradigms can be done with or without integrity, in what I think of as, adapting the language of anthropologist Clifford Geertz (1973), thin or thick versions. The thin versions may take the forms of paternalistic or self-serving charity that imposes services on unreceptive "others"; projects that magnify or institutionalize inequalities of power, produce outcomes that are worse than the original problem, or lead to unrealistic and unsustainable dependencies; social change work that is only rhetorical, narrowly selfish, and against a wide range of offenses without offering alternatives. And any of the paradigms can raise false expectations, inflame social divisions, and leave people tired and cynical.

The thick versions of each paradigm are grounded in deeply held, internally coherent values; match means and ends; describe a primary way of interpreting and relating to the world; offer a way of defining problems and solutions; and suggest a vision of what a transformed world might look like. At their thickest, the paradigms seem to intersect, or at least to complement one another. Insisting on the humanity of another person in the face of sometimes overwhelming pressure to deny that humanity can be a motive for charity, for project, and for social change. The differences begin to emerge at the level of action and efficacy: what changes do I wish to bring about, what effort is most meaningful to me, what outcomes do I expect? While it is not the point of this paper, it is worth noting that at this level the paradigms have profoundly different senses of time and space: charity is out of time and space; projects divide time and space into rational and manageable units; and social change places one squarely in the stream of history leading up to and through the world as it is.

My point in these descriptions has been to raise the possibility that we do not necessarily experience service as growth along a continuum, but that we come into service with a primary orientation, and work out of this orientation. Only occasionally, I would hypothesize, is a primary orientation given up for an alternative. Certainly an organizer (as I have suggested) can have a strong faith basis for her or his work; certainly a project manager can be committed to long-term economic development; certainly an individual act of caring can be done in such a way as to have long-term community impact or historic resonance. My sense is that while we can do work across these paradigms, we are most at home in one or another, and interpret what we do according to the standards of the one in which we are most at home. Growth, or development, I suspect, occurs mostly within a given paradigm. Studies such as *Some Do Care* (Colby, 1992) and *The Altruistic Personality* (Oliner, 1988) suggest, for example, that deep versions of charity can be personally sustaining and lead to significant public acts. And, done well, I would argue that all three paradigms lead ultimately toward the transformation of an individual within a community, and toward the transformation of the communities themselves.

Ernesto Cortes describes the transformation of the Industrial Areas Foundation as it changed from issues-based organizing to values-based organizing. Noting that the power base for the IAF in San Antonio is the Catholic church, he describes "role playing" the letters of the apostle Paul with community members. "The point was to help people . . . to find integrity in their own lives." This integrity, grounded in the traditional, church-based values of the Hispanic community Cortes was organizing, helped, in the words of author Mary Beth Rogers, "to end their [parish members'] isolation from each other, and they began to develop a vision of community in which they initiated action instead of waiting passively for something—good or bad—to happen to them" (1990, p. 134).

While charity, project, and social change paradigms may lead ultimately to the transformation of the individual and the community, they suggest different ways of defining issues and understanding change over time. The irony of service, in service-learning, is enacted when we do not recognize these differences and teach accordingly. The irony of service-learning in higher education is that we assume that the learning consequences of service may differ significantly from the nature and immediate purpose of the service itself. In my own courses, for example, my assumptions about a continuum of service have led me to incorporate "movement" politics and address knotty issues such as racism while having students engage in tutoring or care for infants at an AIDS center. The students, who grasp the content intellectually, ask over and over again what their service has to do with the course content. While I can justify some of their "confusion" as simply a step in learning, they seem to me to be raising an appropriate question, and one which gets at the heart of experiential education: If experience is a way of knowing, then why do you have us doing service that is at best only partially consistent with what you are teaching? Why do you teach change and have us help manage programs or do direct service? A second, related, problem arises as they resist the logic of the continuum, saying, in essence, "That is not me. I'm not moving." How do I respond to what they are saying?

Part of the answer is, no doubt, to expand their—and my—notion of what service is. Students in an introductory service-learning course at the Feinstein Institute, for example, had as their service assignment conducting oral histories that were to be used by a parish planning committee as a step in organizing their community. In classroom discussion sessions, they compared their experiences with those of students who were tutoring children, and said, "What we are doing isn't service." In fact, the oral histories needed and requested by the parish initiated dialogues that crossed over "town-gown" boundaries, and identified a core organizing group for the parish planning committee. Similarly, students from a marketing course developed and implemented a research project for a children's museum. Useful, carefully done, and delivered on time, the students resisted the idea that this "professional" experience could be a form of service.

Certainly, students need to understand that several forms of service exist; that they can all be meaningful; and that they have choices about what they will do and how they will do it. And they need to be challenged to make those choices consciously, based on experience and reflection. The irony is that unless we can adequately describe the range of service that exists, students will continue to work with a narrow and artificial definition of service that polarizes into a limited domain of service and an expansive domain of not-service.

PRACTICAL IMPLICATIONS

At the Feinstein Institute for Public Service we have created a new major and minor in Public and Community Service Studies. As we develop the service sites and placements that are integrated into the courses comprising the program, we have to articulate the relationship between service and learning, and establish opportunities that will undergird the program: Is our objective to challenge and move students along a continuum or to the upper right-hand quadrant of a grid where they are engaged in the work of social change? Or is it to help them articulate more fully what they believe and think about the practice and meaning of service, and to challenge them to work with ever-increasing integrity and insight? While both options assume that educators are fit to change people, the latter approach seems to me more appropriate.

The questions are not rhetorical, and have immediate practical implications: Do we develop service placements for introductory courses that begin with service placements that are structured, focused on direct service to other individuals, and introduce in a very personal way what our community partner Jim Tull has called "the meanest problems of our society"? Do our 200 and 300 level courses increase the stakes, offering placements that require more leadership, somewhat greater responsibility, and an introduction to the institutions that structure our communities and channel the bulk of community service? Do our capstone courses invite students to work with people and organizations committed to some sort of systemic change?

Or, do we privilege what I am calling "paradigms" of service, fitting all three into each level in appropriate ways, and employ a comparative approach that sets up a creative tension leading students (and faculty) into deeper understanding of those paradigms? At this point in time, I lean toward the latter approach. While I know (or think I know) what sort of service I personally find most engaging and meaningful, I believe a comparative approach opens up dialogue and creates an opportunity for learning that would be stifled if we began with an end point in mind.

How we answer the question also has implications for the community partnerships we develop. At the Feinstein Institute we have made two strategic decisions regarding community partners. First, we differentiate between "core" and "placement" partners. Second, we engage our core partners in reviewing and delivering our curriculum. Placement partners, as the name implies, simply serve as placement sites for students in our courses. Their work and needs match the experiences we are seeking to develop for our students. Core partners also serve as placement sites for our students. In addition, however, we make significant staff commitments to learning about, supporting, and working directly with a limited number—four or five—of core partners. Over our first year, these commitments have taken the form of doing strategic planning together, intentionally developing interdependent agendas; supporting the work of the partner by actively developing other campus-based resources; and it may, down the road, take the form of swapping or sharing (formally or informally) staff. Our goal in developing core and placement partnerships is to explore the strengths, weaknesses, commonalities, and contradictions inherent in a comprehensive range of service.

Our core partners are selected on three loose guidelines: the partner is involved in work that is in the self-interest of the college to support; the partner affects the communities immediately surrounding the college; and the partner is willing to make itself an ally in the education of our students.

This approach has been recommended to the Feinstein Institute by a community advisory group (Tull, 1995), composed of four individuals drawn from different types of service organizations. Their recommendations to us were based upon their reading and critique of our major proposal and our course syllabi; visits to classes (minimally four visits each); one individual co-teaching a pilot course with a faculty member; and a series of conversations they held with faculty and other community representatives. They recommended establishing formal agreements with core partners, based on the following elements:

- The cooperative development of service site projects by students and agency staff

- Formal human resource exchanges between the Feinstein Institute and community organizations (staff and faculty contribute as board members, on planning committees and other work, while agency staff, board, and members participate in teaching and other Institute work)

- Orientation, training, and education of students at the agencies as a context for service

- Provision of service by the Institute to the agencies using the expertise and unique resources of the Institute and college

- Guaranteed minimum commitment of students' service hours to agencies

- Agency commitment to a serious student internship program that would allow advanced Institute students to perform longer term, in-depth, and more advanced service.

CONCLUSION

In a discussion of service at the 1994 Conference of the National Society for Experiential Education, Nadinne Cruz (1994) offered what seems to me the best definition of service I have heard. "Service," she said, "is a process of integrating intention with action in the context of a movement toward a just relationship." If we are to educate ourselves and our students in ways that lead us toward just relationships, one of the first steps must be developing our collective capacity to describe and analyze the intentions and actions that inform our work. Irony is, simply, the gulf between intention and action. In this paper I attempt to describe a central irony that can (and does) emerge in service-learning: the gap between the content and outcomes of our teaching, on the one hand, and the type of service in which we engage on the other. Should we approach service as a continuum or as a set of related paradigms? Is authenticity—the reverse of irony—to be found by structuring service-learning so that we grow or move in a particular direction, or so that we are challenged to self-consciously name and work more consistently within a paradigm of service? As educators, do we make explicit (and try to model) the need to change, or the need to become more ourselves? Do we advocate a way of doing service, or do we hold up choices? Is our concern the type of service activity that is done, or the integrity with which it is done? How do we know if we are moving toward justice? Imagining service as a set of related paradigms, each with the potential to move by a different path toward justice, seems to me a step toward overcoming the irony of service-learning, a way of stepping into and embracing the contradictions that often separate our intention from our action. And it seems to me that an understanding of service that is simultaneously more inclusive and deeper can open spaces for all of us to find more allies, deepen the conversations in the service-learning community and find new ways to express and hear the hopes we have for the impacts we might make.

REFERENCES

Boss, J. (1994). The effect of community service work on the moral development of college students. *Journal of Moral Education*, 23(2), 183–197.

Breuer, R. & Nelson, F. (1992). Building ownership: A coach's guide to teaching politics. Minneapolis: Project Public Life.

Catholic Church (1994). *Catechism of the Catholic Church*. United States Catholic Conference, Inc.

Christian Conference of Asia (1980). *Guidelines for development*. Singapore: Christian Conference of Asia.

Cohen, J. & Kinsey, D. (1994). 'Doing good' and scholarship: A service learning study. *Journalism Educator*. 48(4), 4–14.

Colby A. & Damon, W. (1992). *Some do care*. New York: The Free Press.

Cruz, N. (1994). Notes of the author, Reexamining service-learning in an international context, workshop. Annual Conference of the National Society for Experiential Education, Washington, D.C., November 11.

Dewey, J. & Tufts, J. H. (1908, 1932). *Ethics*. New York: Henry Holt and Company.

Dimock, H. G. (1981). *Intervention and collaborative change*. Guelph, Ontario: Office for Educational Practice.

Elden, M. & Chisolm, R. (1993). Emerging varieties of action research: Introduction to the special issue. *Human Relations*, 46(2), 121–142.

Geertz, C. (1973). Thick description: Toward an interpretive theory of culture, in *The interpretation of cultures*. New York: Basic Books, Inc. 3–32.

Giles, D. E. & Eyler, J. (1994a). The impact of a college community service laboratory on students' personal, social, and cognitive outcomes. *Journal of Adolescence*, 17, 327–339.

Giles, D. E. & Eyler, J. (1994b) The theoretical roots of service-learning in John Dewey: Toward a theory of service-learning. *Michigan Journal of Community Service Learning*, 1(1), 77–85.

Goodwyn, L. (1978). *The populist moment*. New York: Oxford University Press.

Griffith, E. (1984). *In her own right: The life of Elizabeth Cady Stanton*. New York: Oxford University Press.

Illich, I. (1968, 1990). To hell with good intentions, in J. Kendall (Ed.), *Combining service and learning*. Raleigh: National Society for Internships and Experiential Education, 1, 314–320.

Johnstad, K. (1991). Conversation with the author, University of Minnesota YMCA, May 18.

Lackey, A. S., Burke, R. & Peterson, M. (1987). Healthy communities: The goal of community development. *Journal of the Community Development Society*, 18(20), 1–17.

Markus, G., Howard, J. P. F. & King, D. C. (1993). Integrating community service and classroom instruction enhances learning: Results from an experiment. *Educational Evaluation and Policy Analysis*, 15(4), 410–419.

McKnight, J. (1995). Politicizing health care, in *The careless society: Community and its counterfeits*. New York: Basic Books. 80–90.

McKnight, J. (1989). Why servanthood is bad. *The Other Side*, 25(1), 38–42.

Morton, K. (1989, May). The politics of service. *Democracy Notes*, 1, 3.

Neusner, J. (1988). Righteousness, not charity: Judaism's view of philanthropy. *Liberal Education*, 74(4), 16–18.

Oliner, S. P. & Oliner, P. M. (1988). *The altruistic personality: Rescuers of Jews in Nazi Europe*. New York: The Free Press.

Project Public Life. (1991). *Teaching politics: A report from the third annual project public life working conference*. Minneapolis: Project Public Life.

Rogers, M. B. (1990). *Cold anger: A story of faith and power*. Denton: University of North Texas Press.

Schultz, S. (1993). Notes of the author from Democracy and Service, preconference workshop, Annual Conference of the National Society for Experiential Education, San Francisco.

Shaha, B. (1989). Notes of the author, from Training in Community Organizing, Bangladesh YMCA, Daka, Bangladesh, September 16–30, 1990.

Taylor, G. (1989). Notes of the author from a seminar, Project Public Life, Humphrey Institute for Public Affairs, University of Minnesota, January 27.

Tull, J., Hill, A., McElroy, C., & Zagoudis-Eastrich, L. (1995). *Report from the community advisory group.* Providence: Feinstein Institute for Public Service.

Tunick, S. (1994). Notes of the author, conversation at preconference workshop, From Service Learning to Education for Democracy, Annual Conference of the National Society for Experiential Education, Washington, D.C., November 8.

United Way of Minneapolis (1991). *Face of the twin cities: United Way planning document.* Minneapolis: United Way of Minneapolis.

11 Community Service and Critical Teaching

BRUCE HERZBERG

"Capitalism with a human face," said our new provost, Phil Friedman. This was the way he hoped the United States would model capitalism for the new democracies in eastern Europe. It was, therefore, a motto for what the students at Bentley College, a business school, should be learning. My English Department colleague Edward Zlotkowski challenged the provost to put a human face on the students' education by supporting a program that would make community service part of the curriculum. Friedman agreed and Zlotkowski took on the massive job of linking courses with community agencies. At first, the projects were simple: Students in writing courses visited soup kitchens and wrote up their experiences. Later, as the service-learning program developed, students in accounting classes helped revise the accounting procedures of non-profit community-service agencies and audited their books for free. Students in marketing and business communication designed advertising and public relations materials to improve the distribution of agencies' services. And the students in one freshman composition class— mine—learned to be adult literacy tutors and went weekly to a shelter in Boston to offer their help.

There are many obvious benefits, to students and to the agencies and individuals they serve, from service learning. Many students become eager volunteers after the ice is broken by class projects and they see where they can go, how they can help. A surprising number of the students in my class, for example, did some volunteer work in high school, but would not be likely to do so in college—in a new city, without contacts—were it not for the liaison provided by service learning. Most agencies are eager for new volunteers.[1] And of course, the students perform real and needed services. Faculty members, too, report a new sense of purpose in their teaching. This is, perhaps, most striking at a school like Bentley, where students are not only majoring in business but often seem to have fallen into the narrowest view of what that means, adopting a gray and jaded image of the businessman, scornful or

From *College Composition and Communication* 45.3 (1994): 307–19.

embarrassed by talk of social justice and high ideals. Edward Zlotkowski describes his teaching efforts at Bentley in the years before he founded the service learning program as attempts "to help my students break out of the intellectual and moral miasma in which they seemed to me to wander."

I should interject here that the idea of service learning did not originate at Bentley. There are well-developed community service projects at several colleges and universities. Stanford has made extensive use of service learning in freshman English courses. And Campus Compact, an organization of college presidents that promotes public service in education, has been in existence since 1985. The observations I have made about the venture at Bentley are echoed in reports from other schools.

There is a good deal of evidence from our program that service learning generates a social conscience, if by that we understand a sense of the reality and immediacy of the problems of the poor and homeless along with a belief that people in a position to help out should do so. Students report that their fears and prejudices diminish or disappear, that they are moved by the experience of helping others, and that they feel a commitment to help more. This is a remarkable accomplishment, to be sure.[2] But it is important to note that these responses tend, quite naturally, to be personal, to report perceptions and emotions. This is where my deepest questions about service learning lie.

I don't mean to belittle the kind of social awareness fostered by service learning, especially with middle-class students. Students in business courses are discovering real applications of their knowledge in the organizations they serve. More importantly, they are learning that they can use their knowledge not only to get jobs for themselves but also to help others. But what are they learning about the nature of the problems that cause these organizations to come into existence? How do they understand the plight of the people who need these services? I worry when our students report, as they frequently do, that homelessness and poverty were abstractions before they met the homeless and poor, but now they see that the homeless are people "just like themselves." This, they like to say, is something that could happen to them: They could lose their jobs, lose their houses, even take to drink.

Here, perhaps ironically, is a danger: If our students regard social problems as chiefly or only personal, then they will not search beyond the person for a systemic explanation. Why is homelessness a problem? Because, they answer, so many people are homeless. The economy is bad and these individuals lost their jobs. Why are so many people undereducated or illiterate? Because they didn't study in school, just like so-and-so in my fifth grade class and he dropped out. Community service could, as my colleague Robert Crooks puts it, "work in a larger way as a kind of voluntary band-aiding of social problems that not only ignores the causes of problems but lets off the hook those responsible for the problems."[3] Campus Compact director Susan Stroud voices the same kind of concern: "If our community service efforts are not structured to raise the issues that result in critical analysis of the issues, then we are not involved in education and social change—we are involved in charity" (3).

I agree. I don't believe that questions about social structures, ideology, and social justice are automatically raised by community service. From my own experience, I am quite sure they are not.

Such questions can and should be raised in a class that is engaged in a community service project. Here, too, there is no guarantee that students will come to see beyond the individual and symptomatic. But that is what I wish to discuss at greater length. I don't see why questions like these cannot be raised in any course in the university, but if there are prime locations, they would be (and are, at Bentley) courses in economics, political science, sociology, and composition.[4] The connection to composition is by no means obvious. It is all too easy to ask students to write journal entries and reaction papers, to assign narratives and extort confessions, and to let it go at that. A colleague reported overhearing a conversation between two students: "We're going to some shelter tomorrow and we have to write about it." "No sweat. Write that before you went, you had no sympathy for the homeless, but the visit to the shelter opened your eyes. Easy A."[5] Even for those whose awakening is genuine, there is reason to doubt that the epiphany includes an understanding of the social forces that produce and sustain poverty, illiteracy, discrimination, and injustice. There is little evidence that students spontaneously gain critical self-consciousness—an awareness of the ways that their own lives have been shaped by the very same forces, that what they regard as "choices" are less than matters of individual will. Writing personal responses to community service experiences is an important part of processing the experience, but it is not sufficient to raise critical or cultural consciousness.

Writing about the actual experience of doing community service, then, does not seem to me to be the primary work to be done in a composition course like mine. Instead, we study literacy and schooling and write about that.[6] At this point, I need to explain some of the mechanics of the course, but I will keep it short.

Students are invited to be in this project and we have had no difficulty raising enough volunteers from the pool of incoming students. I have run the project in a one-semester version, but the two-semester sequence that I will describe here is far better. During the spring semester, the students are also enrolled together in a section of introductory sociology.[7] In the fall semester, the students are trained to be adult literacy tutors, and in the spring semester they do the actual tutoring.

The composition course is not devoted to literacy tutoring, but rather to the study of literacy and schooling, as I have mentioned. This is an important distinction: We do not set out to study teaching methods or composition pedagogy. The students learn some of the teaching methods they will need in tutor-training sessions that take place largely outside of class time. But in the class itself, our goal is to examine the ways that literacy is gained or not gained in the United States and only in that context do we examine teaching theories and practices.

During the fall semester, we read Mike Rose's *Lives on the Boundary* and a number of selections from *Perspectives on Literacy*, an anthology edited by

Kintgen, Kroll, and Rose. In the spring semester, we read Kozol's *Savage Inequalities* and more of the essays in *Perspectives on Literacy*. The students write many summaries of sections of these books as well as several essays drawing on what they learned from them. In the spring semester, they write research papers on topics that arise from our studies.

Toward the end of the fall semester, the students have about ten hours of tutor training designed to sensitize them to the problems and attitudes of illiterate adults as well as to provide them with some teaching materials and methods. These sessions focus on the need to respond to the concerns of the learners and to understand the learners' reasons for seeking literacy education. The sessions also help the tutors generate ideas about teaching materials and how to use them. While the tutoring is going on, we devote some class time each week to questions about how to handle interpersonal problems or obtain appropriate teaching materials.

In the 1992–93 session, the sociology professor and I took the students to the shelter at the beginning of the spring semester for an orientation session. The following week, the students returned to the shelter without us and started the actual tutoring. At the start, the students were naturally apprehensive about tutoring adults in a shelter. Most of them had done some volunteer work before, but not in settings like that. They were very nervous when we actually went to the Pine Street Inn. We left Bentley's clean, well-lighted suburban campus and drove the ten miles into downtown Boston after dark, parked under the expressway, and went past a milling crowd of men into a dreary lobby. We watched the men being checked with a metal detector while we waited for John Lambert, the director of the shelter's education program. The students clumped together around Dave, a football player. Dave wrote in his field notes that he was conscious of this attention and that it made him even more nervous than he already was.

We went upstairs for our orientation, stepping over some sleeping men stretched out on gym mats in the dining hall. Upstairs, we met a number of men who had been working with volunteer tutors. The students later said that they were impressed by the effort that these men were making to try to improve their lives. They did not seem attentive, though, to the analysis offered by the shelter's assistant director, who explained that while the shelter provided critically needed services, it also undermined any sense of independence the residents might have. Their self-esteem seemed to be under constant attack by all the social institutions they came in contact with, including the shelter itself. When I brought it up in class, the students had little memory of this discussion. On their first visits to the shelter, they were simply more concerned with negotiating the immediate physical and psychic environment. Soon, however, they became accustomed to going to the shelter. Two or three of the boys in the class, including big Dave, did not get learners right away and instead walked around the shelter, visiting with the residents and trying to recruit them into the literacy program. Some of the girls did this on occasion, too. The students were irritated that they did not have learners but eventually realized that their presence in the shelter was a valuable advertisement for the literacy program.

The learners' needs are various: Some are almost completely illiterate, some are schizophrenic, a few need ESL teaching, some read well but need help with higher-order skills. Many of the learners come irregularly; many are easily distracted. One woman is pregnant, another is ridiculed by her boyfriend for needing help with phonics. One young woman is prevented by her mother (who also lives at the shelter) from taking tutoring because, the mother insists, she doesn't need it. But many of the students developed excellent tutoring relationships and all learned how to draw on their own resources both psychologically and pedagogically.

The students tended to see their learners, quite naturally, as individuals with personal problems—alcoholism and drugs, mental breakdown, family disintegration, or some nameless inability to concentrate and cope. It is quite easy to see these problems as individual ones. Very few of the students ever became indignant about what they saw. They hoped to help a few people as much as they were able. They would like to know if there is a "cure," but they don't regard that as a realistic hope. What I want to focus on here is how difficult my students find it to transcend their own deeply ingrained belief in individualism and meritocracy in their analysis of the reasons for the illiteracy they see.

They do become indignant when we discuss *Lives on the Boundary*, which describes the ways that schools systematically diminish and degrade culturally disadvantaged students, or when we read *Savage Inequalities*, which tells about the structural inequities in the funding of public education and the horrible consequences of that inequity. The students are indeed distressed by systemic discrimination against poorer people and disenfranchised groups. In their responses to these books, it is clear that they understand the class discrimination inherent in tracking and the effect of tracking on self-esteem. But they do not seem to see this discrimination in the lives of their learners. One reason, perhaps, is that the learners themselves regard their situations as personal problems. They, too, have imbibed the lessons about individualism and equal opportunity. The traces have been covered over. Thus, in order to understand that they are in the presence of the effects they have been reading about, the students must also understand—viscerally if not intellectually— the nature of what Gramsci called hegemony: the belief that one participates freely in an open and democratic system and must therefore accept the results it produces. They must see, in other words, that the people in the shelter believe the same things that they, the students, do—that there is equal opportunity to succeed or fail, to become literate or remain illiterate. They need to analyze the way that schools and other institutions, like the shelter itself, embody those beliefs.

Here is a passage from *Lives on the Boundary*. We spent a lot of time with this:

> American meritocracy is validated and sustained by the deep-rooted belief in equal opportunity. But can we really say that kids like those I taught [as a Teacher Corps volunteer] have equal access to America's educational resources? Consider not only the economic and political barriers

they face, but the fact, too, that judgements about their ability are made at a very young age, and those judgements, accurate or not, affect the curriculum they receive, their place in the school, the way they're defined institutionally. The insidious part of this drama is that, in the observance or the breach, students unwittingly play right into the assessments. Even as they rebel, they confirm the school's decision. They turn off or distance themselves or clam up or daydream, they deny or lash out, acquiesce or subvert, for, finally, they are powerless to stand outside the definition and challenge it head on. . . . [T]he children gradually internalize the definition the school delivers to them, incorporate a stratifying regulator as powerful as the overt institutional gatekeepers that, in other societies, determine who goes where in the educational system. There is no need for the elitist projections of quotas and exclusionary exams when a kid announces that he just wants to be average. If you want to insist that the children Joe and Monica and the rest of us taught had an equal opportunity in American schools, then you'll have to say that they had their equal chance and forfeited it before leaving the fourth grade. (128)

Elsewhere in *Lives on the Boundary*, Rose speaks sensitively about the difficulties freshmen have with academic discourse, a discourse "marked by terms and expressions that represent an elaborate set of shared concepts and orientations" (192). Rose himself is a brilliant stylist of academic discourse, as the passage I've quoted reveals. Rose advises that students need many opportunities to become comfortable with this discourse, and I take his advice seriously. There is much that my students cannot fathom in his book, many references to abstractions and complex terms (such as "incorporate a stratifying regulator as powerful as the overt institutional gatekeepers"), so we spend time talking and writing about important passages like this.

"American meritocracy is validated and sustained by the deep-rooted belief in equal opportunity." This sentence is a complete stopper. My students consistently claim that they have never heard the word "meritocracy" before. Once defined, though, the idea is perfectly obvious to them: of course those who are smartest, most talented, and work hardest rise to the top. What else? "Equal opportunity" is also initially difficult for them—not because it is unfamiliar but because it never seemed to require definition or reflection. This is not the first place in *Lives on the Boundary* that the students have encountered a challenge to the idea of equal opportunity: The challenge is both implied and explicitly stated many times. Yet, even 128 pages into the book, their first reaction is to regard this sentence as a positive statement about a noble ideal, an American virtue. It costs them a great effort to see that Rose is saying that one false idea is sustained by another, that the very words "validated and sustained" carry a negative connotation, that "deep-rooted belief" means self-deception. It costs them more than intellectual effort: It means a re-evaluation of the very deep-rooted beliefs that Rose is discussing here. It means seeing that Rose is talking about their beliefs and criticizing them.

When Job, the righteous man, loses his property, his children, and his health, he angrily questions the belief that God is just and gives people what they deserve. He lashes out at his friends, the false comforters, who stead-fastly maintain that the good are rewarded and the wicked punished (and thereby imply that Job is suffering for some sin). Yet Job is in a terrible dilemma. He is frustrated and angry, convinced that the comforters are wrong, yet unable to explain his situation—for he believes precisely the same thing the comforters believe. When a belief is deeply rooted, alternatives are inconceivable.

How do my students abandon their comfortable belief in equal opportu-nity and meritocracy? Did they not deserve, did they not earn their place in school and society? They have the greatest respect for Mike Rose and want to believe what he says, but it isn't easy. As education critic Colin Greer says, tra-ditional historians of education "mistake the rhetoric of good intentions for historical reality" and persist in believing, against all evidence, that schools are the instruments of social change (4). We can hardly fault students for clinging to such a belief. We ran into a similar problem discussing a passage earlier in Rose's book:

> We live, in America, with so many platitudes about motivation and self-reliance and individualism—and myths spun from them, like those of Horatio Alger—that we find it hard to accept the fact that they are seri-ous nonsense. (47)

Here, too, we had worked on the definition of "individualism" and the nega-tive connotations of "platitudes" and "nonsense." The students never heard of Horatio Alger. After I explained about Alger, Lynne told us, without the least self-consciousness and without comment, that her grandfather came from Italy without a cent and became a success in America all on his own, without help from anybody.

In their fall semester papers, the students tested out the ideas they were learning about systemic discrimination through schooling. They were very tentative about this at first. Kyle wrote:

> In America today, we find that how an individual will do in school is often dependent upon what economic class they come from. Through studies of literacy, experts have found that there are different levels of success in school among individuals of diverse socioeconomic back-grounds. . . . Children of [the] middle- and upper-class are able to attend better schools and have greater access to books and other reading mate-rials. Therefore, they tend to feel more comfortable with the material in school while lower-class children, whose parents are not so well off in terms of money, are more inclined to be insecure. In addition, in situa-tions where parents of poor children have had low levels of education, there is a good possibility that their children will also have low levels of education. While at the same time the situation is reversed with children of well-to-do parents.

These ideas are clearly unfamiliar to Kyle, and so he needs to repeat them and carefully spell out the steps in the process of discrimination, while holding onto the possibility of individual differences. "Experts" have discovered this injustice—it is not immediately accessible to experience. The parents of lower-class children are not so well off "in terms of money"—though they may, I think Kyle implies, have good intentions.

It is difficult, as I have said, for my students to understand these ideas, let alone deal with them critically. In the spring semester, for example, while we were studying Kozol's *Savage Inequalities*, a book that describes and decries the differences between well-funded suburban schools and their decrepit and overcrowded counterparts in the cities, Lynne (who told us about her grand-father) suggested that the students in south Chicago's schools were probably just not personally motivated to do school work, like the kids in her high school who flunked. Several students murmured in agreement, though when I challenged her, several others expressed dismay about Lynne's assumptions. Lynne is not a conservative ideologue. As with the comments about her grandfather, she was simply being unself-conscious. Her comment helps us see how hard it is to understand the social nature of experience and to accept the idea of structural injustice.

In an essay called "Critical Teaching and Dominant Culture" in *Composition and Resistance*, a volume of essays on critical teaching, Cy Knoblauch describes his attempts to bring his students to some consciousness of the injuries of class. He tells how his students were unmoved by "The Lesson," Toni Cade Bambara's story about poor black children visiting F.A.O. Schwartz. Knoblauch quotes a student response that he characterizes as typical: "If you strive for what you want, you can receive it." As Knoblauch cogently argues, the goal of critical pedagogy is to help students see and analyze the assumptions they make in comments like these. Still, it takes a lot of time and work to do this and Knoblauch is honest enough to say that he did not have the success he wished for.

Time and work were on our side, though, in the literacy-tutoring project—we had two semesters of composition, a sociology course, and the project itself. At the time that Lynne made her comment about Chicago schoolkids, the students had been tutoring at the Pine Street Inn shelter for several weeks. There was, apparently, nothing automatic or instantaneous about that experience that helped them understand Rose or Kozol. The community service experience doesn't bring an epiphany of critical consciousness—or even, necessarily, an epiphany of conscience. The effect was slow and indirect. In time, the students began to realize that the people at Pine Street were *not* like them. They did not, finally, conclude that "this could happen to me." Though they were not allowed (by the wise rules of the shelter and good sense) to quiz their learners on their personal lives and histories, they had learned enough about the learners' family distress and social isolation, their disconnection from community, lack of individual resources, and reliance on charitable institutions and the effects of those conditions on their self-images—to realize that "this could happen to me" is a shallow response.

The tutoring, as best we could determine, appeared to be productive for the learners at the shelter. In many ways, the best help that tutors can provide in such a setting is to come regularly and respond sensitively to the learners' concerns. The learners are coming to the literacy program at the end of what is typically a long series of personal and social failures, and though they expect—and often demand—a school-like experience again, the tutors are there to humanize it as much as they can.

The final research papers for the composition course show a growing sophistication about the social forces at work in the creation of illiteracy. Students visited nursery school classes to see how children learn, returned to their own high schools to find out what happened to the kids who flunked, corresponded with convicts in prison-education programs. In his paper, "The Creation of Illiteracy through Tracking," Dave (the football player) writes, "Tracking tends to maintain or amplify differences in socioeconomic status, the opposite of 'equalizing' these differences as schools should." Schools can't be held responsible for prior economic discrimination, Dave argues, but they must be held accountable for reinforcing it. Kevin borrowed several history textbooks used over the last ten years in the Waltham High School, counted the number of pictures and other references to African-Americans and compared them to the number of pictures and similar references to whites, analyzed the images, and tried to imagine what a black student would learn about American culture from an education in Waltham, Massachusetts (Kevin is white). Our friend Lynne asked how school systems with the money to do so were addressing the needs of disadvantaged students. She concludes that "the systems with the extra money to spend on special programs are not facing these types of problems." She points out that there is no lack of information about how to spend this money well and describes the settled and unreflective attitudes about schools and teaching that prevent the adoption of new methods.

Some students referred to their tutoring experience in their papers. Mark, for example, noted the kind of knowledge his learners sought—sentence-diagramming and algebra—and commented that their frustrating search for credentials, fostered by traditional (and failed) schooling, had left them without job skills on the one hand and with an artificially low sense of their own abilities on the other. Most of the students did not, however, incorporate the tutoring experience in the research papers they wrote for my class. This was as it should be: The goal of the course was not, as I have explained, to facilitate the tutoring experience, but to investigate the social and cultural reasons for the existence of illiteracy—the reasons, in other words, that the students needed to perform the valuable service they were engaged in. In that sense, the tutoring project was constantly present in our class. In the sociology course, the students used their visits to Pine Street more directly as the object of field observations and analysis.

The effort to reach into the composition class with a curriculum aimed at democracy and social justice is an attempt to make schools function the way Dave and my other students want them to—as radically democratic institutions, with the goal not only of making individual students more successful, but also of making better citizens, citizens in the strongest sense of those who take responsibility for communal welfare. These efforts belong in the composition class because of the rhetorical as well as the practical nature of citizenship and social transformation.

What the students' final papers show, then, is a sense of life as a communal project, an understanding of the way that social institutions affect our lives, and a sense that our responsibility for social justice includes but also carries beyond personal acts of charity. This is an understanding that has been very rare among Bentley students. Immersed in a culture of individualism, convinced of their merit in a meritocracy, students like those at Bentley need to see that there is a social basis for most of the conditions they take to be matters of individual choice or individual ability. As Kurt Spellmeyer says, "the university fails to promote a social imagination, an awareness of the human 'world' as a common historical project, and not simply as a state of nature to which we must adjust ourselves" (73). Students who lack this social imagination (most of them, according to the study Spellmeyer cites) attribute all attitudes, behavior, and material conditions to an individual rather than social source. Students will not critically question a world that seems natural, inevitable, given; instead, they will strategize about their position within it. Developing a social imagination makes it possible not only to question and analyze the world, but also to imagine transforming it.

NOTES

1. A successful program requires a great deal of coordination between the school and the community agencies. Individual teachers working on their own to arrange contacts will find the task exhausting and daunting. While many agencies welcome short-term volunteers, some cannot. Literacy tutoring, for example, requires consistency over time, so that tutors can establish a relationship with the learner. In short, the school-agency ties must be well developed before the students show up. I don't wish to discourage such programs, but to suggest that good planning can prevent many problems and frsutrations. See Cotton and Stanton, "Joining Campus and Community through Service Learning," in *Community Service as Values Education*.

2. The advocates of service learning assume that values must be taught in college. I'm comfortable with that assumption and won't try to make the case for teaching values or critical consciousness here. The question of whether to teach values at all is by no means settled. It has been raised persistently as a general question in education and it has been a topic of hot debate in composition studies. Patricia Bizzell argues cogently for the importance of teaching values in *Academic Discourse and Critical Consciousness*. C. H. Knoblauch and Lil Brannon's *Critical Teaching and the Idea of Literacy* is a recent and valuable contribution. Maxine Hairston dissents in "Diversity, Ideology, and Teaching Writing." Paulo Freire, Henry Giroux, and Ira Shor have long been advocates of teaching values through the development of critical consciousness. And I have something to say about the issue in "Composition and the Politics of the Curriculum."

3. Crooks goes on: "Let me hasten to say that by 'those responsible' I mean all of us, who through direct participation in institutional actions, policy-making, ideas, attitudes, or indirectly, though silence and compliance, offer support to pervasive economic, social, political, and cultural systems that produce the kinds of problems that community service addresses."

4. At some universities, the theology department is the primary location for these courses. Georgetown University, Boston College, and Marymount College link community service to theology courses on injustice and social responsibility, for example.

5. I reported this conversation to Zlotkowski, who responded that he believed that many students remained defensive about the fact that they really did have their eyes opened. In anonymous student evaluations that have no effect on grades, he finds a predominance of sincere reports of changed attitudes.

6. The courses in the Stanford program tend to focus on writing to or for the agency being served. Such projects are undertaken at Bentley by more advanced classes. See *Let 100 Flowers Bloom* for a description of Stanford's rationale. A high-school writing course in which students

work as literacy volunteers is described by Norma Greco in "Critical Literacy and Community Service: Reading and Writing the World."

7. The benefits of "clustering" courses are described in *Learning Communities* by Faith Gabelnick et al. When students are co-registered in two or more courses, instructors can develop common themes, draw on material taught in each other's courses, explore shared readings from different perspectives, and have some common writing assignments. While my students were working on their writing with me and doing their tutoring at the shelter, in the sociology course they were learning about the effects of social and institutional forces on the formation of identity. Their final research papers were submitted in both courses.

WORKS CITED

Bizzell, Patricia. *Academic Discourse and Critical Consciousness.* Pittsburgh: U of Pittsburgh P, 1993. 277–95.

Cotton, Debbie, and Timothy K. Stanton. "Joining Campus and Community through Service Learning." *Community Service as Values Education.* Ed. Cecilia I. Delve et al. San Francisco: Jossey-Bass, 1990.

Crooks, Robert. "Service Learning and Cultural Critique: Towards a Model for Activist Expository Writing Courses." Conference on College Composition and Communication, San Diego, CA, March 1993.

Friedman, Phil. "A Secular Foundation for Ethics: Business Ethics and the Business School." *EDP Auditor Journal* 2 (1989): 9–11.

Gabelnick, Faith, Jean MacGregor, Robert S. Matthews, and Barbara Leigh Smith, eds. *Learning Communities: Creating Connections Among Students, Faculty, and Disciplines.* San Francisco: Jossey-Bass, 1990.

Greco, Norma. "Critical Literacy and Community Service: Reading and Writing the World." *English Journal* 81 (1992): 83–85.

Greer, Colin. *The Great School Legend: A Revisionist Interpretation of American Public Education.* New York: Basic, 1972.

Hairston, Maxine. "Diversity, Ideology, and Teaching Writing." *CCC* 43 (1992): 179–93.

Herzberg Bruce. "Composition and the Politics of the Curriculum." *The Politics of Writing Instruction: Postsecondary.* Ed. Richard Bullock and John Trimbur. Portsmouth, NH: Boynton, 1991. 97–118.

Kintgen, Eugene R., Barry M. Kroll, and Mike Rose, eds. *Perspectives on Literacy.* Carbondale: Southern Illinois UP, 1988.

Knoblauch, C. H. "Critical Teaching and Dominant Culture." *Composition and Resistance.* Ed. C. Mark Hurlbert and Michael Blitz. Portsmouth, NH: Boynton, 1991. 12–21.

Knoblauch, C. H., and Lil Brannon. *Critical Teaching and the Idea of Literacy.* Portsmouth, NH: Boynton, 1993.

Kozol, Jonathan. *Savage Inequalities.* New York: Crown, 1991.

Let 100 Flowers Bloom: Community Service Writing Curriculum Materials Developed by the Stanford Freshman English Program. Stanford U, n.d.

Rose, Mike. *Lives on the Boundary.* New York: Free, 1989.

Spellmeyer, Kurt. "Knowledge Against 'Knowledge.'" *Composition and Resistance.* Ed. C. Mark Hurlbert and Michael Blitz. Portsmouth, NH: Boynton, 1991. 70–80.

Stroud, Susan. "A Report from the Director." *Campus Compact* (Fall 1992): 3–4.

Zlotkowski, Edward. "Address to the Faculty of Niagara University." Niagara, NY, April 1993.

PART THREE

Rhetoric, Civic Writing, and the Public Sphere

12 Rogue Cops and Health Care: What Do We Want from Public Writing?

SUSAN WELLS

On February 24, 1991, Arthur Colbert, a Temple University criminal justice major, was stopped by two Philadelphia police officers as he looked for his date's address. They accused Colbert of running a crack house under the name "Hakim," and took him to a deserted building. He was beaten; a gun was pointed at his head. Colbert spent the rest of the night at the 39th District Headquarters on Hunting Park Avenue, being questioned, slapped around, and threatened. They let him go in the morning, warning him to stay out of the area.

The next day, Colbert returned to the headquarters and filled out a "Citizen's Complaint" form. He wrote the story of his night, filling three sheets of paper, printing in capitals, and concluding, "The above events happened violently and brutally. . . . I am a Temple student and will be around that area quite frequently. It seems as though the people who are supposed to be protecting my civil rights are the ones who are violating them. I can't say this for every police officer, but this is the case with these two cops" (Bowden and Fazlollah). The officer in charge was impressed: unlike other complaints against these policemen, Colbert's was "coherent and concise, loaded with details." The subsequent investigation uncovered (eventually) a pattern of frameups, bribes, and abuses of power by the Philadelphia police; it led to charges, suspensions, transfers, and other reforms.

I was fascinated by this story in the September 10, 1995 *Philadelphia Inquirer*. As a citizen, I was angry; as a teacher, I was upset that a student had been brutalized. But as a writing teacher, I was triumphant. Colbert had probably learned to write strong narrative in *our* program; his complaint sounded like a successful basic writing assignment—good sequential order, lots of detail and elaboration, a clear, supportable conclusion. Someone had done good work with this student. And his text had been efficacious: it had turned around the whole police department, delivered innocent grandmothers from unjust imprisonment, and set aside scores of false convictions.

From *College Composition and Communication* 47.3 (1996): 325–41.

My triumph settled down with my next cup of coffee—Colbert's complaint had been the twenty-third filed against these cops, and the Rodney King incident probably prompted the department's investigation. But my moment of exhilarated delusion speaks about the desire for efficacious public writing, particularly as it is invested in students. It speaks of that desire's urgency; the response to Colbert's writing seemed to rectify his terrifying experience. It speaks of that desire's poverty: I once had stronger hopes than helping my students write good complaints if they were beaten up by the cops.

I want to investigate this desire, in its urgent poverty, more fully. If we want more for our students than the ability to defend themselves in bureaucratic settings, we are imagining them in a public role, imagining a public space they could enter. I argue that we need to build, or take part in building, such a public sphere; that the public sphere is always constructed; and that it cannot, in our society, be unitary. These exigencies are not limited to academic settings: any speaker must work to build a public. I base my arguments on Jürgen Habermas's treatment of the public sphere, as modified by Oskar Negt and Alexander Kluge, and illustrate them by examining President Bill Clinton's construction of a public in his 1993 Health Care Speech.

Rhetoricians and compositionists have turned toward the public, for the best of reasons. But we have some problems locating the public—knowing exactly where should we turn. In the Charles Kneupper Memorial Address to the Rhetoric Society of America, Edward Schiappa argued that "the place for cultural critique by teachers and scholars of rhetorical studies is not only the classroom or academic books and journals, but also 'in the streets' and other nonacademic public and private forums" (21). Schiappa rounds up the usual suspects: letters to the student newspaper, or even the hometown newspaper, speaking before city council or the state assembly. For Schiappa, and for most of us, when we think about "public discourse," the public appears as a preexisting forum where citizens make decisions face to face. That space is so intensely imagined that we think it must be real—just a little inaccessible, like live theater or downtown department stores.

But our encounters with even a local civic space—the place where we decide a strike vote, hire a new minister, form a block watch—are discontinuous and associated with crises. These scraps of discursive space are not just pale descendants of the *agora* or the Enlightenment coffee house; they are something else entirely. Public speech is a performance in time, located at specific historical junctures, temporary and unstable, even though it is imagined as a location in space, always available, with secure and discernable borders. We feel guilty for our absence from the public; we suspect that it has been usurped by political functionaries and spin doctors. As compositionists, we apply a deficit model to public discourse: it is one more thing students don't know, one more thing we have trouble teaching (Smith; Farrell, *Symposium*). But public space is not available, at least not in the form we have imagined it.

It might be helpful to see the public and public speech as questions, rather than answers, and to consider how they are understood in contemporary cultural theory. The central theorist of the public is Jürgen Habermas, specifically in his *The Structural Transformation of the Public Sphere: An Inquiry into a Category of Bourgeois Society*. Like so much of Habermas's work, *The Structural Transformation of the Public Sphere* is both deeply problematic and astoundingly fruitful. Originally published in 1962, it was translated and re-issued in 1989, and has provoked serious debate in the United States on both theoretical and historical grounds (Robbins; Calhoun). Scholars have criticized Habermas's historical analysis (Ryan, "Gender"; Eley) and argued that he failed to understand domination (Aronowitz; for responses, see Habermas, "Concluding"; Wells). In Germany, the theory of the public sphere was criticized, extended, and developed by Oskar Negt and Alexander Kluge, whose *The Public Sphere and Experience: Toward an Analysis of the Bourgeois and the Proletarian Public Sphere* is finally available in English twenty years after its original publication. Within rhetorical theory, Thomas Farrell's *Norms of Rhetorical Culture* takes up Habermas's analysis from an Aristotelian perspective, treating the public as a pre-existing audience, formed by a more or less developed rhetorical culture.

Habermas defines the public sphere as a discursive domain where private individuals, without the authority of state office, debate the general conduct of social and political business, holding official bodies accountable at the bar of reason. The public sphere promises equality of access and discussion governed by rationality, with no holds barred, no topics off limits. But it is not without its contradictions. We come to the public sphere with an orientation to reciprocal exchanges formed in a capitalist economy, and an orientation to subjectivity formed in the intimate world of the family. The public, like representative democracy, secularism, or experimental science, emerges as a richly determined practice that produces both knowledge and ignorance, both domination and a diffusion of power.

The Structural Transformation of the Public Sphere serves both as a historical reconstruction and as an aid to critical reflection. As a historical reconstruction, *Structural Transformation* considers the conditions for the possibility of democratic institutions; as an aid to critique, it contrasts actual decision making with the ideal of emancipated participation. Nor is Habermas's a utopian account: the public, for him, has always implied exclusion and domination as well as openness and reason, since it assumed precisely the distinctions of wealth and property from which the concept of the private citizen is abstracted. For Habermas, the public is not a pre-existing site, a place to be entered by good citizens or seized by insurgents. Public discourse is not a kind of writing, or an ensemble of genres (letters to the editor, campaign leaflets, letter to Congress). Public discourse is a complex array of discursive practices, including forms of writing, speech, and media performance, historically situated and contested. The public is not, as in some forms of Marxism, a reflex of productive relations, although public discourse does circulate as a commodity among others, even as it makes an exorbitant demand for dissemination outside the commodity system. Speakers and writers come to the public with a weight of personal and social experience; to speak in public is to render those experiences intelligible to any listener whatever, and therefore to compromise their private density. Finally, the public is not simply a neutral container for historical events: it has its own history, its own vexed construction, its own possibilities of growth and decay.

We do not do justice to this history, this set of possibilities, when we assign students generic public writing, such as an essay on gun control, or a letter to a nonexistent editor. In such assignments, students inscribe their positions in a vacuum: since there is no place within the culture where student writing on gun control is held to be of general interest, no matter how persuasive the student, or how intimate their acquaintance with guns, "public writing" in such a context means "writing for no audience at all." It is not some deficit on the part of students that makes such writing impossible. The space within which a new kind of public writing might be read, and therefore the incitement to read it, must be constructed, just as the culture of workingmen's colleges and ladies' physiological societies was constructed in the nineteenth century, just as MOO's and newsgroups are being constructed now. Such construction is difficult, and the teachers' role in it is contradictory. This essay frames those difficulties, and provisional attempts to resolve them, including such tactics as the Howard University "broad sympathy" pedagogy, which locates students within a public tradition of writing by Howard alumni, the many attempts at classroom magazines, including Randall Popken's practice of publishing a yearly research journal through Tarlton State University classes, and courses like Karyn Hollis's Writing for Social Change, which places student writers as interns in community organizations.

The difficulty of constructing a public is not an accident attached to our cloistered academic status. We are not uncertain in our treatment of public writing because we have been sheltered from a vibrant public sphere. Our public sphere is attenuated, fragmented, and colonized: so is everyone else's. All speakers and writers who aspire to intervene in society face the task of constructing a responsive public. Nobody, not even the president speaking on national television, enters it without difficulty. Clinton's Health Care Address (September 22, 1993) was a remarkable example of how these and other difficulties operated on the most sanctioned of speakers, supported by all the media of publicity and the ethos of high public office.

The Clinton Health Care Plan was a major priority of his new administration. Clinton's speech explained to Congress and the television audience the provisions of the plan and argued for its central principle, universal coverage. But the passion of this speech was directed, not at health care reform, but at the debate that would make reform possible: "I want to say to all of you, I have been deeply moved by the spirit of this debate, by the openness of all people to new ideas, to argument and information" (1836).[1] The desire to learn and the willingness to argue engage some of the deepest energies of this speech, and rightly so. A debate within some accountable public space was a precondition for any of the specific propositions about health care reform Clinton advocated. Clinton needed something like a Habermasian public sphere: a space that could sustain and adjudicate a debate on evidence.

But the health care debate could not be restricted to members of Congress. Somehow, the "voices of the people" had to be included. And there is a venerable figure, in presidential rhetoric, for those voices—the representative citizen, an ordinary person whose experience demonstrates the policy-maker's point. We meet many such citizens in the Health Care Address—the small businessman with insurance problems, the nurse called from a patient's bedside to fill out forms. These figures have been investigated in the rich literature on presidential rhetoric in speech communication, where they are seen as attempts to simulate or create a public (Ryan, "Harry"; Medhurst; Bochin; Ritter and Henry; Weiler and Pearce, *Public*; Jamieson, *Eloquence* 1992). Here we read, for example, of the "hero in the balcony," a representative citizen who exemplifies public support for a policy. Ideally, the citizen is present at the speech, invited to stand for applause: the citizen can also be quoted, invoked, made present by a letter or artifact. Living or dead, the "representative citizen" has been a staple of presidential rhetoric since Reagan (Weiler and Pearce, "Ceremonial"; Carter; Blankenship and Muir; Ritter and Henry). Quoted or cited, such figures operate on multiple levels: within the authoritative discourse of the president, the audience sees and hears itself. Within the discourse of power, the figure of the ordinary citizen offers the audience identification with a name, town, and an occupation rather than a faceless "silent majority." Pictures of the representative citizen function as an inartistic proof of the proposition being advanced. Aristotle grudgingly conceded visual displays a place, alongside oaths and confessions obtained by torture, in the arsenal of persuasion; on television such images are obligatory—the saintly Mother Hale, the diabolical Willy Horton (Jamieson, *Eloquence*, 90–118). Reagan raised the use of representative citizens to a minor presidential art form, introducing Clara Hale during his first State of the Union Address, reading a letter from the daughter of a veteran at the Point du Hoc dedication in Normandy, and commemorating individual soldiers—Lt. Trujillo from Grenada, Sgt. Benavidez from Viet Nam—during congressional addresses. As Jamieson has demonstrated, the heroic individual can be a powerful metonym for a whole line of public policy, so that admiration for Trujillo or Benavidez implicates an audience in a specific and controversial foreign policy (*Eloquence* 157, 122). Representative citizens do not grow like mushrooms in the House balcony: they are invented, according to very precise specifications. After the Panama invasion, the Pentagon was directed to find a military hero who had saved lives rather than taking them; they searched long and hard before they found Trujillo (Ritter and Henry 106).

The representative citizen is a location, a "topic," functioning both as a heightened example of public virtues or vices, and also as a prop for identification. The representative citizen carries the quasi-sacred functions of savior or scapegoat—nobody questions Mother Hale's virtue, or Willie Horton's guilt—and is also one of us, enjoying fifteen minutes of fame. In either role, the representative citizen displaces argument. The representative citizen is someone who is supposed to know, who has been delegated to understand, through intense experience, complex public issues. In the presence of such figures, it is impolite to discuss policy, since to oppose the Grenada invasion or voluntarism as a solution to drug abuse, or to support prison furlough programs, would be to affront those heroes and victims who look down from the balcony. To quote the representative citizen is to speak with a voice that imitates everyday talk, while precluding argument. The heroic citizen becomes the mouthpiece of monologic public policy discourse. Quoting the citizen suggests that any of us, talking through policy issues in terms of our own experience, will be more profound for being less professional.

In quotation, ordinary citizens seem to whisper in the corridors of power. The heroic citizen allows the political speaker to represent public policy as a conversation that anyone could enter. The professional discourse of public policy frames complex political and social issues as soluble problems, issues that can be resolved with the available evidence (Ohmann). Since public administration, like science and education, has become professionalized, opportunities for informed debate on central questions of policy have diminished (Habermas, *Legitimation*). Instead, simulacra of the public haunt the presidential address.

Clinton used the small businessman Kerry Kennedy, whose insurance company wanted to drop his parents, to support a central argument of the speech. Kennedy's dilemma demonstrated the need for far-reaching change in the health care delivery system. Reagan had used representative citizens to introduce deliberative materials into epideictic contexts, but Clinton's exigencies were quite different. Since Clinton was proposing sustained political debate, he needed a more complex figure than Reagan's citizen hero; rather than a ceremonial confirmation, he needed a representation of voice, of argument. These are not easy functions for the figure of the representative citizen: a monologic figure, capable of speech but not reply, stands uneasily for a dialogic situation. This contradiction, I would emphasize, was no mistake of Clinton's: it bears the marks of difficulty and labor that distinguish all contemporary attempts to construct or approach a public.

Clinton drew the lesson from Kerry Kennedy's experience: "This story speaks for millions of others, and from them we have learned a powerful truth. We have to preserve and strengthen what is right with the health care system, but we have got to fix what is wrong with it" (1838). This conclusion was at once tautological and controversial. No one would argue against preserving the good and reforming the bad, or propose that we change the good and keep the bad; Clinton invoked a maxim, a commonplace. Only in the context of an address to Congress on health care is such a proposition arguable: it shifts the debate's burden of proof from the status quo, assuming instead the need for serious reform. (See Jacobs on declining public confidence in health care in Fall 1993.) Further, Clinton imagined—created, in the course of the speech—a discursive site where Kerry Kennedy, Congress, and the president could agree on reform. This configuration of the public sphere is strategic: since Congress had a long history of rejecting health care reforms, Clinton wanted to build an alternate space of political deliberation where the need for change in the health care system is assumed.

But, of course, this work of construction did not hold. In spite of Clinton's palpable desire for a broad public debate, and the force with which he expressed it in the health care speech, we had no debate, no health care reform. Rhetorically, the Clinton administration entered a long period of feverish improvisation and mobile advocacy. We would not hear a call for debate again; and all possible readers of this essay will know better than I the outcome of Clinton's improvisations. While the failure of health care reform was not primarily rhetorical, it suggests that figures like the representative citizen, adapted to spectacle and refeudalized passivity, do not advance the labor of rationality that could sustain a contemporary public sphere.

And probably not a single public sphere, as Oskar Negt and Alexander Kluge suggest in their *The Public Sphere and Experience*. Putting in motion the contradictions in Habermas's theory of the public, exploiting them to indicate openings, absences, and possibilities within contemporary public life, their public sphere is understood as contradictory to "proletarian experience." (The term is deliberately anachronistic.) The proletariat is characterized by negation, by opposition to the existing world, and by the need for reflection, for some practice of discourse that can make that negation explicit. Proletarian life is not a cohesive whole, and therefore cannot be expressed in the abstract rationality of the bourgeois public sphere, since within the public sphere, the class experiences of subaltern groups become private, commodified as interest group politics. At the same time, public institutions are shaped by a commonality of everyone's historical experience. Institutions like the university, representative democracy, and the press certainly perpetuate hierarchy, but they have also been shaped by cultural struggles, and preserve historical experiences that we may want to claim.

Abstaining from public life or public discourse severs our connections to those histories. For Negt and Kluge, no revolutionary paroxysm can resolve these contradictions: "If the masses try to fight a ruling class reinforced by the power of the public sphere, their struggle is hopeless; they are always simultaneously fighting against themselves, for the public sphere is constituted by them" (xlvii). The public sphere, however alien, cannot be simply opposed, but must be reconstructed and colonized. It will neither go away nor leave us alone.

Negt and Kluge's public is contradictory, overdetermined, insoluble, and peremptory—and so it is very close to the experience of the classroom. As citizens, we cannot abstain from the public sphere or wish it away; we cannot fight it, although we can fight in it. The public sphere as it has crystallized and shattered in modernity does not represent, and cannot represent, the experience of subaltern classes; it does not even represent all the significant experience of ruling classes. It is a specific, historically textured, means of political representation; partial but not illusory. Our life in the classroom is marked by similar inevitability, partiality of representation, and historical contingency.

Whatever the limits of Negt and Kluge's analysis, with its Marxist vocabulary and its relentless politics, I know of no other theory that does justice to the simultaneous sense of exclusion and attraction that marks our relations to the public as students and teachers: our sense that the broadest political arenas of our society are closed to us, inhospitable; and also our impulse to enter them, or approximate them, or transform them. I have never known a writer, student or teacher, who wanted a smaller audience, or a narrower readership; I have never known a writer who felt unproblematically at home in the discursive forms of broad political or social address.

Unlike Habermas, who sees the displacement of the classic public sphere by media as a "refeudalization" of public discourse, Negt and Kluge see the media as available for alternative publics and counter publics. Allusively, they suggest tactics for creating partial, temporary, and multiple public spheres. Negt and Kluge are less interested in critical diagnosis of the public sphere than in the efficacious production of alternatives (140): the reconstruction of public symbols and monuments, a diverse political press, associations of children, and the development of new forms of sensory experience. None of these theorists sees the public as a benign solution to marginalization or a debased domain of alienated doublespeak: the public is neither noble nor inherently oppressive. The cynicism that we encounter daily in our students and ourselves responds to a fragmented and contradictory public, a public that must be constructed and reconstructed, that requires multiple nego-tiations and positionings for every possible speaker. Cynicism, distrust of politics, even apathy, are neither moral failings nor signs of a romantic (or postmodern) political innocence; they are strategies for addressing a public that no longer supports the illusion of organic integrity.

Such fragmentation has rhetorical consequences. Clinton's choice of health care as the central issue for his first year was an attempt to finesse the fragmented public: all of us, after all, live in vulnerable bodies. But Clinton spoke, instead, of disembodied representative citizens, advocating the careful deployment of resources, an extension of technical expertise and government planning. Clinton argued that in a rational health care system, bodies will no longer be arbitrarily designated as "high risk," or as manifesting a "pre-existing condition": they will instead be abstracted to the rule of universal coverage. The body, like the abstracted citizen of the Enlightenment, achieves agency and efficacy at the cost of everything that had marked it as distinct, particular, individual, corporeal. But bodies are not simply generic containers for an undifferentiated human essence. They are complex, highly mediated, and culturally constituted locations, over which play every possible social division and conflict.

Hence, rather than escaping the contradictions inherent in the concept of the public, Clinton's call for health care reform posed them as issues of naked self-interest. The initial debate on the Clinton plan, therefore, cruised the aisles of the health care K-Mart. What would be covered? Mammograms? Breast cancer surgery? Breast reconstruction? Prenatal care? Abortion? Infer-tility treatment? The body, proposed as an abstract object of "universal cover-age," dissolved at once into a series of contingent, deeply ideological choices, brokered rather than reasoned.

Again, it was not Clinton's mistake that led to this aporia: such contradictions have characterized political discourse and rhetorical theory since the Enlightenment. Clinton's invocations of the body and his utopian call to public debate are both inconsistent, just as our desires for our students are inconsistent, but they are necessarily and unavoidably so. Clinton attempted to manage or contain this aporia, and to construct a public that would not immediately fragment into constituencies or "communities" by displacing the motivation for reform from health to rationality, by relocating our desires from the body to debate. This strategy did not work: there was neither rationalization, containment, nor debate.

Our pedagogy of public discourse does not do much better. On the level of handbook advice, public discourse presents students with problems of abstraction: they must explain everything, assume an audience that knows nothing. Unlike the densely articulated lore that guides students through critical essays, research papers, and other academic genres, textbook advice on public writing is thin and soupy, as if the role were so improbable that no guidance could normalize it.

In *Fragments of Rationality*, composition theorist Lester Faigley convincingly argues for a reorientation to public discourse, a recovery of the emancipatory impulses of the early process movement (71). Faigley joins Halloran in calling for "recovering a lost tradition of rhetoric in public life," noting that while college rhetoric in the eighteenth century was highly politicized and anything but safe, it also excluded women, minorities, and working people. Having replicated Habermas's discussion of the contradictions of the bourgeois public sphere, Faigley proposes that we interrogate the structures of the classroom, opening up a new area of disciplinary investigation within it:

> To challenge the lingering conception of the writer as ungendered, classless, and living outside of history, several scholars in composition have invited students to explore their situatedness as writers and the politics of literacy. These explorations are often aligned with a more general movement known as *cultural studies*. (72)

Faigley is proposing a valuable pedagogical practice, but not a practice of public discourse. Clinton called for debate on health care rather than for improved health care; Faigley advocates the analysis of literacy rather than public literate action. The desire for a public derails the activity that might construct one. Our choice is between the bad abstraction of a publicity which barely disguises privilege, and the concreteness of a self-reflexive practice directed at critique and self-consciousness rather than intervention or agency. Cultural studies has made invaluable contributions to political pedagogy, but it does not answer the question of how students can speak in their own skins to a broad audience, with some hope of effectiveness.

Given the intractable fragmentation of our own public sphere, it is likely that the representations of the public we offer students beyond the classroom will be provisional; we will look for alternate publics and counter publics.

We might be guided by an image from Negt and Kluge's later work, *History and Self-Will*—the prison visiting room.[2] The visiting room allows communication between inside and out. It represents the prisoner's participation in both worlds. The visitor's room is not a free space, let alone a safe house, but a space in which boundaries are put in play for both prisoner and guest (Jameson 72). Would it do too much violence to the utopian energies of our profession if we were to take the visiting room as an image of the discursive spaces we are seeking? Such a metaphor might help us make better use of such ingenious tactics as paired writing classes at different institutions, the collection of oral histories, the establishment of computer networked classes.

The image of the visiting room suggests that our work establishes a point of exchange between the private, the domain of production, and some approximations of the public sphere. It is not directed at the political opinions of students, however progressive or retrograde, but toward the production and reading of texts that move between the public (the political, the abstract, the discussable) and the private. Privacy includes, in our society, both the most intimate experiences of the family and also a railroad's plans for chemical spill containment system. The realignment of rhetorical pedagogy to the public I advocate is not, therefore, a prescription or proscription of a genre of writing. Personal essays are not intrinsically "private"; technical discourse is not necessarily "public." Rather, publicity is constructed as a relation of readers to writers, including notions of rationality and accountability that are continually open to contest.

And here, the image of the prison visiting room breaks down, since public discourse is not face-to-face conversation. Unlike conversation, public discourse cannot be regulated by attending to the responses of a partner. In the public, we encounter proposals rather than intentions, a search for common understanding rather than a desire for expression. The Enlightenment public sphere regulated itself by abstracting its participants to a norm that was male, adult, and propertied. A reconstructed public sphere cannot readopt those norms of abstraction—but it cannot model itself, either, on the deeply situated nuances that shape good talk. The public requires, instead, an understanding of what is assumed—and therefore available as a value—by all speakers and writers: of what is universal without being foundational. These discursive norms, Habermas argues, operate counterfactually—we invoke them only when they are not being met. They are universal, not because human nature is unchanging, but because relations of equality and reciprocity are implied when speakers and writers take up the work of persuasion. Nobody can argue that you *ought* to be persuaded by force rather than reason, that a powerful speaker has the *right* to impose ideas on others, or that personal benefit *should* outweigh the interests of a group. We may be scandalized by Habermas's notion of communicative values, and of the subordination of particular interests in the public sphere, but there are good reasons to take these unfashionable ideas seriously. In many ways, we assent to these ideas whenever we undertake the labor of persuasion, a labor we undertake not because we think that society is transparent to rationality,

but because we know that we will live with the outcome of socially constructed decisions. We do not want them to be determined by force or manip-
ulation. As Habermas put it:

> There seems to be in the minds of many of my interlocutors over the past
> years an alternative I've never quite understood: that when there are dif-
> ferences, we also have the choice of escaping these repressive procedures
> [of public discourse] and just going off in peace. That's not a meaningful
> alternative choice. There are problems that are inescapable and can only
> be solved in concert. Who, then, makes up the concert? ("Concluding Re-
> marks" 467)

Public discursive forms share an orientation to action, including communicative action. They require a reconfiguration of the writer, and of agency, beyond the figure of the isolated modernist scribe (Brodkey). Communicative
action is an attempt by speakers and writers to coordinate plans, to come to
agreement, to "make up the concert." Agreement can be articulated in different dimensions: communicative action can be oriented to the objective world,
or to interpersonal relationships, or to the subjectivities of speakers. Habermas's definition of communicative action does not require a warm bath of
mutual understanding among parties, or even, for that matter, much in the
way of mutual understanding or respect. It does not require shared styles of
communication. All that is required is an agreement to undertake reciprocal
action, based on shared problems and possible solutions. David Sebberson
has recently demonstrated that such an orientation to action offers a new understanding of power within rhetorical theory, and therefore a renovation of
the traditional rhetorical issues of *praxis* and *phronesis*.

Habermas's examination of communicative action also enables us to
understand the intractable difficulty of contemporary public spheres. Public
spaces are difficult spaces, and they become more difficult as they become
more inclusive. I am reminded of a meeting in my neighborhood, about
evenly divided between Caucasians and African Americans, to discuss crime.
(Here again, we would deal with the police, but not by writing Citizen Complaints: we identified cops we could work with, offices that were receptive to
our input, cracks in the organizational edifice where we could take root.)
Since we had been meeting for a while, the subject of race did come up. The
gas station owner asked if the white people in the neighborhood just didn't
want to live near black people. We actually discussed that question for about
ten minutes before everyone agreed that the problem of crime was not racial.
(We were trying to become a public, but we were likely to fall back into polite
conversation.) Since we were all frightened, tempers were short; since we
were all frustrated, interruptions were common. Our visitor, a block captain
from a neighborhood a half mile over, shook her head and said, "It's so hard,
just talking in this meeting. It's the mind set." This entirely justified complaint
echoes in the literature of our field, in the rich accounts of how the "mind set"
of the academy is alien to women, working class students, and minorities.
(For examples, see Stockton, Dixon, Brodkey.)

Rhetorics associated with identity politics would prescribe that we resolve that difficulty by searching long and hard for ways of talking that would make things less difficult. Such a reconfiguration of ways of speaking is certainly humane and necessary. But a rhetoric oriented to public discourse might begin by valuing what is difficult, and direct itself to the connection between discourse and action, rather than to the connections among speakers. What was keeping us at the block meeting, after all, was not affection, but our common desire for security. We do not need abstract norms for speech or action, or any essentialist criterion of rationality external to the issues posed by particular discursive situations. Rather, we need to make explicit the forms of agreement, the criteria of interdependence, that support particular communicative situations. These criteria will be formal and universal in their force: the criteria that force not be used to constrain agreement, for example, or that all affected parties speak to a matter being decided, or that decisions be reconsidered when new information emerges. Our problems require that we make up a very broad concert: they will not yield to more politeness rules. We need instead criteria for an agreement that can be sustained through difficulty, that will last out the inevitable day when reliable speakers hold contradictory positions, for good and honest reasons, and decisions must be made. Such formal criteria have critical force and can be used to open broader participation, a fuller resolution of conflicts, and a livelier appreciation of both difficulty and rhetorical skill. Habermas's theory of communicative action can support discussion in various public spheres without requiring an impossible fullness of discourse, that, in its unapproachability, stabilizes the status quo. Nancy Fraser invokes such impossible fullness in her critique of Habermas:

> Participation means being able to speak in one's own voice, and thereby simultaneously to construct and express one's cultural identity through idiom and style. ("Rethinking" 126)

I could not find such a cultural identity for myself, least of all in idiom and style. I am sure that I live in this culture, but I don't seem to be able to do it in a single identifiable way. And so I would hesitate to send students on a search for their identities, a unitary cultural identity is itself an object of labor and struggle. Still less could I identify my "own voice." Fraser expresses the desire for an efficacious speech that mediates subjectivity and the social without labor, the desire for a public sphere where speech and writing would not be difficult. This critique of Habermas relies upon the ideas of a unitary subject and a transparently expressive language that she effectively dismantles elsewhere, in *Unruly Practices*. If our publics will not resonate to such sublimely full voices, what will be read and heard in their stead? As rhetoricians and compositionists, we know that the public will need many kinds of writing—engineering proposals, nurses' notes, memorial poems. Any of these texts can be articulated with the concerns of readers; any could become public writing. But public writing in a composition course, understood as a relation between readers, texts, and actions, can be organized in at least four ways.

First, the classroom itself can be seen as a version of the public sphere: as a model of the public, or a concentrated version of the public. Teachers and students see how classroom rhetorical strategies effect individual projects of persuasion and how they open or foreclose possibilities for common work. The issues of such a class might include connection to an audience, positioning, collaboration, and the articulation of texts in time. A classroom that saw itself as a version of the public might value such skills as focusing discussion, organizing work, tolerating and enjoying difficulty, and renunciation of safety and comfort. Such a classroom would develop and extend the pedagogical innovations of cultural studies (Giroux).

As I argued earlier in this essay, the main weakness of such an approach as a way of learning public writing is that the writing classroom has no public exigency: the writing classroom does important cultural work for the million and a half students it serves each year, but it does not carry out that work through the texts it produces. However, the experience of critical teaching in cultural studies (see, for instance, the essays in Fitts and France) suggests when students have come to understand their culture critically, the class's exigency shifts. If the work of the class is reading culture, and if cultural appropriation is, as Habermas suggests, one of the first forms of the public, then the exigency of the cultural studies class—and by extension, the literature class—is potentially public.

A second strategy for teaching public writing would begin with the analysis of public discourse, including the texts produced in alternative and counter publics. Analytic genres would include not only the critical essay but also the genres of the contact zone: parody, dialogue, unedifying comparison. Skills for teachers and students to cultivate would include an orientation to performance rather than disclosure, and a broadened appreciation of performance inside and outside of texts; such a classroom would search for forms of effective public advocacy that are not immediately reducible to brutal rhetorical advantage (Kennedy). Such a strategy locates the composition class within the powerful traditions of rhetorical study; it also mortgages composition to the analytic bias of such study, rather than encouraging the production of alternatives.

A third strategy might be to produce student writing that will enter some form of public space. Programs in literacy instruction have explored this terrain, opening to reflection students' experiences writing for others, and watching others write (Minter et al.). Such teaching is firmly located in the social, and moves from a study of what students already know, as apprentices of the academy, to reflection about how that knowledge can be transformed. The real presses on such teaching in many ways: any internship program will face the thorny issues of placing students in political organizations, in advocacy groups that may seem transgressive to the academy, or as writers for controversial public figures. And this strategy necessarily confronts the problem of relentless ideological reproduction: direct experience of the social can be a very convincing argument for the impossibility of change. None of these problems, of course, is itself a reason to foreswear such a teaching strategy.

A fourth possible strategy for teaching public writing is to work with the discourses of the disciplines as they intervene in the public. Habermas uses the notion of differentiation to analyze the disjunctions among mature disciplines, the professions in which they organize knowledges, and the complex public issues that face modern societies: the fate of Clinton's health care plan demonstrates the social cost of differentiation. Differentiation and modernization are not reversible processes: complex issues can be opened to public discussions through a translation or opening of technical specificity, but not by deskilling the professions or evading their expertise.

Particularly in advanced writing classes, students come to composition with an initial socialization in professional forms. We might use that socialization to teach about public writing very concretely in partnership with students from diverse disciplines. A class that included students from political science, sociology, pre-medical fields, actuarial science, planning, and risk management could powerfully address a public issue like health care, an issue that engages each of their disciplines.

Such a class could analyze how, if at all, their discipline speaks to a broader public: what happens at legislative hearings, or in negotiations with granting agencies or regulatory bodies? The class could work collaboratively to produce documents that approximate disciplinary knowledge, but are oriented to broader audiences, and begin to think about how such audiences could be organized. This strategy would take up directly the possibilities and the problems of the university's location in relation to the public and the professions: it would also, at many universities, require serious and sustained organizational work.

These four strategies are schematic and provisional; they are intended to suggest classes or assignments, to help frame a discussion on public writing. All of these strategies assume our continued attention to the writing our students produce, writing that is likely to take on less and less familiar forms as we reconstruct the public. Some of our students' most useful writing might remind us of a 'zine; some might sound like a church bulletin. My guess, though, is that it won't sound much like E. B. White.

Acknowledgments: Many thanks to the CCC reviewers, Steve Carr and Kurt Spellmeyer, and to Judith Rodby, Tom Fox, and their colleagues at the University of California at Chico for their generous, critical, and altogether useful responses.

NOTES

1. Quotations from Clinton are taken from "Address to a Joint Session of the Congress on Health Care Reform," *Weekly Compilation of Presidential Documents: Administration of William J. Clinton, 1993* 29:38 (September 27, 1993) 1836–46. These quotations were checked against the transcript of the speech in the *New York Times,* September 23, 1993, A24–25.

2. This work has not yet appeared in English. My account of the metaphor of the prison visiting room comes from Miriam Hansen's review of Negt and Kluge in "Unstable Mixtures, Dilated Spheres" (*Public Culture,* 1993).

WORKS CITED

Aronowitz, Stanley. "Is a Democracy Possible? The Decline of the Public in the American Debate." Robbins 75–92.

Blankenship, Jane, and Janette Muir. "The Transformation of Actor to Scene: Some Strategic Grounds of the Reagan Legacy." Weiler and Pearce. 11–43.

Bochin, Hal. *Richard Nixon: Rhetorical Strategist.* Westport: Greenwood, 1990.

Bowden, Mark, and Mark Fazlollah. "With '91 Case, Scandal Unfolded." *The Philadelphia Inquirer* 10 Sept. 1995: A1.

Brodkey, Linda. "Writing on the Bias." *College English* 56, (1994): 527–47.

Calhoun, Craig, ed. *Habermas and the Public Sphere.* Cambridge: MIT P, 1992.

Carter, Robin. "President Reagan at the London Guildhall: A British Interpretation." Weiler and Pearce 72–92.

Clinton, William. "Address to a Joint Session of the Congress on Health Care Reform." *Weekly Compilation of Presidential Documents: Administration of William Clinton*, 29:38 (27 Sept. 1993) 1836–46.

———. "Transcript of President's Address to Congress on Health Care." *New York Times*, September 23, 1993: A24–25.

Dixon, Kathleen. "Gendering the 'Personal.'" *CCC* 46 (1995): 255–75.

Eley, Geoff. "Nations, Publics, and Political Cultures: Placing Habermas in the Nineteenth Century." Calhoun 289–339.

Faigley, Lester. *Fragments of Rationality: Postmodernity and the Subject of Composition.* Pittsburgh: U of Pittsburgh P, 1992.

Farrell, Thomas. *Norms of Rhetorical Culture.* New Haven: Yale UP, 1993.

———. "Symposium on Basic Writing." *College English* 55 (1993): 889–92.

Fitts, Karen, and Alan France, eds. *Left Margins: Cultural Studies and Composition Pedagogy.* Albany: State U of New York P, 1995.

Fraser, Nancy. "Rethinking the Public Sphere." Calhoun 109–42.

———. *Unruly Practices: Power, Discourse and Gender in Contemporary Social Theory.* Minneapolis: U of Minnesota P, 1989.

Giroux, Henry. "Who Writes in a Cultural Studies Class? or, Where is the Pedagogy?" Fitts and France 3–16.

Habermas, Jürgen. "Concluding Remarks." Calhoun 109–42.

———. *Legitimation Crisis.* Trans. Thomas McCarthy. Boston: Beacon, 1973.

———. *The Structural Transformation of the Public Sphere: An Inquiry into a Category of Bourgeois Society.* Cambridge: MIT P, 1989.

———. *The Theory of Communicative Action.* Trans. Thomas McCarthy. Boston: Beacon, 1981.

Halloran, Michael. "Rhetoric in the American College Curriculum: The Decline of Public Discourse." *Pre/Text* 3 (1982): 245–69.

Hansen, Miriam. "Unstable Mixtures, Dilated Spheres: Negt and Kluge's *The Public Sphere and Experience*, Twenty Years Later." *Public Culture* 5 (1993): 179–212.

Jacobs, Lawrence R., Robert Y. Shapiro, and Eli C. Schulman, "The Polls—Poll Trends: Medical Care in the United States—an Update." *Public Opinion Quarterly* 57 (1993): 394–427.

Jameson, Fredric. "On Negt and Kluge." Robbins 42–74.

Jamieson, Kathleen Hall. *Eloquence in an Electronic Age: The Transformation of Political Speechmaking.* New York: Oxford UP, 1988.

———. *Dirty Politics: Deception, Distraction, and Democracy.* New York: Oxford UP, 1992.

Kennedy, Alan. "Politics, Writing, Writing Instruction, Public Space, and the English Language." Fitts and France 17–36.

Medhurst, Martin. *Dwight D. Eisenhower: Strategic Communicator.* Westport: Greenwood, 1993.

Minter, Deborah Williams, Anne Ruggles Gere, and Deborah Keller-Cohen. "Learning Literacies." *College English* 57 (1995): 669–87.

Negt, Oskar, and Alexander Kluge. *The Public Sphere and Experience: Toward an Analysis of the Bourgeois and the Proletarian Public Sphere.* Minneapolis: U of Minnesota P, 1993.

Ohmann, Richard. *English in America: A Radical View of the Profession.* New York: Oxford UP, 1976.

Popken, Randall. "Acquiring Academic Genres in Context: A Research Journal in a Freshman Writing Program," Penn State Conference on Rhetoric and Composition, University Park, PA, July 1994.

Ritter, Kurt, and David Henry. *Ronald Reagan: The Great Communicator.* Westport: Greenwood, 1992.

Robbins, Bruce, ed. *The Phantom Public Sphere.* Minneapolis: U of Minnesota P, 1993.

Ryan, Halfod. *Harry S. Truman: Presidential Rhetoric.* Westport: Greenwood, 1993.

Ryan, Mary. "Gender and Public Access: Women's Politics in Nineteenth Century America." Calhoun 259–88.

Schiappa, Edward. "Intellectuals and the Place of Cultural Critique," *Rhetoric, Cultural Studies, and Literacy.* Ed. John Frederick Reynolds. Hillsdale: Erlbaum, 1995.

Smith, Jeff. "Against 'Illegeracy': Toward a New Pedagogy of Civic Understanding." *CCC* 45 (1994): 200–19.

Stockton, Sharon. " 'Blacks vs. Browns': Questioning the White Ground." *College English* 57 (1995): 182–95.

Weiler, Michael, and W. Barnett Pearce, ed. *Public Discourse in America.* Tuscaloosa: U Alabama P, 1992.

———. "Ceremonial Discourse: The Rhetorical Ecology of the Reagan Administration." Weiler and Pearce 11–43.

Wells, Susan. *Sweet Reason: Intersubjective Rhetoric and the Discourses of Modernity.* Chicago: U of Chicago P, 1996.

13 Community Literacy: A Rhetorical Model for Personal and Public Inquiry

LORRAINE HIGGINS
ELENORE LONG
LINDA FLOWER

What is community literacy? Fifteen years ago, when we[1] chose the term "community literacy" for our work in Pittsburgh, we saw it in part as a challenge to the hubris and exclusivity of "cultural literacy," as an affirmation of the social knowledge and rhetorical expertise of people in the urban community in which we worked, and as an assertion that literacy should be defined not merely as the receptive skill of reading, but as the public act of writing and taking social action (Peck, Flower, and Higgins).

As Jeffrey Grabill pointed out in his 2001 analysis of community literacy and the politics of change, our conceptualization of community literacy was, in one sense, an invitation for others in composition/rhetoric to locate the profession's work more broadly in the public realm (89). We located our own projects not in schools or workplaces—at the time, typical sites for composition scholarship and pedagogy—but in a multicultural urban settlement house, a place where private lives and public agendas often merged in social gatherings, youth programs, and community meetings: a place of community-building.[2] But our understanding of the term community literacy referred to more than the need to expand our *sites* of practice. It stood in contrast to cultural and critical literacies as a new kind of rhetorical *activity* encompassing a unique set of goals, literate practices, resources, and relationships. Community literacy was, for us, "a search for an alternative discourse," a way for people to acknowledge each other's multiple forms of expertise through talk and text and to draw on their differences as a resource for addressing shared problems (Peck, Flower, and Higgins 205). Thus, we were not describing an existing community but aspiring to construct community around this distinct rhetorical agenda, to call into being what Linda Flower has more recently described as "vernacular local publics" ("Intercultural" 252; "Can You Build").

The projects that sprang from our collaboration have taken us in many different directions: developing programs for college students who mentor urban youth (Long, "Rhetoric of Social Action"); helping parents and inner-city

From *Community Literacy Journal* 1.1 (2006): 9–43.

teens collaborate on life-project plans (Long, Peck, and Baskins); organizing marginalized groups such as welfare mothers or free-clinic patients to address conflicts through grassroots publications (Higgins; Higgins and Brush); and documenting the expertise of low-status workers, welfare-to-work employees, and disabled students in the public policy discussions of a university think tank (Flower, "Intercultural"). And, as this journal itself will attest, many others in composition and rhetoric have expanded the practices and sites for what is now broadly referred to as community literacy. As Cushman, Barbier, Mazak, and Petrone have noted, this work tends to fall under two rubrics: service learning and action research (209). Many service learning projects foreground the twin goals of public contribution and personal growth. Such programs enhance the rhetorical skills and critical awareness of student interns or mentors who work in non-profits, churches, and after-school programs (e.g., see Deans; Goldblatt, "Van"; Herzberg; Schutz and Gere; Stock and Swensen; Swan). Taking another tack, university scholars and teachers engaged in action research often draw on their disciplinary expertise to intervene in the literate practices of communities, foregrounding aims of social justice and scholarship. They analyze their own interventions to contribute to disciplinary knowledge about the relationships among literacy, education, social policy, and democratic participation (e.g., see Coogan, "Service"; Cushman, *Struggle*; Goldblatt, "Alinsky's"; Hull and James). Other compositionists have conducted ethnographic and other naturalistic studies of literacy within communities and families (e.g., see Brandt; Cintron; Grabill; Moss; Smitherman), contributing to an interdisciplinary strand of scholarship that began several decades ago in education and sociolinguistics (e.g., see Barton and Hamilton; Farr; Freire; Harris, Kamhi, and Pollock; Heath; Hull and Schultz; Scribner and Cole; Street; Zentella).[3]

Community literacy now refers to this whole family of literate and social practices that draw their strength from different theoretical frameworks— from progressive pedagogy, to community organizing and action research, to discourse analysis, cultural critique, and theories of organizational change. This paper sketches a rhetorically centered model of community literacy as personal and public inquiry. Our approach to community literacy

- uses writing to support collaborative inquiry into community problems;
- calls up local publics around the aims of democratic deliberation; and
- transforms personal and public knowledge by restructuring deliberative dialogues among individuals and groups across lines of difference.

A rhetorically grounded community literacy opens up a unique space where intercultural partners can inquire into and deliberate about problems, working toward both personal and public change. At the same time, our approach entails a distinctive form of praxis that guides rhetorical theory building. Our action research with local publics allows us to work toward a model of local public discourse, one that fills the gap between descriptive accounts of situated literacy and more abstract theories of public discourse. In comparison to both *formal* (Barton and Hamilton) and *adversarial* or *subaltern* publics (Roberts-Miller), the *local* publics of community literacy extend Fraser's notion of *alternative* publics. Located in place and time, they offer fine-grained images of spaces where ordinary people develop public voices, letting us characterize the distinctive features of these discursive spaces, the discourses they circulate, and the literate practices that sustain them.

Analyzing the work of local publics extends Iris Young's philosophical theory of communicative democracy, which attempts to overcome the barriers to substantive dialogue between people who do not typically talk with one another. In our experience, such aspirations need to be even more operational. A rhetorical model would guide the development of new practices of collaboration, argument, and problem solving across hierarchical and diverse publics. Finally, accounting for inquiry in this rhetorical model shows us a process of invention and knowledge building more public than that of the classroom, more collaborative than that of media communication (cf. Hauser). And it shows us a new kind of counterpublic (cf. Warner) that attempts to transform the usual patterns of public knowledge building.[4]

In the spirit of Deweyan pragmatism, we want to move toward a grounded, observation-based theory of community literacy as personal and public inquiry by examining its rhetorical features in practice. The work of developing, implementing, and testing literate practices for intercultural inquiry and deliberation is a response to the specific challenges we have observed in schools, institutions, and individual lives in our multicultural urban contexts. The kinds of problems that erupt at this intersection of private and public lives are deeply complex and persistent. Moreover, they involve multiple and diverse stakeholders—a wide array of individuals and groups involved in, affected by, or able to do something about a problem. Such groups rarely share common perspectives on problems, much less a sense of what constitutes the common good. They may not envision themselves as a community, yet if they hope to address complex and far-reaching problems that cross interest groups and demand shared resources and knowledge, they will need to face the deliberative question: *What should we, as a community, do?* And in the face of incredible differences in power, in perspectives, and in discourse styles, they must ask: *How can we, as a community, reason together?* The answer to these open questions shapes not only future action but, we will argue, shapes relationships as well. We seek an inquiry-based, deliberative process that can help stakeholders frame open questions as a community, elicit their multiple—often conflicting—perspectives, and put those perspectives into generative dialogue that promotes change.

In this paper we want to talk about this rhetorically centered approach in terms of critical practices that support inquiry and deliberation. In fifteen years of action and reflection on a variety of projects, we have identified four distinct literate practices that have helped us articulate, support, and rethink the goals of this rhetorical model:

1. assessing the rhetorical situation,

2. creating a "local public,"

3. developing participants' rhetorical capacities, and

4. supporting personal and public transformation through the circulation of alternative texts and practices.

In this article, we articulate this four-part model for community-centered personal and public inquiry.

1. ASSESSING THE RHETORICAL SITUATION

The process of writing about community problems begins, as all writing does, with an analysis of the rhetorical situation—identifying the nature of the exigency that prompts response and the potential audiences that might be addressed (Bitzer). Careful assessment of the rhetorical situation is particularly critical and complex in multicultural and hierarchically organized communities, where different stakeholder groups with unique social perspectives will likely perceive the problem in different ways and will recognize different audiences as appropriate. In this context, there are no "insiders" who possess the means to analyze the situation "correctly." It is not the activist researcher's job to define "the" problem on her own or with "insider" assistance and then impose a solution from without.[5] Rather, when writing about community problems in an intercultural context, all participants enter a discourse and address a situation they do not fully understand—including groups with direct experience, experts who have studied the problem, political leaders with the power to shape public policy, and literacy workers who are there to support change. Any *one* group's perspective on a problem will always be partial— both limited and biased toward its own interests. That is not to devalue the contributions of any one group, but to insist on genuine collaboration across groups, for all stakeholders have knowledge, cultural capital, material resources, and experience that can be critical to assessing the rhetorical situation. In the community literacy work we have done, diverse stakeholders shape the parameters of each project—the often shifting sense of the problem the group addresses, its rhetorical goals, the potential audiences whom they call upon to listen and act, and the outcomes they produce. Literacy leaders, researchers, and student mentors who work in these projects contribute not by defining the problem for others or offering prepackaged responses, but by helping groups articulate, document, and update their sense of the rhetorical situation as it unfolds and develops. Moreover, they prompt stakeholder groups to reflect on the partiality of their own perspectives and on the inclusiveness of the collaborative process. They are particularly attuned to the ways in which some stakeholder groups or perspectives might be excluded, and they support groups by helping them develop strategies that might foster inclusion and more reflective inquiry.

This ongoing interpretation of the rhetorical situation itself is as important as the public proposals and positions that might grow out of collaborative inquiry. Prior to claims and proposals that circulate in public deliberation are tacit perceptions, assumptions, and experiences that inform them. And yet groups who engage in public deliberation often do not have access to the unique social perspectives of others. Thus, they cannot understand the logics behind others' viewpoints. When diverse groups collaborate in analyzing the rhetorical situations that motivate public debate, they unearth tacit perceptions and experiences that underlie others' claims, creating grounds for building future understanding and agreement.

Thus far, we have argued how important it is for stakeholders and literacy leaders to assess and document the rhetorical situation they perceive throughout the process of collaborative inquiry. But what should they assess, and how, and for what purposes? Rhetorical analysis means, for us, not only identifying the exigency—the perceived problems—and audience—potential stakeholders addressed—as Bitzer argued. It also involves reflecting critically on the process of problem solving itself and the ways in which existing practices and histories of decision making and argument might privilege and exclude important stakeholder groups. For us, assessing the rhetorical situation is an ongoing process that involves:

- configuring the *problem space* or object of deliberation,
- identifying relevant *stakeholders* in the community,
- assessing existing *venues* for public problem solving, and
- analyzing *literate practices* used to represent and address problems and the way these practices structure stakeholder *participation*.

Toward this end, it is useful to approach public deliberation as a cognitive-social-cultural *activity*. Yrjö Engeström has argued that activities are systems comprised of *objects*, the problem or material upon which people act; *outcomes*, what is generated by the activity; *tools*, physical and symbolic instruments by which objects are transformed into outcomes; a *community*, those who address the same object; *division of labor*, how tasks, power, and status are apportioned between community members; *rules*, norms, conventions for acting; and *subjects*, the person/group "whose agency is chosen as the point of view for a particular activity" ("Developmental" 67). Activity theory acknowledges the situatedness and materiality of literate practices such as public deliberation, locating practices in particular communities who have particular histories and who draw on particular resources to do their work. Examining these components of an activity system allows for a richer rhetorical analysis that might reveal flaws in the system and points of intervention, as we will illustrate.

Consider how this framework might be used to assess the activity of public deliberation. The object of such activity is a problem that motivates future action by a community, in this case stakeholders who are involved in, affected by, or able to do something about the problem. In a diverse community, problems are hard creatures to pin down; they change shape depending on one's orientation. Various members of a community might have an investment in and a sense of urgency around a particular issue or series of recent events, but the nature of those investments differs, and they will rarely define the problem they "share" in the same way. Problems are not empirical entities "out there"; they are, as so famously argued in the exchange between Lloyd Bitzer and Scott Consigny, interpretations.

In this context, we attempt to configure the problem not from the vantage point of a particular subject but from the less stable, shifting, and complex vantage of a pluralistic community. Thus, we see the object and starting point of deliberation not as a singular problem definition or claim but as a loosely configured *problem space*—a cluster of competing perspectives that circulate in a community, demanding attention, further interpretation, and response.[6] The outcome of deliberation is actionable knowledge—new understandings and arguments that might inform future response to the problem. Such outcomes are achieved by drawing on available resources—the literate tools and established rules for public discussion and decision making. In examining the division of labor in public deliberation, we identify various stakeholders' levels of participation.

In the mid-1990s, for example, talk around landlord/tenant disputes in Pittsburgh's Perry Hilltop neighborhood grew from a low buzz to a distracting chatter that became hard to ignore. This "talk" took the form of gossip, complaint, anecdote among friends, and documented incidents in local news, police records, and court hearings. One would be hard pressed to define *the* landlord/tenant problem, but a familiar set of refrains echoed throughout the community: irresponsible tenants, negligent, insensitive landlords, and unkempt and abandoned buildings that eroded property values and neighbors' sense of safety.[7] This circulating discourse loosely defined the problem space and positioned different stakeholders—subjects with different interests and values—in relation to one another. Analyzing the rhetorical situation meant paying attention to this emerging problem-oriented talk, parsing out who was speaking and listening, and anticipating different perspectives or refrains that might emerge as different stakeholders came together.

In this case, key stakeholders included not only local landlords and tenants but also homeowners and community organizations concerned about the effects of rental disputes on the larger neighborhood. Literacy leaders interviewed these key groups, attending to the history and conflicting values and interests, both economic and social, inherent in the landlord/tenant "problem." Perry was a neighborhood in transition. Recent layoffs by a key employer in the area had put some residents and property owners out of work, and some properties had been sold quickly to absentee landlords with no ties to the community. Owners and residents had known each other well in the past; this was no longer necessarily true. In other cases, the landlord was not an absentee owner, but another mid- to low-income resident trying to supplement his or her own uncertain income with rental money. With little reserve capital, a broken furnace or tenant damage could stretch landlords beyond their resources. Social contracts that had up to this point guided people's behavior toward one another were no longer in place. The only guide available was Pennsylvania (PA) housing law, which one mediator admitted "had a lot of grey areas" in terms of rights and responsibilities. Moreover, appeal to PA law did not address ways to develop better working relationships between tenants and landlords—a proactive strategy for warding off future conflict. In fact, PA law and its application in the courts pitted landlords and tenants *against* one another, eroding relationships further. As one president of a neighborhood association lamented, by the time disputants reached court, too much damage may already have been done to relationships and property. A courtroom is not a venue for proactive deliberation because finding fault— through reconstruction of the facts—takes precedence over forging a plan for the future.

Configuring the problem space in this project and others helped Community Literacy Center project leaders identify stakeholders that needed to be at the table in an intercultural inquiry, and it previewed divergent perspectives that might emerge and be further developed in group writing and discussion.[8] But in an attempt to support genuine dialogue across these perspectives, project leaders, along with various stakeholders, also assessed the existing tools for deliberation in the community—the physical and symbolic mediating instruments typically used to address problems rising to the level of public attention. Specifically, we examined existing venues for deliberation and inquiry and how the literate practices that structured this activity reproduced certain values, norms, identities, and relationships. We considered how tasks and power were divided among stakeholders and examined the rules and conventions that typically structured their work together. These elements of the activity system seemed to converge when we looked specifically at different stakeholders' level of participation in the process. Who was empowered to speak, where, and how? Whose voices were and were not heard? What kinds of practices might foreclose or open up the possibility of inclusive dialogue?

In the landlord/tenant project, we found few venues in which landlords and tenants might engage in sustained problem solving together. One landlord indicated that he had attended meetings with other landlords "just trading horror stories." Although such gripe sessions were cathartic, he acknowledged that they failed to translate grievances into new proposals for action and failed to traverse the limited borders of the self-enclosed landlord group. No tenants attended these meetings. Tenants on Perry Hilltop seemed to lack a public venue even for expressing their concerns, other than at an occasional town meeting where other agendas seemed to dominate and individual voices were often lost. One activist expressed her cynicism about such "open" meetings. Stakeholders are invited to the microphone to contribute ideas, she explained, but too frequently, the organizers "call a meeting, pick your brains, and then do nothing."

Literate practices at play in typical community meetings (e.g., giving oral testimony) rendered less powerful participants invisible. One tenant reported that she had tried to participate but was frustrated with participants not "listening to everyone" and leaders failing to ask "good questions." Talk at such meetings is ephemeral, and divergent viewpoints can easily be dismissed or left out of the public record when the minutes, reports and proposals generated are even made public. This tenant explained: "Sometimes you get in groups, and people don't know you, and when you leave, they don't know you either." More powerful stakeholders with formal education and technical expertise—such as outspoken community leaders with professional knowledge of housing policy and law—can dominate discussion, overshadowing those whose expertise may be grounded in a different set of experiences and in less authorized styles of discourse such as storytelling. Some tenants may opt out for this reason and may instead circulate their concerns and hopes more privately among sympathetic networks of friends. An analysis of these existing practices and their tendency to privilege certain stakeholder groups, silence some perspectives, and promote further factionalism informed the eventual process that participants would use in their CLC landlord/tenant project, a process that included the use of first-person narrative and written documentation of rival interpretations and reasoning that emerged at the table.

In our own work, we have used the components of an activity system to guide our ongoing discussion and analysis of the rhetorical situation with stakeholder groups, both in preliminary interviews and throughout the projects themselves. Other researchers have identified additional methods for analyzing rhetorical situations in unfamiliar and complex community settings. They may conduct formal discourse analysis of key texts and discourses in play, or record the social histories of arguments and ideas that circulate within a community (e.g., see Coogan, "Public," "Service Learning"; Hull and James). It may also be useful to draw on existing written and oral histories or ethnographies of a community to understand emerging problems or to look at empirical studies of the literate practices we hope to support.[9]

Assessing the rhetorical situation in these ways can help us identify key problems and stakeholders, challenges to their deliberating together, and potential sites and strategies for intervention. On Pittsburgh's Northside, our rhetorical analysis helped us understand emerging exigencies and groups vying for public attention as well as those who had been most disenfranchised from public debate: low-income tenants and landlords, African American teenagers facing discrimination and stress in schools and on the streets, patients struggling to be understood in community hospitals and clinics. Our analysis of dominant discourses—in public schools and youth policy, in PA landlord/tenant law, in public discussions of welfare and poverty, and in local emergency rooms—helped us see how power and community relationships were shaped by specific literate practices, to be wary of those practices, and to seek ways to disrupt them in our own projects.[10] Most of all, we realized the need to develop new ways of talking and writing that would document rather than discourage diverse experiences and voices, to create what we call "local publics." In what follows, we describe the requirements of this complex practice.

2. CREATING A "LOCAL PUBLIC": A RHETORICAL SPACE FOR INTERCULTURAL INQUIRY AND DELIBERATION

In contrast to the usual goals of community service, service learning, community organizing, or issue-centered advocacy, our rhetorical model of community literacy seeks to create a *local public*. By this term we mean something more than the public meetings or think tanks we have supported in community centers, church basements, health clinics, and college auditoriums. And we mean something less broad than the imaginary national "public" of the media or the demographic units targeted by marketers. In the rhetorical and philosophical theory on which we draw here, a public is a rhetorical creation; it is called into being by being addressed as a body (i.e., as a public) of interested participants; it exists only if they are willing to lend their attention, to participate in the discourse; and it functions as a public by the circulation of ideas: through reference, response, and rearticulation (Warner 96–114).

Theorists such as Nancy Fraser and Gerard Hauser argue that the public sphere is in fact a network of such publics and that we all participate in multiple publics, from activist readers of *MOVE ON* to football fans. In a democracy, one of the most necessary but problem-ridden functions of a public is to deliberate about shared social concerns, from war, welfare, and public education to local policies—such as the banning of hats in high schools.

The idealized model of the public sphere based on liberal, Enlightenment political theory is best described by Jürgen Habermas. But its assumptions and problems are deeply embedded in our traditions of a liberal, humanistic education (Atwill and Lauer; Roberts-Miller). Called the "bourgeois public sphere" because of its roots in the rise of the middle class and capitalism, this ideal asserts the need to bracket or ignore social difference, to exclude the personal and private in a focus on *common* concerns, and to arrive at consensus through critical-rational argument.

Empirical descriptions of actual publics suggest that the idealized public's wishful fantasy of merely ignoring difference does not work (e.g., see Karpowitz and Mansbridge's study of consensus-oriented public meetings). In practice, the critical-rational argument it privileges can devalue and exclude alternative ways of speaking and knowing—especially those of marginalized groups (Mansbridge). As Iris Young has pointed out, the knowledge produced in a critical-rational framework of deliberation is often partial; in its devaluation of the personal and its quest for generalizability, its claims are often decontextualized; its consensus is often a false one ("Communication"). Critical rationality excludes issues deemed private—consider the battle to recognize domestic violence as a shared, public concern—and dismisses some discourses (e.g., non-schooled, performative, or affective ones) as inadmissible kinds of argument. This in turn has produced a rather limited, selective number of visible publics frequently dominated by elite, male, and capitalistic concerns (Hauser; Warner) that have had the power to style themselves as *"the"* public (Fraser 61). In short, the contemporary critical problem of the democratic public sphere is the problem of dealing—in just and generative ways—with difference.

Deliberative democracy is an ongoing experiment in how to do this. Some theoretical models of deliberation are strictly procedural, while others insist on a *telos* and judge deliberation by its ability to support values, such as liberty, opportunity, or justice. Those who support consensual models fear the divisive effects of diversity, demanding consensus based on the common good. Pluralists, who fear tyranny more than disharmony, ask just who gets to define what is "common" and are willing to seek compromise and live with disagreements (Gutman and Thompson 21–29). But in practice the dominant model of difference management pits publics against one another as special interest groups competing to win. When deliberation is structured as adversarial argument, stakeholders come to open questions and problems with their answers and solutions already formed. The goal, rather than generating knowledge, is to close off discussion and achieve a resolution by force of argument, by market-type interactions such as bargaining, contracting, or by vote (Bohman and Rehg ix–xiii). However, with Iris Young, we believe that a more generative model would call us beyond both identity- and interest-based images of difference into communication with others ("Communication"). It would structure arguments as dialogical reasoning in search of transformed understanding.

These images of a deliberative, democratic public, attuned to communication, inquiry, and justice help us sketch what the local publics of community literacy hope to achieve. First, unlike a discussion group for advocates, such a public actively *seeks out diverse stakeholders and rival perspectives*, but not for the purposes of adversarial argument. Structured around inquiry rather than interest-based persuasion, it helps participants discover what their interests indeed are. Unlike the positioning that identity politics creates, it draws participants into an inquiry in which cultural identity is a source of rival perspectives rather than of rigid positions. Secondly, it *puts participants and their perspectives into generative dialogue*, treating difference as a resource. Dialogue that promotes exchange, consideration of, and response to rival perspectives can unearth unforeseen points of connection and conflict that can enable as well as foreclose future action. Third, such an inquiry *works toward just resolution*. That is, it reaches not for the closure of consensus or the justification for a particular claim but for a working resolution—a contingent agreement on what to do that acknowledges the need for continued negotiation in the face of reasonable difference. Political issues are, as Gerard Hauser and Amy Grim argue, "in the realm of the contingent" and are addressed through rhetoric. Moreover, "for rhetoric to be democratic it must go beyond procedural norms to embrace practices of *democratic inclusion*" (9). Inclusion means not just the expression of ideas but their serious consideration in the deliberative process.

Finally, to achieve these goals, a local public will require two things. First, dominant discourses of deliberative argument have been exclusionary; thus a local public must develop an alternative discourse for doing this work. In turn, participants will require the rhetorical competency to develop and engage in such as discourse. This is not merely the elite competence of critical-rationality that uses universal premises to produce rational, generalizable arguments. A local public communicates in a hybrid discourse: ideas and identities are argued and performed in the languages of its multiple participants. Deliberation in this context is in fact unusually demanding, in that it requires us to listen so well that we can articulate the arguments of others in terms they will accept, to avoid giving or taking offense, and to speak to others who disagree with what they will see as valid reasons, in terms they will understand (cf. Roberts-Miller 207; Young, Becker, and Pike).

That said, one must recognize that the teenagers and college mentors, landlords and tenants, or women from an urban clinic who join a community literacy project come with multiple agendas. But they rarely come prepared to see themselves as problem-solving partners who will be taken seriously. The families, neighborhood advocates, and university types who file into a Community Conversation[11] are rarely prepared to abandon their scripted roles and work with others in new ways—that is, to join a challenging hybrid discourse that values both rational-critical and performative argument, seeks rivals, and works toward collaborative solutions to problems. In short, community literacy enjoins its participants to become a certain *kind* of public, and to engage in rhetorical practices that belong to neither the community nor university. So community literacy must scaffold the rhetorical competence it requires.

And yet, what would turn this unlikely collection of folks in dialogue into a *public*, much less a distinctive one with the power to sustain a discussion? A public exists, Warner argues, not as a material body, but through the process of *circulation*—the flow, cycling, and transformation of *discourse*. And the interesting question becomes, what circulates and how? For example, over a period of five years, the CLC's extended project on "teen stress" put into circulation a distinctive "counterdiscourse," to use Fraser's term (67). This body of texts, thinking tools, ideas, and activities circulated as a chain of CLC projects building on, responding to, and lifting from one another; as a series of booklets printed, distributed, then posted on a website in use by college students 10 years later; as multiple videos and two hypermedia tools that turned up in schools, Planned Parenthood, a detention center, and a hospital clinic; and as dissertation research, academic publication, and local TV coverage. So one test of a public, which we will return to later, is its power to circulate discourse both within a group itself and beyond.

Looking at community literacy from the perspective of rhetoric and political philosophy helps us name this attempt to call into being a distinctive local public: one in which deliberation looks like inquiry, conflicting perspectives and marginalized expertise are a resource, and better resolutions to shared problems are the goal. However, a theory of *local* publics also needs to recognize the very material base of this process—the nitty-gritty work of recognizing the stakeholders, opinion makers, and power brokers and drawing them into this process. It starts, as Eli Goldblatt ("Alinsky's") describes so well, with rubbing shoulders, listening, building networks among the city "suits" and teenagers alike, invitations, the circulation of "news," documents, proposals, and phone calls to those circulators who "spread the word" in the city, the university, and the neighborhood. The process of metaphorical public making depends on the material reality of creating, on the one hand, a welcoming space for its diverse participants and on the other, forums and events that upset people's expectations and draw them into a new kind of discourse which doesn't end when they walk out the door. It depends on the way institutions such as community centers, public schools, universities, and city offices are drawn into the process, offering needed space, money, people, and validation. But sponsorship can change the sponsor as well.

When the graduate students at Carnegie Mellon's School of Public Policy & Management enlisted the Community Think Tank model to hold a conference on imminent changes in welfare policy, their project replaced the traditional meeting of black and white civic "leaders" with a ballroom of people—that included a large contingent of women on welfare—who were engaged in direct deliberation on better options with researchers, policy makers, government officials, and social workers. It produced a substantive report and, what the Dean had asserted never happened with "community" events, a substantive discussion. Deliberative intercultural inquiry is a performative rhetoric that needs to be structured and modeled if we hope to support marginalized voices and avoid the default practices of interest group discourse or of false consensus. And as we will argue in the next two sections, its demanding rhetorical moves need to be both articulated and nurtured.

3. Developing Participants' Rhetorical Capacities

A rhetorical model for personal and public inquiry attempts to overcome the barriers to substantive dialogue that people unaccustomed to speaking with one another are likely to encounter. Others have recognized the need to address such barriers. Iris Young, for instance, has proposed a communicative model for inclusive democracy that "justly requires a plurality of perspectives, speaking styles, and ways of expressing the particularity of social situation" (*Intersecting* 73). In contrast to the more abstract level of Young's political philosophy, however, our own goal has been to theorize rhetorical practices at the local level—to support local deliberation in action. Given this goal, we describe below three rhetorical capacities that might enable people to deliberate across lines of hierarchy and difference:

- eliciting situated knowledge,
- engaging difference in dialogue, and
- constructing and reflecting upon wise options.

In addition, we describe strategies developed in community literacy projects that support stakeholders in this process.

People develop these capacities in collaboration with others; these capacities depend and draw on different kinds of expertise as well as different kinds of social capital. As researchers we cannot nor would we want to impose some stock set of strategies; our model for community literacy is not a formula or set of steps. Rather we must always work *with* participants to find effective tools that groups can adapt from project to project. Such a model locates community literacy in the classical tradition of rhetoric as education for civic participation.

The rhetorical model we propose treats stakeholders' situated knowledge as a resource for transformed understanding and wise action. The term *situated knowledge* signals the perspectival and partial nature of knowing (Dewey 132), the fact that "our knowing is inevitably local knowledge" (Flower, Long, and Higgins 67; cf. Geertz). This fund of knowledge is a rich, experientially based resource for interpreting and problematizing familiar abstractions and stock solutions to problems that have not yet been fully understood. Accessing different stakeholders' situated knowledge can help groups construct and assess the unique situations and "complex social contexts" that lie behind problems (Flower, Long, and Higgins 6).[12] When diverse stakeholders put their situated knowledge into play, the process helps all stakeholders at the table see their own situated knowledge in terms of the larger landscape (Young, *Intersecting* 67)—to recognize that the starting points from which others join the conversation are different from one's own (Langsdorf 316). Accessing the situated knowledge of others helps stakeholders critically assess and expand their own knowledge of a problem in ways that can have important consequences.[13]

Yet there are obstacles to eliciting situated knowledge and to using it both to rethink culturally loaded issues (like respect, responsibility, work, and welfare) and to inform future action. Foremost, situated knowledge is difficult to tap. In day-to-day life, it operates tacitly and often goes unarticulated. Simply asking participants in community literacy projects to share their perspectives in writing and discussion does not guarantee they can or will. As literacy leaders, we have needed to provide a great deal of support to draw out the knowledge that some participants assumed would be obvious to outside readers. Literacy projects that do not provide sufficient scaffolding to elicit this knowledge leave participants vulnerable to being misread or to reproducing dominant discourses already in place.[14] Participants need time, support, and material resources to compose their stories, analyses, and proposals before going public with them.

But to support personal and public inquiry, a rhetorical model has to do more than elicit situated knowledge of problems; it must also recognize and address differences that may emerge in stakeholders' experiences and interpretations. We have found that engaging others—acknowledging, assessing, and substantively responding to their perspectives—helps participants locate generative tensions, misunderstandings, and common assumptions critical to addressing problems in the long term. But the process of engagement entails social, emotional, and intellectual challenges. If we see others as adversaries, or as less authorized to speak, we may resist acknowledging and possibly legitimizing their point of view.[15] Engaging difference in dialogue also makes strong intellectual demands (Flower, Long, and Higgins 121–32). It is difficult to imagine and assess the response of someone else—to project anything but a stereotypical response—when that someone is a socially distant Other, someone whom we would rarely pass on the street, let alone engage in dialogue (Young, *Intersecting* 57–59). The challenge is to recognize Others as so present, so real, that we not only understand but become more able to imagine the unique contributions they make to the inquiry.

People inquire into personal and public problems not simply because they wish to express or share their viewpoints, but because they want change. Ultimately, a rhetorical model of inquiry will create the potential for informed and just action in the future. Yet participants find it challenging to move from expression and analysis to action. One obstacle is that when people think of taking action, they often think of single or simplistic solutions and feel compelled to argue for them as positions. In this move toward action—even after having acknowledged multiple perspectives and having recognized the complexity of the problem and involvement of others at the table in these projects—participants often first reach for default, prepackaged, or stock solutions that already circulate in the dominant discourse (e.g., make moms on welfare go back to work so they won't be tempted to have more babies, or eliminate all work requirements because they are insulting. Throw disruptive teens out of school so they won't bother other students, or eliminate suspension altogether because it is unfair). As these examples show, there is often a disjuncture between the richly nuanced experiences and perspectives that the process of intercultural inquiry creates and these stock answers to the problem.

Below we foreground key discoveries that have emerged from our action research: the kinds of challenges people face in developing these capacities, the kinds of scaffolding that seem to help and why, as well as the need for reflection to hone our own rhetorical capacities for developing these scaffolds from project to project and for increasing our understanding of personal and public inquiry.

Eliciting Situated Knowledge

To develop participants' capacities to articulate, elaborate, and circulate their situated knowledge—both their own and one another's—we have developed several ways to scaffold and support their process.

Problem Narratives   We have found that narrative is a powerful tool for eliciting stakeholders' situated knowledge. Situated knowledge is grounded in lived experience; people often encode and express this knowledge through various forms of narrative—anecdote, dramatic reenactments of a problem, or personal stories they share (Higgins and Brush 11). Furthermore, narrative can make important contributions to deliberative inquiry, turning individual knowledge into a communal resource (Higgins, Flower, and Deems 21); it can provide a means of communication available to all stakeholders at the table to the extent that "everyone has stories to tell . . . and can tell her story with equal authority" (Young, *Intersecting* 71; see also Flower and Deems 116; Higgins, Flower, and Deems 19). Narrative also has a persuasive power that can help unfamiliar audiences identify with the teller's perspective in a way that abstract and generalized positions or claims do not (Higgins and Brush 30). Moreover, narrative helps interlocutors recognize when the differences between their social positions require the "humble recognition" that one cannot fully imagine another's perspective (Young, *Intersecting* 53; cf. Lawrence).

Yet personal stories alone don't necessarily support intercultural inquiry. The challenge is harnessing narrative's capacity to dramatize the reasons behind the teller's values and priorities (Young, *Intersecting* 72) and to illustrate the rich contextual background and social conditions in which problems play themselves out. Narratives that elaborate on stakeholders' reasoning, social positioning, and life contexts generate new information and propel discussion that can move people beyond personal expression to public problem solving.

When narrative is elaborated in this way and focused around the causes of and responses to problems, it can be used for case analysis. In contemporary research circles, John C. Flanagan first identified the power of problem-focused narratives—what he called *critical incidents*[16]—to lay claim to situated knowledge. In the context of community-based deliberative inquiry, critical incidents elicit carefully contextualized accounts of how people actually experience problems involving, for instance, landlord/tenant relations, gang violence, school suspension policies, or welfare reform.

In Community Think Tanks, student researchers do the groundwork for deliberation by collecting critical incidents from a wide range of stakeholders. They use this data to create a briefing book of prototypical problem scenarios (e.g., a conflict between an overworked/behind-schedule nursing aid and an understaffed nursing supervisor). The stakeholders' richly situated interpretations of the scenario allow for a dynamic interchange.

Composed in text, critical incidents translate lived experience into tangible resources for sustained joint inquiry. Participants embed them in articles, dramatic scripts, comic strips, and narratives published in newsletters or handbooks and enacted with the dramatic productions performed within community problem-solving dialogues.

However, using critical incidents and other kinds of narrative to interpret a problem in the service of joint inquiry isn't something that necessarily comes naturally or easily. For instance, to interpret policies for welfare reform in the context of their own lives, welfare moms had to avoid the default schema of popular hero and victim narratives, both of which might erode their credibility and mask the complexity of their lives and decisions (Higgins and Brush 5). Transforming the knowledge of experience into realistically complex problem narratives is demanding work.[17]

Supportive Readers   To support this process of knowledge transformation, we have found it helpful to intervene in several ways.[18] First, as writers begin to construct narratives that illustrate the conflicts in their lives, they benefit from working with supportive readers—college mentors, volunteer readers from the community, or fellow participants in the project. As collaborative planning "supporters," these readers serve as sounding boards, listening to writers' stories take shape (Flower, *Construction* 141–49).[19] A supporter provides not only moral support but also incentive to explain the logic of the writer's experience to a reader who is unfamiliar with her story.[20]

Prompts for Elaboration   Writers' initial stories tend to be under-elaborated, making it hard for readers to understand the motivation behind a narrator or character's actions, their reasoning, or their interpretation of the situation (Higgins and Brush 14). Using supportive readers can help, but we have also supported this process through instructional materials and prompts; for example, a handout listing narrative techniques such as dialogue, inner monologue, or detailed setting descriptions—strategies by which writers might elaborate events and perspectives. We have also found it helpful to prompt explicitly for the story-behind-the-story, a strategy that plumbs for the writer's deeper level of interpretation. Responding to such questions as *What would a teenager see going on here that adults wouldn't? Why did she do that? Why did he say that?*, the writer conveys the "movies of the mind" she may be using to interpret a complex situation. These prompts ask her to set the stage, script the action, assign the roles (Flower, Long, and Higgins 6). Such questions may seem basic enough, but the explanation writers provide can be surprising and enlightening to outside readers.

The story-behind-the-story and other prompts for elaboration reveal the *hidden logic* of often unspoken motives, values, and assumptions that people use to interpret complex situations, a logic invaluable to deliberative inquiry. The impulse for readers to judge and dismiss what they don't understand seems to be a glitch in the human genome, a tendency one has to overtly monitor to hold in check (Gumperz and Tannen 305). As a teenager named Andre pointed out in a newsletter analyzing his city's new curfew policy, "Sometimes adults [police] don't know what teenagers are really thinking, and they misunderstand teenagers' actions and intentions" (*Raising* 2). His article revealed why the curfew policy invoked for him personal encounters with racial profiling, police stopping him because "his hair" made him "look like someone in a picture." Articulated and shared, hidden logic permits other stakeholders to grasp the interpretative power of cultural knowledge other than their own (Flower, "Talking" 40).

Interventions like these do not imply that the people who use them are somehow cognitively or culturally deficient. Quite the contrary. Transforming one's experience into a resource for joint inquiry is often a new enterprise for everyone at the table. Scaffolding that process is a way of honoring the demanding work of transforming lived experience into narrative that serves the aims of problem analysis, collaboration, and argument. Moreover, new situations call for new scaffolds. Adult welfare recipients, for example, needed support to reconstruct chronologies of traumatic life events. The use of "timelines" helped them remember and organize the chronology of their life events for unfamiliar readers (Higgins and Brush).[21]

Engaging Difference in Dialogue

To engage difference in dialogue, it is not enough to invite stakeholders with different perspectives into the room.[22] It is also necessary to represent those not present through outside documents (Flower, "Intercultural" 250), to offer strategies for predicting and engaging rival perspectives, and to use writing to keep difference in dialogue.

Diverse Stakeholders   To make difference real to participants, we have found it useful to create a storehouse of written and visual materials that represent different perspectives on the issue. These may include excerpts from novels, critical incidents that frame the problem, a videotaped interview of someone with firsthand knowledge, published editorials or position statements, even relevant scientific information when pertinent to the project. In the context of deliberative intercultural inquiry, participants analyze these materials not for the internal consistency of their arguments as they might in some writing classrooms; instead, they try to tease out the perspectives of unfamiliar others, representing them not as sound bites or stereotypes but as interested people who inhabit other social positions, each with an internal logic, set of priorities, and commitments of its own. For instance, Amanda Young's interactive multimedia tool on decisions about safe sex entitled *What's Your Plan?* brings to life the faces and voices of multiple boyfriends and girlfriends as well as teens' moms, older friends, and medical advisors. Individually, these materials create a focal point for discussion, but together they grant specificity and grit as well as variation to the abstract notion of multiple perspectives.

Rivaling   We've also seen the generative power of *rivaling*, a strategy that asks writers to imagine alternative interpretations of a question, conflict, or problem (Flower, Long, and Higgins). In some ways, rivaling bears a family resemblance to Young's notion of "greeting" — the recognition and public acknowledgement of others—as a strategy of inclusion (*Intersecting* 70).[23] Young stresses the affective impact of being acknowledged and thus respected by others and the way that greeting creates a respectful climate where people might work together.

An intellectually different procedure, however, rivaling goes beyond the affective moves of establishing goodwill and acknowledging others. It seeks not some quick around-the-table inventory of positions but seriously engages a range of responses to an issue and the reasons behind them. Rivaling often takes the form of talking back to characters in a narrative (who may be other stakeholders), imagining an alternative argument, role playing or inviting the response of other stakeholders, and even articulating the compelling reasons someone might have for responding to problems in ways that seem, from a dominant perspective, unacceptable or against the norm: skipping rent, doing drugs, or not following medical advice. In academic circles, scientists or philosophers examine rival hypotheses in order to eliminate competing arguments; in the context of intercultural inquiry, rivaling first attempts to expand rather than narrow potential interpretations.

For example, in the landlord/tenant project, participants raised rival priorities and concerns, exploring the way different values arose out of stakeholders' different social and economic circumstances and needs. The mediator was concerned with rights and responsibilities, in that these provided criteria for adjudicating conflict. The tenant prioritized closer relationships and better interpersonal communication since she had suffered from the uncaring and uninterested attitude of absentee landlords. A community organizer (and homeowner) focused on property values and the economic health of the Perry Hilltop neighborhood, having seen the consequences of mismanaged apartment buildings (Higgins, Flower, and Deems 26). In putting difference into dialogue, rivaling did not suggest that one appraisal would ultimately prevail over the others but that the participants as writers would need to develop a rhetorical plan that acknowledged these rival concerns.

Rivaling also asks participants to seek out differences and gaps in their interpretation and experience in order to critically assess and expand their own knowledge of a problem. On one hand, rivaling means acknowledging counter-claims that qualify and/or set conditions on one's favored interpretation. Supporters often prompt this move, just as Dan did in the landlord/tenant project when he rivaled Lynn's proposal for a legal process to mediate landlord/tenant disputes. Dan challenged that such counsel would only work if landlords and tenants knew about it, and after years in the community organizing business, the mediation service where Lynn worked was news to him. After Lynn listed legal options for handling late payment of rent, he asked: "How are you gonna *veri*—not *verify*, but *support* your position as to . . . what are the answers about paying rent and the late payment?" In this very moment, however, Dan also rivaled his own tack for engaging with Lynn. He traded a rather challenging and adversarial question that forced her defense ("How are you gonna *veri*[*fy*] . . . ?") with a prompt for more information ("not *verify* but *support*"). Even more to the point, in listening to Lynn, he also recognized limits to his own understanding: "See, now I didn't even know that. I didn't know that." In the context of intercultural deliberation, rivaling fosters sustained inquiry—as it did among these participants—in the midst of difference (Higgins, Flower, and Deems 18).

Teens have taught us to see rivaling—like its counterpart, the story-behind-the-story—less as a set of textual moves and more as an intellectual performance. For teens, performance often provides a window into difference—differences in what people say and how they say it, as well as the nuances of non-verbal communication such as dress, posture, and hand gestures. Teens' performances of interpersonal encounters, for instance, offer interpretations as knowledge that contributes to the group's inquiry. Consider Shaunise's impromptu performance. Shaunise was part of a group addressing the question of how to talk to teens about drugs. On the table was the contention that teens can look to their parents for the "real deal" about drugs. To rival this claim, Shaunise scooted back her chair and stood up. Head bobbing, voice animated, she enacted what it's like to talk to her evasive mother about dicey issues like sex or drugs. Watching teens gravitate to performance in the pursuit of inquiry reminds us to provide the discursive and physical space for the workings of their imagination, for teens new to community literacy can often be quite skeptical that adults, in fact, will listen. They are used to being censored, especially if they express themselves in dramatic ways. They are, of course, onto something. As Young points out, rationalistic norms of deliberation look down on "embodied speech"—and the "valuing and expressing of emotion, the use of figurative language, modulation in tone of voice, and wide gesture" that goes with it (*Intersecting* 65). When teens use this kind of performance as a resource for strategic thinking, they also instantiate a more inclusive model of deliberative democracy.

Writing to Keep Difference in Dialogue   Too often in community meetings difference gets lost or ignored as quickly as it is generated—a problem contributing to the evanescent nature of community talk (Flower and Deems 97) and to the tendency for those who run meetings to selectively record proceedings. Therefore, we see the need for public note-taking that not only records rivals and negotiations as they emerge in discussion but also periodically reviews and consolidates these rivals for the group itself—what Karpowitz and Mansbridge call "dynamic updating" (348). In the landlord/tenant project, for example, the facilitator used a blackboard to keep a running record of the rivals the group generated—the genuine conflicts that arose because of the very real differences in how participants had experienced and interpreted landlord/tenant disputes. Periodically within each session, the facilitator would also review and consolidate these rivals, not to suggest that the differences needed to be resolved in the name of consensus, but that these were the conflicts that the group's joint document would need to address if the text were to represent area landlord/tenant issues fairly and accurately and to be of use to other stakeholders. Consolidating and reviewing rivals also tested the facilitator's representation of the group's emerging rhetorical problem against the others at the table, giving the group members an opportunity to clarify their points before the notes were transferred to the computer, printed, and distributed. Although recording rivals does provide a useful memory aid for the intellectual task at hand, more importantly, the practice serves as a form of respect, acknowledging different perspectives.

Besides keeping track of rivals generated in discussion, another challenge is representing different perspectives in text. We've learned to take an inventive approach to text conventions—and to encourage other writers to do the same. This inventive approach creates a hybrid, multi-vocal text that provides a culturally appropriate way to talk to readers about the issue at hand while inviting readers to negotiate and integrate rival perspectives from the text for themselves. Remember how teens like Shaunise gravitated toward performing rivals? Time and again, we have seen teens demand this same performative capacity from the texts they write. To transform the rivals they've performed into text, teens often borrow and combine text conventions from several interactive genres: an advice column with letters and responses, a skit with multiple characters, or even an internal monologue dramatizing the competing voices inside the mind of a stressed-out teen. Here again, collaborative-planning supporters help writers navigate a decision space filled with an often daunting array of choices. This inventive approach to text conventions brings normally silenced or marginalized voices into a more fully realized intercultural dialogue. For instance, a mother in the Rainbow Health Clinic project wrote about an incident in which she had let her child's prescriptions lapse because they were not covered by her insurance. Text conventions associated with a dramatic script let her represent rival perspectives in dialogue with one another. So her article contextualized typically privileged voices—for instance, the doctors whom she represents in text as "powerful men with long, white beards"—while still giving these voices a way to be present in the inquiry, not in control but in negotiation (*Getting to Know You* 14). When college mentors write multi-voiced inquiries in lieu of the traditional research paper, they, too, often need encouragement to suspend or complicate standard conversations of academic analysis. In classes with our college-student writing mentors, we explore ways that traditional academic research conventions tend to absorb difference, contradiction and complexity—making it hard to express the tentative, experiential, or unresolved aspects that arise when you engage difference in dialogue. We encourage students to draw upon "techniques you know from creative writing and expressive document design" to juxtapose alternative perspectives while offering a running commentary that interprets these voices and their significance to the inquiry (Flower, *Problem-Solving Strategies* 421).

Constructing and Reflecting Upon Wise Options

Finally, participants must be encouraged to generate specific options that grow out of their carefully situated analysis. Whether they propose new responses or interrogate "stock" solutions, they must be encouraged to specify the consequences that might reasonably ensue based on the knowledge they have gleaned from their work together.

Options and Outcomes   To draw people into a deliberative process, the options and outcomes strategy focuses inquiry around choices and their consequences.[24] Rather than offering a single, specific proposal for policy change, these documents pose the question: How can you, the engaged reader, create options in your own sphere of influence that are responsive to the life experiences and social circumstances of others? In this way, the options and outcomes strategy offers a unique version of social action. Instead of eliciting a single solution, the strategy suggests that different stakeholders may need to respond to a problem in different ways, making different trade-offs and choices in the face of no obvious "good" option: *You may be willing to do this, but I would choose this option instead because I fear those consequences more. . . .*

In good pragmatic fashion, the options and outcomes strategy lets decision-makers hear what their decisions might mean in the lives of people affected by them. The test of the decision that a manager or teacher makes will be in its consequences—yet employees or students are often far more able to project those consequences than those in power. At a welfare-to-work think tank session, the human resource manager had a standard "professional" solution to the problems of Melissa, the new hire. Her company's "buddy system" seemed the obvious option, until the union leader at the table began to quietly sketch outcomes from his perspective "on the floor"—such as situations in which race played a quiet but decisive role in what the assigned "buddies" did or in which busy staff were expected to work as trainers, without the pay or prestige of official staff. By the end of the options and outcomes session, the human resource manager had not only suspended her ready solution but had begun to rival herself (Flower, "Intercultural" 260–61).

Imagining a deliberative role for yourself is one challenge; inviting readers to take this deliberative stance is another. When participants in the landlord/tenant project faced the problem of orienting readers of their published Memorandum of Understanding toward future action, they invoked a text convention to structure that deliberative process. You'll recall that the participants' scenarios analyzed the complexity of landlord and tenant problems. Their rich analysis defied simple solutions. To implicate readers, whether landlords, tenants, community organizers or mediators, in wise action in the face of such complexity, the writers followed each scenario with a set of "what-if" questions: *What if the tenant had spoken up about her expectations during her first visit to the apartment?* Under each question, the writers enumerated a set of actions and their consequences, the details of which had been generated over the course of the previous planning sessions. The "what-ifs" implicated all stakeholders in taking wise action, demonstrating that in response to local problems, the deliberative work of the community is to discuss and document an expanded set of options and their consequences in the lives of those affected by them.[25] The *Landlord Tenant Handbook* also included blank pages for notes following each scenario that a reader might take as he or she interpreted the problem and considered the consequences of the "what-if" questions.

In the context of personal and public inquiry, we have found that these text conventions can provide rhetorical cues that expand and shift the standard terms of debate and the standard participants addressed in public deliberation to alternative sets of possibilities, questions, and stakeholders. "What-ifs" generated in the welfare project raised possibilities for *both* personal and structural change, often linking the two in ways rarely acknowledged in public arguments about welfare. These proposals for action do not address welfare recipients as the problem nor do they simply attack current policies or social conditions. As in the landlord/tenant project, individual writers used a variety of "what-ifs" to analyze the implications of their narratives for a variety of stakeholders who might act on the problem.[26] Using narrative and rival interpretation to generate and reason through multiple options instantiates an alternative, more inclusive model of deliberation. In concluding their group document—entitled *Getting By, Getting Ahead*—the group of welfare recipients invoked the same "what-if" convention to form the overarching question that had guided the entire project:

> WHAT IF welfare moms had and took the chance to respond to allegations against them?
>
> THEN the dialogue would go like this. . . .

On the basis of the reasoning the group had articulated over the project's sixteen sessions, the concluding commentary that follows this question shifts public discussion from policy analysts talking among themselves or tax payers pitching insults at welfare recipients (Higgins and Brush 2) to a local public that puts into conversation a range of perspectives and possibilities. The conclusion invokes the repeated phrase "[s]ome have said that welfare mothers" to introduce the most egregious assumptions about welfare recipients in the dominant discourse. The writers then explicitly talk back to these charges, problematizing these claims with counterexamples and rival interpretations that have become shared knowledge from the project itself.

Documents such as the Think Tank "Findings," the *Landlord Tenant Handbook*, and *Getting By, Getting Ahead* are not decision documents or policy statements. Instead, they model an alternative version of argument: deliberative intercultural inquiry. These documents ask people who are decision-makers both in their own lives and on the job to take their experience with collaborative inquiry and the options proposed in a given document back into arenas where they have choices to make. Ultimately, rather than offering a solution, these documents pose the question: How can you create options in your own sphere of influence that are responsive to the life experiences and social circumstances of others?

As researchers we have found that these rhetorical capacities have helped us to adapt scaffolds from project to project and to situate them within a larger working theory of community literacy. For instance, to rival our own socio-cognitive perspective, we look to disciplines outside English studies to inform our study of intercultural deliberation, particularly work in political philosophy and public policy. We don't mean to suggest we are the first to see the need to do so. We trace much of our own appreciation for Iris Young's political philosophy, for instance, to Susan Wells' and John Trimbur's earlier essays and bibliographies in public rhetoric in the early 1990s. We know other readers will recognize the tremendous excitement—the downright gratitude—we feel as we exchange e-mail that cites a quotation, article, or book of a critical theorist or policy analyst who puts a finer point on a problem than we've been able to, or that generalizes more broadly about an issue we've observed firsthand. Consider, for example, Susan Lawrence's study of mentors and teens using a technique called rival readings to grapple with interpretive differences. Often mentors assume they need to establish common ground between their teen writers and themselves; the rival reading technique provided an option for another, often far more generative conversation.[27]

The implications of Lawrence's findings came to life for us against Young's broader treatment of asymmetrical relationships, especially the moral humility that requires people to listen across difference rather than assume they can imagine walking in another's shoes (*Intersecting* 168). Of course, engaging in difference also requires us to consider rivals to our own positions. Currently under debate in public spheres studies are the consequences of deliberation. This debate places our contention that intercultural deliberation builds *new intercultural knowledge* alongside Warner's claim that *deliberation is a fiction* (143), G. Michael Weiksner's claim that deliberation is less about making specific policy changes and more about *conversational exchange* (216), and Carolyn Rude's claim that *more research is needed* to trace the effects of deliberation over time and across circuits of distribution (271). Similarly, comparing options and outcomes lets us grasp what rhetorical studies has to contribute to this growing area of study—particularly its strong methodological tools for sustaining what Hauser calls an "empirical attitude" toward the way "untidy communicative practices" shape public life (275).

We value the distinct capacity of rhetoric to provide principled, adaptive heuristics for treading into unfamiliar intercultural waters. Heuristics like the story-behind-the-story, rivaling, and options and outcomes are the tools of rhetorical invention, but in the context of intercultural deliberation, they help us figure out not just what to say but to invent with others the very discourse in which to say it. We see heuristics like these—with features that can be identified, described, and taught—are a tremendous resource for making good on the promise of intercultural deliberative inquiry and for negotiating its inherent challenges.

4. SUPPORTING PERSONAL AND PUBLIC TRANSFORMATION THROUGH THE CIRCULATION OF ALTERNATIVE TEXTS AND PRACTICES

Calling an intercultural group into a local public is an act of faith and strategic action. Endowing that public with the power to transform anything is working against the odds. But this we believe is at the heart of the model of community literacy theorized here. When the local publics of community literacy launch their counterdiscourse into circulation, they often act as a *counterpublic*, challenging the business of discourse as usual. But, we will argue, they do so with one significant difference from how counterpublics are often theorized.

A Distinctive Kind of Counterpublic

Fraser's and Warner's influential accounts of feminism and queer culture describe counterpublics as critical spaces in which subordinated people formulate oppositional identities and alternative discourses/worldviews. Moreover, they do so through "poetic world making," resisting the exclusionary norms of critical-rational discourse and creating a space for performative, affective, and situated meaning making—central features of community literacy's hybrid discourse.

On one hand, counterpublics work as safe houses, which like the CLC and many other community projects nurture the construction of alternative identities and personal and public voices, empowered to assert oppositional interpretations of their world. On the other hand, they are not merely the expression of a subaltern culture. They are "counterpublics" to the extent that they address, as Warner asserts, a public of "strangers" and that they try to supply different ways of imagining public discourse: "Counterpublics are spaces of circulation in which it is hoped that the *poesis* of scene making will be transformative, not replicative merely" (121–22). In particular, by refusing to adapt to normative discourse, counterpublics are formed in "the original hope of transforming not just policy but the space of public life itself" (124).

Community literacy publics act like a counterpublic—with a critical difference. Current counterpublic theory has attempted to understand the large, national, media-infused discourses of feminism, queer culture, or the black public sphere (Black Public Sphere Collective; Fraser; Gaonkar; Hauser; Warner). Community literacy publics, on the other hand, are local, drawn together by immediate issues and concerns, and are likely to form, dissolve, and reform with an overlapping set of participants—"the usual suspects" of community networks. And unlike strictly textual counterpublics, they thrive on text and talk, on phone calls, face-to-face meetings, church dinners, "just chillin'," local networking, and the work of rainmakers. These counterpublics circulate though myriad paths.

But, we will argue, an even more significant difference is what circulates—that is, the kind of transformation these counterpublics perform and support. Public discourse, Michael Warner argues, call publics into being through address, by saying "not only 'let a public exist' but 'let it have this character, speak this way, see the world this way.' . . . Run it up the flagpole and see who salutes" (114). What is so deeply at stake in these counterpublics—the reason for changing our ways of speaking—is asserting a transformed/transformative *identity* for marginalized, dominated, or devalued peoples. Community literacy publics, by contrast, are not called into being around the aims of a shared identity but are in fact defined by their aspiration to an intercultural, cross-hierarchy composition. What community literacy runs up the flagpole is not the image of an alternative identity, but an alternative discourse. The essential goal of *this* transformative counterpublic is a transformed deliberative practice.

Why is this so important? In currently heated debates over the possibility of deliberative democracy, the central tension is how to deal with the volatile presence of diversity. Should we strive to bracket it, encourage competitive argumentation, or suppress its divisiveness with a focus on the "common" good?[28] The problem, Iris Young points out, lies in identifying difference with identity, as in identity politics ("Difference"). Much as we have done, she argues that difference needs to be treated as a *resource*; not a position, but a source of perspectives. The community literacy stance toward difference asserts the power and necessity of locally situated knowledges. But, with Donna Haraway, we dismiss claims that the identity of the speaker confers a special access to truth. Marginalized knowledge enters discussion as a sought out, valued-but-not-privileged understanding or interpretation that a deliberative democracy needs to consider. In its assertive counterpublic performance of intercultural inquiry, community literacy is less about building oppositional identities than about using difference to articulate silenced perspectives. Rather than dichotomize groups, it challenges the normative exclusionary practices of public talk.

Community literacy acts as a transformative counterpublic when it succeeds in circulating not just fresh arguments, insights, positions, or policies, but an alternative image of public discourse. Its contribution is a transformed model of local public talk. This is a model that actively seeks out difference (in the form of diverse perspectives, rival hypotheses, situated stories-behind-the-story); that insists on the necessity of inquiry before advocacy; and that calls people into a local public charged to imaginative listening and collaborative problem solving grounded in engaged dialogue.

This image of how transformation can work parallels the way Engeström sees activity systems changing in his work in courtrooms, medical clinics, and work teams. Change, he argues, occurs when an idea "is transformed into a complex object, a new form of practice" ("Innovative" 382). In these settings, knowledge building emerges in the "creation of artifacts, [the] production of novel social patterns," and "a re-orchestration" of the voices of participants and the way people work together ("Activity" 27, 35). Looking at community literacy counterpublics as an *activity* also helps us see how that notion of *circulation* works in a *local* public rather than a national or purely media-based one.

This discussion of transformation, circulation, and outcomes is another way of talking about assessment, which is often equated with the narrow evidence of student ratings or the impractically broad result of clear social change, more likely to come from tightly focused advocacy. Within a local public, the indicators of impact can be seen in personal understandings and deliberative performance, and in the more public, multi-faceted evidence of circulation, which we can train ourselves to see (Flower, in prep). Some of these indicators are sketched below.

Supporting Personal Transformation

We have already seen how relatively small, intercultural community literacy groups themselves constitute a productively unsettling public space. Within these locally constructed publics, participants and rhetoricians are inventing new relationships, ideas, and practices that effect personal transformation. One of the most powerful outcomes of this work has been on participants' own sense of agency, particularly their confidence as rhetors—as people with important knowledge who have something to say and a right to say it in the presence of strangers (cf. Hull and Katz). For all the bravado displayed by teens in our projects, for all the self-confidence they exude in each other's company, they often fail to believe that adults can or will listen to them or even that they should. They, and many disenfranchised stakeholders we have worked with, often buy into dominant discourses that construct them as "the problem," rather than people with potential to solve problems, and as incapable or untrustworthy rhetors with nothing worthwhile to contribute. At first tentative about their own ability to speak and be heard, these stakeholders become more confident as they talk across the table, are acknowledged by others, and see their private memories and feelings celebrated in print. Perhaps because of these confidence-building experiences, many participants in CLC projects have joined subsequent projects or participated more actively in their neighborhoods through the networks they established while at the CLC.

Frank Bryan has noted how participating in mixed community meetings can be an important form of civic education—providing a kind of gentle tutelage in how to listen to others with different views, how to suffer the occasional fool, how to take turns and act neighborly to fellow citizens (286–92). But in these projects, participants learn more than the niceties of cooperation on which civil meetings depend; they learn to discover, articulate, and reflect on their own interests which are often put into sharp relief as they listen to others' views. Here, personal transformation goes beyond one's newfound rhetorical confidence and skill in communicating across difference. Articulating and reflecting on one's own situated knowledge can generate surprising insights into one's own beliefs. This type of personal transformation was evident in the welfare writing project, where one participant reflecting on her life history acknowledged—after a great deal of some very difficult and uncomfortable discussion with her peers—a pattern of misplaced trust and naivety in her relationships with men over the course of her life. She titled her section of their publication, "If I knew then what I know now," and called for older women in the community to share their collective wisdom through mentoring young girls.

Caroline Heller, among others, has noted the kind of intimate connections that blossom when disconnected and marginalized citizens come together to write from the depths of their personal experience. This deeply personal and often exploratory writing, discussion, and response takes time and patience, and stakeholders often come to know each other in new ways over the weeks and months they may work together, especially when they assume new roles, such as supporting another's writing. Solidarity building, empathy, and newly forged relationships are often important by-products of the work of local publics.

Discourse shapes identity and structures relationships. We have found that the literate practices and strategies described here can not only transform the way stakeholders think about themselves but also how they relate to one another. The counterdiscourses produced in some projects, for example, challenged professional service discourse in particular. John McKnight has identified the way the discourse of service professions (e.g., in medicine, education, social work, criminal justice) creates asymmetrical relations of power between the "expert" professional and the "passive" and "deficient" recipient of professionalized care or service. When these stakeholders typically come together, for example, when teens talk with principals or when clinic patients confer with medical professionals, their roles, identities, and relationships are shaped by professional conventions that limit the participation of those who are "served" and that filter and frame their knowledge in sometimes disabling ways. Local publics generate counterdiscourses when they set up and enact alternative rules and practices for interacting and thinking together. For example, the Rainbow Health Clinic project demonstrated the transformative power of placing patients' illness narratives, rather than the standard medical chart, at the center of the medical encounter. These narratives solicited psycho-social dimensions of illness that are often bracketed by the traditional practices of taking a patient's medical history;[29] in doing so they transformed the doctor-patient relationship. Patients were not treated as diseases to be cured but as people with illnesses inextricably tied to their complex social and personal histories. As such, their knowledge and expectations were considered critical to diagnosis and treatment, important as the cataloguing of physical symptoms. In this local public, they were active partners with medical staff in interpreting and creating health for themselves and improving the effectiveness of the clinic.

Supporting Public Transformation

Local publics not only spark personal transformation but public change. The challenge here is to recognize the different ways circulation works. The local efforts of the many people cited in this article have led to published essays and new journals such as *Reflections* and the present *Community Literacy Journal*. Our own fifteen years of work have led us from projects and research into theory building. But another obvious form of circulation occurs when documents go beyond publication into practice. For instance, a women's shelter modeled a new writing workshop on the welfare narratives. Medical students prepared for internships in community clinics by learning the socio-cultural aspects of patient care and how to elicit patients' situated knowledge, adapting strategies from *Getting to Know You*. High school teachers used *Whassup with Suspension?* to reflect on how their non-verbal cues might shame, embarrass, and anger some students. And they used Deems and Flower's *Rivaling about Risk* multimedia dialogue to structure a writing/discussion course unit in the public schools. Swan's research created a new course unit in CMU's School of Public Policy and led to a collaborative Think Tank on welfare policy with graduate students. Planned Parenthood used Amanda Young's multimedia *What's Your Plan?: Sexuality and Relationships* to train their teenage peer counselors while a University Hospital Adolescent Clinic used it to collect research data. Moreover, local publics have transformed service learning at Carnegie Mellon, where students in a rhetoric course hone practices such as mentoring teens, developing rivaling readings, and constructing multi-voiced inquiries as a complement to more standard research reports and school-based arguments typically produced in college classrooms. In doing so they sometimes face and negotiate pressures to conform to the writing conventions of their disciplines (Swan), but in the process they learn to consider how the everyday expertise of people they work with connects—or fails to connect—to disciplinary expertise and research findings in their fields. A study of CLC mentors, for example, revealed that the conflicts these mentors negotiated not only paralleled but extended the scholarly debates in Rhet/Comp studies over the contested relationship between literacy and social justice (Long, "Rhetoric of Social Action").

We have argued that one way to understand the transforming work of a counterpublic is to look at how it circulates an alternative discourse and a "new form of practice." Part of this process is to some extent under our control. For instance, in response to a local, unresolved crisis in staffing at long-term care facilities, Flower designed a Community Think Tank that would give voice to the insights of low-wage nurses' aides (the women, usually African American, who worked at the bottom rung of medicine's intensely hierarchical system). Over two semesters, students in a rhetoric class collected critical incident interviews, scripted problem scenarios, and worked with small groups to draw out stories-behind-the story, all of which went into a briefing book that was distributed first at a series of Think Tank sessions with nursing home staff and management and later in a city-wide session with stakeholders from hospitals, agencies, government, policy research, medical education, and nursing homes. This led to the more formal publication and distribution of the Carnegie Mellon Community Think Tank findings on "Healthcare: The Dilemma of Teamwork, Time, and Turnover." Then to make accessible the findings and methods for developing a Think Tank, we developed a university-supported website, http://www.cmu.edu/thinktank, which itself gets put into circulation through use in courses and publications like this one.

This is the kind of textual circulation with which we are all familiar. Although these documents explored options and outcomes for dealing with a particular healthcare dilemma, they raised the flag of a counterpublic by their aggressive focus on the deliberative process itself. The texts modeled—they insistently dramatize in text—an alternative kind of dialogue in which marginalized voices bring significant expertise to solving a shared problem.

Engeström's "new form of practice" may be easiest to see in a text, but the transformations in the relations between people are ultimately more significant, when we can discern them ("Innovative" 382). For instance, students were intimidated by the thought of interviewing nursing aides: "How was I . . . going to offer any useful advice that could possibly change the working conditions for nursing aides?" because they clung to the assumption that they, with the benefits of class, education, income, would need to be the "expert." The transformation came in the recognition of alternative sources of expertise—"I believe the most important thing I learned about the inquiry process was that I knew nothing about the problem"—and criteria for value—"I was shocked . . . to find myself conversing with someone who [working for slightly more than minimum wage] loved their job. It seemed incomprehensible to me."

Other transformations were more clearly "a re-orchestration" of voices and the way people work together (Engeström, "Activity" 35). In one think tank session, the aides and nurses worked out a more equitable way to handle being short-staffed on a given morning, and the Nursing Center CEO, also a participant, adopted it on the spot. At another, the staff thought their idea was good enough to adopt it on a trial basis, without waiting for an administrative order. Needless to say, neither aides nor nurses had been offered this role of collaborative administrative problem-solver before. At the city-wide think tank, when the nursing aide, the head of the city Hospital Council, a policy analyst, and a human resource director sat at a table together, sharing rival interpretations of a problem and testing each other's options with their differently situated insights into possible outcomes, the participants themselves recognized this event as itself the "production of novel social patterns" (Engeström, "Activity" 27).

Stepping back, we would say that the work of inquiry and deliberation rarely leads to such a direct and satisfying change, never mind to revolutionary change on the scale of transforming flawed national policies or eradicating tenacious structural problems like racism. One booklet of welfare narratives will not create a sea of change in welfare reform; *The Landlord Tenant Handbook* will not eliminate the need for mediators and magistrates, even in one small community (cf. Rude). Moreover, reasonable innovations face serious obstacles: physicians, for example, acknowledge the value of soliciting patients' situated knowledge through narrative, but they work in a culture of time-keeping, managed care that constrains their ability to engage in the kind of extended dialogue modeled by the CLC projects. The texts and practices produced in these projects are not ends in themselves but only beginnings, and they work, as publics do, through multiple paths, circulating and re-circulating, evolving and changing—even if incrementally—the way we live and work together as a community. A rhetorically centered model of community literacy proposes one way to keep that important work going.

NOTES

1. In using the collective "we," the authors not only refer to themselves, but to their wider network of partners—literacy leaders, mentors, and project participants—who have had a hand in shaping, implementing, and theorizing community literacy with us at the Community Literacy Center. Although our collaborators are too numerous to mention here, we especially acknowledge the vision and leadership of Wayne C. Peck, Joyce Baskins, Philip Flynn, and Donnie Tucker.

2. Barton and Hamilton draw on a sociological definition of community as the "realm that mediates between the private sphere of the family and household and the public sphere of impersonal, formal organizations" (15–16). Like them, we are drawn to study these local constructions where dominant and marginalized discourses come into contact.

3. Those interested in a review of community literacy scholarship and programs might turn to Cushman, Barbier, Mazak, and Petrone; Deans (for service learning); Grabill; and Long, *Community Literacy and the Rhetoric of Local Publics*.

4. In attempting to sketch a working theory of this rhetorically centered model of community literacy, we will not do justice to the theoretical work of others on which we draw or to what we hope this work adds to such discussions. For a framework that locates this work more broadly in literacy studies in which ordinary people go public, please see Elenore Long's comparative analysis of how different approaches to community literacy imagine their guiding metaphors and context and how they draw on different discourses, literate practices, and inventional processes

(*Community Literacy and the Rhetoric of Local Publics*). For research that positions community literacy within argument theory, rhetorical analysis, and the debates around deliberation, see Lorraine Higgins and Lisa Brush ("Personal Experience Narrative and Public Debate," 2006 and "From Narrative to Argument: Subordinated Rhetors Talk Back," in prep). For a discussion of alternative models of social engagement and empowerment in rhetoric and composition studies and the contribution of contemporary theories of publics and counterpublics, see Linda Flower (*Community Literacy and the Rhetoric of Engagement*, 2008).

5. Scholars in many disciplines have cautioned against this kind of missionary stance, stressing the need to work with community partners (e.g., see Cushman, "Rhetorician"; Flower and Heath; McKnight; Stringer). Brenton Faber has argued that understanding problems and affecting change requires us to be an *engaged* part of a team, not an observing ethnographer, objective consultant, or professional facilitator.

6. In classical rhetoric, deliberative argument begins at the point of stasis, where competing claims about future action are tested by rhetors who are assumed to draw from the same pool of community values and experiences — common *topoi*. But in diverse communities, such argument seems premature; the problem space itself has not been defined. Thus deliberation is a form of inquiry — of discovering the nature of problems and thus plausible responses to them.

7. Coogan demonstrates how these common refrains can be analyzed as ideographs that reveal key arguments and ideologies.

8. In inviting members of representative stakeholder groups to the table, we have found it useful to target what we call second-tier leaders: these are respected individuals who other stakeholder groups have identified as knowledgeable, reasonable, and open to dialogue. First-tier leaders are well-known and highly positioned persons who have already committed publicly to particular positions on community problems. Although their viewpoints are critical and should be considered at the table, the actual participation of first-tier leaders at the table can be disruptive and intimidating to less powerful groups, particularly at the beginning of a project. First-tier leaders are often invited to respond at later stages of community literacy projects.

9. E.g., it was helpful for us to read Mansbridge's analysis of the New England town meeting, in which she notes obstacles to marginalized groups' participation that are similar to those described by participants in the landlord/tenant project (60–62, 109).

10. See Higgins and Brush for an extended discussion of the discourse of poverty and welfare. They identify two common narratives — the hero and victim narrative — that often reproduce dangerous stereotypes of welfare recipients and erode their credibility.

11. Community Conversations are interactive public meetings structured around project participants' writing. They may include performances, readings, panel discussions, and other forms of public presentation and audience interaction.

12. For instance, when female patients from the Rainbow Health Clinic met with medical professionals around the issue of patient noncompliance, the women's situated knowledge shifted the terms of debate (Flower, Long, and Higgins 304; Higgins and Chalich). Initially, the medical professionals at the table pinned the problem of noncompliance on the personality of "difficult patients." In contrast, some of the women interpreted noncompliance in terms of historical and cultural conflicts between African Americans and the medical establishment. It was the situated knowledge of these women writers that recast the dialogue to explore the cultural differences that lead to communication problems.

13. For instance, a doctor who assumes a "noncompliant patient" is belligerent, rather than well versed in the infamous Tuskeegee study (to cite one source of a patient's mistrust) relates to that patient differently than one who considers patient-physician trust to be a complex historical and institutional as well as interpersonal negotiation (Ainsworth-Vaughn; Higgins; Young, and Flower). It's not that the physician's interpretation of noncompliance — focusing, say, on recurring illnesses, avoidable side effects, and more severe outcomes such as heart attack, as well as costs to the health care system — isn't also valid. The point is that a medical point of view is likewise perspectival and partial.

14. The inquiry process we detail here includes both eliciting situated knowledge and testing the adequacy of the interpretive frames that people use to make sense of their own and others' experience. As discussed below, the story-behind-the-story and the rivaling strategy work in tandem to accomplish these two goals. It is not that stakeholders necessarily know from the outset what specific knowledge needs to be elicited and what existing knowledge needs to be reframed — though more marginalized participants often tell us that they have joined a literacy project as a way of challenging negative stereotypes. Joint inquiry is a recursive process of rhetorical invention that the deliberative process itself makes possible.

15. A welfare mom might not want to recognize rival readings that could paint her or others in her situation as irresponsible mothers, for example. And can you blame her? In some cases, dominant discourses have indeed constructed marginalized people as incapable, lazy, inexpert. "Professionals" may also discount the N-of-1, personalized (read: *devalued, biased*) knowledge of their "clients" because their training teaches them to do so. And those who occupy more privileged social positions might feel it dangerous to identify with others whom they assume have not earned "equal" standing.

16. Critical incidents provide specific details and contextual information about the problems people face within complex situations. Critical incidents put pet theories and stereotypes to the test of more operational definitions of a problem. Treated as data, critical incidents show situated cognition in high-stakes contexts where decisions make a difference such as flying a plane in combat or making medical diagnoses.

17. This knowledge isn't necessarily cut off from formal public knowledge. For instance, a tenant may in fact be fluent with many public institutions' forms, regulations, and procedures. But it is also the case that marginalized people often have something to say about institutional discourse that isn't usually part of collective social knowledge; moreover, they know something about the gaps between the professed intent of specific public policies, on one hand, and how they play out in lived experience, on the other.

18. As activist rhetoricians, we have found that designing interventions requires us to refine and articulate our own situated knowledge of community literacy. This action-reflection starts when we actively attend to conflict—the "real life" contradictions, obstacles, and surprises that arise over the course of a project, complicating the story we had previously imagined as to how the inquiry would unfold. Action-reflection then pushes us to construct an explanatory account of the problem, a rationale for the rhetorical design of the intervention itself. Such action-reflection is often recursive as Higgins and Brush found as they tested and refined scaffolding that writers in the Welfare project would find genuinely useful (19). But *useful*, of course, doesn't simply mean that the intervention makes the invention process easier. It means that the rhetorical principles of meaning-making that inform the design of the intervention will help the writer do justice to the expertise she has to share.

19. More specifically, collaborative planning structures the rhetorical thinking typical of experienced writers. The supporter prompts the writer not only to consider content or topic knowledge—the point at which inexperienced writers typically start and stop—but also to construct a more rhetorical plan by actively thinking about key points and purpose in writing, the needs and anticipated responses of readers, and alternative text conventions that might support this increasingly elaborated network of goals, plans, and ideas (Flower, Wallace, Norris, and Burnett).

20. Collaborative planning has been used in a number of academic settings and with participants in a wide range of community literacy projects to teach writing, to support classroom inquiry by teachers and students, and to conduct research into students' strategies. Because this process of articulating a plan helps make thinking "more visible," collaborative planning has been used as a platform for reflection, allowing writers, mentors, and teachers to gain new awareness of writers' goals, strategies, and struggles.

21. Creating such scaffolds is the work of anyone in a project who identifies a rhetorical problem which a bit more structure could help to solve. Mentors often work opportunistically to help writers manage the complex set of goals they often set for their texts (Flower, Long, and Higgins 290–91). In addition, participants often create their own scaffolds with and for one another as they translate a shared problem into a rhetorical plan. For instance, the landlord/tenant group transformed critical incidents into scenarios that blended or realistically modified actual events from anecdotes and personal experience in order to illustrate four "typical" conflicts that could serve as cases against which participants tested their proposals for change (Flower and Deems 118).

22. Here the image of stakeholders seated around a round table first serves as a metaphor and a heuristic, prompting a writer to imagine her perspective as one among others, to figure out how to frame her text in relation to other anticipated perspectives so that hers might not only get a fair hearing but also possibly encourage others to revise their understanding of the problem in light of the situated knowledge she has to offer. Other stakeholders are invited to the table later in the process as writers re-visit their texts to clarify their own experience and interpretations from the perspectives of real, not imagined, readers. By working with community members, we have identified a number of useful criteria for deciding who and how to bring additional stakeholders to the table at this point in the process. For instance, once the Rainbow Health Clinic writers had drafted their contributions to a joint document, but before the texts were finalized for publication, a physician, nurse practitioner, and health administrator were invited to the table not only to listen

to the writers but also to articulate the "movies of the mind" they created in their own interpretative imaginations as they worked through the writers' texts. Again, these were not first-tier leaders in Pittsburgh's healthcare community who had already committed publicly to positions, but rather second-tier leaders—people more likely to know the other points of view well and be able to articulate them, but who also would be more open to hearing new perspectives (Higgins, Flower, and Deems 33). This rival reading session with healthcare professionals put difference into rigorous dialogue, asking writers to re-visit their texts to clarify their own experience and interpretations from the perspectives of engaged and present readers. Often those invited to the table at this time are people whom project participants themselves want to engage in dialogue. In a literacy project on school suspension, for example, teens identified the teachers and administrators whom they wanted to have read and respond to the early versions their documents—adults who were, in the teens' assessment, "at least okay sometimes, and open minded."

23. Young's model of communicative democracy challenges the conventional conception of public deliberation by valorizing the roles that greeting, rhetoric, and storytelling as well as critical argument play in public discourse. For a critique of Young's model, see Seyla Benhabib's "Toward a Deliberative Model of Democratic Legitimacy" in *Democracy and Difference: Contesting the Boundaries of the Political*, also edited by Benhabib.

24. First, the options and outcomes strategy asks participants to generate multiple "real" options—a move designed to counter the common tendency in decision making to consider only one option and decide "yes" or "no." Then, because the responses to complex problems often involve trade-offs—there isn't one "good" option—the strategy asks participants to project and to compare possible outcomes, weighing values and the probability of an outcome.

25. The "what-ifs" allowed the group to share and distribute their expertise; participants actually waited to develop their "what-ifs," not in preparation for a session, but over the course of the session itself (Higgins, Flower, and Deems 32).

26. For instance, following the problem narrative she wrote for the group document, a writer named Jules considered options and outcomes in the "Taking Action" section of her article:

> WHAT IF . . . Young women and men were more savvy about using protection that works for them?
>
> THEN they would have more control over their finances and future.
>
> WHAT IF . . . The older women/teachers/mentors in Jules's life had counseled her earlier about relationships?
>
> THEN she might have felt more secure and savvy when dealing with her boyfriends.
>
> WHAT IF . . . All young women were counseled in this way?

In these action plans, the writers don't reach a decision or one claim about what to do. That is, they don't solve anything *per se*. Instead, they generate multiple, plausible, informed proposals built on the reasoning they have done together. And they consider the consequences of these possibilities for all stakeholders.

27. For a description of the rival reading technique, see Flower's *Problem-Solving Strategies for Writing in College and Community* 415–18.

28. If one locates the hope of a democracy in a common commitment to the common good, acknowledging, much less enfranchising, difference opens the Pandora's box of divisiveness and interest group bargaining. Yet, if our ideal is a disinterested concern, who defines this common good, especially if you and I hold racially different notions of what it is, and some of us lack the cultural capital to assert our vision as the common one (cf. Bohman and Rehg; Gutman and Thompson; Roberts-Miller)?

29. Medical rhetoricians, anthropologists, and practitioners have written extensively on patient-physician communication and the way standard medical practices create what Parson has called a "sick role" for patients (also see Higgins; Hunter; Kleinman).

WORKS CITED

Ainsworth-Vaughn, Nancy. *Claiming Power in Doctor-Patient Talk*. Oxford Studies in Sociolinguistics. New York: Oxford UP, 1998.

Aristotle. *Art of Rhetoric*. Trans. J. H. Freese. Cambridge, MA: Harvard UP, 1982.

Atwill, Janet, and Janice Lauer, eds. *Perspectives on Rhetorical Invention*. Knoxville: U of Tennessee P, 2002.

Barton, David, and Mary Hamilton. *Local Literacies: Reading and Writing in One Community*. New York: Routledge, 1998.

Bitzer, Lloyd. "The Rhetorical Situation." *Philosophy and Rhetoric* 1 (1968): 1–14.

Black Public Sphere Collective, ed. *The Black Public Sphere: A Public Culture Book.* Chicago: U of Chicago P, 1995.

Bohman, James, and William Rehg. *Deliberative Democracy: Essays on Reason and Politics.* Cambridge, MA: MIT P, 1997.

Brandt, Deborah. *Literacy in American Lives.* Cambridge, MA: Cambridge UP, 2001.

Bryan, Frank. *Real Democracy: The New England Town Meeting and How it Works.* Chicago: U of Chicago P, 2004.

Carnegie Mellon Community Think Tank. "Healthcare: The Dilemma of Teamwork, Time, and Turnover." *The Community Think Tank.* Spring 2002. Carnegie Mellon University. 19 September 2006 <www.cmu.edu/thinktank/docs/healthcare.pdf>.

Cintron, Ralph. *Angel's Town: Chero Ways, Gang Life, and Rhetorics of the Everyday.* Boston, MA: Beacon P, 1997.

Consigny, Scott. "Rhetoric and Its Situations." *Philosophy and Rhetoric* 7 (1974): 175–86.

Coogan, David. "Counter Publics in Public Housing: Reframing the Politics of Service- Learning." *College English* 67.5 (May 2005): 461–82.

———. "Service Learning and Social Change: The Case for Materialist Rhetoric." *College Composition and Communication* 57.4 (2006): 667–93.

Cushman, Ellen. "Rhetorician as Agent of Social Change." *College Composition and Communication* 47.1 (1996): 1–28.

———. *The Struggle and the Tools: Oral and Literate Strategies in an Inner-City Community.* Albany: State U of New York P, 1998.

Cushman, Ellen, Stuart Barbier, Catherine Mazak, and Robert Petrone. "Family and Community Literacies." *Research on Composition: Multiple Perspectives on Two Decades of Change.* Ed. Peter Smagorinsky. New York: Teachers College P, 2000. 187–217.

Deans, Thomas. *Writing Partnerships: Service Learning in Composition.* Urbana, IL: NCTE, 2000.

Deems, Julia, and Linda Flower. *Rivaling about Risk: A Dialogue Tutorial.* Pittsburgh, PA: Carnegie Mellon, 1996.

Dewey, John. *Quest for Certainty.* Vol. 4 of *John Dewey: The Later Works 1925–1953.* Ed. Jo Ann Boydston. Carbondale: Southern Illinois UP, 1988.

Engeström, Yrjö. "Developmental Studies of Work as a Testbench of Activity Theory: The Case of Primary Care Medical Practice." *Understanding Practice: Perspectives on Activity and Context.* Ed. Seth Chaiklin and Jean Lave. Cambridge, MA: Cambridge UP, 1996.

———. "Activity Theory and Individual and Social Transformation." *Perspectives on Activity Theory.* Ed. Yrjö Engeström, Reijo Miettinen, R.-Leena. Punamäki, and Roy Pea. Cambridge, England: Cambridge UP, 1999. 19–38.

———. "Innovative Learning in Work Teams: Analyzing Cycles of Knowledge Creation in Practice." *Perspectives on Activity Theory.* 375–404. Ed. Yrjö Engeström, Reijo Miettinen, R.-Leena. Punamäki, and Roy Pea. Cambridge: Cambridge UP, 1999.

Faber, Brenton. *Community Action and Organizational Change: Image, Narrative, Identity.* Carbondale: Southern Illinois UP, 2002.

Farr, Marcia, ed. *Latino Language and Literacy in Ethnolinguistic Chicago.* Mahwah, NJ: Erlbaum, 2005.

Flanagan, John C. "The Critical Incident Technique." *Psychological Bulletin* 5.4 (1954): 327–58.

Flower, Linda. *Community Literacy and the Rhetoric of Public Engagement.* Carbondale: Southern Illinois UP, 2008.

———. "Can You Build a Transformative (Local) Public Sphere? Spaces for Alternative Representations of Identity and Agency in Marginalized Youth." Berkeley, CA: NCTE Assembly for Research. February 19–21, 2004.

———. *The Construction of Negotiated Meaning: A Social Cognitive Theory of Writing.* Carbondale: Southern Illinois UP, 1994.

———. "Intercultural Knowledge Building: The Literate Action of a Community Think Tank." *Writing Selves and Society: Research from Activity Perspectives.* Ed. Charles Bazerman and David Russell. Fort Collins, CO: WAC Clearinghouse, 2002.

———. "Partners in Inquiry: A Logic for Community Outreach." *Writing the Community: Concepts and Models for Service Learning in Composition.* Ed. Linda Alder-Kassner, Robert Crooks and Anne Watters. Washington, DC: American Association for Higher Education, 1997. 95–117.

———. *Problem-Solving Strategies for Writing in College and Communities.* Fort Worth, TX: Harcourt Brace, 1998.

———. "Talking Across Difference: Intercultural Rhetoric and the Search for Situated Knowledge." *College Composition and Communication* 55.1 (2003): 38–68.

Flower, Linda, and Julia Deems. "Conflict in Community Collaboration." *New Perspectives on Rhetorical Invention.* Ed. Janet Atwill and Janice Lauer. Knoxville: U of Tennessee P, 2002. 96–130.

Flower, Linda, and Shirley Brice Heath. "Drawing on the Local: Collaboration and Community Expertise." *Language and Learning Across the Disciplines* 4.3 (2004): 43–45.

Flower, Linda, Elenore Long, and Lorraine Higgins. *Learning to Rival: A Literate Practice for Intercultural Inquiry.* Mahwah, NJ: Erlbaum, 2000.

Flower, Linda, David Wallace, Linda Norris, and Rebecca Burnett, eds. *Making Thinking Visible: Writing, Collaborative Planning, and Classroom Inquiry.* Urbana, IL: NCTE, 1994.

Fraser, Nancy. "Rethinking the Public Sphere: A Contribution to the Critique of Actually Existing Democracy." *Social Text* 25/26 (1990): 56–80.

Freire, Paulo. *Pedagogy of the Oppressed.* Trans. M. B. Ramos. New York: Continuum, 1989.

Gaonkar, Dilip P. "The Forum. Publics and Counterpublics: Introduction." *Quarterly Journal of Speech* 88.3 (2002): 410–12.

Geertz, Clifford. *Local Knowledge: Further Essays in Interpretive Anthropology.* New York: Basic Books, 1983.

Getting to Know You: A Dialogue for Community Health. Pittsburgh, PA: Community Literacy Center and The Rainbow Health Center, 1996.

Goldblatt, Eli. "Alinsky's Reveille: A Community-Organizing Model for Neighborhood-Based Literacy Projects." *College English* 67.3 (2005): 274–94.

———. "Van Rides in the Dark: Literacy as Involvement." *Journal for Peace and Justice Studies* 6.1 (1994): 77–94.

Grabill, Jeffrey T. *Community Literacy Programs and the Politics of Change.* Albany: State U of New York P, 2001.

Gumperz, John, and Deborah Tannen. "Individual and Social Differences in Language Use." *Individual Differences in Language Ability and Language Behavior.* Ed. Charles Fillmore, Daniel Kempler, and William S.Y. Wang. New York: Academic P, 1979. 305–25.

Gutman, Amy, and Dennis Thompson. *Why Deliberative Democracy?* Princeton, NJ: Princeton UP, 2004.

Habermas, Jürgen. *The Structural Transformation of the Public Sphere: An Inquiry into a Category of Bourgeois Society.* Cambridge, MA: MIT P, 1989.

Harris, Joyce L., Alan G. Kamhi, and Karen E. Pollock, eds. *Literacy in African American Communities.* Mahwah, NJ: Erlbaum, 2001.

Hauser, Gerard. *Vernacular Voices: The Rhetoric of Publics and Public Spheres.* Columbia: U of South Carolina P, 1999.

Hauser, Gerard, and Amy Grim. *Rhetorical Democracy: Discursive Practices of Civic Engagement.* Mahwah, NJ: Erlbaum, 2004.

Heath, Shirley Brice. *Ways with Words: Language, Life, and Work in Communities and Classrooms.* New York: Cambridge UP, 1983.

Herzberg, Bruce. "Community Service and Critical Teaching." *College Composition and Communication* 45.3 (1994): 307–19.

Higgins, Lorraine. "Revising the Medical Encounter," in prep.

Higgins, Lorraine, and Lisa Brush. "From Narrative to Argument: Subordinated Rhetors Talk Back," in prep.

———. "Personal Experience Narrative and Public Debate: Writing the Wrongs of Welfare." *College Composition and Communication* 57.4 (2006): 694–729.

Higgins, Lorraine, and Theresa Chalich, eds. *Getting to Know You: A Dialogue for Community Health.* Pittsburgh, PA: Community Literacy Center and Rainbow Health Center, 1996.

Higgins, Lorraine, Linda Flower, and Julia Deems. "Collaboration and Community Action: Landlord and Tenants." Pittsburgh, PA: Carnegie Mellon, 1996.

Hull, Glynda, and Michael Angelo James. "Geographies of Hope: A Study of Urban Landscape and a University-Community Collaborative." *Blurring Boundaries: Developing Writers, Researchers, and Teachers: A Tribute to William L. Smith.* Ed. Peggy O'Neill. Cresskill, NJ: Hampton Press, in press.

Hull, Glynda, and Mira-Lisa Katz. "Crafting an Agentive Self: Case Studies of Digital Storytelling." *Research in the Teaching of English,* forthcoming.

Hull, Glynda, and Katherine Schultz. *School's Out! Bridging Out-of-School Literacies with Classroom Practices.* New York: Teacher's College P, 2002.

Hunter, Kathryn. "Remaking the Case." *Literature and Medicine* 11.1 (1992): 163–79.

Karpowitz, Christopher F., and Jane Mansbridge. "Disagreement and Consensus: The Need for Dynamic Updating in Public Deliberation." *Journal of Public Deliberation* 1.1 (2005): 347–64.

Kleinman, Arthur. *The Illness Narratives: Suffering, Healing, and the Human Condition.* New York: Basic Books, 1988.

Langsdorf, Lenore. "Argument as Inquiry in a Postmodern Context." *Argumentation* 11 (1997): 315–27.

Lawrence, Susan. *Reading Other's Realities: Double-Sided Discourse Moves.* Ms. Pittsburgh, PA: Carnegie Mellon, 1996.

Long, Elenore. *Community Literacy and the Rhetoric of Local Publics.* West LayFayette, IN: Parlor Press, in prep.

———. "The Rhetoric of Social Action: College Mentors Inventing the Discipline." *Inventing a Discipline: Rhetoric Scholarship in Honor of Richard E. Young.* Ed. Maureen Daly Goggin. Urbana, IL: NCTE, 2000. 289–318.

Long, Elenore, Wayne C. Peck, and Joyce Baskins. "Struggle: A Literate Practice Supporting Life-Project Planning." *School's Out! Bridging Out-of-School Literacies with Classroom Practice.* Ed. Glynda Hull and Katherine Schultz. New York: Teachers College P, 2002. 131–61.

Mansbridge, Jane. *Beyond Adversary Democracy.* Chicago, IL: U of Chicago P, 1983.

McKnight, John. *The Careless Society: Community and Its Counterfeits.* New York: Basic Books, 1995.

Moss, Beverly. *A Community Text Arises: A Literate Text and Literacy Tradition in African American Churches.* Cresskill, NJ: Hampton P, 2003.

Peck, Wayne, Linda Flower, and Lorraine Higgins. "Community Literacy." *College Composition and Communication* 46.2 (1995): 199–222.

Roberts-Miller, Patricia. *Deliberate Conflict: Argument, Political Theory, and Composition Classes.* Southern Carbondale: Southern Illinois UP, 2004.

Rude, Carolyn. "Toward an Expanded Concept of Rhetorical Delivery: The Uses of Reports in Public Policy Debates." *Technical Communication Quarterly* 13.3 (2004): 271–88.

Schutz, Aaron, and Anne Ruggles Gere. "Service Learning and English Studies: Rethinking 'Public' Service." *College English* 60.2 (1998): 129–50.

Scribner, Sylvia, and Michael Cole. *The Psychology of Literacy.* Cambridge, MA: Harvard UP, 1981.

Smitherman, Geneva. *Talkin' That Talk: African American Language and Culture.* New York: Routledge, 1999.

Stock, Patricia, and Janet Swensen. "The Write for Your Life Project: Learning to Serve and Serving to Learn." *Writing the Community: Concepts and Models for Service Learning in Composition.* Ed. Linda Adler-Kassner, Robert Crooks, and Ann Waters. Washington: American Association for Higher Education and NCTE, 1997. 153–66.

Street, Brian. *Literacy in Theory and Practice.* Cambridge UP, 1985.

Stringer, Ernest. *Action Research: A Handbook for Practitioners.* Newbury Park, CA: Sage, 1996.

Swan, Susan. "Rhetoric, Service, and Social Justice." *Written Communication* 19.1 (2002): 76–108.

Trimbur, John. "Consensus and Difference in Collaborative Learning." *College English* 51: 602–16.

Warner, Michael. *Publics and Counterpublics.* New York: Zone Books, 2005.

Weiksner, G. Michael. "E-THE PEOPLE.ORG. Large-Scale, Ongoing Deliberation." *The Deliberative Democracy Handbook: Strategies for Effective Civic Engagement in the Twenty-First Century.* Ed. John Gastil and Peter Levine. San Francisco, CA: Jossey-Bass, 2005. 213–37.

Wells, Susan. "Habermas, Communicative Competence, and the Teaching of Technical Discourse." *Theory in the Classroom.* Ed. Cary Nelson. Urbana: U of Illinois P, 1986. 245–69.

Whassup with Suspension? Pittsburgh, PA: Community Literacy Center, 1992.

Young, Amanda. *What's Your Plan?: Sexuality and Relationships. A Multimedia Dialogue/Tutorial.* Pittsburgh, PA: Carnegie Mellon, 1996.

Young, Amanda, and Linda Flower. "Patients and Partners, Patients as Problem-Solvers." *Health Communication* 14.1 (2001): 69–97.

Young, Iris Marion. "Communication and the Other: Beyond Deliberative Democracy." *Democracy and Difference: Contesting the Boundaries of the Political.* Ed. Seyla Benhabib. Princeton, NJ: Princeton UP, 1996. 120–35.

———. "Difference as a Resource for Democratic Communication." *Deliberative Democracy: Essays on Reason and Politics.* Ed. James Bohman and William Regh. Cambridge, MA: MIT P, 1997. 383–406.

———. *Intersecting Voices: Dilemmas of Gender, Political Philosophy, and Policy.* Princeton, NJ: Princeton UP, 1997.

Young, Richard, Alton Becker, and Kenneth Pike. *Rhetoric: Discovery and Change.* New York: Harcourt Brace, 1970.

Zentella, Ana Celia, ed. *Building on Strength: Language Literacy in Latin Families and Communities.* New York: Teachers College P, 2005.

14 Maybe the Reason Why

MARK HOWARD

At the Community Literacy Center (CLC) in Pittsburgh, Carnegie Mellon students, community leaders, and local citizens together practice "rivaling," "exploring the story behind the story," and several other rhetorical strategies described by Lorraine Higgins, Elenore Long, and Linda Flower in "Community Literacy: A Rhetorical Model for Personal and Public Inquiry" (p. 167 in this volume). The CLC emphasizes the uses of rhetoric, writing, intercultural conversation, narrative, argument, drama, and publication to explore and address local problems.

Weeks of collaborative inquiry and writing culminate in a "Community Conversation" on a topic of local concern. Community Conversations are live performances that feature readings, speeches, videos, scripted skits, and spontaneous dialogue among the various stakeholders who attend. They are also the occasion for releasing multi-voiced publications that reflect the weeks of discovery, conversation, and writing that lead up to each Community Conversation. Street Life: Dealing with Violence and Risk in Our Community *is one such publication from 1993, and Mark Howard's "Maybe the Reason Why" is one of six pieces—most of them written by Pittsburgh youth in collaboration with Carnegie Mellon students—that appeared in it. Sixteen-year-old Howard explains to adults how fear of violence*

FIGURE 14–1   Howard's Piece as It Appeared in *Street Life*.

From *Street Life* (Fall 1993): 4.

202

and the rules of the street govern everyday decisions, from the clothes he wears to the places he can be seen. Consistent with the CLC approach, Howard also explores several possible options available to him and other urban youth for responding to such challenges.

Readers who are interested in the complete version of this publication—and others like it—can access the Community Literacy Center archives online. Those seeking a fuller discussion of the theoretical context for the CLC can consult Linda Flower's book Community Literacy and the Rhetoric of Public Engagement *(Carbondale: Southern Illinois UP, 2008).*

W HY DON'T YOU . . . Want to go with me to visit your aunt anymore?

WHY DON'T YOU . . . Want to wear your new outfit? . . . Do you know how much I paid for that?

WHY DON'T YOU . . . Go to the basketball court anymore? . . . All you do is sit around the house all day.

WHY DOESN'T HE . . . Come over here anymore? . . . He used to come from the other side of town just so you two could hang out.

WHY DO YOU . . . Think you need to change schools all of the sudden? . . . What makes you think that you will do any better there?

These are just a few examples of the questions that parents, guardians, and concerned relatives ask their kids because they may not understand the new pressures arising from gangs and other forms of violence. I feel that it is very hard for parents to understand what teenagers are going through these days, simply because they do not see and hear a lot of the things that go on between them. *MAYBE THE REASON WHY* . . . the person in the first instance may not want to go visit a certain relative is because the relative may live in a neighborhood where this person is unknown or not liked (gang members react to unfamiliar faces almost as badly as to wearing the wrong colors). *MAYBE THE REASON WHY* . . . the person in the second instance may not want to wear that certain outfit is because of the color of the outfit. It is a lot easier to get shot over wearing the wrong color in the wrong neighborhood in Pittsburgh now than it ever was. As things progress, it seems as though it will never get better . . . just worse!!!! *MAYBE THE REASON WHY* . . . the person in the third instance does not go to the basketball court anymore is because there could have been a drive-by done by a rivaling gang there before, but it does not necessarily have to be gang related. This person also could have possibly been worried about getting harassed by the police because the basketball court may be considered *"HOT."* The term *"HOT"* refers to a certain area that may be known for its heavy drug selling activities. *MAYBE THE REASON WHY* . . . the person in the fourth instance does not come from the other side of town anymore is because the people in the part of town that he wants to go to may harass him because they do not know him, or they know where he is from. It could also be that the two people just do not get along with each other anymore because their two neighborhoods do not get along. *MAYBE THE REASON WHY* . . . the person in the last instance feels that he has to change his school is because something could have happened recently between two neighborhoods that attend that school and it could have caused new problems. Some of the possible problems could be that some of the students are bringing the violence into the school because of something that may have happened on the street. Another reason why someone might want to change schools is because there could be two (or more) different gangs in one school. This could very easily result in constant arguments and fighting between them. The last reason I can think of is, if someone attends a school which is made up of mainly one neighborhood but that person is from a different neighborhood, that person could feel very threatened if the two neighborhoods did not get along. It would be very hard to try to remember what was for homework when you are worried about getting jumped by fifteen or so people after school. Here is one big example of how neighborhood stereotyping limits teenagers today and puts them in possibly violent situations:

I am now 16 years of age and if I was to go to the Hill, Garfield, East Hills, Homewood, and certain parts of Northside, I would get jumped and possibly shot because they don't know me, or because they know where I'm from and they automatically assume I am in L.A.W. (a Larimer Ave., Wilkensburg gang). I am affiliated with a lot of the people in L.A.W. as friends but I don't participate in hunting down or looking for people in different gangs to beat up or start trouble. I am not even "in" the gang, but I stay over at my friends' houses and go places like the movies or mall with them, but I don't just hang around on the corner with them. My friends sometimes say about me to other people in their neighborhood that "He's in JD" (a member of the JD set) just to protect me, but then other people know me as being in JD and that could, in turn, cause more problems for me. I did not really choose to hang with these people, but it seems as though I am limited to few neighborhoods—Wilkinsburg mostly. Another reason that I hang with these people is because our friendship is stronger than with people in my old neighborhood. For example, we are all too good of friends to let the colors of our clothes get in the way. One time I went to Wilkinsburg and I had on all blue (that is one of the colors that the rivaling gangs wear). None of my friends really said anything about it. They actually joked about it, "What . . . you a CRIP?"

WHAT ARE MY CHOICES HERE?

CHOICE: Since everybody thinks I'm in it anyway, and they label me that way, I might as well be in the gang. I feel that is why 90% of gang members join. To me, that is peer pressure, though, and it hasn't caused me to join a gang.

CHOICE: Move to the area where your friends are, but watch what you get into. I think this is the best idea, but not everybody can just get up and move. What I mean by "watch what you get into" is: If they want to do drive-bys or beatings of other gang members, I would just stay in the house and play Nintendo. It does help to tell people you disapprove of beating people up for no reason—especially when girls disapprove—because most girls don't like dudes that bully. It might get the gang members to think twice about it if people from their own neighborhoods say this. One time I talked my friends out of fighting another group.

CHOICE: Don't hang on the corner with known gang members because if someone sees you there, you could be the innocent victim of a drive-by. Go other places. If we see someone from a rivaling neighborhood, I tell my friends not to say anything. Going to parties in our own neighborhood is usually safe.

15 FROM *Naming the LD Difference*

CARNEGIE MELLON COMMUNITY THINK TANK

Naming the LD Difference: Dilemmas in Dealing with Learning Disabilities *documents the collaborative work of students, teachers, school administrators, parents, college professors, local business people, and other stakeholders who came together in 2003 as part of a Carnegie Mellon Community Think Tank.*

Community Think Tanks are designed to create cross-age, intercultural dialogues among people who solve problems. Many of the strategies that Lorraine Higgins, Elenore Long, and Linda Flower discuss in "Community Literacy: A Rhetorical Model for Personal and Public Inquiry" (p. 167 in this volume) are evident in these selections.

FIGURE 15–1   FIGURE 15–2

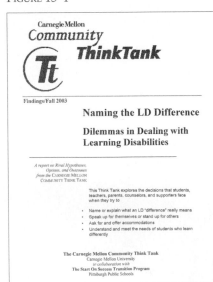

From *Naming the LD Difference: Dilemmas in Dealing with Learning Disabilities* (Fall 2003): iv, 3–6.

Readers who are interested in the complete version of this publication — and others like it — can access the Carnegie Mellon Community Think Tank archives online. Those seeking a fuller discussion of the theoretical context for this and similar projects can consult Linda Flower's book Community Literacy and the Rhetoric of Public Engagement *(Carbondale: Southern Illinois UP, 2008).*

How Does a Think Tank Dialogue Work?

A diverse set of participants join each other at round tables as problem-solving partners. Working with our representative problem cases, we *use* our differences

- To discover the "story-behind-the-story" from different points of view
- To draw out alternative, "rival hypotheses" from each other
- To propose workable options for dealing with this problem

The Carnegie Mellon team documents this problem-solving dialogue and publishes the findings on the Community Think Tank website (www.cmu.edu/thinktank). . . .

Decision Point 1. Exposed!

In a Mainstream Classroom

TEACHER: *(Passing out sheets of paper)* Okay, class, today we will be reading the Bill of Rights Each of you needs to choose a partner and split up the reading. Then, once you have finished the reading, you will need to work with your partner to answer the questions on this handout.

SHAUNA: *(Speaking flirtatiously to Joel, who is sitting next to her)* Hey Joel, do you want to be my partner?

JOEL: *(Shy and hesitant)* Umm . . . Yeah, sure.

BILLY THE BULLY: *(Laughing)* Uh-oh, look who Shauna got stuck with.

SHAUNA: *(Paying no attention to Billy)* Okay, great, Joel! How about I read the first paragraph and you read the second one. Then we can work together to answer the questions on the handout?

JOEL: *(Not making eye contact)* Whatever . . . that's cool. . . .

NARRATOR: Joel has had a crush on Shauna for three weeks. . . . He doesn't want her to know that he has a little trouble with reading.

SHAUNA: Okay, great! *(She begins to read)*

NARRATOR: A few seconds pass in silence. . . . Shauna reads with great interest. . . . Joel looks around the room, and taps his pencil; he is having a hard time. Joel doesn't want to read anymore, so decides to talk to Shauna. . . .

JOEL: So, Shauna, you going to the game on Saturday?

SHAUNA: *(Looking up, confused)* Um, I'm not sure yet. . . . *(Goes back to reading)*

JOEL: Oh, it should be a good one.

TEACHER: *(Interrupting Joel)* Joel, shh! Do your work.

NARRATOR: Joel picks up the paper and tries to read it, but gets frustrated and puts it down after a short while . . . the teacher notices him struggling and walks over to his desk. She takes him aside and tries to speak to him one on one, but the other students overhear.

TEACHER: Joel, are you having a difficult time with the reading?

THE STORY BEHIND THE STORY

What Is Joel Thinking?

A parent says:
- Sometimes my son tries to get out of a hard task by causing a disruption.

A student says:
- Personally, if I'm in this situation and I like the girl, I'm not going to tell her anything at all. I'll make up a lie or something . . . I'm not going to straight up tell her.

Whose Problem Is This—the Student's, the Teacher's, the School's?

An administrator says:
- Teachers should know if they have a student with an IEP. They shouldn't have to ask the student, "Are you having trouble?" Like I said before: pre-planning!

A student says:
- The teacher didn't know that he had a disability, and she should have been told at the beginning of the year. I let the teacher know when I go in that class; they know I have an LD. Some teachers ask me, and I tell them to read my IEP or something. So then I can say it's the teacher's fault for everything!

An administrator says:
- I don't think this is Joel's fault, but I think it is a problem for Joel, because his teacher is not really engaging where she should. And really, the bottom line here is that you guys in school are the people we are supposed to take care of. The teacher is there to support you.

The Think Tank says:
- You can't just blame Joel. He might be inexperienced and new to this. He doesn't stand up for himself well, and he needs help along the way.

The Think Tank says:
- The problems are multiple, because the bully's problem becomes Joel's problem and that becomes the teacher's problem. Eventually, it's going to be the whole class's problem! The class won't be able to progress if it's dragging an anchor.

OPTIONS AND OUTCOMES

Decision Point #1: Exposed!

Joel's standard strategies to avoid exposure have failed. He is suddenly marked as a personal failure and the teacher and students are forced to deal with an issue they too had avoided—naming the meaning of a learning disability.

Option #1: The Teacher Manages the Situation.

A teacher says:
- She needs to tell him to hang in there and that she'll talk to him later. When a student is stuck like that, the stress can be unbelievable, but she needs to calm the other kids down as well.

A student says:
- The teacher probably didn't think she was talking loud enough so that other kids could hear, but that didn't help any.

A college student says:
- She needs to handle the problem removed from the situation. For example, she might take the bully aside to talk to him.

Option #2: The Student Takes Responsibility to Get His Needs Met.

A teacher says:
- I think that Joel needs to advocate for himself. In high school, no one is going to do it for you. He needs to pull the teacher aside and say, "Look, I have a disability. These are the accommodations I need." Unfortunately, in high school, you pave your own road and it is sink-or-swim with a lot of things.

A student says:
- I don't think that all teachers really do know about students with LDs, because I had a situation kind of like that, but the teacher didn't know. He just didn't know and I had to give him my IEP paper so he could finally know. Not all teachers already know, being that they get a large amount of students in every single class. For every student, it's kind of hard to know everything about them. And also they might know that you have a learning difficulty, but they might not know what it is, how it affects you. It comes down to defining it and learning about it too.

A parent says:
- Is it really the student's responsibility to let the teacher know? There is a line.

Option #3: The Teacher Prevents These Problems in Advance.

An administrator says:
- There needs to be professional development. This is a teacher issue; this is not a student issue. This is something that could be captured, brought better to the classroom, if the teacher had more sensitivity and better strategies.

An administrator says:

- Teachers may know that you are on the list as having an LD, but they really haven't read the IEP, and sometimes quite frankly, the IEPs aren't written very well. They don't give you the information you need.

A parent says:

- If you're the teacher and you see this, you can partner a student willing to help with a student who needs help, in a positive environment. A lot of progress can be made.

A teacher says:

- A support aide would be useful, just to pass out papers and give attention to students so the teacher can deal with everything going on at once.

Option #4: The School System Takes Responsibility for Responding to the Student's Needs.

A teacher says:

- My goal is to educate you about your disability, but I need supporting documentations. When students are on the move, a lot of the paperwork doesn't follow them like it should. It's an administrative issue, like getting the housekeeping together so that there is a paper trail with the kids.

A teacher says:

- I have been able to see the paper trail that follows, and it is amazing how it differs from school to school. In some of the schools, it's been really difficult to find the supporting documentation other than an IEP that explains the disability and really pinpoint where the student has trouble. In other schools, it's no problem whatsoever.

An administrator says:

- I think it's also important to remember that so many of our teachers, especially the ones that have been around for a while and are burnt out, really believe that this is not something that they "signed on for." They are saying, "I am really not interested in it, or I shouldn't have to make these accommodations because I am a science teacher, and teaching science is what I'm trained to do."

A teacher says:

- The problem is that control is being removed from the local level. It used to be that the principal set the tone for how the teachers should behave. But now, that control is being removed, and departments regulate everything. Because things are becoming so standardized, and the teachers are evaluated by how well their students do on standardized tests, the pressure is on the teachers to do everything by the book.

16 Service Learning and Social Change: The Case for Materialist Rhetoric

DAVID COOGAN

David Fleming, perhaps, did not have service learning in mind when he proposed "rhetoric as a course of study," but even a cursory glance through the literature suggests that many of these courses are beginning to fulfill what Fleming defines as "the promise of all paideutic rhetorics": the making of good citizens ("Rhetoric" 180). In fact, I would put an even finer point on the claim. The promise is not just to make good citizens but to enable student-citizens to write for social change. When methods of effecting change include public advocacy, community organizing, or collaborative writing with non-profit groups, these courses may be further defined in rhetorical terms as efforts aimed at discovering the available means of persuasion. In that case, the question is not whether service learning has a rhetorical dimension but how we construe the public sphere in which change occurs and what role rhetoric plays in the change process.

Framing the question this way takes us beyond the related but ultimately more restrictive question of teaching students to address "real" audiences. Well-reasoned arguments appropriately addressed are an important goal of any public writing. But, as Susan Wells points out, the public is not a "neutral container" for students to fill: "it has its own history, its own vexed construction, its own possibilities of growth and decay" (328). Effective advocacy does not begin with the principles of good argument, then, but with an analysis of those historical and material conditions that have made some arguments more viable than others. The appeal of service learning, in this light, is that it offers rhetoricians a unique opportunity to *discover* the arguments that already exist in the communities we wish to serve; *analyze* the effectiveness of those arguments; collaboratively *produce* viable alternatives with community partners; and *assess* the impact of our interventions.

The most innovative approaches to service learning and community-based writing have already shown us a path from the classroom to the community. But no approach that I am aware of has shown us a path from

From *College Composition and Communication* 57.4 (2006): 667–93.

rhetorical discovery to practical outcomes in quite the same way that I am theorizing it here. Bruce Herzberg, for example, teaches students to analyze social problems such as homelessness. But he defers community-based, rhetorical production to the teaching of critical consciousness. Students who took his course and volunteered at a homeless shelter were not taught how to advocate for changes in the way the homeless are treated in Boston but how to think about the social causes of homelessness. In this context, Wayne Campbell Peck, Linda Flower, and Lorraine Higgins have suggested that the problem with critical consciousness in community-based writing projects is that it does not offer "strategies for change beyond resisting dominant discourse practices" (205). What they recommend instead is a practice of "community literacy" that establishes the conditions in which students and community partners can jointly "pose and analyze problems, set goals, stimulate readers, generate options, and test alternatives" (214). While this clearly enables rhetorical production, it also limits the scope of rhetorical analysis to the process of deliberation, itself, setting aside the larger rhetorical history that has shaped—and is likely to continue shaping—those same deliberations.

A tempting way to merge rhetorical discovery, analysis, production, and assessment would be to place students in community-based organizations (CBOs) and, in this way, limit the scope of rhetorical activity to a study of how each organization produces persuasive community texts. Nora Bacon has advocated this approach and claimed success for students who wrote for an organization aiding Central American immigrants in the San Francisco Bay Area of California: they succeeded because they appropriated the voice, the genre, and even the production schedule of the newsletter that they were asked to create. A second group of students—asked to write fact sheets for an anti–Gulf War organization—did not do as well, according to Bacon, because they supported the war and were thus unable to successfully inhabit the ethos of the organization. The problem here is not that Bacon is up front about the politics of writing partnerships but that she simply substitutes the CBO for the student and, in this way, evades the more challenging questions about social change: whether we ascribe authority to CBOs or to students, we still need to know how that authority translates into arguments that make a difference in institutional practices, governmental policy, public opinion, or some other sector of the public sphere.

To travel the path from discovery to outcomes, then, we need more than critical consciousness, community literacy, or an acculturation of CBO rhetoric. We need to know how the materiality of discourse intersects with human agency at unique, historical moments and produces changes that communities can really see. Or to put it plainly, we need a materialist rhetoric. Although I am not aware of any attempts to extend theoretical discussions of materialist rhetoric, which originated in departments of speech/communication, to the pedagogy of service learning in English departments, I believe it can be so extended and, in many ways, enriched by the practical challenges of teaching students how to position themselves on the ideological battleground of claims and warrants on public issues facing our communities. My case for materialist rhetoric, then, is not just a case for rhetorical activism in service learning but a case for rhetorical scholarship in the public sphere: a challenge to test the limits of rhetorical theory in the laboratory of community-based writing projects in order to generate new questions for rhetorical theory, rhetorical practice, and rhetorical education.

Materialist rhetoric raises the question of social change by extending the unit of analysis well beyond the text. Michael McGee, an early and influential figure here, says that in this formulation rhetoric is not a technique for producing or analyzing texts but "a natural social phenomenon in the context of which symbolic claims are made on the behavior and/or belief of one or more persons, allegedly in the interest of such individuals, and with the strong presumption that such claims will cause meaningful change" ("A Materialist's" 38). While this formulation of rhetoric clearly identifies it as "a species of coercion" (40), it does not define it as a neutral tool for the exercise of power. It is a form of power, itself. Celeste Michelle Condit and John Louis Lucaites explain that this is the case because in a democracy

> There is no dominant ideology that inexorably governs social and political action. Instead there is the rhetorical process of public argumentation in which various organized and articulate interest groups negotiate the problems of resource distribution in the collective life of the community, and there is a shared rhetorical culture out of which they all draw as they strive to express their particular interests. (xiv–xv)

Expression may take a variety of forms,[1] including narratives, characterizations, allusions, metaphors, and coded expressions, but ideographs dominate because, while they *appear* to "be drawn from ordinary language" and may also appear to express the speaker's intentions in an original way, they in fact "represent in condensed form the normative, collective commitments of the members of a public, and they typically appear in public argumentation as the necessary motivations or justifications for action performed in the name of the public" (xii–xiii). Ideographs are not full arguments, then, but ideological icebergs: the visible bump of what lies beneath. To analyze an ideograph is to take the ideological pulse of the community. In ordinary times, McGee explains, ideographs "remain essentially unchanged" ("The Ideograph" 431) and become "definitive of the society we have inherited" (430). "But when we engage ideological argument, when we cause ideographs to do work explaining, justifying, or guiding policy in specific situations, the relationship of ideographs changes" (434). What once were reliable signposts on the road of public discourse become blurry symbols of dissensus. Disagreements about an ideograph are not discrepancies over its formal properties but its formative power to contain our commitments, "as when awareness of racism" at mid century raised a "contradiction between [the ideographs of] 'property' and 'right to life' " in public debate over open housing (434). The contradiction between "property" and "right to life" was much more than a verbal dispute but a vigorous contest over actual properties, banking practices, neighborhood borders, and the physical safety of African Americans.

When the goal is to intervene in public discourse and social practices—to influence change in unfair housing practices, for example—academics are obviously on shaky ground. "Scholars are all analysts at heart," writes McGee in "Text, Context, and the Fragmentation of Contemporary Culture," "but nothing in our new [postmodern] environment is complete enough, finished enough to analyze" (75). What we have in the nonacademic world are not master texts that name our condition but "fragments of 'information' that constitute our *context*" (75). Successful rhetoricians here are not expert dissectors of texts but agile performers who cue their audience with a "dense reconstruction" of the fragments (70).

If McGee is right that in a postmodern world, the fragment packs more punch than the text, and we want our own work in the community to "cue" the audience in such a way that they will do something or even believe something, then it seems we need to stop doing criticism and start doing rhetoric. But how—and where—would we "do rhetoric"? And how would we know when we've done it well? McGee's materialism runs into trouble here because it juxtaposes rhetoric—a "natural social phenomenon"—with discourse—"an 'archeological' remnant" of that "larger phenomenon," rhetoric ("A Materialist's" 39). This enables McGee to clarify rhetoric as something more than a type of discourse but disables what Ronald Greene has called "an analytic search" for the "specific ways in which the techniques of power and the techniques of rhetoric intersect to regulate a population" (32). McGee's materialism, according to Greene, concerns itself too much with "the representational politics of practical reasoning" (30): it imagines power as a primordial force that is coded into language (into ideographs, narratives, and characterizations) and then decoded by analysts. Greene's take on materialism, which he bases on Althusser and Foucault, is that power does not well up in individuals who then code that force into words so much as it wells up in a "structure of signification" that "stabilizes meaning by distributing populations and institutions onto a terrain of a governing apparatus" (30). The difference here is that Greene's materialism shifts the burden of proof away from changes in public discourse—the publicity effect of rhetoric—and toward changes in institutional practices.

To illustrate how these concepts might be used in service learning and related community-based writing courses, I need to elaborate the way in which ideographs name ideological practices and illustrate the link between these "techniques of rhetoric" and "techniques of power." This will be done through a case study of public school reform in Chicago that began in the mid 1980s. The case study shows how "local control" and "accountability" functioned as ideographs in the public debate, enabling provocative characterizations of stakeholders and compelling narratives of change. After I show how "local control" and "accountability" were deployed in the 1980s and 1990s, I will then discuss a service learning project that I directed at the Illinois Institute of Technology in 2002 that used the same arguments for "local control" and "accountability" to advocate—unsuccessfully—for increased parent involvement in seven public schools on the South Side. In my analysis of this rhetorical failure—at best, a partial success—I explain how arguments for parent involvement were produced and received by parents in the community and why our attempts at rhetorical production were not supported by the kind of rhetorical analysis that I believe materialism can provide. I end by generalizing from the Chicago story an approach to service learning that would enable us to discover, evaluate, produce, and assess rhetorical interventions in the public sphere.

THE RHETORIC OF SCHOOL REFORM IN CHICAGO, 1988–1995

At the heart of the school reform controversy in Chicago are competing constructions of how change occurs and who has the authority to change an institution. "Local control," I argue below, functioned as an *ideograph*, warranting a multiclass and multirace coalition of parents, activists, politicians, and academics to *characterize* parents as capable political actors and to *narrate* school reform as a bottom-up, revolutionary process of infusing the system with parents' common sense and compassion for their children. Mechanisms of control made available to parents by the Illinois State Legislature in 1988 included the power to direct school policy, to fire/hire the principal, and to approve (or veto) the school budget.

Unaccustomed to seeing these technologies of power as anything other than the substance of their own professional privilege, many school administrators actively resisted the 1988 law. After seven years of protracted struggle wagered in the courts, the schools, the media, and in the legislative process, a new law was passed in 1995 that recentralized the system. The main premise of the new law was that professionals know best how to run the schools and professionals needed to be accountable to the mayor. What we see in this seven-year controversy, then, is not rational deliberation about how to improve the schools but what Kendall Philips, in another context, has called the "struggle for dominance" in public rhetoric, which attempts to "dislocate or disorient dominant systems of discourse" and often succeeds by threatening "decorum, assumptions, and [the] subject positions of opponents."

To understand why "local control" and "accountability" emerged as viable ideographs in the controversy, we need to look at the material conditions at CPS during the years leading up to the legislation. And these conditions are grim. According to G. Alfred Hess, an educational researcher and proponent of reform, half of all minority, low-income students in Chicago were over-age in the 1980s, having been retained in grade school at least once; only one in three high school seniors could read at national norms; and the dropout rate was 56 percent—as high as 67 percent in the inner city (Hess, *Restructuring* 16–18, 34). It was this school system that then U.S. Secretary of Education William Bennett famously characterized as the "worst in America," following the release of *A Nation at Risk* (Banas and Byers 1). And it was the publicity of the comment, as opposed to Bennett's solution (vouchers, back to the basics), that generated the most controversy in Chicago. The *Chicago Tribune* amplified Bennett's criticism with a series of reports on students' experiences in failing schools:

> The majority of Chicago high school students are consigned to dilapidated, mostly segregated neighborhood schools serving a course of study that prepares them neither for college nor the world of work. They are the discards in a three-tiered system of wildly inconsistent quality, a system of educational triage that results in a separate and unequal education for the city's 111,891 high school students. (Goozner, Norris, and Griffin 11)

At stake in the public outcry, however, was not just the poor performance of the students or the poor conditions of the buildings, but the poor performance of the administrators and teachers. Hess shows that roughly half of the elementary schools awarded federal, antipoverty money did not receive their allocations from the Central Board of Education. The money had been illegally diverted by the board to fund operating costs, including some administrative positions (Hess, *School* 146). Reformers also characterized administrators as uncaring or inept when they reported that the Chicago Public Schools (CPS) "regularly short-changed their students through 20% shorter subject periods, chaotic classrooms, and phantom study halls" (Hess, *Restructuring* 21) and had misclassified 7,000 (of 12,000) students as "educationally mentally retarded," triple the rate of other large urban school systems such as New York or Los Angeles (Designs for Change). These allegations characterized the central bureaucracy as out of control and unresponsive to student needs. The main target for school reform, then, was the Central Board of Education. Or as Bennett put it when asked where to begin with reforming Chicago's schools: "Explode the blob" (Banas and Byers 1).

When confronted with allegations of corruption or mismanagement— these negative characterizations of his staff and facilities—Superintendent Manford Byrd reacted defensively, saying that researchers and reporters were just trying to "trash" CPS (Hess, *Restructuring* 21). Byrd also rationalized poor student achievement, pointing helplessly to all the low-income students with which he had to contend. Or, as Hess puts it, Byrd adopted a strategy of blaming the victim and, in so doing, set an example of lowered expectations that contradicted research on effective schools (21). Capitalizing on the public's discontent with CPS, Mayor Harold Washington, Chicago's first black mayor, created the Parents Community Council (PCC): a committee that would guarantee ordinary citizens a voice in the emerging reform debate. The move was popular: a thousand citizens showed up for a meeting designed to accommodate five hundred (Hess, *School* 69). Washington also encouraged business leaders to join the PCC in a coalition that would push for site-based management at the state legislature. Business leaders committed to decentralized structures and "horizontal" management techniques responded well to the mayor's invitation. But these moves were seen as controversial in the black community; they challenged not only the authority of Byrd and the president of the Chicago Teachers Union (both of whom were black) but also the authority of established leaders in the black community, who were bypassed by the mayor.

It is worth pointing out here that the issue was not so much what to do for the schools but who had the authority to do it. In order to establish the legitimacy of the "local control" and its cognate "site-based management," reformers had to seize the exigency created by the mismanagement and poor performance of CPS and negatively characterize the board as incapable, insensitive, and corrupt. This made room for positive characterizations of business leaders as progressive purveyors of good management techniques and parents as people of common sense and compassion. It also made room for a range of narratives on how to improve each school—a distrust of top-down programs for change. As I mentioned earlier, the main vehicle for making parents visible as political actors in school governance was the local school council (LSC). Seats on the LSC had to be won in a political campaign, but the structural design of the councils gave parents the majority vote. As the activist researcher Don Moore explained, "because school staff are more assertive and more familiar with educational issues, parents and community must have a numerical majority of council seats to hold a rough equivalence of power" (147). The assumption here is that legislators can empower parents by leveling the political playing field and, in this way, encourage democratic deliberation.

The politics of "local control," however, quickly became apparent. As Hess explains in *Restructuring Urban Schools*, for all intents and purposes, devolving authority (and resources) down to the local level meant supporting schools that were either 100 percent black and poor or some combination of black and other minority groups. The intention, however, was not to create racial division but to rearticulate Johnson-era liberalism and civil rights activism during the era of Ronald Reagan. Critics of "local control," however, did not quite see it this way. To them, "local control" meant a return to the folly of "maximum feasible participation" and the paradox of state-sponsored "community action."[2] Because the law did not advocate forced integration through busing, a change in the relationship between property taxes and school funding, or preferential treatment for African Americans over other large minority groups (such as Latinos), these criticisms were not easily substantiated. Racism and classism played a part in the controversy, nonetheless, when the dean of a local school of education in Chicago characterized the boldness of the '88 reform law as the equivalent of "giving the keys of the asylum to the inmates" (Hess, *Restructuring* 22), a comment that—given the high proportion of black inmates in Illinois and in the nation—could hardly be interpreted as race neutral.

Other concerns were raised about the legal rights and moral authority of parents. Lieberman, writing a year after the reform law was implemented, questioned the logic behind the preference afforded to "parents" in the legislation.

> Why a biological parent who never showed the slightest interest in his
> offspring is accorded a preferred legal status over other citizens escapes
> me. . . . In many families, in-laws or friends play the role which parents
> play in idealized, two parent families, but such caring individuals are
> relegated to 2nd class citizenship. A fourteen-year-old mother has the
> legal right to be a member of the LSC but not someone who has effec-
> tively raised children in a healthy environment in some other school. It is
> difficult to understand how or why anything so preposterous on its face
> could be politically viable. (28)

Lieberman takes issue with the positive characterization of parents not because he wants to dismiss their potential but because he wants to extend the
material resources made available by the legislation to other caregivers in a
family. Others took a less-nuanced view. One teacher, in a questionnaire about
reform, wrote that "it is difficult to imagine a sudden parental competence or
educational interest" emerging as a result of reform (Hess, *Restructuring* 88).
But to Moore, the reform legislation was designed to address exactly this sort
of negative characterization or low expectation of parents.

> It does not take an advanced degree in education to recognize, for ex-
> ample, that a school cannot follow up on absent students if it doesn't
> have an accurate attendance-taking system, that outsiders roaming the
> halls without challenge pose a threat to student safety, that late buses rob
> children of learning time, and that leaky roofs and long delays in the
> arrival of textbooks make it difficult to teach. (150)

In this passage, Moore narrates the process of school reform as a process of
rational deliberation that cuts against differences in status (e.g., the difference
between having or not having "an advanced degree in education"). Rational
people can solve school problems provided they have the right tools to do it.
In the short run, Moore and his coalition of reformers were successful. A
major push by the business community succeeded in generating candidates
to run for the LSCs and getting parents to come out and vote for the candidates (Hess, *School* 178; *Restructuring* 57). Early assessments about reform
made reference to these election results in order to claim that "local control"
could work.

A few years later, however, voter turnout and candidate applications both
dropped and student achievement remained stagnate. One of the ways of
empowering parents was to train them to participate in LSC meetings. Yet in
the years following the 1988 legislation, the Central Board of Education held
back the reallocated federal money that was supposed to go to the local school
councils, reserving it instead for a raise in teacher salaries. This had a dramatic effect on the ability of councils to function, as one reformer recalled in
an interview with Stephanie Chambers.

> Think about what happened in 1988. We (black community activists) fi-
> nally had some say in the schools. But the legislation came back revenue
> neutral. So you had all these really interested parents who felt the energy,

and they were elected to LSCs. Many of them had no experience with budgets or curriculum or hiring a principal because they'd never been invited in the past to do these things. Without the money for training and because the system was in bad shape in terms of money, it seemed as if they wanted us to fail. That way the blame could be placed on these unqualified, undereducated activists. (655)

In addition to being stonewalled by the Central Board of Education, reformers had to contend with a lawsuit by the Chicago Principal's Association (CPA) challenging LSC authority to fire principals. The lawsuit reinforced existing perceptions about the racial politics of reform when news reports played up situations in which black LSCs had fired white principals and replaced them with black principals (Hess, *Restructuring* 72–73). A closer look at the actual operation of LSCs also raised doubts about the very possibility of open deliberation at LSC meetings. While one quarter of the LSCs appeared to be engaged in group problem solving, closer to half appeared to be engaged in "consolidated principal power" and the remaining one quarter seemed to have changed not at all (Bryk, Sebring, Kerbow, Rollow, and Easton 83). Since the reform process had not targeted particular changes in the curriculum, it has likewise been difficult to link changes in school governance to academic achievement (Shipps, Kahne, and Smylie). Or, to put it another way, the reform movement was, in 1995, vulnerable to a rollback by the new mayor, Richard M. Daley.

In order to effect this takeover of CPS, the mayor had to limit the financial and governmental responsibilities of the LSCs in the name of increased "accountability." Because the rhetoric of "local control" was already well established among educators and politicians, however, the new legislation advocating "accountability" could not just get rid of the LSCs. It had to work indirectly to strip them of their powers. This was achieved by dissolving the Central Board of Education, creating a new "management team" that reported directly to the mayor, and reclaiming control of the federal money that had been lost under reform. With control of top management and the budget, the mayor could dissolve LSCs it deemed ineffective or unaccountable and reverse their decisions on sensitive issues such as hiring/firing of principals (Shipps, Kahne, and Smylie).

In these ways, the new management team effectively gutted the governing powers of LSCs without challenging rhetorical consensus about the value of "local control." Publicly, the administration continued to support the LSCs. Dan Weissmann quotes Paul Vallas, then chief academic officer of CPS, as saying, "We respect them, we work with them, and they add an awful lot of value to the system, and that's our official position. That's the way it is." However, long-time Bronzeville community activist Sakoni Karanja contends that's the way it is "as long as [councils] don't act up. As long as we act like we don't know what we're doing, they're comfortable with us. But the minute we start acting like a democracy, calling things into question, that's when LSCs become targets." Or as one member of the administration frankly put it to Chambers, "The administration would like to eliminate LSCs. What would be ideal is to have LSCs like the reconstituted LSCs, because they have no power. They are more advisory boards" (Chambers 661).

Having recharacterized parents as subordinates in the structure of signification governing school resources, the mayor's coalition could go on to narrate a different link between reform and academic achievement. Where the 1988 law deliberately resisted standardized curricula and benchmarks, the 1995 law pressured teachers into using "scripted lesson plans" (Shipps, Kahne, and Smylie). They also instituted high-stakes testing, with remedial summer school or grade-retention as the punishment for those who scored poorly. Daley and Vallas have argued that these changes have resulted in Chicago's steady (but incremental) improvements in test scores. Reform advocates argue the opposite position using the same evidence. They claim that improvements in academic achievement are a result of the decentralization process that began in 1988 (Bryk, Sebring, Kerbow, Rollow, and Easton). Either way, the academic improvements are not considered by educational researchers to be substantial.[3] What is substantial is that the 1988 law did not just articulate a preference for "local control" in public education but collective commitments to minority empowerment and self-determination. The significance of the 1995 law, from a materialist perspective, then, is that it challenged those commitments and, for the most part, succeeded by characterizing LSCs as inefficient or unaccountable and characterizing the mayor's management team as efficient and accountable; by narrating school reform in terms of efficiency instead of equality.

LOOKING FOR "LOCAL CONTROL" IN 2002: THE PROJECT ON PARENT INVOLVEMENT

This is not to suggest that "local control" is dead. The mechanism of the local school council is still there, and the schools are still failing to improve. All that's needed is community organizing. Or so it seemed to the staff at Urban Matters when they set out to increase parent involvement in the South Side neighborhood of Bronzeville by partnering with students at the Illinois Institute of Technology (IIT). The project, which we called Community Leadership in Bronzeville Public Schools, was a two-semester course conducted in the spring and fall of 2002, with roughly a dozen students each semester. Mrs. Brown, the African American Director of Urban Matters,[4] coordinated a half dozen community organizers and one education consultant for the project. The goal during the first semester was to persuade community residents to run for seats in LSC elections at six elementary schools and one high school. During the second semester, which I focus on here, the goal was to drum up support for an umbrella organization—a parents' union, we called it—that would advocate for improvements in all seven schools.[5]

It is not hard to see why the premise of "local control" and the mechanism of the LSC would be appealing to a nonprofit organization that, according to its mission statement, aims "to transform extremely low-income African American communities through leadership development" in the

Afrocentric tradition. "Local control" warrants a grassroots effort to narrate social change from the bottom up. It characterizes even the most significantly marginalized people as capable political actors. Urban Matters likewise locates itself within an Afrocentric philosophy of "Nguzo Saba" (or, the "seven pillars of strength") that values (among other things) *Umoja* (unity) and *Kujichaugulia* (self-determination). These values resonate especially well with the ideograph of "local control": Practicing Umoja means "guiding critically needed investments by the community's own vision"; believing in Kujichaugulia means believing that "cultural identity is necessary for any group to mobilize on its own behalf." These two pillars of Nguzo Saba foreground that side of "local control" that calls upon African Americans to narrate a culturally empowering process of change that comes from the lived experience of their people.

It is not hard to see why Urban Matters would welcome the assistance of even non-African American college students. For while Urban Matters does profess an Afrocentric philosophy of community development, they also point out in their mission statement "African-centeredness does not suggest cultural exclusionism." They recognize the importance of coalition-building across racial and economic lines in much the same way the school reform movement discussed above succeeded primarily as a racially and economically diverse group of parents, politicians, activists, and academics. This relationship with Urban Matters was developed in a previous service learning project that I organized to document styles of successful leadership in public housing. In that project, students interviewed graduates of Urban Matters's leadership training course and created portraits of them as community leaders, which were later used to help the organization document their impact in the community.[6] Community Leadership in Bronzeville Public Schools grew out of this project but also departed from it in significant ways by involving the students directly in the practice of leadership. Instead of doing research on the community so that others could make effective presentations to funders, students "did rhetoric" alongside their community partners.

Before I explain what the students and their community partners actually did to increase parent involvement in the schools, however, I should say something about IIT and the surrounding neighborhood of Bronzeville, since the conditions at the institute and in the neighborhood are highly relevant to my analysis of our rhetorical intervention. Although IIT does not have an official service learning program, English majors, or even a critical mass of students and faculty in the humanities or social sciences, it does have an Office of Community Development[7] that links faculty and students with service opportunities in the community and an Interprofessional Research Program (IPRO) housed in the undergraduate college. The IPRO program "engages multidisciplinary teams of students in semester-long undergraduate projects based on real-world topics from sponsors that reflect the diversity of the workplace: corporations, entrepreneurial ventures, nonprofit organizations, and government agencies."[8] Because IIT is a technical university, most of the IPROs tend to address technical problems in engineering or science for corporate sponsors. However, a small group of "community connections" projects are offered each semester for nonprofit organizations that address issues such as economic development, public education, and health care.

Bronzeville, the South Side neighborhood in Chicago that was once filled with many black-owned businesses and characterized favorably at mid-century as the site of the second Harlem Renaissance, is today filled with public housing developments. Nearby the poor African Americans living in these developments are middle-class, white, and international students and faculty at IIT as well as a middle-class network of African American community organizers and nonprofit organizations. Because the boundaries between IIT and the community are distinct, incoming students are advised not to walk on certain streets and to avoid whole areas—and the boundaries are rarely crossed. The IPRO program facilitated border crossing but also focused expectations narrowly on problem solving in the "real world." Students who sign up for IPROs sign up with the understanding that these are not courses driven by assigned readings, lectures, or prearranged writing assignments—they are research projects driven by the client's needs. In this case, those needs were discussed by me and Mrs. Brown before the semester began. I then wrote them into the syllabus and gave them to students.

> The goal of this semester's project is to assist our client in creating an agenda for school reform in conjunction with the LSC's of seven of Bronzeville's public schools. Each newly elected LSC member needs to lionize parent/constituency support for reform, ideally around a set of curricular, financial, or policy issues. Our main goal is to assist these LSC members get a better handle on school reform issues—to develop a practical way of talking about it so they can better address their constituents. Once each LSC has generated support for reform, Mrs. Brown and I hope that they will go on to create a parents union: an independent network of parents and community organizers working in concert with the local school councils (LSCs) to improve all Bronzeville public schools.

In their final report on the project, the students explained how they translated these goals into a workload that they could all share.

> The group [of twelve students] was divided into three teams to conduct research on each of the schools. The initial groups were focused on the political, social, and educational aspects that govern the schools. After many hours of research were completed, each person was assigned to one of the schools, to do more specific research into that school's particular problems. A meeting was then organized with Urban Matters in the hopes of encouraging parents to play an active role in their schools.

At one of these organizing meetings attended by parent volunteers and several newly elected LSC members, the needs of the emerging union were identified—e.g., the need for a name, the need for a mission statement, the need to identify advocacy issues at each school—and, where appropriate, these needs were translated into writing tasks for the students. Representative tasks included creating fact sheets on each of the seven target schools for the LSC members to use as talking points with parents; a visioning statement on the union itself; the naming and graphical representation of the union; a guidebook for parents of school-age children; a PowerPoint presentation on how to read and interpret a school budget; and flyers, posters, even magnets advertising upcoming union meetings. Urban Matters set the schedule for completing the documents, provided feedback on the drafts, and shared responsibility for the cost and distribution of the final copies.

Two documents in particular were widely circulated in the community—the brochure about the union and the flyers advertising union meetings. These texts made indirect use of "local control" and "accountability"—the two ideographs that formed the backbone of the rhetorical controversy discussed above. Although we did not name these terms ideographs or evaluate their careers, the terms nonetheless enabled us to characterize parents as capable and compassionate and to narrate school reform as a process of holding teachers and administrators accountable to the process of shared governance made legal in 1988.

In the three-fold brochure that we designed to announce the union and its mission (Figure 16–1), the argument for "local control" can be discerned in the name, "Parent's Organization Working for Educational Responsibility, for our kids." In choosing this name, participants at the organizing meeting (parents, students, Urban Matters staff) sought to emphasize the autonomy

FIGURE 16–1   Outside Section of the Brochure *POWER, For Our Kids*

of parents, (it would be *their* organization, not Urban Matters's organization) as well as the parents' interest in holding educators "accountable" (to be *responsible* for providing a quality education). These claims for "control" and "accountability" were made more immediate by the tagline "for our kids," scrawled in a graffiti-style font. The long and somewhat prosaic name was made memorable, then, both graphically and by its acronym: "POWER, For Our kids."

The inside section of the brochure (Figure 16–2) likewise emphasized the need for solidarity. It presented the organization not as a solution provider but as a forum for discovering solutions. For example, in a section called "Visions for the Future" the platform for POWER is presented in a series of "We must" statements, such as "We must gain knowledge about the legal and financial aspects of the schools within our community." Importantly, these statements did not specify a timetable for achieving specific reform goals, because Mrs. Brown's intent was not to impose an agenda on the parents but to build unity around a set of shared principles, including the value of controlling school governance and finance, the need for new educational resources, and the importance of holding educators and administrators accountable for action or inaction on behalf of their children. The brochure thus established a need for "local control" by affirming the capacity of parents to deliberate among themselves about what's right for their children and to advocate with others in positions of power.

FIGURE 16–2   Inside Section of the Brochure *POWER, For Our Kids*

Not surprisingly, the brochure was approved by Urban Matters and mailed to community residents along with a notice of the first POWER meeting. Attendance at that next meeting, however, was disappointingly low: the IPRO students outnumbered the parents 2 to 1. Part of the problem was logistical. As the students explain in their final report on the project, "Mrs. Brown had a mailing list for three hundred parents, which we heavily relied upon. Later, we found that the list was not updated. As a result, not all parents received the brochures that advertised the date of the next POWER meeting." Subsequent analysis of the recruitment problem during class meetings with Mrs. Brown, however, raised the possibility that the brochure presented a problem as well. Mrs. Brown felt that the brochure's diction was too formal and that some of the information it contained might have been better presented in bullet points. To remedy this situation, the students decided to change the style and substance of the advertising campaign. When the next POWER meeting was chosen, students created a series of flyers and posters about the organization and hand-distributed them in the community. Figure 16–3 represents this phase of the project. The flyers and posters took a more aggressive stance on the rhetorical strategy of empowerment, challenging parents to form a "united front to fight the corruption in our schools and the unjust treatment of our children." While the visual representation of the union changed somewhat, the major change was in this negative characterization of the school system.

FIGURE 16–3   Back-side of Flyer Advertising an Organizing Meeting for POWER, For Our Kids

Parents, are you concerned about the education your child is receiving in the Chicago Public School System?
Think about it...

Should our public schools have 12 year-olds in the 3rd grade?
They do.

Should they carelessly place our kids in Special Ed. without notifying parents? **They are.**

Should students who have passed 5th grade have to retake it jst because there isn't a 6th grade teacher available? Ridiculously enough, **they are.**

Should our schools be claiming that our children are incapable of learning while they are dumbing down the curriculum? **They are.**

Should our schools be claiming that they cannot afford to improve when they never seem to have trouble funding excessive standardized testing and faculty pay raises? **They are.**

Should our schools be complaining about staff shortages when we, as parents, are no longer welcome to even set foot inside the classroom, let alone volunteer? **They are.**

Do you want to ensure that your child is getting the quality education that he or she deserves?

Well, you're not alone...

The back of the flyer offered several reasons for forming a united front against CPS. Parents generated these reasons at POWER meetings, and the students transformed them into a series of provocative questions to be answered in the negative: "Should our students who have passed fifth grade have to retake it just because there isn't a sixth-grade teacher available?" This question was based on the experience of one irate parent in Bronzeville whose child was asked to repeat fifth grade due to a teacher shortage. (She transferred the child to another school.) Similar abuses reported at these meetings included inappropriate retention of students (twelve-year-olds who were still in the third grade); the careless diagnosis of learning disabilities and subsequent placement of students into special education programs without parental notification; a curriculum driven by standardized tests; and hostility toward parent volunteers.

In addition to posting the flyers in storefronts and train stations, students went to all seven of the schools to hand them out to parents. In their final report, they explain what happened on those days:

> While passing out the flyers at each school, we found that there was an immediate reaction by the school. Some schools said we should have called them ahead of time to arrange a date for distribution, and some IPRO members were told to only pass out flyers outside of school grounds. In other schools, we were better received, and in the case of one school, they even gave one member a tour of their parent's resource room. Overall, we found mixed reactions from the school and faculty about our presence at the schools.

Unfortunately, this second advertising campaign also failed to boost attendance at the next meeting, and it soon became unclear to the students and the handful of parents who did attend these meetings regularly what POWER might actually accomplish. In their final report, the students discussed how these circumstances changed the work of the project during the second half of the semester:

> Due to the lack of parent participation some of our IPRO team members took a more direct approach with their respective schools. This included going to one of the school's LSC meetings and obtaining a copy of the Minutes of the last meetings and, in another case, speaking directly with the principal on the phone. At a previous POWER meeting we had found that all LSC parents present had not received or ever read a copy of the *Handbook of Model Rules of Procedure for Meetings for Chicago Local School Councils* [a document the principal was required to give them]. Parents were also not aware of how the *No Child Left Behind Act (NCLB)* affects their respective school. As a result, several projects by our IPRO team were started in order to address these issues including a report on NCLB and a resource book for LSC members.

While these projects gave the students a sense of purpose and were applauded by the staff at Urban Matters, they could also be seen as a retreat from rhetorical work in the community: a substitution of public advocacy with behind-the-scenes writings that, however educational, were quite easy to file away and ignore. Who, after all, was on hand to read them?

This is not to suggest that no advocacy took place during the semester and nothing positive happened as a result of our collaboration with Urban Matters. At one POWER meeting, a school uniform issue emerged. The parent leading the discussion explained that the principal had forbidden the boys to wear their hair in braids and that her son, who had long hair, was now wearing it in an Afro. The mother questioned the principal's reasoning that seemed to imply that "messy" hair is better than clean braids, as she put it. The principal's argument that braids were a sign of gang affiliation was dismissed by the parents in the room, and the parents resolved to go to the next LSC meeting to confront the principal. The small-group campaign to change the policy was short and successful: parents made a brief presentation at the LSC meeting and convinced the principal to rescind her decree. And then the semester ended.

A MATERIALIST ANALYSIS OF THE PROJECT

Because we had set out to organize seven schools around substantive issues related to parental involvement, it was disappointing both to the students and the staff of Urban Matters that only one issue emerged at the very last minute after all of that work. Lee Artz, who has organized service learning projects on the North Side of Chicago through the Department of Communication at Loyola University, has argued that, in situations like this, "students working with social service agencies experience" less "the reality of the disadvantaged" and more "the constraints on the agencies." Admittedly, Urban Matters was understaffed and, in some ways, unprepared for the task of organizing a school reform project of this scale. But IIT was also constrained by its mission as a technical institute and its lack of a critical mass of students in such fields as urban planning or rhetoric. It would be too easy, however, to simply conclude that a different CBO group and a different university, perhaps one with English majors, could have achieved more than we achieved. What really went wrong in the project was that the students and staff were thrust into rhetorical production—coming up with good arguments for "local control"—before they had done any rhetorical analysis.

By failing to analyze "local control" and "accountability" within the history of the school reform movement, we failed to discover the most probable means of persuading parents to get more involved in their children's education. Moreover, we assumed a style and substance of involvement—attending organizing meetings, working with LSCs, etc.—that was either unrealistic or irrelevant to the life experiences or priorities of the parents. This limited us to the most obvious pathways into the public sphere and the most difficult measures of tracking our work. The students were always looking for more direct measures of their impact: increased numbers at POWER meetings, innovative leadership from LSC members, and the identification of a broader range of curricular or budgetary issues to address. Yet because our evaluation of "local control" only emerged *in situ*, we had neither the insight nor the capacity to recommend alternative rhetorical strategies much less alternative ways of tracking their impact. All we could do was redouble our efforts, which only widened the gap that we now all saw between the rhetoric and the reality of "local control" in 2002.

The problem that the students faced, in other words, was that they had not been taught to read public discourse as an historical project. Nor had they been taught how to discern the link between techniques of rhetoric and techniques of power. Rhetoric becomes powerful when it articulates hegemonic consensus *and* manages to use that consensus as a lever to pull down material resources. Our project was instructive, in that regard, because it managed a partial success: in the first semester (not discussed here), all seven of the schools with which we collaborated had contested LSC elections and most of the newly elected LSC representatives were elected on account of Urban Matters and the IPRO students. Arguments for "local control" had produced seats on the local school councils: techniques of rhetoric had been connected to techniques of power in CPS. The difficulty came about in the second semester when we assumed that these LSC representatives in fact constituted a base of support or a resource for leadership in the schools.

As I suggested above in my discussion of Daley's takeover of CPS in 1995, "accountability" did not succeed by openly challenging hegemonic consensus surrounding "local control." It chipped away instead at the governing powers of the LSCs, making a seat on the LSC about as powerful as a seat at the train station. What changed, as a result of the Daley/Vallas intervention in 1995, then, was not so much hegemonic consensus about reform but the less visible structure of signification governing the apparatus of CPS: administrative posts, supplemental budget, curricular policy, and so on. Had we studied these structural changes in power, which now favored a discursive formation of "accountability," we would have most likely discovered alternative pathways into the public debate. We then would have understood why our ability to win LSC elections one semester did not automatically translate into the ability to do much more. This, in turn, would have prompted a discovery of alternative methods for persuading parents to take a more active role in their children's education based on "accountability" and "local responsibility," ideographs now dominant in Chicago school reform.

Preliminary evidence that rhetorical criticism of ideographs can improve the design and delivery of service learning projects comes from an analysis of the third semester of the project, where I shifted the rhetorical work away from "local control" of the schools and toward the "local responsibility" of parents, teachers, and administrators to create programs to address student achievement. From a tactical point of view, this shift entailed working with another CBO that took a less adversarial approach to community organizing and establishing a partnership with fewer and more needy schools, in particular, those facing punitive action as a result of the recently passed No Child Left Behind (NCLB) law. By shifting the rhetorical work of the project away from "local control" of the schools and toward the "local responsibility" of all stakeholders in public education, we have made public advocacy less glamorous but also less risky. Instead of appealing to parents as disenfranchised political actors who need to organize *against* something, we have created the conditions in which members of the community, the schools, the university, and the nonprofit world can organize *for* something.

So far, this approach has gotten results. Initial contact with the principals at our two target schools quickly escalated into formal meetings with the teachers, staff, and parents to brainstorm appropriate programs for parent involvement. For the students, this necessitated field work at the schools—meeting with the stakeholders and determining their needs and current resources—and collaborative research online and in the library to discover what sort of parent involvement programs work in low-income, African American communities. Their work culminated in a set of recommendations for each school, formal, group-written reports that were reviewed by our community sponsor and the two schools, revised, and approved.[9]

THE CASE FOR MATERIALIST RHETORIC IN SERVICE LEARNING

It could be argued, of course, that in hindsight, our vision is always perfect—that a materialist analysis of the project certainly clarifies what went wrong but does not necessarily translate into a pedagogy. In the remainder of this essay, then, I want to elaborate my pedagogical framework of discovery, analysis, production, and assessment and show how it can be used to identify reasonable measures of change.

Discovering the arguments that already exist in the communities we wish to serve means listening closely to our community partners and corroborating what they have to say. Ideographs need to be traced to more than one person, more than one text, and more than one setting. Cognates of the ideograph need to be identified and distinguished as well, because they may signal a rift in consensus, as I have tried to illustrate in the overlap between "local control" and "local responsibility." This should not force us into unusual research methods or replace rhetorical production with criticism. We simply begin with the everyday texts made available through our partnerships in the community—newsletters, newspapers, meeting announcements and minutes, training programs—and use these to identify the key organizations, individuals, and arguments. As Wells reminds us, a public is an historical project. And many CBOs keep a paper trail of their projects. We need to find out who has been here before us and what they've argued before we propose doing anything new.

We need to do more than just identify ideographs, narratives, and characterizations, however. We need to link these and other techniques of rhetoric to techniques of power—to analyze how well public discourse has fared. The emphasis in our analysis, in other words, must remain on outcomes. In the last semester of the school reform project, for example, I did not say to students "we need to do an ideographic analysis of local responsibility" but that "we need to find out what sort of parent involvement programs work in low income, African American, urban communities (in general) and which ones might work here." The students did not know they were taking a materialist approach to rhetorical analysis, but they were. The broadness of the research task forced them to break down how "parent involvement" was constructed, rhetorically, in the research and how it might lead to desirable outcomes in Chicago, e.g., increased student achievement, decreased disciplinary referrals, etc.

In "The Rhetorician as an Agent of Social Change" Ellen Cushman (p. 235 in this volume) makes a parallel case for an outcomes-based approach to community writing projects that, perhaps, deliberately leaves the revolution to revolutionaries. She argues that we need to find ways of enabling people in under-served communities to "use language and literacy to challenge and alter the circumstances of daily life" (12). In her case, this meant writing documents with and for poor, African American women seeking changes in housing, employment, and other areas of their lives. She did not seek a sea-change in public policies affecting these women. She simply wanted to "facilitate actions" (14) for individuals in need; to perform, rhetorically with these citizens and learn from their performances.

It would be easy to draw a less hopeful conclusion about these kinds of collaborative, rhetorical performances, especially in light of the school reform controversy where rhetoric often felt like "a species of coercion," as McGee puts it, albeit one that is "comfortable" and obviously preferable to "a gun shoved in the ribs" (40). It would seem from this characterization of rhetoric that professors, college students, and small nonprofit groups are simply outgunned on the political battleground and should either get out of the way or go get a bigger gun. Such cynicism about the very idea of change would be unavoidable in a Foucaultian view of discursive regimes unattached to real agents. Knowing the agents and their constraints does not make intervening any easier. But a materialist approach to community-based writing projects does give us something concrete to work with, somewhere to begin.

Acknowledgments: I want to thank Linda Flower, David Fleming, and Nancy Welch, who read several versions of this manuscript. Their tough questions and generosity gave me good cause to revise and great strength in the process. I would also like to thank Cheryl Spivey-Perry at the Lugenia Burns Hope Center.

NOTES

1. See Condit *Decoding Abortion Rhetoric* for a full glossary of terms and definitions.
2. See Moynihan for a critique and Zarefsky for a rhetorical analysis of community involvement in the war on poverty.
3. See Shipps, Kahne, and Smylie for a discussion of substantial and insubstantial criteria.
4. The real name of this organization is the Lugenia Burns Hope Center, which is directed by Cheryl Spivey-Perry, and which I got permission to use only after this essay had already gone into production.
5. For more information on the two semesters of the project, see http://www.iit.edu/~coogan/service_learning.html.
6. See Coogan "Counter Publics in Public Housing" for a discussion of this project.

7. For more information on IIT's Office of Community Development, see http://www.iit .edu/~iitcomdev/.

8. For more information on the IPRO program, see http://ipro.iit.edu.

9. See http://www.iit.edu/~ipro303s03 to read the recommendations for increasing parent involvement in two of Bronzeville's public schools.

WORKS CITED

Artz, Lee. "Critical Ethnography for Communication Studies: Dialogue and Social Justice in Service-Learning." *The Southern Communication Journal* 66.3 (2001): 239–50.

Bacon, Nora. "Community Service Writing: Problems, Challenges, Questions." *Writing the Community: Concepts and Models for Service-Learning in Composition.* Ed. Linda Adler-Kassner, Robert Crooks, and Ann Watters. Washington, D.C.: American Association of Higher Education, 1997. 39–56.

Banas, Casey, and Devonda Byers. "Chicago's Schools Hit as Worst." *Chicago Tribune,* November 7, 1987. Edition: Sports Final. Page 1.

Bryk, Anthony S., Penny Bender Sebring, David Kerbow, Sharon Rollow, and John Q. Easton. *Charting Chicago School Reform: Democratic Localism as a Lever for Change.* Boulder, CO: Westview Press, 1998.

Chambers, Stephanie. "Urban Education Reform and Minority Political Empowerment." *Political Science Quarterly* 117.4 (2002/2003): 643–65.

Chicago Tribune. "How To Fix America's Worst Schools." Final Edition. May 29, 1988: Section 2. Editorial Page 2.

Condit, Celeste Michelle. *Decoding Abortion Rhetoric: Communicating Social Change.* Urbana: University of Illinois Press, 1990.

———. "Democracy and Civil Rights: The Universalizing Influence of Public Argumentation." *Communication Monographs* 54 (1987): 1–18.

Condit, Celeste Michelle, and John Louis Lucaites. *Crafting Equality: America's Anglo-African World.* Chicago: University of Chicago Press, 1993.

Coogan, David. "Counter Publics in Public Housing: Reframing the Politics of Service Learning." *College English* 67 (2005): 461–82.

Cushman, Ellen. "The Rhetorician as an Agent of Social Change." *College Composition and Communication* 47.1 (1996): 7–28.

Designs for Change. *Caught in the Web. Misplaced Children in Chicago's Classes for the Mentally Retarded.* Chicago, IL: Designs for Change, 1982.

Fleming, David. "Rhetoric as a Course of Study." *College English* 61.2 (1998): 169–91.

Goozner, Merrill, Michele L. Norris, and Jean Latz Griffin. "Chicago Schools: 'Worst In America': Tenth in a Series on the Chicago Public Schools, the System Called the Worst in the Nation by the Secretary of Education: System Can Make Cruelest Cut of All." *Chicago Tribune,* 25 May 1988. Sports Final Section: News Page: 11.

Greene, Ronald. "Another Materialist Rhetoric." *Critical Studies in Mass Communication* 15 (1998): 19–29.

Herzberg, Bruce. "Community Service and Critical Teaching." *College Composition and Communication* 45.3 (1994): 307–19.

Hess Jr., G. Alfred. *Restructuring Urban Schools: A Chicago Perspective.* New York: Teachers College Press, 1995.

Hess Jr., G. Alfred. *School Restructuring, Chicago Style.* Newbury Park, CA: Sage, 1991.

Lieberman, M. "A Brief Analysis of the Illinois Education Reform Act." *Government Union Review* 10.2 (1989): 23–30.

McGee, Michael. "The 'Ideograph': A Link between Rhetoric and Ideology." [*Quarterly Journal of Speech* 6 (1980): 1–16] *Contemporary Rhetorical Theory.* Ed. John Lucaites, Celeste Condit, and Sally Caudill. New York: Guilford, 1999. 425–40.

———. "Text, Context, and the Fragmentation of Contemporary Culture." [*Western Journal of Speech Communication* 54 (1992): 97–119] *Contemporary Rhetorical Theory.* Ed. John Lucaites, Celeste Condit, and Sally Caudill. New York: Guilford, 1999. 65–78.

———. "A Materialist's Conception of Rhetoric." *Explorations in Rhetoric: Studies in Honor of Douglas Ehninger.* Ed. Raymie McKerrow. Glenview, IL: Scott Foresman, 1982. 23–48.

Moore, Donald R. "The Case for Parent Involvement." *Empowering Teachers and Parents: School Restructuring Through the Eyes of Anthropologists.* Ed. G. Alfred Hess, Jr. Westport, CT: Bergin & Garvey, 1992. 131–55.

Moynihan, Daniel P. *Maximum Feasible Misunderstanding: Community Action in the War on Poverty.* New York, Free Press, 1969.

Peck, Wayne Campbell, Linda Flower, and Lorraine Higgins. "Community Literacy." *College Composition and Communication* 46.2 (1995): 199–222.

Philips, Kendall. "A Rhetoric of Controversy." *Western Journal of Communication* 63.4 (1999): 488–510.

Shipps, Dorothy, Joseph Kahne, and Mark A. Smylie. "The Politics of Urban School Reform: Legitimacy, City Growth, and School Improvement in Chicago." *Educational Policy* 13.4 (1999): 518–45.

Weissmann, Daniel. "Balancing Power." *Catalyst*, April 1998. Retrieved April 10, 2002, from <http://www.catalystchicago.org/news/index.php?item=1716&cat=35>.

Wells, Susan. "Rogue Cops and Health Care: What Do We Want from Public Writing?" *College Composition and Communication* 47.3 (1996): 325–41.

Zarefsky, David. *President Johnson's War on Poverty: Rhetoric and History.* Alabama: University of Alabama Press, 1986.

PART FOUR

The Ethics of Engagement

17 *The Rhetorician as an Agent of Social Change*

ELLEN CUSHMAN

In his "Afterthoughts on Rhetoric and Public Discourse," S. Michael Halloran finds that "the efforts of citizens to shape the fate of their community . . . would surely have been of interest to American neoclassical rhetoricians of the late eighteenth and early nineteenth centuries" (2). Unfortunately, he sees an "apparent lack of interest in such 'Public Discourse' among new rhetoricians of late twentieth-century English departments" (2). One way to increase our participation in public discourse is to bridge the university and community through activism. Given the role rhetoricians have historically played in the politics of their communities, I believe modern rhetoric and composition scholars can be agents of social change outside the university.

Some critical theorists believe that the primary means of affecting social change is to translate activism into liberatory classroom pedagogies. This paper seeks to address other ways in which we can affect social change, something more along the lines of civic participation. As Edward Schiappa suggests, "pedagogy that enacts cultural critique is important but it is not enough. . . . We should not allow ourselves the easy out of believing that being 'political' in the classroom is a substitute for our direct civic participation" (22). I agree. I hope here to suggest ways we can empower people in our communities, establish networks of reciprocity with them, and create solidarity with them. Using a self-reflexive rhetoric, I'll describe the limitations of my own role as a participant observer in a predominately Black (their term) neighborhood in a city in upstate New York. I hope to reveal a tentative model of civic participation in our neighborhoods which I believe illuminates some paradoxes in postmodern approaches to composition.*

From *College Composition and Communication* 47.1 (1996): 7–28.

*This paper is a multivoiced, self-reflexive look at our roles as rhetoricians. As such, I hope to turn our work as scholars inside out, upside down, back in upon itself. I've included many voices in this paper because this was the only way I seemed able to capture the range of reactions I've had to the theories and practices of critical pedagogues and cultural studies theorists—from initial enthusiasm to disillusionment to frustration and anger. And so I've organized this paper as a hall of mirrors. The central

Approaching the Community

One of the most pressing reasons why composition scholars may not work in the community has to do with deeply rooted sociological distances between the two. Many universities sit in isolated relation to the communities in which they're located—isolated socially and sometimes physically as well. Rensselaer, for example, where I'm a fourth year aPhiD candidate,# is isolated socially and physically from the community.

The Hudson borders Troy on the East, rolling hills on the West. Most of downtown developed along the river valley, while RPI expanded up one of these hills. People in the city generally call those associated with RPI "higher ups." Rensselaer students often call people in Troy "Troylets," "trash," or "low lifes." RPI was originally built closer to the city, beginning at the West edge of the valley, but for reasons too complicated to go into here, RPI expanded up the hill. The relationship between Rensselaer and Troy is best symbolized by the Approach, what used to be a monument of granite stairs, pillars, and decorative lights, but is now barely recognizable as a walkway.[1] (See Figure 17–1.)

The city gave the Approach to Rensselaer in 1907 as a sign of the mutually rewarding relationship between the two. Once an access way to the university on the hill, literally and figuratively, the stairway was pictured on many of the notebooks of students in the Troy City school district. Walk into any diner in the city and folks can remember the Approach pictured on their notebooks when they were growing up. Even in the late 1950s, students and city officials

---

image is the argument that rhetoricians can be agents of social change outside the university and a brief explanation of how this plays out in research. To create this image, I use a narrative voice to tell a story of possibility. The footnotes with various markers are the next set of mirrors and reveal more background for my argument. In these footnotes, I use a self-critical voice hoping that we will pause for a brief moment to examine our discourse. The numbered endnotes include the theorists I find most useful in reflecting my argument. Here I use an academic voice in a conscious effort to work within the system. Finally, we have the appendices. In these I don't want to cite specific authors because the onus to consider the ramifications of using critical discourse remains on all of our shoulders. Yours and mine. With these asides, I want to point to trends in the discourse I've heard at conferences and read in the work of many composition scholars. I've appended these, first, because they reflect the main argument by revealing my initial frustration and, many times, anger, which prompt this paper; and, second, because they're written from this anger, I risk being dismissed as inflammatory, a risk I hope to reduce by making them an aside; third, these asides have significant personal value to me. They're the best translation of my street-tough, face-breaking, fight-picking voice that I can manage for an academic audience. Given this activist research, my white trash history, and being only one pay check away from returning to the streets, I'm never very far from that voice, that way of being, no matter how many books, computers, students, and teachers I sit in front of.

#An aphid is a type of louse. So an aPHiD brings the "lo" together with "use." The plural of louse is lice. When I graduate, I'll have a License to create knowledge from the people I study. Do da. Do da.

FIGURE 17–1   View of "The Hill" and the Approach in the Early 1900s.

(Source: Institute Archives and Special Collections, Rensselaer Polytechnic Institute, Troy, NY)

FIGURE 17–2   Rensselaer Students Clean Up the Approach in 1959.

(Source: Institute Archives and Special Collections, Rensselaer Polytechnic Institute, Troy, NY)

worked together to maintain this connection as part of a "civic betterment project." (See Figure 17–2.)

Unfortunately, the Approach fell into disrepair during the early 1970s as a result of disagreements between the city and university about who should have responsibility for maintenance. Now angry graffiti, missing stairs, and overgrowth symbolize the tattered relationship between the city and RPI. (See Figure 17–3.) Young fraternity boys are rumored to use the Approach for initiation during rush week, and certain ski club members have skied down the

FIGURE 17–3   The Approach in 1995.

(Photo courtesy of Chris Boese.)

Approach as a testament to their ability and courage. While Troy natives look at the Approach in fury and disgust, the city and RPI continue to negotiate over its upkeep and hopeful repair.

I spend time describing this symbol of the relationship between the university and the city because I don't think this relationship is an isolated example of the sociological distance between the university and the community. It's precisely this distance that seems to be a primary factor in prohibiting scholars from Approaching people outside the university. Every day, we reproduce this distance so long as a select few gain entrance to universities, so long as we differentiate between experts and novices, and so long as we value certain types of knowledge we can capitalize on through specialization.[2] This history of professionalization might be one reason academics have so easily turned away from the democratic project that education serves to ensure— civic participation by well-rounded individuals.[3]

Malea Powell, an Eastern Miami and Shawnee Indian, suggests that the theorizing of academics necessitates a distance from the daily living of people outside academe, particularly those people we study. Although she's found "a location for healing in theory," she also knows these theories are used to "civilize unruly topics," with a similar assumption of manifest destiny that colonists use(d) to civilize unruly Native Americans. "Central to telling the 'American' story is the settlers' vision of the frontier, a frontier that is 'wilderness,' empty of all 'civilized' life." In order to colonize, the settlers denied the very existence of Turtle Island's original people. Powell sees that this denial, this un-seeing . . . characterizes our "American" tale. For the colonizers it was a necessary un-seeing; material Indian "bodies" were simply not seen . . . the mutilations, rapes, and murders that made up "the discovery" and "manifest destiny" were also simply not seen. Un-seeing Indians gave (and still gives) Euroamericans a critical distance from materiality and responsibility, a displacement that is culturally valued and marked as "objectivity."

Scholars reproduce this colonizing ideology when we maintain a distance from people. In search of an area of interest, we look to stake our claim over a topic, or in Powell's words, "define a piece of 'unoccupied' scholarly territory . . . which will become our own scholarly homestead." If the scholarly territory happens to be occupied by other scholarly endeavors, our job demands that we show how these original scholars fail to use their territory well, thereby giving us manifest justification for removing their theories from the territory through expansion, co-option, or complete dismissal. In some fundamental ways, we shirk our civil responsibility and always already enact violence under the guise of objective distance, and the thin veil of "creating" knowledge.

Powell (and I) "don't mean to disable scholarly work here." But I believe that in doing our scholarly work, we should take social responsibility for the people from and with whom we come to understand a topic. I'm echoing Freire who shows that when we theorize about the oppressed, we must do "authentic thinking, thinking that is concerned about *reality*, does not take place in ivory tower isolation, but only in communication" (64). Once we leave the classroom, we're again in ivory tower isolation, unless we actively seek our students in other contexts— particularly the community context.

Activism begins with a commitment to breaking down the sociological barriers between universities and communities. And if we see ourselves as both civic participants and as preparing students for greater civic participation, then activism becomes a means to a well defined end for Approaching the community. Recent work by Bruce Herzberg reveals one model for how rhetoricians can enter into the community. His thoughtful article on "Community Service and Critical Teaching" shows how he manages to link his writing courses with community agencies.

> The effort to reach into the composition class with a curriculum aimed at democracy and social justice is an attempt to make schools function . . . as radically democratic institutions, with the goal not only of making individual students more successful, but also of making better citizens, citizens in the strongest sense of those who take responsibility for communal welfare. (317)

I'm not asking for composition teachers to march into the homes, churches, community centers, and schools of their community. I'm not asking for us to become social workers either. I am asking for a deeper consideration of the civic purpose of our *positions* in the academy, of what we do with our knowledge, for whom, and by what means. I am asking for a shift in our critical focus away from our own navels, Madonna, and cereal boxes to the ways in which we can begin to locate ourselves within the democratic process of everyday teaching and learning in our neighborhoods. For the remainder of this paper, let me offer some brief considerations of what such activism might ideally entail, as well as some practical limitations of trying to live up to this ideal. For these considerations, I draw upon my own activist research in a primarily African-American inner city.

SHORT CHANGED

Most current accounts of activism in cultural studies don't do justice to social change taking place in day-to-day interactions. I think activism can lead to social change, but not when it's solely measured on the scale of collective action, or sweeping social upheavals. (See the appendix on "Slippery Discourse.") Rather, we need to take into our accounts of social change the ways in which people use language and literacy to challenge and alter the circumstances of daily life. In these particulars of daily living, people can throw off the burdens placed upon them by someone else's onerous behavior. In other words, social change can take place in daily interactions when the regular flow of events is objectified, reflected upon, and altered. Daily interactions follow regular patterns of behavior, what sociologist Anthony Giddens terms "routinization." These interactions result from every individual re-enacting the social structures that underpin behaviors. Giddens's notion of the "duality of structure" captures the ways in which individuals' behaviors manifest overarching social structures. When the routine flow of events is impeded or upset, we have an example of deroutinization—of what can be the first steps to social change on micro levels of interaction. I've found that people disrupt the status quo of their lives with language and literacy and that the researcher, when invited to do so, can contribute resources to this end.

For instance, Raejone, a 24-year-old mother of two, applied to a local university. As she composed her application essay, I offered some tutoring and access to Rensselaer computers. This was the first time she had applied to college. In another example, Lucy Cadens moved to a safer, suburban apartment complex. With my (and others') letters of recommendation, she obtained decent housing that accepts her Section 8. To facilitate the process of transferring her social services from one county to another, she asked me to complete a letter of certification which stated how many children she has in her new apartment. This is the first time Lucy has lived outside of the inner city. These precedents mark the very places where people deroutinize the status quo of wider society, together, during activist research.[4] Over the course of two and a half years of research, these people and I have worked together during numerous literacy events to create possibilities, the promising, if minute, differences in opportunity: together we've written resumes, job applications, college applications, and dialogic journals; when asked to do so, I've written recommendations to landlords, courts, potential employers, admissions counselors, and DSS representatives; one teen and I codirected a literacy program that allowed six children to read and write about issues important to them and that united resources from Rensselaer, Russell Sage College, the public library, and two philanthropic organizations. Since together we unite resources and grease the mechanisms of wider society institutions, all of these literacy acts carve possibilities from the routine ways these institutions, agencies, courts, and universities have historically worked in constraining ways.

I need to emphasize the difference between missionary activism, which introduces certain literacies to promote an ideology, and scholarly activism, which facilitates the literate activities that *already* take place in the community. For example, the Cadens' household had become too crowded with extended family. Lucy's daughter, Raejone, and her two children decided to seek housing from the philanthropic organization that rented to Raejone's mother. This agency had many units available and a short waiting list, but as the months passed, Raejone realized that her name never moved up the list. Her sisters also applied for housing but encountered similar foot dragging. Raejone found housing through a private landlord and then wrote a letter to this housing agency. In it she protested the inadequate treatment she received. Raejone and the directors of this housing program met to discuss the letter, and since then, Raejone's sisters have been offered housing by this agency. Raejone's letter caused the people who were simply reproducing their typical behavior to pause and consider the impact of their actions. In effect, the people in this housing program have altered the ways in which they treat Raejone and her family. Raejone, without any of my assistance, potently enacts her agency in order to challenge the routine foot dragging she faced.

Often this type of social change would be overlooked or underestimated with the emancipatory theories we currently use. Those who choose to say resistance only counts when it takes the form of overt and collective political action might describe us as using nothing more than coping devices with this literacy. Choosing to see this interaction in isolation, they may be correct; however, Scott reminds us that thousands of such " 'petty' acts of resistance have dramatic economical and political effects" (*Domination* 192). These daily verbal and literate interactions mark the very places where composition teachers can begin to look for the impact of our critical pedagogy and activism, both in the classroom and when we approach the community.[5]

RED ROBIN HOODS

If we view social change at a micro level of interaction, we can begin to see where activism fits into the particulars of daily living. Activism means accepting a civic duty to empower people with our positions, a type of leftist stealing from the rich to give to the poor. To empower, as I use it, means: (a) to enable someone to achieve a goal by providing resources for them; (b) to facilitate actions—particularly those associated with language and literacy; (c) to lend our power or status to forward people's achievement. Often we are in a position to provide the luxuries of literacy for people. Since we're surrounded with the tools for literacy all day long, we often take for granted the luxury of the time and space needed for our literacy events. We schedule our work days around papers we read and write; our research is often carried out in libraries—clean, well lit, with cubicles and desks to use as we silently mine books for information;✧ and we return to our homes or offices to trace out an idea with pen and paper or at the keyboard. Our time is devoted to reading and writing with spaces and institutional resources often provided for us. But when we approach the community, often we will be forced "to recall the material conditions of writing," to remember that "we do confront such complex material questions as how to provide equality of access to computers for word processing" (Gere 87).

The reading and writing used for individual development in many communities is a valued, scarce, and difficult endeavor. We may say to ourselves that reading and writing is more important than some daily worries, such as cleaning, taking care of children and grandparents, and cooking, but often one of the primary ways people build a good name for themselves outside of work is to be solid parents, providers, doers. Mike Rose reminds us in *Lives on the Boundary* as he describes Lucia, a returning student and single mother, and notes "how many pieces had to fall in place each day for her to be a student. . . . Only if those pieces dropped in smooth alignment could her full attention shift to" the challenges of literacy for her own development (185). In *All Our Kin*, Carol Stack also describes similar domestic demands which must take priority over time for oneself in order for people to maintain their social networks of reciprocity. In other words, before people can devote their time to reading and writing to improve themselves, their social and family duties must be in place. Many women in the neighborhood in which I am immersed say they "wish there were more than 24 hours in a day," or they qualify their literate goals with, "if I had time, I could study that driver's manual." Yet, for a researcher, seeing the need for time is only half of the equation; the other half is doing something about those needs.

Empowering people in part enables them to achieve a goal by providing resources for them. Since it's difficult for many of these women to clear time alone while they're at home, we often schedule one or two hours to be together during the week when they know they won't be missed. We've spent time in places where we have many literate resources at our disposal including bookstores, libraries, my apartment (not far from this neighborhood), as well as the Rensselaer computer labs and Writing Center. During these times we've cleared together, we've studied driver's manuals, discussed books, gone through the college application process, as well as worked on papers, resumes, and letters they wanted to write. Because we have worked together, these people who want time away from the neighborhood have achieved their literate goals.

✧ We mine data in our scholarly homeplots looking for a gem of an idea others will value.

Empowerment also happens when we facilitate people's oral and literate language use as well as lend our status for their achievement. The people in this neighborhood recognize the prestige of the language resources and social status I bring from Rensselaer and ask for assistance in a number of their language use activities.+ One woman had just received an eviction notice and asked me to "help [her] get a new place." She asked if we could practice mock conversations she might have with landlords over the phone. She thought this practice would "help [her] sound respectable, you know, white." As we practiced in her dining room, she wrote what we said on the back of a Chinese take-out menu for future reference. Once she set appointments to see an apartment, she contacted me so we could view the apartments together because "having you with me will make me seem respectable, you being from RPI and all." She differentiates between the social languages we speak and she wants to practice these languages with me.[6] She also identifies one way she can use my position for her own ends. She eventually got an apartment and thanked me for what she saw as my contribution. (See the appendix on "False Consciousness.") I've found that the luxury of literacy can easily be transferred from the university to our neighborhoods when we expand the scope of our scholarly activities to include activism. While empowerment may seem one sided, as though the scholar has a long arm of emancipating power, the people in communities can empower us through reciprocity.

MUCH OBLIGED

The terms governing the give-and-take (reciprocity) of involvement in the community need to be openly and consciously negotiated by everyone participating in activist research. As Bourdieu terms it, reciprocity describes a gift-giving and receiving behavior which can produce a mode of domination if the gift is not returned. "A gift that is not returned can become a debt, a lasting obligation" (126). Depending on the terms of the exchange, this obligation can either be in the form of a monetary debt, which imposes "overtly economic obligations by the usurer," or, in the form of an ethical debt, which produces "moral obligations and emotional attachments created and maintained by the generous gift, in short, overt violence or symbolic violence" (126). Reciprocity in exchange networks quickly produces power relations where the likelihood of oppression depends upon the terms of the giving and receiving.

While Bourdieu depicts reciprocity networks by studying the bonds maintained in relations between kin-people and tribal chiefs, this notion of reciprocity applies to the ways in which we enter into the community. With an idea of how exchanges create and maintain oppressive structures, activists can pay conscious attention to the power structures produced and maintained during their interactions with others outside of the university. Reciprocity

---

+ In addition to language resources, I make available many of my material resources: clothes, small amounts of money, food, and rides to the doctor, stores, and DSS offices.

includes an open and conscious negotiation of the power structures reproduced during the give-and-take interactions of the people involved on both
sides of the relationship. A theory of reciprocity, then, frames this activist
agenda with a self-critical, conscious navigation of this intervention.

Herzberg's work exemplifies reciprocity well when interpreted in terms
of the give-and-take relationship between the researcher and community.
Through a "service-learning program," students at Bentley became adult literacy tutors at a shelter in Boston and wrote about their experiences in Herzberg's composition classroom. At the outset, the rules were established for
what types of information could be exchanged between the tutor and learners. The students "were not allowed (by the wise rules of the shelter and good
sense) to quiz their learners on their personal lives and histories" (315). Before
these tutorial sessions began, the boundaries for exchange of information
were set. Students tutored, wrote, and received college credit; Herzberg gave
his time and energy, which eventually earned him a spot in this journal; and
although this article does not make clear what the people in the shelter received and gave from this involvement, he indicates "the tutoring, as best
[as they] could determine, appeared to be productive for the learners at the
shelter" (316). From his work, we begin to see how bridging the university
and community establishes give-and-take relationships that must be openly
and carefully navigated.

It may seem that the activist research I described in the previous section is
one-sided, that I may sound like a self-aggrandizing liberator of oppressed
masses. But this just isn't the case, since, these people empower me in many
ways. Referring back to my original definition of empowerment, they've enabled me to achieve a primary goal in my life: getting my PhD. They've let me
photocopy their letters, personal journals, essays, and applications. They've
granted me interviews and allowed me to listen to their interactions with
social workers, admissions counselors, and DSS representatives. They've told
me stories and given me the history of this area through their eyes. They've
fed me, included me in their family gatherings for birthdays and holidays,
and have invited me to their parties and cook outs. They've read my papers
and made suggestions; they listened to my theories and challenged them
when I was off mark. (See the appendix on "In Ivory Towers, We Overlook.")
As I write my dissertation, they add, clarify, and question. In some very important ways, we collaborate in this research. In fact, the two women whose
writing I refer to most frequently in this article, signed a release form so that
you may read about them today. To quote from the *CCC* "consent-to-reprint"
forms, Raejone and Lucy understood that they "will receive no compensation" for their work and that they "assign publishing rights for the contribution to NCTE, including all copyrights." They have given me the right to
represent them to you and have facilitated my work in doing so. They've also
lent me their status. They've legitimized my presence in their neighborhood,
in masque, and in some institutions simply by associating with me. Through
reciprocity, they've enabled me to come closer to achieving my goal every
day; they've facilitated my actions; and they've lent me their status.

THE ACCESS IN PRAXIS

Often we don't have to look far to find access routes to people outside of the university. Any kind of identification we may have with people in our communities, to some extent, acts as a point of commonality where our perspectives overlap, despite our different positions. These points of convergence, I think, come closest to Freire's notion of solidarity. Solidarity manifests itself when there are common threads of identity between the student and teacher. To achieve empowerment through critical consciousness, the teacher "must be a partner of the students in his relations with them" (62). A partnership connotes people working together toward common goals. Freire finds "one must seek to live with others in solidarity . . . [and] solidarity requires true communication" (63). I believe that access to people with whom we identify is the initial building block for the solidarity and communication needed in activism.

Many access routes into the community have been established by philanthropic organizations, churches, community centers, and businesses. Before an access route is chosen, though, significant research needs to be done to see how the community developed, what types of contributions are needed, and whether or not there's precedent for the work proposed. After I spoke with representatives in many philanthropic and social service agencies, I volunteered in a bridge program between Rensselaer and a community center. Once there, I proposed a summer literacy program, but when this was over, I soon realized that I needed to reposition myself in the community. When I stopped volunteering, the women in this community found it easier to identify with me as a person and not as an organizational member.

Although I'm white, the women in this neighborhood and I identify with each other in many ways: we're no strangers to welfare offices, cockroaches, and empty refrigerators. We've held our chins out and heads up when we haven't had enough food stamps at the check out line. We've made poor (and good) choices in men and have purple and pink scars to prove it. We know enough to take out our earrings before we fight. We know abuses and disorders and the anonymous places people turn to for them. Since many of these people came from the Carolinas, and since my great-great-grandparents were in the Trail of Tears, we know why, on a crisp January day, a cardinal in a pine tree gives us hope.

Once we locate an access route into the community, we can begin the long process of self disclosure and listening from which we can begin to identify with each other. For Freire, communication is the main way to achieve this identification: "Through dialogue, the teacher-of-the-students and the students-of-the-teacher cease to exist and a new term emerges: teacher-student with students-teachers. The teacher is no longer the-one-who-teaches, but one who himself is taught in dialogue with the students, who in turn while being taught also teach" (67). Through communication, the exchange of questioning and asserting, we come to identify with each other and challenge the bases for our differences.

While this type of dialogue can take place in the classroom, the very power structure of the university makes it difficult to establish and maintain dialogue and solidarity. There's only so much we can get to know about our students within the sociological confines of the academic composition classroom. (See the appendix on "Freired Not.") Yet when we approach the community, we maneuver around the sociological obstacles that hinder us in the classroom from communicating with our students in ways that show our identification with them. Said another way, activism starts with some kind of identification with people outside of the university, an identification that often can flourish in a context where both the scholar and people together assess and redraw lines of power structures between them.

NO MOTHER TERESAS HERE

With the initial components of activism roughed out this way, I need to provide some important caveats. Let me show a few of the limitations of this kind of praxis with reference to shortcomings and mishaps in my own ethnographic fieldwork. My first concern in folding open activism this way is that these principles will be read as altruistic, when in my experience activism establishes an interdependency. Activism can't be altruistic because we have to be in a position to participate in our communities. The very same position as scholar which distances us from the community also invests us with resources we can make available to others. And we need these luxuries in order to be stable enough to give our time, knowledge, and resources. This means we must work very hard in the academy with the support of our community in order to garner the status and resources that we then return to the community.

I don't mean to simplify the process of gaining luxury here because I recognize that becoming an agent of social change in our neighborhoods requires time and energy. As a funded graduate student, I'm particularly fortunate to have the time and money to do this activist research. My teaching assistantship requires an average of twenty hours of work per week, and since I'm through with course work, I'm only on campus when I'm teaching, writing on the computers, or researching in the library. While I know my professors have 3/2 and 3/3 course loads, I've heard of other professors who have 5/5 course loads and hundreds of students every semester.[7] Yet, at the risk of sounding Pollyannish, we've already seen precedents for the type of scholarly civic participation I suggest. Perhaps through the reciprocity of activism, we might fold together our scholarly and civic duties.

Since the relationship established in activism centers upon reciprocity, an interdependency emerges. One of the ways in which we've maintained a mutually empowering relationship is through open and careful navigation of the reciprocity we've established. While this reciprocity may sound easy to maintain, many times requests have to be turned down. I've asked to record certain people and have been refused; I've also asked for examples of certain types of writing people didn't feel comfortable giving me, so I went without. Likewise, one person asked me to co-sign on a car loan (which I couldn't); and another person asked me to sign over any royalties I receive from a possible book to the families on the block (which I'm still considering). Everyone in this research realizes what we stand to gain from the work, and reciprocity helps prevent the work from becoming altruistic.

If we ignore the give-and-take established in activist research and instead choose to paint ourselves in the bright colors of benevolent liberators, we risk becoming what Macedo so delicately terms "literacy and poverty pimps" (xv). When we adopt a fashionable theory of emancipatory pedagogy and activism without considering the structural constraints imposed by reciprocity, we capitalize on other's daily living without giving any of these benefits in return. But here's the paradox—we need to make activism part of our research and teaching, so that we can make a living in the university. How else will we be able to give in equal amount to what we take?

ACCESSIVE FORCE

The degree to which we gain entrance into the daily lives of people outside the university in some measure depends upon who we are. The boundaries of our access must be negotiated with the people. Often, leftist posing assumes a here-I-am-to-save-the-day air, takes for granted immediate and complete entrance into a community, presumes an undeniably forceful presence. In my own work, I've overstepped the boundaries of my access working under similar assumptions. Six months into this research on a summer afternoon, I joined a large group of teens and adults playing cards, sipping beer, and talking on a front stoop. I was dealt into a game of 21 and listened to gossip and news. Lucy Cadens had a boyfriend (Anthony) who was seated in one of the folding chairs at the end of the stoop. Lucy had been gone for a few minutes, and he and I chatted until it was my turn to deal.

Later that day, Lucy called me away from the stoop and asked, "You want to tell me about Anthony?" I thought she was referring to a complaint a parent made to the center staff about him, and told her I wasn't at liberty to talk about it. She looked confused and asked me if I was talking to him that day. I told her of what I thought was an innocent conversation about gambling in Atlantic City. "They told me he was fishing with you," she said with her hands on her hips. I was shocked; what I thought was a simple conversation was actually him flirting with me. I told Lucy that I would keep a much safer distance from him and asked if she thought I should make that a unilateral decision about interacting with men in the neighborhood. She said I should be careful about who I talked to and about what, but that I could be polite to them. Since then, I've negotiated this boundary much more carefully and have gathered the majority of my notes from the children and women of the neighborhood. In this way, the access I presumed I had was fundamentally limited along gender lines. The lines of access must be charted, recharted, and respected in activist research. I had overstepped a boundary, albeit unintentionally, and realized my liberal presumption of unlimited access was pompous and shortsighted.

THE BEST LAID APPROACHES

Civic participation requires careful understandings of how our position will work, or not, within the given organizations of people. As mentioned earlier, I originally gained access to this neighborhood as a literacy volunteer and researcher through a bridge program between Rensselaer and the neighborhood center located in the heart of this community. As a volunteer, the social workers expected that I follow the same rules of conduct that they were institutionally bound to follow. However, I soon realized that the roles of researcher and volunteer contradict each other in important ways.

As a volunteer, a team player, I was expected to tell the social workers any details I might be privy to which concerned the private lives of the people in this neighborhood. I often visited the homes and sat on the stoops with people when the social workers were bound to stay in the center—their liability insurance did not cover them if something happened to them outside the center. As a researcher, though, I needed to walk between both worlds, the home and community center, but I was bound to the ethics of participant observation which dictate I cannot reveal information about my informants. Unfortunately, the center staff felt threatened by my peculiar position and worried that I would jeopardize their standing within the community with the information I had about the workings of their institution. As a result, they asked me to discontinue my volunteer work with them.

When we first consider bridging with communities, especially if we hope to do research at the same time, we must chart the internal workings of the institutions in order to see the ways we might, or might not, fit in. I initially believed I could simply volunteer and do research—"surely people will welcome the time and resources I offer." Here I was guilty of leftist posing disguised as philanthropy. Because I assumed this, I didn't negotiate my role within this organization well at all.

Even with these limitations, we can begin to participate in our communities despite (to spite) the sociological distances we must cross. Cultural studies models of empowerment and critical pedagogues are derelict in their civic duties by not including an expanded version of activism. Through activism, we've taken the first, tentative steps toward social change outside of the social confines of the university classroom. Finally, we not only fill a civic responsibility with activism, but also inform our teaching and theories with the perspectives of people outside the university. We begin to see just how deficient our estimations of our students are when we immerse ourselves and contribute to their everyday literacy and hidden belief systems.

The roads into the communities aren't paved with yellow bricks and sometimes may seem unapproachable, but access can generally be gained with observation and informal interviews to see who is already in the neighborhood and how they got there. Along the way relationships need to be navigated openly and consciously with close attention paid to boundaries and limitations in our access and intervention. Of course, I'm ignoring one potential means of access into the community—our students. But then, this assumes that we have solid enough relations with them to be able to follow them beyond the moat surrounding the ivory tower.

———

APPENDICES

Slippery Discourse

Many researchers believe that they can promote *social change* and *empower* students through critical literacy and emancipatory pedagogy. Yet we often hear the terms *social change* and *empowerment* used as though the nature of their outcomes is clearly established and reflected upon. This slippery discourse leads us to believe that we're all after the same ends: "enfranchising outsiders," having "social impact," creating a more "just society," offering a "liberating ideology," honing students' "awareness and critical consciousness," challenging "the oppressive system," "encouraging resistance," and of course, "interrogating dominate hegemony."† Just how these end products of critical pedagogy lead to social change and empowerment isn't clear to me from these discussions. In fact, some scholars make no distinctions between social *change* and *empowerment*, as though to empower is to liberate, and to liberate is to produce social change.[8] Underpinning this slippery discourse is an equally slick assumption—*social change* and *empowerment* lead to some kind of collective action or resistance involving the masses of people we teach.[9] When we view the impact of critical pedagogy from these grand levels, though, we miss the particular ways in which our teaching and research might contribute to students' abilities to take up their civic responsibilities once they leave our classrooms. We need a theory of social change and empowerment that captures the complex ways power is negotiated at micro levels of interaction between people, which would allow us to better characterize the impact of our work. With such a theory, we're less likely to paint ourselves as great "liberators of oppressed masses."

False Consciousness

Many critical theorists portray themselves as brokers of emancipatory power, a stance that garners them status at the expense of students. One way to make a position for themselves in the academy is to diagnose their students as having "false consciousness." Once labeled as having "false consciousness," students can be easily dismissed and diminished by critical theory.[10] Yet, the many scholars who do immerse themselves into the daily living of people find, predictably, hidden ideologies—belief systems that contain numerous, clever ways to identify and criticize onerous behavior.[11] In some fundamental

———

†These trends in discourse I culled from many of the collected essays in *Composition and Resistance*. Since these discourses often make one think of saviors, the footnote marker seems particularly apt.

sense, the discursive posturing we so frequently hear would not be able to legitimize itself, if it didn't diminish others in its wake. The label of false consciousness, then, reveals more about the speaker's limited access to students and communities, than it reveals about the level of people's critical abilities. If cultural studies theorists were to visit the homes and streets of the people attending their classes, they would likely hear critiques of the dominating sociological forces.[12] Therein we see the fundamental problem in building our models of cultural studies: we're sociologically distanced from the cultures we study.

In Ivory Towers, We Overlook

When we fail to consider the perspectives of people outside of the academy, we overlook valuable contributions to our theory building. Without a praxis that moves between community and university, we risk not only underestimating our students' pre-existing critical consciousness, but we also risk reproducing the hegemonic barriers separating the university from the community. That is, we become guilty of applying our theories from the sociological "top-down," instead of informing our theories from the "bottom-up." In fact, it appears many value the idea more than the people, a value that bolsters the sociological distance of the university from the community. I've even read arguments *supporting* the social isolation of theorists in the academy from people in communities. In other words, we exclude many of the people we're trying to empower for the sake of positing (what we sure as hell hope will be) liberating ideas. The flaw in this logic seems so obvious: How can we study ideologies, hegemonies, power structures, and the effects of discursive practices when we overlook community discursive dispositions—the place where these language practices are first inculcated, generated and consequently reproduced in the social habitus?[13] Thus, many postmodern theorists remain tucked within their libraries and don't engage the very people they hope to help. They will send their theories down to the people and engage each other in postmodern conversations (over pomo tea perhaps) in their postmodern universities.

Freired Not

When we begin to turn cultural studies in on itself in a self-reflexive manner, we see its limiting assumptions and paradoxical stances as it's applied to composition studies. And this is indeed a shame, because the political and sociological theories it employs are very useful in expanding our roles as rhetoricians to include more perspectives from the margins. In the opening of *Pedagogy of the Oppressed*, Freire evaluates the oppressors in society: "To affirm that men are persons and persons should be free, and yet, to do nothing tangible to make this affirmation a reality, is a farce" (35). What he means by tangible is left up to interpretation; I suggest he means activism.[14] If we let *tangible* be synonymous with activism, then to what extent is promoting critical consciousness in our classrooms "activist"? My sense is that we're not doing enough because we're acting within the role of the teacher that has been perpetuated by the institution, and thus keeps us from breaking down the barriers between the university and community. In fact, many critical pedagogues have betrayed their activist agenda in their classrooms by characterizing their students as "dull," "numb," "dumbly silent," "unreflective," "yearning" and/or "resentful."‡ They place themselves in the oppressive position by relegating students to the category of the "unfortunates." Pedagogues are only two letters shy of becoming demagogues. About these characterizations, Freire might say: "No pedagogy that is truly liberating can remain distant from the oppressed by treating them as unfortunates" (39). What these researchers fail to remember is that the students they teach are in a prime position for critical reflection precisely because they are disenfranchised: "Who are better prepared," Freire asks, "than the oppressed to understand the terrible significance of an oppressive society?" (29).

NOTES

1. While this idea of the physical surroundings having significance isn't novel, it is often overlooked as a tool to critique our own context, the university setting. Bakhtin, for example, finds that "everything ideological possesses semiotic value" ("Marxism" 929). In other words, "any physical body may be perceived as an image. . . . Any such artistic-symbol image to which a particular physical object gives rise is already an ideological product. The physical object is converted into a sign" (928). This allows us to critique how even the construction and setting of the Approach can take on significance. Thus, "a sign does not simply exist as a part of a reality—it reflects and refracts another reality" (929). The stairway is a sign of the connection between the city and university, a connection that needs maintenance.

2. Cheryl Geisler offers a cogent summary of these ideas in the second chapter of her recent book on expertise in the academy. Further, Bowles and Gintis present a Marxist analysis of the ways in which schooling serves to perpetuate the class hierarchies necessary for modern capitalism to flourish.

3. Mike Rose's latest work reveals the rich and complicated ways in which primary and secondary school teachers still move toward this democratic principle. His book challenges the country's impoverished discourse used to describe education, and takes steps toward envisioning a discourse of possibility centered on a fundamental belief in the strong ties between education and democracy.

4. Activist research expands upon notions of *praxis*. Originally developed by Aristotle, praxis resembles "phronesis, action adhering to certain ideal standards of good (ethical) or effective (political) behavior" (Warry 157). Marx embellished this political agenda for participation in his "Eleventh Thesis," and some applied anthropologists have since adopted praxis as a term describing, loosely, ethical action in the research paradigm geared toward social change. For example, Johannsen brings postmodern critiques to ethnography and finds that research as praxis demands that we actively participate in the community under study. While expanding the participant side of social science research is necessary in order to achieve praxis, examinations of praxis in social sciences are for the most part "wholly theoretical and with only occasional reference to methodological or pragmatic concerns associated with planned change, intervention, or action research" (Warry 156). Even though applied anthropology, a subfield of anthropology, provides theoretical models for how praxis enters into the research paradigm (see Lather), many scholars still need to do the work of intervention at the community level.

5. Some may question the potency of such activism and the extent to which these literacy events really did challenge the status quo. In his classic social scientific study entitled *Black Families in White America*, Andrew Billingsley depicts some of the historically rooted everyday struggles of African-Americans in achieving social and geographic mobility. Education "is a most reliable

---

‡ As found in the popular collection of essays *Contending with Words*.

index and a potent means of gaining social mobility and family stability in our society. The absence of systematic training and education during slavery and reconstruction depressed the social structure of the Negro people most, just as the presence of education in small and scattered doses proved such a powerful source of achievement" (79). Raejone's application essay for college suggests one way we worked against this historically rooted absence of education that Billingsley mentions in an effort to create the presence of higher education in her family. Similarly, the literacy which contributed to Lucy's relocation to a suburban area loosens "the tight white noose around the central cities [that] has kept Negro families from being able to penetrate suburbia in any appreciable numbers" (74).

6. Different types of discourses constitute different contexts, an idea Bakhtin described well as the difference between "everyday genre" ("what ordinary people live, and their means for communicating with each other)" (*Dialogic* 428) and "social languages" ("the discourse peculiar to a specific system of society (professional, age group, etc.)" (430). Thus, "heteroglossia" allows us to understand how "language is stratified, not only into linguistic dialects . . . but also— and for us this is the essential point—into languages that are socioideological: languages of social groups" (272).

7. I found Pauline Uchmanowicz's recent article particularly disturbing. She describes her "dog years" as a part-time college writing instructor at two institutions where she teaches "between twelve and sixteen scheduled classes per week" and is paid "a little over half the salary of a full-time teacher for teaching double the course load" (427). Add to this burden her commute of five hundred miles every week and lack of job security, and I begin to worry that the luxury needed for activism is out of reach for many composition teachers.

8. Jennifer Gore insightfully critiques "some shortcomings in the construction of 'empowerment' by critical and feminist educational discourses which create problems internal to their discourses" (54). For example, she identifies how the agency of empowerment stems from the teacher, while the subject of empowerment is usually the student. As the center of activity in these discourses, the teacher is more important than the students—a practice that contradicts the theoretical emphasis on the student.

9. I think many of us work so closely from Freire's model of pedagogy we believe the impact his literacy projects have will be in equal kind and type to the impact our classes may have. However, Freire cautions "it is impossible to export pedagogical practices without re-inventing them. Please, tell your fellow American educators not to import me. Ask them to recreate and rewrite my ideas" (Macedo xiv).

10. James Scott, a political scientist, makes a convincing argument against the label of "false consciousness." His ethnographic fieldwork in Malaysia depicts not only the social forces which daily influence Malay peasants, but also reveals their unseen defiance and hidden ideology used to challenge these forces. He differentiates between those public and private behaviors that relate to power struggles. The peasants appear to cordially accept the authority of landlords in their public encounters with them; however, they actually fought this oppressive ideology in private spheres. This resistance Scott terms as the difference between "public and hidden transcripts," and reveals how these peasants have devised a number of ways to challenge their subordination. These forms of often "low profile, undisclosed resistance" create the infrapolitics of larger society (198), but also suggest the limitation of the notion of false consciousness. Since most researchers and teachers aren't privy to the hidden ideologies of their informants/students, we miss the ways in which resistance and critical consciousness are constructed in subtle, often unnoticed ways.

11. For example, Keith Basso found that Western Apaches have clever, elaborate systems of mocking "the Whiteman." Luis Moll immersed himself in a Mexican-American community in Tucson, Arizona, and characterized complex systems of knowledge and strategies shared by households in order to "enhance survival within harsh social conditions" (225). Carol Stack in *All Our Kin* found African-Americans devised many strategies to undermine the welfare institution's influence in their fund allocation, including withholding information, foot dragging, and misrepresenting census data. Perhaps with more access to their students' communities, critical scholars would not be so quick in their dismissal of their students' critical abilities.

12. Fundamental to activism, I believe, is not only a basic trust in the potential and abilities of people, but also a basic mistrust of assessments that diminish and dismiss others. Brian Fay, a philosopher of social science, describes the ontological values of critical social science this way: "An active creature . . . is intelligent, curious, reflective, and willful" (50). All people have these qualities regardless of their socio-cultural circumstances. Activism has roots in a genuine care and respect for all people. Anything short of this and our work quickly takes on a paternalistic, patronizing, and ingenuine flavor.

13. Pierre Bourdieu's sociological model of the *habitus* describes dispositions as patterns of behavior, such as language behaviors, which then combine to make the "acquired system of generative schemes, the habitus" (54).

14. As Giroux points out, "though Freire provides the broad theoretical framework needed to help bridge the gaps that plague radical education in North America, his analysis in key places warrants further substantiation and depth" (136). For the sake of this argument, I believe that in North America, teaching is different from activism. Teaching is institutionalized because a certain social status is constructed around the knowledge used in this role (see Berger and Luckmann). Yet, activism in the politics of the community is not institutionalized, per se, rather, it's a civic duty that all people can potentially fulfill without needing specialized knowledge related to schooling (Geisler; Bowles and Gintis). So activism is more closely related to civic duty and teaching related to an institution. I see these two activities on the same continuum of the democratic process, as potentially mutually informative, but not interchangeable projects of democracy.

WORKS CITED

Bakhtin, Mikhail. *The Dialogic Imagination.* Ed. Michael Holquist. Austin: U of Texas P, 1981.
———. "Marxism and the Philosophy of Language." *The Rhetorical Tradition.* Ed. Patricia Bizzell and Bruce Herzberg. Boston: St. Martin's, 1990. 924–63.
Basso, Keith. *Portraits of "The Whiteman."* Cambridge: Cambridge UP, 1979.
Beach, Richard, et al., eds. *Multidisciplinary Perspectives on Literacy Research.* Urbana: NCTE, 1992.
Berger, Peter, and Thomas Luckmann. *The Social Construction of Reality.* New York: Anchor, 1966.
Billingsley, Andrew. *Black Families in White America.* New York: Simon, 1968.
Bourdieu, Pierre. *The Logic of Practice.* Stanford: Stanford UP, 1990.
Bowles, Samuel, and Herbert Gintis. *Schooling in Capitalist America.* New York: Basic, 1976.
Fay, Brian. *Critical Social Science.* Ithaca: Cornell UP, 1987.
Freire, Paulo. *Pedagogy of the Oppressed.* New York: Herder, 1971.
Geisler, Cheryl. *Academic Literacy and the Nature of Expertise.* Hillsdale: Erlbaum, 1994.
Gere, Anne Ruggles. "The Extracurriculum of Composition." *CCC* 45 (1994): 75–92.
Giddens, Anthony. *The Constitution of Society.* Berkeley: U of California P, 1981.
Giroux, Henry. *Ideology, Culture, and the Process of Schooling.* Philadelphia: Temple UP, 1981.
Gore, Jennifer. "What We Can Do for You! What *Can* 'We' Do for 'You?'" *Feminisms and Critical Pedagogy.* Ed. Jennifer Gore and Carmen Luke. London: Routledge, 1992. 54–73.
Halloran, S. Michael. "Afterthoughts on Rhetoric and Public Discourse." *Pre/Text: The First Decade.* Ed. Victor Vitanza. Pittsburgh: U of Pittsburgh P, 1993. 52–68.
Herzberg, Bruce. "Community Service and Critical Teaching." *CCC* 45 (1994): 307–19.
Johannsen, Agneta. "Applied Anthropology and Post-Modernist Ethnography." *Human Organization* 51 (1992): 71–81.
Lather, Patti. "Research as Praxis." *Harvard Educational Review* 56 (1986): 257–77.
Macedo, Donald. Preface. *Politics of Liberation.* Ed. Peter McLaren and Colin Lankshear. Routledge: London, 1994. xiii–xix.
Moll, Luis. "Literacy Research in Community and Classrooms: A Sociocultural Approach." Beach et al. 211–44.
Powell, Malea. "Custer's Very Last Stand: Rhetoric, the Academy, and the Un-Seeing of the American Indian." Unpublished essay. 1995.
Rose, Mike. *Lives on the Boundary.* Boston: Penguin, 1989.
———. *Possible Lives: The Promise of Public Education in America.* New York: Houghton, 1995.
Schiappa, Edward. "Intellectuals and the Place of Cultural Critique." *Rhetoric, Cultural Studies, and Literacy.* Ed. Frederick Reynolds. Hillsdale: Erlbaum, 1995. 26–32.
Scott, James C. *Domination and the Arts of Resistance.* New Haven: Yale UP, 1990.
———. *Weapons of the Weak.* New Haven: Yale UP, 1985.
Stack, Carol. *All Our Kin: Strategies for Survival in a Black Community.* New York: Harper, 1974.
Uchmanowicz, Pauline. "The $5,000–$25,000 Exchange." *College English* 57 (1995): 426–47.
Warry, Wayne. "The Eleventh Thesis: Applied Anthropology as Praxis." *Human Organization* 51 (1992): 155–63.

18 *"The Rhetorician as an Agent of Social Change" in Action: Online Cherokee Nation Educational Projects*

CHEROKEE NATION
MICHIGAN STATE UNIVERSITY STUDENTS

Since 2004, Ellen Cushman has been working with her tribe, the Cherokee Nation, located in Tahlequah, Oklahoma. She serves as one of six Sequoyah commissioners who form a scholarly think tank for the Nation, and she's taught in the Nation's Youth Leadership Institute. Between 2005 and 2007 students in her Michigan State University multimedia writing classes developed two educational resources for the tribe that are available under the history section of their Web site, http://www.cherokee.org/Culture/Default.aspx

These educational modules provide an overview of two eras in Cherokee history related to tribal laws and treaties and to the allotment. Use the following URLs to view the full documents.

http://www.cherokee.org/Culture/treaties/toc.htm

http://www.cherokee.org/Culture/allotment/Default.htm

Students in Cushman's other outreach classes have developed Web sites, digital videos, promotional materials, and needs assessments for community organizations and start-ups. These works have served to further the goals of community organizations and have trained students in the types and kinds of writing and research that they will do as professional writers.

From *Cherokee Nation Laws and Treaties, 1684–1907* and *The Allotment Era in Cherokee History, 1887–1914.*

FIGURE 18–1   Cherokee Nation Laws and Treaties, 1684–1907

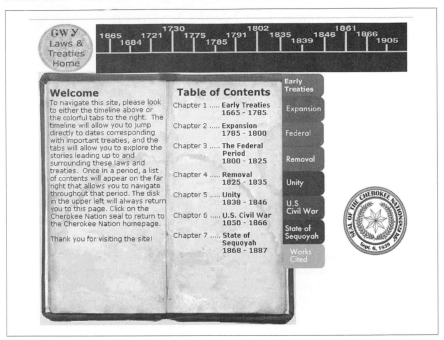

(Image courtesy of Ellen Cushman.)

FIGURE 18–2   The Allotment Era in Cherokee History

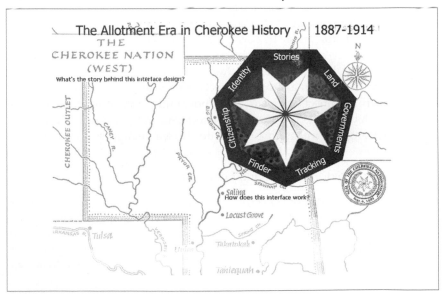

(Image courtesy of Ellen Cushman.)

19 Service-Learning as a Path to Virtue: The Ideal Orator in Professional Communication

JAMES M. DUBINSKY

In a recent article, V. A. Howard, relying on a detailed study by Engell and Dangerfield (1998), decries "the market-model university" and its adverse effects on the humanities. According to Howard (1999), the market-model leads to "Peg-Board vocationalism," a term he coined to describe a belief held by many students and parents that higher education's primary responsibility is to prepare students to fit into an array of job slots. In Howard's opinion, this view has led to a decline in the enrollment in and a devaluing of the humanities, resulting in coarsening values and a general loss of concern for public service ideals (p. 125).

As a professional writing program director in an English department at a major technological, research-oriented university, I read Howard's article with interest. The modifier "professional" is integral to my work: I am responsible for preparing students for "job slots." Yet, while acknowledging that responsibility, I reject the notion that what my colleagues and I teach, despite its clearly practical nature, must be vocational in Howard's pejorative sense. Nor do I believe that, even if a field has a practical approach toward the economy, such a field must, by its nature, devalue the ideals of public service. My beliefs are predicated upon a strong connection between my field and classical rhetoric. Such a connection opens up opportunities for examining the civic values of rhetoric extolled by classical rhetoricians (e.g., Aristotle, Quintilian, Isocrates, Cicero) and integrating them into current pedagogy.

CLASSICAL RHETORIC AND SERVICE-LEARNING

Classical rhetoricians were concerned with preparing young men[1] for their roles as citizens by teaching them to be skilled persuasive speakers in various situations (e.g., legal, political, and ceremonial) for both public and private audiences. They taught practical skills to be used for the common good. For instance, in *Rhetoric*, Aristotle addressed human conduct in relation to activi-

---

From *Michigan Journal of Community Service Learning* 8.2 (2002): 61–75.

ties that maintain community life (1954; Miller, 1989). He spoke of the orator's duty to "attempt not only to prove the points mentioned but also to show that the good or the harm, the honor or disgrace, the justice or injustice, is great or small" (1954, 1359b19–23). Learning rhetoric was "useful" (1355b9), but it also had a "moral purpose" (1355b19).

Other classical rhetoricians and educators, such as Isocrates and Quintilian, had similar goals for teaching rhetoric. Isocrates (1990) sought to use rhetoric and oratory to advocate interests that bind communities together (Papillon, 1995), arguing that the "art of discourse . . . is the source of most of our blessings. . . . and if it were not for this we should not be able to live together" (p. 50). In *De Oratore*, Cicero (1969) builds on Aristotle and Isocrates by promoting the need to prepare orators—citizens who, by uniting wisdom and eloquence and integrating theoretical and practical knowledge, work to shape the community's political life. According to Cicero, the orators' importance lies in their ability to "bring help to the suppliant, to raise up those that are cast down, to bestow security, to set free from peril, to maintain men in their civil rights" (I, viii). Quintilian (1972) extended Cicero's ideals to produce speakers and writers who had their communities' best aims at heart (Murphy, 1987). In his *Institutes of Oratory*, Quintilian explained that he wanted each orator, "whose character [he was] seeking to mould, [to] be . . . a true statesman, not in the discussions of study, but in the actual practice and experience of life" (p. 126). In his mind this could only happen with "the broadest education," (p. 126) which would be applied to human affairs. All these rhetoricians are part of a tradition that helped to shape our western educational system's core (Barber, 1992, 1994; Halloran, 1976; Marrou, 1964), a tradition rich with evidence that higher education's mission in general is to be of practical service to society (Boyer, 1990; Wallenfelt, 1986; Waterman, 1997).

Many scholars and educators in my field see professional communication as classical rhetoric's direct descendant (Deans, 2000; Halloran, 1976; Johnson, 1998; Miller, 1989; Reynolds, 1992; Whitburn, 1984). As a result, we see our mission as practical in what Richard Bernstein calls the "high" sense: we see it tied to the Aristotelian notion of *praxis*, which involves human conduct (C. Miller, 1989; T. Miller, 1991). This connection has led a recent movement for many in our field to consider service-learning as a pedagogical strategy, which enables us not only to teach our students practical skills but also to address the civic issues involved in using those skills. Thus, we see our goals for implementing service-learning as similar to those of Isocrates and Quintilian: we want to teach a useful skill set, but we also want to inculcate a sense of civic idealism.

Many educators, to include Howard, see service-learning as having a strengthening effect for the humanities and liberal education in general (e.g., Barber, 1992; Checkoway, 2001; Taylor, 1994, to name just a few). I have seen its positive effects, and in this article, I interrogate the value of service-learning pedagogy as a bridge between a practical, "market-driven" focus and a humanistic, service-oriented one when teaching a practical course. In so doing, I outline ways in which service-learning has been used, discuss problems and concerns with its use, and offer, by presenting a case study from my own use, how service-learning may serve to unite conflicting goals embedded in the terms "service" and "learning." My goal is to address the tensions at the hyphen—between service and learning, organizations and clients, workplace preparation and civic literacy, and to show that, when used with care and reflection, service-learning can be a bridge or a path toward virtue and can create ideal orators in the classical sense defined by Quintilian (1972): orators and citizens who put their knowledge and skills to work for the common good.

Because the study of rhetoric has been intimately connected with civic participation and service since the fifth century B.C.E., an infusion of contemporary theory and practice of service-learning does not revitalize my field so much as it builds upon a pedagogical goal and praxis that is two-and-a-half millennia old. By integrating the "two complex concepts: community action, the 'service,' and efforts to learn from that action and connect what is learned to existing knowledge, the 'learning'" (Stanton, Giles, & Cruz, 1999, p. 2), we in these more professional, market-driven fields can create a "symbiotic relationship" (Migliore, quoted in Jacoby, 1996, p. 5) not only between the two concepts, but also between those served and those serving (Coles, 1993).

THE DEBATE ABOUT VOCATIONALISM

The accusation that my field, professional communication,[2] is utilitarian or vocational is quite common, particularly among members of my own department, many of whom teach literature, one field that Howard points to as declining or threatened. It is interesting that concerns about the professional communication field do not come just from those outside our field. In a recent article in *Technical Communication Quarterly*, one of the field's top journals, Jack Bushnell (1999) argues that we in professional communication have "become training departments for corporate 'clients' who provide us with internships and fellowships for our students, and ever increasing numbers of good-paying jobs for our graduates" (pp. 175–76). As "training departments," he believes that we are losing sight of our "mission as college and university teachers . . . to prepare our students to be critical thinkers," who are responsible not only for reporting information to serve their companies but also for writing future decisions that could affect larger communities (p. 177). Bushnell's concerns are neither new nor unique to members of our field. Others who approach our field from very different theoretical positions, such as Patrick Moore (1999), have raised similar concerns about our role as teachers, about "how professors define technical communication," and about how that definition influences what gets taught (pp. 211–12). Moore, for example, also addresses the issue of training; however, he is concerned that, due to an over-emphasis on rhetoric and theory, we are not preparing our students effectively enough to enter the job market, a position almost diametrically opposite, in aim and curricular emphasis, from Bushnell's. Taken as two competing positions inside our discipline, Moore and Bushnell represent the horns of a dilemma that Carolyn Miller (1989) described over a decade ago when she explained that "courses and programs in technical writing are both praised and damned for being 'practical,'" which to Miller, "suggests a certain attitude or mode of learning" (p. 14).

As a teacher and program administrator, I take the debate about training and learning seriously. The three issues outlined above—our "mission as college and university teachers," the question of "how professors define technical communication," and the attitudes we have toward learning—are concerns, I would argue, that we cannot afford to take lightly. We in professional communication are at a critical place in our discipline's development (Staples, 1999), and I am thankful for voices such as Bushnell's and Moore's. They are creating necessary conversation about our disciplinary goals, conversation that is also applicable beyond our field. Because our programs are growing and our status in and out of the academy is increasing, along with the status of our graduates (Geonetta, 1997), those of us in the more practical fields need to talk about curricula and come to definitions we can agree upon in order to "meet the disciplinary responsibility of preparing students to meet citizenship and workplace responsibility with integrity as well as with knowledge and skill" (Meyer & Bernhardt, 1997; Staples, 1999, p. 161). Meeting this responsibility is critical as we work to create what Billie Wahlstrom (1997) calls a "unified vision of our discipline" (p. 303), one in which professional communicators "emerge as educated decision maker(s) whose professional decisions are informed by critical thinking skills, theory, application, ethics, communication ability, and knowledge about technology" (Staples & Ornatowski, 1997, p. xii), so that they may be valued members of their workplaces and society.

Service-learning is a topic in recent curricular discussions outlining ways we in professional and technical writing might prepare students to think critically and become educated decision makers. In the past five years, educators have begun to demonstrate that service-learning, used in what Deans (2000) has called "writing for the community," has the potential to improve academic learning for, and inculcate civic ideals in, students in professional communication courses (Hafer, 1999; Heilker, 1997; Henson & Sutliff, 1998; Huckin, 1997; Matthews & Zimmerman, 1999).[3] Based upon the case studies I have read and my own experience with this pedagogy, I am convinced that service-learning, used fully and reflectively, helps students develop the critical thinking skills Bushnell advocates; it also prepares students for the workplace in a more comprehensive way than many other pedagogical strategies because students apply what they have learned by working with real audiences. Most importantly, it helps students to meet their citizenship responsibilities. Service-learning pedagogy enables us to make our courses "a matter of *conduct* rather than of production" [italics in original] and to bridge the theory/praxis and academe/workplace splits Miller (1989) highlighted because it is practical in the fullest sense (p. 23). Students learn the skills they'll need in the workplace, and they gain a practical wisdom (*phronesis*) that enables them to be critical citizens.

Service-learning is a valuable and powerful pedagogy, but integrating it fully and reflectively into professional/technical communication courses is not easy. Even as the evidence for its value mounts, so does the evidence for problems and concerns associated with it. For example, the logistics of working with organizations in the community are complicated; and coordinating projects requires significant effort and time from teachers, students, and community partners. There are also problems associated with projects that are not done well. Such problems may increase the divide between academe and community, particularly if the students' projects are done poorly or if the students believe that their projects would have been better if the community partner had been more available.

Logistics and time are just a few of the problems. Others include asking students to write for communities they do not know, which can lead to frustration for both the students and the community partners (Bacon, 1997). Then there are problems in motivating students to go beyond the instrumental course goals. Sometimes, even when a course is well planned, some students will see service as "lame" because they see the course's goal (or their own) is limited to "improv[ing] [their] technical skills" (Matthews & Zimmerman, 1999, p. 391). If we, as educators, accept that argument about the centrality of technical skills and production, still more problems may occur because of the vocational or credential building emphasis. With that emphasis, students may miss the point of the service altogether, or so minimize its value that the civic learning is limited (Adler-Kassner & Collins, 1994; Lisman, 1998; Mattson, 1998). Finally, if we emphasize service, but refer to it as volunteering rather than as working to effect change, students may simply see their service as a charitable contribution. While charity has positive features, focusing on volunteering tends to result in a sense of altruism in students—they "feel good about themselves and their work," (as did one of my business writing students), but few long-term benefits for the community or society result (Kahne & Westheimer, 1996; Morton, 1995; Rhoads, 1997).

These problems and concerns are real; I have experienced them all in courses I have taught using service-learning pedagogy. But they can be overcome, and when they are, the benefits to students, the community, and our discipline are worth the effort. Students who participate in a class that balances service and learning and establishes partnerships with community organizations with change, not charity, as the goal are more likely to become citizens who use their rhetorical abilities for society's good. They become rhetoricians for change (Cushman, 1996).

I intend for this essay to continue the conversation about the need for curricular reform by extending and modifying the argument advanced by Matthews and Zimmerman (1999) that we integrate service-learning into our curricula. Some of their suggestions are excellent, particularly the recommendation to "develop and maintain close relationships with . . . nonprofit organizations" over extended periods (p. 401). Other suggestions about how to accomplish this integration, however, such as requiring students to apply for these service-learning courses or offering a two-semester sequence, are problematic (pp. 397–400). If the reason for integrating service-learning lies in our desire to prepare students to meet citizenship and workplace responsibilities, limiting enrollment defeats that goal. As for having a two-semester sequence, such a solution could work for our professional communication majors/minors (and we should consider it), but it would be a luxury that most students who take our technical and business writing courses and their departments cannot afford. Thus, instead of complicating the curriculum by adding hurdles or additional courses, I argue that most solutions lie within individual teachers' grasps: many problems outlined result from the ways in which service-learning is defined, framed, and taught.

To make my argument, I begin by defining service-learning, focusing on the need to achieve a balance between service and learning. In a classroom that achieves such a balance, students shift from a perspective that focuses more on production to one that focuses on conduct by developing reciprocal relationships with their organizations. An interesting point to note is that when the balance is achieved, the emphasis on conduct does not diminish students' enthusiasm for the course nor does it result in students losing sight of the positive benefits they gain from this experiential learning type. Finally, I suggest that service-learning should be mandatory for all professional communication curricula if we are interested in bridging academe and workplace and assisting our students to become ideal orators who meet their citizenship responsibilities.

WHAT IS SERVICE-LEARNING?

Service-learning is neither easily defined nor practiced (Adler-Kassner, 2000; Kendall, 1990). As I have come to understand and practice it, the pedagogy combines three axes: *learning* (establishing clearly defined academic goals), *serving* (applying what one learns for the communal/societal benefit), and *reflecting* (thoughtful engagement about the service-learning work's value). Service-learning is *learning-by-doing* for others.

When students participate in service-learning, they

> participate in an organized service activity that meets identified community needs and then reflect on the service activity in such a way as to gain further understanding of course content, *a broader appreciation of the discipline, and an enhanced sense of civic responsibility* [italics added.] (Bringle & Hatcher, 1996, p. 222)

In order to meet the needs of their community, students must learn to deepen connections and relationships with their partners. As they deepen these relationships, they gain a better understanding of others and the contexts in which they live. Then, because they develop these relationships, they begin to *care* about their community and seek to improve it. Kahne and Westheimer (1996) call this model of service-learning the "change" model, explaining that change, as opposed to charity, adds a political dimension to the learning and helps students become more civic-oriented by asking them to think more critically about their role in society as they develop a reciprocal relationship with their organizations (p. 595). The emphasis on service's civic nature addresses arguments that challenge using the word "service" because it "suggests in-equality among the participants," implies oppression, or connotes charity in a negative, self-righteous sense (Jacoby, 1996, p. 8). This emphasis also renews the universities' civic mission and prepares students to more fully participate in our social institutions (Barber, 1992, p. 248).

By providing opportunities for our students to work with community partners, we prepare them to participate in society, helping them become what Quintilian (1972) calls "ideal orators." Service-learning in the change model is the vehicle for such preparation; it involves connecting our class-rooms to the world beyond campus while creating an ethical base for learning (Boyer, 1994; Coye, 1997). It focuses on "how-to" *and* restores a link between citizenship and service that has historically been a concern of our educational system (Barber, 1992; Barber, 1994; Boyer, 1990; Boyte, 1993; Miller, 1989; Staples, 1997; Waterman, 1997). Because service-learning is concerned with getting things done for the common good, students gather the necessary "know how" along with an opportunity to bridge theory and practice by tak-ing the knowledge they accumulate and applying it to human affairs (Whit-burn, 1984, p. 229).

I draw on Quintilian (1972), specifically, because I have come to believe, as Whitburn (1984) did, that the "beginnings of a model for addressing our current problems in professional communication" are present in his works (p. 228). According to Quintilian, the ideal orator was "a good man, skilled in speaking" (p. 118). Quintilian's emphasis was on goodness and skill, and on an inherent virtue that the orator uses for the common good. The ideal orator is "no specialist"; rather, because "all knowledge is his province" and because he is willing to put that knowledge to work for the common good, the orator reveals himself, as I indicated earlier, " 'in the actual practice and experience of life' " (Quintilian, quoted in Whitburn, p. 228). He bridges gaps by reaffirm-ing human capability and "performing well in particular cases" (p. 233).

By emphasizing the importance of working with community members and applying what is learned in the classroom to "particular cases" in order to solve problems, service-learning becomes the path to virtue that Quintilian advocates. This work recognizes how knowledge is situated and the need for individual rather than prescriptive solutions. Problem-solving in these in-stances is not a narrowly utilitarian term (Boyte, 1993, p. 63); nor is it linked to charity, a common complaint about service-learning (Kahne & Westheimer, 1996; Matthews & Zimmerman, 1999; Morton, 1995). Instead, solving prob-lems engages students as both practitioners and citizens who use their knowl-edge and skills to work for their organizations and for the entire society (Whitburn, 1984).

FROM CHARITY TO CHANGE

Thus far, I have mentioned two competing models for service-learning: char-ity and change. As I indicated earlier, I borrow these models from Kahne and Westheimer (1996), who by asking "in service of what?" define goals in terms of learning and community change. In their "charity" model, learning focuses on giving, and the service aspect adds to the learning experience. It is this model that I see many in our discipline practicing. While there is nothing inherently wrong with this model, it is incomplete if we are seeking to meet our civic responsibilities by helping students gain a "broader appreciation of the discipline" and become educated citizens who participate actively in their communities to solve problems and effect change (Cushman, 1996).

In Kahne and Westheimer's "change" model, learning focuses on caring, which is linked to creating more lasting relationships among service-learning participants in order to encourage students to reflect critically on social conditions and individual responsibilities. This model is better suited to achieving the goals outlined by Meyer and Bernhardt (1997), Staples (1997), Wahlstrom (1997), and others because the service experience, valued equally with the learning, enhances how students understand citizenship and helps them shift from a self-oriented to an other-oriented focus. Students not only see the benefits inherent in this kind of learning-by-doing; they also see the value inherent in working with community partners to solve problems, and they begin to recognize that they have a responsibility to continue that work as they move from academia to the workplace.

For the past two years, working to move from a charity model to a change model, I have seen this model's benefits for students and their service-learning partners. In this section, by describing changes in student attitudes between two successive workplace writing course semesters, I illustrate the differences between the two models. These differences manifested themselves in three ways: 1) students emphasized their contributions to the community instead of emphasizing how the course prepared them for the workplace; 2) students and the service-learning partners worked more closely together, and by doing so, eliminated some of the problems dealing with coordination and commitment; 3) students did not see the work as charity, as something they were "giving" to those less fortunate; instead they saw the work as an opportunity to get involved in their community and work to solve problems.

Basic Course Structure

In both semesters the major project in the course was a collaborative project involving a community organization. In the first semester, there were 24 students; in the second semester, 23. I designed the course so that the service-learning projects were worth 45 percent of the semester grade. In the first semester, I offered students the option to choose a project involving a nonprofit organization or an unsolicited recommendation report with an invoked client (a college administrator responsible for the promotional materials of any college in the university); in the second, the service-learning was mandatory. All of the students in both semesters chose the service-learning project. They worked in teams and completed service-learning agreements with our University Service-Learning Center. These agreements outlined their responsibilities and provided an opportunity for them to conduct an initial audience analysis by learning about their organization's mission, history, and structure.

The project followed Huckin's model (1997), with some checks and balances that I added throughout the semester: a bid proposal that the client has to approve, a progress report—sometimes two, the project itself, an oral presentation, and a reflection report submitted at semester's end. All interaction with organizations was conducted on site (at the YMCA for instance) or at a site chosen by the team and the site representative (sometimes the site representative would meet the students on campus to save them a long drive). I stayed in touch with the organizations throughout the semester by phone and email, asking them to complete evaluations on the teams' progress during the project, but I didn't participate in the teams' meetings. At the term's end, the students presented their finished projects to the class, got feedback, and then revised them for their organizations. After the students presented their projects to the organizations, I asked for and received evaluations from the organizations, which I factored into the project grade.

My students worked with six organizations each term (e.g., YMCA, the Free Clinic of the New River Valley, the Montgomery County Office of Youth, and Giles County Housing Development Authority) to produce a range of products (e.g., annual reports, newsletters, brochures, Web sites). All of these organizations had requested help via the University Service-Learning Center because they were short-handed, and they were glad to have collaborative teams of three to five students offer whatever help we could give them.

Documenting Change

My course structure and the project design, as outlined above, remained constant. However, as I became aware that my students were focusing more on self than on others and were not developing reciprocal relationships with their organizations—in essence, as I became aware that we were not really involved in service-learning as I defined it earlier, I altered my course materials, my approach (such as making it mandatory rather than optional), and even the language I used to describe service-learning. The revisions resulted in significant changes in the students' perceptions of, and attitudes to, their projects and to service-learning. To illustrate how the students' perceptions about the value of the service-learning projects stem, to a large degree, from my emphasis and focus rather than from any problems or deficiencies in the students, let me offer a table and two stories.

First, the table (see Table 19–1). In it, I categorize comments from two successive semesters that students made on anonymous, end-of-course questionnaires that accompany the instructor evaluation form. I use the end-of-course evaluations because, more so than in reflection reports and journals, students tend to be frank and less likely to tone down any criticism; they know that I am not the primary audience. In addition, these forms, unlike the reflection reports, are not evaluated, and I do not see them until after the semester is over. In these questionnaires, standard in our department, students are asked only

TABLE 19–1   Changes in Student Perception

	Value of service-learning project	Service-learning as career enhancement	Service as valuable (in general)	Service as "helping"	Service as solving problems and/or meeting needs
Before (charity model) (24 students)	22	19	5	5	1
After (change model) (23 students)	23	20	17	3	9

two questions: 1) "What has been most beneficial to you about this course, and why?" 2) "What suggestions do you have, if any, for improving it?"

To distinguish among their comments about the project's value, I created five categories: 1) comments about the project's value; 2) comments about career enhancement as an important benefit; 3) comments about service's value in general; 4) comments about service being perceived as a means to help others, as charity; and 5) comments about service being valuable because problems affecting quality of life and ability to support others' needs in the community are solved.

The table provides comparative data on responses to the first questions. In both semesters, most students mentioned the project as the course's most beneficial aspect. The differences, however, are in the nature of the benefits. In the first semester, labeled my charity model, nearly 90 percent of the students mention the career-enhancing benefits, but only 20 percent mention the value of the service, and these students frame that value in terms of helping or charity (one student talked about it as both helping and solving problems). In the second semester, however, after I redefined the course goals and shifted my emphases, the number of students mentioning service as a valuable benefit increased nearly 60 percent (to 78 percent from 20 percent). About 40 percent of those students saw the value of the service in terms of problem-solving or change. Most interesting is that even with this shift in emphasis toward service, there is little change in the emphasis the students placed on the project's practical, career-enhancing value. Elevating the importance of service did not result in any corresponding diminishment in learning or the benefits of production.

Now the two stories — the first from the fall semester, the second from the spring. Here I rely on student comments from their written work: reflection reports, journals, and online discussion lists. The first story is about a group of young women who worked with the YMCA to learn about the different programs that the YMCA offered and the ways in which the YMCA serves the community in order to create an annual report. These students began by meeting with the associate director to understand what the YMCA wanted in terms of content and layout. Then, after learning what programs were offered, they began a long process of interviewing program directors, volunteers, and participants in programs in order to write articles for the report. By semester's end, they had put a lot of time in the fact-finding, writing, designing, and editing. The end result, minus the budget, which was not ready by semester's end, was an annual report that was clear, well organized, and professional. The YMCA published the report (adding only the budget) as written and designed by the students. The associate director said that the "report helped to bring a new perspective, which was needed." She also said that the "writing style made reading enjoyable."

All told, the students were understandably proud of their accomplishment. But how they described their achievement is telling. Their emphasis was primarily on career enhancement and secondarily on "helping." Only once, in a six-page reflection report, did they mention any benefits that the YMCA would accrue or anything about the populations that the YMCA served. Here are a few excerpts, including the one reference to "helping":

> Through this project, we both have gained the knowledge we did not have coming into the project that we will be able to take with us as we pursue our careers. We have an activity to put on our resumes that we can discuss with a potential employer so that they can see that we have had experience in the workplace.

> We learned real-world concepts and applied them. We liked working for an organization, but at times, we felt distanced; even though they were our client, we didn't feel a strong commitment.

> We learned other things as well. By actually creating the product, we were able to see how the YMCA helps people, and we were also helping people by writing articles about the success of the YMCA.

Reading their report and working with them during the semester, I believe that they learned about an organization that works to "empower others to achieve shared goals that promote the common good" (interview with director). But, based on their comments, it appears that what they valued most was what they learned in terms of skills, having an opportunity to practice those skills in a "real" setting, and how that experience would help them in the future. They did gain some larger perspective about the YMCA's place in the community and derived satisfaction from "helping people," but this benefit was clearly secondary. And, when I look for any indication that they perceived their work as effecting change, I found none.

The second story is about a group of three students who worked with the YMCA to write a grant proposal to help fund an after-school program for low income children. These three students had to work closely with the YMCA director to find a granting agency, evaluate the request for proposal, assess the needs of the community being served, and write the grant. This team spent a lot of time working out of class; they had to contact the granting agency, the school where the program would be implemented, and community members who would be affected. In addition, they had to research the issue of childcare availability and cost in order to make a strong case. This work meant digging into county and state statistics and conducting interviews with parents and administrators. By semester's end, they too had a finished product, and they too were proud of their work. However, their reflection report and journal entries had a different slant. Instead of focusing on the benefits they accrued, they focused on the problem they were trying to solve and how their grant proposal might accomplish the task. Here are a few of their comments:

> Our task wasn't easy. Unlike some of the other groups, we had a very restricted format for our grant. That said, we learned how to come to terms with a problem. Many families in our community (mostly single moms) who need childcare can't afford it. The YMCA, in one of its many efforts to reach out and help people in our community, saw this problem and worked to solve it. We were glad to be a part of this team, and we hope that the grant is funded. Those kids need it!

> Service-learning opened up working and the community; it was real work for people. Not only will I use what I learned, but I feel good about learning—a bit of a new feeling. The organization we worked for has some real needs and few resources. I was surprised to see this; I didn't expect to see poverty here, and children going without. Working with these people and this organization has given me a new set of lenses to see the world outside, a world too few students ever see while in school.

Looking at these excerpts from their reflection report, it seems clear that this group had a different take on the service-learning project than the previous semester's group. Their emphasis is on how their work would serve the community's needs. They talk about being part of a "team" with the organization, rather than having a client relationship. One could argue that the project type they were involved in played a role, and I would have to agree that it may have contributed to their attitude. However, when I take the statistics from the table into account, I know that there is more to it than just the project type. And I believe that the difference lies primarily in the approach I took.

My Approach

My teaching philosophy is predicated on the notion that teaching is a *teche* (an art with a focus on the end—in this case, civic values and practical skills), and that to be successful, teachers must be reflective practitioners who are capable of recognizing problems and who, after identifying problems, work to solve them by making changes in their pedagogy (Cochran-Smith, 1999; Schön, 1995). In the two stories and the table above, I offer evidence that documents some changes in my students' attitudes about service-learning. In the brief section that follows, I describe the process that led to those changes.

I began working with service-learning pedagogy a year prior to the two semesters I discuss above. At first, due to not completely understanding the need to balance service and learning (and the methods necessary to achieve that balance), I treated service-learning as a kind of experiential learning with an added value. I "sold" it to students by emphasizing the practical (instrumental) advantages and added that they would learn to help others. We worked hard, produced good products, and were successful. Our clients used most of the documents we produced, and nearly every client was satisfied; some so much so that they requested more help in subsequent semesters (e.g., the YMCA, as illustrated above). In general, the students and I felt a sense of accomplishment.

We were especially pleased because the organizations we assisted responded positively. For instance, a senior staffer at the Montgomery County Department of Social Services sent her student team and me an email describing the work the student team had done to create a newsletter:

> We are pleased with the newsletter your students have created for us. . . . Their choice of layout, folding design, graphics, and paper resulted in a slick, professional newsletter. . . . We appreciate the students' efforts in giving us ideas and suggestions on how we can improve. All in all, they did us a great service.

I received similar statements from other agencies such as the Village of Newport, which needed newsletters produced in order to seek funds to continue their work to restore their three covered bridges, and from the Blacksburg Senior Center, for whom we produced a basic instruction manual about computer and email use. The work my students produced had tangible effects on the community, bringing people together, sharing news, raising funds for essential human services, and providing necessary instruction.

This success of creating deliverables that met certain criteria and satisfied the clients we worked with was seductive. So were the positive comments from my students, who, in person and on the anonymous course evaluations, emphasized that they learned what they came to learn (to produce professional documents for clients) and gained experience they could use later. In addition, many noted that their work, the documents they produced, was helpful, which made them feel good.

The success made it harder for me to see the shortcomings in terms of service-learning pedagogy. We were being useful; we were doing good work, work that furthered the organizations' goals we supported. That said, I could see, based upon those same comments, that while what we were doing was good work, we were not "doing good" in the fullest sense. The emphasis for most students was on how the projects benefited them, not on how, through the projects, they were solving problems for others and making a difference in their communities. And virtually no one talked about change; instead, the few who mentioned service did so by talking about how they felt good because they helped others. While helping is good, it is not sufficient if we seek to develop civic ideals fully. As Cushman (1996) says, "service focuses not on 'helping' others but on joining them as relative equals in a common project of social change" (p. 199).

To shift the emphasis from charity to change, I looked at my course in the mirror. When I did, I saw the reflection of someone who had focused far too much on the instrumental sense of being practical by emphasizing experiential learning's advantages in terms of future employability. In addition, I realized that I had not included the service as a text; instead, I had treated it as an outcome (Morton, 1996). The result? My students were not mentioning service or problem-solving because we were not engaging with the community; I was not helping them achieve reciprocal relationships with their community partners. As far as I could tell, the heart of the problem lay in the course design itself and the manner in which I had implemented service-learning pedagogy.

Definition

As I re-visioned the course, the first problem I addressed was definition. What was service-learning and how did my students understand it? As I examined their course evaluations and reflection reports, I looked for clues that might explain why students seemed to say so little about the projects' civic benefits and/or why they focused so prominently on the instrumental benefits. My first clue had to do with how they defined the relationships with the organizations. All but one of the students talked about the organizations they worked with as "clients." By talking about clients, they were following my lead (I had used the term "client project" in my syllabus and in class), and I was following others' lead in our discipline (Crawford, 1993; Henson & Sutliff, 1998; Huckin, 1997). I believe that the term "client project" worked to undermine the service aspect. Students acted more like consultants for hire. They talked about *working for* clients rather than *working with* partners. In general, this language to some degree predefined the relationship. As a result, an essential element in the service-learning definition—developing a reciprocal relationship with their organization—was not met.

In addition, as stated earlier, I promoted the pedagogy's learning side to motivate the students to tackle the additional work involved with these projects. Looking back at my course documents, my emphasis is evident. The course description emphasizes that students will

> learn how to communicate effectively in the workplace. By reading and writing the kinds of "real-world" texts that professionals use daily and having opportunities to work collaboratively with organizations/ businesses in the community, [they will] learn the essentials of writing clearly, correctly, and concisely.

From stem to stern, from syllabus to semester evaluations, my focus was on the work's practical benefits of what they produced and how it would benefit them and their future careers. The students responded by telling me how they had met the course goals that I had laid out.

Finally, I had not helped them see a full context for service. I had portrayed their work as volunteering, as giving. As a result, students developed an attitude that, while altruistic and noble, did not engage them in citizenship, in being responsive to the community needs by first understanding those needs and then seeking to change the situation to meet those needs (Barber, 1998; Kahne & Westheimer, 1996; Shutz & Gere, 1998).

Service as Text

Another problem in the way in which I framed the course was that I did not give enough attention to the concept of "service." Keith Morton (1996) argues that if we think of service as a text, we suggest that service is equal to written work in its learning potential. Students also give service more weight when confronted with it in a manner equal to readings about, say, proposal writing (p. 282). During those first semesters, I focused far more attention on the course texts and the student texts than I did on *service as text*. I spent the majority of my time helping students learn the necessary skills in order to ensure that we met the organizations' needs by creating the best documents/products. I did not discuss the idea of service, or issues surrounding the service (e.g., why these organizations had such insufficient resources or why some organizations were funded sufficiently but others were not) until the course's end (to prepare them for the reflection report). Nor did I discuss the actual documents they were preparing, in regards to biases or social and political agendas. By ignoring the service, I gave priority to the texts we were using, thus contributing to the emphasis on producing deliverables. The result was to diminish the concept of service and to emphasize the instrumental tasks. In addition, when combined with my emphasis on a business rather than a social relationship with the organizations, my students had little to guide them toward establishing reciprocal partnerships.

Course Re-Design

To counter this over-emphasis on training and working toward civic goals, I redesigned the course by refining the service definition, shifting my emphasis, and using service as a text in the course. In so doing, I was able to transform a course that was more heavily weighted on training to one that balanced training and service, and my students' attitudes toward the course improved, even though I required them to serve.

In my redesign, one goal is to expand the notion of service by working at the hyphen. I am convinced that achieving service-learning is most explicitly difficult at the hyphen, a symbol of the reciprocity or "symbiotic relationship" (Migliore, quoted in Jacoby, 1996, p. 5) not only between the two concepts, but also between those served and those serving (Coles, 1993). I have also found that by including an emphasis on the hyphen and thus on my goals for both service and learning, I help my students see the need for achieving reciprocity.

Achieving reciprocity is essential, as is making the course goals explicit I have come to agree with Joan Schine (1997), who explains that service-learning should begin with clearly stated educational objectives. For her, service-learning must:

- Be rooted in the conviction that schooling at its best concerns itself with the humane application of knowledge to life
- Be carefully introduced and creatively promoted
- Be directed not just to the community but also toward the school itself
- Be focused on something more than preparation for a career
- Be set up so that students not only be asked to go out to serve; they should also be asked to write about their experience and, if possible, discuss with others the lessons they have learned. (p. 187)

These objectives are foundational as I seek to balance service and learning and succeed in helping students grow as citizens, the university and community grow as partners, and all three come together to achieve a version of democratic caring and a true union of the liberal arts and vocational education to achieve a humane direction to education (Dewey, 1944).

To close the gap between service and learning, to work toward reciprocity, I make my pedagogy more explicit. First, I share the objectives listed above with both my students and their "service-learning partners," a term I have adopted to highlight the work's reciprocity and the need to achieve a deeper level of intimacy with the organizations we are supporting. I also add more explicit discussions of the nature of service, addressing its many forms and uses. By introducing readings and short, reflective writing assignments in addition to the final reflection report, I make service a text in the course. With service as a text, we not only talk about how to produce better documents; we also talk about why and for whom. I challenge my students to think about the role(s) they will play in their communities and their obligations to those communities. By integrating the concept of service into the course, students see that it has the same weight and value as layout or style issues.

One of the most important issues that we address is the distinction between charity and change. Focusing on what service means, we discuss how one's attitude toward the work predefines, to some extent, the results. In addition, we also talk about language, focusing on terms such as "client" and "partner." I ask students to write informally about these issues in a NetForum (an online discussion area), then we discuss their responses in class. With a clearer sense of service as change, we talk about the social issues surrounding their projects, highlighting the problems and frustrations that they see their partners, and the individuals their partners serve, experience.

To deepen the relationship with, and encourage more involvement by, the community partners, I have asked the partners to come to class at the semester's beginning and end to share in roundtable discussions about the projects. Having the community members come to class at the beginning helps to bridge the distance between academe and community, and everyone involved gains an understanding for what the semester relationship will entail; at the end our meetings help us see what we have accomplished and what remains to be done. The course-ending meetings are more of a celebration than a briefing, sharing work done well for some greater good. My goal is to make the relationships (between students and agency, faculty and agencies, students and faculty) more in line with Robert Coles's (1993) suggestion that service requires *connections*.

Conclusion

After working with this pedagogy for nearly three years, I have learned that to succeed at service-learning students must build a bridge between service and learning, one that they may have to cross many times before actually reaching knowledge. The bridge is not uni-directional; in fact, I am convinced that the hyphen in the term "service-learning" applies not only to the space between service and learning for the student; it also applies to the space between the student and the agency or organization the student supports, between the students and the teacher, and between the teacher (as the academy's representative) and the organizations (as the community's representatives). The more omni-directional the movement (between service and learning, student and organization, organization and educational institution), the more likely that reflection, and therefore service-learning, will occur.

Earlier, I shared a few of my students' comments that pointed to their satisfaction and their focus on career building first, and service second. Then, I showed how the changes I made increased the balance between service and learning. I cannot claim that the changes I have begun to make have transformed my classes completely. I do not think transformation happens overnight, and I am still not sure that I have found the right balance of service and learning. That said, I can say that many more students now seem to see their work differently and recognize their civic responsibilities. They also are learning that the work they will do has the potential to effect change. Some students actually write mini-epistles about this change in attitude. Here are two students' ideas about the value of service-learning:

> Many Americans today lose sight of the importance of community service. Distracted by our busy lives, we overlook the positive role we can play in the betterment of our neighborhoods, and how this effort can lead to a happier, healthier America. For much of my college career, I was among those students whose busy lives cause us to be myopic. However, my involvement with the Christiansburg Managing Information in Rural America (MIRA) Team through a service-learning project changed my outlook. My work with MIRA has had a profound impact on my commitment to volunteerism and has solidified my plans to become an active member of my community.

> Service-learning projects offer students a chance to give to the community. Students receive a number of benefits from the New River Valley community, enjoying the transportation system, local libraries, parks, emergency services, and a number of other services that are provided or underwritten by the local governments. Service-learning projects provide a chance to work for a community organization, enabling students to join with community members and participate more fully with them.

These two students worked hard to give something to their partners and their community. They worked to develop a reciprocal relationship. Although it was quite difficult at times (due to group dynamics and the nature of the organization they supported), they still came to see that there is a larger purpose to their service and their schooling.

Asking students to consider a larger purpose to their service and schooling is just the beginning. As we consider curricular questions, we must answer: what is our discipline for? and by extension, what is college for? The answers to those questions vary, naturally, upon whom you ask. However, given service's long tradition at many higher learning institutions and the service tradition that we, in our discipline have, I would argue (as I have elsewhere) that

> The tacit tradition linked to the pejorative term of "service" needs to be brought out into the open for examination and discussion. We need to "see" the text that was first written around the time of the Morrill Act, and we need to argue that the very forces that produced the universities and colleges many of us teach in are the same forces that created the need for our courses. We should wear the mantle of *service* [italics in original] proudly as we demonstrate the value of service to the university. We need not hide our relationship with service in order to claim disciplinarity. (1999, p. 42)

If we accept this service mantle, we might also want to expand what that service means and for whom.

Taking the cue from Quintilian, I believe the service is to our students and to society at large. According to Barber, "the university [does not have] a civic mission . . . the university *is* [emphasis added] a civic mission, is civility itself defined as the rules and conventions that permit a community to facilitate conversation and the discourse upon which all knowledge . . . depends" (1992, p. 186). Our mission is to help our students become valuable, viable orators who see their work as important to the communities in which they live. We are responsible for more than giving them skills and knowledge; we need to help them learn to "act through" that knowledge with a sense of responsibility (Johnson, 1998, p. 155). One of the best ways I have found to accomplish that goal is the service-learning pedagogy.

As I have come to understand it, service-learning pedagogy can bridge the gaps and the horns of the dilemma Miller described. Implemented reflectively, it creates a learning attitude that enables students to boost critical thinking skills and improve the integration of theory and practice. They learn to do *for* others and themselves by *working with others* in a reciprocal relationship, thus preparing themselves for the workplace and for their place as citizens. As such, the work they produce is truly a matter of conduct. I have also learned that one must be very aware of the tensions inherent in our curriculum and the pedagogy, particularly the tensions at the hyphen—between service and learning, organizations and clients, workplace preparation and civic literacy. The key to success is to make those tensions explicit to students and the agencies they work for by creating truly reciprocal relationships.

NOTES

1. In ancient Greece, only young men were given rights to be citizens, and citizenship was determined by birthright, not wealth (Crowley & Hawhee, 1999).

2. Professional communication as a term describes the various ways the field in which I work is identified (technical writing, technical communication, technical and scientific communication, business communication, professional writing, and so on). While there are some distinctions that are important (see Sullivan & Porter, 1993, for an overview), they are not essential to the argument that I am making here about vocationalism, service-learning, and civic idealism.

3. That a major publisher, Allyn and Bacon, has contracted to produce a textbook focusing on service-learning pedagogy in professional communication testifies to its growing stature. This text will follow in the footsteps of the earlier text by Watters and Ford (1994), which focused on service-learning strategies in writing-across-the-disciplines.

REFERENCES

Adler-Kassner, L. (2000). *Service-learning at a glance. Reflections on community-based writing instruction, 1,* 28–29.

Adler-Kassner, L., & Collins, T. (1994). *Writing in service-learning courses: Technical report no. 9.* Minneapolis: University of Minnesota's Center for Interdisciplinary Studies of Writing.

Aristotle. (1954). *The rhetoric and poetics of Aristotle.* (W. R. Roberts, Trans.). New York: Modern Library.

Bacon, N. (1997). Community service writing: Problems, challenges, questions. In L. Adler-Kassner, R. Crooks, & A. Watters (Eds.), *Writing the community: Concepts and models for service learning in composition* (pp. 39–55). Washington, DC: AAHE/NCTE.

Barber, B. (1992). *An aristocracy of everyone.* New York: Oxford University Press.

Barber, B. (1994). A proposal for mandatory citizen education and community service. *Michigan Journal of Community Service Learning, 1*(1), 86–93.

Barber, B. (1998). Civic mission of the university. In B. Barber (Ed.), *A passion for democracy* (pp. 178–86). Princeton, NJ: Princeton University Press.

Boyer, E. (1990). *Scholarship reconsidered: Priorities of the professoriate.* Princeton, NJ: Carnegie Foundation.

Boyer, E. (1994, March 9). Creating the new American college. *Chronicle of Higher Education,* A48.

Boyte, H. (1993). What is citizenship education? *Rethinking tradition: Integrating service with academic study on college campuses* (pp. 63–66). Denver, CO: Education Commission of the States, 1993.

Bringle, R. G., & Hatcher, J. A. (1996). Implementing service learning in higher education. *Journal of Higher Education, 67,* 221–39.

Bushnell, J. (1999). A contrary view of the technical writing classroom: Notes toward future discussions. *Technical Communication Quarterly, 8,* 175–88.

Checkoway, B. (2001). Renewing the civic mission of the American research university. *Journal of Higher Education, 72,* 125–47.

Cicero (1969). *De Oratore, Books I & II.* (H. Rackham, Trans.). Cambridge, MA: Harvard University Press.

Cochran-Smith, M. (1999). Learning to teach for social justice. In Gary A. Griffin (Ed.), *The education of a teacher* (pp. 114–44). Chicago: NSEE.

Coles, R. (1993). *The call of service: A witness to idealism.* Boston: Houghton Mifflin.

Coye, D. (1997). Ernest Boyer and the new American college. *Change, 29,* 20–29.

Crawford, K. (1993). Community service writing in an advanced composition class. In J. Howard (Ed.), *Praxis I: A faculty casebook on community service learning* (pp. 75–83). Ann Arbor, MI: OCSL Press.

Crowley, S., & Hawhee, D. (1999). *Ancient rhetorics for contemporary students* (2nd ed.). Boston: Allyn and Bacon.

Cushman, E. (1996). The rhetorician as an agent of social change. *College Composition and Communication, 47,* 7–28.

Deans, T. (2000). *Writing partnerships: Service-learning in composition.* Urbana, IL: NCTE.

Dewey, J. (1944). Exchange with Alexander Meiklejohn, in Fortune. In J. A. Boydston (Ed.), *The later works of John Dewey: Vol. 15* (pp. 250–337). Carbondale, IL: Southern Illinois University Press.

Dubinsky, J. (1999). Making the invisible discourse of service visible. In *CPTSC '98 Proceedings* (pp. 40–44). Lubbock, TX: Council for Programs in Technical and Scientific Communication.

Engell, J., & Dangerfield, A. (1998). The market-driven university, humanities in the age of money. *Harvard Magazine*, 100.5: 48–55, 111.

Geonetta, S. C. (1997). Designing four-year programs in technical communication. In K. Staples & C. Ornatowski (Eds.), *Foundations for teaching technical communication: Theory, practice, and program design* (pp. 251–58). Greenwich, CT: Ablex.

Hafer, G. R. (1999). Making the connection: Desktop publishing, professional writing, and *pro bono publico*. *Technical Communication Quarterly, 8,* 405–18.

Halloran, S. M. (1976). Tradition and theory in rhetoric. *Quarterly Journal of Speech, 62,* 234–41.

Heilker, P. (1997). Rhetoric made real: Civic discourse and writing beyond the curriculum. In L. Adler-Kassner, R. Crooks, & A. Watters (Eds.), *Writing the community: Concepts and models for service-learning in composition* (pp. 71–78). Washington, DC: AAHE/NCTE.

Henson, L., & Sutliff, K. (1998). A service-learning approach to business and technical writing instruction. *Journal of Technical Writing and Communication, 28*(2), 189–205.

Howard, V. A. (1999). The humanities and service-learning: Whence and whither? *Michigan Journal of Community Service Learning, 6,* 123–33.

Huckin, T. (1997). Technical writing and community service. *Journal of Business and Technical Communication, 11,* 49–59.

Isocrates. (1990). From *Antidosis*. In B. Herzberg & P. Bizzell (Eds.), *The rhetorical tradition* (pp. 50–54). Boston: Bedford Books.

Jacoby, B., and Associates. (1996). Service-learning in today's higher education. In B. Jacoby & associates (Eds.), *Service-learning in higher education: Concepts and practices* (pp. 3–25). San Francisco: Jossey-Bass.

Johnson, R. R. (1998). *User-centered technology*. Albany: SUNY P.

Kahne, J., & Westheimer, J. (1996). In service of what? The politics of service learning. *Phi Delta Kappan, 77,* 593–600.

Kendall, J. C. (1990). Combining service and learning: An introduction. In J. C. Kendall & Associates (Eds.), *Combining service and learning: A resource book for community and public service*. Raleigh, NC: NSEE.

Lisman, C. D. (1998). *Toward a civil society*. Westport, CT: Bergin and Garvey.

Marrou, H. (1964). *A history of education in antiquity*. (G. Lamb, Trans.). New York: New American Library.

Matthews, C., & Zimmerman, B. (1999). Integrating service learning and technical communication: Benefits and challenges. *Technical Communication Quarterly, 8,* 365–83.

Mattson, K. (1998). Can service-learning transform the modern university? A lesson from history. *Michigan Journal of Community Service Learning, 5,* 108–13.

Meyer P. R., & Bernhardt, S. A. (1997). Workplace realities and the technical communication curriculum: A call for change. In K. Staples & C. Ornatowski (Eds.). *Foundations for teaching technical communication: Theory, practice, and program design* (pp. 85–98). Greenwich, CT: Ablex.

Miller, C. (1989), What's practical about technical writing? In B. E. Fearing & W. K. Sparrow (Eds.), *Technical writing: Theory and practice* (pp. 14–24). New York: MLA.

Miller, T. (1991). Treating professional writing as social praxis. *Journal of Advanced Composition, 11,* 57–72.

Moore, P. (1999). Myths about instrumental discourse: A response to Robert R. Johnson. *Technical Communication Quarterly, 8,* 210–23.

Morton, K. (1995). The irony of service: Charity, project and social change in service-learning. *Michigan Journal of Community Service Learning, 2,* 19–32.

Morton, K., (1996). Issues related to integrating service-learning into the curriculum. In B. Jacoby & Associates (Eds.), *Service-learning in higher education: Concepts and practices* (pp. 276–96). San Francisco: Jossey-Bass, 1996.

Murphy, J., Jr. (Ed.) (1987). *Quintilian on the teaching of speaking and writing: Translations from books one, two, and ten of the Institutio Oratorio*. Carbondale: Southern Illinois University Press.

Papillon, T. (1995). Isocrates' techne and rhetorical pedagogy. *Rhetoric Society Quarterly, 25,* 149–63.

Quintilian. (1972). *Institutio Oratorio*. (H. E. Butler, Trans.). In T. W Benson & M. E. Prosser (Eds.), *Readings in classical rhetoric*. Bloomington: Indiana University Press.

Reynolds, J. F. (1992). Classical rhetoric and the teaching of technical writing. *Technical Communication Quarterly, 1,* 63–76.

Rhoads, R. A. (1997). *Community service and higher learning: Explorations of the caring self*. Albany: SUNY Press.

Schine, J. (1997). Looking ahead: Issues and challenges. In J. Schine (Ed.). *Service Learning* (pp. 186–99). Chicago: NSSE.

Schön, D. (1995). Knowing in action: The new scholarship requires a new epistemology. *Change*, 27(6), 27–34.

Shutz, A., & Ruggles Gere, A. (1998). Service learning and English studies. *College English, 60*, 129–49.

Stanton, T. K., Giles, Jr., D. E., & Cruz, N. I. (1999). *Service-learning: A movement's pioneers reflect on its origins, practice, and future*. San Francisco: Jossey-Bass.

Staples, K. (1999). Technical communication from 1950–1998: Where are we now? *Technical Communication Quarterly, 8*, 153–64.

Staples, K., & Ornatowski, C. (1997). Introduction. In K. Staples & C. Ornatowski (Eds.), *Foundations for teaching technical communication: Theory, practice, and program design* (pp. xi–xxi). Greenwich, CT: Ablex.

Sullivan, P., & J. Porter. (1993). Remapping curricular geography: Professional writing in/and English. *Journal of Business and Technical Communication, 7.4*, 389–422.

Taylor, J. (1994). Service Learning: Education with a purpose. In A. Watters & M. Ford (Eds.), *A guide for change: Resources for implementing community service writing* (pp. 165–70). New York: McGraw-Hill.

Wahlstrom, B. (1997). Designing a research program in technical and scientific communication: Seeing standards and defining the agenda. In K. Staples & C. Ornatowski (Eds.), *Foundations for teaching technical communication: Theory, practice, and program design* (pp. 299–316). Greenwich, CT: Ablex.

Wallenfelt, E. C. (1986). *Roots of special interests in American higher education*. Lanham, MD: University Press of America.

Waterman, A. (Ed.). (1997). *Service learning: Applications from research*. Mahwah, NJ: Lawrence Erlbaum Associates, Inc.

Watters, A., & Ford, M. (Eds.). (1994). *A guide for change: Resources for implementing community service writing*. New York: McGraw-Hill.

Whitburn, M. (1984). The ideal orator and literary critic as technical communicators: An emerging revolution in English departments. In R. J. Connors, L. S. Ede, & A. Lunsford (Eds.), *Essays on classical rhetoric and modern discourse* (pp. 226–47). Carbondale and Edwardsville: Southern Illinois University Press, 1984.

20 FROM *Students in the Streets*

PAULA MATHIEU

True democratic campus/community partnerships—partnerships that strive to meet the needs of a community, as defined by the community, that are of high quality and sustained involvement, that involve students, faculty, and staff and community members—will be a key marker for higher education in the millennium.
—THE CAMPUS COMPACT WINGSPREAD CONFERENCE

I've learned the hard way. Now when I get a phone call from a university professor or student, I don't reply.
—FRAN CZAJKOWSKI, Executive Director, Homeless Empowerment Project

. . . [T]he "right" form of service learning can only be decided upon by specific actors in particular contexts struggling with the possibilities and dangers involved in acting in communities beyond their classrooms.
—AARON SCHUTZ AND ANNE RUGGLES GERE

THE PROMISE AND PERILS OF INSTITUTIONALIZED SERVICE LEARNING

Even though many scholars connect service learning to past educational initiatives founded by educators like John Dewey[1] or Jane Addams[2] or point to the early use of the term *service learning* in the 1950s,[3] and even though the roots of service learning can be traced to countless grassroots projects developed by dedicated teachers and students,[4] the contemporary push toward institutionalized programs of service learning can be dated to the selfish decade of the 1980s and was born, in part, from public relations concerns. Patricia Hutchinson (2002) notes that "a desire for college students to challenge the common perception that young adults were self-seeking and out of touch with social issues" led to the development of the Campus Outreach

From *Tactics of Hope: The Public Turn in English Composition* (Portsmouth, NH: Heinemann, 2005), 85–115.

Opportunity League (COOL) by a Harvard graduate in 1984. A year later, the presidents of Brown University, Georgetown University, and Stanford University founded Campus Compact to counter public images of college students as "materialistic and self-absorbed, more interested in making money than in helping their neighbors" by identifying service learning as a primary strategy for advancing a more positive image of college students (Campus Compact 2004a). H. Brooke Hessler (2000) asserts that desires for publicity and marketing continue to underscore many universities' interest in service learning:

> At a time when many colleges and universities are vying to differentiate themselves from competing institutions, it is no coincidence that service-learning programs are gaining administrative attention. Service learning represents a way to demonstrate institutional generosity and historical ties with the local community, presumably in contrast with the soul-less online and proprietary enterprises. (28)

In other words, service learning is, in the eyes of many academic administrators, an important marketing tool, a "unique selling point" for the institution.

Interestingly, however, service learning is becoming less unique and more the norm in higher education. As of 2004, Campus Compact lists as members the presidents of more than 900 two- and four-year private and public colleges and universities in 46 states and the District of Columbia. The conferences and publications of Campus Compact are funded by large corporations and foundations like General Electric, the Ford Foundation, the Johnson Foundation, and the Corporation for National Service (Campus Compact 2004a; Campus Compact "Wingspread"). Campus Compact supports the development of service learning through a variety of initiatives: by promoting the growth of service learning on member campuses (through the creation of guidelines, rubric, and syllabi); by creating campaigns that support the passage of federal legislation promoting community service; by forming partnerships with business, community, and government leaders; by organizing conferences and meetings that provide information to members; and by awarding grants and awards to member schools (Campus Compact 2004a).

Without drawing quick or simple conclusions, I think it's worth asking some hard questions about the value of the rapid expansion of service-learning programs fueled by organizations like Campus Compact. What difference does it make that such organized and well-funded support for service learning has its roots in elite institutions and is being promoted in a top-down model through a network of college presidents? What difference does it make that the motivation to create both the Campus Compact and COOL networks was grounded in a desire for better public relations for ivy-league college students? What models of service learning do national organizations promote? What needs get prioritized and what concerns receive little attention?

In today's colleges and universities, the trend seems to be toward creating long-term, top-down, institutionalized service-learning programs; or to continue with Michel de Certeau's terminology, universities privilege *strategic* rather than *tactical* service programs (1984). Strategies, according to de Certeau, seek to create stable spaces that can overcome temporal changes. Creating strategies means institutionalizing, creating official spaces, like service-learning offices or university-controlled community centers in local neighborhoods. As de Certeau shows, seeking and creating strategic power has certain benefits: Actions can be calculated, continuity can be assured, and broader spaces can be claimed or controlled.

Clearly, predictability, continuity, and funded positions and spaces can benefit service-learning programs a great deal. Scholars like Linda Flower (2003) and Ellen Cushman (2002b, 2002a) make compelling cases for the advantages that institutionalized and long-term service-learning projects can yield. My concern, however, is that we must also consider the disadvantages of institutionalized models and consider more local *tactical* options as well.

Much scholarship related to service learning equates institutionalization with success. Statements such as these are commonplace: "The success of service learning will depend on the level of its institutionalization and how the faculty accepts, adopts, and implements it within the university" (Scapansky 2004); ". . . to foster the institutionalization of service learning . . . gives service learning advocates an ongoing voice in *CCCC*" (Deans 2000a); "Institutionalizing service-learning can be a critical strategy for mobilizing students as agents of social change who will also serve as positive representatives of higher education" (Hessler 2000). "In other words, service learning must become institutionalized within higher education" (Hutchinson 2002).

Campus Compact produces a variety of reports and documents encouraging institutionalization, including an annually updated report entitled *The Self-Assessment Rubric for the Institutionalization of Service-Learning in Higher Education*. This multivariable rubric is "designed to assist members of the higher education community in gauging the progress of their campus's service-learning institutionalization efforts" (Furco 2003). In short, the prevailing tenor of the discussion of institutionalizing service-learning programs frequently begs the question of the value of institutionalization, by assuming it as a natural and important goal.

In contrast, little scholarship raises critical questions about the value of creating institutionalized service projects. Margaret Himley (2004) does raise difficult ethical problems related to service learning, by placing fundamental questions about the shape and direction of service learning at the center of her inquiry:

> . . . [F]aced with so many dilemmas, I want to ask, what should we do as community service learning teachers? Institutionalize long-term relationships with agencies in the community (Flower "Partners"; Hessler 2000)? Become public intellectuals who conduct research in the community as

collaborative inquiry (Cushman 2002b)? Abolish student-based service-learning courses? Replace journals with well-defined methodologies such as case-studies and ethnographies and make service learning more explicitly like ethnography? Never have students write about the service experience (Herzberg, cited in Welch 2002)? Always have students write about the service experience (Welch 2002)? . . . Get rid of service learning in first-year composition? Get rid of it altogether? (432–33)

Himley's openness both to questioning the foundations of service learning itself and to considering a range of options—of which institutionalization is only one—promotes a useful willingness to remain open to a variety of possible service models, or to move away from service if certain troubling problems can't be resolved.

A fairly direct critique of top-down institutionalized service programs is articulated by Bruce Herzberg in an interview with Tom Deans, in which he expresses concern "about the shift from grassroots to top-down implementation" in service learning:

> I have encountered more and more people who said that they are being forced to implement service learning. The shift began at the close of the 1990s, I think. In the 1980s to early to mid-nineties, implementation was only made possible through huge and often self-sacrificing efforts by individual faculty members who believed in and were excited by community-based work. . . . So it's ironic that by the end of the 1990s we are in a situation where "the provost told me to do service learning." That's what I hear in workshops: "The dean mandated it"; "I was chosen to head up the project"; "I don't know anything about it, and I'm here to find out." And "I have to do assessment." And "I have no idea about what my budget is or how I'm supposed to promote this." And "There's a student requirement that they have to do service learning." . . . I haven't seen much written about this problem and I'm concerned that our community address this issue forcefully. (Deans 2002a, 75)

As Herzberg's comments suggest, service-learning programs that began because of the "huge and often self-sacrificing efforts" of individual instructors are being supplanted in many cases by top-down institutionalized efforts. To be fair, upper-level administrative support of service-learning programs can benefit existing service programs by sanctioning academic and staff time for the cultivation of service projects, establishing longer-term connections with community, and building in institutional rewards for faculty and staff engaged in service programs. An institutionalized service program can often claim measurable successes, be visible, and replicable.

While institutionalization of service learning is not evil on its face, it is risky and not necessarily beneficial, especially when universities institutionalize well-intentioned but top-down relationships. The very advantages of institutionalized service learning—measurable success, broad institutional presence, and sustainability—create a generic set of needs and priorities that make it difficult to respond to communities' needs and ideas. Rather than advocating institutionalization of service learning per se, we should ask, what values are we institutionalizing? What needs are we prioritizing? What risks do we incur when we seek to create broad, measurable, sustainable programs that claim institutional resources and space?

Harper, Donnelli, and Farmer (2003) warn that "institutions of higher learning risk becoming benevolent tyrants who injure the community by trying to save it." They describe the transition from "small independent service-learning projects into large administrative programs" in which "the institution is enriched through something of a colonizing enterprise, no matter how well intentioned such an enterprise may seem to individual students, teacher, and administrators." A partnership becomes exploitative, they claim, when power is viewed as "unidirectional, flowing from a root source to its branches" creating a sense of the university that "gains a greater understanding of itself as it interacts, appropriates, and projects itself onto the other" (619).

In seeking sustainability of strategic service programs, we need to critically examine the kinds of projects or relationships we are seeking to inscribe and repeat. The very need to repeat service projects in many different course sections, semester after semester, may predetermine what kinds of projects are created. To decide a year ahead, for example, what needs several hundred college students can fulfill in a limited amount of time, determined by the academic schedule, makes it more likely that the projects will be somewhat generic and not responsive to the particular rhetorical moment. Strategic planning, by definition, means securing stable continuity over time, and in many ways resists local rhetorical responsiveness. When service learning is a predetermined goal, *kairos*, or timeliness is sought—if at all—only after a decision is made that students must find some service to perform. When a program prioritizes continuity, it risks solving the difficult task of finding service sites for students semester after semester by relying on models that define service as a generic and benign task—like tutoring or serving a meal at a soup kitchen. Such models proceed from a problem approach, in which the community is defined as the source of the problem, which the university defines and on whose behalf the students work.

Finally, when seeking to promote top-down, ongoing service-learning programs, one risks glossing over or overlooking the real limitations of time and of the projects themselves. The people we work with in the streets don't live or think in terms of semesters or quarters or finals or spring breaks. The rhythms of the university do not necessarily harmonize with the rhythms and exigencies of community groups. If the impetus driving service learning is a desire to promote the university as a site of good work, how likely is it that universities will do multiple, meaningful service projects semester after semester, classroom after classroom, in exactly the amount of time a semester allows? As the following examples show, it is not very likely.

Too-Common Examples?

What would happen to our theorizing and principles about service learning if we listened to the community more? How effectively are top-down programs "serving" our partners? I asked some nonprofit workers and community friends around the United States and in the United Kingdom to talk to me about their experiences of working with university students. Sadly, it was easy to gather the following stories.

Example 1: What the Student Wants

The following email was sent to the offices of *Spare Change News*, Boston's street newspaper, on January 29, 2003:

> Hi,
>
> My name is April[5] _____ and I am a senior at _____ University. I am currently in a writing course and have been assigned your organization as my client for the semester. Through this course, I must produce various assignments that involve media proposals/campaigns to educate people about *Spare Change* and homelessness. I was wondering if it would be possible for you to send me any information your organization has, i.e. flyers, brochures, organizational material, etc, that you have in your office (that are unavailable online)? Even better, would it be possible for me to come in and meet with someone to talk about your organization so I can better understand how to represent you? Or attend any meetings you have scheduled? When you have the opportunity, please get back to me.
>
> Thank you,
>
> April _____

I ran across April's email as part of my regular volunteer editorial work at *Spare Change*, having been asked by the editor to go through the email and sort out the important pieces. I printed it out and brought it to Fran Czajkowski, executive director of the organization. She read it, laughed, and threw it aside, saying, "No thanks. Help like that is no help at all."

April may have been surprised that her email never received a reply. She might have felt frustrated or angry that her classwork became more difficult than she had hoped, since she did not get the meeting she requested. She might have even felt resentful that a course required her to offer what she considered help to the homeless and no one ever got back to her. Her teacher might even write someday about the difficulty of getting service organizations to cooperate.[6] This was clearly not a successful community-university partnership.

More than just a stray example, this story exemplifies the problems that can occur when teachers themselves are not connected to the community and *assign* organizations to students or ask students to *seek out* sites themselves. I think it's useful to interrogate why the nonprofit saw this as an undesirable offer and imagine how April's teachers could have set up a more successful experience.

When I interviewed Fran about the situation, she remarked that the student's email announced that she was assigned this nonprofit for the semester yet she had no information about the paper. This was, as all staff confirmed, the first contact anyone in the organization had received from anyone at April's university relating to this course. Who was the instructor who *assigned* April this organization? What responsibilities did he or she have to that organization when it became required course content? April's email indicated that she *must* produce media proposals/campaigns to educate *people* about this local nonprofit and homelessness. Whether or not such documents would be useful to this organization seems not to have been considered at all.

April's request represents not only a logistical failing but a rhetorical one as well. Throughout her email, April wrote only about *her* needs and what *she* must do for *her* class. She expressed that she couldn't find the information she needed on the Web and made three requests of the organization, two which would be time consuming (send documents and meet with her), and a third that seems inappropriate altogether: to allow the student to attend internal meetings. Fran remarked that this third request seemed surprisingly forward and was typical of other students' attitudes toward community nonprofits. "Could you imagine a student making the same request of IBM or even a local tax agency? It wouldn't happen," she said (Czajkowski 2003).

Fran also expressed frustration because the student could have learned more about the organization prior to contacting her. Street newspapers are sold on the streets by vendors who are homeless or low-income; their pages provide information about homelessness and the organizations themselves. So, for a dollar, April could have better prepared herself before contacting *Spare Change.*

In addition to lacking a rhetorical sense of her audience, April's email also lacked *kairos* or a sense of timeliness, in terms of what was currently going on in the organization. If she had read the paper, she would have learned that the development committee at *Spare Change* had been cultivating a relationship with a local advertising agency to develop a public-awareness campaign, which would be hitting the streets around the time she sent the email. Such campaigns take a great deal of time and expertise to develop and implement, more than one semester's work from one undergraduate student. April herself offered nothing to the organization in exchange for her requests. She did not even try to make the case that her assignment might be useful to the organization.

In one sense, April's teacher put April in a difficult and a rhetorical situation, requiring her to create documents for an organization with no sense of its current needs, just a generic imperative to *help*. Along with this imperative, the instructor granted the students at least the hypothetical right to publicly represent a community organization. Fran was surprised that April was asked by her instructor—and seemed comfortable claiming—this right without knowing the organization or even asking their consent.

In a perfect world, small nonprofits like *Spare Change News* would have enough staff to keep their website fully up to date and to reply to even unhelpful requests like April's. The very fact that they can't shows that nonprofits often lack the material resources that would make quick and easy "student service" useful. Fran describes the situation this way:

> It's often more work to explain what we need to a class of unprepared students than to do it ourselves. Especially when students are just interested in us because of one course or one project, it's not worth our time. I get about 30 phone calls each semester from college students wanting to do final projects for some course or another on *Spare Change* and they all want to meet with me, and I just say no. Even when teachers try to set it up, they approach me as a stranger. They often know so little about our organization or our needs that the time required makes it not worth it. Plus as an organization, we've been burned too many times by promises. (Czajkowski 2003)

Fran's remarks attest to problems that result when partnerships are not grounded in ongoing local relationships, and connections with local organizations occur after a service-learning course is designed. Courses that ask students to choose sites of service not only risk framing service as a generic good, they also risk providing a disservice to community partners.

Example 2: Burn Me Twice—Master's Student Doesn't Deliver

Fran mentioned being "burned" by other university partnerships, and when I asked her to explain, she easily found examples. She described a project that seemed carefully planned to have a reciprocal and positive outcome for all involved. A graduate student in communications and her advisor contacted the organization, hoping to produce a documentary video about the newspaper and its vendors. The student planned the project as her master's thesis and the organization would receive a professionally made video about itself. The professor promised that *Spare Change* would have a say in determining the length, angle, and participants in the video. The student promised to stay out of the way and to be a minimal intrusion on the organization. Fran agreed to give the student access to staff, vendors, volunteers, meetings, and upcoming events. Based on all principles of community partnerships, the planning seemed sound.

In reality, the project required much more time of staff, vendors, and volunteers than originally proposed. "That was all right, though," Fran said. "We were hoping for a video we could really use." Some months after the filming ended, Fran received an email indicating that the video was complete; the thesis project had been passed. She was assured that "after a few final edits" the organization's video would arrive.

As of this writing, more than two years after the video was promised to the organization, nothing has arrived. Repeated efforts to contact the student and her advisor have resulted in promises but no video; the student received her master's thesis but the organization received no film.

When instructors set up projects that advocate "writing for the community" (Deans *Writing*), how careful and sure are we that the final work arrives and is assessed by the organization? Once grades are handed in and we move on to the next semester or project, how carefully do we follow up to be sure the student work has met a specific need?

Example 3: No One Burned, But No One Helped Much Either

A business writing faculty member approached a large street paper and asked if her students could develop new project ideas and write up marketing proposals for the publication. Lisa, one of the paper's staff members, made herself available to answer questions from students and the faculty member; she offered to visit the class to discuss the publication and its current projects. After the term ended, the instructor arrived carrying a box filled with glossy-covered reports, recommending a variety of projects for the publication. After the instructor left, I asked the staff member, "What will you do with all of those?"

"Honestly," she replied, "Probably not much. I'll glance through them, but there's probably not much here that will be of use to us."

I then asked about the instructor. Lisa said, "The instructor is a very nice woman. Spoke to me a few times. But in the course of a few conversations, it was hard to imagine what kind of projects students could do that would also be directly relevant to us in one term. We've met this faculty member, but she didn't know our organization all that well. None of these student projects will be specific enough to really meet any of our needs."

Finally, I inquired as to what might have made this connection more useful. Lisa said, "I'm not sure, because I don't know the needs and requirements of the class very well. Maybe if [the faculty member] had spent some time, even doing some volunteer work, she could have suggested more specific projects. Or even better, it might be interesting to plan a class together."

The good news of this example is that the teacher did speak with the organization before the semester. She did follow through. She drove with a box of reports to the community organization, and she honestly hoped they would be useful. The course was set up, however, to teach students to write marketing proposals. The assessment of the course did not include attention to whether or how the proposals were useful or timely in the eyes of the organization.

As I'll discuss near the end of this chapter, establishing another model of community partnerships might mean taking the partnership idea even more seriously. Specific courses could then be planned around specific needs of specific groups at specific times.

Example 4: The Case of the Vanishing Intern

A midwestern university's internship office arranged a required undergraduate service internship for a student to spend a summer working 20 hours a week for an East Coast nonprofit that had a paid staff of four. Megan Mahoney, one of the staff members, spoke with the internship advisor, exchanged emails with the student, and made plans for his arrival. Megan spent much of the first day with him, teaching him about the organization, offering different projects or areas where he could work, and getting him set up on the computer system. On his next scheduled day in the office, he did not arrive or call. Concerned phone calls and emails to both the student and the faculty advisor weren't returned. He never returned for a second day of work.

More than two weeks later, an email arrived at the organization that read, in its entirety, as follows:

> Hi, It's [first name]
>
> Please tell [staff member] and whoever else needs to know that I can't volunteer for you anymore. I'm sorry that I didn't tell you this beforehand, and I'm sorry if there are complications. I can explain this at some other time.
>
> Thank you
>
> [first and last name]

After Megan forwarded me this email, I asked her about the experience, including how much time was lost. "It could have been worse," she said. "He was only in the office for a day." Since he had committed to 20 hours per week, however, the organization had planned for him to pick up slack left by the prolonged illness of a part-time staff member. Because of his abrupt withdrawal and the two-week gap before telling them he wouldn't return, the organization had to scramble to fill the holes.

I asked if she would be willing to partner with this university again. "I'd be reluctant," she said.

When universities require service of students — in the form of mandatory service-learning classes or internship — the service opportunity is designed to offer the student a specific kind of experience. At the same time, however, such a requirement displaces the responsibility of educating college students on community organizations not compensated for, and often inconvenienced by, such work.

Example 5: The Tutee Talks Back

Charles Ferguson, a *Spare Change News* vendor, has "been served" by students at several Boston-area shelters and service organization. He told me that, like many people he knows, he has grown wary of students and sometimes even deceives them:

Sometimes college students come into the neighborhood or the shelter for a class. They're just putting in their time or collecting their information, and that's it. They want to have an experience with me quick, write an essay, get in and get out. Study our behavior. Probably to laugh at you. There are plenty of writers. They want to exchange emails, get my phone number. As soon as they've got what they need, they're gone. I don't know if they think we notice, we do. People I know make up stories, lies, to tell them. They call it "game," something to do to pass time, to play back when someone is doing something to you. Recently, a [university] student told me that he wanted to write a story on homeless people. I had a question for him, why should he get my story? (Ferguson 2004)

I asked Charles if he felt that the kind of troubles he experienced indicate that it would be better not to send students into places like shelters. He thought about it, and offered the following advice, underscoring a belief that all useful connections depend on why students are sent, for how long, and what they know about a neighborhood or community:

What advice would I give? Be in no hurry, be cool. Spend some time. Don't show people you are so intense wanting something from them. Also, many of the students are white, and many of them have never been around too many black people. When white people are nervous around black people, we can tell. Don't just show up a few times, make a real commitment to a neighborhood, be part of it. (Ferguson 2004)

The scholarship in service learning has already addressed the need for service projects to be integrated into communities (Flower 1997), to attend to student attitudes (Herzberg 1994; Schutz and Gere 1998; Green 2003) and to include long-term commitments by faculty (Cushman 2002b). One could argue that the examples I offer occurred only because someone merely did not keep up with current scholarship or follow the rules of accepted Campus Compact protocol[7] in working in service-learning contacts.

Yet I argue that the problem goes beyond individual mistakes. The gaps between theory and its practice should not be overlooked or glossed over but rather foregrounded as what Carrick, Himley, and Jacobi (2000) describe (borrowing from Paulo Freire) as *ruptura*, "conflict[s] that force us to make a decision, to act, to break away from the old and familiar" (57).

Even isolated cases of campus community work gone wrong cast long shadows for everyone involved in university-community partnerships. It takes just one experience of "being burned" for a community group to sour on the idea of working with our students. Especially in smaller communities, how many annoyed nonprofits will it take before universities have trouble finding "placements" to help educate their students? And even when partnerships run more smoothly—when the video does arrive or the marketing proposals do show up—how much do the projects really benefit the community groups? How good are we at asking and finding out? It is worth considering whether the costs to community groups justify the perceived benefits of

top-down service programs that require sending students into the streets semester after semester.

A CASE FOR LOCAL, TACTICAL COMMUNITY PROJECTS

Given the powerful institutional needs, material supports, and a wide body of
scholarship promoting institutionalized service learning,[8] it seems likely that
such initiatives will grow or at least persist in the near future. Whether such
strategic development of service learning in the long term is viable will depend on local and institutional relationships, antagonisms, personalities, and
material supports. While I doubt this chapter will stem the tide toward broad,
strategic service projects, I would like to take up Harper, Donnelli, and
Farmer's call to "imagin[e] possible other futures for how service-learning
might be manifest within and beyond institutions of higher learning" (2003,
636) by advocating localized, *tactical*, and carefully—if at all—institutionalized projects. These projects should develop and grow from the bottom up,
not the top down, nor mandate service of students, consider the community
as a source of expertise, and acknowledge and seek to work rhetorically
within the specificity and limitations of space and time. Before elaborating on
these characteristics of *tactical projects*, I share one example.

One Tactical Project: Kids' 2 Cents

Before arriving at *Spare Change News* in the fall of 2001, I foolishly and incor-
rectly assumed that I might be able to "leverage" the time I had spent at the
street paper in Chicago and move smoothly and quickly into engaged projects
in Boston. After all, I knew street papers, plus I knew the Boston staff somewhat from annual street-paper conferences. When I traveled to Boston for my
campus job interview, I spent one afternoon at the street-paper office talking
over needs, projects, and ideas.

Once I relocated, however, I realized that, just like in Chicago, I needed to
spend time keeping my mouth shut and doing whatever work needed doing
before understanding the local setting well enough to help create anything
new. For the first year, I made myself a general workhorse—mostly writing
grants and news stories, copyediting, or doing other grunt editorial work.
Fran, the organization's director, and I would talk about possibilities as I got
to know—and to be known by—the vendors and staff of the paper. I learned
that just because I was familiar with the work they did didn't mean they
would be familiar or comfortable with me.

Occasionally Fran would mention an idea that interested her, a desire to
help the roughly 9,000 readers of the fortnightly newspaper understand that,
in Massachusetts, *homeless* is a term that often means children and families,
even though most people you see on the streets are men; rarely one can identify homeless families on the streets. We talked about the values underlying a

street paper, of wanting not merely to report *about* homeless children but to hear *from* them, to demystify the concept "homeless child" by embodying it with words, stories, and images. One night, Fran said, "I imagine a supplement to *Spare Change* called *Kids' 2 Cents*" (Czajkowski 2003). She said she knew an organization that worked with children in area shelters. I said, "This might be a project to connect my students with." The organization Fran spoke with recommended that we contact a shelter in Waltham, Massachusetts; Fran called the director and the three of us agreed to meet.

The shelter director told us that she read *Spare Change*, which is why she agreed to meet with us. At first she was gruff and skeptical, which I understood, but she said she liked the paper and heard good things about the organization. Even though I represented my university in that meeting, I was also a *Spare Change* trustee and volunteer. After a long discussion of rules, CORIs,[9] and preparation, she agreed to let us test out weekly meetings of the Kids' 2 Cents Writing Group with the school-age kids living at the shelter, although she warned us that there might not be any interest.

I didn't want "service" to be mandatory in my fall-semester Literatures of Homelessness class. Once we got the approval from the shelter, I announced the Kids' 2 Cents project to the class as one possibility for the students' course project, asking interested people to see me. We ended up with a group of seven who signed on and attended an orientation held by the director, Fran, and me. None of us knew how well the weekly project would work. I told the students, "No one might want to work with us. The kids might not like the idea of a writing group or the idea of university kids coming to hang out with them. Whatever happens happens. Your grade will be determined by your participation in setting up and attending the project and your presentation to our class about the project—not by whether this project works. Failure or lack of continuation are both viable options." The freedom for the project not to succeed was important for me, and for the students. I didn't want us to find ourselves in a situation where we felt we *had* to make homeless kids work with us.

My students and I met before our first writing-group meeting, made books for each child to fill, and bought art supplies—gel pens, fruity-smelling erasers, paper bags, construction paper, even paint. We assembled some story and poetry books for reading aloud. We hoped for the best.

Our first evening, in October, we set up in a family meeting room in the shelter, which houses 38 families. Soon a stream of children came running in, and with simple questions like "Would you like to draw?" or "Want to write a story?" we had a writing group. During the twenty-minute ride to the shelter each week, our group would plan activities. On the way home we would review the evening and consider changes.

As the semester neared its end, we had barely talked with the kids about *Spare Change* or publishing their writing. We had mentioned it—to them and their moms--but in the weekly flurries of drawing, writing, and reading aloud, publishing hadn't taken center stage. While we had enough writing to assemble an issue of the paper, the timing seemed wrong.

I talked with the students, and they shared my apprehension. I said that whatever was completed by the end of the semester would be fine in my eyes in terms of grades. Their obligation to the course would end in December. But I also said, "I think I'd like to keep coming after break. To work a few more months and wait until the time feels right for publishing an issue of the paper. No one is required to keep coming. But, if anyone wants to, you're welcome."

Five of the seven students decided to keep coming to the writing group each week, along with the two English graduate students who had been helping from the beginning. Three more months of weekly visits after the semester ended, the time felt right. Kids were often asking about the publication of the newspaper. We typed up all of the writing and assembled artwork and photographs. The director read through the entire manuscript and the moms gave permission to publish each piece of their child's writing and a photograph. The kids' writing and images filled eight of the newspaper's sixteen pages. The rest of the paper was filled with articles completed by students in the Literatures of Homelessness class, contextualizing the issue of homelessness and families with articles about housing costs and state policies for schooling homeless kids, reviews of children's books about homelessness, and background pieces about the writing group itself. The issue was published at the end of March 2003 and sold out before the two-week run had finished.

At the end of the year, I had three meetings—with the students, the shelter director, and the staff at *Spare Change*—to discuss the project's successes and problems. All expressed a desire for the project to continue, but Literatures of Homelessness was not being offered the next year.

All of the groups decided to continue the project. The second year of Kids' 2 Cents took place absent a direct connection to a single course: Some students from the class continued our weekly visits, and some first-year writing students taught by the participating graduate students or me signed on too. Everyone involved agreed to attend the writing group and to write one article for the newspaper. We published another "Kids' 2 Cents" issue in the spring of 2004. At the time of this writing, another series of meetings is planned for all parties to decide if and how the project should continue.

I describe this project as *tactical* in that it originated not from university needs but from the articulated needs of one community group (*Spare Change*), and involved another community group as well as university students. The project was connected to a class with a topic specifically dedicated to issues of homelessness and writing. Asking homeless children to share their stories was an attempt to frame the community as a source of knowledge, not a source of deficit. The project was framed as an artistic project, encouraging kids to write, draw, take photos, and tell stories about whatever it was they wanted to write, draw, or tell about.[10] Since neither the course nor the project was defined by institutionalized service-learning structures, it could be adaptable in seeking to negotiate the time frame between the university schedule and the organic needs of the project itself—the best way to build trust, continuity, and enough momentum. Continuity of the project is a question, not an imperative; the project will continue or not continue in the future, depending on the desires of all parties.

Tactical projects have their limitations as well as their strengths. For the children's writing group, the onus of organizing and logistics remained with me, the project director. I raised small amounts of cash from the university and through the street paper. After the first semester, my car was the only vehicle to get students to the shelter. That meant I could never miss a week—and there were many Thursday nights when I had hoped or needed to do just that. In the second year, I lent my car on the nights I had a meeting conflict, and a few graduate students helped share the burden of organizing and driving. The street paper approved a small budget, but the students and I purchased all supplies and struggled to keep track of receipts in order to be reimbursed. In tactical projects, resources and efforts are highly localized. A more institutionalized program might have provided transportation and supplies and helped expand the program.

My question, though, has been and remains this: At what cost would institutionalization have helped this project? If Kids' 2 Cents were a larger, more institutionally sanctioned program, it likely could not have remained as flexible. If it became ongoing and expected, how quickly or easily could it decide to no longer publish the writing of children living in a shelter, if it seemed the newspaper or university were benefiting more than the children? How likely is it that an institutionalized version of this project would decide that a new project with the same kids—or no project at all—would be better . . . for now? And who would make that decision in an institutional program—an instructor, a service-learning coordinator, a dean? And what values or urgencies would get prioritized?

While much scholarship touts the value of institutionalizing projects, it is equally worth noting the value of creating local, tactical projects. Tactical projects view the community as a source of expertise, foreground specific community needs, involve students in work that has specific rhetorical exigencies, and acknowledge their own limitations. Individually, these characteristics can be found in many existing service-learning projects and could be adapted into more strategic initiatives.

Viewing the Community as a Source of Expertise

As I described in the Introduction, a project orientation, as opposed to a problem orientation, views the constituency—whether it be students or a local community group—as a source of knowledge and expertise. Tactical service-learning projects may be grounded in ongoing, pressing social concerns; but rather than adopting a problem approach that frames the community as a site of deficit or need, they seek ways to construct projects that acknowledge the expertise and capacity existing there.

Many examples of *writing for the community* and *writing with the community*, as outlined by Thomas Deans, construct partnerships that highlight the expertise of communities. Even more so would be projects that I would like to call *writing by the community*, which include projects that assist in community publishing and oral-history publishing (see. e.g., Owens 2001; Cassell 2000; Goldblatt and Parks 2000) as well as a wide range of academic research exploring extracurricular literacy (such as Gere 1994; Brandt 2001; Cushman 1998; Mathieu 2003; Powell and Takayoshi 2003). The value in all of this work is to create relationships that not only claim reciprocity in a general way, but create bodies of knowledge that undercut elitist notions that frame communities, especially in urban areas, as sites of problems that only academic experts can fix. Tactical projects prioritize an exchange of skills or ideas over ameliorating a problem.

Foregrounding Community in Project Creation and Assessment

In many service programs, projects or ideas initiate within the institution and extend outward. Teachers or administrators often decide, first, that service is a good idea, then seek connections to allow service to take place. Tactical projects begin or are grounded early on in locations outside the university or result from relationships that exist for other reasons than the research or service connection. While the goal of strategic programs is to be organized and efficient, tactical projects are anything but efficient. Efficiency might develop over time, if a specific project warrants efficiency, but the process itself is not methodical or specific. For example, a graduate student might decide to start volunteering with a local environmental organization because he or she cares about the work the organization does. He or she might hope that a service-learning connection might develop over time. It would only develop, however, if and when an appropriate match is made between local needs and the university classroom.

Ideas for tactical projects can generate inside or outside the university and can be fueled by students, teachers, or nonprofit staff. For example, an undergraduate at the University of Washington, Erin Anderson, worked as a volunteer at *Real Change News* and became excited about the possibilities of making greater connections between her university and the newspaper. She brokered an introduction between the paper's director and a faculty member, which led to continued meetings. Throughout it all, Erin served as an important liaison and source of information as future projects developed. The university approved a two-credit course, Street Papers, Poverty and Homelessness, which the nonprofit director taught as an adjunct faculty member and involved University of Washington students. Plans are under way to further develop this partnership throughout the street-paper network with a developing university global classrooms project.[11]

Understanding That Service/Activism Is Never Neutral

Tactical courses acknowledge that no act or deed is neutral and that any act of service promotes certain needs while undermining others. Serving a cup of soup at a shelter provides immediate needs to a hungry person but does nothing to change the system that makes that person hungry in the first place. Lobbying for affordable housing seeks to change the system that makes people homeless, but does nothing to meet immediate needs. In a tactical view, all projects are incomplete.

One example of a service course that approaches decisions about service as value-laden is Peter Vandenberg's course on the rhetoric of graffiti at De-Paul University (see Chaden et al. 2002). In this course, students study and photograph local graffiti and begin to understand it as a phenomenon over which people disagree. Students learn that the city wants to paint over all graffiti, including murals. Graffiti artists see their work as making important public statements. Community residents have varying opinions, designating some graffiti as worth preserving and other graffiti as gang tagging that needs to be covered over. The students in Vandenberg's course document all the graffiti that they find and study on a website, acknowledging its value and the need to archive it. Yet students also work with local community groups to help them either preserve or cover over specific graffiti. This might mean writing city officials regarding preservation permits or painting a sealant over a mural wall. On the other hand, it might mean whitewashing garage doors or painting spray-painted bricks. Either way, students realize that they are working in a contested space and honor the opinions of certain community members regarding the graffiti, well aware that others (including themselves) may feel differently about the decisions being made. In this example, students serve a limited and specific rhetorical function.

Using Space and Time Rhetorically

Whereas a strategic development of service learning seeks to create institutional spaces that sanction and allow for the development and sustainability of service projects, a tactical approach works within and learns from the belief that local streets and communities are not controlled by any university. Rather than seeking to control or institutionalize space, a tactical orientation privileges timeliness and sensitivity to space. As Michel de Certeau (1984) asserts, tactics are rhetorical acts that rely on and take advantage of opportunities that present themselves; one pins one's hopes not on control but on using time in clever ways (37–39). The limitations and artificiality of time, especially as it is doled out in a university setting, define the limits of all service-learning enterprises; in a tactical orientation, the radical insufficiency of the acts we perform is foregrounded, not as a critique of a project but as a necessary component of remaining accountable as teachers and students.

Any project will feel sand in its gears when the time frames of daily life and university life meet. In the Kids' 2 Cents project, the college students need to keep to a schedule to allow themselves to include work with homeless children in a writing group each week. But to the children, our scheduled interaction includes large and often artificial gaps: missing weeks at Thanksgiving, spring break, Easter; a missing month in December; entire disappearances in the summer. Even though it was planned this way, even though the organization understands, and even when we explain to the kids why we'll be away and when we'll be back, there's pain there, or at least disruption, in the lives of kids who've already experienced profound disruptions. A tactical approach prompts me to think about and discuss this issue for next year: Are there ways to minimize the gaps, or try to make better plans with the shelter so our absences can correspond with other activities they schedule for the kids? While my students and I appreciate and benefit from the rhythms of a university's cycle, that cycle doesn't always fit with the rhythms of life in the streets outside of campus. Rather than merely accepting this disconnect, a tactical orientation seeks clever ways to work around such limitations—such as continuing projects beyond a semester—or at least to acknowledge the real limitations of time.

Acknowledgement can be as simple as rhetorical awareness. For example, when service-learning coordinators used to contact me at the street paper seeking "placements for next semester," I happened to know approximately when that might begin and for how long that would last. But the language of credit hours and semesters is not as meaningful as actual days, dates, number of weeks, or even fiscal years to some nonprofits. A tactical approach reminds us that the university does not control the turf nor the discourse and that learning to work in the streets requires such sensitivity and awareness.

Beyond Binaries: How Can Strategic Programs Act More Tactically?

In this chapter I have described service-learning projects along a spectrum ranging from strategic—focused on institutionalization and sustainability—to tactical—prioritizing bottom-up, time-contingent, flexible development of projects. Clearly, as I hope some of these examples show, this strategic-tactical binary serves a more rhetorical purpose rather than a descriptive one; approaches to doing neighborhood projects range from large top-down, mandatory, general service programs to extremely ad hoc unfunded labors of love that last for a short time and then disappear. By exploring the strategic-tactical binary, I hope to have made the case for the values inherent in more tactical projects: organic origins, a project orientation that frames the community as a source of knowledge, genuine community involvement in planning and evaluation, and a rhetorical sense of timeliness and the limitations of time.

Tactical projects are grounded in timeliness and hope and as such seek not measurable outcomes but completed projects. The projects have value in themselves but hope for intangible changes— in students, in community members, in the university itself. The key to that hope, however, is an acknowledgment of the radical insufficiency of any single project.

Such subjective and rhetorical values might not be practical or easy to implement within university administration. If universities are serious about walking the walk of "serving" the community and getting beyond public relations catchphrases, however, we need to find ways to make and keep community projects local, specific, responsive, and timely. Such a commitment may require forgoing institutionalized service-learning projects altogether or insisting that programs are only institutionalized from the bottom up, project by project, relationship by relationship. This kind of a commitment would also require significant questioning or redefining of the work of teachers, writers, and scholars in the university.

NOTES

1. See Deans 2000b.
2. See Flower 1997.
3. See Hutchinson.
4. See Schutz and Gere; Deans 2000b; Zlotkowski.
5. The name has been changed but the rest of the content is not altered.
6. Some service-learning scholarship reports complaints by students or instructors about community groups either not returning calls or being resistant to suggestions by the students or faculty. See for example Cullum or Bennett.
7. See Campus Compact "Wingspread."
8. A recent Google search resulted in 3,720 hits for the phrase "institutionalized service learning"; adding "English" and "college" or "university" to the phrase still generated 1,520 hits. While not conclusive, this search shows that, at least on websites, there is a lot of discussion about institutionalized service learning, nearly none of which is critical of the trend.
9. Criminal Offender Record Information (CORI) is the name given to the standard criminal background check currently required for anyone wanting to work with children staying in state facilities.
10. We never asked students to write specifically about homelessness or the difficulties in their lives. The majority of the writing never touched on difficult issues, but was mostly about things like space aliens or dogs named Christina Aguilera. A few older kids did choose to write about life in a homeless shelter or about poor people in general. The mothers of each child read— or were read—every piece of writing, and we only printed work that they had approved.
11. For more information about the Global Classrooms Initiative, visit http://www.washington.edu/oue/faculty/globallearn.html.

WORKS CITED

Bennett, B. Cole. 2000. "The Best of Intentions: Service-Learning and Noblesse Oblige at a Christian College." *Reflections* 1(2): 18–23.
Brandt, Deborah. 2001. *Literacy in American Lives.* New York: Cambridge University Press.
Campus Compact. 2004a. "About Campus Compact: What We've Done: An 18-Year Retrospective." http://www.compact.org/aboutcc/retrospective/retrospective.html.
———. 2004b. "Benchmarks for Campus/Community Partnerships." http://www.compact.org/ccpartnerships/benchmarks-overview.html.
Campus Compact. 1999. "Wingspread Declaration on the Civic Responsibilities of Research Universities." http://www.compact.org/civic/Wingspread/Wingspread.html. 14 April 2004.
Carrick, Tracy Hamler, Margaret Himley, and Tobi Jacobi. 2000. "Ruptura: Acknowledging the Lost Subjects of the Service Learning Story." *Language and Learning Across the Disciplines* 4:3 56–75.

Cassell, Susie Lan. 2000. "Hunger for Memory: Oral History Recovery in Community Service Learning." *Reflections* 1:2. 12–17.

de Certeau, Michel. 1984. *The Practice of Everyday Life.* Translated by Steven Rendall. Berkeley, CA: University of California Press. 1988.

Chaden, Caryn, Roger Graves, David A. Jolliffe, and Peter Vandenberg. 2002. "Confronting Clashing Discourses: Writing the Space Between Classroom and Community in Service-Learning Courses." *Reflections* 2(2): 19–39.

Cullum, Linda. 2000. "Surprised by Service: Creating Connections Through Community-Based Writing." *Reflections* 1(2): 5–11.

Cushman, Ellen. 2002b. "Sustainable Service Learning Programs." *College Composition and Communication* 54(1): 40–65.

———. 1998. *The Struggle and the Tools: Oral and Literate Strategies in an Inner City Community.* Albany, NY: SUNY Press.

———. 2002a. "Service Learning as the New English Studies." In *Beyond English, Inc: Curricular Reform in a Global Economy.* David Downing, Claude Mark Hurlbert, and Paula Mathieu, eds. Portsmouth, NH: Boynton/Cook Heinemann.

Czajkowski, Fran. 20 August 2003. Personal interview.

Deans, Thomas. 2000a. "CCCC Institutionalizes Service-Learning (Interview)." *Reflections* 1(1): 3–4.

———. 2000b. *Writing Partnerships: Service-Learning in Composition.* Urbana, IL: National Council of Teachers of English.

———. 2003. "Community Service and Critical Teaching: A Retrospective Conversation with Bruce Herzberg." *Reflections* 3(1): 71–76.

Ferguson, Charles. 28 May 2004. Personal interview.

Flower, Linda. 1997. "Partners in Inquiry: A Logic for Community Outreach." In *Writing the Community: Concepts and Models for Service-Learning in Composition.* Linda Adler-Kassner, Robert Crooks, and Ann Watters, eds. Washington, D.C.: American Association for Higher Education Press. 95–119.

———. 2003. "Talking Across Difference: Intercultural Rhetoric and the Search for Situated Knowledge." *College Composition and Communication.* 55(1): 38–68.

Furco, Andrew. 2003. "Self-Assessment Rubric for the Institutionalization of Service Learning in Higher Education (Revised 2003)." Campus Compact at Brown University. http://www.tulane.edu/~ServLrng/Rubric_Background_rev2003.doc.

Gere, Anne Ruggles. 1994. "Kitchen Tables and Rented Rooms: The Extracurriculum of Composition." *College Composition and Communication* 45(1): 75–92.

Goldblatt, Eli, and Stephen Parks. 2000. "Writing beyond the Curriculum: Fostering New Collaborations in Literacy." *College English* 62(5): 584–606.

Green, Ann. 2003. "Difficult Stories: Service-Learning, Race, Class and Whiteness." *College Composition and Communication.* 55(2): 276–301.

Harper, Todd M., Emily Donnelli, and Frank Farmer. 2003. "Wayward Inventions: He(u)retical Experiments in Theorizing Service Learning." *Journal of Advanced Composition* 23(3): 615–640.

Hessler, H. Brooke. 2000. "Composing an Institutional Identity: The Terms of Community Service in Higher Education." *Language and Learning Across the Disciplines* 4(3): 27–42.

Herzberg, Bruce. 1994. "Community Service and Critical Teaching." *College Composition and Communication* 45(3): 307–319.

Himley, Margaret. 2004. "Facing (Up To) 'The Stranger' in Community Service Learning." *College Composition and Communication* 55(3): 416–438.

Hutchinson, Patricia. 2002. "Service Learning: Challenges and Opportunities." New Foundations: Organizational Issues and Insights. http://www.newfoundations.com/OrgTheory/Hutchinson721.html.

Mathieu, Paula. 2003. "Not Your Mama's Bus Tour: A Case for 'Radically Insufficient' Writing." In *City Comp: Identities, Spaces, Practices.* Bruce McComiskey and Cynthia Ryan, eds. Albany, NY: SUNY Press. 71–84.

Owens, Derek. 2001. *Composition and Sustainability: Teaching for a Threatened Generation.* Urbana, IL: National Council of Teachers of English.

Powell, Katrina M., and Pamela Takayoshi. 2003. "Accepting the Roles Created for Us: The Ethics of Reciprocity." *CCC* 54(3): 394–422.

Scapansky, Tim. 2004. "Service Learning and Faculty in the Higher Education Institution." New Foundations. Organizational Issues and Insights. http://www.newfoundations.com/OrgTheory/Scepansky721.htm.

Schutz, Aaron, and Anne Ruggles Gere. 1998. "Service Learning and English Studies: Rethinking 'Public' Service." *College English* 60(2): 126–149.

Welch, Nancy. December 2002. "'And Now That I Know Them': Composing Mutuality in a Service Learning Course." *CCC* 52(2): 243–263.

Zlotkowski, Edward. 2000. "Service-Learning and Composition: As Good as It Gets (Interview)." *Reflections* 3(1): 1–3.

21 Ruptura: Acknowledging the Lost Subjects of the Service Learning Story

TRACY HAMLER CARRICK
MARGARET HIMLEY
TOBI JACOBI

I am sure that one of the most tragic illnesses in our society is the bureaucratization of the mind. If you go beyond the previously established patterns, considered as inevitable ones, you lose credibility. In fact, however, there is no creativity without *ruptura*, without a break from the old, without conflict in which you have to make a decision. I would say there is no human existence without ruptura (38, emphasis added).

–PAULO FREIRE, *We Make the Road by Walking*

As members of the Service Learning collective in the Writing Program at Syracuse University, we have been actively designing and teaching a sequence of undergraduate writing courses that integrate community service in various ways—by asking students to write *about* the non-profit agencies where they participate, to write *for* those sites by producing brochures and websites, and to write *with* people as tutors in adult literacy programs or in local urban high schools.[1]

Along with the successes, we have encountered recurring challenges: In what ways do we intellectually and politically frame the service learning requirement? How do we write course rationales? How do we encourage students to talk in the classroom about their experiences? How do we theorize the ethical and rhetorical complexities of student volunteers as they represent people at the sites, many of whom may differ from the students in significant ways? Is reciprocity a main goal of service learning?[2] What sorts of reciprocities can and do (and do not) emerge? What disjunctures and crises, or ruptura, occur when the ideals of service learning are put into practice? How can we as teachers, students, and community participants acknowledge them?

From *Language and Learning Across the Disciplines* 4.3 (2000): 56–74.

After several semesters of teaching community-based classes, we notice our students (and selves) challenging the comfortable narratives (e.g., accounts of reciprocal learning, tallies of student service hours or monies raised) in service learning discourses and recognizing moments when neatly planned activities fall away, rupture. It is in moments such as these that we (teachers and students) experience what Paulo Freire named ruptura, a conflict that forces us to make a decision, to act, to break away from the old and familiar. Rather than finding tidy answers to our questions in existing service learning theories of reciprocity and representation, we advocate a rhetoric of acknowledgement across community service learning relationships, an articulation of the tensions that occur when we require that students leave the classroom and go into various neighborhoods and non-profit agencies.

As students meet people and enter places that put pressure on their sense of who they are and how the world is, we set in motion processes of identification and disidentification, moments of comfort and discomfort. Risky encounters such as these mark not only service learning but also the project of education more generally. As teacher-scholars, we need always to attend to the ways narratives of progress structure our understanding of what we do and of what students learn, narratives that make it difficult to recognize the anxieties, fears, and conflicts that are also so much a part of the story. In acknowledging the tensions that arise out of these service learning pedagogies, a method of collaborative inquiry emerges. We not only attend to traditional structures of representing "others," but also call them in question by refracting one story with another.

As writing teachers, we notice that these struggles often emerge at the point when students have to write about their service learning site and experiences—that is, when they face the very real responsibility of representing for academic consumption events and people they are just beginning to get to know. In the following reflective class writing, Kaye, a first-year student, discusses her struggle to compose a descriptive and analytical profile of the afterschool program she worked with:[3]

> Here I am trying to fulfill the requirements of this portfolio and my mind draws a blank. This is not to say that I have nothing to write about; I just don't know what I feel good writing about and what I think should not be brought across on paper. I know that some experiences are ones that I want to tell about and at the same time I don't feel right telling them. . . . [I realize that] I am not someone who feels comfortable writing about other people. . . . I do not like the idea of creating an image or situation for [others] to picture in their mind. If this were to be fictional, I could create enough work to keep you reading for hours but I cannot find a way to honestly show you who these people are because they are just that, people. . . . I [have] tried not to just define these people as characters but show them to you as they are, real people that made me think. (Kaye Berube)[4]

This student self-consciously and responsibly grapples with the temptation to merely textualize the people at her site, to see them as characters.

Moments like this interrupt the safety of a printed syllabus, skew the trajectory of a carefully crafted assignment, and make all kinds of problems visible. Fundamental to the process of learning, because they put in motion—and keep in motion—the situated, complex, and difficult (re)learning that educators locate at the center of all pedagogy, rupturas like these become a method of acknowledging the project of critical education in the world.[5]

In this essay we turn to the crisis of representation in ethnography and to stories of rupturas from our own experiences as service learning teachers to explore the discursive, institutional, and psychological reasons why these breaks may be difficult to analyze, easy to suture over, and necessary for understanding the intellectual project of service learning theory and pedagogy.

REPRESENTING (AND BEING REPRESENTED BY) OTHERS

Ethnographers have been confronted for years with the awesome responsibility of representing others; of making sense of what they have seen, were told, or read in their sites; and then of making it available for distant readers. One telling account of this struggle is Margery Wolf's *A Thrice Told Tale: Feminism, Postmodernism & Ethnographic Responsibility* (1992). In this book Wolf describes how she stumbled upon a short story she had written about events in the spring of 1960, which had occurred while she was living with her anthropologist husband in a small village in northern Taiwan. Having forgotten the story, she then searched through old files for her original field notes and personal journals from that period of time, and discovered they told different stories. In her book, she acknowledges how the telling of these stories has changed for several reasons: she is now an anthropologist herself; questions of reflexivity now preoccupy the discipline; problems of appropriation and representation now undermine the very project of the discipline. Indeed some postmodern critics have challenged the very possibility of ethically representing others, while other critics have claimed that the ethnographic process itself "is an exercise in colonialism" (p. 5). In order to further explore this complex problem and to argue that these criticisms should make feminist ethnographers more aware and careful but should not stop them altogether, Wolf presents three texts she wrote about this one event (the short story, her unanalyzed field notes, and an essay she published in *American Ethnologist*), with commentaries that illustrate and argue with the problems and promises "this new period of reflexivity [have] brought to the fore" (p. 7).

The differences and conflicts and problems of representation and responsibility that haunt ethnographic encounters also trouble community activism and service learning.

Robert Coles (1993), for example, recounts how Ruth Ann, a nine-year-old girl in a 4th grade composition class he was teaching, challenged his assumptions about himself, when she asked questions like, "We were wondering why you come over here to us. We thought, he must be busy with his regular life, so why does he take time out to come visit here, when he could be someplace else that's more important. . . . Did you hear something bad about us?" (Coles, p. xvii). Her questions unsettled his "well-intentioned, earnest affirmation of good intent," forcing him to construct in his mind "a devastating critique of myself and my kind—confirming her uncompromising appraisal of me as yet another slummer, eager to wet his feet in a fashionably different terrain, all the more to inflate his sense of himself and the view others had of him" (p. xvii). Linda Flower (1996) demonstrates too the hard work of negotiating differences through her analysis of the community/university collaboration between Pittsburgh's Community House and the Center for the Study of Writing and Literacy at Carnegie Mellon. She discusses how incommensurate discourses across lines of difference may make a shared social reality impossible, a deeper reciprocity unlikely (p. 66). Participants have to be willing to persist with conflict, with a sustained engagement with multiple voices and perspectives, where there will be no "master narrative that resolves the complexity into a unified, thematic story" (p. 88).

Both ethnography and community activism depend upon moving into intersubjective relationships with others across lines of difference, relationships fraught with anxiety, frustration, partial communication, rough spots, and tough times.

We have to remain alert to the power asymmetries and different discursive and material realities of the people involved in community-based projects. We risk confusing our ethical and political desires for reciprocal and mutually beneficial relations with the much messier realities that those relations often (re)enact. We risk masking rather than unmasking power dynamics. We risk mis-recognizing our own desires and needs. If we move too quickly toward discursive constructions such as the reciprocity narrative, which then suture over these difficulties, we risk *fixing* complexities rather than *acknowledging* them as central to and part of learning.

In Wolf's tradition of thrice told tales, we seek ways to structure methods into our service learning courses that offer ample opportunity to tell *and retell* the many diverse stories of service learning—by giving voice to the visceral and frightening, by holding off easy answers, by acknowledging the unhappy as well as happy endings, by questioning our selves and own positionality, by developing self-reflexive ways of receiving stories—that is, by excavating the lost subjects.[6]

MARGARET'S STORY: "REQUIRING" TRANSFORMATION

"... to excavate the lost subjects in a story until what is uncanny can be engaged" (p. 15)

—BRITZMAN, *Lost Subjects, Contested Objects*

There are several familiar versions of the service learning story. In one, "students will come to recognize their privilege and in the sad, troubled lives of others find that they, by contrast, are still living in the land of the free, the home of the brave. Armed with a point of light, they will lead just one person, often a very cute child, out of the darkness their parents willfully cast her into. . . . They will feel compassion and wish life were better for those they serve" (Stanley, p. 60). This caricature of what some call "volunteerism lite" points to the concern that students will enact charity as a kinder and gentler form of imperialism rather than as a starting point for a systemic analysis of the social. Nothing changes structurally: the poor stay poor, the privileged stay privileged. Or, in another version of the story, students come to recognize the value of conflict and difference, enter the contact zone, and come to embrace the different meanings of an apparently shared experience, as they may "move from the academic armchair of liberal goodwill or radical critique to an intercultural collaboration" (Flower, p. 45).

These stories focus on endings, and may say more about teachers' expectations than about all that happens to student volunteers. We foreclose important possibilities when we tell the service learning story teleologically, especially in terms of final or failed transformations.

I propose that we look instead at other moments in the service learning experience: when the volunteers or community members do not like each other, when volunteers resent the time they are forced to give up, when participants develop antipathies that don't make their way to consciousness, when students have visceral reactions to their sites, and so on. The student volunteer may hate being the only white person in the room, or community participants may resent the superior attitude of the kids who come "off the hill" to "help" them as "role models." Lots of scenarios come to mind. But it would be "uncivil" or "ungrateful" for service learning participants to admit to any of these things. Thus the public discourse of service itself—"giving back to the community" or "helping others" or "forming partnerships"— may make the problem worse. One way to avoid these discomforting feelings is to cover them over with the language of altruism, which provides a defense against the depth and complexity of feelings and responses evoked by the service learning experience.

How do we get students to talk about these difficult subjects in the classroom? How do we get ourselves to? How might we have conversations with community participants about the complexities of these encounters?

As I reflect back on the syllabus for my service learning course last fall (WRT 105: Citizenship, the Narrative Imagination, and Good Writing), I'm struck by the problematic way I too cast the service learning story. The syllabus was eight pages long. To set up the course rationale, I first pulled seven quotations from the local paper that illustrate discord along lines of difference (e.g., the controversy over the Boy Scouts and homosexuality, federal hate crime legislation, the skirmishes between India and Pakistan). I raised questions about how we come to know others in an increasingly media-saturated world where figures such as "the welfare mother" or "the Islamic militant" or "violent teen superpredator" serve as our only reference points. Then I proposed three hypotheses for us to test through the service experience and through our discussion of course readings such as Benjamin Barber's "Teaching Democracy through Community Service" and "Bowling Alone" by

Robert D. Putnam: [1] fundamental to questions of citizenship and to good writing is respecting others as capable and contributing members of a multi-cultural society, [2] the act of narration is a basic way that we understand ourselves and others, and [3] service learning is one way to accomplish the civic learning necessary for a multicultural democracy. It took me four pages to lay out these hypotheses. I defined students as citizens and rhetors, who must recognize "others . . . without denigrating . . . differences or reducing [them] to caricature." I argued for cultural narratives that do not "perpetuate hegemonic power relations, social injustice, and material inequity." I relied on discourses of abstract values like "good citizenship" and "good rhetors"—and so on and so on.

In retrospect, I read my own syllabus as defensive, addressed not only to my students, but also to other audiences—teachers in the Writing Program who openly question the value/s of service learning (which they see as un-paid labor, as irrelevant to the teaching of writing, etc.), parents who might not think service could be a serious part of academic study, other service learning practitioners whom I had been reading and among whom I wanted to locate myself. I see too the high handed moralism of the discourse, which explains how students did come to read the course as about becoming "bet-ter" people—with "better" coming to mean not selfish, not lazy, not morally indifferent, not immature (if class debates are any indication).

Students resisted the terms by which the syllabus interpellated them. They were right.

The discourse of my syllabus addressed the superego: it just wasn't okay to be "good enough" students and volunteers.[7] We had to be spectacular. I was calling for the heroic, the utopic, the patriotic in a way, out of my own anxiety about justifying service learning in a first year writing course for the first time. I locked us into a very particular discourse of service learning, which addressed students in moralistic ways, which they could either accept or reject, but not easily or openly negotiate. On the first day of class I expected students to challenge the 20 hour service requirement. Instead, they sat there, silent, passive, obedient. A very serious student who fretted, "But what if nothing happens to us at our sites" initially raised the only concern. He rec-ognized that transformation and moral improvement—not just 20 hours of service—was being required.

Ironically, of course, it is this very discourse of moralism that keeps everyone in their socio-economic place and that perpetuates the status quo—and that undermines the very project I tried to initiate. The privileged con-tinue to enjoy their privilege because they have now taken time out of their busy lives to help those less fortunate than themselves, and the less privileged feel, or ought to feel, gratitude.

I might now tell the story of the service learning rebellion, which hap-pened slowly and quietly over the course of the semester, as students couldn't find time to get to their sites, as they argued that required service was "forced volunteerism" and so not volunteerism at all, as they crabbed about the transportation problems, etc. Yet when I encouraged a class debate, students withdrew from any invested discussion or alternative projects. Some students completed the service requirement (some very "successfully"), while most barely squeezed in enough hours to have something to write about and to not flunk the course.

But what I want to consider here is how to write my next syllabus. What discourses will I draw on—and why?[8] What if I say something like, "Students will donate 20 hours of their time to overworked and understaffed not-for-profits, which will give us in return more to talk about and more to write about, as we study the many arguments for and against service learning." Would that be a way to avoid demanding "a learning" or "a service learning narrative"? Or would it be possible to start the course by asking students to workshop the syllabus and develop and debate "our" course rationale—and then return to it across the semester for discussion, analysis, critique, qualification? Or would it be productive to provide many rationales—mine, service learning theorists, the community non-profits? That is, how can I get the course started without trying to "fix" the meaning of the service learning ahead of time?

More importantly, how can I resist my own teacherly impulses to write "the" narrative of the course? How can I resist the rescue fantasy "that education can be made from the proper teacher, the proper curriculum, or the proper pedagogy so that learning will be no problem to the actors involved"? (Britzman, p. 5). How can I open up space, for myself and for students, to recognize the anxieties, fears, contradictions, and conflicts that are always already a part of the education narrative?

TRACY'S STORY: IF CHILDREN ARE HOMEWORK, WHAT AM I?[9]

> "If you have come to help me, you are wasting your time. But if your liberation is bound with mine, then let us work together."
>
> –SADIE BROWER NEAKOK

One afternoon, about six weeks into the semester, as my freshman writing course, Literacy and Community,[10] was ending, a student reluctantly lingered behind. Bright and creative, she was typically outspoken, so I was quite surprised when she hesitated to speak. Her words, which appear in a paper she eventually wrote, capture the essence of our discussion:

> The first time I saw this place I was taken aback. My naïveté had me envisioning brightly colored walls, toys and everything else I had while I was growing up. I was out of my element from the very beginning. Even before viewing the facility, I had been uneasy with the knowledge of what I must do to complete my Writing 105 course. It was disconcerting to my sensibilities that I would be working here for 20 hours over the next few months, and then I inevitably would be leaving, never to see these kids again. How could this possibly be fair to them? What exactly were they to me? A homework assignment? I began to wonder if it af-

fected the kids to see so many volunteers come through the organization about the same time each year, and then to watch as the workers dwindled back down to permanent employees as the holiday season neared.

As her words carefully and tentatively rolled off of her tongue, I sensed how difficult this conversation was for her. Margaret Dana Singsen[11] knew she was revealing something that would make her vulnerable—as a student, as a community participant, as a human being. But despite the risks involved in confronting her teacher, an authority who had both put her in this position and would eventually assign her a grade, Dana was committed deeply to expressing the discomfort, the conflict she felt with the community project she was charged with. Her bold critique implicated nearly every institutional structure she was working within—the course, the Center for Public and Community Service, the community agency itself.

During the private moments of our conversation, I listened. I admired. I heard.

How could I invite and sanction such a troubled practice? What right did I have to push students into such anxiety-ridden moral dilemmas? To encourage such a potentially careless mis-use of others? How does this affect the children?

How could I not invite and sanction such active participation in the community? What right did I have to refuse precious resources to community agencies that depend in part upon the university? To deny students and children in the community opportunities to cross the often sharply drawn lines between communities of difference, to forge human relationships, to become active learners both inside and outside of the classroom?

She was surprised, I think, when I not only admitted that I shared her concerns, but also invited her to bring them into the classroom, to make them public, and to allow others to consider them. As far as she knew, her peers had bought into the celebratory discourse of community service. No one else had spoken out against the ways that it had been framed in our course syllabus, the university's mission statement, any of the agency mission statements, the public media, or political propaganda. In these documents, service was good. Dana believed that if she spoke up, she might stand alone.

Students did not necessarily disagree with Dana's concerns. Many were also frustrated, confused, or shocked by their experiences in the community. They did not, however, take up her request to consider the ethical implications of the community work that was required of them. Instead they saw the space she opened up as an invitation to share their own rupturas—the moments of anxiety, conflict, or discomfort they were experiencing.

One student, for example, who was working at the same agency as Dana, told us of a young child who had endearingly latched herself onto her leg, refusing to let go. While the student was a little surprised by the child's behavior, she was even more stunned by the agency director's response—punishment. Other students at the agency corroborated this story by sharing others that illustrated the director's strict policy about any physical contact.

How could a child be punished for seeking out affection?

Amidst a clamor of horrified voices, a single voice emerged. It suggested that maybe the director was worried about the children getting too attached to people who would soon leave the agency and them. The voice was Dana's.

"Say more about that," I urged.

Reiterating her concern with the inevitable reality that she would be leaving the agency at the end of the semester—*if children are homework, what am I?*—she explained that her ideological resistance to the project itself would not permit her to initiate or accept any human contact. Though she desperately felt the need to reach out and hug a child, it was because of her concerns for the children that she resisted her human urges.

The class was silent.

A student working at a different agency whispered, "I hug the children," and like water being released from a dam, others joined her. Louder now, she added, "They need love. They need to know we care."

Dana's brow wrinkled. I asked the class, "Why?"

Students retorted with predictable and troubling claims about disadvantaged children, unfortunate home lives, broken homes, and poor people. The pervasive belief seemed to be that the kids they were working with—because they wore the same clothes every day, ate food voraciously, and/or smelled like they weren't bathed often—needed their love and affection because they "don't get it at home."

This time my brow wrinkled. *What assumptions are embedded in those claims?* I raised a litany of questions: "Why are you assuming that the kids you are working with are not getting love and affection at home? What do you mean by love and affection? What makes you claim that children need it? Need it the way you give it? Need it from transient volunteers?"

As students recalled stories of their own early childhoods—the small private daycare programs staffed with doting, trained professionals, the loving relationships they developed with live-in nannies, the comfort of knowing a parent would be waiting after-school—a theme emerged: students were making assumptions about the non-profit agencies they worked with based upon their own personal experiences. As one student proclaimed, "This is how I grew up and look where I am now!"

This was a difficult discussion.

As the next few weeks passed, students wrote journals and a series of mini-essays, one–two page papers that described different aspects of their community agencies.[12] The culminating assignment asked them to compose an agency profile, a five–seven page paper, which synthesized and expanded upon the writing they had already done. They were asked not to just describe the agency, but also to discuss why and how it functioned as it did.

I brought an agency profile written by a former student for the class to consider and discuss. They were appalled. One student exclaimed, "She's not telling it like it is. She's evaluating it based upon her own middle-class upbringing." He went on, joined by others, to observe that while she described the agency, its members, and what happened during her visits, she did not explore deeply enough why the agency needed to respond to the community and function the way that it did based upon what the community itself valued and needed. They felt that the essay was more about the student writer than the agency and people she worked with.

Things were getting complicated; they were getting more interesting. *Did Dana set this important discussion into motion?* I looked forward to reading their profiles. I looked forward especially to Dana's.

Like many of her classmates, Dana did not really write an agency profile. Her paper started by describing the ways she reacted to and interacted with the agency and proceeded to narrate her process of coming to know and understand the community she was working with. And while she did reveal many details about the agency and its members in this section, the "profile" itself really began several pages later when she wrote:

> And then it dawned on me that [the agency director] shared many of the same feelings about volunteers as I did. She too knew that this was a class obligation, and that we would be leaving just as abruptly as we had come.

As the rest of her paper unfolded, she identified and illustrated unwritten policies which forbade physical contact between children and volunteers; which intentionally rotated volunteers through different activities and age-grouped rooms; and which encouraged older children to become mentors and university volunteers to become facilitators who ran activities, but did not necessarily participate in them. Dana, like many of her classmates, needed to look inside of herself, to talk about and write about what she saw on the inside, before she could profile what she saw and experienced on the outside.

I have a lot to learn from this class and from Dana. Why did this group of students critique their peers for writing themselves into the communities they worked with, yet, in the end, in at least some ways, produce that kind of writing themselves? What am I asking of students when I assign an agency profile? What are they telling me they need instead? As I consider these questions in the context of the narrative I have just shared, I realize the need to reframe the writing assignments I impose upon students, assignments which require them to achieve scholarly distance from their communities just as they are imagining ways to locate themselves within them.

As I plan my revisions, I am compelled to flip through pages of student writing; Dana's writing in particular has influenced me deeply. Over the course of the semester she told many stories: stories about herself, stories about herself in the community, stories about others in the community, stories about how she read her community, stories about reading herself. None of her narratives, however, tell "the real story"; none of them are complete. My students join Wolf in teaching me that all stories can only ever be partial narratives, and remind me that I cannot, and should not, expect or even desire "the real, complete story" from students.

Tobi's Story: Into the Community[13]

Ruptura #1

> "She came once, was afraid to touch the children and got on her cell phone to get a ride home."
>
> —Community evaluation form, Fall 1999

This assessment came from the daycare center director at the end of the semester. I've gone over again and again how I could have recognized this student's experience earlier. None of her papers reflected this lack of engagement; in fact, they pointed to investment. She wrote passionately about the lack of screening and safety precautions required for volunteers. I knew that she hadn't spent as much time in the community as her peers, but it wasn't until the last day of the class that I realized something was really wrong.

This student taught me a valuable lesson. If I were to continue teaching service learning courses, a shift had to occur. I hadn't realized clearly enough what students might be going through even though I'd been a volunteer at one organization or another for much of my life. I needed to understand the frustration and excitement my students were writing about in their journals, what it felt like to carve 20 hours out of a semester in a new and uncomfortable setting, and, most importantly, why this student had identified and argued an agency issue, fulfilling all of my assignments, without spending more than one hour at "her" site. The only contact I had with agency placements came in the form of a brief evaluation at the end of the course. It was not enough. As I struggle to find ways to understand the experience of students like this one, I am reminded of the lake at my childhood home.

> I grew up in rural Wisconsin, in a place, as my father says, where most people come to vacation. There is a lake and acres of land. The seasons marked our activities, and, as autumn turned to winter, the lake changed, the water freezing in interestingly layered configurations. And while wind or snow robbed us of a see-through clarity most years, windows into these depths did appear. Sunburst shapes ranging from the size of a quarter to a bowling ball offered dark openings through which to examine a silent lily pad, the dappled sand bottom. Inevitably, our breath would steam the holes, blur our vision.

Like those frosted icy windows, my experience in the service learning classroom became clouded with questions of representation, authority, and inexperience as students began raising ethical questions in journals and essays and as the evaluations from agencies came in. I decided if I was to understand the complexities of the task I was engaging my students in, the coded language in their writing, I needed to occupy a place in the community along with them. If we were going to talk about and study the community in class, I too had to be in the community. It wasn't enough to rely on the university placement office and their writing; I had to redefine boundaries with students.

I began working with an adult and family literacy center about a year ago.

Ruptura #2

Since, like many of the Syracuse students, time dictated the hours I could spend at the center, the volunteer coordinator paired me with another tutor. She worked with our student Ann[14] on GED-level reading skills, and I was to follow with a half-hour of writing tutoring each Tuesday. The volunteer coordinator suggested I meet the reading tutor to discuss how we might support each other, and I agreed, certain that tutor collaboration could maximize Ann's chances of passing the GED. I was also interested in meeting a long-time volunteer tutor, in looking for mentoring, as I imagined my students might as they encountered established site volunteers and staff members.

Except the reading tutor didn't want to meet me. She wouldn't shake my hand or even look at me directly. Eyeing the tape recorder in my hand, she would have nothing to do with what she saw as a university researcher coming down from the hill to study this student, this center, and her.

I was stunned. Why wouldn't she meet me? Was it because of the difference in our education? She was being tutored in math while she tutored Ann in reading. Was it because I looked young, like a college student? She was in her forties. Was it because I looked too white? She was an African American. Was it somehow class-based? I had dressed in my casual teaching clothes. She wore jewelry and painted nails. What had I done? This had never happened before.

––––––––––

Was this the kind of experience my students were having? What had I done in the classroom to prepare them for this? I went home and journaled, writing through my anxieties of rejection. My students were required to maintain one journal page per community hour, but these were collected only three times over the semester. This hardly seemed the most effective way to bring these issues into the classroom. How could I use these moments to teach?

Ruptura #3

> *Journal entry: Can we please just work on writing?*
> *I went to the center today a little late, around 5:40 by the time I got there. I find myself very cognizant of the time I'm occupying with Ann. I know that she expects to be able to leave by 6 pm. I know that her daughter needs to go home, to get away from school. The curious thing is that this time I didn't want her stories of child suicide and the emergency room. I didn't need them the way I did the last few times. I had been willing, even eager, to take on some of her emotional weight before, but today I was tired. I had my own problems. I really just wanted to think about how adult literacy could work, about writing. What am I saying? I already feel guilty for sort of experimenting with different strategies "on" her, and now I'm rejecting her stories? Her need to share her life with me? How can I even write this? How would Ann feel about this representation?*

As I drafted my story for this essay, this particular telling elicited lots of response. "Explore what you mean when you say you didn't *need* her stories." "Yes, the courting ritual of coming to know someone demands this sort of engagement." "Say more about Ann—where does she enter this conversation?" In many ways, their retelling of my story—a retelling itself—has had a paralyzing effect. Which one should I tell?

The one about a teacher-scholar needing affirmation outside the university? Like students who long for "real world" experience, I needed Ann's stories because I needed to get off campus, to ground a world of literacy theory in a world of place and practice. Ann's stories offered me a way to renew my faith in myself as a teacher, to legitimize my place at the university in the world.

The moment when I couldn't hear any more of Ann's stories because I couldn't stop dreaming them at night? I couldn't stop retelling myself her stories. I lived them again and again as I struggled to come to terms with middle-class guilt and resist trying to find solutions. I couldn't sleep for weeks.

The one about using story to teach writing and then switching gears when that didn't work? Ann and I listened to her stories. We tape recorded them and wrote them down. I wanted her to feel the same investment in writing that I wished for my students. I thought the stories might be a way in. They certainly shocked and "invested" me. My own distance from the material reality of her life was undeniable. She talked of slum landlords and lost security deposits; I listened, talked to her about how learning to write might help her fight the system. Then it stopped working. The stories became our time together. As much as she needed a listener, she also needed a reading and writing teacher. Soon thereafter, we devoted the first few minutes of each encounter to talk and then turned to her books and writing assignments.

The moment of fascination turned to boredom? In many ways my journal reveals a fascination, a rapture, with the stories the site had to tell, a collection of lives so different that voyeuristic participation was almost too much to bear. I couldn't help but desire membership. But eventually those feelings subsided. What happens when comfort/discomfort is brought back into equilibrium? Like the ice holes that are inevitably abandoned after a couple of days for the thrill of another winter activity, our experiences in the community risk becoming "average," burden instead of novelty. This introduces a new crisis: boredom. Is this the point at which students turn in blank entries? How can I help them understand that comfort doesn't mean that there is nothing left to write about?

The story of false stability? As I came to know Ann and her stories, as we developed our own rituals and methods of interaction, I recognized a sense of stability in my place at the center. And yet stability is the last label that comes to mind as I characterize how service learning relationships exist in my classroom. It is difficult for students, teachers and community participants to escape the reality of our transient roles, the physical migration between the community and classroom in a short 15-week season.

How can I/we tell these stories? How do I encourage students to choose? What do I do with the journals my students turn in? As I redesign curriculum, which story do I ask for next? Like Margaret and Tracy, I need to ask this question again and again.

Ruptura #4

As I grapple with this cacophony of voices, I'm realizing that Ruptura #3 is really just a small part of Ruptura #4, a questioning. Where do I locate ruptura? Was it in the act of journaling—is that where I allowed myself to pause between my knowing and the unknown? Was it in the questions of my essay-writing peers? Is it caught somewhere between my retellings? How can I help students get hold of these things, name them? How can we learn from them? Amid the choice and trauma of retelling, we can come to understand the complexities of the relationships—student-student, student-community, student-writing—service learning pedagogies and practices develop. In the chaos, a method begins to emerge.

And so ruptura becomes a constant rebirth of the telling, and I'm back to ice. Conditions affect what was once clarity all season long, but, in the end, there is movement. Pools of water form along the surface. Sharp cracks ripple into fracture as the sun dapples in physics, challenges a solid into flux, re-introducing the chaos of motion. I'm wrong about the windows. Rupturas aren't about clearing the frost away. Rupturas melt ice, shift the shape of what we know into what we can know. That, then, is my goal as a service learning teacher of writing, to help students engage in the act of ruptura without reaching for a cell phone.

Toward a Conclusion: Acknowledging Ruptura

The method we are developing for recognizing the value/s of ruptura in our service learning writing classes follows from Wolf's trope of thrice told tales: we are using representation to understand representation.

We are arguing that service learning courses should not be measured by one narrative, one paper alone, one final account. Rather, multiple narratives, together with journals and other notes, should be set side by side, seen as partial pieces of an unfolding inquiry and reflected upon not as finished products, but as layers of coming to know and understand. By varying the genre and the audience, by analyzing stories collectively, by excavating the less visible or even hidden dimensions of the story (like the unacknowledged audiences), we understand texts as polyvocal, contextual, always meaning more and always meaning less than writers intend.

We are advocating for a method of narrative refraction—not treating stories as foundational, but as complex, meaningful, ongoing events that can be told and retold to keep learning and teaching in motion.

Recognizing ruptura allows us to resist the master narratives of service learning, reciprocity, happy endings, and the public discourse of activisms. Representing ruptura through telling and retelling makes visible the ways service learning is a contested terrain, a complex social, economic, and political field, in which all participants face challenging interpersonal interactions and representational responsibilities. In acknowledging ruptura, we locate these struggles—the ways course rationales interpellate students, the ways students negotiate service learning assignments, the ways we have to choose which stories to tell—at the heart of the intellectual project of service learning and critical experiential education.

Acknowledgments: We wish to thank Eileen Schell and Maureen Fitzsimmons for their generous and helpful feedback on early drafts and our service learning writing students and community partners for their thoughtful contributions to this project.

NOTES

1. We recognize here the work of Tom Deans (*Writing Partnerships: Service-Learning in Composition*, NCTE, 2000) and Linda Adler-Kassner ("Inner Landscapes, Outer Worlds: Mapping the Territory of Service-Learning and Composition." Keynote, Spring Conference, Writing Program, Syracuse University, Feb. 1999), and the support we have received for these courses from the Center for Public and Community Service and from the University Vision Fund for improving teaching and learning at Syracuse University. For more information and to read our course syllabi, see our website at (http://wrt.syr.edu/service.html).

2. Barbara Jacoby, in her well-known book, *Service Learning in Higher Education: Concepts and Practices*, for example, defines service learning as "a form of experiential education in which students engage in activities that address human and community need together with the structured opportunities intentionally designed to promote student learning and development. Reflection and *reciprocity* are key concepts of service-learning" (p. 5, emphasis ours). As we explored the presence of service learning in higher education through institutional websites, this last line was cited again and again. Reciprocity, in some incarnation, is almost always present in the rhetoric of service.

3. At Syracuse University, we have an on-campus office, the Center for Public and Community Service (CPCS), which negotiates, manages, and maintains links with community non-profit agencies. Each semester CPCS distributes an extensive list of 150 possible community placements. Students send a wish list of three selections and CPCS coordinates placements for them. Students are required by CPCS to work for at least twenty hours over the course of the semester at the agencies.

4. Data for this article was collected during the service learning writing courses taught in fall 1999. All student work has been used with the permission of the writers. Student writers were consulted and elected to use their real names.

5. In their doctoral work, Tracy and Tobi are researching and developing ethical practices of service learning curriculum, sustained community partnerships, and critical pedagogy. We look forward to additional research which will continue to enlarge the dialogue to include student learners and community collaborators.

6. If space permitted, we would extend Britzman's discussion of self-subversive narratives of education: "to explore those other dimensions, that other story, the story of one's own otherness" (p. 16). She describes the three versions or retellings of a story as the ethnographic, the reflective, and the uncanny. We also draw attention to *Political Moments in the Classroom* (Himley, et al.), an account of a group of teachers in the Syracuse University Writing Program who used collaborative story-telling as a method for refracting and understanding the many aspects of challenging classroom events, or ruptura, that roughly fell under the rubric of "the political."

7. See Britzman for a discussion of Bruno Bettelheim's notion of the good enough teacher, who transfers not learning, but a demand that students learn to make their own demands in learning (p. 41).

8. There are many structural changes too: the service learning course I designed is focused specifically on having Syracuse students tutor in the public high schools in the city. With advice from faculty in the School of Education, I have met and talked with high school teachers interested in having these tutors. The project is much more narrowed and focused in its relationship with the community, in its goals, in its tasks.

9. I acknowledge the academic and ethical work of Margaret Dana Singsen, Kaye Berube, and the rest of my Fall 1999 WRT 105 class that I have represented in this article.

10. This course was designed by two of this article's authors, Tobi and Tracy. It was taught during the Fall 1999 semester and was populated with students who had been enrolled in a section which required them to spend at least twenty hours outside of class working with a local non-profit agency of their choice, preferably on literacy-related projects. By the fifth week of the course,

students were assigned to after-school tutoring programs like the Boys and Girls Club and public school classrooms where they assisted teachers with music education, drama, and art. All students worked directly with children.

11. For clarity and with her permission, we use Margaret's middle name in this story.

12. The mini-essay prompts asked students to: analyze agency mission statements; describe physical locations; identify, categorize, and describe agency members; capture and explain some dialogue and agency-specific language.

13. This is a story of corners, of shape-shifting and breaks, one teacher's sequence of motion, representation, and reformulation. Like all rupturas, the beginning is one of many and, while this text must stop, it does not conclude.

14. A pseudonym.

REFERENCES

Berube, K. (1999). Reflection in Unit #2 Portfolio, WRT 105, Writing Program, Syracuse University.

Britzman, D. P. (1998). *Lost Subjects, Contested Objects: Toward a Psychoanalytic Inquiry of Learning.* Albany: SUNY Press, 1998.

Carrick, T. H. (1999). WRT 105: Literacy and Community. Writing Program, Syracuse University.

Coles, R. (1993). *The Call of Service.* New York: Houghton Mifflin Co.

Flower, L. (1996). Negotiating the Meaning of Difference. *Written Communication 13*(1), pp. 44–92.

Himley, M. (1999). WRT 105: Citizenship, the Narrative Imagination, and Good Writing. Writing Program, Syracuse University.

Himley, M., Le Fave, K., Larson, A., Yadlon, S. & the Political Moments Study Group. (1997). *Political Moments in the Classroom.* Portsmouth, NH: Heinemann/Boynton Cook.

Horton, M. & Freire, P. (1990). *We Make the Road by Walking: Conversations on Education and Social Change.* Philadelphia: Temple University Press.

Jacobi, T. (1999). WRT 105: Literacy and Community. Writing Program, Syracuse University.

Jacoby, B. (1996). *Service-Learning in Higher Education: Concepts and Practices,* ed. by B. Jacoby and Associates. San Francisco, CA: Jossey-Bass.

Singsen, M. (1999). Unit #2 Portfolio, WRT 105, Writing Program, Syracuse University.

Stanley, M. (1993). "Community Service and Citizenship: Social Control and Social Justice." In T. Y. Kupiec (Ed.), *Rethinking Tradition: Integrating Service with Academic Study on College Campuses.* Providence, RI: Campus Compact, pp. 59–62.

Wolf, M. (1992). *A Thrice Told Tale: Feminism, Postmodernism & Ethnographic Responsibility.* Stanford, CA: Stanford University Press.

22 Alinsky's Reveille: A Community-Organizing Model for Neighborhood-Based Literacy Projects

ELI GOLDBLATT

Who serves whom in community-based composition courses? Our field has taken a well-meaning and enthusiastic interest in this combination of writing instruction and service-learning over the last few years. Studies in the mid- to late nineties described courses and institutional arrangements and began to explore the ramifications for composition and English studies (Schutz and Gere; Herzberg; Peck, Flower, and Higgins). Linda Adler-Kassner and her colleagues edited an influential volume in 1997 that signaled the arrival of this new approach as a major pedagogical movement, and in 2000 Tom Deans's *Writing Partnerships* gave us a basic framework for thinking about the cooperative relationship between students and the organizations they encounter in these courses. More recent work has focused on how community-based learning can be sustained over time through faculty research (Cushman), how to address the gap between community and academic discourses (Chaden, Graves, Jolliffe, and Vandenberg), and what contradictions we must struggle with in intercultural inquiry (Flower), each study highlighting strategies for respecting the needs and abilities of participating community partners. In a crucial step toward establishing the institutional structures necessary for sustained partnership, Jeffrey T. Grabill and Lynée Lewis Gaillet have urged us to focus on the interface between writing programs and community partners. The need for a balanced and nonexploitive relationship in community-based learning asserts itself insistently in our discussions of this approach, and clearly at this stage writing program administrators must become much more active in developing institutional models that promise true mutual benefits for postsecondary schools and their off-campus partners.

Because the literature is heavily oriented toward student- and faculty-based outreach into underserved communities, we seldom hear of community-based learning projects initiated by community partners themselves. The Community Literacy Center in Pittsburgh may be one exception (see Peck, Flower, and Higgins), but even that landmark partnership arose as much out of the social commitments of faculty at Carnegie Mellon University as out of

From *College English* 67.3 (2005): 274–95.

the community's needs articulated by their Settlement House collaborators. The fact is that universities and colleges seldom develop plans based on suggestions that originate off-campus. Faculty and students devise projects based on research into local citizens' needs or approach recreation centers and libraries to house tutoring projects or screening programs. Neighborhood centers with no official link to a university are less likely on their own to take the steps necessary to bring a cooperative project with a university into being: contacting the right academic units; working with faculty to develop a plan the center's board would approve; and carrying forward the project using university personnel, facilities, and resources.

Neighborhood centers often have energetic and creative people on staff, but they usually face high demand for services, few resources, limited training of support staff, and no time to develop projects with partners in an entirely different work culture like a university. Academics get tenured and promoted for asking questions and proposing interpretations, for publishing and teaching. By publishing this article on community-university partnerships and teaching community-based courses, for example, I add lines to my vita and earn points in the economy of my college and profession. In contrast, directors of neighborhood centers must produce programs and services for their constituents with minimal expense and little room for experimentation, keeping one eye on their boards and the other on funding sources at all times. Manuel Portillo, the neighborhood center director I describe in this article, gains no tangible advantage in his organizing world for appearing in a learned publication; he still cannot get health benefits from the board of his small nonprofit organization until he brings in sufficient grant money in the next fiscal year.

This difference of time and emphasis stacks the cards toward university-initiated projects that are research-driven and aimed at providing undergraduate and graduate students community-based experiences. As academics passionately interested in literacy—and professionals invested in literacy as the medium of our own careers—we see reading and writing as the heart of our involvement with communities. But organizers see literacy as one of many issues they must address with their constituencies, and the people who attend adult basic-education programs or welfare-to-work projects see literacy as one of many needs in their lives along with health care, housing, food, child care, and employment. Is there a way that neighborhood centers themselves could pursue agendas that universities would respond to on terms dictated by the neighborhoods? Can writing programs in particular foster such arrangements? Could a different model of research and outreach support community-based agendas?

To formulate a new model of university-community connections based more in the latter's reality, we might focus on a theory of action devised for neighborhoods rather than for higher education. Educators tend to imagine their work with students within a traditional pattern—let's call it the "throughput" model. We move students along a path marked by diplomas and certificates, occupy them with reading and writing tasks, determine their achievements with tests or papers. Above all, throughput requires that we keep them at desks and tables, in libraries or at computer workstations, with the occasional field trip or lab to indicate that the learning they do has application in a world outside school. After four or five years of this, they graduate and move on to jobs or further study. Even most community-based learning courses follow this model; they simply substitute engagement with genuine outside learners for the texts that might otherwise represent the outside world. Ellen Cushman notes the prevalence of what she calls the "end-of-the-semester project model of service learning" (59), a model that allows courses with significant off-campus experience to approximate the shape and policy of classroom-based courses. As Cushman is careful to emphasize, this model is by no means wrong or inappropriate, but the traditional approach may not be the most suited for the needs of adult learners in a neighborhood literacy center or children in an after-school program. They need teachers who are not just passing through and programs that do not appear one year and evaporate the next. They need literacy programs that take into account the array of demands on a stressed community. Most of all, they need tutors who see individual learners as whole people and university partners sensitive to the entire missions of local agencies, not just researchers studying subjects in sites or educators supervising students in field placements.

SAUL ALINSKY: A COMMUNITY-ORGANIZING MODEL

Let us consider what a community-based model might look like if founded on principles derived from the work of Saul Alinsky, the influential community organizer whose career spanned the period from the 1930s through the 1960s. Longtime organizer and activist Heather Booth has said, "Alinsky is to community organizing as Freud is to psychoanalysis" (qtd. in Slayton 198). His work can serve as a lens for reorienting our vision, shifting the setting for our model building from the campus to the streets.

Alinsky was not an educator, if by that we mean a person concerned with schools and schooling, but he cared a great deal about how ordinary people learn to act for their own good and the good of their neighbors. Like the work of two other theorists who have had a tremendous impact on the field of composition/rhetoric—John Dewey and Paulo Freire—Alinsky's writing is highly suggestive about ways to get students to work together on common projects and take responsibility for their own educational process. Unlike Dewey, however, Alinsky was mainly concerned with organizing disenfranchised people so that they could exercise more political power (or, as Charles Silberman has put it, so that "banding together will give them the capacity to alter the circumstances of their lives" [335]). Unlike Freire, Alinsky said little directly about literacy and more about strikes, actions, and alliances that would shake the established powers from their exploitive and paternalistic habits. Unlike both Dewey and Freire, Alinsky was more a fighter than a writer in his career; his two books on organizing are polemical, sometimes to the point of being obnoxious. Yet Alinsky's commitment to empowering people has much in common with these two better-known twentieth-century figures, and his faith in the democratic process resonates with an abiding faith in our field that access to disciplinary knowledge and authority comes through support for students' composing processes.

Saul Alinsky was born in 1909 to immigrant Russian Jewish parents living in a small flat in a three-story tenement on the Near West Side of Chicago. His family wasn't destitute—his father owned a small garment sweatshop in the building where they then lived—but Alinsky grew up in a tough neighborhood where gangs of Jewish kids fought against Polish kids in the bordering slum (see Finks or Horwitt for this and much of the following biographical information). He attended the University of Chicago, studying archaeology and sociology as an undergraduate and graduating in 1930. He continued in Chicago's sociology department for graduate work in criminology, but, partly because of financial pressures and partly because of his own temperament, he left academic studies to work full-time in the field. By the time he had reached his late twenties, Alinsky had developed a tough but open and effective intellectual style of working with a wide range of people. He had accrued some reputation as a promising young criminologist, and in 1938 he was offered a lucrative job running the Probation and Parole Board in Philadelphia and teaching at the University of Pennsylvania. He decided, however, to forgo the temptations of secure government and academic employment in order to organize on the streets of Chicago (Finks 12–13; Sanders 44–45).

Alinsky's talents as a community organizer began to emerge when Clifford Shaw sent him in 1938 to a neighborhood on Chicago's West Side called Back of the Yards. Alinsky's biographer Sanford Horwitt describes this place "as perhaps the nadir of industrial slum life," an immigrant neighborhood putrid with the stench of meatpacking houses and stockyards (57); thirty years before, Upton Sinclair had written scathingly about this same neighborhood in *The Jungle*. Alinsky himself said that Back of the Yards "was not the slum across the tracks. This was the slum across the tracks from across the tracks" (Sanders 45). Organizing in the Back of the Yards was a daunting task. On top of the poverty and political powerlessness of the area, the warring factions and the relative neutrality of the Roman Catholic Church—the dominant social organization in the area—made the prospects look dim from the start (Horwitt 55).

Alinsky began organizing as he had been trained to do in other neighborhoods: hang around and get to know the people and resources in the area. In an earlier study of Chicago's "Little Italy," Alinsky had developed a technique for interviewing kids, and fifteen teenagers had written their life histories for researchers with his help (Finks 11; Horwitt 25). But in Back of the Yards, his job was to use his information to organize a juvenile recreation and counseling center under the auspices of Shaw's Chicago Area Project (CAP). What made CAP different from other settlement-house programs was that Shaw's approach emphasized "citizen participation." As Horwitt puts it, "When the people realized they could change local conditions, Shaw theorized, they would then feel more responsible for doing something about the problems that plagued them" (53). This required Alinsky to develop relationships with all the community's churches and other institutions, in the hopes of getting them to cooperate on CAP. Cooperative effort seemed impossible at first because—although the area was entirely white and Eastern European—the Poles, Slovaks, Bohemians, and Lithuanians traditionally did not get along with one another, and their respective churches showed no interest in meeting together, let alone joining hands to accomplish something for all the residents. But Alinsky developed a powerful working friendship with lifelong neighborhood resident and local park director Joseph Meegan, and together they formed the Back of the Yards Neighborhood Council (BYNC) that succeeded in bringing the factions together to fight for the common good.

The BYNC proved a powerful model of what neighborhood organizations could do when they worked together. Developing close ties with labor leader John L. Lewis as well as progressive Catholic Bishop Bernard J. Sheil, Alinsky built a power base and a national reputation that made him both loved and loathed. Always using Chicago as his base, Alinsky in 1940 founded a national organization called the Industrial Areas Foundation (IAF) (Horwitt 91) and through IAF he or his few organizers led successful organizing efforts in South St. Paul, Los Angeles, Rochester, and Buffalo. With the help of future journalist Nicholas Von Hoffman and others, Alinsky organized the black neighborhood of Woodlawn in the South Side of Chicago. To be sure, they also failed rather spectacularly in New York City's Chelsea district and never made much headway on a project in Kansas City, Kansas. Alinsky's organization trained César Chávez, and Chávez later used Alinsky's techniques to organize California farm workers. Alinsky worked with Ivan Illich in the early 1950s when the young priest was first starting to be active with the Puerto Rican community in New York City.

Not only did his organizing activities touch many between 1938 and 1970, but also Alinsky's thought and writing influenced many in the field of urban politics and labor activism. The man *Harper's* called "the professional radical" deeply impressed the journalist and economist Charles Silberman, whose popular 1964 book, *Crisis in Black and White*, offers Alinsky's organizing approach as the main hope for solving the tensions in urban neighborhoods of the time. In addition to his best-selling book on organizing, *Reveille for Radicals*, and his reprise book for a new generation, *Rules for Radicals*, Alinsky also wrote a sympathetic portrait of his friend and mentor, CIO founder John L. Lewis. As *Time* magazine noted in 1970, "Like Machiavelli, whom he has studied and admires, Alinsky teaches how power may be used. Unlike Machiavelli, his pupil is not the prince but the people" ("Radical" 56). Alinsky was one of the outstanding radical, noncommunist figures on the left for over thirty years of the twentieth century.

Throughout his career, Alinsky was often regarded with disgust by the right, wariness by the left, and downright exasperation by many in between. In the sixties, the conservative *Christian Century* made a habit of attacking this man and his "bizarre, anti-Christian doctrines of power" ("Episcopal" 1452).

Further to the right, in the late 1960s the Ku Klux Klan twice picketed his arrival at airports, and the FBI warned him of death threats from the reactionary militia called the Minute Men (Horwitt 539). On the liberal left, *The Nation* said in a 1946 review of *Reveille* that "in some parts of the world fascism has made use of exactly this sort of 'radical' talk," and *The New Republic* that year said that Alinsky's book "expresses a point of view which runs the risk of developing *away* from the democracy that the author speaks of with such fervor" (qtd. in Horwitt 183). For those further left, throughout his career "Alinsky's disavowal of a class analysis made him and the importance of his work suspect" (Horwitt xv). The last chapter of *Rules for Radicals*, in which he outlines a campaign to work with the middle class, has a whiff of compromise that New Left radicals must have found repugnant. Moderate critics found his famous dictum that organizers of the poor must "rub raw the sores of discontent" particularly objectionable ("Gadfly" 30).

No matter what audience he addressed, Alinsky was, as biographer P. David Finks remarks, "hard-nosed, outspoken, and profane; when he wanted to be, he could be loud, bullying, impatient, and scornful of questions he thought stupid or elementary" (266). Like many men of his generation, he was not particularly open to contributions to the work by women (Horwitt 289), and one comes to suspect that his notorious hostility to social work was at least in part a reaction to a profession that women had largely invented, especially in the Chicago of Jane Addams's Hull House settlement movement (see Horwitt 127). In his books Alinsky gleefully tells about manipulating and lying to individuals and groups (*Reveille* 106–28), shows disdain for conventional ideas of morality (*Rules* 24–47), revels in conflict and battle with his enemy (*Reveille* 132–54), scorns liberals (*Reveille* 19–23), and takes great pride at being hated wherever he is called to organize (*Rules* 136). In short, he could be an irascible and ornery guy, even to his friends and family.

And yet there is a compelling sweetness to his vision. In *Reveille for Radicals* Alinsky defines a radical with reference to Revolutionary War–era democrats who "really liked people, loved people—all people. They were the human torches setting aflame the hearts of men so that they passionately fought for the rights of their fellow men, all men" (9). For him, a radical "places human rights far above property rights" (16) and—with an undistracted intelligence "not fooled by shibboleths or facades" (15)—fights both to achieve "economic welfare" and "freedom of the min[d]" for oppressed people (16). Alinsky was never a member of the Communist Party, and indeed resisted any program of principles that might override a more compelling philosophical consistency: "The radical is deeply interested in social planning but just as deeply suspicious of, and antagonistic to, any idea of plans that work from the top down. Democracy to him is working from the bottom up" (17). The straight-talking, blunt tone of Alinsky's prose can sometimes obscure the complexity of his social thought; he regarded the abilities to compromise and to develop relationships as crucial qualities in an organizer, just as he called for organizers to show courage and candor in the face of corporate threats.

A SET OF PRINCIPLES

From Alinsky's *Rules for Radicals* I have culled a set of principles for community organizing that also make sense for community-based learning approaches in rhetoric-composition. Those with experience in organizing may find these rules commonplace and even old-fashioned, but for the field and for those teachers and administrators anxious to develop ties with stressed neighborhoods and failing schools, Alinsky's principles can provide useful guidance. The list isn't exhaustive, but I think these principles can help us formulate a new model of university-community connection that is less focused on service and traditional notions of education and yet more effective in promoting productive learning for all involved.

1. Draw on the inevitability of class and group conflict as well as the unpredictability of events for your creativity to invent tactics that fit the moment (19).

2. Be guided by a broadly defined sense of self-interest, taking on multiple issues, and encourage all other participants to do the same (23, 53–59, 76).

3. Try to see every situation in as stark a light as possible, unblurred by ideological imperatives, traditional hatreds, or conventional moralities (12–15).

4. Communicate with others on their own ground, amassing personal experience and solid relationships among the people with whom you intend to work (70, 81–97).

5. Respect people's dignity by creating the conditions for them to be active participants in solving their own problems rather than victims or mere recipients of aid (123).

6. Shape educational experiences that matter in people's lives by helping individuals identify issues they can grasp and do something about (106, 119, 124).

7. Build the leadership capacity of the group being organized and take as the goal the independent functioning of that community (92, see also *Reveille* 64–75).

These seven principles frame learning in the context of doing. Dewey could have written some of these principles, and Freire could have written others. Yet the community organizer embodies a late-twentieth-century radicalism Dewey does not, and the Jew from multiethnic Chicago adds an American social context to pedagogy, as Freire could not. Thomas Deans has pointed out that Dewey emphasizes education as a means to achieve democratic unity to such an extent that "we hear little about race, ethnicity, and cultural difference in Dewey's writings" (35), and he remarks that though "both Dewey and Freire are progressive in their theories and practices [. . .] only Freire can be considered radical" (41). As radical as Freire's approach to literacy is—serving as the basis for literacy campaigns among the dispossessed of Brazil, Cuba, Nicaragua, and elsewhere in the developing world—in the United States Freire's thought has become so abstracted that his ideas often translate into little more than a preference for discussion over lecture in college classrooms. His contribution to American progressive educational theory

is invaluable, but Freire did not design his literacy programs for the contradictions of education in American cities, where kids game on PlayStations
in unheated apartments with peeling, lead-based paint and attend schools
where state-of-the-art computers sit untouched because no one has the time
or technical knowledge to set them up. Perhaps because Alinsky is not expressly an educational philosopher, his work provides a striking challenge to
those of us who want to conceptualize the role of literacy education within the
context of university-community relationships.

Kate Ronald and Hephzibah Roskelly have noted that "philosophical
pragmatism"—as practiced by Freire, Dewey, and others—"makes experience and consequence integral to epistemology and inquiry" (620). Alinsky
demonstrates this same restlessness to know and to try limits, but he takes
his philosophy to the streets. Alinsky's goal is organizing first and foremost;
even though education was an important part of his overall program, he
was not especially concerned with schooling or literacy. He wanted to make
lives better by bringing people together in a working organization so that
they could change their own living conditions and gain dignity. As he puts it
most succinctly, "Change comes from power, and power comes from organization. In order to act, people must get together" (*Rules* 113). Alinsky has a
bite to him that Dewey and Freire no longer have after so many educators
have borrowed from their work, applied their theories to practice, and argued
their merits and limitations. Alinsky's principles are perhaps more difficult to
domesticate into a pedagogical approach, not because his language is arcane
or his philosophy abstract but because his politics are consistently blunt and
confrontational.

At the heart of Alinsky's approach to organizing is his concept of self-
interest. To those who worry that self-interest as a motivational force would
lead to individual greed and communal disintegration, he answers: "The fact
is that self-interest can be a most potent weapon in the development of cooperation and identification of the group welfare as being of more importance
than personal welfare" (*Reveille* 94). The proper function of the organizer, in
Alinsky's view, is to identify problems that affect people individually but help
them see these problems as issues they can do something about collectively
(*Rules* 119). This requires from the organizer a view of daily life undistracted
by the lure of fast money or political position and a faith that people will elaborate a program that will be good for all (*Reveille* 56).

Alinsky stresses that nothing can be accomplished without tremendous
effort to build relationships with local leaders (*Reveille* 188), factions in a
group (*Reveille* 125), and indeed anyone the organizer wants to work with or
influence (*Rules* 93–94). However, he also urged his organizers to *disorganize*
old and unproductive ways a community works (or doesn't work) in order to
build a stronger, more participatory organization later (*Rules* 116). Alinsky
organizers are agitators because they provoke conflict for the purpose of
drawing people into action together: "The job then is to get the people to
move, to act, to participate; in short to develop and harness the necessary
power to effectively conflict with the prevailing patterns and change them"

(*Rules* 117). Reading Alinsky now, years after his initial successes in the late 1930s as well as his revival during the radical 1960s, one can feel both the love and the hatred the man could inspire.

The picture Alinsky paints of the organizer clashes with the image most of us hold as proper for a teacher. In popular opinion, teachers shouldn't be overtly political, shouldn't manipulate their students, and shouldn't reach beyond the discipline or skill set they are hired to teach. In fact many of us would feel uncomfortable acting like Alinsky's organizers in the classroom. Yet we might wish to be more creative and responsive to the particular situations our students find themselves in, hope to build the leadership capacity of the communities we serve, and desire to communicate based on better knowledge of our students' lives and more respect for their dignity. I am not suggesting that we convert undergraduate tutors into young Alinsky agitators stirring up trouble in schoolyards and street corners. Nor do I urge professors to don leather jackets and give up their tenure to work in storefront literacy centers. Radical fantasies are appealing, but to rush off in that direction is to mistake Alinsky's style for his politics. To me Alinsky is calling for a deeper commitment to change than fantasy allows. He challenges us in post-secondary positions to think like organizers rather than academics when we devise models of university-community relationship.

As academics, even if we want to put neighborhood needs first, we cannot but start with the demands of our classrooms or the requirements for promotion. But what if we start from the activist's ground in this instance, learning before we act, developing relationships and commitments before we organize classes and set up research projects? When we have established these relationships, we may be able to help the community partners identify problems and transform these problems into issues to act upon, only later considering how students in courses fit in and what university resources could be helpful in addressing the issues. In short, what if we use our research, teaching, administrative, and writing abilities for the sake of the people our students tutor, not only for the sake of the college programs we run? What if the "throughput" model didn't dominate our program designs, but instead we followed a model of long-term investment in the neighborhoods where we work and centers with which we form partnerships? This thinking leads to a model of community-based learning and research in which students and their teachers are not so much providing services as participating in a collective effort defined by academics and local citizens alike.

THE OPEN DOORS COLLABORATIVE

At Temple University in 1998 we started a component of the writing program called the Institute for the Study of Literature, Literacy, and Culture (see Parks and Goldblatt). The College of Liberal Arts supports the institute with a very small budget, a stipend for one graduate assistant, course reductions for the director, and, some years, reductions for a faculty fellow or two. Whatever other funding we need comes from grants. After about four years we gave the institute a simpler name for regular usage: New City Writing. The stream-lining of the name reflects changes in the mission. New City Writing is still an academic unit in which scholars and students interested in the cultural formation of literature and literacy can pursue special projects, but our focus is on community-based writing and reading programs that lead to publi-cations as well as educational ventures whereby schoolteachers, neighbor-hood people, and university-related people can learn together. We have published a magazine called *Open City* that collected writing by homeless people, school kids, and local writers on subjects like food or shelter. We founded New City Press to publish book projects related to specific commu-nities in the Philadelphia area, such as a series of interviews with residents of a historically integrated working-class South Philadelphia neighborhood called the Forgotten Bottom (Tarrier), a collection of essays by activist dis-abled people talking about their lives and campaigns (Ott), and a bilingual oral history of Mexican mushroom workers in a rural area west of the city (Lyons and Tarrier).

New City Writing works as a partner with local schools and neighbor-hood organizations. We develop projects with community arts organizations such as Art Sanctuary, serving primarily an African American population, and Asian Arts Initiatives, a group focused on Asians and Asian Americans in Chinatown as well as areas in the southern and western sections of the city. We place undergraduates and graduates from courses and with independent projects in various school and community sites, focusing especially on writ-ing centers that can be developed and supported by the organizations involved but can serve as a settled location for visiting tutors and speakers. We participate in writing grant proposals with our partners, acting as the ad-ministering agents for some grants and providing resources and assistance for grants held by other groups. Always we try to respond creatively and coop-eratively to needs articulated by neighborhood organizations, and we try to emphasize building institutions and leadership that will allow long-term relationships and trust to grow among partners.

As in the composition instruction paradigm shift led by Peter Elbow, Don-ald Murray, Nancy Sommers, and Sondra Perl during the 1970s, community-based learning and research has shifted focus from product to process because, as Alinsky would say, the democratic process is paramount. Not that the grant proposals we write and the projects we design aren't important—just as the final version of a student's paper matters much more than early process rhetoric admitted—but the unfolding effort to brainstorm ideas, draft proposals, revise our sense of what matters to us, and recommit ourselves to collaborative work leads us to stronger final projects than anything that any of the partners could have devised in our offices alone. Compositionists should recognize the logic of this approach; it is resonant both with the pro-cess movement and with the principles of community organizing articulated by Alinsky. Building capacity, forming relationships, communicating across institutional boundaries—these processes ultimately shape the nature of the solutions any community can design and support.

As an example of the way a project might be developed under Alinsky's model, I offer a brief account of Open Doors, a cooperative effort among directors of three adult-education centers in North Philadelphia and New City Writing. To me, Open Doors suggests a new model emerging at this stage of the community-based learning movement, one that comes from neighborhoods and draws on the university without being controlled by its demands. I entered into conversations with my partners on this project with few expectations and no particular goal except that I wanted to meet some people working at the nexus of ESL, technology, and literacy issues within small agencies in the North Philly community. After more than two years of meetings and listserv exchanges and grant applications, I hope that Open Doors will lead to a loose network of programs that can serve as a kind of alternative or preparatory community college. We see a need among people in the neighborhoods who have a desire to try college and perhaps seek a degree but who need a transitional year or two before they enroll in traditional postsecondary education. I would not be surprised, however, if a year from now some other formation that my collaborators or I cannot yet imagine arises from our work.

In January 2002 I called on Manuel Portillo at his office next door to St. Ambrose Episcopal Church in a Latino neighborhood of North Philadelphia. The priest of the church, Father Carlos, had approached Temple's Community Partnerships Office to get ESL teachers from Temple for the church's new educational program, Proyecto sin Fronteras, which Manuel directs. Community Partnerships had arranged to have a few TESOL students work at Proyecto as a part of their graduate program in the previous year. My colleague Steve Parks had met Manuel at a Temple event, and he praised Manuel and his program. I had also heard of Manuel from an organizer who worked with him in another neighborhood, and I knew Manuel had a strong interest in educational programs that encourage greater civic participation in the community. I put aside everything else one afternoon and went to see him in the Proyecto office, a converted rowhouse in a portion of North Philly largely Latino but, unlike most of the Latino areas, not exclusively Puerto Rican. Manuel is a slender man in his mid-forties, a refugee from Guatemala who left at the height of the government war against dissenters in the mid-1980s. He is intense but a good listener. He had nearly finished a college degree in his country before being forced to flee and had studied social work in Connecticut and Boston, worked in an organizing campaign for people living with HIV in South Chicago, and then come to Philadelphia in the 1990s to work at various community-development jobs.

That first visit Manuel and I talked over hamburgers and coffee at a lunch counter around the corner from his office. He told me about the Guatemalan paramilitary's having killed his father—a leader in the resistance forces based in the capital—and kidnapped his nieces before he and his siblings fled the country. I had studied Spanish in Guatemala in 1980, and so at least I knew something of the situation there at the time. I talked about my mother's struggle with lung cancer, and we discussed the effect that personal traumas have on one's vocational choices. Manuel recounted the problems of a married couple—both doctors from Colombia—who had just asked him for help finding work in Philadelphia. He described the computer-literacy class that he himself taught three times a week in the center's computer lab. We shared ideas about teaching and organizing and speculated on why people in the neighborhood wanted so much to "learn computers" and what we could do in response to that strong demand. It turned out we had some friends in common in the Guatemalan refugee community and in the foundation world. (Despite being the fifth-largest city in the United States, Philadelphia often shows itself to be a very small town.) We left with no particular plan but the start of a working friendship.

The next time Manuel and I met, Steve Parks came along, too, and brought his new baby, Jude. Jude was in on the conversation, gumming crackers and magnanimously accepting attention from us and other patrons at the lunch joint. We told Manuel about New City Writing and he told us about his conversations with Johnny Irizarry, a director of an adult-education program in the heart of the Puerto Rican community. I got excited about bringing Johnny into the picture because not only had we worked with him closely before on a couple of projects with New City, but also he is one of the best-known figures in the community arts and cultural organizations of Philadelphia. When he resigned from the Puerto Rican arts organization he had run for many years, the city's main paper ran a front-page article about him, a very rare recognition for a community activist. We had helped Johnny get free tuition to finish a master's degree at Temple during a time when he needed an advanced degree to work with the school district and we needed his guidance to work effectively in the Puerto Rican community. I had always admired Johnny's combination of undying good humor and fierce commitment to social justice, and he knew just about everyone doing anything progressive in Philadelphia neighborhoods. Johnny and Manuel had been talking about developing an approach to literacy and education based on the realities of the Latino neighborhoods, an approach with the liberation attitude of Freire but a feel for the economics on Fifth Street, the heart of Philadelphia's Puerto Rican community. Steve, Manuel, and I all agreed that working together could really be fun.

Let me pause at this point and glance back at the Alinsky principles. Stitched into the story about our unfolding relationship with Manuel are approaches to organizing that differ from what we do in the university. In school there are classes, schedules, books on syllabi, concepts to cover. In a neighborhood there are alliances and enmities, jobs and welfare, abandoned houses and fenced-off gardens. The terrain is less defined and the time isn't parceled out in fifteen-week intervals, but the needs are tremendous and the urgency persists like the stench of a hundred old oil-burning furnaces laboring in winter. Steve and I meet Manuel on his ground, not primarily as professors representing a major institution but as interested people with lives of our own. As we talk we learn more about the challenges people around Proyecto face, what the funding issues are, who teaches and studies there regularly, how the church relates to the school it founded but must let grow independently.

I listen for the self-interest of the neighborhood within multiple issues, I express my own self-interest in the project, and I try to see *this* neighborhood specifically as opposed to others in the city or an abstract concept of poor communities. Most of all I allow myself to be guided by Manuel, to learn to trust his vision while still recognizing where I have useful observations to add of my own. We are working together to identify underlying themes that can form the basis of future projects, and both of us eventually agree that building leadership capacity among the people who go to Proyecto is a central objective.

Soon after that conversation, I visited Manuel's computer class. Twelve people worked at fairly up-to-date computers in a little lab on the second floor. The learners were all women except for one man in his twenties; the women ranged in age from early twenties to late fifties, and all were Latina except one older white woman who spoke no Spanish. Manuel introduced me and I talked a bit about our idea that students need a bridge between where they are now and the community college or Temple courses they might take at the beginning of a college career. Two women spoke to me after class about the possibilities of further links between their computer class and college programs. Rosa was in her early thirties, spoke English with a strong Spanish accent—she had come from Venezuela within the last couple of years—and showed great determination to make a new life for herself and her children. She wanted to know if we were sending tutors right away to Proyecto. She had tried community college one semester and decided it wasn't right for her—too confusing, too much English—but she felt she needed more skills and a better job, and she was anxious to get started right away. I met her again later that week in Manuel's office. Rosa was dressed for an interview, talking to Manuel about work prospects anywhere in the area.

Isabel was a bit younger than Rosa. She asked questions for herself and others in class, and quizzed me afterward about the admission policy at Temple. It turned out she was from a well-known Dominican family that owned a number of grocery stores in the area. She had gone to high school not far away but had moved to the suburbs after her father was murdered in the course of a robbery at one of their corner stores. Her sisters had gone to college but, when Isabel got to the city community college, she felt totally overwhelmed by the work her teacher assigned her in the first remedial writing course, though she had earned good grades in her public school. She dropped out, but not before she'd battled through two remedial reading and writing courses and gotten credit for the first college composition course; by that time she'd met and married a doctor from another Dominican family and was raising two young children in a nearby suburb. She came back to the old neighborhood almost every day, and she wanted to get back to college now, probably at night. Manuel told me later that she was quite capable of doing college work and could pay for it, but she lacked confidence in her abilities at school. Isabel was a powerhouse in her community, raising funds for college scholarships for Dominican students, but her fear of academic work held her back.

At Proyecto later that week, Manuel and I met with Johnny and his assistant director Marta, a Latina woman in her mid-twenties who announced that her aunt had once owned the rowhouse where we were meeting. Also attending were two white women from an adult-education program called Urban Bridges connected to St. Gabriel's, another Episcopal church, less than a mile northeast of Proyecto in a section of the city called Olney. Felice Similaro, Urban Bridges' director, and her assistant director MaryAnn Borsuk ran a center that served a very mixed community, including Haitians and Puerto Ricans, Cambodians and Africans, with youth programs as well as literacy and technology courses. With a very small paid staff, Urban Bridges depended heavily on the tutoring provided by undergraduates in service-learning classes at a few different regional colleges. Felice and MaryAnn knew a great deal about the range of approaches to adult basic education and also about the support available from the state Department of Education and other government and private agencies. Everyone from the three centers had extensive experience with foundations, but no one felt that their center was on very stable financial ground in this period when an uncertain stock market made grant money tight and foundations unpredictable.

We talked about what we'd like to work toward, and Johnny spoke movingly about learners needing a curriculum suited to their lives and languages. A small, incredibly energetic man, Johnny is quick to smile but speaks with great seriousness and passion about the work needed in his community. He stressed the need to address the pressures neighborhood center students experience—the urgent demand for marketable skills and serviceable English, as well as the confidence and contacts to get them work outside the neighborhood—but at the same time he felt we had to be committed to building leadership in the community and emphasizing the way people can work together to make things better for all. He clearly had a vision of the kind of organizations that work best in Puerto Rican neighborhoods, but at the same time his years of cooperative work made him respectful of other opinions and careful not to dismiss anyone.

At this meeting I took notes on what people wanted us to work toward. The next day I set up a listserv through Temple for the six of us and sent to the list a one-page statement of our purpose and goals, based on my notes from the meeting. At subsequent meetings we talked through the document I had produced. The focus was not only on a "reality-based and transformative" curriculum for information-technology literacy, but on an organizing strategy that would enhance the perspective of teachers in these small computer labs and directors of the programs about what adults could learn from the neighborhood environment. One big issue that emerged for all three centers—and others that people knew about in the area—was the need for more qualified teachers to make the best use of the computer labs they had built with capital grants earlier. We joked about the irony that centers could get money for computers and connectivity, but few foundations or state agencies would pay for the teachers that made those labs useful to the neighborhoods. This was to become a crucial issue for the collaborative to address.

We held a meeting at Johnny's center near the Fifth Street hub of the Puerto Rican neighborhood. Here we revised our document to focus less on technology and more on cooperative support and curricular reform. Here are the first two paragraphs of the document after that meeting:

> The Open Doors Collaborative is a consortium of adult-education programs in North Philadelphia concerned with establishing a comprehensive approach to literacy instruction that is reality-based and transformative for learners. We propose to develop teaching and learning practices that engage learners in active civic participation. In addition to sharing ideas on curriculum and policy, the collaborative hopes to share resources in our effort to maintain computer services, attract and retain excellent staff, and buy hardware and software at competitive rates.
>
> As a first project, we will develop a curriculum that promotes critical thinking, independent inquiry, communication skills, and leadership ability within the specific context of North Philadelphia neighborhoods. This curriculum would also integrate the information technology students are learning in the small computer labs that have grown up in many community centers and churches. It could function as a stand-alone course or as a component of a GED program.

We decided to resist the temptation to look for funding from a foundation for the moment. Almost everybody had a story about foundations that asked their organization to follow all kinds of planning and evaluation procedures, only to find that most of the money in the grant went to experts who planned and evaluated but added nothing to the work with learners. In my minutes of the meeting, I wrote down this remark from Felice: "The problem is that it's so multilayered that by the time the money gets to the base there's little left." Everyone agreed that we would not "chase the money" in this new alliance but formulate our plans and goals first, before we began talking to anyone about funding.

I recount the details of our beginnings in Open Doors not because the specifics matter very much to those who didn't live through it, but to illustrate both the complexity and the pleasure of working in partnership across the university-community divide. To make a new organizing effort go, as Alinsky would say, you have to identify the true self-interest of the communities involved and figure out how to get resources to address those needs. You have to identify well-connected leaders with an effective approach to actual problems in the neighborhood. You have to talk through conflicts and negotiate any tensions among organizations each of which is struggling for its existence. Our meetings continued through the spring and summer, with the group deciding to stay small; an idea of sponsoring a retreat for North Philly community agencies was transformed into an effort to write a grant proposal to support a collaborative project just among our organizations. Felice, who kept Urban Bridges afloat by paying close attention to funding opportunities, ran across a Request for Proposals (RFP) from the U.S. Department of Education that seemed tailored for us. As she put it at the meeting where we shifted from the retreat idea to the grant, "We don't want to run after the money, but we have to run our organizations, don't we?" We worked intensively on that grant proposal and, though we ended up not submitting it, we weathered some conflicts across our programs arising from personal styles and organizational cultures. The language we produced for that proposal looked as if it would work for other grants in the future, but the founding ideas were taking shape with each iteration.

Open Doors came to recognize that the most pressing need for small neighborhood adult-literacy centers is more well-trained and committed teachers who know the communities in which they work. This is particularly true where information technology is part of the core teaching skill; the best-qualified teachers prefer higher-paying work at for-profit trade schools or community colleges if they can't get solid full-time work in neighborhood centers, even if they are sympathetic to the missions of the centers. We developed a two-pronged approach to this problem. First, we would try to get funding for attractive teaching positions—full-time and with good benefits—for teachers whom our coalition of centers could share. Individual centers might not be able to afford a full-time teacher, but a consortium could share costs, write grant proposals together, and divide the supervisory responsibilities so that all centers would benefit and services to people in the area could increase in scope and quality. Second, we hoped to develop a model of "community educator" on the Latin American model: indigenous education and health workers trained to provide services to their neighbors by the few educated teachers and health-care workers available in the countrysides of many poor nations. We felt this model would also work well for technology and literacy training in underserved urban neighborhoods in the United States.

After about a year and a half of meeting together, the Open Doors group broke up. Johnny was under heavy pressure from his agency to write grant proposals that would save them, and he no longer had time to meet with us. Felice resigned to pursue other projects, and MaryAnn stayed on at Urban Bridges as the group made the transition to connect with a larger social service agency called Episcopal Community Services. Manuel and I, however, continued to meet and develop the concepts. I joined his board as chair and began the job of pulling together community members with little organizational experience and outsiders with expertise but no direct ties to the neighborhood. The Open Doors experience gave concrete expressions to the problems and possible solutions we could apply to neighborhood literacy centers. I taught a class at Temple where I invited four students from Proyecto to participate, and these Proyecto students became our first class of community educators. We are writing grant proposals for Open Borders now that we hope will eventually allow us to go back to our Open Doors partners and develop both the sharing of professional staff and the training of community educators. In addition, we've worked out a plan for service-learning experiences in Proyecto classes. Community technicians, like community educators, could be paid a stipend to help maintain computer labs in local churches and centers as a means of combining on-the-job training with neighborhood collaboration. I regard the Open Doors project not as a failure but a long-term investment in helping neighborhood leaders identify problems related to literacy and work toward local solutions that eventually will change the way North Philadelphians move through training programs and the way Temple students relate to centers like Proyecto.

Perhaps the most compelling element for me of the approach we developed in Open Doors is the shift in focus from individual to collective improvements. This speaks to the last three principles of Alinsky's organizing approach; the shift honors the experience of disenfranchised people while it points toward greater independence for groups *and* individuals who must see themselves as agents of their own future rather than victims of their history. Manuel has been particularly strong in his argument that, in his own center, the stress should be on how any individual functions within his or her multiple communities. "What are the communities from which you come and to which you wish to return?" he asked a group of his students when I brought rhetoric-composition graduate students from Temple to visit Proyecto. A student I will call Lourdes answered by saying she had three communities. One was in the block or two around her house, a microneighborhood in North Philly populated by immigrants from the Dominican Republic like herself but also by people from Puerto Rico and other Latin American countries. Another was the neighborhood around her husband's little grocery store, a renovated building in an African American neighborhood where the drug trade is intense but where people had been friendly to her and her husband. Lourdes noted that many neighbors there helped her learn English, and now she felt a commitment to make life better in that community, too. Finally Proyecto itself served as a crucial community for her. She was attending classes in computer literacy there three times a week so that she could help her children with their homework. She said at first she couldn't do more than turn her computer on and off, but now she could set up a system and handle word-processing software. She had developed a strong bond with the others in her advanced technology class and wanted to continue working with them. She took great pride in her growing abilities to speak English and manipulate a computer system, but she realized that she had much more to do if she wanted to contribute in significant ways to all these communities. Her own self-interest was intimately tied to the well-being not only of her family but also of the friends and neighbors who have helped make her life since arriving in this country more hopeful and productive.

Soon after that session, Manuel asked Lourdes to train as a community educator with me. In that role, she worked for eight weeks writing and reading with my undergraduate senior seminar. We also invited her to join the board of Proyecto. Alinsky would have loved her story, for it illustrates not only the effort to help individuals grasp issues they can do something about but also the way to build leadership capacity, hers and those of people who encounter her. She is becoming a leader in her home communities, but—believe me—Lourdes's remarks were not lost on the grad students who heard her, either.

KNOWLEDGE ACTIVISM

But how is this story relevant to college writing instructors and program administrators? What's so valuable about hanging around in North Philly, making fun of foundations and swapping family stories? And what role does a university writing program play in organizing a neighborhood around literacy? Perhaps the most telling question is the one with which I began this article: Who is serving whom? One can never answer the question definitively, even in a single, seemingly static, situation; even the worst university-community relationships can change with the weather. A state-funded research university might pay little attention to the needs of poor neighborhoods— or those scholars who interact with them—until a legislator from an urban district takes over the committee that decides higher-education funding. Suddenly faculty who do community-based work can become important to the university's central administration and the way researchers relate to community needs can come under intense scrutiny. No matter which way the wind blows, the question of who is serving whom needs to be asked again and again.

I served my community partners with an approach I've come to think of as knowledge activism. My experience, the resources I could contribute, and my noninterventionist approach gave me a certain credibility to participate in the organization-development process. I helped found and nurture the Open Doors Collaborative, and I continue to work with Manuel and Proyecto. A study leave from my university when we first got started gave me time that others in the group did not have, and I have contacts in the city literacy network and foundations that proved useful from time to time. My writing skills allowed me to take good notes and shape them into a document we could rework collectively. My experience with literacy instruction and research helped because I could suggest language in grant proposals that might convince funders. I spoke Spanish passably and taught high school in the neighborhood; this local knowledge allowed me to listen intelligently to the conversation. Most important, I was willing to invest time and energy without being in charge, to build alongside others working in the neighborhood rather than enter the scene with a plan already formed. As Alinsky would have it, I met people on their own ground and observed the situation without preconceived notions of what they needed or who they were.

Another aspect of knowledge activism is that I could bring to bear institutional resources that I had at my disposal for my partners' needs. The Temple University Writing Program had received grant money to participate in community projects, and I was able to provide some funding to start the community-educator training project. I brought graduate and undergraduate classes in contact with Proyecto, and in the last few years my Temple colleagues and I have arranged assistantships, internships, and volunteer positions to aid small nonprofit organizations with few resources of their own. Alinsky's principles, however, operate as useful reminders when knowledge activists begin to draw on their institutional affiliations. University resources, available to us because of our professional (and privileged) positions, must be offered responsibly and cooperatively. It helps no one to give aid without a clear purpose or with no commitment to build relationships across institutions, and it is cynical exploitation to offer resources with hidden agendas based primarily on university-determined objectives.

At the same time, Manuel, Johnny, Felice, and MaryAnn had a store of experiences and allies to share with me. The work they do challenges any narrow understanding of reading and writing confined to the college campus. Rosa, Isabel, and Lourdes reminded me just how broad the spectrum of literacy really is and how high the stakes are for those who do not have full institutional access to literacies of the dominant culture. Literacy researcher Deborah Brandt has noted that "despite ostensible democracy in public education, access to literacy and its rewards continue to flow disproportionately to the children of the already educated and the already affluent" (197). This same heritage of class advantage follows literacy educators as well. Unlike college writing administrators like me at large research universities, directors of adult-education centers do not have tenure or a large institution's budget behind them as they build their programs. Their students and clients often live precariously and must succeed or face welfare cutoffs, unemployment, deportation, or prison. The mission of my partners' adult-education centers forces me to conceive of writing and reading beyond the boundaries of undergraduate and graduate curricula, even when I sit in university committee meetings or hold conferences with dissertation advisees. Located only inside my campus, I can either come to believe my job is terribly exalted, the top of the literacy food chain, or I can despair that I make no difference in the life of anyone. Again, the "throughput" system defines our consciousness and masks the reality of other community and individual objectives in settings off campus. After every Open Doors meeting I remembered that I function inside an institutional framework for literacy that is merely one among many.

In the long run, the shift to a more collective view of education is profound for a college writing program. It can cause us to question the throughput model of education, in which the writing program plays such a prominent part. Of course we want individual students to succeed as they move from general education to major, from wide-eyed (and scared) first-year student to world-weary (and scared) senior. We have a responsibility to help students move through their school careers and be able to function in jobs afterward. But this model is almost entirely focused on individuals developing a knowledge base and skill set. How do a writing program, a general education curriculum, and a department-based major foster a sense in individuals that they are connected to other citizens in large and small ways? How do we in writing programs make manifest our understanding of literacy as social, local, or efficacious beyond having students read articles that say so? The crucial thing is that we need not see our programs as merely forming a conduit; instead we can position our entire institution as one among many that engage with a wide range of people. When we think of ourselves as members of more than an academic community, our neighborhood connections should be constituted in such a way that students encounter partners engaging in substantial work rather than clients receiving aid.

My encounters with Manuel, Johnny, Felice, MaryAnn, Rosa, Isabel, and Lourdes give me concrete moments for understanding Alinsky's "rules." The time demanded to apply these principles overwhelms me occasionally; the conflicts between the needs of different neighborhoods and the real or perceived goals of the university can seem quite impossible to reconcile. Alinsky stresses that conflict is inevitable and that out of it must arise creative solutions and greater perspective. At the same time, for all his emphasis on conflict, Alinsky's greatest organizing was built on well-tested friendships. Like organizing, literacy work can be sustained by such friendships even amidst conflict. On the other hand, the specialization and risk-aversion common in university life, the narrow formulations of self-interest and turf protection that seem inevitable in every adult endeavor—these are ways of handling conflict that can exhaust the spirit and wither the mind completely. If we are willing to accept roles as participants or even knowledge activists rather than detached observers or paid consultants, we can reframe for ourselves the sites and texts of literacy instruction through satisfying and reciprocal relationships with our neighborhood partners.

NOTE

1. I want to thank my partners at the Open Doors for their cooperation on this article and their willingness to allow me to publish their real names and the names of their organizations. This naming allows the piece to function less as an ethnographic study and more as a critical history. I am also grateful to Linda Adler-Kassner and two anonymous readers from *College English*, who gave me excellent editorial suggestions. I want to dedicate this piece to my mother, Selma Kushner Goldblatt, who worked briefly with Alinsky in the late forties and died in the first year of the Open Doors project.

WORKS CITED

Adler-Kassner, Linda, Robert Crooks, and Ann Watters, eds. *Writing the Community: Concepts and Models for Service-Learning in Composition*. Washington, DC: American Assn. for Higher Education, 1997.
Alinsky, Saul. *Reveille for Radicals*. New York: Vintage, 1946.
———. *Rules for Radicals*. New York: Vintage, 1971.
Brandt, Deborah. *Literacy in American Lives*. Cambridge: Cambridge UP, 2001.
Chaden, Caryn, Roger Graves, David A. Jolliffe, and Peter Vandenberg. "Confronting Clashing Discourses: Writing the Space between Classrooms and Community in Service Learning Courses." *Reflections* 2.2 (2002): 19–39.
Cushman, Ellen. "Sustainable Service Learning Programs." *CCC* 54 (2002): 40–65.
Deans, Thomas. *Writing Partnerships: Service-Learning in Composition*. Urbana, IL: NCTE, 2000.
"Episcopal Editor Denounces Saul Alinsky." *Christian Century* 15 Nov. 1967: 1452.
Finks, P. David. *The Radical Vision of Saul Alinsky*. New York: Paulist, 1984.
Flower, Linda. "Intercultural Inquiry and the Transformation of Service." *College English* 65 (2002): 181–201.
"The Gadfly of the Poverty War." *Newsweek* 13 Sept. 1965: 30–32.
Grabill, Jeffrey T., and Lynée Lewis Gaillet. "Writing Program Design in the Metropolitan University: Toward Constructing Community Partnerships." *Writing Program Administration* 25.3 (2002): 61–78.
Herzberg, Bruce. "Community Service and Critical Teaching." *CCC* 45 (1994): 307–19.
Horwitt, Sanford D. *Let Them Call Me Rebel: Saul Alinsky—His Life and Legacy*. New York: Knopf, 1989.

Parks, Steve, and Eli Goldblatt. "Writing beyond the Curriculum: Fostering New Collaborations in Literacy." *College English* 62 (2000): 584–606.

Peck, Wayne C., Linda Flower, and Lorraine Higgins. "Community Literacy." CCC 46 (1995): 199–222.

"Radical Saul Alinsky: Prophet of Power to the People." *Time* 2 Mar. 1970: 56–57.

Ronald, Kate, and Hephzibah Roskelly. "Untested Feasibility: Imagining the Pragmatic Possibility of Paulo Freire." *College English* 63 (2001): 612–32.

Sanders, Marion K. "The Professional Radical Moves In on Rochester: Conversations with Saul Alinsky, Part 2." *Harper's Magazine* July 1965: 52–59.

Schutz, Aaron, and Anne Ruggles Gere. "Service Learning and English Studies: Rethinking 'Public' Service." *College English* 60 (1998): 129–49.

Silberman, Charles E. *Crisis in Black and White*. New York: Vintage, 1964.

Slayton, Robert A. *Back of the Yards: The Making of a Local Democracy*. Chicago: U of Chicago P, 1986.

PART FIVE

Writing Programs as Community Engagement

23 Writing Beyond the Curriculum: Fostering New Collaborations in Literacy

STEVE PARKS

ELI GOLDBLATT

"In dreams begins responsibility."

–W. B. Yeats

As Susan McLeod noted more than ten years ago, the movement for writing across the curriculum at its best has been about "change in the entire educational process at the university level" ("Defining" 23). From its inception in small liberal arts colleges to its broad application in land grant universities and Ivy League schools, WAC has challenged teachers in every discipline to think more about the context and nature of student learning than they might within the traditional content-driven model of college teaching. WAC's attention to students' learning precedes the recent drive in higher education circles to shift universities "from teaching to learning" (Barr and Tagg; M. Miller; Schneider and Shoenberg).

Indeed, WAC practitioners have become institutional leaders in faculty development and activist program design. Writing program administrators (WPAs) are often asked to participate in service learning task forces, teaching excellence advisories, technology roundtables, and core revision committees. Writing programs are now involved in service learning projects that connect the classroom to the community (Adler-Kassner, Crooks, and Watters; Cushman "Public"; Herzberg; Schutz and Gere) and in new instructional initiatives that draw on information technology and the Internet (Anson; Faigley; Hawisher et al.; Walvoord; or see on-line journals such as *Kairos*). Our colleagues in the National Writing Project have for many years been working with teachers on writing pedagogy in elementary and secondary school (Silberman).

The growing involvement of college writing teachers in various community, technology, and school initiatives signals a shift in writing program emphasis that invites us to reconsider the original social compact out of

From *College English* 62.5 (2000): 584–606.

which WAC was formed. David Russell has suggested that WAC combines elements of competing camps in early twentieth century education: progressive educators' concern for "child-centered teaching" and the modern consolidation of disciplinary knowledge. In Russell's view, WAC strikes a balance between those two, reflecting John Dewey's vision that "students' use of language must lead systematically from the experience of the individual to the collective experience of the culture as represented by organized disciplines" (26). However, his history of WAC also emphasizes the extent to which "writing" thus became tied to the university's structure of specialized departments. The movement won battles to shift instruction away from mechanical "skills" and toward the discourse of text-based disciplinary communities (25), but it gained its success because it "linked writing not only to learning and student development but also to the intellectual interest of specialists" (39). At the end of the century, universities are changing again, and the deal WAC struck with departments and disciplines—to train students in the major and forward the move to specialized education—may not generate and sustain the sort of literacy instruction necessary for students in universities of the next century.

Even from the point of view of faculty, maintaining an uncritical alliance with disciplines does not serve the interests of many colleagues. Faculty who collect folklore or oral histories, sponsor community writing projects, or facilitate school-based publications often have no forum within the university's disciplinary structure to share the results of their research with colleagues of like mind but different discipline. Indeed, absent a central site to explain and develop a broader conception of writing and reading, traditional models of literacy and faculty collaboration dominate. If compositionists reframe WAC to reach beyond university boundaries, we can foster cross-pollination and interdisciplinary discussion of how knowledge is shaped and conveyed in culture. In short, WAC could integrate a multiplicity of writing and reading modes with a conception of literacy instruction not limited to serving the needs of established disciplines.

This article begins by reviewing calls for an expanded conception of WAC and looks at the tension between the standard structure of college writing programs and the increasing external demands on these programs. We then describe an example of a program that carries writing instruction and literacy research beyond university boundaries. Finally, we suggest problems and benefits that may accompany this change of orientation for writing programs. The argument is not that WAC needs to abandon its traditional support for writing in the disciplines, but that we should imagine our project as one that combines discipline-based instruction with a range of other literacy experiences that will help students and faculty see writing and reading in a wider social and intellectual context than the college curriculum. Such a reconceptualization of WAC requires increased collaborations among university, school, and community partners as well as a greater sense of commitment by writing program administrators to literacy in the regions where our institutions are located.

INSTITUTIONAL DEMANDS AND NEW CHALLENGES FOR STUDENTS

An expanded conception of WAC responds both to current institutional demands and to new challenges in literacy faced by undergraduate students. In a sense, both involve recalibrating the "balance" David Russell describes in WAC "between the individual student's experience and the collective experience that a discipline and its teachers represent" (41). Institutionally, universities are under enormous pressure to provide a wider range of study to a more diverse population through an extended spectrum of instructional modes, while the financial resources for the universities—especially public universities—contract. As Anne Herrington and Charles Moran have warned, WAC grew as funding for the universities expanded after World War II, and if "such expansion was a factor in the origin and development of writing in the disciplines, then the present contraction may be a factor in its demise" (236). WAC will need to suit itself to the changing conditions of university funding, and in many ways an expanded conception of WAC is quite suited to the new environment in which recruitment and retention of students gains importance and undergraduate student learning is valued over research and graduate education.

At the same time, students are facing new challenges in terms of what they must know in work and civic life. They often think they are looking for vocational training, but they must be prepared for much more complicated demands than job preparation. They must learn abilities that will sustain them through multiple career changes, new roles in marriage and community life, and forbidding political crises in the environment, economy, and social justice. If compositionists and rhetoricians are to act upon the current research and theory in our own journals, writing programs can no longer be limited to introducing students to the rhetoric of academic fields and majors. Our attention to public discourse (e.g., Cushman "Public"; Mortensen; Wells), critical literacy in schools and community settings (e.g., Cushman "Critical"; DeStigter), cultural studies (e.g., Berlin and Vivion), and the weaving of personal stories into academic argument (e.g., Brodkey; Goldblatt; R. Miller) suggests that writing and rhetoric teachers have much to offer students beyond either traditional belletristic notions of the essay or discipline-specific understandings of effective prose.

First, consider the institutional demands on writing programs. In her 1996 meditation on "The Future of WAC," Barbara Walvoord issued this challenge: "WAC programs, which have traditionally focused on micro issues, must now devote significant attention to macro issues. The first macro challenge is the need to work with other organizations" (68). She pictures WAC as a social movement and recommends that WPAs should work more directly with national organizations such as the American Association for Higher Education, university-based institutes for higher education research and leadership such as those at Syracuse and elsewhere, foundations such as Pew Charitable Trusts, and governing bodies such as accrediting agencies, boards, and legislatures. She recognizes that WAC has lost some of its early vigor but calls on us "to act now as a mature reform organization" and take a role in "what history may call the era of teaching" (74).

An alliance among university instructors and teachers both in K–12 and adult basic education is particularly crucial, even if it appears today to be quixotic. Too often university faculty do not frame even our teaching mission in such a way as to class ourselves with schoolteachers or community educators. The differences in privilege and autonomy make such alliances seem impossible. There is also little in the tenure or promotion reward structure to encourage long-term engagement by faculty with public school or community organizations (see "Making Faculty Work Visible"). In addition, the decisions made by both public schools and universities (for example, curricular initiatives or building projects) often alienate neighborhood residents and take no account of community literacy projects.

And yet "teaching literacy" is a term under which a considerable range of educational efforts—from graduate school to adult job training to daycare— could be united. This term authorizes educators to work on vexing community problems by joining hands and minds across institutional boundaries. To take a particularly striking example, in one Philadelphia public high school that serves a predominantly Latino population, the average entering 9th grade cohort is approximately 1,200 students. On average, only 200 students receive diplomas (North Philadelphia Community Compact Data Report). Of those, few were capable of entering a four-year college program without tremendous transitional support. Numbers like these—tantamount to genocide in poor neighborhoods throughout the United States—have significant impact on college enrollments as well as welfare and crime statistics, but in human terms educators simply must develop a principled and effective response to such a social catastrophe. Mike Rose has written eloquently about the good to be found in American public schools in the most stressed neighborhoods, and he has called for

> a different kind of critique, one that does not minimize the inadequacies of curriculum and instruction, the rigidity of school structure, or the "savage inequalities" of funding, but that simultaneously opens discursive space for inspired teaching, for courage, for achievement against odds, for successful struggle, for the insight and connection that occur continually in public school classrooms around the country. (4)

A network of people concerned with literacy in a region could develop a supportive and constructive critique of public education that would make solutions possible across traditional educational and community boundaries.

Nor should the banding together of teachers at all levels be seen as inimical to research. One might argue that today, when productivity is the main measure of work, teaching in the humanities looks more defensible than unfunded research in all but the most elite institutions. But the making of knowledge should not be split off from the conveying of it. Our hope lies in the opposite direction: just as we foster better teaching at all levels, we should also support more educators and students in the project of inquiry. By asserting the place of writing not only within the curriculum but within the local social context, academics will be in a better position to explain to a skeptical public just why research and publication really do matter to the society at large.

Urging us from a more practical direction is Susan McLeod in a recent article on the nature of WAC. Even more directly than Walvoord, she focuses us on what it takes to create programs that survive: "Wise WAC directors will also look for outside funding for their programs . . . and will integrate their programs with important campus initiatives—assessment, technology, general education reform, so as to braid WAC into ongoing issues rather than having it as a free-standing (and more vulnerable) entity" ("WAC at Century's End" 72). Her metaphor of "braiding" seems particularly appropriate for describing the way WAC can become involved with a variety of projects not immediately associated with writing. As her 1997 work with Eric Miraglia makes clear, enduring WAC programs need strong administrative funding, grassroots support, and consistent leadership that remains active and vibrant over time (Miraglia and McLeod 48). Of course there is great danger in paying for a writing program through grant money, but McLeod makes an important point when she urges that writing programs must seek funding for projects to make new contacts and to achieve the proper integration into the fabric of a particular university and a specific region.

The grant-writing process has the added advantage that, by articulating new goals and re-creating established programs, it can help reinvigorate a program staff or oversight board, consolidate faculty support, capture administrative attention, and broaden the role of community and public school participants. Grant writing leads the writing program beyond the curriculum, for funders are often looking for novel approaches to link programmatic efforts that have heretofore operated in isolation. This is not to say we should work beyond disciplines in order to chase money, but the funding possibilities can be a good incentive to contact the people we have long regarded as allies but we were always too busy to meet.

Another voice calling for compositionists to reach beyond campuses and traditional roles is Kurt Spellmeyer's. He echoes Walvoord's call in a very different key:

> We will need to become ethnographers of *experience*: I do not mean armchair readers of the "social text," but scholar/teachers who find out how people actually feel. And far from bringing English studies to a dismal close, the search for basic grammars of emotional life may give us the future that we have never had, a future beyond the university. (911)

Spellmeyer is addressing compositionists as members of an English faculty engaged in a large-scale cultural undertaking. He seems to be advocating that writing teachers become peacemakers with colleagues in literary studies, that we search for common ground—to use the title metaphor of his 1993 book—on which to revive the teaching and production of written language.

As Spellmeyer suggests, reasons for reaching beyond the curriculum are not purely programmatic or institutional. Increasingly, theorists in composition have described writing and writing classes in terms of identity formation and transformation in ways that supersede the old debate between expressivist and social models of writing pedagogy. Richard E. Miller suggests that writing is "a place where the personal and the academic, the private and the public, the individual and the institutional, are always inextricably interwoven" (267). Through a meditation that is both intensely personal and markedly academic, he calls for writing and writing instruction that allow students and authors to test out various discourses against one another and thereby use language that demonstrates "an ability to imagine a transformed reality" in lived experience (284).

Both Spellmeyer and Miller might be dismissed as simply repackaging the belletristic tradition, but despite traces of Emersonian yearning for transcendence, both develop a view of literacy more capacious and tolerant than is usual in our limited academic horizon. They willingly step beyond skepticism and the narrow politics of theory debates, and this opens writing instruction up to a world beyond academic discourse while not denying the importance of knowledge as it is practiced and elaborated inside universities. Conceiving of writing beyond the curriculum does not deny the value of disciplinary knowledge, but it allows us to think through and across and outside disciplines so that, as Miller hopes, "the personal and the academic are set loose and allowed to interrogate one another with no predetermined outcome" (284).

An expanded WAC draws on Ernest Boyer's vision of a renewed higher education in this country. When the late president of the Carnegie Foundation described a model of postsecondary school that stands apart from the two traditional American models of excellence in higher education—the small, high-priced liberal arts college and the large, research-intensive land grant university—his words seem now to apply to our own endeavor:

> What I'm describing might be called the "New American College," an institution that celebrates teaching and selectively supports research, while also taking special pride in its capacity to connect thought to action, theory to practice. This New American College would organize cross-disciplinary institutes around pressing social issues. Undergraduates at the college would participate in field projects, relating ideas to real life. Classrooms and laboratories would be extended to include health clinics, youth centers, schools and government offices. Faculty members would build partnerships with practitioners who would, in turn, come to campus as lecturers and student advisers.
>
> The New American College, as a connected institution, would be committed to improving, in a very intentional way, the human condition. (A48)

Boyer calls for an engaged institution, one in which research informs community service as well as teaching and disciplinary knowledge production, one for which the campus is just one of many learning sites possible for student and teacher alike. As our epigraph and title suggest, our dream leads us to new responsibilities but also to new cooperative partnerships. In the succeeding section, we describe institutional structures designed expressly for the purpose of bringing university students and faculty into collaboration with community groups and schoolteachers and their pupils in order to foster new cultural practices and more active types of learning. Building that ambition into the WAC program is what will take writing beyond the curriculum.[1]

STRUCTURE VERSUS FUNCTION: MODELS FOR A DREAM

The basic outline of writing programs has settled into a pattern over the last years since Susan McLeod outlined the components of WAC in 1987 ("Defining"). Figure 23–1 presents a four-component writing program. Sometimes schools may be missing upper-division courses, and sometimes writing centers are underdeveloped or absent. Even the first-year writing course—the mainstay of writing programs—has occasionally been excised in favor of a broader WAC effort. Some schools have initiated WAC programs tied to public speaking and communication, a move not reflected in our diagram. But we think the diagram indicates a basic structure for writing programs.

Figure 23–2 indicates a constellation of functions possible for most writing programs. This is hardly an exhaustive list, and yet any WPA will feel exhausted just contemplating such an array of demands. Not all writing programs serve all of these purposes, but most are under pressure to serve many purposes, and—at least in an informal way—most programs do more than the basic structure in Figure 23–1 would suggest. WPAs and their assistants or allies regularly field community phone calls, give local talks, write grant proposals, serve on boards and committees, organize symposia, or consult with schools for purposes not reflected in our basic structural diagram. For this reason, the basic structure may no longer be meeting the demands of contemporary writing programs. At Temple University, we are rethinking the

FIGURE 23–1   A Common Configuration for WAC/WID Programs

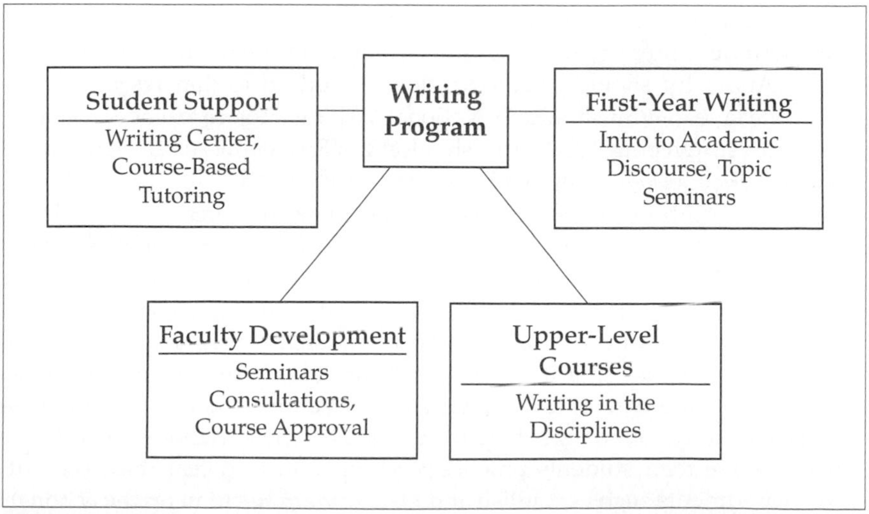

FIGURE 23–2   Functions for Writing Beyond the Curriculum

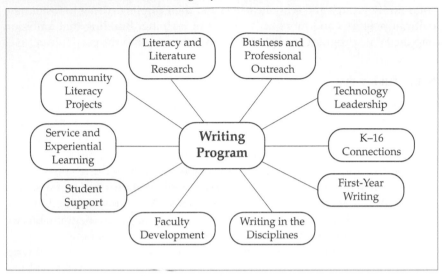

purposes for the writing center, recognizing its growing importance as an information technology leader and faculty teaching resource. We are developing service and experiential learning within advanced writing and rhetoric courses and establishing the Institute for the Study of Literature, Literacy, and Culture to support these courses as well as research and outreach in the regions and the schools (Sullivan et al.).

One outcome of our new orientation is a set of questions we have begun to ask about the relationship between English education teacher training programs and WAC. Typically, these two have little to do with one another because one is based in a university's education school and the other in its college of arts and sciences. But why shouldn't future teachers work as tutors in the writing center or as fellows for writing-intensive courses in the disciplines? And why shouldn't compositionists and education researchers be close colleagues? Why shouldn't National Writing Project teachers converse with first-year writing TAs? Why shouldn't WPAs know about high school writing curricula in their regions?

Several painful conflicts emerge when we talk to professors and administrators on both sides of the institutional divide at other universities. One is that too often compositionists and literature faculty in English either don't know or don't respect their colleagues in English education, and this sets up a corresponding resentment among education faculty against anyone in English. Another is that education majors are not highly respected as students and thus are not recruited to be writing tutors. A third source of mutual hostility is that education colleges tend to be jealous of their relationships with the schools where their students practice teaching, and they fear that "content-area" departments such as English and history want to cut in on the action.

At the same time, both education and liberal arts colleges are in serious crisis at the moment. Education programs are under intense pressure nationally from legislatures and the public to produce more knowledgeable and effective beginning teachers (witness the recent outcry in Massachusetts over teachers' performance on standardized certification tests). Meanwhile, in a recent national survey of public attitudes toward liberal arts education, researchers found that only about "one-third of parents and a quarter of high school students and university graduates view the liberal arts positively" (Hersh 19). In composition, English-trained and education-trained writing specialists read much the same literature but do not recognize each other as colleagues often enough. Literature faculty and education professors who teach the teaching of literature rarely, if ever, even meet one another, let alone talk about their fields together. Certainly we all face very real problems, but we simply cannot solve them without each other.

Recently, Peter Rabinowitz from literary studies and Michael Smith from English education collaborated on *Authorizing Readers*, a fascinating consideration of how current literary theories can be productively and ethically applied in secondary school classrooms. This kind of cooperative project is all too rare in the fields of literary and literacy studies. There should be more alliances of this sort—in research, teacher training, and program design— within and without the college campus. One means by which the writing program at our university has reached out and across boundaries is the founding of the Institute for the Study of Literature, Literacy, and Culture. The institute is by no means the only instance of our writing beyond the curriculum effort, but we think it is perhaps the most innovative and indicates the possibilities that open once we reconceptualize WAC. We turn to a description of the institute now.

THE INSTITUTE FOR THE STUDY OF LITERATURE, LITERACY, AND CULTURE

The Institute for the Study of Literature, Literacy, and Culture is an alliance of university, public school, and community educators. Housed in the Departments of English, the institute sponsors courses, seminars, workshops, and lectures designed to bring together the educational community surrounding Temple University around a common set of principles:

- Every student should have the support necessary to achieve at high standards and gain an understanding of the social context of literacy instruction.

- A collaborative relationship should exist among knowledge-producing institutions and disciplines.

- Communities should have the means to produce and distribute written and artistic materials that can present and shape group identity as well as forward civic debate.

These goals are based upon the belief that an integrated and productive educational environment requires an active dialogue between educators, neighborhood members, and students about the future of their region.

The institute is governed by an advisory board, fellows, and a director. The advisory board is structured to ensure representation from all aspects of the educational community surrounding Temple University. At present, the board has representatives from the city school district, a network of community-based teachers, the arts community, Temple's School of Education, and faculty from the humanities and social sciences. Their role is to consider how a particular project from one site can be "braided" into other existing projects or goals. For instance, we recently strengthened a proposal to create a service-based cultural studies program at Temple through discussions with board members about work being done in the public schools and the community. What might have remained a "strictly academic" enterprise was reformulated as a tool to create common educational objectives across institutions.

Institute fellows are responsible for the actual work of producing inter-disciplinary and interinstitutional programs. They create and oversee projects that bring different elements of the community into contact with each other. For instance, one fellow organized a national conference on Alain Locke, the African American philosopher of the Harlem Renaissance. Another developed a lecture series titled "Converging Cultures in Urban Environments," while a third conducted seminars on Shakespeare and performance in public schools. A fourth fellow, who holds a position in the provost's office, helps us link our activities with the city school district. This year, fellows will expand the institute's connections to cultural and literacy centers in the greater Philadelphia region and create service-learning courses around issues such as homelessness and urban housing. The work of the fellows is supplemented by the work of the institute-affiliated faculty and teachers, whose research, disciplinary knowledge, and classroom practice serve as the basis for much of the institute's programmatic development.[2] The director is responsible for maintaining alliances with community and school organizations, providing support for fellows, exploring new connections, and discovering funding sources.

Although the institute's overall goal is to integrate different educational communities, its projects might be broken into four distinct areas of work: schools, communities, university, and research and publication.

Schools

One guiding principle of the institute is that every student should have the support necessary to achieve at high standards. The institute has made a conscious decision to frame its work with teachers around the demands of their classrooms, and it has also made an effort to work with school districts that have revised their curriculum along the lines of the national standards movement. One of the outcomes of this decision is that university faculty who partner with teachers must focus on the application of even the most sophisticated analysis or theory to secondary and undergraduate classrooms.

One example of this effort linked the standards' language of "interdisci-plinarity" and "cross-competencies" in a workshop focusing on Shakespeare and performance.[3] The seminar was led by a university faculty member and two public school teachers. Its participants included high school teachers, principals, graduate students, and undergraduate education majors. Participants read different historical accounts of Shakespeare's time, decided how this information might alter the reading of a text, and then performed that interpretation using limited props. Participants then blended this technique of performance with historical study to generate standards-based lesson plans. These plans were taken into the classroom, tested, and evaluated by participants. Here it was particularly important that the workshop included high school teachers who could evaluate whether the standards were addressed by the assignment and who could explain the value of this technique to university faculty and students. In the next stage of this project, a few participating teachers will have their students perform a Shakespeare play for their local community.

This focus on hands-on learning, links between the university and schools, and standards-based applications appears in our teachers' writing groups as well. Composed of public school teachers and led by a graduate of the English Department's creative writing master's degree program, the seminar encourages teachers to explore their own writing lives and then bring their writing experience into the classroom. Participants read fiction, write their own stories and poems, and discuss their work with each other. Some bring in half-written manuscripts, and others come with ideas for writing projects they have long harbored. As with the Shakespeare and performance seminar, participants eventually develop lesson plans which can carry the excitement and intensity of a creative writing workshop into their classroom (and perhaps into the community, too, with readings and publications). The process is similar to approaches developed in National Writing Projects across the country. The innovation here is that the institute opens a doorway between teacher development and the creative writing program, where earlier there had been no connection.

Community

The institute's primary objective in working with community groups is to ensure that collaborative relationships develop among knowledge-producing institutions. Our current programs include the Norris Homes Girls' Group and the revitalizing of Teachers for a Democratic Culture. The girls' group consists of ten preadolescent and adolescent girls and is held in a local health center near Temple University. Originally, this was a support group for girls where they could discuss health and sexuality issues, but it soon became apparent to the leaders that "health" and "sex" were wrapped up in complex social and emotional issues not easily explored in a weekly discussion. At the request of the health center's director, the institute arranged to have a graduate assistant—as it happens, a student from the Department of African-American Studies who had previously tutored in a Chicago housing project—meet weekly with the group and encourage them to write about their lives.

Here the goal was not only to generate a sense of group identity, but to publish that identity as a way to spark community awareness. Within a year, the students had published their first collection, *United Sisters*. It contains personal observations, poems, and essays about growing up in their community. During the course of this project, the girls' group also participated in university programs and events. The girls were offered use of Temple University's writing center and math resource center for academic help. Students from the African-American Studies program attended girls' group meetings to share their insights about growing up in an urban environment. Academic events, such as a tribute to the poet Sonia Sanchez, allowed the girls to meet established African American writers.

Central to the institute's work is the belief that the coordinated efforts of educators, students, and community members across institutions help to promote social justice. For this reason, the institute also agreed to take on the task of revitalizing Teachers for a Democratic Culture (TDC). Growing out of the culture wars of the early 1990s, TDC quickly became an organization in which over 1,600 faculty and graduate students organized their responses to attacks on multiculturalism, feminism, and progressive scholarship. As with most progressive faculty organizations, however, TDC soon suffered from its own success. The burdens of maintaining such a membership and struggling against well-funded right-wing organizations such as the National Scholars Association or Lynne Cheney's Alumni Association soon led to its faltering. In addition, an inability to focus the organization's activities on transforming actual educational practices both within classrooms and in local communities led to a lack of purpose once the initial burst of activism had ceased.

Now housed in the institute but separate from it, TDC (www.temple .edu/tdc) is a nonprofit organization linked with other progressive faculty groups. It has also expanded its vision to include teachers from a wide range of educational institutions. More to the point, TDC now uses its membership dues to initiate local and regional alliances and joint projects among literacy institutions. For instance, working from the premise that literacy education should also occur within the struggle for basic community rights, TDC cosponsored the Poor People's Summit in Philadelphia. This two-day conference was designed to highlight the effects of welfare reform in one local neighborhood and to educate community members about how to organize politically. Speakers and activists from all over the country came to share information, teach organizing techniques, and create alliances. TDC has also created a Progressive Information Network (www.temple.edu/tdc/pin) to supply progressive editorials for use by members in local newspapers as well as Labor Matters (www.temple.edu/tde/publications.html), a weekly e-paper on labor activism. Finally, it is developing a Faculty Activist Directory as a resource for teachers nationwide (www.temple.edu/tdc/fad). Positioning itself as an alternative professional organization, TDC works to foster and link local moments of struggle to national efforts to expand citizen rights. We hope it will carry the mission of the institute into a national arena.

University

The institute has worked to develop both undergraduate and graduate courses that focus on service-learning projects linked to acknowledged community needs. For instance, the Shakespeare and performance seminar was also linked to an undergraduate literature class for future teachers. In addition to the seminar, some undergraduate students led a Shakespeare drama club at a city public school. In other classes, oral history projects at nearby public schools were linked to an undergraduate English class developing an anthology of "City Voices," and a communication studies course enabled students to formulate "guerrilla" media projects around community needs. In a project planned for next year, student ethnographers will investigate public housing and social justice issues for an anthropology course. Others will work with a welfare rights organization to produce newsletters and information packets.

Each of these courses provides valuable learning and research possibilities for those involved. We believe, however, that the ability of future faculty to teach such courses depends upon graduate education taking on an interdisciplinary and service-learning focus. For this reason, the institute has developed a certificate open to graduate students in any discipline. Students will take courses in cultural theory, community politics, and the politics of literacy institutions. They also must serve an extended internship at a local literacy or cultural center, applying their course knowledge to the dynamics of actual community politics. In addition, many of the courses offered are designed to allow students to link their study with literacy institutions. Blending academic knowledge with community involvement, students will leave the program with the skills necessary to support such work, whether inside or outside academic careers.

Research and Publication

We believe that cultural work should be shared across communities. A community should be able to produce written and artistic materials which can develop and enrich its own identity and at the same time spark productive political debate in the larger social arena. In order to circulate a variety of materials to local and national audiences, the institute established a publishing house called New City Press and TDC aligned itself with the academic journal *Annals of Scholarship.*

New City Press was designed to publish community-based histories and narratives as alternatives to the ones fostered by the mainstream media. The press was patterned in part on the *Journal of Ordinary Thought*, a grassroots publication associated loosely with University of Illinois-Chicago. Each issue of *JOT* focuses on a different neighborhood writing group. For example, in one issue, "Mixed Feeling" (No. 3, Oct. 1995), people who had lived in or around a housing-project building slated for demolition wrote about their memories and frustrations associated with its closing. We also admired the activist publishing done at the Community Literacy Center in Pittsburgh (Peck, Flower, and Higgins). Another source of inspiration was the Federation of Worker Writers and Community Publishers (FWWCP). This organization links, advertises, and distributes the work of community presses in the United Kingdom. Rather than sponsor any particular publication, the FWWCP provides expertise to community groups who wish to start writing groups and publishing ventures. They work with presses that enable local communities to recount and preserve their history. For instance, an affiliated press in Brighton, Queenspark Books, regularly publishes histories of its port community and its residents. Queenspark is currently developing a "countermap" for tourists who wish to understand Brighton as more than a beachtown.[4]

New City supports a variety of community projects. For instance, one of its first publications was a coaches' handbook for a city neighborhood baseball league (www.temple.edu/isllc/ncp). The handbook, written and compiled by volunteers in that community, offers tips to new coaches on practice organization and skill building, and it not only serves to instruct coaches and parents in the league, but models teaching and organizing skills for neighborhoods that want to start their own leagues. A future project will feature oral histories of a local neighborhood completed by public school students. Working with Asian Americans United, the press will also publish a folktale-based story written about the need to keep a local library open. In these and other projects, New City Press provides publishing expertise to local organizations and the legitimacy of publication to nontraditional histories and small-scale but vital civic projects.

New City also supports the institute's general effort to link educators from a variety of communities. A prime example of this is *Urban Rhythms* (*UR*). This publication was the idea of students in a service-learning literacy course sponsored by the institute.[5] Originating as a class project, *UR* has become a collaborative project linking faculty, students, and community members from the schools, colleges, and neighborhood organizations surrounding Temple University. Similar to the *Foxfire* magazine of the early '70s (see Wigginton), *UR*'s goal is to document and disperse the insights, folk traditions, and community visions of city neighborhoods. Although the journal is less than one year old, it has already become a means by which teachers from a variety of institutions can share the work of students. One middle school class uses the journal as a weekly exercise in creative writing. Another school incorporates the journal into the mentally gifted curriculum. Several university classes have allowed students to focus their work around guest editing special editions. Finally, graduate students and visiting faculty have come to see the journal as a way to expand their links with the schools and communities.

This push to link the production of knowledge to community activism also marks TDC's alignment with *Annals of Scholarship* (*AOS*). While *AOS* has a long history of publishing academic articles on multiculturalism, global studies, and critical theory, the journal will now feature an additional section each issue which links such scholarship with local and national activism.

We hope that what *UR* does at the local level with college students and city schools, *AOS* will do on a national level with faculty, universities, and the regions they serve.

Crossing Categories

The activities described in the preceding sections would be of little value if they remained isolated in their distinct categories (schools, community, university, publication and research). While we have tried to suggest that every project challenges the categories, it is important to realize that each project allows other links to occur within the institute. In Figure 23–3 we list many of the projects discussed earlier.

One way to read the figure is left to right. The emphasis on local stories runs through the Norris Home Girls' Group, student oral histories, literacy classes, and New City Press. Similarly, a focus on community activism runs through the Poor People's Summit, the Alain Locke Conference, TDC, and NCP/*UR*/*AOS* publications. It is also possible, however, to move from the Poor People's Summit to neighborhood histories, literature/education courses (taking education to mean community goals), and NCP publications. That is, the goal of the institute's activities is to allow alliances and partnerships beyond traditional town–gown or disciplinary boundaries. Fellows, students, community members, and affiliated faculty are able to use the institute as a place to weave together community, university, school, and publication projects. Possibilities for collaboration are created where individuals who may not have thought of each other as allies can find a space to work together. Essays formerly available only to academics can now be read and discussed by teachers and health care workers; communities can assemble histories which academic and civic leaders might need to read. Through this work, we hope to achieve the "braiding" McLeod describes as the next step for WAC programs.

FIGURE 23–3   Current Projects of the Institute for the Study of Literature, Literacy, and Culture

Community	Public Schools	University	Publication/Research
Norris Homes Girls' Group	Oral Histories	Literacy Courses Service Learning	New City: Individual Histories
People and Stories	Multicultural Curriculum	Multicultural Lit/Service Learning	New City: Community Histories
Public Theater Performance	Shakespeare	Lit/Ed Courses	*Urban Rhythms*
Activists' Network	Neighborhood Histories	Project SHINE	New City: Guidebooks
Poor People's Summit	Alain Locke Conference	Teachers for a Democratic Culture	NCP/*AOS*: Academic Texts

The figure also highlights the potential political conflicts that emerge when forming alliances with community, regional, and (in the case of TDC) national partners. By cosponsoring the Poor People's Summit or the standards-based lesson plans, the institute clearly positions itself within the local and academic community. By helping to organize the poor, for instance, the institute is sending a signal about current welfare legislation and local homeless laws. By supporting efforts to bring standards-based education into the Philadelphia school system, the institute may alienate teachers and community members who perceive standards as bad pedagogy and potentially racist. Even choosing a Shakespeare workshop over one on Toni Cade Bambara could potentially send troubling signals to certain constituencies.

As the scope of these projects indicates, however, it is difficult to reduce the institute to any one ideological flavor. Standards might seem to contradict progressive editorials; a poor people's summit might seem an odd pairing with Shakespeare. This is as it should be. Communities are politically complex. There is no single ideological navel from which all institute programs derive. They emerge from the combined insights of the institute's community, university, and public school members. This process is not always pretty. Participants argue, worry, storm out, compromise, then drink coffee together. There is dialogue and there is debate. Hard feelings emerge and, sometimes, are smoothed over. People come to a place where they disagree with a particular program but continue to participate. The idea of a broad, integrated educational community has slowly transcended any one person's objections to a program. The political test has become whether the imagined community that brought us around the table is becoming a reality.

Conclusion

A vision of university writing programs that stretch beyond the curriculum and campus presents exciting possibilities to program designers and administrators. As this vision becomes reality, it is important to be explicit about the potential problems as well. While the hope still remains that this direction will lead to a richer environment for literacy instruction, the shortcomings and inherent limitations in the venture can sometimes appear painfully obvious. In this conclusion, we share some of our questions about writing beyond the curriculum, speculating on the reward structure and the approach to graduate education necessary to sustain the sort of program we have set out to construct.

For the sake of brevity, we limit ourselves here to three problematic areas for our writing program and the institute: maintaining focus, gathering support, and building alliances. In some sense they are all a function of the same virtue, arising from the explosiveness and multidirectionality of a new, unfolding idea. It is easy to get lost in the array of paths that could be taken once you step off the sidewalk. It is even easier to overreach resources in the rush to try too many projects at once. And it is perhaps easiest of all to affront potential allies in your eagerness to make a new program succeed.

One of us gave a talk about our program at a major southwestern university last year. Afterward, one sympathetic faculty member asked this simple question: "If you follow up on all these new directions for WAC, how do you prevent yourself from getting distracted from the business of writing instruction and assure your home constituency that first-year students are still learning to write for their college courses?" We find ourselves returning again and again to this question, and not only because it stands as a warning for us when we contemplate yet another cross-institutional project. It also makes explicit certain terms underlying writing pedagogy that we must interrogate in order to move into a new phase. What, for instance, is our "home constituency" and what "business of writing instruction" are we in? Does an orientation toward "academic discourse" in our first-year course sequence preclude or require a counterbalancing emphasis on writing outside the walls of the academy? Is it possible to explore many new institutional connections and still maintain a focus in a reconfigured writing program? And what if we feel we have maintained our focus, but our colleagues—inside and outside the English department—perceive us as impossibly scattered and quixotic?

We cannot answer all these interrelated questions here. Our best provisional response to the whole complex is that we must be committed to assessment and reflection—always interrogating ourselves, our colleagues, our project partners, and our students about what learning is taking place inside and outside the classrooms. Does the imagined program actually help anybody, or does it just rack up more lines on the program track record? Does a proposed project support agreed-upon or implicit community goals? Does it support the integrative vision of diverse groups within a region? Is something older but more valuable lost in the rush to shape something new? Enthusiasm for the large-scale goal should not blind us to crucial little failures along the way.

At the same time, it would be unwise to be bound by the expectations of a higher education system that no longer exists. As Richard Hersh has noted, fewer than 5 percent of college students attend small liberal arts colleges, still the "gold standard for undergraduate education" for most liberal arts administrators (16). In a study that Hersh's Hobart and William Smith Colleges commissioned, a large majority of high school students and their parents indicated that "college is important because it 'prepares students to get a better job and/or increases their earning potential'" (20). Students are more and more conscious of their college education as an investment in a future they cannot fully predict but are wary about nonetheless (see Carnevale; Menand). If they ever did, certainly today universities no longer function primarily as that Shakespearean green world to which young swains and damsels repair for a night of revelry, in preparation for their dawn weddings and coronations. At our own university, more than 80 percent of students work twenty hours a week or more; they have precious little time for midsummer night dalliance.

Meanwhile, graduate education cannot simply churn out young adults who have served five to eight years of indentured servitude in exchange for their degrees, only to have them undertake more servitude in the adjunct mills. The MLA says that "fewer than half the seven or eight thousand graduate students likely to earn PhDs in English and foreign languages between 1996 and 2000 can expect to obtain full-time tenure-track positions within a year of receiving their degrees" (Gilbert 4). To the extent that the job crisis is caused by the deliberate downsizing of all human services in U.S. society today, graduate students and faculty must engage actively in debates and protests over public priorities if we wish to rectify this situation. However, are even those who find employment being prepared for the kind of employment they will find in the next century? As Chris Anson has pointed out, "technology will soon change not only how we work within our institutions but also how 'attached' we may be to an institution, particularly if we can work for several institutions at some physical (but not electronic) remove from each other" (274).

If preparing for the struggles and the opportunities in the days to come means a little distraction, it must be risked. In a publication of the Association of American Colleges and Universities, Carol Schneider and Robert Shoenberg put the situation this way:

> The shift from a teaching to a learning paradigm of instruction, the incorporation of information technology and all it makes possible into the fabric of the institution, the increasing engagement with the local and global community, the new awareness of an assertive and rapidly expanding for-profit higher education sector and the reconsideration of such issues as tenure collectively exemplify the quite profound transformations now in process. We are indeed in the midst of a time of great change. (3)

While such futurist rhetoric in higher education circles might itself be cause for concern—sometimes the prophetic tones mask corporate attitudes and expectations among some deans and provosts—there can be no doubt that major changes are occurring. Writing programs are often the first places in a school to feel the tremors. What may look like distraction in WPAs now may eventually seem a principled (if feverish) response to challenges others have not yet recognized or are trying desperately to ignore.

Consider the work of gathering support and building alliances. Both the liberal arts college and the central administration at Temple University have been supportive of the writing beyond the curriculum efforts because they perceive such work as attractive to new students, friendly to service-learning initiatives, helpful for faculty development, and timely as a connection between and among colleges that need to find ways to work together.[6] At the same time, we have been concerned from the start that any particular move might be perceived by factions within English and in other areas of the college and university as empire building. In such a context, it has been important to negotiate with every center, institute, department, or program that has a common interest in projects we propose, always stressing mutual benefits over turf battles. We have approached a number of local and national foundations, first informally to let them know our new direction and then through proposals for one or another project. Where we have worked with school districts or community organizations, we have stressed partnership over paternalism and slow building of trust over quick deal-making.[7]

Working with the College of Education has been particularly gratifying. The Writing Program and Education had only a very scant history of cooperation until recently, but today planning has begun on a number of joint projects. We have key allies in the education faculty, and we work closely with the Professional Development Schools, the committee that oversees relations with schools where students practice teaching. The First-Year Program cooperates with the Teaching English as a Second Language program in Education to provide ESL versions of our writing courses. The Writing Program and Education collaborated on a conference this year for high school teachers and college WPAs on expectations for student writers in college and secondary school; next year another conference is planned that addresses assessment issues. The more work done side by side, the easier it will be for graduate students and undergraduates to understand the intimate connections between literacy and literature on the one hand and pedagogical theory and practice on the other.

Finally, we must add a word about the reward structure and graduate training that underpins faculty life. People tend to do what they are most rewarded for and what they are trained to expect rewards for. In any academic field the rewards traditionally go to those who do research or creative work; grants for such work are the highest form of legitimization, and—in fields where grants are scarce and small—publication, exhibition, or performance records stand for achievement in one's field. Teaching has come to be more valued in many schools in recent years, but publishing still determines tenure and promotion in research universities and many teaching colleges. Our institute arose in part from discussions supported by a grant from the Fund for the Improvement of Postsecondary Education (FIPSE) on the reward structures for faculty (see Gips and Stoel). Members of the Temple FIPSE group quickly came to the conclusion that, rather than working against the commitment to research in our Research I institution, we should work with that commitment but support new directions in which faculty and graduate students could grow. Thus arose the fellowships and graduate certificate program described earlier.

Our next step is to think more expansively about graduate training and teacher preparation. Jerry Gaff and Leo Lambert have pointed out how important it is to train students not only to be "better students" and "better teaching assistants" but to prepare them to be "better assistant professors" (44). It seems necessary to go beyond this goal, admirable as it may be, because the job placement statistics suggest that at least some of our graduates will choose to seek employment outside the college classroom. We are developing connections so that graduate students in literature and creative writing, as well as in composition/rhetoric, could explore work in communities and schools, in unions and businesses, in government agencies and hospitals. This is not an attempt to short-circuit the traditional training they receive, but to build upon it, to widen the context in which students learn to interpret and generate written texts.

Peter Mortensen has recently suggested that "teacher/researchers should search for ways to accommodate their writing about college composition to broader, nonacademic audiences" (198). He wants us to enter debates, such as the current controversy over remediation in the City University of New York system, because we can offer a perspective on students and literacy often missing in the popular press. He warns, though, that "for such writing to be ethical, it may indeed be anchored in national concerns, but it must attend to the local because it is there that political and social issues of great consequence can be deliberated and acted upon" (198). In a sense, the Institute for the Study of Literature, Literacy, and Culture and the idea of writing beyond the curriculum is our version of that ethical commitment. We are building on the insights of social theory in composition research by engaging in the world our students come from and go to, and we intend to add our voices especially in the local scene because that is where we teach, raise our kids, and pay taxes. In this sense, writing and literacy instruction go beyond the "beyond." This is simply where we live.

NOTES

1. Paul Heilker seems to be the first to use the expression "writing beyond the curriculum" in print, though he did not specifically apply the expression to WAC programs.

2. Faculty interest in the institute has been quite strong. An initial call for participation resulted in over forty faculty from a variety of departments, all affiliating with the institute in the space of three weeks.

3. Cross-competencies is the term used by the school district to denote lesson plans which ask students to perform to several standards across subject and skill areas. For instance, students working on a science project which will be presented to a city council representative will be expected to meet science, writing, applied learning, and public-speaking standards.

4. We must also mention here another remarkable journal. *Rising East: The Journal of East London Studies* is a research journal overseen by an advisory board of faculty, teachers, government representatives, and community members from the East London area. Its aim is to bring the collective insights of literacy and community experts to bear on discussions of East London's future. Each issue carries political, economic, and cultural analysis of the area. Although the journal demands a high level of literacy in its readers, it is written free of specialty terminology. It represents the collective voice of a community speaking out about its future—a voice to which local politicians and business leaders often feel the need to respond.

5. This project would not have been possible without the outstanding work of students such as Mike Carter, Ribu John, Alima Saffell, Brian Sammons, and Robyn Wilcox or without the cooperation of teachers such as Sharmaine Ball and Joel Moore.

6. For instance, from the College of Liberal Arts, the institute has received course reductions to support fellow positions as well as a small annual budget. The graduate school has funded a graduate student assistant. In addition, the institute has received grant support from the John S. and James L. Knight Foundation, the Fund to Improve Postsecondary Education, the Philadelphia Higher Education Network for Neighborhood Development, Philadelphia Education Fund, and the Community Outreach Partnership Center, among others.

7. We have been particularly aided in this process by Lori Shorr, Director of School/Community Partnerships. She has been energetic and creative in making durable connections with teachers and administrators, enabling us to develop exciting projects in a very short period of time.

WORKS CITED

Adler-Kassner, Linda, Robert Crooks, and Ann Watters, eds. *Writing the Community: Concepts and Models for Service-Learning in Composition.* Washington, DC: AAHE/NCTE, 1997.
Anson, Chris M. "Distant Voices: Teaching and Writing in a Culture of Technology." *College English* 61.3 (1999): 261–80.

Barr, Robert B., and John Tagg. "From Teaching to Learning—A New Paradigm for Undergraduate Education." *Change* (Nov./Dec. 1995): 15–25.

Berlin, James A., and Michael J. Vivion, eds. *Cultural Studies in the English Classroom*. Portsmouth, NH: Boynton/Cook Heinemann, 1992.

Boyer, Ernest L. "Creating the New American College." *Chronicle of Higher Education* (March 9, 1994): A48.

Brodkey, Lynda. "Writing on the Bias." *College English* 56.5 (1994): 527–47.

Carnevale, Anthony. "Liberal Education & the New Economy." *Liberal Education* (Spring 1996): 4–11.

Cushman, Ellen. "Critical Literacy and Institutional Language." *Research in the Teaching of English* 33.3 (1999): 245–74.

———. "The Public Intellectual." *College English* 61.3 (1999): 328–36.

DeStigter, Todd. "The Tesoros Literacy Project: An Experiment in Democratic Communities." *Research in the Teaching of English* 32.1 (1998): 10–42.

Faigley, Lester. *Fragments of Rationality: Postmodernity and the Subject of Composition*. Pittsburgh: U of Pittsburgh P, 1992.

Gaff, Jerry G., and Leo M. Lambert. "Socializing Future Faculty to the Values of Undergraduate Education." *Change* (July/Aug. 1996): 38–45.

Gilbert, Sandra. "Final Report: MLA Committee on Professional Employment." New York: MLA, 1998.

Gips, Crystal, and Carol F. Stoel, eds. *Making a Place in the Faculty Rewards System for Work with K–12: A Report of Four Universities*. Washington, DC: American Association for Higher Education, 1999.

Goldblatt, Eli. "Writing Home: A Literacy Autobiography." *Writing on the Edge* 9.1 (1997/98): 41–50.

Hawisher, Gail E., Cynthia L. Selfe, Charles Moran, and Paul LeBlanc. *Computers and the Teaching of Writing in American Higher Education, 1979–1994: A History*. Norwood, NJ: Ablex, 1996.

Heilker, Paul. "Rhetoric Made Real: Civic Discourse and Writing beyond the Curriculum." Adler-Kassner, Crooks, and Watters, 71–77.

Herrington, Anne, and Charles Moran. "Writing in the Disciplines: A Prospect." *Writing, Teaching, and Learning in the Disciplines*. Ed. Anne Herrington and Charles Moran. New York: MLA, 1992. 231–44.

Hersh, Richard H. "Intentions and Perceptions: A National Survey of Public Attitudes Toward Liberal Arts Education." *Change* (March/April 1997): 16–23.

Herzberg, Bruce. "Community Service and Critical Teaching." *College Composition and Communication* 45.3 (1994): 307–19.

"Making Faculty Work Visible: Re-interpreting Professional Service, Teaching, and Research in the Fields of Language and Literature." *Profession* (1996): 161–216.

McLeod, Susan. "Defining Writing across the Curriculum." *WPA: Writing Program Administration* 11.1–2 (Fall 1987): 19–24.

———. "WAC at Century's End: Haunted by the Ghost of Fred Newton Scott." *WPA: Writing Program Administration* 21.1 (Fall 1997): 67–75.

Menand, Louis. "Everybody Else's College Education." *New York Times Magazine* (April 20, 1997): 48–49.

Miller, Margaret A. "The Advancement of Teaching: An Interview with Lee Shulman." *AAHE Bulletin* (September 1997): 3–7.

Miller, Richard E. "The Nervous System." *College English* 58.3 (1996): 265–86.

Miraglia, Eric, and Susan McLeod. "Whither WAC? Interpreting the Stories/Histories of Enduring WAC Programs." *WPA: Writing Program Administration* 20.3 (Spring 1997): 46–65.

Mortensen, Peter. "Going Public." *College Composition and Communication* 50.2 (1998): 182–205.

North Philadelphia Community Compact Data Report: 1995–1996.

Peck, Wayne Campbell, Linda Flower, and Lorraine Higgins. "Community Literacy." *College Composition and Communication* 46.2 (1995): 199–222.

Rabinowitz, Peter J., and Michael W. Smith. *Authorizing Readers: Resistance and Respect in the Teaching of Literature*. New York: Teachers College P/NCTE, 1998.

Rose, Mike. *Possible Lives: The Promise of Public Education in America*. Boston: Houghton Mifflin, 1995.

Russell, David R. "American Origins of the Writing across the Curriculum Movement." *Writing, Teaching, and Learning in the Disciplines*. Ed. Anne Herrington and Charles Moran. New York: MLA, 1992. 22–42.

Schneider, Carol G., and Robert Shoenberg. *Contemporary Understandings of Liberal Education.* Washington, DC: Association of American Colleges and Universities, 1998.

Schutz, Aaron, and Anne Ruggles Gere. "Service Learning and English Studies." *College English* 60.2 (1998): 129–49.

Silberman, Arlene. *Growing Up Writing: Teaching Our Children to Write, Think, and Learn.* Portsmouth, NH: Heinemann, 1991.

Spellmeyer, Kurt. "After Theory: From Textuality to Attunement with the World." *College English* 58.8 (1996): 893–913.

Sullivan, Frank, Arabella Lyon, Dennis Lebofsky, Susan Wells, and Eli Goldblatt. "Student Needs and Strong Composition: The Dialectics of Writing Program Reform." *College Composition and Communication* 48 (1997): 372–91.

Walvoord, Barbara. "The Future of WAC." *College English* 58 (1996): 58–79.

Wells, Susan. "What Do We Want from Public Writing?" *College Composition and Communication* 47 (1996): 325–42.

Wigginton, Eliot. *Sometimes a Shining Moment: The Foxfire Experience.* Garden City, NY: Anchor/Doubleday, 1986.

24 *A Tattoo's Story*

JAKK G. III

What's in a name? For Jakk, an eleventh-grader from Syracuse, New York, the answer is more than skin deep, for his identity is literally and figuratively embodied in his tattoo. This poem is part of the New City Community Press book Soul Talk: Urban Youth Poetry, *which features the voices of students in Syracuse public schools. As Steve Parks and Eli Goldblatt note in "Writing Beyond the Curriculum: Fostering New Collaborations in Literacy" (p. 337 in this volume), the New City Community Press was born of their efforts to publish community voices in the Philadelphia area. Believing that stories of local communities matter in addressing issues of national and global significance, the New City Community Press has expanded to provide opportunities for a variety of local communities to represent themselves by telling their stories in their own words.*

FIGURE 24–1
(Source: New City Community Press.)

From *Soul Talk: Urban Youth Poetry* (Syracuse, NY: Syracuse University Press, 2008), 4.

I have a tattoo and it tells a story.
My tattoo says "Jakk" with two k's
You're supposed to spell it with a "ck," but not me
That's how my father spells it
And how my grandfather spells it
My grandfather is an old, mean, selfish drunk
I don't see any of him in me
Not one bit
My father also spells it with a "ck"
But once again, not me
My father is a dead-beat dad
A drunk, a drug addict, abusive, a liar and much more
So I don't see any of him in me either
That's why I spell my name differently
The only thing I got from my father
Is my physical strength
Everything else comes from my mother
Maybe I should change my name to Brenda
Like my mom

25   *My Decision*

JESÚS VILLICANA LOPEZ

This autobiographical narrative is excerpted from Espejos y Ventanas/Mirrors and Windows, *a New City Community Press anthology that presents the stories of three generations of Mexicans who migrated to Kennett Square, Pennsylvania, to work in the mushroom industry. As Steve Parks and Eli Goldblatt note in "Writing Beyond the Curriculum: Fostering New Collaborations in Literacy" (p. 337 in this volume), the New City Community Press was born of their efforts to publish community voices.*

FIGURE 25–1

(*Source: New City Community Press.*)

FIGURE 25–2

she gave to us to spend outside of school or to go out to a party or something like that, right? I admire my mother very much because in spite of being a woman, she held the family together without depending on anyone. with nothing more than her own strength, her will, and her work. Because we are very poor there in Mexico.

"IN MEXICO, WE LIVED IN A STONE HOUSE PATCHED WITH CLAY THAT HAD A DIRT FLOOR, WITH ONLY ONE ROOM FOR THE ENTIRE FAMILY."

In Mexico, we lived in a stone house patched with clay that had a dirt floor—it was tiny, with only one room for the entire family. We made our living growing corn and beans to eat—this is a staple food of the region. Most of the time my grandparents grew the food since my mother insisted that I go to school. She wanted me and my brothers to improve our lives and she believed very strongly that school was the best route to do that. But I helped my grandparents when I wasn't in school and on the weekends. I tried very hard to do my best, to put a lot of passion into my work. I know that school is very useful, but I didn't have the resources to continue my studies and neither did my mom or my grandparents. So I decided to leave school and come up here. I believe that by doing this work here in the US, I can help my brothers and sister get ahead in life and provide them with a better education, a career, so that they won't have to make the same sacrifice that I made when I came here for them. I send my family four or five times as much as they used to earn each month. Every three or four weeks I send around $1000 to Mexico.

My trip North was very—how can I explain it!—it wasn't a very happy trip, but it was something I had to endure in order to go on. I had to face dangerous situations, like crossing the border, sleeping under the moon at night, and then in darkness in the forest. I was afraid that if I were to go out, some strange animal might come to kill us. There were all sorts of dangerous animals in the forest—snakes, bears, things like that.

I left Moroleón for the North at daybreak, with great sadness. I was with a group—my uncle and some friends of his, all older. I was the only young person in the group. The night before I left I tried and tried to get to sleep so that I could leave easily in the morning, but I couldn't sleep the

(*Source: New City Community Press.*)

From *Espejos y Ventanas/Mirrors and Windows* (Syracuse, NY: Syracuse University Press, 2008), 201–19.

Espejos y Ventanas/Mirrors and Windows *features both Spanish and English versions of Lopez's piece as well as the oral histories of retirees who came north twenty-five years ago, mothers and children who stayed in Mexico and finally made it over, and children graduating from college, their feet planted in two worlds. It provides a window into the general struggles of immigrant populations for social, political, and economic rights.*

M y decision to come here caught me by surprise. The truth is that I hadn't really thought about coming here. But as I grew up I looked around and the idea came to me that I had to find a way to better myself so that someday I could start my family. And then an uncle of mine and a cousin helped me decide if I wanted to come here, no? They were already here in the United States.

My mom was against my coming because I was still very young. I came here against her will, so to speak, because she didn't like the idea that I would be so far away from them. She told me to think very carefully about things: if I felt able to move away from them and come here to confront new challenges, new things in life, then I would be living a life I wouldn't even be able to imagine. I would be far from my family, from my home, from my country, without knowing anybody or knowing where I would end up or who would come to visit me. In the end, I made the decision on my own because I wanted to find a new way of life or a future for myself. I wanted to be self-reliant and also to help my family—my mom and my siblings. I have four siblings, all younger than I: my sister is 8 years old and I have one brother who is 14 and another who is 12. Because I am the oldest, I have a great responsibility to be with them, to protect them and my mom. It's my duty to give them the best, to create opportunities for them so that they can get ahead. I am responsible for showing them how to live life.

Unfortunately, my father is sick. He lost his memory—he doesn't remember anything. He's like, traumatized, or something. He's around 40 and is gradually losing his intellect. His illness is sapping his abilities little by little—his mind and his body. Even though my father has no memory, I think that he knows that I am here. I don't know if I can express it very well, but I think he must have some strong feelings for me. In other words, it's like I can feel what he feels, but I don't know how to describe it.

My mother works in the city of Moroleón in a tortilla shop—she makes sandwiches and cooks. She is paid 100 pesos a day, about $10. Almost all of what my mom made went toward buying things for us and she also paid for our studies. If she made around 500 pesos [$50] a week, about 200 of that she gave to us to spend outside of school or to go out to a party or something like that, right? I admire my mother very much because in spite of being a woman, she held the family together without depending on anyone, with nothing more than her own strength, her will, and her work. Because we are very poor there in Mexico.

In Mexico, we lived in a stone house patched with clay that had a dirt floor—it was tiny, with only one room for the entire family. We made our living growing corn and beans to eat—this is a staple food of the region. Most of the time my grandparents grew the food since my mother insisted that I go to school. She wanted me and my brothers to improve our lives and she believed very strongly that school was the best route to do that. But I helped my grandparents when I wasn't in school and on the weekends. I tried very hard to do my best, to put a lot of passion into my work. I know that school is very useful, but I didn't have the resources to continue my studies and neither did my mom or my grandparents. So I decided to leave school and come up here. I believe that by doing this work here in the U.S., I can help my brothers and sister get ahead in life and provide them with a better education, a career, so that they won't have to make the same sacrifice that I made when I came here for them. I send my family four or five times as much as they used to earn each month. Every three or four weeks I send around $1,000 to Mexico.

My trip North was very—how can I explain it?—it wasn't a very happy trip, but it was something I had to endure in order to go on. I had to face dangerous situations, like crossing the border, sleeping under the moon at night, and then in darkness in the forest. I was afraid that if I were to go out, some strange animal might come to kill us. There were all sorts of dangerous animals in the forest—snakes, bears, things like that.

I left Moroleón for the North at daybreak, with great sadness. I was with a group—my uncle and some friends of his, all older. I was the only young person in the group. The night before I left I tried and tried to get to sleep so that I could leave easily in the morning, but I couldn't sleep the whole night. I stayed up all night with my mom and then it was time for me to prepare to leave. My uncle came to the house and said that they had come for us. I left with my suitcase and then, with the blessing of my mother, I climbed into the car and we left. Crying, with great sadness, we left our families and the village where we lived behind.

We left focused on our future, with the intention of finding a new way of life and confronting new problems. But, then, at the same time, it was a risky and very dangerous adventure. Friends had preceded me to the North and they told me that I was going to experience the adventure of a lifetime. They talked about what was in store for me—crossing rivers, escaping from different animals, climbing mountains, and making my way through the cacti. They said that in the desert there would be times when we wouldn't have enough food or water for maybe six, seven, or eight days. In fact, the main thing we carried with us was water because it is true what they say—that water is life.

We crossed the border with a *coyote* that my uncle had found. This *coyote* wasn't bad—in fact, he was kind. He helped us and went through everything with us, until we reached the border. My trip cost 1,500 Mexican peso—$150—and later, when I had already arrived here at the border, I asked my relatives here in the United States for another $1,500 to come from the border up here to Pennsylvania. Yes, it's a lot of money, but as I told you, I have

FIGURE 25–3

Jesús delante del mural de una casa de hongos, pintado por César Viveros-Herrera.

Jesús in front of César Viveros-Herrera's painting of a mushroom barn.

(*Source: New City Community Press.*)

friends here—uncles, aunts, cousins. In five months I finished paying back the money that was raised for me.

I left my town on August 6th and I arrived here on North American soil on August 13th. There were around 17 of us; about six were from my group, from La Ordeña. When we arrived at the border we came through a wooded mountain range in Arizona. It was cool, with many tall trees that blocked the sun. I entered the forest and started to walk for a long time. We walked all afternoon and all night and suddenly it started to rain and we continued walking in the rain. At night we rested and slept for maybe three hours—say, from midnight to 3:00 a.m. We walked the whole day and we rested for a short while to eat. We also slept sometimes during the day. Then I arrived at a town called Phoenix. Some of the others got separated from us—we went through the mountains and they went through the desert—but we all arrived at a designated time at the same hotel in Phoenix. When I got to the hotel, I found all the different groups gathered together in small rooms. And they had locked us in and we didn't sleep. Finally, at daybreak they fed us.

It's true that I was hungry during the trip; we had some food, but it wasn't enough. We survived, thank God. The main thing was that we carried water—it was more important than food. We were lucky to go through the mountains because there were fresh-water streams where we could fill our gallon jugs.

When I was in the forest, I happened to see two bears—they were small, but I was scared that the mother was around. I saw a snake—it crossed my path and I got scared and ran away. Also, there were caves in the middle of the forest. The government had put up boards, like wooden signs with a skull and crossbones, that prohibited entrance to the caves because there might be toxic materials inside. We continued on and we didn't even look at the caves.

When we were crossing the border, I saw the border patrol, but they didn't see us. I could see them at night from far away on the highway. When we crossed the highway, they were passing by, but they didn't see us. I didn't see them face to face. It wasn't my turn for them to catch me.

I didn't have too many problems during the crossing because I was accustomed to walking and running—I played sports. Some of the others had a hard time—they were tired and exhausted. Some weren't able to walk or climb the mountains, but I kept moving forward. I tried to help my uncle at times: I carried some of his gear because he wasn't accustomed to walking so much. He even told me that it seemed like I had come before because I didn't have any problems. I was advised before the trip that I would have to learn to separate the good from the bad and I was able to discern the difference for myself, so—thanks to that—I was overcoming difficulties and helping the rest of the people on the trip.

The whole trip took six days—three days walking in the mountains and three days there in Phoenix at the hotel waiting for my cousins to send me $1,500 so I could leave Phoenix and come here to Philadelphia. With this money the *coyote* got his pay for bringing us to the United States and he bought us a plane ticket to come from Phoenix to Baltimore. After arriving in Baltimore, we took a taxi to Kennett Square.

I am one of the younger people in the camp, but there are others younger than I—some are friends and one is my cousin, who is 14. When I first came here the truth is that I felt an enormous fear inside of me, since I didn't know where I was and I knew no one except my uncle, who came with me. At night I felt this profound loneliness because I was in such a big place without knowing anybody. At first my uncle lived with me in the same camp, but after awhile he left and went to work in another place. In a few months, another uncle came and is here with me. He gives me advice about how to get along with the others here, so that everyone can be friendly. My uncle is my guiding light.

Actually, I was very surprised at the conditions here in the camp. When I left Mexico, I thought that I was coming to a place where we were going to be, well, free, with a big living space. But when I got here, I realized that it wasn't that way—it was a small place where many of us were cramped together. At times we really have to make an effort to get along, since there are so many of us —we are 16 now, and in the summer there will be 20. The camp is one long room, an open dormitory, without separate bedrooms. Each of us has our own space where we sleep, but there is no real private space. We make sure to respect each other's things, though. With so many people living to-gether, there are bound to be conflicts sometimes, but we know that we have to try to avoid them. If someone tries to attack you, you just have to put up with it. . . .

I get up faithfully at daybreak, at 2:00 in the morning. Before I leave for work I eat a little. If I want to, I can rest one or two days a week, but since I'm not that tired, I figure I should put more energy into work. I work seven days a week, 12 or 13 hours a day. Some days, when there isn't much work, I might be done by 8:00 in the morning. Today, I worked until 4:00 in the afternoon—13 hours. The only thing that affects you is lack of sleep because you have to wake up so early. That's the one bad thing about harvesting mushrooms—you wake at dawn and are nearly always sleep deprived.

It's piecework—they pay me by the box—so if I want to make more money, I have to force myself to try to harvest more mushrooms. They ask you to pick an average of six boxes an hour—they pay $1.00 a box. Each box holds ten pounds of mushrooms. There are times when I fill eight or ten boxes an hour—so I pick 80 to 100 pounds of mushrooms each hour. There are weeks when there is a lot of work, which means you get a bigger check. And when there are very few mushrooms you leave early and don't earn much. When there's no work, you make $100 or $200 a week, but when there's work, most workers get $500. Me, I've gotten four-hundred-dollar checks. After working awhile, it's not that hard anymore—you get used to picking mushrooms.

When I first started to work in the mushroom plant, it was very difficult for me to learn to pick mushrooms. You have to harvest the mushroom by cutting it with a knife and it was hard for me to get a good grip on the knife, so I kept dropping the mushrooms after I cut them. Sometimes I cut myself and even now I still do, but not so often. When we cut ourselves, the wounds aren't so deep—they are only scratches and we keep on working. Now when I cut myself I don't worry, since my fingers are used to it.

The bosses don't pay much attention to the health of the workers. At the company, for example, we don't even have a medicine cabinet. If one of us had the misfortune to take a fall or cut ourselves, we would have to resort to driving ourselves to the hospital or demanding that the boss help us. At first when I was working on the upper mushroom bed I was afraid to walk because I was way up high. But I'm no longer afraid. Sometimes people do slip and fall, but usually they're OK. Once my cousin fell and ended up missing several weeks of work, but he had health insurance. I don't have insurance.

There are lots of chemicals that cause irritation or rashes, but the bosses say that there is no problem. I remember that when I first started working here, they had me sign a contract—they gave me a list of what I should do before coming to work and after leaving. Like, I should take a bath, or I should wash my hands before I eat.

In my free time, I go out with friends to the stores or something or I hang out with them in the house, chatting or watching TV. There are different cable channels. I like to watch sports—I often spend Saturday and Sunday watching the soccer teams with everyone, My favorite team is "America" from Mexico City. During the time that I have been here, I haven't gone out much—most of us are not accustomed to going out. We're somewhat iso-

FIGURE 25–4

Segundo piso de una casa de hongos.

Second story of mushroom barn.

(Source: New City Community Press.)

lated because we're not familiar with how to travel in this country, to go to the city or other places. . . .

The most difficult thing about living here is that you're not close to your family and loved ones. That's what you think about most—your family, your brothers and sisters, your relatives, the people you love the most. I miss my family in Mexico, but I've been here just a short time, so I don't feel that I'm very far away from them. Also, I talk to them every week on the telephone, which makes me feel close to them. And they write to me. In her letters, my mother tells me to take care of myself, to save my money, to put passion into my work, and to avoid getting into scrapes. She reminds me of what she taught me well—to choose my friends wisely.

When I talk to my mother on the phone, she tells me to save my money so that I can get ahead and to think about making a house for myself some-day. I want my house to be in the town where I grew up, in La Ordeña. My dream is to try to save a lot of money here and someday go back to Mexico and get a house. I'd like to get married, have children, and live happily, to just live my life.

I would like to say something to all the people who might think that being here in the United States is easy. I want them to know it isn't that way because you don't necessarily know what you're up against. You think you will come here and find happiness, a new world full of marvels—but it isn't

FIGURE 25–5

Jesús y su familia vivieron en esta casa de un cuarto hasta la primavera de 2004, cuando él pudo construir una nueva casa de 3 cuartos en el terreno vacío visto aquí, usando el dinero que ganó pizcando hongos.

Jesús and his family lived in this one-room house until the spring of 2004 when he was able to build a new three-room house on the empty lot pictured here, using the money he earned picking mushrooms.

that way. You will face tremendous loneliness with a great many problems, large and small. And you have to be responsible for yourself instead of expecting to rely on others.

I would advise all who are thinking of coming here to think carefully about things. First, think about what you will do when you are here, who might accompany you on your trip, and if you are mentally and physically prepared, if you are strong enough to face your personal and social problems. Because if you are not prepared to face life, to face new challenges, it will weigh very heavily on you over time. Often it is misfortune that makes us unable to bear this burden and that gets us into trouble. And everything that you hoped for when you came here can turn out quite differently than you planned. You can succumb to temptation, like alcohol or drug addiction, and all the desires and dreams that you came here with can so quickly disappear into oblivion. If a person comes with desire, with interest, and if he knows why he's coming, what he's coming to and what he intends to accomplish here, then yes—it's worth it.

[In the fall of 2003, Jesús' father died. Jesús was not able to return to Mexico for his burial. In the Spring of 2004 his mother, two brothers, and sister moved into their new three-room house in La Ordeña—paid for with the $10,000 that Jesús had sent home.]

26 Writing Across Communities: Diversity, Deliberation, and the Discursive Possibilities of WAC

MICHELLE HALL KELLS

This land is a poem of ochre and burnt sand I could never write, unless paper were the sacrament of the sky, and ink the broken line of wild horses staggering the horizon several miles away. Even then, does anything written ever matter to the earth, wind, and sky?

–Joy Harjo

In the ecology of human experience, writing matters. For Composition Studies, Writing Across the Curriculum (WAC), service learning, and professional and technical communication, writing matters because it authorizes writers and readers to take action.[1] Dynamic, changing, and endlessly creative, language contours our spheres of belonging. As Anis Bawarshi argues in "The Ecology of Genre," writing reflects "the habits and the habitats for acting in language" (71). Moreover, writing connects us to a world of relationships (Cooper, "Ecology"; Dobrin and Weisser; Owens; Syverson; Weisser). We write to sustain our connections with the people, living spaces, and work processes shaping our local and global communities. Literacy educators play critical roles as cultural mediators helping students contend with the imperfect world of human communication, offering them choices about how to use language. In this role, teachers must continually negotiate between two challenges: finding out how writing matters to students and helping students find out how writing matters in the university, in the workplace, and in their diverse communities of belonging. Whether our students become professional writers or professionals who write, they will operate in interdisciplinary, intercultural, and international spaces where the resolution of competing goals and interests is situational and often elusive.

College students of the new millennium face a future of increasing regional and global economic disparity, declining natural resources, international

From *Reflections* 11.1 (2007): 87–108.

political tensions, off shore labor outsourcing, rapidly shifting job markets, and transnational migration patterns. The uneven distribution of wealth, services, and resources across social groups is among the enduring problems our students confront as future leaders. With these changes, the demands for rhetorically efficacious writers will continue to grow. By promoting opportunities for context-based writing, WAC programs can facilitate students' civic, academic, and professional engagement with diverse discourse communities.

Cultural change and the challenges of scarcity are ancient realities in the Southwest United States where I live and teach, and where many students at the University of New Mexico are descendents of indigenous tribes, the earliest inhabitants of the Americas. First peoples have been adapting to climate and socio-political shifts for thousands of years, and lessons from the past are very present here. As University of New Mexico anthropologist David Stuart suggests in *Anasazi America*:

> As America matures it must work at the arts of survival if it is to be the model of prosperity, democracy, and stability a century from now that it is today. The model of prehistoric Pueblo society—efficient, egalitarian, homogenous, and self-sufficient—is not one we can or should mimic in detail. The United States is far too large, heterogeneous, polyglot, and growth-oriented to justify such mimicry. We probably cannot achieve their level of efficiency or egalitarianism. . . . But the means of Pueblo success at survival points the way toward some essential improvements. (199)

The erosion of natural resources and the inequitable distribution of wealth represent the primary factors leading to the decline of the once highly adaptive, culturally and technologically developed Chacoan prehistoric culture. As Stuart notes, these are the same issues facing the U.S. and our future national leaders—the students we are teaching in our classrooms today. Stuart recommends, "We can start by accepting the lesson left to all of us by the Anasazi of Chaco Canyon and their adaptable descendants—that survival means establishing a durable community. A durable community is one that balances growth with efficiency and refuses to be seduced by greed and power." I argue that literacy education programs that foreground the values of community and sustainability enhance students' initiation into a complex ecology of human relationships.

WRITING ACROSS COMMUNITIES: WAC WITH A DIFFERENCE

When I joined the faculty at the University of New Mexico in 2004, the chair of the Department of English asked me to start a conversation about WAC. Over the next two years, we launched the Writing Across Communities initiative based on a series of inter-disciplinary discussions about cultural diversity and academic, professional, and civic literacies. In this article, I examine how the process of seeding a WAC initiative within the social and environmental context of the Southwest extends and enhances current approaches to WAC. I focus on the two-year coalition-building process of the UNM Writing Across Communities initiative that has incorporated as key elements identifying stakeholders, assessing needs, and theorizing WAC for ethnolinguistically diverse student populations. For us at the University of New Mexico, WAC is more than teaching writing across the curriculum; it is an advocacy initiative promoting conditions in our educational system that encourage learning, authorship, and connections to multiple contexts. The distinguishing feature of the Writing Across Communities model is our integrated focus on student diversity and the overall cultural ecology of our regional environment.

We began with the recognition that to be successful, WAC program development would need to be organic (community-based), systemic (institutionally-distributed), and sustainable (flexible and responsive). We understood that the writing lives of ours students will not be limited to academic and work-place environments but will also be exercised in pueblos, villages, and other communities in and beyond the university. In an environmental context ever-concerned about the protection and use of scarce resources (land, water, and energy), we live in a delicate ecology shaped by the political histories of sovereign Indian nations, Spanish land grants, federal appropriations for military and land management projects, and the growing encroachment of outside developers. The legacy of colonization conditions not only the collective memory, but the material and social realities of our region. In an educational context where nearly half of the high school graduates require remedial education upon entering college and live in communities ranked the poorest in the nation, issues of scarcity and social justice are central. Implementing WAC from a cultural ecology approach can help to frame new conversations about the dimensions of communicative competence or what Bawarshi calls "rhetorical ecosystems." A Writing Across Communities approach to WAC foregrounds the dimensions of cultural and sociolinguistic diversity in university-wide writing instruction.

The exigencies for WAC at the University of New Mexico are many. Reflective of students in other ethnolinguistically diverse, economically challenged regions in the country, post-secondary students in New Mexico are not equally and effectively acquiring the literacy practices they need to successfully negotiate the pathways to civic, academic, and professional leadership. The progressive educational legislation of Governor Bill Richardson instituted the Lottery Scholarship in New Mexico, making access to higher education tuition-free for every high school graduate with a GPA 2.5 or higher. However, the absence of support mechanisms across the curriculum for emerging college writers exacerbates students' lack of preparation for the demands of college-level writing. Entry-level college students often struggle to acquire academic discourse conventions in first-year college composition courses and other disciplines. Shifting retention and graduation rates suggest that more than a third of our first-year college students fail to finish their degrees and graduate. UNM also holds the distinction of being the only R1 Hispanic-serving, open-admissions institution that also serves one of the largest Native American student populations in the nation.

Thus, the complex cultural ecology of this institution is shaped not only by the broad ethnolinguistic heterogeneity and economic challenges of the region, but historical class, cultural, political, and environmental divisions. New Mexico remains one of the poorest states in the nation. Seeking ways to connect students' home communities to college literacy education calls for a reconceptualization of WAC through a deliberative process that engages diversity and the discursive possibilities of representation. It is a process that must directly involve students themselves. Moreover, it is a process that should include consideration of the range of rhetorical resources influencing students' lives in and beyond the academy.

Additionally, we realize that conversations about writing instruction and student diversity demand not only sustained consideration of writing practices across academic, civic, and professional contexts, but require systematic assessment of how we teach writing within the Department of English. As such, establishing the UNM WAC initiative along side the programmatic revision of our first-year composition sequence appears to be a mutually beneficial enterprise. In "Reinventing WAC (Again): The First-Year Seminar and Academic Literacy," Doug Brent's examination of the relationship of WAC to the first-year writing sequence suggests that the strategic alignment of the two "can only be to the advantage of students" (274). We reason that if the first-year composition sequence is a critical point of entry into academic discourse and writing across the disciplines, then a WAC-enhanced first-year sequence should be a central feature of our new WAC initiative.

Determining the shape of such a WAC-enhanced first-year sequence has been an exercise in negotiating dissent. Critical self-reflection about how we teach writing (and how we think we teach writing) has begun in our own backyard in the Department of English and the Rhetoric and Writing Program, where attitudes and assumptions about student literacy are as disparate and sometimes divisive as in any other department. What I have learned as initiator and program chair for the 2005–2006 Writing Across Communities colloquia series at UNM is that WAC is not a single conversation. WAC is a ganglion of conversations that links to an ever-expanding range of practices and intellectual pursuits: computer-mediated writing instruction, service learning, writing-intensive courses, first-year writing seminars, technical and professional writing, interdisciplinary learning communities, writing centers, ESL and bilingual education, and many more. The process of critical self-reflection is not a once-and-for-all enterprise; we need to engage faculty, graduate teaching assistants, undergraduates, administrators, and community members in the conversation all along the way.

Amidst this complexity, we ask: What is the unifying exigence for WAC? Elaine Maimon muses about the future of WAC and suggests, "As the new century moves along, we might even say that writing across the curriculum occurs at the point where chaos meets common sense" (x). As a newcomer to the WAC conversation, I would argue that the chaos instigated by implementing any WAC program—and a "Writing Across Communities" model in particular—emerges whenever we transgress the ethnocentric biases that permeate every field and discourse community, including Composition Studies, itself. The greatest resistance I have encountered in conversations about ethnolinguistic and textual (or genre) diversity seems to come from compositionists intent on protecting the primacy of essayist literacies in the academy. Recognizing that students need to write for and to audiences other than insider experts in English Studies not only destabilizes how we teach first-year college students but challenges how we teach graduate teaching assistants charged with introducing novice writers to academic discourse. The prospects of both endeavors are daunting for any WAC program, but are especially problematic for an initiative that seeks to interrogate what Christopher Thaiss identifies as the first principles of WAC.

Thaiss maps the future of WAC by reflectively weaving the threads of the past thirty years of WAC scholarship to define both "a core of consistent WAC principles over the span, and the theoretical influences that have worked changes on the concept" (299). Central to his analysis are the key terms, or first principles of WAC: "writing" "across" and "curriculum." Noting that both "curriculum" and "writing" are ambiguous and highly contested terms, Thaiss observes that " 'the curriculum' is subject to the same destabilizing forces that make the definition of 'writing' so volatile" (314). And, the term "disciplines" is no less problematic. Thaiss concludes that we cannot assume "fixity" in the concept of either "writing across the disciplines" or "writing across the curriculum."

Victor Villanueva further questions traditional WAC models, arguing that "WAC . . . has tended to be assimilationist, assimilation being a political state of mind more repressive than mere accommodation" ("Politics" 166). For Villanueva, even the concept of "writing to learn" does not "go far enough, doesn't historicize our conceptions of language and knowledge, keeps us tied to a Platonic mind-set" (166). How might we move beyond traditional WAC perspectives toward a "Writing Across Communities" perspective that is first and foremost a context-based WAC initiative serving ethnolinguistically diverse student populations, a model that is not assimilationist in intent?

Like Villanueva, I contend that traditional models of WAC too narrowly privilege academic discourse over other discourses and communities shaping the worlds in which our students live and work. Although WAC seeks to make visible the codes, genres, media, and purposes of the knowledge-making systems of the university to novice writers, historically WAC has not been called upon to interrogate the additional knowledge-making systems and discourses students seek to acquire. Traditional WAC approaches replicate and reaffirm dominant discourses by socializing new writers into established systems. By contrast, Writing Across Communities as a cultural ecology approach seeks to cultivate critical awareness of the ways that literacy practices are shaped by ever-shifting sets of economic, political, social, cultural, and linguistic factors.

"ATTENDING TO THE MARGINS:" TEXTS AND CONTEXTS

In *Attending to the Margins: Writing, Researching, and Teaching on the Front Lines*, Valerie Balester, Victor Villanueva, and I argue that "we need to de-marginalize (or re-center) our thinking about educationally underserved students—the social, linguistic, cultural (racialized and genderized)" individuals who fill our classroom (Kells and Balester xix). The "marginal" or non-traditionally prepared (or what Villanueva calls "historically excluded") students are increasingly becoming the "core" of U.S. higher education demographics (Villanueva "Edge City" 1). Assumptions about who our students are and what they need should change with these demographic shifts. We need to be teaching students across contexts how to pay attention to texts—critically, reflectively, and ethically. Equally important, we need to be listening to our students concerning the consequences of texts on their lives and spheres of belonging. For historically underserved student populations such as Latino and Native American groups in the Southwest United States, exercising authorship across genres and contexts is central to representing the interests of their communities. "The discursive practices, spoken and written, of traditionally excluded writers, situated in diverse sites, demand to be heard" (Kells, Balester, and Villanueva 3). A culturally sensitive approach to writing instruction accepts that genres are more than just forms, but represent social practices that have consequences—social, political, cognitive, moral, and material consequences and effects.

Examining the linkages between WAC, Composition Studies, and service learning, David Jolliffe argues that an understanding of genre "holds great potential for explaining how students learn to 'behave' as functioning, intellectual adults in the discourse communities they encounter in college and beyond" (96). Similarly, Norman Fairclough contends, "It is vital to understand these consequences and effects [of genre] if we are to raise moral and political questions about contemporary societies" (14). Those of us doing the work of text production and exegesis too often shortchange our students, especially those students who belong to historically disempowered groups, when we fail to call attention to the role text and genre play in growing, sustaining, and dismantling communities as well as the role that texts play in the circulation of such social goods as knowledge, wealth, resources, power, and prestige. As Bawarshi asserts, "Genres do not simply help us define and organize kinds of texts; they also help us define and organize kinds of social actions, social actions that these texts rhetorically make possible" ("Genre Function" 335).

The genres of academic research and discourse tend to mystify social hierarchy and to distance, or even efface, the means by which we produce and reproduce knowledge and power. Writing Across Communities, as a resistance discourse, can function as a mechanism for transdisciplinary dialogue to demystify the ways we make and use knowledge across communities of practice. The act of writing is more than a skill, it is also an occasion for agency, or in some cases, a loss of agency. It is important to recognize the rhetorical resources students bring to the classroom and affirm the tacit knowledge they already have about the way the world works for them. Consistent with the historical aims of WAC, we need to help students bridge the knowledge they have with the knowledge they need for success in college and beyond. But we need to do more, especially when we are mediating academic discourses for historically excluded students.

Ronald Scollon and Suzanne Scollon's study of Native American students (Athabaskans of Canada and the U.S.) indicates that academic discourse practices, particularly essay writing, can stir considerable conflicts of identity as well as transgress boundaries of belonging for indigenous student writers. The authorial stance and structure of the thesis-driven essay as genre demands a measure of self-display inconsistent with Athabaskan cultural practice. The students in Scollon and Scollon's study describe themselves as stuck in an ethical and social dilemma inside the academic setting. This challenge is very real at the University of New Mexico, where we serve students from Laguna, Acoma, Zuni, Navajo, and fifteen other pueblos from around the region. Students coming to UNM from these pueblos describe memories and cautionary tales that echo Luci Tapahonso's reflections on the legacy of "formal education" in New Mexico boarding schools and the enduring impact on her family and Navajo (Diné) community:

> My childhood is intertwined with memories of various relatives "talking" to me and sharing by the implication the value of silence, listening, and observation. We spoke Diné from birth, but because of our parents' negative experiences in school, they taught us basic English concepts like the alphabet, our American names (which we didn't use at home), our birth dates, and census numbers before we entered public school. . . . My first memory of speaking English in school consists of three words— "what," "yes," and "no." When a white adult spoke to me, I would say, "What!" not as question but as a loud and emphatic answer. Since speaking Diné was forbidden, many of us did not talk at school or in the presence of whites. . . . It became clear that the two settings, school and home, were distinctly different places and incompatible. (343–44)

The consequences of engaging in academic genre practice such as essayist literacy need to be acknowledged and addressed by university writing programs. To write a successful ENGL 101 essay can represent an affront to the tribal authority structures to which these students belong. And yet, to fail to engage in rhetorical self-promotion in the classroom represents failure in ENGL 101 essay writing. James Paul Gee points to this difficulty when he argues that in essayist prose both the audience and the author are fictionalized and "the text is decontextualized from specific social networks and relationships" (25). The social artificiality of essayist literacy as a genre practice can reinforce social distance rather than mitigate alienation for culturally diverse students. Moreover, the dialogue and deliberation of the academic classroom can pose a real dilemma to our students whose primary communities of belonging privilege silence and listening over rhetorical self-display and verbal engagement. For example, in my upper-division honors course, Rhetorics of

Place and Belonging, a young woman from the Acoma pueblo thoughtfully educated me about this constraint in a recent email:

> My apologies for missing class today. I just received your e-mail class agenda, so I decided to write you back to let you know why I missed class. We (Acoma people) have just begun our Indian Lent which is a time when we are supposed to put all of our drums and storytelling away for at least a month before Easter. For us it is a time of reflection upon our religion. The Yellow Woman story that we read in class talks about a pueblo figure which right now I am not allowed to hear about or read about. I hope this is no problem for you.

There would have been no way for me to know how this student was negotiating the conflicts imposed by my lesson plan unless she took the risk to tell me directly. Scollon and Scollon point out that students from many different groups encounter similar forms of cultural alienation in the academic classroom. If we cannot produce a one-size-fits-all model of teaching writing across the disciplines, what can we realistically and productively do to address the heterogeneity in our classrooms?

WAC and the Possibilities of Ecocomposition: Aligning Advocacy and Engagement

The challenge for the Writing Across Communities initiative at UNM is enhancing opportunities to build identification with the cultures of the academy as well as to cultivate appreciation across the university for the cultures and epistemologies our students bring with them. By taking an advocacy role in the university for ethnolinguistically diverse students, WAC can help to mediate and educate faculty and administrators about the constraints and concerns facing college writers. Communicative competence depends upon complex strategies of shuttling between ideas and audiences, a challenging, culturally dependent process.

To date, however, WAC leaders have primarily charted the course and described the shape of WAC in university contexts. For example, in "Clearing the Air: WAC Myths and Realities," Susan McLeod and Eileen Maimon articulate the principles and practices of WAC from the points of view of teachers and administrators in established curriculum-centered WAC programs. Absent from their discussions, however, are the perspectives of undergraduate students themselves, the beneficiaries of WAC programs. Similarly, David Russell's *Writing in Academic Disciplines: A Curricular History* attends to trends and developments in the practices of disciplinary writing through the evolutionary history of university education between 1870 and 1980, focusing inquiry primarily on institutional sites of power and prestige. In *WAC for the New Millennium: Strategies for Continuing Writing-Across-the-Curriculum Programs* (McLeod, Miraglia, Soven, and Thaiss), the editors celebrate the staying power of WAC and, at the same time, acknowledge the gap in WAC literature focusing on the issues and needs of historically excluded student populations.

We know very little about how WAC shapes and responds to local conditions in institutions serving historically excluded student populations.

What might WAC look like if we concerned ourselves with not only the discourses our students acquire in the classroom, but the rhetorical resources they bring to the university? What might WAC look like if we open the conceptual umbrella to include engagement with a broad range of cultural, civic, and professional discourses? How can we map the challenges students confront in the university? Even more importantly, how do we include students in the meta-discursive process of inventing WAC?

In their article "Writing Beyond the Curriculum: Fostering New Collaborations in Literacy," Steve Parks and Eli Goldblatt (p. 337 in this volume) call for an expanded conception of WAC that includes more than disciplinary and academic literacy practices. They propose a model of WAC that is capacious enough to include not only writing in the disciplines but service and experiential learning, community literacy projects, business and professional writing, as well as public school outreach. Parks and Goldblatt prefigure a "Writing Across Communities" model by challenging WAC theorists and administrators to look beyond academic discourse communities as generative sites for student engagement. What is still missing even from this model is a vision of WAC from the point of view of students as citizens of multiple spheres. Models that fail to connect the dimensions of human interaction with local and global environments obscure the interdependence and interrelationships integral to community development and survival. In our twenty-first century globalized, hyper-cyber-mediated communicative context, rhetoric is more than the art of persuasion; it is an art of survival.

If community and sustainability are the central values for literacy education, ecocomposition offers a productive framework from which to reconsider and situate WAC within a broader cultural ecology of human communication. In a conference paper connecting WAC to ecocomposition theory and practice, graduate student and charter member of the University of New Mexico WAC project Carson Bennett asserts, "Indeed ecocomposition is designed to enable students to use critical thinking and writing to breach boundaries of place, community, politics, and academic subjects." Putting ecocomposition ideas into practice through the Writing Across Communities initiative, Bennett describes the range of communities, issues, and discourses his first-year composition students have engaged. Bennett describes how one Native American student in his course wrote a letter, published in the local newspaper, opposing a proposed road extension through the Petroglyph National Monument, sacred lands to his pueblo. Bennett concludes, "The project I have described was a success, not because a few letters were published and few heads were turned, but because students learned that writing matters. Through writing, they can breach the boundaries between discourse communities, and they can make a difference."

Ecocomposition anticipated nearly two decades ago the need for culturally-sensitive approaches to engaging students in the recursive process of inquiry and document production (Cooper, "Forward"; Dobrin and Weisser;

Owens; Syverson; Weisser and Dobrin). Marilyn Cooper's early proposal suggests that an ecological model of writing offers a way to conceptualize composition as a social practice of "dynamic interlocking systems that structure the social activity of writing" ("The Ecology of Writing" 7). Similarly, Syverson suggests that writers, readers, and texts operate as a kind of ecological system capable of becoming self-organizing, adaptive, and dynamic (4). Rassool defines literacy practice as an organic "cultural activity that involves people in conscious and reflective action within a variety of situations and everyday life" (25). Owens expands on this notion of cultural interdependence and calls attention to students as a "threatened generation," arguing for a pedagogy of sustainability that foregrounds the relationship between culture, survival, body, and place in the teaching of writing (23). Elaborating further on the ecology metaphor of writing, Cooper observes that "it is through an ecological understanding of writing that the field aligns itself with the dominant paradigm of the last century" ("Forward" xi). Extending this claim, I argue that it is through an ecological understanding of culture and communication that WAC specifically, and English Studies generally, can help to realign communicative dynamics in the twenty-first century university. Ecocomposition can inform WAC and service learning programs, moving us toward an interdisciplinary vision of sustainability.

In "Breaking Ground in Ecocomposition," Dobrin and Weisser articulate two models gaining attention in Composition Studies. The first model, "an ecological literacy approach," stresses the natural world and role of human beings in the environment. The second model, a "discursive ecology approach," recognizes that words and writing are integral to sustaining human systems. Synthesizing these two approaches, I propose that a cultural ecology approach to WAC can help to foreground context as a way to understand and use the genres of academic, professional, and civic/community literacies. Cultural ecology resists a culture-blind mode of document production and seeks to guide students to critically respond to the cultural and symbolic systems within diverse contexts. Practicing cultural ecology in the classroom challenges writers to recognize that every rhetorical situation represents complex social configurations and interdependent relationships.

The circulation of discourse is to a cultural ecology what energy flow is to environmental ecology. The communication life cycle sustains community, initiating, maintaining, and regulating relationships. Cultural health, like environmental conservation, emerges from a "capacity for self-renewal" (Leopold 221). An ethic of sustainability, therefore, evolves out of an ecological conscience of human interaction, or as Aldo Leopold charges, an "effort to understand and preserve that capacity" for renewal (221). The metaphor of a cultural ecology of communicative action offers us and our students a productive way to conceptualize the contexts in which we work and live. Citizenship (belonging and allegiance), environment (the physical and social biota), ethics (values and behavior), and communicative action (rhetoric and symbol-making) become intricately linked in the practice of writing. To teach writing removed from this complex web of relationship is to risk replicating exploitation and misinformation. As Denise Tillery argues, "We need to teach our students that ethical writing entails a delicate negotiation between the demands of the workplace and the demands of the greater society, and no writing task, no matter how seemingly trivial, is immune from the pressures of the power structure" (113).

Under the rubric of Writing Across Communities, the scope of WAC enlarges to engage not only ideas across the disciplines, but the dissonance and dissent concomitant to the democratization of academic discourse. Engaging dissonance is precisely the work of civic and academic discourse, of taking on the role of citizen and scholar, of belonging to a human community. Writing is the act of negotiating difference through language.

MAKING A PARADIGM SHIFT

Building upon the theoretical foundations of ecocomposition, Writing Across Communities represents a shift in paradigm. Informed not only by WAC and Composition Studies, but by the critical perspectives of New Literacy studies and Sociolinguistics articulated by such scholars as Barton, Gee, Fairclough, and Johnstone, a Writing Across Communities approach to literacy education foregrounds dimensions of ethnolinguistic diversity and civic engagement. Coalescing conversations among faculty, administrators, graduate students, and undergraduate students in and beyond the Department of English, we began by hosting a colloquia series over three semesters beginning in spring 2005 and culminating in the fall of 2006. The organizing themes of the colloquia series included: "Knowing Our Students," "Inviting Our Students to Academic Literacies," and "Preparing Pathways to Professional Literacies." Keynote panelists have included Juan Guerra (University of Washington), Susan McLeod (University of California, Santa Barbara), and Barbara Johnstone (Carnegie Mellon) along side local faculty, administrators, and students. We have involved stakeholders at multiple levels of the institution, including the UNM provost, the tutoring center director, the vice president of student affairs, as well as faculty from Spanish, Native American Studies, Linguistics, Earth and Planetary Sciences, Communication, Education, English, Architecture, and Library Sciences. The WAC dialogue has also involved representatives of programs such as Freshman Learning Communities, Service Learning, College Enrichment, and the newly established New Mexico Teacher Exchange initiative.

Shifting from a historically prescriptive stance to a descriptive perspective, we began by asking questions in a series of interdepartmental conversation-builders. We shifted perspectives by asking teachers both inside and beyond the Department of English to describe their students. We posed questions such as: What are the characteristics of the discourse communities (personal, civic, and academic) that our students bring to the university? How diverse are these practices and how does that diversity affect curriculum? Rather than perpetuating a discourse of deficiency, we invited the university into dialogue about the wealth of cultural resources our students possess and the challenges they face in their academic journey. We asked graduate students and first-year writing teachers to engage in the same exercises with their students. We provided focused writing exercises and group process protocols. Finally, we asked undergraduate students themselves to participate in a series of focus group and roundtable discussions about their writing experiences both before and after coming to UNM. We encouraged teachers to write along with their students and to share their own responses to such questions as, Why are you here at UNM? Where are you going? How can writing help you be what you want to be and get you where you want to go? Findings from these classroom-based discussions are available online at the UNM WAC archive (*Writing Across Communities*).

In April 2005, we hosted the first Writing Across Communities Collo-quium, "Knowing Our Students," featuring as keynote speaker Professor Juan Guerra. His address, "Creating Pathways to Academic Literacy and Be-yond: Situating the Personal, Professional, and Political," asserts that we must work to dismantle the barriers dividing the university from local communi-ties. Guerra reinforces the role of the university as an agent of service to the larger community in forms of research, education, and distribution of infor-mational resources. He challenges WAC advocates to engage in a shared and mutually productive critique of public education kindergarten through col-lege. Finally, Guerra offers the concept of "transcultural repositioning" as a way to conceptualize the act of moving across discourse communities with authority and integrity ("Putting Literacy"). He argues that in order to move across cultural boundaries, rhetorically efficacious individuals, especially individuals from historically-excluded groups, cultivate adaptive strategies that help them to negotiate new and different contexts and communicative conventions.

In October 2005, we extended the discussion by launching WAC Week and hosting symposia featuring WAC scholar Susan McLeod and sociolinguist Barbara Johnstone. In the deliberative process of WAC Week, we asked stu-dents to name their experiences at UNM. The centerpiece of WAC Week was a serendipitous and celebrative event we called the Write On! Workshop (WOW!), a gathering of over 200 undergraduates from across the disciplines who came to workshop papers, dialogue about their writing practices, cri-tique the first-year writing sequence, respond to a student questionnaire, and listen to local spoken word poets. The enthusiastic response from undergrad-uate students is best summed up in the comments from anonymous partici-pants who wrote the following responses on student questionnaires. One student commented:

> It was an extremely pleasant surprise to realize just how much all of the people from the English Department cared about what students thought. It was nice to feel like I was involved, and I could voice my opinion. I liked the atmosphere of the small table discussions and the opportunity to hear what other students were doing and thinking when it came to their English classes. The experience was a real eye opener.

Another undergraduate reflected on the daily literacy practices affecting students' writing experiences:

> I attended a roundtable discussion where thoughts, ideas, and experiences on English were discussed. I was impressed to see such a great turnout in the number of attendees, so many that people were just sitting there waiting for a spot to open up. The discussion gave me ideas of what students in other English classes were going through. One subject that stayed caught in my mind after leaving the roundtable was our discussion about our communication to one another like email and text messaging. Never did I ever think that these two subjects would be a topic of our discussion. Our communication to one another has a great deal to do with English and I never viewed it that way. The English department did a great job on providing help to all students with English classes. I am glad that I was able to be apart of the writing across communities week.

We have gathered the findings from WAC Week events to inform the current revision of the first-year writing sequence which we will pilot in the fall 2007.

At the close of the 2005–2006 Writing Across Communities Colloquia series, organizers extended the conversation by forming the WAC Alliance as a way to formalize dialogue about writing at UNM. Members drafted a constitution and by-laws. In the spring of 2006, the WAC Alliance grew into a chartered, student-directed organization inviting students and faculty to talk together about what they know, what they need to know, and how we as their teachers can help them. The WAC Alliance is currently governed by a head council of eight elected members representing graduate students, undergraduate students, lecturers, part-time instructors, representatives of other community entities and a non-voting faculty advisor. The mission and purpose of the WAC Alliance is as follows:

> The WAC Alliance is a forum for the conversation regarding writing, a think tank of and for the UNM learning community. We advocate active, engaged writing-to-learn processes across disciplines through innovative teaching in order to cultivate a culture of writing and inquiry. Our goal is to engage the campus in dialogue regarding writing-to-learn and writing-to-communicate while addressing the changing needs of the student body to ensure academic as well as professional success at all levels.
>
> The three main components of Writing Across Communities include civic, academic, and professional communities. The WAC Alliance seeks to bridge these communities and maintain communication between the various entities on and off campus while cultivating discussion and pedagogical support for diverse literacy practices across UNM discourse communities. (Writing Across Communities)

This student-centered Writing Across Communities infrastructure has branched into various sub-sets or interest groups such as the WAC Peer Tutoring team that is drafting a proposal for a "Writing Center Without Walls."

Other WAC interests extend into First-Year Learning Communities, the Undergraduate Creativity and Research Colloquium, and Service Learning. Alliances between WAC, the first-year writing sequence, and a new Service Learning program are currently being established. We are also growing alliances with the Spanish Heritage Language program and the Peer Mentoring for Graduates of Color (PMGC) Special Initiatives under the Office of Graduate Studies. For the UNM WAC initiative, the challenges of economic scarcity and the possibilities of democratic leadership have translated into a growing creative and collaborative movement.

REVISIONING "FIRST PRINCIPLES" OF WAC

A Writing Across Communities approach to college writing instruction invites students to consider how an understanding of the dimensions of cultural diversity enhances their ability to write and communicate: *Appropriately* (with an awareness of different conventions); *Productively* (to achieve their desired aims); *Ethically* (to remain attuned to the communities they serve); *Critically* (to learn to engage in inquiry and discovery); and *Responsively* (to negotiate the tensions caused by the exercise of authority in their spheres of belonging). This reconceptualization of WAC from a cultural ecology model helps to frame new conversations about WAC and the dimensions of intercultural communication shaping the writing contexts in which students exercise authority. The underlying assumptions of Writing Across Communities assert that:

- Students arrive already embedded in complex discourse communities;

- Membership in different discourse communities is a dynamic (ever expanding and receding) process, as students shift among the communities to which they already belong and those to which they seek to belong;

- Students bring discursive resources and literacy practices that are variably conditioned by the cultural and intellectual communities of the academy;

- Agency in language does not begin and should not end in the college classroom;

- WAC, writing programs, and writing centers should serve as advocates of literacy and language awareness for speakers of English as well as members of other ethnolinguistic communities present on and around campus;

- Teachers in WAC programs, writing classrooms, and writing centers serve an important role as cultural mediators between the academy, students, students' homes, and their target academic and professional discourse communities.

The Writing Across Communities project at UNM is first and foremost an advocacy initiative. We are deeply and unabashedly invested in the mythos of education and the belief that greater access to a range of knowledge systems enhances the agency of individual students as well as their communities. Higher education represents more than a personal asset, emblem of entitlement, or marker of prestige. The work of teaching civic and academic literacy across communities represents the democratization of knowing.

Only by knowing the local condition can we and our students contemplate the implications and challenges of global intercultural communication we face. Every human interaction—whether in person, print text, cyberspace, or visual media—is a form of intercultural communication. Region of origin, family position, gender, ethnolinguistic identity, nationality, age, and religion are only a few of the variables that constitute one's culture or systems of belonging. Students cannot begin to reconcile differences in cultural systems beyond their own circles of affiliation if they have not critically reflected on their own. In order to cultivate cross-cultural competence, WAC needs new ways to think about the heterogeneity of the rhetorical situation.

Writing Across Communities as cultural ecology integrates the dynamics of community, culture, knowledge-making systems, and the environments in which students and teachers together participate in the intellectual life cycle. Writing Across Communities as a cultural ecology of intercultural communication invites writers into a new system of metaphorical thinking that involves the interpretation and negotiation of different sets of expectations. As such, WAC as an approach to intercultural communication and text production involves learning new strategies in conflict resolution and meta-discourses to help communicators mediate and negotiate inevitable conflict. Students across the disciplines need to cultivate the kind of rhetorical alacrity that emerges from principled participation in deliberative action within and across diverse discourse communities.

"Perhaps the most radical decision that educators can make," argues Owens, "is to remain convinced that they and their students can literally reconstruct their worlds for the better" (19). I would like to expand on Owens' assertion by arguing for the adoption of a cultural ecology model of WAC to help students recognize that culture is not something "out there" that belongs to the "other," but something around and inside of them. A cultural ecology approach invites writers into new systems of metaphorical thinking that make empathy possible.

Finally, writers need "boundary-spanning ability" (Coppola and Karis xiii). Only by knowing the local condition can students contemplate the global nature of intercultural communication. Recognizing, responding to, and accommodating resistance are pivotal concerns if we are to play a role in facilitating an ecology of intercultural communication across communities. Future WAC scholarship needs to address the interests and challenges of historically-excluded student populations where varied literacy practices demand the accommodation of difference. As their teachers and university program directors, we will need to learn the rhetorical arts of community praxis and intercultural communication along side of our students.

NOTE

1. A version of this article was presented in the panel, "Writing Across Communities: A Cultural Ecology of Language, Learning, and Literacy," featuring Michelle Hall Kells, Juan Guerra, Carson Bennett, Scott Rogers, Beverly Army Gillen, Dana Salvador, and John Bess for the 2006 Conference of College Composition and Communication in Chicago. A special thank you to

Carson Bennett for his thoughtful suggestions to earlier drafts of this article. I would also like to extend my appreciation to my colleagues at the University of New Mexico, especially Scott Sanders, Chuck Paine, David Jones, and to our graduate student, Leah Sneider, who has faithfully served as our WAC events coordinator for the past two years. Their enthusiastic support and leadership is making the vision possible.

WORKS CITED

Barton, David. *Literacy: An Introduction to the Ecology of Written Language.* Cambridge, MA: Blackwell, 1994.

Bawarshi, Anis. "The Genre Function." *College English* 62.3 (January 2000): 335–60.

———. "The Ecology of Genre." Weisser and Dobrin 69–80.

Bennett, Carson. "Writing the Web of Influence: Connecting Students to Their Cultural Environments through Ecocomposition." Conference of College Composition and Communication. Palmer Hotel, Chicago. 24 March 2006.

Brent, Doug, "Reinventing WAC (Again): The First-Year Seminar and Academic Literacy." *CCC* 57.2 (December 2005): 253–76.

Cooper, Marilyn M. "The Ecology of Writing." *Writing as Social Action.* Eds. Marilyn M. Cooper and Michael Holzman. Portsmouth, NH: Boynton/Cook, 1989. 1–15.

———. "Forward: The Truth Is Out There." Weisser and Dobrin xi–xviii.

Coppola, Nancy W., and Bill Karis, eds. *Technical Communication, Deliberative Rhetoric, and Environmental Discourse: Connections and Directions.* Stamford, CT: Ablex, 2000.

Dobrin, Sidney I., and Christian R. Weisser. "Breaking Ground in Ecocomposition: Exploring Relationships between Discourse and Environment." *College English* 64.5 (May 2002): 566–89.

Fairclough, Norman. *Analyzing Discourse: Textual Analysis for Social Research.* New York: Routledge, 2005.

Gee, James Paul. *An Introduction to Discourse Analysis: Theory and Method.* 2nd ed. New York: Routledge, 1999.

Guerra, Juan C. "Creating Pathways to Academic Literacy and Beyond: Situating the Personal, Professional, and Political." Spring 2005 Literacy Symposium. University of New Mexico, Albuquerque, 25 Apr. 2005. <http://www.unm.edu/~wac/Spring2005/Spring2005.htm>.

———. "Putting Literacy in Its Place: Nomadic Consciousness and the Practice of Transcultural Repositioning." *Rebellious Reading: The Dynamics of Chicano/a Literacy.* Ed. Carl Gutierrez-Jones. Center for Chicana/o Studies: University of California at Santa Barbara, 2004. 19–37.

Harjo, Joy. "This Land Is a Poem." *How We Became Human: New and Selected Poems: 1975–2001.* New York: Norton, 2002.

Johnstone, Barbara. *The Linguistic Individual: Self-Expression in Language and Linguistics.* New York: Oxford UP, 1996.

Jolliffe, David. "Writing Across the Curriculum and Service Learning: Kairos, Genre, and Collaboration." McLeod, Miraglia, Soven, and Thaiss 86–108.

Kells, Michelle Hall, and Valerie Balester, eds. *Attending to the Margins: Writing, Researching, and Teaching on the Front Lines.* Portsmouth, NH: Heinemann-Boynton/Cook, 1999.

———, Valerie Balester, and Victor Villanueva, eds. *Latino/a Discourses: On Language, Identity, and Literacy Education.* Portsmouth, NH: Heinemann-Boynton/Cook, 2004.

Leopold, Aldo. *A Sand County Almanac and Sketches from Here and There.* New York: Oxford UP, 1949.

Maimon, Elaine P. "Foreword." McLeod, Miraglia, Soven, and Thaiss vii–x.

McLeod, Susan, and Elaine Maimon. "Clearing the Air: WAC Myths and Realities." *College English* 62.5 (May 2000): 573–83.

———, Eric Miraglia, Margot Soven, and Christopher Thaiss, eds. *WAC for the New Millennium: Strategies for Continuing Writing-Across-the-Curriculum Programs.* Urbana, IL: NCTE, 2001.

Owens, Derek. *Composition and Sustainability: Teaching for a Threatened Generation.* Urbana, IL: NCTE, 2001.

Parks, Steve, and Eli Goldblatt. "Writing beyond the Curriculum: Fostering New Collaborations in Literacy." *College English* 62.5 (May 2000): 584–606.

Rassool, Naz. *Literacy for Sustainable Development in the Age of Information.* Philadelphia, PA: Multilingual Matters, 1999.

Russell, David. *Writing in Academic Disciplines: A Curricular History.* 2nd ed. Carbondale: Southern Illinois UP, 2002.

Scollon, Ronald, and Suzanne B. K. Scollon. *Narrative, Literacy, and Face in Interethnic Communication.* Norwood: Ablex, 1981.

Stuart, David E. *Anasazi America*. Albuquerque: U of New Mexico P, 2000.

Syverson, Margaret A. *The Wealth of Reality: An Ecology of Composition*. Carbondale: Southern Illinois UP, 1999.

Tapahonso, Luci. "They Moved Over the Mountain." *Here First: Autobiographical Essays by Native American Writers*. Ed. Arnold Krupat and Brian Swann. New York: Random House, 2000. 338–51.

Thaiss, Christopher. "Theory in WAC: Where Have We Been, Where Are We Going?" McLeod, Miraglia, Soven, and Thaiss 299–325.

Tillery, Denise. "Power, Language, and Professional Choices: A Hermeneutic Approach to Teaching Technical Communication." *TCQ* 10.1 (Winter 2001): 97–116.

Villanueva, Victor. "Edge City: Class and Culture in Contact," Kells and Balester 1–5.

———. "The Politics of Literacy Across the Curriculum." McLeod, Miraglia, Soven, and Thaiss 165–78.

Weisser, Christian R. *Moving Beyond Academic Discourse: Composition Studies and the Public Sphere*. Carbondale: Southern Illinois UP, 2002.

———, and Sidney I. Dobrin, eds. *Ecocomposition: Theoretical and Pedagogical Approaches*. Albany: State U of New York P, 2001.

Writing Across Communities. Home page. 24 Oct. 2006. University of New Mexico Department of English. 1 Mar. 2007. <http://www.unm.edu/~wac/index.htm>.

27

When the Community Writes: Re-envisioning the SLCC DiverseCity Writing Series

TIFFANY ROUSCULP

The uses of language are what teachers of literacy teach (or should teach), which means that how we teach is at least as important as what we teach—maybe, in fact, more important.

–JAY ROBINSON, "Literacy and Lived Lives"

Since opening in the fall of 2001, the Salt Lake Community College's Community Writing Center has re-conceptualized the potential of writing centers and writing programs to move beyond the academy's walls and to interact with their surrounding communities. The Community Writing Center is informed by a pedagogy that re-envisions the relationships between literacy and society and attempts to acknowledge and support a range of literate practices and events. It is a site where the multiple needs for literate actions can find their beginnings, journeys, and fruition.

Previously housed in a low-income, multi-use community development project, and now located off-campus in a two-room space adjacent to the Main City Library in downtown Salt Lake City, the Community Writing Center welcomes all city residents to participate in its programs. Originally founded to provide one-on-one writing assistance to the public—just as campus writing centers do for students across the country—the Community Writing Center (CWC) has evolved over the past four years into five distinct programs:

- *The Center:* "A place to write," with technological, textual, and learning resources, space to compose and receive feedback, and room to meet about writing. The CWC is located in downtown Salt Lake City and open to all greater Salt Lake metropolitan residents 16 years old and older.

- *Writing Coaching:* Free one-on-one assistance on any writing task from start to finish: résumés, poetry, letters, articles. Located at the CWC, in libraries and community centers around the valley, and on-line.

From *Reflections* 5.1 (2006): 67–88.

- *Writing Workshops:* Workshops for the public and for local organizations, on topics ranging from grant-writing to poetry, journaling to press releases.

- *Writing Partners:* Long-term collaborations with local organizations to develop sustainable change through writing.

- *DiverseCity Writing Series:* A multi-group, cross-valley writing and publication project to build bridges over social chasms such as economic disparity and racial intolerance.

The Community Writing Center is staffed by six part-time Writing Assistants, who are most often also students from the community college and nearby colleges and universities; I have been the director since its inception.[1] So far, the CWC has worked with over 1,200 individuals and 80 community organizations through these collaborative and adaptable programs that partner the community college in learning relationships that Thomas Deans might refer to as "writing *with* the community." Situated outside the kinds of course curriculum requirements and constraints that influence service-learning partnerships, and free of the research requirements necessary within many university-community collaborations, the CWC has responded in an organic way to the diverse writing and literacy needs and requests of Salt Lake City's adults. Stephen Ruffus, SLCC English Department Chair, observes, "There is a different pedagogical context at the CWC, separate from the rhythms inherent in a classroom setting. Akin to a jazz improvisation, the participants in CWC programs draw on themselves, on the project itself, and riff into new and exciting literacy events, helping themselves to deal with dominant discourses."

The CWC's development, from the beginning, drew heavily upon the work of Wayne C. Peck, Linda Flower, and Lorraine Higgins at the Community Literacy Center (CLC) in Pittsburgh, especially their explorations of "community literacy" as "a search for an alternative discourse." Intending to create a hybrid space, drawn from campus writing centers, CLC research, and the community college mission to meet a broad range of community-identified writing needs in Salt Lake City, the Community Writing Center identified its mission as follows:

> Because writing effectively is a means to improving people's lives, the mission of the SLCC Community Writing Center is to support the writing goals of out-of-school adults. We fulfill this mission by initiating and developing short- and long-term writing programs and by collaborating with working alliances to identify ways that our resources can serve the community. The CWC also provides training and opportunities for college students and the general public to contribute to our mission.

In Fall 2004, this mission statement was revised to read:

> The SLCC Community Writing Center promotes the improvement of writing abilities for personal, economic and social goals. To achieve this mission, the CWC sponsors innovative outreach programs and collaborates with community partners to identify the best use of its educational resources.

One of the Community Writing Center's programs, the DiverseCity Writing Series, demonstrates how skilled uses of language bridge differences and foreground discourse practices that too often go unrecognized as the fabric of community building. Initiated before the CWC actually opened its doors, the DiverseCity Writing Series is the CWC's longest-standing program. Over the past six hears, it has evolved from a single-partner short-term community writing project into a year-round, multi-group collaborative community writing and publishing project.

The DiverseCity Writing Series started in the fall of 2000, as a "sequel" of sorts to the *Bridges* newsletter—a service-learning partnership between the SLCC English Department and Artspace, Inc., a non-profit arts and neighborhood developer (see Figure 27–1). The *Bridges* newsletter was produced by SLCC students in an English Special Topics course that I taught in which they researched and wrote about the people and histories of an essentially abandoned neighborhood in downtown Salt Lake City that Artspace was in the process of re-building. The non-profit had approached the college to develop a narrative record of the neighborhood to supplement its own community-building efforts. Each semester, for three years, English students went into the community to gather stories, and students from the College's printing apprenticeship program produced the newsletter which was distributed to residents and organizations in the community. The on-going project received an outstanding service-learning award from the Utah Campus Compact and provided a tangible resource for Artspace in its fundraising efforts.

While the *Bridges* newsletter evolved, the Community Writing Center also continued to develop. As SLCC faculty worked to establish the initial programming that the CWC would provide to the community, we examined the rapidly changing demographics of Salt Lake City. Predominantly a settlement for members of the Church of Jesus Christ of Latter-Day Saints (Mormons) for over a century, the population of the Salt Lake valley had increased (mostly due to immigration from other states and countries) at three times the national average: 25% between 1990 and 2000. While Mormons still make up a significant portion of city residents (approximately 35%) and the community remains predominantly Caucasian, the diversity of the metropolitan area is increasing faster than it had for decades; in fact, the Hispanic community

FIGURE 27–1   The DiverseCity Writing Series Time Line

1998	1999	2000	2001	2002	2003	2004	2005
	Bridges Newsletter						
		DiverseCity Writing Series					
		Single Partner					
					DiverseCity Writing Series (Multi-Group)		

has doubled over the last ten years. This dramatic change has brought with it growing pains similar to those many Mountain West states are facing. Most notable are challenges about who belongs in the community—and to whom the community belongs—leading to conflict and isolation.

Spinning off of the *Bridges* newsletter's purpose to interview residents and share the stories of the community—in essence, writing *for* or *about* the community—the DiverseCity Writing Series moved the college into writing *with* the community (Deans). In this new version of community building, the words and writing would be those of the people who lived in the community, rather than enlisting students to interview residents and interpret and present their stories. In some ways, the new project moved towards what Jay Robinson describes as "the empowerment of individuals to speak freely in such voices as they have about matters that concern them, matters of importance, so that conversation may be nourished" (*Conversations* 284). The initial purpose was to move from the student-interpretations of community presented in the *Bridges* newsletter, to self-presentation of those voices by the people in the community. Many higher education-community partnerships have been started with similar intentions, such as the one described in "Unsheltered Lives" by Carol Winkleman, who facilitated a writing project with a battered women's support group. This intention appears to lead to many such projects focusing on "life stories" or narrative writing, which, interestingly, in many institutions has been mostly removed from academic writing curricula.

The initial proposal for the pilot DWS, submitted to the college's administration for financial support, included the following language:

> The DiverseCity Writing Series aims to provide individuals with opportunities to express themselves and to be understood by their communities. People who have been silenced by cultural, institutional or historical forces need a safe, encouraging, and educational environment in which to create their stories. When people write about their lives, and are valued for doing so, confidence and personal insight grow. Analysis of the surrounding community can lead to increased interest in, and dedication to, participating in that community. Also, when those stories are shared, we will raise awareness--and hopefully understanding—of the myriad of people in this community who make Salt Lake their home. (Rousculp)

Although two students were involved with the project (English majors earning credit through the college's Co-operative Education program), the DiverseCity Writing Series was established outside the typical service-learning course paradigm. Together, the two students and I met three times with the staff of a local low-income women's advocacy organization, Justice, Economic Dignity and Independence for Women (JEDI), to explore the possibilities for a writing partnership between the organization and the college. We agreed on a proposal that would establish an eight-week writing workshop for six to eight of JEDI's clients and/or staff. The participants would write in response to informal writing assignments that explored themes of self and community. At the end of the project, the CWC would produce a 'zine of their writing and sponsor a reading held for their families, friends, and the general public.

Over the next year and a half, the DWS program partnered the college with three additional community organizations: 1) The Road Home homeless shelter, 2) the Liberty Senior Center, and 3) the Cancer Wellness House. Each eight-week workshop focused on assignments with themes of self and community and culminated in 'zine publications and public readings. During this same period of time, the Community Writing Center had opened its space downtown. After the fourth round of the DWS, students who staffed the CWC felt that the program had reached a type of stasis and began to brainstorm ways to revise it. Sara Gunderson, a CWC Writing Assistant from Salt Lake Community College, researched alternatives and learned about two model programs: Write around Portland, in Oregon; and the Neighborhood Writing Alliance, in Chicago. Both had multiple groups that met regularly and came together for anthologized publication and communal presentation. The Write around Portland program partnered with non-profits, while the Neighborhood Writing Alliance facilitated public writing groups in community locations such as libraries. We thought that the DiverseCity Writing Series might be able to evolve into something similar. As I was by then directing the Community Writing Center and was occupied with its multiple programs, Gunderson took on the task of expanding the DiverseCity Writing Series as a part of her work as a CWC Writing Assistant. Working about ten hours a week together, Gunderson and I spent the next six months revising it into a multi-group year-round writing program.

The expansion of the DiverseCity Writing Series started with five writing groups—three associated with local organizations (an adult literacy center, a senior center, and a teen arts program), and two "public" groups (one meeting at the Community Writing Center and the other at a city library). Volunteers from the community were trained by the CWC to mentor the groups using collaborative, non-directive approaches. To recruit volunteers, we utilized local newspapers, radio stations, and community service websites. A typical volunteer donates approximately four hours a month to the DiverseCity Writing Series and remains with the program for 18 months (Figure 27–2).

The groups met every other week and at the end of six months, participants submitted their writing to an anthologized publication; each submitter was guaranteed to have at least one piece of writing published. As with the previous version of the DWS, these submissions were left unedited by the DiverseCity Writing Series coordinator; the words of the community were to be presented as is, not interpreted by another party. With funding from an SLCC grants program, the anthology, designed and laid out by myself and Gunderson, was printed professionally and distributed to workshop participants, city and county libraries, and area community centers. (To offset some of the publishing expenses, copies of the anthology are sold at the public reading events and on consignment at bookstores.) To celebrate the publication, all participants were invited to share their work in a public reading held at a local art gallery.

During the past two and a half years, the DiverseCity Writing Series has published five anthologies of community writing, staged five public readings

FIGURE 27–2   Roles of Community, Students, and Faculty in DWS Evolution

	Bridges Newsletter	DiverseCity Writing Series (Single Partner)	DiverseCity Writing Series (Multi-Group)
Community	Subjects	Writers	Writers and Volunteer Group Mentors
Students	Writers (Service Learning)	Assist writers and DWS facilitator (Co-op Education and CWC Writing Assistants)	DWS Program Coordinator (CWC Writing Assistant)
Faculty (myself)	Course Instructor (Service Learning)	DWS Facilitator	CWC Director

(each attended by nearly 100 community members), and expanded to eight writing groups including the Liberty Senior Center, the Literacy Action Center, the Gay, Lesbian, Bi-Sexual and Transgendered Community Center of Utah, Centro Civico Mexicano, an Adult Day Treatment Center, and an environmental writing public group at the local REI retailer. It has received four small grants from private and governmental foundations and a fair share of positive publicity from the local media.

With these revisions in place—multiple writing groups, varied distinctions of diversity, and workshops led by mentors from the community instead of students and faculty from the college—we felt we had taken a step beyond Deans's construction of writing *with* the community into a new model of a higher education-community partnership. Currently, the DWS appears to be emerging as its own set of multiple discourse communities, supported, but not constructed, by an educational institution. Each writing group is developing its own identity and style of interaction, while at the same time remaining a part of the matrix of groups within the larger program. Some have organized open houses to showcase their writing groups to their communities; others have established open mic evenings; and still others have created their own "mini-'zines" on a particular theme. No longer are the DiverseCity Writing Series groups the province of the community college; rather they constitute a matrix of dynamic partnerships between the Community Writing Center and the writers and volunteers who mentor them, a sum of multiple distinct participants.

REVISING TOWARDS SUSTAINABILITY

For the DiverseCity Writing Series to reach sustainability, extensive commitment from Salt Lake Community College and community partners (collaborating organizations and individual participants alike) has been required, which, as I argue below, has evolved through critical revision into fully shared ownership of the program by the community and the college. At the same time, the DiverseCity Writing Series, as a part of the Community Writing Center, has met the needs of the community college as well, thus securing its continued funding.

FINDING MUTUALLY BENEFICIAL RELATIONSHIPS

With the emergence of service-learning and other community-based educational approaches, working beyond the institutional walls is becoming more and more pervasive at colleges and universities across the nation. According to the American Association for Community Colleges, in 2004, 600 out of the 1,200 community colleges offered service-learning already within their curriculum and at least 35–40% of the rest were considering it. These programs often emerge from community "service commitment to the local community" (Serow and Calleson 5). This "service commitment" was a key rationale for the Community Writing Center's development. As Dr. Helen Cox, SLCC Associate Academic Vice President noted, "[The college had] a desire to serve presently un-served diverse populations." SLCC is similar to most community colleges across the nation, whose missions include the creation of access, educational opportunity, centers of adult education, and community outreach.

While community colleges have a longstanding tradition of responding to community needs through non-credit and/or certificate courses, four-year colleges and universities also provide multiple learning opportunities to the public through lectures, life-long learning programs, and other specialized instructional programs, including a dramatic increase in service-learning. At many institutions, faculty awards, recognition, and requirements for tenure now include service components. In 2004, Campus Compact noted at least thirteen four-year college/university model programs focusing on writing outreach. A significant portion of these outreach programs is based in a service-learning model, which is understandable, given that most four-year colleges and universities have student-centered missions that require innovations to tie directly into their students' learning experiences.

Regardless of the motivation to move outside of the institutional walls, one hurdle that colleges and universities often face when working with the community is the negative perception from past experiences. Sometimes, an institution's research goals can unintentionally override the mutually-beneficial relationships that colleges and universities can have with their surrounding communities, thus alienating the community partner who may end up feeling objectified by the partnership. As Ellen Cushman notes in her article "Sustainable Service Learning," "Mistrust of university researchers is not uncommon in the communities where universities are located" (40). Cushman skillfully argues for a model of sustainable university-community partnerships that requires service-learning professors to view the "community site as a place where their research, teaching, and service contribute to a community's self-defined needs and students' learning" (40). However, community colleges can draw upon a model different from that of the university. In fact, one advantage that community college faculty may have in working with the community is that research and publication are not typically requirements for tenure. By following collaborative methods, and expecting fully-shared commitment and responsibility from its partners in reaching mutually-determined educational goals, higher education institutions can undo previous experiences (Peck, Flower, and Higgins; Judkins and LaHurd). When a partner organization realizes that a proposed collaboration is not a pretext to research, barriers can drop and positive experiences go a long way to spreading the word to other community organizations and individuals.

Another factor that influences the community's perception of the higher educational institution is the extent to which the college is committed to the partnership—particularly by providing resources for its continuance. However, a college (specifically its administration and/or boards of trustees and regents) must be able to see clearly how the institution benefits from a community partnership in order to commit its resources for more than an interesting new trial run. Tapping into the institution's publicly promoted values and mission, and drawing overt attention to the ways the community project helps the college fulfill that mission can be a strong argument for continued support.

At Salt Lake Community College, the Community Writing Center has received support from all levels of administration. In addition to community-minded college leaders, I believe this support has been partly due to our vigilance in showing how the Community Writing Center, and especially the DiverseCity Writing Series, directly promotes SLCC's mission, values, and goals, which include:

- Community: We value community involvement and economic development.
- Creativity: We value creativity, innovation, and responsible risk-taking.
- Diversity: We value personal, cultural, and ethnic diversity.

In addition, we have drawn constant attention to three of the college's six goals—A Learning College, Diversity, and A Partner in the Community— throughout the development of the Community Writing Center and the DiverseCity Writing Series. Seemingly, our efforts to do this have resonated with the college leaders. What started five-and-a-half years ago with a one-time $500 matching contribution from the School of Humanities for the Utah Humanities Council grant request that started the DiverseCity Writing Series has evolved into a annual six-figure hard-funded budget. The college also proudly "claims" the Community Writing Center; on the "Community Services Education" page of the SLCC website, along with two other community-focused programs, it reads: "SLCC's award-winning Community Writing Center brings together new and experienced writers, blending diverse voices in community publications, readings and discussion groups."

While the institutional support for the CWC and the DiverseCity Writing Series has continued to grow, commitment from the community partners has been equally important. For this to be achieved, it was necessary that the DiverseCity Writing Series be jointly owned by both the college and the community; it needed to move into a completely shared partnership, not one offered to the people by the college. As I describe in the paragraphs that follow, we made significant revisions to the DiverseCity Writing Series between the single-group and multi-group versions—based on close analysis of the first version—that attempted to balance the agency of the college and the community. It appears, based on the continuation of the program and its steady growth, that we have come a significant way towards reaching this goal.

INTERROGATING OWNERSHIP

While the first version of the DiverseCity Writing Series intended to move ownership of the community-based writing from students to the community itself, upon reflection, the Community Writing Center retained significant agency over the process and presentation of the writing. In the first version, the CWC proposed for the partner's acceptance that the writing in the workshops—designed to "help" the participants "find their voices"—would "explore self and community" through a series of informal writing assignments. One reason this approach was taken was that we had to do so in order to receive a small grant from the Utah Humanities Council (the local National Endowment for the Humanities branch), which required that a "scholar" lead community members through their learning experiences. As can be seen in a passage from that grant proposal, the CWC is clearly the active agent in the collaboration: "In this partnership, [the CWC will] provide opportunities and assistance for the individual writer to create written records of life stories, personal and political opinions, and self/community reflection." In addition to the grant requirements, this was the first time I had stepped fully outside of the discourses of the classroom environment into writing with the community, and the structure provided by the workshop approach was a more accessible bridge to the writing than the completely open forum into which the DWS has evolved.

Even so, as the first DiverseCity Writing Series writing workshop progressed, it appeared that the participants were taking the "assignments" into their own hands for their own purposes. With the typical motivating factors of compliance that influence students (grades, credit, career goals) removed, the participants changed the dynamics of the teacher-learner relationship, attending sporadically and selectively responding to the writing prompts. I was concerned that the project was doomed to failure, but at the end, the project evaluation indicated, "Although the project seemed tenuous at times during our eight-week workshop, the resulting 'zine and public reading exceeded all expectations. Seven writers contributed eleven pieces of writing to the 'zine and over 50 people attended the public reading at a local café." Some of the writers jumped at the chance to write about themselves: two women combined all of the writing prompts into extended memoirs and self-analyses. However, others went in their own directions: one woman wrote an elegy for her recently deceased mother; another included a manifesto of sorts about the state of women in poverty. In the three other partnerships in the first version of the DWS, the CWC still provided writing prompts to elicit writing about the relationship between self and community, but encouraged the participants to use them only as starting points as was useful for them; "personal story" began to expand into fiction, parody, essay, and verse.

Upon reflection, Sara Gunderson and I agreed that the thematic focus of the writing workshops in the first version of the DiverseCity Writing Series was assuming too much agency in the partnerships. As we re-envisioned an expanded DWS, we considered expanding the themes, or soliciting project-wide themes from the multiple writing groups, like "power" or "freedom" in order to unite the participants in purpose and discussion. However, in the end we decided that the individual participants, and the writing communities that would emerge from them, should determine both genres and topics.

Another way we discovered that the Community Writing Center assumed too much agency in the first version of the DiverseCity Writing Series was in the presentation of the publications. I, and the students assisting me, tended to "interpret" the writings in the 'zine publications in the introductions that we wrote for them. As Todd DeStigter notes in his article, "Good Deeds: An Ethnographer's Reflections on Usefulness," "Any cross-cultural 'translation' . . . includes potentially oppressive self-representation: that is, usurping the ownership of another person's experience and putting it into our own terms" (36). These introductions, which we thought of as "frames" for the participants' writing, unintentionally interpreted the community's voices, just as service learning students had done with the stories in the *Bridges* newsletter. For example, in the publication from The Road Home workshop, the Introduction begins "In this, the second DiverseCity Writing Series publication, writers from The Road Home describe what it's like to be a member of a homeless community, and also what it takes to remain an individual in this most transient of populations." While this may seem benign, and even though we were vigilant about keeping the writing "as is," leaving misspellings and creative grammar choices intact, this introduction categorized the writing contained within the publication into two specific foci, and perhaps diverted attention from a reader's ability to perceive the wider range of topics and contributions that were present within it.

In the second version of the DiverseCity Writing Series, in which the publications anthologized writing from the multiple groups, we still included an introduction, but stayed away from interpreting or categorizing. The Introduction that Gunderson wrote to the first collective anthology demonstrates this:

> A couple of times while compiling this anthology, I called my brother in Tucson and said, "Okay, I have to read this to you—it's so good." Other times, I stopped colleagues of mine and asked if I could read them an excerpt from a particularly provocative piece. There is some excellent work in **Sine Cera**, and that's cool because it's all written by people from our community—people we stand in line with at the grocery store, people we sit next to on the bus.

And hopefully what this shows is that anyone can write. So many people believe that the only good writers are published writers, and that just isn't true. Yes, some of the authors in this anthology have been previously published, but the majority of them have not. In fact, for some, the work found here is their first ever writing endeavor.

With this in mind, we titled the anthology **Sine Cera** (SInay-Kera). The term is Latin and means "without wax." And as the story goes, "sine cera" was used to describe a sculpture created without flaws, thus not needing wax to fill-in fissures or chips. It is believed that "sine cera" is the Latin root of the word sincere. A sincere sculpture. A sincere effort. And so, we adopted this term to be the name of the DiverseCity Writing Series Anthology.

Anyone can write. That's what the DiverseCity Writing Series shows. And with writing comes power. Power to move your reader, power to express yourself. Power to take small black symbols and incite rage, lust, or nostalgia. Power to heal.

So, read on and enjoy. And maybe sometime, if you feel like it, pick up a pen and try scribbling something down. Who knows, it might even be good.

It is possible that the participants in the first version of the DiverseCity Writing Series could have written the introductions to their 'zines themselves. But, at the end of each eight week workshop, the writers were so busy finishing up their own pieces for the 'zine and preparing for the public reading, that there was no desire to focus on a piece of collaborative writing. This was not surprising to us, given the resistance that students in writing classes often express about collaborative writing projects. Outside of the classroom space, the DiverseCity Writing Series participants took what they wanted from these workshops, rather than engaging in collaborative writing to analyze and present their writing. Based on the development of the writing groups during the second version of the DiverseCity Writing Series, it seems that community writers—in order to collaboratively write—need a motivating factor that emerges from within the group, rather than one of "empowerment" as defined by an educational institution. Recently, some of the groups, in what we loosely call the "third version" of the DiverseCity Writing Series, have determined their own themes of writing for a period of time and compiled their own mini-'zines that they have collaboratively designed and produced outside of the DWS program.

Another issue that we confronted in the revision of the DiverseCity Writing Series, was that the partnerships always focused on a disenfranchised group, an "other." We analyzed the groups with whom we had partnered, and noticed that through the selection of "oppressed" or "othered" populations (low-income women, the elderly, the homeless, the ill), that we were, in fact, making a determination of what diversity meant, and, again unintentionally, falling into the kinds of exploitive relationships that higher education-community collaborations can engender. This revealed itself, again, in the introductions to the 'zines, as can be seen in the Liberty Senior Center publication:

In many other cultures, stories from elders are sought out for guidance, comfort, and life lessons. In our country, senior citizens are often ignored, much less listened to for the wisdom in their stories. Sometimes they are dismissed as unwise or thoughtless, their opinions irrelevant to our harried lives. However, it takes less than a short second to realize these stories come from mindful and experienced people, stories that flow from the thoughts and memories, and sometimes painful hands, of our senior writers.

On the surface, this type of presentation appears to be merely respectful of a population that is often dismissed in our culture. However, as bell hooks eloquently presents in *Yearning: Race, Gender and Cultural Politics*:

> No need to hear your voice when I can talk about you better than you can speak about yourself. No need to hear your voice. Only tell me about your pain. I want to know your story. And, then I will tell it back to you in a new way. Tell it back to you in such a way that it has become mine, my own. Re-writing you as I write myself anew. I am still author, authority. I am still colonizer, the speaking subject, and you are now at the center of my talk. (151)[2]

To avoid this dynamic, we decided to construct a combination of the programs that we'd researched by including some writing groups associated with local organizations that supported "othered" communities, such as the Literacy Action Center (a non-profit dedicated to helping adults learn to read) and the Gay, Lesbian, Bi-sexual, Transgender Community Center of Utah; yet we also established public groups open to anyone, located both at the CWC and at one of the city's libraries. We decided that a truly diverse program was one that honored the complex subtleties of a community, rather than relying on culturally-determined identity politics to select who would be invited to participate. In fact, the program has since evolved to include what might be considered a "privileged" demographic—environmentalists—with the establishment of a sustained environmental writing group that meets at the local R.E.I. retailer.

FOLLOWING THE COMMUNITY'S LEAD

One other revision to the DiverseCity Writing Series as it moved from the first to the second versions was that the volunteer group mentors were expected to share their writing with the writers in equal ways. In the first version, none of the participants in the DWS groups had expected me or the student assistants to share our writing with them as they were with us, with one exception: the Road Home homeless shelter writing group, which was made up of current and previous shelter residents along with shelter staff members (social workers and case managers). The staff members participating in the workshop all had similar education to me—master's degrees or higher—and their professions were socio-economically similar to mine. Perhaps this contributed to their awareness of the inherent contradictions that were being made when I referenced collaborative practices and critical pedagogies of empowerment, yet was not sharing my own writing with them. They requested that I write something for the public reading, because if they had to get up in front of people and bare their souls through writing, then I did too. Although I emotionally resisted this request, they were right, and I shared a personal essay at the reading. In the current version of the DWS, the group mentors (volunteers from the community) are expected to write along with the people who participate in the groups. Not surprisingly, just as writing center tutors often report that tutoring helps them improve their own writing as much as their tutees', the mentors note that the writing groups help with their own writing.

In some ways, these writing groups have created versions of "habitable spaces" as coined by Jay Robinson, and noted by Cathy Fleischer and David Schaafsma in their "Introduction" to *Literacy and Democracy*. "What is crucial to the fostering of such a conception [of literacy]," they explain, "is the development of a 'habitable space,' a common place, a safe place, where conversation can begin and where meaning might be negotiated to create communities in which literacy might flourish" (xx). David Gravelle, a mentor for the GLBTCCU writing group said, "The writers in my group really value the space we've created, and I feel fortunate to be helping to sustain that space. Watching them work with each other, and watching them give and be influenced by each other's feedback, has inspired me in my own writing."

Even though writing with the group is a type of requirement, or expectation, of the mentors, we have found that it is easier for some of the mentors to disregard these expectations than it is for the writers. Melissa Helquist, a mentor for the Literacy Action Center writing group, noted a moment when she elected not to follow the assignment that her group had established for itself:

> The writers decided that their writing topic would be "abandonment," something they all felt they'd encountered in their lives: in personal relationships, in the education system, etc.—that the abandonment they'd encountered had in some way halted their learning process. Often, I'll also write on whatever topic was chosen, but this time, I felt that the topic was too challenging, only presenting uncomfortable emotional disclosure. So, I wrote nothing. One of the writers took on the topic and wrote a very thoughtful and painful reflection on abandonment throughout her life. She had not necessarily wanted to write about abandonment, but that was, as she said, simply "the assignment." This was a writing-related and personal challenge, but only the writers made the effort. The two facilitators did not do the work. Even though writers in the group always have the choice not to write on a specific topic, as *students* they feel more pressure than we as teachers feel. The risk is much less significant for us.

I believe that this construction of "students/teachers" in this particular group is a response to its evolution as a type of "hierarchical collaboration" as described by Andrea Lunsford and Lisa Ede as interactions between learner and teachers that are unambiguous in terms of authority and responsibilities

(153). While most of the writing groups operate in a collaborative feedback model—participants bring in their writing for feedback from the group and work collaboratively on revisions, and sometimes topic generation—two of the groups, the Literacy Action Center and the Valley Mental Health group, have requested more "classroom-based" instruction in the partnerships. The adults in the Literacy Action Center see themselves as needing to learn from their mentor. The case workers with whom we collaborated on the development of the Valley Mental Health group felt a classroom-based workshop would fit in with their daily schedule of life skills courses.

In addition, the illnesses and brain injuries the writers in the Valley Mental Health group are coping with prevent them from engaging in most levels of revision; nearly all of their writing is done in the moment, and then turned in for consideration for publication in the anthologies. This also runs counter to the process in all of the other groups, which spend a majority of their time on the processes of revision and feedback. While it may appear that this type of collaboration contradicts the CWC's intention to transfer the agency from itself to the participants in the writing groups, it is actually a manifestation of just that purpose; similar to the discovery that Thomas Philion made in his literacy work with middle-school urban students that, "While I retained a commitment to the idea of making dynamic connections between classrooms and the larger world, I began to conceive the need to subordinate this goal to the less ambitious but equally vital aim of involving students actively in reading, writing, listening and speaking" (67). The CWC responded to the expertise of the adult literacy and mental health professionals and co-constructed writing groups that could accommodate their clients' needs, rather than adhering to our own assumptions about the best approaches to creating writing communities.

As we revised the DiverseCity Writing Series, we wanted to move away from the focus on the individual's relationship with the community and towards the relationships that exist within a community, the shared-ness of writing and its power to bridge differences. The first expansion goal stated, "The DiverseCity Writing Series operates under the idea that writing has the power to unite a community and build bridges over social chasms such as economic disparity and racial intolerance." We wanted to move in a direction similar to the one described by Jay Robinson in "Literacy and Lived Lives," about his work with high school writing and publishing collaborations:

> We wanted these publishing projects, these introductions into the uses of written language, to serve as antidotes to debilitating forms of separation, isolation and loneliness [between two high schools]. . . . We were seeking to make and remake a public, through engagement in a common project, in which language could be used to translate the deeply personal, which can only be deeply felt, in to the public character words can achieve as readers open their minds to worlds authors can shape for them. (7)

As we worked through the experiences and products of the first version of the DiverseCity Writing Series, however, we realized it was not possible for the Community Writing Center, as an institution of the community college, to continue to be the primary agent and meet these goals. The project had to become jointly shared by the college and the community and provide mutually-beneficial ends to each. Over the past two and a half years, it seems that this has been achieved.

NOTES

1. Between 1997 and 2001, I worked with Stephen Ruffus, Chair of the SLCC English Department, to found the CWC. Though I am currently the director of the CWC, I have maintained my faculty status at the college and still teach for the English department. As this article shows, this work has given me the opportunity to interact with the community in several different roles (service learning faculty, community publishing facilitator, and director).

2. Interestingly, one popularly successful documentary, *What I Want My Words to Do to You*, details a writing group in a women's prison facilitated by writer Eve Ensler (author of *Vagina Monologues*), in which the participants' writing was "read back to them" in a final performance by Hollywood celebrities.

WORKS CITED

American Association for Community Colleges. *Horizons Service Learning Project*. (2004). http://www.aacc.nche.edu/Content/NavigationMenu/ResourceCenter/Projects_Partnerships/Current/HorizonsServiceLearningProject/HorizonsServiceLearningProject.htm. 22 Jun. 2004.

Cox, Helen. Personal Interview. 22 May 2004.

Cushman, Ellen. "Sustainable Service Learning Programs." *College Composition and Communication*, 64.1 (2002): 40–65.

Deans, Thomas. *Writing Partnerships: Service Learning in Composition*. Urbana, IL: NCTE, 2000.

DeStigter, Todd. "Good Deeds: An Ethnographer's Reflections on Usefulness." Fleischer and Schaafsma, 28–52.

Fleischer, Cathy, and David Schaafsma. "Introduction: Further Conversations: Jay Robinson, His Students, and the Study of Literacy." Fleischer and Schaafsma, xiii–xxxii.

Fleischer, Cathy, and David Schaafsma. *Literacy and Democracy: Teacher Research and Composition Studies in Pursuit of Habitable Spaces: Further Conversations from the Students of Jay Robinson*. Urbana, IL: NCTE, 1998.

Gravelle, David. Personal Interview. 12 May 2005.

Helquist, Melissa. "No subject." Personal e-mail sent to author. 25 July 2005.

hooks, bell. *Yearning: Race, Gender and Cultural Politics*. Boston: South End Press, 1990.

Judkins, Bennet M., and Ryan A. LaHurd. "Building Community from Diversity: Addressing the Changing Demographics of Academia and Society." *American Behavioral Scientist*, 42 (1999): 780–93.

Lunsford, Andrea, and Lisa Ede. *Singular Texts/Plural Authors: Perspectives on Collaborative Writing*. Carbondale: Southern Illinois Press, 1990.

Peck, Wayne C., Linda Flower, and Lorraine Higgins. "Community Literacy." *College Composition and Communication*, 46 (1995): 199–222.

Philion, Thomas. "Three Codifications of Critical Literacy." Fleischer and Schaafsma, 53–81.

Robinson, Jay. *Conversations on the Written Word: Essays on Language and Literacy*. Portsmouth, NH: Boynton/Cook, 1990.

———. "Literacy and Lived Lives: Reflections on the Responsibilities of Teachers." Fleischer and Schaafsma, 1–27.

Rousculp, Tiffany. "Pilot Project: DiverseCity Writing Series-JEDI for Women." Proposal to Salt Lake Community College Administration. 29 September 2000.

Ruffus, Stephen. Personal Interview. 12 August 2004.

Serow, Robert C., and Diane C. Calleson. "Service-Learning and the Institutional Mission of Community Colleges." *Community College Review*, 23 (1996): 3–14.

Winkleman, Carol L. "Unsheltered Lives: Battered Women Talk about School." Fleischer and Schaafsma, 104–34.

PART SIX

*Pedagogies
in Action*

28

Tapping the Potential of Service-Learning: Guiding Principles for Redesigning Our Composition Courses

CHERYL HOFSTETTER DUFFY

I was nervous because I thought some American people didn't like Asian people and my English skill was quite bad, so I was afraid that I could not make a good conversation with them. Before "get-together," I had never had a conversation with American students. I was afraid that they spoke too fast and I might not understand them. However, I was wrong. After I talked with them, I found that they were very nice.

It was fun to get to know a student that is from another country. That was the closest I ever got to another student that wasn't my own culture.

Based in part on student reflections like these, I deemed my first foray into service-learning a success. Our "International Connections" project linked one section of English 101 (first-year composition) students at Fort Hays State University with students from the nearby Hays Language Institute, where international students come to learn English. We invited international students to our classroom for an initial meeting and listened while they introduced themselves and participated in a question-and-answer session. Later, we hosted a more social get-together, where U.S. students brought food and everyone participated in getting-to-know-you activities. Ultimately, FHSU students each drew the name of an international student to interview one-on-one, later using that information and experience as the basis for a paper in their composition class. Thus, international students had the opportunity to practice their English and socialize with U.S. students, while U.S. students broke down some cultural barriers and ended up with content for their writing as well.

I was glad to be finally participating in service-learning (or *community-based writing*, the terminology preferred by many who fear the word service places too much emphasis on server expertise and the neediness of the

From *Reflections* 3.1 (2003): 1–14.

served[1]). It is an increasingly enticing option for composition faculty drawn to the promises of greater student engagement and more meaningful learning. Service-learning is clearly established and growing within the field of composition studies.

Ideally, composition faculty would avail themselves of this wealth of thinking and theorizing before ever attempting to teach a service-learning class, to ensure a coherent, thoughtfully critical program. Ideally. I, however, was eager to begin and too overwhelmed as a newly appointed director of composition to do much delving beforehand. Within the series of developmental stages through which Chris Anson asserts that service-learning teachers pass, I was definitely at stage one: full of initial enthusiasm and commitment (177). So, based on a couple of conference sessions attended, a couple of workshops on service-learning at neighboring Kansas State University, and a couple of articles out of *Reflections*, I dived in. And that might be what most of us have to do—after all, how many of us who teach composition for a living have the time to do a complete review of the literature? Unless one focuses on service-learning as part of his or her doctoral work or, perhaps, as part of one's sabbatical research, gathering the necessary background information and insight to implement service-learning may well seem too daunting a task.

This article, then, is an attempt to provide some of that background and insight in one place, and to do so in the context of my own evolving service-learning course. During the semester immediately following my first attempt at service-learning with the International Connections project, I had the good fortune of going on sabbatical to (among other things) research service-learning. It was a humbling experience. The more I read, the more I saw what I should have done differently. Despite its limited success, my first community-based writing project could have been so much more—for both the international students and my composition students. The purpose of this article, then, is to give a nod to that success and, more importantly, to trace the shortcomings of that first attempt and the subsequent improvements made in light of the thoughtful service-learning work that has gone before me. That is, I follow the advice of B. Cole Bennett, who reminds service-learning faculty of how crucial it is "that we continue to critically monitor our progress, investigating our failures while we rejoice in our successes" (18).

THE SUCCESSES

The most positive result of the International Connections project was the (albeit limited) achievement of both academic and cultural goals. Through their participation in this project, 101 students honed their interviewing and note-taking skills as they worked one-on-one with the international students. Later, 101 students focused their ideas and organized them into academic papers—perhaps a comparison/contrast piece, a profile of an international student, or a critical analysis of U.S. life through international eyes. Their work on these papers followed common writing classroom practices: discussing ideas, drafting papers, giving and receiving peer response, and revising final drafts.

A primary cultural goal of the project was to begin bridging the gap of "otherness," especially prevalent at a rural institution like Fort Hays State University in western Kansas. The Midwest is not known for its diversity, and many students come to FHSU having had little or no contact with someone from a different culture. Although international students—both those enrolled at FHSU and those from the nearby language institute—are a fairly common sight on campus, they often cluster in groups, and U.S. students, while ready to smile and offer a quick Midwestern "hi," rarely move beyond that superficial greeting into real conversation. In "Surprised by Service: Creating Connections through Community-Based Writing," Linda Cullum writes of "the melting away—at least temporarily—of stereotypes, fears, and ignorance of the 'other'" when students meet and work "with people with whom they might otherwise never come into contact" (9).

That melting away process certainly began during our International Connections project. For example, before we began the project, a U.S. student wrote in his reflection journal that international students "don't seem very friendly. They aren't the type of people that would say hi as they pass you on the sidewalk." That misperception was cleared up at our first question-and-answer session when a 101 student asked the international students, "What has surprised you the most since you've come to Hays, Kansas?" and a Korean student volunteered, "I was so surprised that people here say 'hi' to strangers! In my country, you only greet people you know. At first, I am thinking students who say 'hi' are talking to someone else, not me!"

Similar instances suggested that students were at least beginning to move beyond entrenched stereotypes and ignorance. After some initial silence at an early get-together—and a clear division of groups (with U.S. students huddled on one side of the room and international students on the other)—the room eventually filled with students mingling, talking, and laughing. A U.S. student wrote in his reflection journal: "One question seemed to lead to another and then it seemed that we were just talking. . . . We were able to laugh and joke around with each other." (Note the undertone of surprise that one could actually talk easily and have fun with someone from a different culture.) Another student wrote of the experience: "It got rid of any stereotypes that were wrongly in my head, like, you can't talk to one [an international student] because they don't know English." (I suspect, though, that the experience more realistically *challenged* a few stereotypes, rather than "got rid of" them all.) I found the following two entries from separate students to be especially heartening: "I probably would have never met any international students if we didn't have this activity" and "We've been e-mailing back and forth every night since [the get-together]." The international students overcame a few fears as well, as noted in the opening quotation of this article and in the following reflection: "I thought I couldn't understand well what students say because they speak so fastly. But I could more understand than I thought it. It was very helpful to me. It was easier than I thought it. I enjoyed it."

Finally, students began addressing their stereotypes and assumptions as they wrote their papers for class. One student, Rhonda, originally planned to write a paper about the *differences* between Japanese and U.S. education. After her interview session, however, she decided instead to write on the *similarities* between Japanese teenagers and her own teenaged children here in the U.S. Another student, Charlotte, opens her paper with the line, "The first thought that comes into my head when I see a person of a different race or ethnic background is that I more than likely don't have a lot in common with that person." Throughout her paper, though, she traces the many similarities she shares with Pok, a student from Thailand, and in her conclusion she writes:

> I used to think that because people did not speak the same language as I did, that they would have nothing in common with me. I now realize this is not the case. Pok comes from halfway across the globe and we still have so much in common, and our cultures are really not as different as I thought that they would be. Many countries may seem far from similar to America; however, that may not be the case. People simply need to take the time and initiative to figure that out.

Though somewhat naive, such thinking is also tentatively encouraging. The Thai student's otherness has been reduced in Charlotte's eyes—because of her discovery that he shares interests and experiences consistent with her U.S. experience. A next step might be for her to accept and appreciate those aspects of Pok's experience that do not coincide with her own—for her to move beyond her notion of "whiteness [. . . as] the unexamined norm," a concept addressed in the insightful book *Why Are All the Black Kids Sitting Together in the Cafeteria?* by Beverly Daniel Tatum (93).

THE FAILURES

On the whole, however, the papers were disappointing. Only one student chose to tackle the challenging topic of looking at the U.S. through international eyes; everyone else opted for the simpler approaches of narrative, comparison/contrast, or biographical profile. Those genres do not necessarily preclude critical analysis, but for this particular assignment, sadly, almost all such papers lacked critical depth. I blame that in large part on my own uninformed planning. First of all, there was not enough *time*. The International Connections project was a two-and-a-half-week unit tucked into the middle of the semester, unrelated topically to what had gone before and what would follow. The only required contact with international students was the initial panel discussion and the get-together with a follow-up interview. Most 101 students started their interviews toward the end of the get-together, and some even *finished* them on the spot—meaning they had only two meetings with the international students before beginning to write. Is it any wonder, then, that many 101 students at the writing stage complained that they did not have enough material for my modest 2–5-page requirement?

In an article in *Reflections* Hannah M. Ashley reports on her service-learning endeavors in Philadelphia, where first-year writers are linked with older adults to participate in literacy tutoring. After "an initial getting-to-know-you and match-up luncheon," students meet numerous times with the seniors to collaborate with them on memoirs, letters, and other literacy projects (11). What for her students was merely an introduction to the service-learning project (the get-acquainted activity and luncheon) was, for my students, almost our entire project. We simply did not have enough of the "person-to-person dialogue" necessary for intercultural understanding (Flower, "Partners" 107).

We also did not have enough opportunities for the kinds of critical reflection that might have informed the 101 students' writing, fostering greater critical depth. As Bruce Herzberg warns us, "The community service experience doesn't bring an epiphany of critical consciousness—or even, necessarily, an epiphany of conscience" (315). Instead, that experience must be couched in some sort of intellectual context, surrounded by readings, discussion, and critical reflection. Without such careful attention to analysis, Aaron Schutz and Anne Ruggles Gere assert, "we may end up reinforcing ideologies and assumptions we had hoped to critique" (147). Such was the case in at least one instance during the International Connections project, when cultural awareness seemed to be lacking entirely. One U.S. student used his paper to contrast Japanese and American food—emphasizing the weird and substandard nature of the other culture's diet. His paper dripped with sarcasm: "Who *wouldn't* prefer slimy raw fish to a thick, juicy steak?" He might have thought he was being funny, but he was actually being ethnocentric and unthinking. Rather than bridging gaps, our project—with its inadequate reading/thinking/discussing—in this case had only reinforced notions of superiority and "otherness."

Hand in hand with critical pedagogy is Edward Zlotkowski's call for greater academic rigor within service-learning programs. The success of such community-based programs over the long haul, Zlotkowski contends, will hinge on their ability to link community experience with traditional academic goals. While International Connections students did write traditional classroom papers, their learning and the project itself could have been enhanced by the kinds of readings, intellectual collaboration, and traditional research practices common in the academy. Without such rigor, the program might be guilty of what Laura Julier calls "feel-good pedagogy" (135), or it might find itself on the low end of the dichotomous description of service-learning offered by Alice Reich: "from a warm-fuzzy to an academically rigorous experience; from course add-on to an integral component" (5).

MOVING IN THE RIGHT DIRECTION

My first step toward revision was to expand the scope and time factor of the project. While I would not have needed to take such an extreme step, I decided to spread the International Connections project essentially over the course of the entire semester, fully integrating the project into the design of the course and allowing plenty of opportunity for intellectual preparation and reflection. Preparation began the first week of class as students freewrote about a time when they felt themselves to be "the outsider"—writing they later developed into a personal essay. During that first week students also began reading selections from *Crossing Customs: International Students Write on U.S. College Life and Culture*, a collection of essays by international college students (Garrod and Davis). The readings explore notions of self and personal identity, and they also offer varying critiques of U.S. culture. These themes, then, informed the work of the semester as students read, reflected in their journals, participated in small- and large-group discussions, and wrote papers ranging from expressive to academic.

Expressive papers came early in the semester—the first narrating feelings of exclusion, and a second exploring how each individual student's past had shaped his or her identity (recurring themes in *Crossing Customs*). As Patricia Stock and Janet Swenson note, starting with personal writing is a logical first step, for students "learn more easily and better when they undertake a new study in terms of the images and experiences they bring to it from their home communities" (154). Moreover, concepts that might otherwise seem abstract or distant when encountered in the readings have more relevance and meaning if students have first explored those concepts in relation to their own stories (155).

My students moved into academic writing as they summarized selected essays from our reading that they anticipated using as outside sources in a later academic paper critiquing American society, compiling an annotated bibliography in MLA format. Before writing that essay, however, 101 students spent four weeks getting to know international students from the Hays Language Institute (HLI) and working on collaborative writing projects with them. (Logistically, I had to coordinate this timing with the HLI instructors, as they run four-week sessions that needed to coincide with our International Connections project; otherwise, some international students might have finished their program of study and moved on before completing the collaborative work with my 101 class.)

Aside from spending more time with the international students, composition students also spent that time in a way different from before. Our approach during the first go-around was simply too one-sided, without much mutuality. *We* questioned *them* during the initial visit, *we* planned a get-together and brought refreshments for *them*, *we* interviewed *them*, and then *we* wrote papers about *them*. Clearly, we were the agents and they were the subjects. This time we began with a reciprocal question-and-answer session, with both groups of students asking questions of each other, demonstrating that we all have much to learn *from one another*. Cooperatively, we planned the get-together, with both groups contributing ideas for the get-acquainted activity, and both groups bringing favorite foods to share.

The most significant difference, however, was the writing accomplished. This time, students formed writing teams comprised of U.S. and international students to work collaboratively on newsletters covering mutually decided-upon topics. Adam, a U.S. student, and Naruemol, a Thai student, wrote an article comparing and contrasting their two respective countries. Erika (U.S.) interviewed Takanori (Japan) and wrote a profile of him and his experiences as an international student. One team's newsletter was devoted entirely to surviving as a college student in Hays, since many HLI students go on to enroll at FHSU after completing their language study. Articles ranged from "How to Meet New People" to "How to Get a Job in Hays." Extra copies of the newsletters—printed with funds from a Learn and Serve mini-grant I secured—went to the Hays Language Institute for use with future classes, which always need high-interest, relevant reading materials in English. Writing teams in similar service-learning classes could collaborate on projects other than newsletters—perhaps a survival manual for incoming international students, or an article (or series of short articles) for the campus newspaper on such possible topics as "How to Get to Know an International Student" or "International Students Reflect on American Life." Unlike the papers students handed in the first time I attempted service-learning—papers written to the teacher—the writing done collaboratively in the revised course has a richer and more authentic rhetorical situation, with clearly defined audiences and purposes.[2]

Throughout this interaction, students kept work logs (recording the meetings held, work assigned, team deadlines set, work completed, and so on) so that the HLI instructor and I could monitor and evaluate the work of the collaborative teams. Students in English 101 also kept journals, in which they recorded their experiences, observations, and reactions. Chris Anson has cautioned that "[j]ournal writing in many service courses may serve the purpose of creating a log or record of experience, but falls short of encouraging the critical examination of ideas" (169). To avoid this pitfall, I required that students tie their journal observations whenever possible to the reading, thinking, and discussion begun during the first half of the semester. In particular, 101 students were encouraged to use readings, observations, interactions with international students, and emerging analyses to, in the second half of the semester, develop an academic argument critiquing some aspect of American culture. That paper was essentially a research paper drawing upon readings, interviews, observations, and personal experience.

The final paper for the semester was a capstone essay reflecting on the entire semester: types of writing accomplished, thinking that had expanded or changed, as well as self- and other-awareness that had developed. Students wrote about acquiring specific writing skills—like incorporating details or using MLA format. They also wrote about changes in their own thinking. Kelli wrote, "This semester of English Composition had more of an effect on me as a writer than any English class I have ever taken. . . . [W]e focused on writing in a way that forced me to realize my own personal outlook on life."

Of course, there is always the danger that students are savvy enough simply to tell us what we want to hear. At least in one case, however, a student offered tangible evidence of her changed perspective. In her capstone essay, Erika wrote of her earlier thinking: "Before our newsletter project, I was not fond of people from other countries coming to America to use our school and our money, and to steal our jobs. I could not care less whether or not I had a friend from another country." She later came to feel "truly ashamed" of that attitude. "The students I worked with were hilarious and made me laugh every day. They taught me about their country, food, and life back home. I still talk to some of the students I met through this project. . . . I respect the international students who study in America, and I am pleased they are here." The truest indication of her changed perspective came at a Student Government Association meeting where international students were requesting travel funds to attend a conference on American culture over Christmas break:

> Some of my fellow senators in Student Government felt the students were asking for a free vacation. I quickly spoke up on behalf of the international students, explaining how hard these particular students work and how much effort they put into studying in America. I also pointed out that these students have no place to go during Christmas break. The outcome to our heated debate was extremely unusual. Student Government could not grant the requested amount to the group because they were not registered as a Fort Hays State University student organization on campus. I was terribly upset by this predicament, as were many other senators. To solve this problem, several senators donated enough money to send this group of international students to their Christmas conference. If this situation had taken place before my lesson in diversity, I would have lacked involvement in this debate.

Now, I am not arguing that Erika's experience was typical, but I do offer it as evidence of the *possibilities* for real change and informed action that can emerge from a thoughtfully developed service-learning course. This example also illustrates how the capstone essay allowed Erika to process her evolving attitudes—and to link them to her service-learning experience.

Writing for the semester, then, ran the full gamut of discourse from expressive (journal entries, narratives, personal essays) to civic (collaborative projects with public purposes and audiences) to academic (annotated bibliographies and research papers) to some sort of blend (capstone essays). Students surely benefit from such a wide array of writing experience that differs from the traditional writing classroom, for as Nora Bacon reminds us, "[A]s long as we design our courses around personal and literary essays, we are teaching a tiny corner of the world of discourse" (52). While we cannot "teach it all" in one short semester, we *can* provide a variety of writing opportunities, exposing our students to more than that tiny corner.

Tom Deans gives us another way of classifying discourse within the service-learning curriculum. He organizes his book, *Writing Partnerships: Service-Learning in Composition*, around three types of service-learning writing: writing *about* the community, usually in journals and academic essays; writing *for* the community, usually nonacademic writing such as manuals, newsletters, etc.; and writing *with* the community, usually collaborative inquiry and writing (16–20). In light of these classifications, the writing within the newly revised English 101 course with the International Connections theme still includes writing *about* the community (in journal entries and course papers), and because of the increased critical pedagogy, that writing demonstrates greater intellectual depth than similar writing done during the pilot service-learning project. (For example, in writing the "Critique of American Culture" essays, students drew upon their classroom reading and their interaction with international students to write on topics ranging from educational opportunities to materialism to the American work ethic.) The course now also includes a mixture of writing *for* and *with* the community as teams of international and U.S. students put together their collaborative projects.

Closing Thoughts

Do I regret diving in without adequate theoretical grounding in service-learning? No . . . and yes. No, because I discovered that you can do almost everything wrong and still have some good results. With that first, flawed attempt, students were still engaged, wrote interesting and appropriate papers overall, cleared up certain cultural misperceptions, and began forming connections and even friendships across cultures.

But yes, I do have some regrets because I am now aware of the rich possibilities inherent in service-learning when we consciously apply the theoretical principles that composition researchers and practitioners have advanced in recent years. We owe it to ourselves and our students to tap into those principles as we design our courses:

Integration—The syllabus needs to allow enough time for meaningful interaction, and students need adequate preparation for and reflection about the service-learning project.

Critical Pedagogy and Academic Rigor—Outside readings, critical discussions, guided reflection, and use of academic discourse can ensure that the service-learning project accomplishes academic and not just altruistic goals.

Mutuality/Reciprocity—Faculty should look for ways to recognize and utilize the contributions of all parties involved, members of the community as well as members of the academy.

Diverse Discourses—Service-learning offers a ripe opportunity for students to explore varieties of written discourse (expressive, civic, and academic) for a variety of purposes (writing about, for, and with).

Certainly, trying service-learning in the first-year writing course can be a risky and time-consuming venture. Following these guiding principles, though, we can enrich our classrooms and our teaching. Alice Reich writes of investigating service-learning "in order to stay alive as a teacher" (3). When we design a course that incorporates the best of what practitioner-researchers have to tell us about community-based writing, we do indeed "stay alive," and our students discover the power of writing to reveal the world—and even transform it.

NOTES

1. See, for example, Linda Flower, who writes, "I am cautious with the word 'service.' I don't want my students to see themselves as the donors of knowledge or expertise to others in need, but as partners in collaborative planning and mutual learning" ("Evolution" 4).

2. Some will contend that the academic essay occurs within a true enough rhetorical situation—after all, can the teacher not be a "real" audience? Are the purposes of demonstrating mastery of academic discourse conventions not "real" purposes for a student? Even if we grant such claims, an argument can still be made for introducing students to rhetorical situations outside the classroom to broaden their repertoire of writing skills. Perhaps Nora Bacon says it best: "[W]e cannot expect a body of skills and knowledge about writing developed in a single rhetorical context to have universal application" (53).

WORKS CITED

Adler-Kassner, Linda, Robert Crooks, and Ann Watters, eds. *Writing the Community: Concepts and Models for Service-Learning in Composition.* Washington, DC: American Association for Higher Education and NCTE, 1997.

Anson, Chris M. "On Reflection: The Role of Logs and Journals in Service-Learning Courses." Adler-Kassner, Crooks, and Watters 167–80.

Ashley, Hannah M. "True Stories from Philadelphia." *Reflections on Community-Based Writing Instruction* 1.1 (2000): 10–13.

Bacon, Nora. "Community Service Writing: Problems, Challenges, Questions." Adler-Kassner, Crooks, and Watters 39–55.

Bennett, B. Cole. "The Best Intentions: Service-Learning and Noblesse Oblige at a Christian College." *Reflections on Community-Based Writing Instruction* 1.2 (2000): 18–23.

Bowdon, Melody, and Blake Scott. *Service-Learning in Technical and Professional Communication.* New York: Longman, 2003.

Cullum, Linda. "Surprised by Service: Creating Connections through Community-Based Writing." *Reflections on Community-Based Writing Instruction* 1.2 (2000): 5–11.

Deans, Thomas. *Writing and Community Action: A Service-Learning Rhetoric with Readings.* New York: Longman, 2003.

———. *Writing Partnerships: Service-Learning in Composition.* Urbana, IL: NCTE, 2000.

Flower, Linda. "The Evolution of 'Intercultural Inquiry.'" *Reflections on Community-Based Writing Instruction* 1.2 (2000): 3–4.

———. "Partners in Inquiry: A Logic for Community Outreach." Adler-Kassner, Crooks, and Watters 95–117.

Ford, Marjorie, and Elizabeth Schave. *Community Matters: A Reader for Writers.* New York: Longman, 2002.

Garrod, Andrew, and Jay Davis, eds. *Crossing Customs: International Students Write on U.S. College Life and Culture.* Garland Studies in Higher Education. New York: Falmer, 1999.

Herzberg, Bruce. "Community Service and Critical Teaching." *College Composition and Communication* 45.3 (1994): 307–19.

Julier, Laura. "Community-Service Pedagogy." *A Guide to Composition Pedagogies.* Eds. Gary Tate, Amy Rupiper, and Kurt Schick. New York: Oxford UP, 2001. 132–48.

Reich, Alice. "Call and Response: Service-Learning in a Liberal Arts Curriculum." *Building Community: Service-Learning in the Academic Disciplines.* Eds. Richard J. Kraft and Marc Swadener. Denver: Colorado Campus Compact, 1994. 3–6.

Ross, Carolyn, and Ardel Thomas. *Writing for Real: A Handbook for Writers in Community Service.* New York: Longman, 2003.

Schutz, Aaron, and Anne Ruggles Gere. "Service Learning and English Studies: Rethinking 'Public' Service." *College English* 60.2 (1998): 129–49.

Stock, Patricia Lambert, and Janet Swenson. "The Write for Your Life Project: Learning to Serve by Serving to Learn." Adler-Kassner, Crooks, and Watters 153–66.

Tate, Gary, Amy Rupiper, and Kurt Schick, eds. *A Guide to Composition Pedagogies.* New York: Oxford UP, 2001.

Tatum, Beverly Daniel. *"Why Are All the Black Kids Sitting Together in the Cafeteria?" And Other Conversations About Race.* New York: Basic Books, 1997.

Zlotkowski, Edward. "Linking Service-Learning and the Academy." *Change* 28.1 (1996): 20–27.

29 *Service Learning and First-Year Composition*

BROCK HAUSSAMEN

INTRODUCTION

"Service learning" refers to the use of voluntary community service as an integral part of an academic course. In a cycle of experience and reflection, students apply their skills and knowledge to help people, and in the classroom, they reflect on the people, social agencies, and communities they have encountered and on the nature of service. Service learning is not primarily social assistance; it is a pedagogy, one that addresses not only the issue of how best to learn but also the question of the best purposes of learning. The words of the Rutgers University service learning motto express the good will, "Serving to Learn. Learning to Serve."

As one of Raritan Valley Community College's trio of service learning coordinators, as well as an English professor, I encourage colleagues to try service learning, and I help find appropriate agencies for their students. The applications of service learning extend all across the curriculum. Accounting students help agencies keep their financial records. Students in physical education courses conduct exercises with children or the elderly. Students in sociology and psychology courses observe social and individual behavior while they help at adolescent drop-in agencies, community mental health centers, and group homes for the developmentally disabled. Students in the sciences, math, communications, education, computer science, and marketing have all volunteered for service that has augmented their academic training, their career preparedness, and their community awareness.

Service learning is a new branch of experiential education. It differs from the two older branches of internships and cooperative education in that service learning is unpaid, requires fewer hours—at Raritan Valley, usually 30 hours a semester or less, depending on the faculty member's specifications—and is only one of the components within a course instead of being a course or program unto itself. Service learning has taken root at all levels

From *Teaching English in the Two-Year College* 24.3 (1997): 192–98.

of education since the 1980s as many educators have acknowledged that while graduates may go forth successfully trained as aspiring private professionals, many are also unprepared and unwilling to accept roles in the public community. Racism on campuses, the national cynicism about politics and government, and the decline of volunteerism have forced a recognition that in a democracy citizenship education cannot remain merely an extracurricular activity.

In the field of English, literature often lends itself to community experiences. The literature of women, of law, of AIDS, of African American and Eastern cultures can all lead to service learning projects. However, here, I describe service learning in first-term composition, where it has rich potential to affect many college students.

OPTIONAL SERVICE LEARNING IN ENGLISH I

Service learning can be organized in two basic ways in any course. It can be an optional project, or it can be required or strongly recommended for all students. In English I at Raritan Valley, service learning fits well as an optional alternative for the research paper assignment that is the culminating course project. Different instructors approach the research assignment in different ways, but the community can be a resource for most of them. Over the years, I have usually assigned a biographical essay about a member of the student's family, a paper drawing on both interviews and library sources. Now, with the service learning option, an alternative assignment is for the student to spend at least fifteen hours in a nursing home in conversation with a senior citizen and to write the researched biography about that person instead of a family member. To prepare for this project, I telephone the volunteer coordinators at several nursing homes, ask whether they can arrange suitable pairings if students contact them, and then give the students the list of nursing homes, contact persons, and phone numbers to select from on their own. Generally, about half the students in a class express initial interest in this assignment, and half of those complete it.

One problem with service learning as an option is the compensation for the additional hours it requires. In actuality, most students completing service learning do not look back on the time spent as onerous at all, and many put in additional hours. But at the start of the semester, for community college students holding jobs, thirty hours, even fifteen hours, sounds like a lot. So an incentive helps. The carrot I offer is that the students completing the nursing home project will be excused from the final exam. The omission of the exam does not compromise the course for those diligent enough to finish the required paper, and it does not, for that matter, save students much time, but it is an attractive incentive. In other courses across the college, and at other colleges, faculty often adjust the writing requirements of those students choosing a service learning project or give them extra credit in some form. This element of service learning management, however, is unsettled and controversial, for on the one hand, the student's time commitment should be acknowledged, and yet faculty should seek to adhere to the principle of giving academic credit only for the evaluated academic results of service, not for the time alone.

The students at Raritan Valley who volunteer for the nursing home project spend an hour or two at a time during the middle portion of the semester befriending an elderly man or woman. Each week I ask a couple of these students to talk in class about what the resident is like, what the home itself is like, how they feel about being there, how they think they are perceived, and what sources they are finding in the library that amplify the life stories they are hearing. Such reflection is indispensable to service learning as a pedagogy, for students, although they usually feel good about their community work, are not particularly inclined to contemplate it after they leave it behind each week. Reflection—through discussions, journals, and research—prompts the student to unpack a host of impressions and to reach for an understanding of them. Service by itself is not learning; the learning occurs in the examination and analysis of the service.

Listen to student Marie Hocker, who juxtaposed historians' accounts of the Battle of Guadalcanal with the reminiscences of World War II veteran, Stan, now 80 years old,

> mostly deaf, single-legged, nearly blind without bottle-thick glasses. . . . He speaks his mind bluntly. "Anybody don't want to hear, don't have to listen." I have listened to Stan for the past two months, and have learned more than I had imagined I would.

In hearing and telling the story of Stan's life and of Guadalcanal, Marie saw the issues of human need that permeate both the past and the present. She concluded:

> "One of these days you'll come to see me and I won't be here," he tells me. "Where're you going, Stan?" I ask. "I don't know. Somewhere where the food is good and people treat you decent." I think back on his time on Guadalcanal. He was fighting then for "somewhere where the food was good and the people treat you decent. . . ." I want to believe that the odds are not as overwhelming now and that the spirit of those who fought at Guadalcanal lives on in those who take care of the Guadalcanal survivors. I want to believe that Stan's American Dream will still come true. Stan, may the food be good and the people treat you decent, always.

ENGLISH I WITH REQUIRED SERVICE LEARNING

The optional mode of service learning of the sort I have described has advantages and disadvantages. It gives the faculty member who is trying the method for the first time an opportunity to get the feel of it, to see how it fits with the course objectives, and to see how the students respond. On the other hand, when only a few students in a class are carrying out such involved projects, those students require extra time and attention, and their experience of the course may become significantly different from that of the other students.

For these reasons, many faculty who have tried the optional model have gone on to teach sections in which service learning is a standard requirement of the course. Raritan Valley now offers as many as a dozen such classes across the disciplines each semester.

One of these has been a section of composition subtitled "Writing and Learning in the Community." The service requirement is indicated in the published course schedule so that students are aware of it when they select that section. The course draws students who have volunteered in the past or have wanted to do so—and predictably others as well who arrive at the first class claiming that they had no idea what that service thing meant but the section fit in their schedules. A few of the disenchanted ones drop the course, but more often those who grudgingly start the service go on to become fully engaged. While one might expect that altruism or at least a sharp sense of responsibility would be a criterion for successful service learning, in fact a student does not need either in order to find service learning eventually gratifying.

The partnership between a composition class and the community can be of different kinds. One relationship has come not from service learning at all but from the study over the last couple of decades of the role of community in the nature of discourse and the writing process. Writers, it has been emphasized, write not just as individuals but as members of communities. (Joseph Harris has surveyed this topic in a fine essay.) The awareness of discourse communities has inspired service courses organized around writing that is needed in and by community services and groups—newsletters, pamphlets, flyers, histories. The anthology *Writing for Change*, edited by Ann Watters and Marjorie Ford, includes examples of such projects.

Another connection between the writing class and the community is through tutoring. Composition students explore the theme of literacy and, with some basic training in tutoring, help high school students or other community members to improve their writing skills. Bruce Herzberg has written about a fully developed version of this approach at Bentley College in Massachusetts.

But my design has been simpler, because I wanted a model that other English faculty could easily adopt and, if they did so, for which community placements could be found in large numbers. I invite students to pursue any kind of community service they are interested in, as long as it is unpaid (so a current job in a care center doesn't qualify), is helpful in nature, and is likely to be something the student would learn from (I allowed one student in his third year with a volunteer fire company to use that as his service, but it never became a new experience for him in any way; I should have established more particular goals with him at the start). The minimum time required for students is thirty hours over the semester; students hand in a time sheet, initialed by a supervisor, at midterm and at the end.

Often their service interests turn out to be career-related; they check out what it is like to work in hospitals or day care centers or county government or art therapy. Sometimes they follow up a community involvement that they are already familiar with—a nursing home around the corner from their house, a service program at the family church. I describe a variety of agencies on the first day of class and evaluate the students' own suggestions for placements, and I press them all to make phone calls for interviews quickly because getting started can easily consume three weeks. (At colleges without a service learning or other volunteer office, faculty can obtain listings of volunteer opportunities from local governments, from comprehensive agencies such as United Way, and sometimes from local newspapers.)

The writing assignments for the course parallel those given in other composition sections; final papers emerge from the same process of drafts and peer discussion, and they are held to the same standards. The difference is that all of the papers are about community and service. They include narratives and essays on such topics as an incident in the past when the student did or did not help someone, definitions of community, a description of the volunteer site and its clients, and arguments on whether service should be required or not. The students also keep a journal. I give them a list of questions to consider such as, "What did someone say to you that surprised you?" "If you were in charge, what changes would you make at the agency?" "What conflicts did you experience or observe at the agency? What caused them?"

The research assignment is a problem-solution paper. Students select some element of the social problem that their agency is dealing with. They research the sources of the problem, the conflicting points-of-view involved, and the possible solutions. Grasping such complexity does not come easily to most of them, and I emphasize the multiple nature of causes and options. They interview the director of their agency, and they include their experiences at the agency in their discussion. Their writing process often includes coming to grips with contrasts between the written sources and their first-hand impressions. They are expected to draw conclusions and make recommendations.

Here are some examples of their topics: One student at a day care center with children from distressed families did her research on problem children in a preschool setting, on how to humanely control and discipline children who may have become accustomed to neglect and harsh punishment at home. A student coaching a Pop Warner football team studied the dilemma of competitive, high-pressure parents on the children's playing field. Another student helping at a community theater compared the complaints from local arts and theater groups about lack of government funding with demands from individuals about their entitlements to welfare.

For readings in the course, I sometimes use *Writing for Change*, at other times my own assortment of essays and stories. (The old chestnut "The Lottery" by Shirley Jackson takes on new life in discussions about community involvement!) Many teachable essays about social problems appear on newspaper op-ed pages. *Education for Democracy*, by Benjamin Barber and Richard Battistoni, is a large, exemplary collection that includes readings about service learning itself. (See the appendix for organizations that provide extensive information about service learning, including sample course syllabi.)

SERVICE LEARNING, ENGLISH, AND DEMOCRACY

As the semester progresses, students ask pointed questions about why community service is part of their English course. I tell them that the purpose is not to solve community problems but to improve their education. I tell them that I believe their education ought to promote not only their professional and personal development but their development as community members as well. That is accomplished by using their communication skills to reflect on their community experience. And indeed, students not only have plenty of material to write about, but as any teacher of service learning quickly discovers, students need to do a great deal of talking about their first encounters with hyperactive children, or frail elderly, or the poor. Students have much to say about the agencies themselves, the confusions of getting started there, their verdicts about whether people are being helped effectively or not. But as they talk in class, write about their experiences, give each other advice and support, and read related narratives, their frequent comment is that the course acquires a reality for them that other courses have not had. They, like service learning students in general, report increased confidence in themselves both as learners and as someone "who can make a difference." All this is their way of expressing the fulfillment of the primary goal of service learning: to bing the academic world and the democratic community into a closer relationship.

Benjamin Barber of Rutgers University is an eloquent advocate of citizenship education in a democracy, and among what he considers to be the political benefits of service learning, two are also curriculum goals of English. First, service learning students listen. They must pay careful attention to the unfamiliar words they hear from the unfamiliar people they work with. And listening, Barber points out, is an essential but endangered skill in our talkative, media-dominated democracy; it is through listening that people understand each other and find the possibilities for political compromise. The other skill is imagination. Successful service learning students must stretch their vision in their study of people from different backgrounds, and such imagining, the capacity for informed social empathy, is a critical art in a democracy ("The Democratic Imperative").

Occasionally, of course, listening and understanding go awry, and service learning does not work well for a student. Some students do not become engaged at their agency. They report that they stand around a lot or are bored or that no one is telling them what to do. Asking them to explain in detail what the situation is—who the people are and exactly what they are doing—is a helpful preliminary step in encouraging participation. Only once have I encountered the opposite sort of difficulty: a girl was so involved in listening to the overwhelming problems of young teenagers at an after school center that she herself began to feel overwhelmed. She willingly wrote in her journal about what she was hearing (and asked me not to read certain pages), and I encouraged her to talk in class, where she felt supported by the other students. She gradually found her bearings at the agency and has since become a peer counselor in a high school.

In such cases, and whenever I think it might be worthwhile, I telephone the volunteer's supervisor around mid-semester to share information and suggestions. These calls sometimes uncover another problem that can arise, which is that the agency is not using or supervising volunteers effectively. This may occur in a large organization such as some hospitals, or in any agency that is not prepared to provide volunteers with some structure. For a while, I steer volunteers elsewhere.

Let me conclude by pointing out that while many four-year institutions have service learning programs, service learning has a special impact at community colleges, where students come from the local community and, to a large extent, will remain in it. Community service is integral to the notion of the community college. Many service learning students say they want to continue working at their agencies after the semester ends; some of them do for a while, and a few go on to take regular positions there. But for all of them, service learning deepens their relationship to their home community and increases the chance they will participate in that community again in the future.

APPENDIX

Several major organizations provide information about service learning:

Corporation for National Service/1201 New York Avenue, NW/Washington, DC 20525/202-606-5000, Ext. 136. http://www.cns.gov/learn.html. The federal agency that directs Americorps also provides grants for collegiate service learning through its program Learn and Serve America: Higher Education.

Campus Compact Center for Community Colleges/1833 West Southern Avenue/Mesa, AZ 85202/602-461-7392. http://www.mc.maricopa.edu/academic/compact

American Association of Community Colleges/One Dupont Circle, NW, Suite 410/Washington, DC 20036-1176/202-728-0200, ext. 254. http://aacc.nche.edu/speproj/service/resource.html. A center for information about both selected model service learning programs as well as service learning in community colleges nationwide.

National Society for Experiential Education/3509 Haworth Drive, Suite 207/Raleigh, NC 27609/919-787-3263. http://www.tripod.com//nsee. An organization that predates the service learning movement, NSEE publishes excellent materials on teaching through service learning.

National Service Learning Cooperative (K–12) Clearinghouse/University of Minnesota/1954 Buford Avenue, Room R290/St. Paul, MN 55108/800-808-7378. http://www.nicsl.coled.umn.edu A clearinghouse for a wide range of information about organizations, materials, and specialists.

WORKS CITED

Barber, Benjamin R. "The Democratic Imperative for Civic Education." Address: Princeton University. 16 Nov. 1995.

Barber, Benjamin R., and Richard M. Battistoni. *Education for Democracy: Citizenship, Community, Service: A Sourcebook for Students and Teachers.* Dubuque: Kendall, 1993.

Harris, Joseph. "The Idea of Community in the Study of Writing." *College Composition and Communication* 40 (1989): 11–22.

Herzberg, Bruce. "Community Service and Critical Teaching." *College Composition and Communication* 45 (1994): 307–19.

Watters, Ann, and Marjorie Ford. *Writing for Change: A Community Reader.* New York: McGraw, 1995.

30 Text-Based Measures of Service-Learning Writing Quality

ADRIAN WURR

INTRODUCTION

The rapid rise in the popularity of service-learning over the last decade has led to increased calls for evidence of its effect on student learning. Edward Zlotkowski, a senior associate at the American Association for Higher Education and author of numerous books and articles on service-learning, has repeatedly asserted that more academics would be swayed by empirical evidence showing gains in cognitive learning. Unless service-learning advocates become far more comfortable seeing enhanced learning as the horse pulling the cart of moral and civic values, and not vice versa, service-learning will continue to remain less visible and less important to the higher education community as a whole than is good for its own survival (Zlotkowski 24–25).

The study described here takes this charge seriously. As part of a larger dissertation study investigating the impact of service-learning on social, cognitive, and personal domains of learning, this paper describes a comprehensive writing assessment model used to measure the effects of service-learning on the writing performance of first-year college composition students. The model considers linguistic and rhetorical features in writing that can be compared to holistic evaluations of student writing and other qualitative assessments. Such direct measures of the writing produced by students in service-learning and comparison composition classes can help shed light on the potential academic benefits of service-learning in composition by answering the question: Does service-learning contribute to improved student writing, and if so, in what ways?

Context

The service-learning curricula examined in the study were designed as part of a larger Southwest Project linking students and teachers at the University

---

From *Reflections* 2.2 (2002): 40–55.

of Arizona with their counterparts in two local elementary schools to teach and learn about the land and people of the Southwest. Students in participating sections of first-year composition read and wrote about issues related to the Southwest in their college composition classes while also leading small group discussions on the Southwest in classes at two local elementary schools. The students were not only meeting community-defined needs by participating in this project, they were also meeting the goals of first-year composition by researching, designing, and drafting texts to meet the needs of multiple audiences.

The goals for first-year composition, as outlined in *A Student's Guide to First-Year Composition* and excerpted below, are as follows. Students will:

- Read texts to assess how writers achieve their purposes with their intended audiences.

- Learn the conventions of scholarly research, analysis, and documentation.

- Learn other conventions of academic writing, including how to write clear and correct prose.

- Learn to revise and respond to feedback from readers to improve and develop drafts.

- Learn to develop ideas with observations and reflections on [their] experience.

- Learn to analyze and write for various rhetorical situations.

- Develop a persuasive argument and support it with evidence and effective appeals that target [their] intended audience. (Wurr, Eroz, and Singh-Corcoran, 175)

Three major essay assignments—a rhetorical analysis, documented analysis, and reflective essay—are typically required of all first-year composition students and provide a basis from which to assess the degree to which curricular goals are met. In the service-learning courses, these assignments were designed to encourage students to reflect on the work in their community. Table 30–1 outlines the major writing assignments for service-learning courses in the study.[1]

TABLE 30–1   English 101/107 Southwest Project Essay Assignment Sequence and Descriptors

1. Rhetorical Analysis Essay (5–7 pages), in which students research a local environmental problem from various viewpoints.
2. Persuasive Essay (4–6 pages), in which students suggest ways to solve or reduce the impact of the environmental problem they researched.
3. Reflective Essay (4–6 pages), which introduces a portfolio of students' accomplishments over the semester, and within which students explain why they chose the texts they did, for whom they are intended, and what purpose the texts or portfolio is meant to serve.

RESEARCH DESIGN

The primary participants in the study were a diverse mix of students enrolled in parallel first-year composition courses for native (NS) and non-native (NNS) English speaking students.[2] Students did not know about the service-learning component in these courses before enrolling, but were informed of this and other work related to the course in the first weeks of the semester. Each class section (labeled C1–C4 in Table 30–2) had a total enrollment of between 17 and 20 students[3] and one graduate student or adjunct faculty instructor.

Male and female participants were roughly equal in numbers and age, yet came from diverse linguistic and cultural backgrounds. Although a sample of convenience, the participants in this study are representative of the diverse student populations typically found on large, urban college campuses in America today.

Previous studies attempting to show gains in student writing as a result of teacher intervention and/or curricula have been largely unsuccessful in part because much of what is taught in freshmen composition (e.g., research and library skills) is not easily documented or measured in the writing students produce (Haswell). A secondary purpose of the present study, therefore, was to investigate valid and reliable methods for describing writing quality based on current linguistic and rhetorical theories for analyzing student writing, with particular regard given to the persuasive essay writing emphasized in many writing courses incorporating service-learning. Holistic scores and primary trait analyses that had been used reliably to measure the use of rhetorical appeals, reasoning, coherence, and mechanics in other writing contexts were used as a means for documenting the impact of service-learning on student writing performance.

Holistic Writing Assessments

Holistic assessments of writing provide some advantages over primary trait scoring. In addition to accounting for the interaction of elements within a text, holistic or impressionistic scoring also allows for a greater degree of interaction between the reader, writer, and text than evaluations based on the enumeration of linguistic and rhetorical features in a text. Also, since the weight of any one element within a text is always relative to other factors, holistic assessments are less likely than primary trait scales concerned with accuracy and mechanics to penalize writers, particularly second language writers, for surface level errors.

TABLE 30–2   Language by Curricula Factorial Design

	NS (English 101)		NNS (English 107)	
Service Learning	C1	(N=19)	C2	(N=16)
Comparison	C3	(N=19)	C4	(N=19)

Since the essays in the present study were drafted over time, students had the opportunity to revise and edit all writing samples submitted for evaluation. This reduced the likelihood of fossilized errors appearing, as they often do in timed essay writing, by allowing students to avail themselves of a variety of resources including peer tutors, writing center consultants, the teacher, and computer grammar and spell check programs before they submitted their writing for evaluation. It is more likely, then, that the writing sample came closer to representing the student's true writing ability for the task.

All essays were rated by a team of qualified independent evaluators using the five-point scale presented in Table 30–3. Using exact and adjacent scores, where up to a 1-point difference between scores is regarded as signifying agreement, the rubric resulted in an inter-rater reliability rate of .83 in the present study.

Analysis of Rhetorical Appeals

Ulla Connor and Janice Lauer developed scales for judging the persuasiveness of student writing for use in the International Study of Written Composition (commonly referred to as the IEA study because of its sponsor, the

TABLE 30–3   Holistic Scoring Guide for Persuasive Essays

Score of 5: Excellent

Strong, clear focus and thesis. Effective organization—including a beginning, middle, and end—with logical grouping of ideas into paragraphs. Lots of details and relevant examples from outside sources and, when appropriate, personal experience to support main ideas. Discussion shows a clear understanding of issue and texts, as well as a sense of purpose and audience. Few errors.

Score of 4: Good

Clear focus and thesis. Overall coherence with paragraphs to group similar ideas. Some examples and supporting details. Discussion demonstrates a good understanding of the issue and integrates ideas from primary and secondary sources of information. Occasional errors.

Score of 3: Adequate

Weak focus and thesis. Some coherence and logical grouping of ideas. Some examples and details, though connections may not always be clear. Discussion demonstrates a basic understanding of the issue and texts. Multiple errors.

Score of 2: Poor

No clear focus or message. Few appropriate examples or details. Discussion relies on a limited number of sources of information and overlooks complicating evidence. Serious errors which interfere with meaning.

Score of 1: Failing

Writing is seriously incomplete or does not address the assignment prompt. Errors prevent communication.

International Association for the Evaluation of Educational Achievement) conducted by Alan Purves and other researchers around the world. Starting with the use of ethos, pathos, and logos as persuasive appeals first identified in Aristotle's *Rhetoric*, and integrating the work of more modern rhetoricians such as James Kinneavy and Janice Lauer, Connor and Lauer describe measures for identifying and rating the use of three persuasive appeals: rational, credibility, and affective, as shown in Table 30–4 ("Understanding").

The IEA study achieved inter-rater reliability rates for the rational, credibility, and affective appeal scales of .90, .73, and .72 respectively (Connor, "Linguistic/Rhetorical" 76). As will be discussed more completely at the end of this paper, it is not clear from the literature if these figures represent exact or adjacent-score agreement between raters. Using adjacent-score agreement, as is done in large-scale writing assessment programs such as the Test of Written English and others administered by the Educational Testing Service, the present study achieved inter-rater reliability rates of .94, .94, and .93 for the rational, credibility, and affective appeal scales respectively.

TABLE 30–4   Rhetorical Appeals Scale

Rational

0   No use of the rational appeal.*

1   Use of some rational appeals, minimally developed or use of some inappropriate (in terms of major point) rational appeals.

2   Use of a single rational appeal* or series of rational appeals* with at least two points of development.

3   Exceptionally well developed and appropriate single extended rational appeal* or a coherent set of rational appeals.*

Credibility

0   No use of credibility appeals.

1   No writer credibility but some awareness of audience's values; or some writer credibility (other than general knowledge) but no awareness of audience's values.

2   Some writer credibility (other than general knowledge) and some awareness of audience's values.

3   Strong writer credibility (personal experience) and sensitivity to audience's values (specific audience for the solution).

Affective

0   No use of the affective appeal.

1   Minimal use of concreteness or charged language.

2   Adequate use of picture, charged language, or metaphor to evoke emotion.

3   Strong use of picture, charged language, or metaphor to evoke emotion.

*Rational appeals were categorized as quasi-logical, realistic structure, example, analog.

Note: From Connor, Ulla, and Janice Lauer. "Cross-Cultural Variation in Persuasive Student Writing." *Writing Across Languages and Cultures.* Ed. Alan C. Purves. Newbury Park, CA: Sage, 1988. 138. Reprinted with permission.

Analysis of Reasoning

In *The Uses of Argument*, Stephen Toulmin presents a model of informal logic to assess the soundness, strength, and conclusiveness of arguments that is comprised of three main parts: claims, data, and warrants (1). Claims are defined as conclusions whose merits we are seeking to establish (97). Data provide support for the claims in the form of experience, facts, statistics, or events. Warrants are rules, principles, [or] inference-licenses that act as bridges between claims and data (98). In "Cross-Cultural Variation in Persuasive Student Writing," Connor and Lauer describe a three-point analytic scale to rate the quality of reasoning in persuasive essays using Toulmin's categories of claim, data, and warrant. Shown in Table 30–5, Connor and Lauer's scale assesses both the quality and the quantity of the logic used. Using this scale, the present study achieved an average inter-rater reliability rate of .89.

TABLE 30–5   Criteria for Judging the Quality of Claim, Data, and Warrant

Claim

1   No specific problem stated and/or no consistent point of view. May have one subclaim. No solution offered, or if offered nonfeasible, unoriginal, and inconsistent with claim.

2   Specific, explicitly stated the problem. Somewhat consistent point of view. Relevant to the task. Has two or more subclaims that have been developed. Solution offered with some feasibility, original, and consistent with major claim.

3   Specific, explicitly stated problem with consistent point of view. Several well-developed subclaims, explicitly tied to the original major claim. Highly relevant to the task. Solution offered that is feasible, original, and consistent with major claims.

Data

1   Minimal use of data. Data of the "everyone knows" type, with little reliance on personal experience or authority. Not directly related to major claim.

2   Some use of data with reliance on personal experience or authority. Some variety in use of data. Data generally related to major claim.

3   Extensive use of specific, well-developed data of a variety of types. Data explicitly connected to major claim.

Warrant

1   Minimal use of warrants. Warrants only minimally reliable and relevant to the case. Warrants may include logical fallacies.

2   Some use of warrants. Though warrants allow the writer to make the bridge between data and claim, some distortion and informal fallacies are evident.

3   Extensive use of warrants. Reliable and trustworthy allowing rater to accept the bridge from data to claim. Slightly relevant. Evidence of some backing.

Note: From Connor, Ulla and Janice Lauer. "Cross-Cultural Variation in Persuasive Student Writing." *Writing Across Languages and Cultures.* Ed. Alan C. Purves. Newbury Park, CA: Sage, 1988. 138.

Analysis of Coherence

Research indicates that topical structure can be an important indicator of overall writing quality (Witte, "Writing Quality"; Connor, *Contrastive*; Connor and Farmer; Cerniglia, Medsker, and Connor). In "Topical Structure and Writing Quality: Some Possible Text-Based Explanations of Readers' Judgments of Students' Writing," Witte found that high-quality essays had more parallel and extended parallel progression than low-quality essays.

Building on this idea, Betty Bamberg developed a system to help students revise their essays and improve coherence using topical structure analysis. Connor and Lauer adapted this into a 4-point rubric to measure text cohesion, and achieved an inter-rater reliability rate of .93 (Connor and Lauer 311). Shown in Table 30–6, Bamberg's system was chosen for the present study and resulted in an inter-rater reliability rate identical to that achieved by Connor and Lauer.

TABLE 30–6   Bamberg's 4-Point Holistic Coherence Rubric

The writer

4
- identifies the topic and does not shift or digress.
- orients the reader by describing the context or situation.
- organizes details according to a discernible plan that is sustained throughout the essay.
- skillfully uses cohesive ties (lexical cohesion, conjunction, reference, etc.) to link sentences and/or paragraphs.
- often concludes with a statement that gives the reader a definite sense of closure.
- makes few or no grammatical and/or mechanical errors that interrupt the discourse flow or reading process.

3
- meets enough of the criteria above so that a reader could make at least partial integration of the text.

2
- does not identify the topic and inference would be unlikely.
- shifts topic or digresses frequently.
- assumes reader shares his/her context and provides little or no orientation.
- has no organizational plan in most of the text and frequently relies on listing.
- uses few cohesive ties (lexical, conjunction, reference, etc.) to link sentences and/or paragraphs.
- makes numerous mechanical and/or grammatical errors, resulting in interruption of the reading process and a rough or irregular discourse flow.

1
- essay is literally incomprehensible because missing or misleading cues prevented readers from making sense of the text.

Note: From Connor, Ulla, and Janice Lauer. "Understanding Persuasive Essay Writing: Linguistic/Rhetorical Approach." *Text* 5.4 (1985): 311. © Mouton Publishers. Reprinted with permission.

Analysis of Mechanics

Following Yili Li's dissertation study on the effect of computer-mediated communication activities on student writing, the present study measured the effective use of mechanics using the grammar checker of Microsoft Word 2000 (version 9.0.2720) to identify the following types of deviation from the conventions of standard academic English in the students' essays:

Adverb: He writes bad.

Article: A honest person would not do that.

Capitalization: he took it.

Comma use: It was late, the boys were hungry.

Commonly confused words: Who's is that?

Comparative: Writing is more easier than we expect.

End-of-sentence preposition: She got the job she applied for.

End-of-sentence punctuation: My bus had left!.

Extra word: The boat in the the basement was too big.

Fragment: The rock samples.

Negation: We couldn't hardly keep up with the orders.

Number agreement: These banana are almost ripe.

Parallelism: He should either pass or should bid.

Possessives: The mans jacket was never found.

Question mark: Who said that.

Quotation marks: John said, I can't abide by that.

Relative pronoun: One person which I respect was Jim.

Spelling (Confirmed manually): His assesment of the situation wasn't popular.

Subject-verb agreement: One of the most important files are missing.

Tense shift: He left and takes a nap.

Verb form: She had ran out of time.

The grammar checker on Microsoft Word 2000 was customized to identify only these types of errors. Because of the limitations of grammar checkers, manual confirmation was still necessary to avoid, for example, an in-text citation being counted as a fragment. The total number of confirmed errors in each student essay was divided by the total number of words to arrive at an errors-per-word ratio. This ratio represented the level of adherence to formal conventions such as mechanics and style in a given essay. Using this method, the present study found the essays written in service-learning sections to have significantly fewer mechanical errors than those written in traditional comparison sections of first-year composition ($p < .04$).

SUMMARY OF FINDINGS

The results from the holistic and analytic assessments of writing ability indicate a strong relationship exists (p<.01) between a reader's holistic assessment of an essay's quality and the effective use of rhetorical appeals, logical reasoning, and cohesive devices in that same essay, as shown in Table 30–7. The high correlation between the primary trait and holistic scores suggests that rhetorical appeals, reasoning, coherence, and mechanics are not only significant variables to consider in assessing writing quality, but also important concepts to cover in teaching students how to become better writers. Composition students and teachers can benefit from gaining a more informed understanding of the most salient writing traits in holistic judgments of writing quality, while those more interested in service-learning can gain empirical support for their practices.

The study also found that the frequency of mechanical errors was inversely related to these same primary trait and holistic measures, suggesting the difficulty of assessing any one primary trait without some intervening influence from other factors. Though the use of highly trained raters may have reduced this effect somewhat, the mild correlation between mechanics and other writing assessment measures raises the question of how best to account for such interaction when using analytic scoring mechanisms. In my dissertation, I suggest chaos theory can help account for such interactions through its description of complex and dynamic systems. I develop this idea by applying chaos theory to both writing assessment and service-learning program evaluation.

Does Service-Learning Contribute to Improved Student Writing?

One of the most significant findings of the study was documenting a significant between-group difference on every writing assessment measure. The

TABLE 30–7   Holistic and Analytic Writing Assessment Correlations (N=75)

	Holistic	Appeals	Logic	Coherence	Mechanics
Holistic	1.00				
Sig. (2-tailed)					
Appeals	.337	1.00			
Sig. (2-tailed)	.003				
Logic	.507	.548	1.00		
Sig. (2-tailed)	.0001	.0001			
Coherence	.390	.448	.509	1.00	
Sig. (2-tailed)	.001	.0001	.0001		
Mechanics	−.219	−.316	−.338	−.260	1.00
Sig. (2-tailed)	.059	.006	.001	.024	

results shown in Table 30–8 indicate that independent raters judged the essays produced by students in service-learning sections of first-year composition to be superior to those produced in comparison sections in a variety of ways. These scores are mean scores for each group that were computed by averaging the scores individual raters assigned each essay on holistic and primary trait analyses. The scores given for rhetorical appeals and reasoning also represent mean scores for the three separate analyses and scores within each rubric (i.e., rational, credibility, affective rhetorical appeals, and claim, data, warrant scores respectively), but each of these components was scored separately by raters so that an essay could, for example, receive a score of 3 for warrants and a score of 1 for data.

Converting the 5-point holistic scale to letter grades, for example, reveals that service-learning essays were judged to be better than comparison essays by about half a letter grade. Analytic assessments of each group's use of rhetorical appeals, logic, coherence, and mechanics show service-learning essays to be superior to comparison essays on every measure. The data presented in Table 30–9 indicate that the possibility of these results occurring by chance was small.

TABLE 30–8 Between-Group Comparison of Writing Assessment Scores

	Group	N	Mean*	Std. Deviation	Std. Error Mean
Holistic	SL	36	3.4722	.7923	.1321
	Control	39	3.0385	.8459	.1355
Appeals	SL	36	2.1750	.3544	5.906E-02
	Control	39	1.8810	.4214	6.748E-02
Logic	SL	36	2.2417	.3948	6.579E-02
	Control	39	1.7623	.3916	6.271E-02
Coherence	SL	36	3.1436	.5508	9.179E-02
	Control	39	2.6410	.6277	.1005
Mechanics	SL	36	3.16E-03	2.402524E-03	4.00E-04
	Control	39	4.67E-03	3.647087E-03	5.84E-04

*Note: The range of possible scores for each variable above was 1–5 for holistic scores, 0–3 for appeals, 1–3 for logic, and 1–4 for coherence.

TABLE 30–9 Independent Samples T-Test for Equality of Means Between Groups

	T-Value	Degrees of Freedom	Significance (2-tailed)
Holistic	2.287	73	p<.025
Appeals	3.255	73	p<.002
Logic	5.276	73	p<.0001
Coherence	3.673	73	p<.001
Mechanics	–3.767	73	p<.04

These results provide empirical support for including service-learning in college composition curricula. While other studies have demonstrated the positive impact service-learning can have on the community (e.g., Gelmon et al. and Gray), this study has shown that incorporating service-learning in college composition improves student writing, and has provided a viable model for assessing this growth in student writing.

Suggestions for Future Research

The primary trait and holistic assessments of the writing produced by students in service-learning and comparison sections of first-year composition were conducted with readers familiar with the institutional context of the present study and with the institution's writing assessment procedures. As a result, inter-rater reliability rates were .83, .94, .89, and .93 for holistic, rhetorical appeals, reasoning, and coherence respectively. These results compare favorably to those reported in other studies (see Table 30–10) that involved larger samples drawn from diverse instructional and cultural settings. The range of writers and writing contexts represented in Connor and Lauer's two studies, for example, may have complicated the assessment task for their raters. The cohesiveness of the educational setting in which the present study occurred may have had a positive impact on the outcomes and help account for the high inter-rater reliability rates achieved (White).

It is important to note, however, that these inter-rater reliability rates are for adjacent-score matches. When inter-rater scores were two or more points apart, the raters were said to have disagreed in their assessment of the essay and a third reader would read the essay. An average of all three raters' scores would comprise the essay's final assessment score. Since it is not clear from other published studies using similar holistic and primary trait instruments exactly how they determined their reported inter-rater reliability rates, I have included both sets of figures in Table 30–10. The results from the comparison studies mentioned above are listed in the third column. Inter-rater reliability rates for mechanics are not included since these were calculated by computer.

Each rating session in the present study began with an explanation of the assessment procedure and scoring guide to be used, followed by practice in scoring several sample essays in order to reinforce the points outlined on the scoring guide. Nevertheless, some problems arose in interpreting and

TABLE 30–10   Inter-Rater Reliability Rates from the Present and Comparison Studies

	Exact Match	1-Point Difference	Comparison Study
Holistic	.38	.83	.83b
Appeals	.50	.94	.78b
Logic	.54	.97	.66c
Coherence	.47	.93	.93a

Note: a = Connor and Farmer; b = Connor and Lauer "Understanding"; c = Connor and Lauer "Cross-Cultural" applying at least two of the rubrics. The 3-point scales for judging the quality of claims, data, and warrants in the analysis of reasoning rubric all seemed to contain a gap between scores 1 and 2. One rater, for example, asked how she should score an essay with an easily identifiable argument structure, but one in which the writer's ethos undermined the argument's credibility. After discussing the point, all three raters seemed to agree in word but not deed as their differing scores on such essays led to several 1–3 splits, particularly on claims and warrants. The 4-point rubric for analyzing coherence was also problematic. Only one of the 75 papers in the study received a score of 1 since the descriptor, essay is literally incomprehensible, rarely applies to college level writing; softening this criterion to mostly incomprehensible might be more effective and appropriate. Also, with the practical elimination of a score of 1 from the coherence scale, many essays ended up receiving a score of 3 since this represented the middle ground between two more thoroughly defined alternatives. The descriptors for scores of 2 and 4 could benefit from being defined more narrowly, and the descriptor for 3 needs to be described in more detail, not just in opposition to adjacent scores. Although refining the rubrics in these or other ways more applicable to the local context may lead to higher inter-rater reliability rates, some variance in scoring is inevitable given the individual nature of reader responses.

Process vs. Product

One drawback of focusing on text-based measures of writing quality is that it may have the undesirable effect of emphasizing written products over composing processes. It would be interesting to investigate the composition strategies students in campus and community-based writing courses used as they completed their writing assignments. Protocol analysis might be one way in which to investigate this topic (see, for example, Flower and Hayes; Penrose and Sitko).

Another limitation of the writing assessment model described here is that focusing on a single or even multiple writing sample collected within a semester may not capture long-term effects on writing performance. One would hope to see changes in participants' attitude and behavior concerning writing as well as in the actual writing produced before concluding that a particular course or methodology had an impact on student writing performance. To address this concern, teacher-researchers might also consider the students' own self-assessment of their writing development as a result of the course, as indicated by reflective journal writing, writing portfolio, end-of-the-semester course evaluations, and interview data. All of these components were included in my dissertation study, but space limitations prevent describing them in detail here. The results, however, were generally encouraging with regard to the positive impact service-learning can have on students' beliefs about writing and research. A longitudinal, multi-institutional study of service-learning might reveal the extent to which these results accurately describe the outcomes for writers working in other service-learning teaching and learning contexts.

NOTES

1. The writing portfolio mentioned in assignment #3 consisted of journal assignments, research, and writing done for community partners, and a multi-drafted essay. These portfolios were scored holistically using a 6-point rubric. The holistic scores for writing portfolios and persuasive essays were strongly correlated, so only the persuasive essay scores and rubric are discussed in this paper. See my dissertation for more on the writing portfolios (133–4).

2. See Wurr (We Are) for more on the comparison of the impact of service-learning on NS versus NNS students.

3. One student in C2 and C4 declined to participate in the study, hence the difference in the number of enrolled students and study participants.

WORKS CITED

Bamberg, Betty. What Makes a Text Coherent? *College Composition and Communication* 34 (1983): 417–29.

Cerniglia, C., K. Medsker, and Ulla Connor. Improving Coherence Using Computer-Assisted Instruction. *Coherence in Writing: Research and Pedagogical Perspectives*. Eds. Ulla Connor and A. M. Johns. Arlington: TESOL, 1990. 227–41.

Connor, Ulla. Linguistic/Rhetorical Measures for International Persuasive Student Writing. *Research in the Teaching of English* 24 (1990): 67–87.

———. *Contrastive Rhetoric: Cross-Cultural Aspects of Second Language Writing*. New York: Cambridge UP. 1996.

———, and Mary Farmer. The Teaching of Topical Structure Analysis as a Revision Strategy for ESL Writers. *Second Language Writing: Research Insights for the Classroom*. Ed. Barbara Kroll. New York: Cambridge UP, 1990. 126–39.

———, and Janice Lauer. Understanding Persuasive Essay Writing: Linguistic/Rhetorical Approach. *Text* 5.4 (1985): 309–26.

———, and Janice Lauer. Cross-Cultural Variation in Persuasive Student Writing. *Writing Across Languages and Cultures*. Ed. Alan C. Purves. Newbury Park, CA: Sage, 1988. 138–59.

Flower, Linda, and John R. Hayes. Images, Plans, and Prose: The Representation of Meaning in Writing. *Written Communication*, 1.1 (1984): 120–60.

Gelmon, Sherril B., et al. (1998). Community-University Partnerships for Mutual Learning. *Michigan Journal of Community Service Learning* 5 (Fall 1998): 97–107.

Gray, Maryann J. Assessing Service-Learning: Results from a Survey of Learn and Serve America, Higher Education. *Change* (March/April 2000): 30–39.

Haswell, Richard. *Gaining Ground in College Writing: Tales of Development and Interpretation*. Dallas: Southern Methodist UP, 1991.

Kinneavy, James L. *A Theory of Discourse*. Englewood Cliffs, NJ: Prentice Hall, 1971.

Lauer, Janice M. et al. *Four Worlds of Writing*. 2nd ed. New York: Harper and Row, 1985.

Li, Yili. Using Task-Based E-mail Activities in Developing Academic Writing Skills in English as a Second Language. Diss. U of Arizona, 1998.

Penrose, Ann M., and Barbara M. Sitko, eds. *Hearing Ourselves Think: Cognitive Research in the College Writing Classroom*. Oxford: Oxford UP, 1993.

Purves, Alan C. *Writing Across Languages and Cultures: Issues in Contrastive Rhetoric*. Newbury Park, CA: Sage, 1988.

Toulmin, Stephen E. *The Uses of Argument*. Cambridge: Cambridge UP, 1958.

White, Edward M. *Personal Interview*. 11 Nov. 2000.

Witte, Stephen P. Topical Structure and Revision: An Exploratory Study. *College Composition and Communication* 34 (1983): 313–41.

———. "Topical Structure and Writing Quality: Some Possible Text-Based Explanations of Readers' Judgments of Students' Writing." *Visible Language* 17 (1983): 177–205.

Wurr, Adrian J. The Impact and Effect of Service-Learning on Native and Non-native English Speaking College Composition Students. Diss. U of Arizona, 2001.

———. We Are (Not) One: Managing Diversity in Community-Based Writing Programs. Paper presented at the Annual Conference on College Composition and Communication, Chicago, IL 2002.

———, Betil Eroz, and Nathalie Singh-Corcoran, eds. *A Student's Guide to First-Year Composition*. 21st. ed. Edina, MN: Burgess, 2000.

Zlotkowski, Edward. Linking Service-Learning and the Academy: A New Voice at the Table? *Change* (January/February 1996): 21–27.

31

The Trouble with Transfer: Lessons from a Study of Community Service Writing

NORA BACON

Because service-learning programs straddle two worlds, they bring into sharp relief a set of stubborn questions about the transfer of knowledge. School, we all know, is not quite like the world outside: when students leave campus to engage in community service, they are making a significant transition that prefigures, in many respects, the transition they make upon grad uation from "school" to "real life." As educators and researchers, we have long wondered about such transitions. What exactly is the relationship between the knowledge students develop in school and the knowledge they need in other settings? Do the skills and knowledge we value here have value in the community and the workplace as well? Do students learn them well enough to make use of them? Do they transfer automatically, or with effort, or not at all?

It was questions like these that motivated the study discussed below. Specifically, I had reason to doubt that the skills and knowledge students develop in college writing classes are relevant to the writing adults are asked to do in nonacademic settings. This doubt took root during the years when I taught Community Service Writing courses at Stanford University, teaching my students to write essays while observing their efforts to produce press releases, fact sheets, and brochures for community organizations; it was deepened by a review of the literature on nonacademic writing. To learn more about the relationship between college writing instruction and the knowledge required for nonacademic writing, I worked with a team of teachers and administrators to create a Community Service Writing program at San Francisco State University, then observed the participants over a period of three semesters.

What I found was that, while the question of whether skills and knowledge taught in writing classes transfer to community settings seems, on the face of it, critically important, it is not in fact an adequate way to conceptualize students' transitions from school to community contexts for writing. As

From *Michigan Journal of Community Service Learning* 6.1 (1999): 53–62.

the study progressed, one of the lessons suggested by the growing body of literature on "situated learning" found an insistent echo in my own data. It was not always the case (as some theorists of situated learning would predict) that skills and knowledge failed to transfer. But it was the case that looking for transfer failed to direct my attention toward the most suggestive aspects of the students' experience.

TRANSFER AND ITS DISCONTENTS

The concept of "transfer" has been problematic at least since 1901 when E. L. Thorndike and R. S. Woodworth conducted a series of experiments to determine whether training in one "mental function" (for example, estimating the area of a rectangle) improved a subject's performance in tasks requiring a similar mental function (estimating the area of another geometric shape). In "The Influence of Improvements in One Mental Function upon the Efficiency of Other Functions," they report their findings as follows:

- Improvement in any single mental function need not improve the ability in functions commonly called by the same name. It may injure it.

- Improvement in any single mental function rarely brings about equal improvement in any other function, no matter how similar, for the working of every mental function-group is conditioned by the nature of the data in each particular case. (pp. 249–50)

Thorndike later objected when others said that no transfer of knowledge occurs, but he observed that it is better for educators to assume too little than too much (Joncich, 1962).

Researchers of the next generation turned their attention to investigating the circumstances under which transfer takes place. A key variable is task similarity: if a subject practices Task A, the practice will affect performance on Task B if the two tasks are similar. Transfer is also promoted if the practice task is performed many times, if the time interval between tasks is short, if the subject practices on a variety of related tasks before attempting the target task, and if the similarity of tasks and the goal of transfer are explicitly pointed out (research reviews appear in Ellis, 1965; Gick & Holyoak, 1987).

Transfer theory is attractively neat and clear. If the experience of Community Service Writing students is analyzed in terms of this theory, writing in school is characterized as a practice task, writing in the community as a target task. The question of knowledge transfer, then, looks like this: Does practice writing essays in a composition course improve students' performance on community-based writing tasks? Unfortunately, this simple formulation of the question ultimately proves unsatisfactory.

Problems arise, first, because neither writing in school nor writing in the community is an activity as simply defined or carefully controlled as a laboratory task. When Thorndike and Woodworth studied the effect of estimating the area of rectangles on subjects' ability to estimate the area of triangles, they began with the assumption that all area estimation is similar enough to be comparable but that rectangles and triangles are different enough to make estimating the area of one a different task from estimating the area of the other. Rectangles are in one category, triangles in another.

With writing tasks, it is difficult to defend a similar kind of reasoning. Every text is different from every other text. The personal essay that students write in week 1 of a typical composition course may be so different from the argumentative essay they write in week 15 that it is misleading to characterize writing these papers as practicing a single task. Similarly, nonacademic texts vary too widely to be lumped into one category; a given nonacademic paper might well have more in common with a school essay than with another nonacademic paper. It is difficult, then, to delineate the categories "practice task" and "target task."

A second problem arises from the fact that writing is a multi-layered activity requiring simultaneous use of many kinds of skills and knowledge. We know that some "basic writing skills" do indeed transfer; handwriting, spelling, and punctuation require attention only among very inexperienced writers (Scardamalia & Bereiter, 1986). By the end of elementary school, children may not have perfected their spelling and punctuation, but most will have made them automatic. Given this automaticity and given the uniformity of conventions for handwriting, spelling, and punctuation across virtually all kinds of writing, it is not surprising that skills developed in one context are easily operationalized in other contexts.

However, when we shift our attention from mechanical to substantive matters, we enter the territory where the writer faces choices, and the notion of transfer is inadequate to describe how writers make use of what they know. Consider the simplest case—a writer who knows just what she wants to say crafting a single sentence. The writer makes lexical and syntactic choices governed by an enormously complex set of constraints. These include limits on her vocabulary and control of sentence structure; the mood and persona she wishes to create; how she wishes to manipulate emphasis within the sentence; how she hopes to connect the sentence to the text before and after it. For the writer who does not begin with an idea on the brink of expression, the choice-making is further complicated by the simultaneous effort to create and to articulate a meaning.

Furthermore, writers' choices depend upon their understanding of the genre and the rhetorical context in which they are working. If a writer learns in school that she should develop her ideas thoroughly, she may well carry this proposition—"when writing, I should develop my ideas thoroughly"—to another setting, say to a community agency where she agrees to write a fundraising letter. She may keep the proposition in mind and attempt to employ it. But how is she to judge the meaning of "thorough" in this context? Standards for thoroughness differ across settings, and they differ across writing tasks even in a single setting. If the writer does remember that she should be thorough and does make an earnest attempt at thoroughness but writes too long a letter because she has misjudged the requirements of the context, what can we say about the transfer of knowledge? Whether we say her knowledge transferred (because she remembered and attempted to use it) or did not transfer (because it did not serve her well), we have failed to capture the salient point about the relationship between this writer's prior knowledge and the choices she made.

Cases like this, which transfer theorists characterize as "negative transfer," arise because knowledge is intricately bound up in the social contexts in which it is developed, shared, and employed. While it is certainly possible, and sometimes necessary, for theorists to discuss knowledge as if it were a collection of particles that could be stored up within an individual mind, the reality for the knower is not nearly so simple. Knowledge comes colored by circumstances and laden with social and cultural significance. The understanding that "when writing, I should develop my ideas thoroughly" involves a concatenation of concepts—about what counts as writing, about what it means to develop an idea, about the generation and possession of ideas, about the relevance of "shoulds" to writing—so complex that a full portrait of the understanding would have to include not only a detailing of the situations where our hypothetical writer has heard and practiced the principle but also a social history of the principle itself.

In the end, the trouble with transfer is that it encourages us to think of knowledge as a set of particles to be acquired, transported, and applied rather than as the consequence of socially-situated learning. Jean Lave (1991) describes the problem in a memorable metaphor:

> The vision of social existence implied by the notion of transfer . . . treats life's situations as so many unconnected lily pads. This view reduces the organization of everyday practice to the question of how it is possible to hop from one lily pad to the next and still bring knowledge to bear on the fly, so to speak. (p. 79)

As an alternative, Lave offers a view informed by her own and others' empirical studies of apprenticeship learning. In *Situated Learning: Legitimate Peripheral Participation* (1991), Lave and Wenger characterize apprentices as newcomers to "communities of practice," and they stress that the newcomers gain full membership in the community by engaging in the practice with the guidance of more experienced members. In apprenticeship learning, explicit teaching is rare. Experienced practitioners frequently do not explain the principles that guide their practice; in fact, it is not necessary that newcomers and old-timers share the same mental representation of the work. What matters is that apprentices undertake the simultaneous processes of performing an increasing share of the work, participating in the social world in which the work is embedded, and constructing an appropriate "identity of mastery."

Situated learning theory, then, differs from transfer theory in several significant respects. It emphasizes the particularity of knowledge, reminding us that many cognitive skills appear to be context-specific and that even general knowledge "can be learned only in specific circumstances" and "must be brought into play in specific circumstances" (Lave & Wenger, p. 34); it highlights the importance of activity in learning, de-emphasizing the role of rules,

schemata, and explicit instruction; and it focuses less on the mind of the individual learner than on the social world in which learning takes place, suggesting a complex set of relationships among the individual, the members of
communities of practice, and the culture as a whole.[1]

In service-learning programs, we create opportunities for students to
move back and forth between the campus and the community in the hope
that each setting will grant them access to insights that enrich their experience
of the other. As service-learning research develops, it seems likely that we will
frequently face questions about how knowledge is developed and used across
multiple contexts. Though these may present themselves as questions about
transfer, my experience studying young writers suggests that we are better
served by a framework that directs our attention to the social and cultural circumstances in which learning occurs.

OBSERVATIONS OF COMMUNITY SERVICE WRITING

In my observations of the Community Service Writing program at San Francisco State University, I found that faculty participants frequently spoke as if
the practice of writing involved wielding a set of discrete skills and/or understandings that could be mastered in school and universally applied. Teachers
frequently referred to students as "strong writers" or "weak writers" based
on their performance with classroom writing tasks. For a few weeks, those of
us who planned the program considered limiting enrollment to students who
had earned high grades in earlier writing courses. Our plan was predicated
on the assumption that people who earned high grades in writing courses
would write successfully in community settings as well, while those who
earned low grades might, in one teacher's words, "embarrass the university"
by producing unacceptable papers. In other words, faculty participants in
the Community Service Writing Program expressed the beliefs that have
informed writing instruction for more than 100 years. As Smagorinsky and
Smith (1992) observe, both the writing-process approach that dominates composition instruction today and the earlier, product-oriented approach begin
with a similar view of writers' knowledge: "The two focuses do share a common assumption that general knowledge is sufficient and that writers can
transfer it spontaneously from situation to situation with relative ease"
(p. 285). It is this assumption that accounts for the persistence of composition
courses as a near-universal freshman requirement.

It is precisely this assumption that I hoped to investigate. To this end,
I designed a comparative assessment of students' papers.[2] I selected the 25
students participating in the study whose Community Service Writing documents had been written individually rather than collaboratively. For each
student, I constructed an Academic Writing Proficiency profile which, on the
basis of a collection of papers assessed by the teacher, rated the student's
overall proficiency on a six-point scale and identified strengths and weaknesses consistently exhibited in the papers. The same students' Community
Service Writing documents were assessed by three readers experienced in

evaluating nonacademic texts. These readers also assigned an overall score on a six-point scale and identified strengths and weaknesses.

When the two overall scores for each student were compared, a pattern emerged: in general, the most proficient academic writers produced the most successful CSW documents. The correlation of the scores is $r_{xy} = .7626$, which is significant at $\alpha < .05$. This result is consistent with the expectation of the faculty participants.

However, a closer look at the students' experience calls into question the reasoning behind our prediction. I collected an extensive body of qualitative data: field notes recording meetings, conversations, and class sessions; interviews with teachers and site supervisors; essays from fifty students reflecting on their experience writing for community agencies; a series of interviews with each of six focal students (one interview focusing on the student's writing background, one on his or her experience at the community organization, one on choices made in writing specific passages); copies of the focal students' course portfolios, including multiple drafts of most papers; and printouts of hundreds of email exchanges among the participants.

Of the steps taken to analyze these data, two are relevant to the findings reported here. First is analysis of the interview data, which yielded insights into students' efforts to make use of prior knowledge, experience, and instruction as they undertook unfamiliar writing tasks. Using established interpretive methods (Bogdan & Biklen, 1992), I read the interview transcripts to identify recurrent themes, labeled and listed the themes, then used the labels as categories for coding the data. I examined the coded data for patterns, generated hypotheses about what the patterns might mean, and tested the hypotheses with subsequent readings of the transcripts, the students' papers, and my field notes. Second is analysis of the reflective essays, which yielded insights into students' efforts to make use of the social milieu of the community agencies to build knowledge about their topics and about the genres in which they were asked to write. This analysis involved a similar process of identifying salient themes, coding the data, identifying patterns, testing my interpretation of the patterns in further readings, and triangulation with other data sources.

The findings which emerge from this analysis suggest that the correlation in students' performance as writers in academic and nonacademic contexts involves several factors in addition to the transfer of knowledge. While it is surely true that many of the skills and understandings that enable good writing in school are similarly useful in nonschool settings—that is, that the relevant knowledge transfers—other features of the students' cognition, attitudes, and behavior have more power to explain the correlation.

By way of example, let me introduce a young woman who was enrolled in a Community Service Writing course in the fall of 1995. Pamela,[3] a Filipina who had lived in this country for fifteen of her nineteen years, was an avid writer. She had a favorite aunt with whom she had corresponded since she was a child; she wrote weekly letters to her parents, who had returned to the Philippines, and to her sisters in Los Angeles; and she kept a diary where she wrote whenever she felt the need to work through her thoughts and feelings about events in her life.

Pamela was judged, by her teacher and by the readers who assessed her work, to be an above-average writer. Although she had some trouble with sentence structure, she earned high marks for content, organization, and development. These strengths appear to be based, in part, on knowledge about writing acquired in school; Pamela understood and made an earnest effort to apply lessons about organizing her essays, developing paragraphs, and combining sentences. The strengths also appear to be linked to what she describes as "a passion for writing." Pamela loved to write because, she explained, "it's like, a piece of yourself. It's letting you give your perspective on things, and it's like a way for me to vent myself. . . . I can say whatever I want on a piece of paper and, you know, I don't have to show it to anybody." Pamela was an engaged writer. She never wrote about a topic until she had found a way to make it matter, to establish an intellectual and emotional point of connection.

When asked to write an essay about a personal experience, Pamela chose to write about the Northridge earthquake of 1993. Pamela lived in Los Angeles at the time. The quake awakened her from a sound sleep, and she watched in terror as the furniture in her apartment was flung about the room. After the earthquake, her apartment was uninhabitable, and her workplace was reduced to rubble.

When I asked Pamela why she wrote the essay, she responded with the puzzled pause that usually greets such a question. Surely I knew that she wrote the paper because it was an assignment. But she quickly shifted to an explanation of why she had chosen the earthquake as her topic.

> My purpose of doing it was, I think a lot of things happened that two weeks that I tried to just shove in the back of my head. And I wanted to take all of it out. I wanted to recall that time because I think it gave me such a reason to, it just totally motivated me after that earthquake. I could die, you know? . . . that's why for the paper I wanted to kind of delve into the back of my head and kind of remember that hey! Life is really short. So I wrote about it.

Pamela is a serious, thoughtful young woman whose understanding of life was a work in progress; she actively and deliberately drew lessons from her experiences, and the lessons informed her behavior from day to day.

For her community service placement, Pamela chose to write for the San Francisco Tenants' Council because, having endured roommate troubles the year before, she appreciated the importance of their work. Although Pamela approached school writing assignments with confidence, she felt "overwhelmed" at the prospect of writing for a community organization. She found Jennifer, her supervisor at the Tenants' Council, to be extremely patient and helpful; nevertheless, the assigned task puzzled her. "It's really scary because I've never had to write a press packet before. I don't know what it is!"

While teachers expected students' school-based knowledge about writing to carry over into the community setting, very few students shared that expectation. Pamela was typical in believing that she had entered a whole new world where her knowledge and experience had little relevance. Her concern stemmed in part from her own assessment of her strengths and weaknesses as a writer. She wrote best, she said, when she could convey to her reader that the writing was coming from inside herself. She had trouble with research papers where her personal concerns could not take center stage, and she found the press packet to be similarly challenging.

Pamela's first task was to write an overview of services offered by the Tenants' Council. Jennifer gave Pamela a stack of materials—pamphlets, newsletters, ordinances and legislative propositions the Council had sponsored—and Pamela read them with genuine interest, motivated not only by the need to understand her topic but also by the desire to learn about her rights as a tenant. Still, she felt uninspired. "After trying, like reading everything over and over and over again, and thinking it over and over in my head, I just couldn't come up with anything. And so finally, I was just like, okay, I gotta go and see this for myself."

Pamela took the initiative to attend a drop-in counseling session, where she listened to conversations between tenants and counselors and took detailed notes. "That really, really, helped out a lot, because then I got to see first hand what exactly it is that they do, what it is I'm going to be writing about." Both Pamela and Jennifer remarked on how valuable Pamela's first-hand experience was in supplying specific, accurate detail for her description of tenant counseling. When she reflected on the experience later, Pamela articulated a lesson for community writing that echoes her belief about academic writing: "I think you just have to get really involved with it."

When it came time to pull the information she had gathered into a coherent whole, Pamela relied upon the organizational structure she knew best. The first draft of her document is a textbook example of a five-paragraph essay, with an introduction that ends in a three-part thesis statement, three middle paragraphs headed by topic sentences, and a brief conclusion. In later drafts she added headings but continued to present each section as a single paragraph.

While Pamela's academic essays won high marks for their organization, readers who assessed her Community Service Writing document did not single out organization as a strength. One reason may be that readers have different expectations for the design of nonacademic documents. Pamela, too, was dissatisfied with her document design, particularly when Jennifer told her that, instead of including the piece in a press packet, she might turn it into a brochure. "If it's like this," Pamela said, "and you hand it out to people, they're not going to want to read it." Some information in the document might have been included in a bulleted list rather than paragraph form. But, Pamela observed, "I just didn't think of doing it that way because . . . I just think I'm not really used to doing things in a form like that. I felt like it had to be a paper."

The skills, understandings, attitudes, and habits of mind that shaped Pamela's work on school writing tasks were clearly salient to the choices she made when she wrote for the Tenants' Council. But the question of how her prior knowledge affected her community-based writing has no simple answer. Pamela's love for writing, her commitment to finding a personal connection with the topic, and her willingness to throw herself into the work seem to account for her success in generating well-developed content in both settings. By contrast, she had a limited set of strategies for organizing and presenting material, and its limits were more severely strained by the community writing (which, after all, she was doing for the first time) than by school writing tasks. Pamela persisted, working side by side with Jennifer until — after four drafts — both of them were pleased with the document.

Central to Pamela's success as a writer is her habit of analyzing her experience. She was proud of the text she had created, but she was not uncritical. In fact, she noted the same weaknesses observed by readers with expertise in nonacademic writing, recognizing that she needed a tighter design and a more "professional" tone. Her work for the Tenants' Council broadened Pamela's view of writing. Like school writing tasks, Community Service Writing was folded into the cycle of experience and reflection by which Pamela shapes her education and her identity as a capable adult.

THE SCHOOL-TO-COMMUNITY TRANSITION

I've described Pamela's experience at some length because it illustrates several features of Community Service Writing that, throughout data collected from dozens of student writers, appear to warrant close attention. If we are to understand the transition from school to community contexts for writing, we must attend to a broad range of cognitive, affective, and social factors that influence writers' behavior. Eight of these are listed below. Each item in the list might be viewed as a continuum along which writers vary as they work to produce functional texts in unfamiliar settings. Taken together, they begin to account for the dynamics of the transition.

1. Knowledge about Writing

Knowledge about writing is of two types. First is propositional knowledge, familiarity with a set of principles describing conventions for written language and strategies for composing texts. When Pamela explained to me that an opening sentence should entice the reader or when she said that long sentences were less likely to sound choppy than short ones, she was exhibiting propositional knowledge about writing. Of course, it frequently happens that writers know principles and fail to follow them when they write, and it happens still more frequently that they adhere to principles they could never articulate. As a consequence, propositional knowledge about writing is of less interest than writing proficiency.

By writing proficiency, I mean simply the cluster of abilities required to produce texts. To find out what someone knows about writing, we look at the texts they write. Although any text can give only an approximate and incomplete glimpse of the writer's underlying knowledge, patterns that obtain across many texts are revealing.

Texts are typically evaluated for their content, overall organization, paragraph organization and development, sentence structure and fluency, and mechanics. Generally, the larger and more substantive the unit of discourse, the more likely it is that criteria for success vary across contexts and genres: what counts as good content or an effective organizational plan will be different in a brochure than in a personal essay. Smaller units of discourse are more constant across contexts and genres: we almost always expect verbs to agree with subjects, for example, and conventions for spelling and punctuation show little variation. As a result, the concept of transfer may be a useful theoretical tool in studies of basic skills while it has limited value for understanding writers' control over discourse styles.

2. Theory of Writing

By "theory of writing," I mean a writer's conception of what writing is and what it is for. Some theories of writing seemed helpful to students in transition while others were dysfunctional. Pamela, for example, viewed writing as self-expression. While this theory seems ill-suited to nonacademic writing (and to most academic writing outside of English departments), it did not in fact prove damaging, perhaps because it was accompanied by the habits of deep personal engagement and critical reflection.

Other students I interviewed had characteristic ways of talking about writing, too—as communicating with readers, as filling up a form according to the rules, as demonstrating knowledge and intelligence. One student, for example, who had always been identified as a "weak writer," had a "just the facts, ma'am" theory of writing. In her view, the essential purpose of writing was to provide an accurate record of information, and she had a strong preference for brevity. Since she did not see writing as an occasion to explore her own thinking, she was out of step with the purposes of writing in school, and she had trouble earning a passing grade in composition courses. In her Community Service Writing, she remained a "weak writer," but she did piece together a usable document. Her theory of writing as getting down the facts was less disabling in this context.

In short, students varied in their conceptions of what writing as a practice is all about. Theories of writing that promoted or impeded success in school did not necessarily have the same effect outside the classroom. In addition to their skills and knowledge, students' theories of writing affected their performance in school and community settings.

3. Rhetorical Awareness

By rhetorical awareness, I mean the writer's sensitivity to the fact that different rhetorical contexts call for different choices about what to say and how to say it. Some CSW students, particularly those who had experience writing outside the classroom (on high school newspapers or speech teams, for example), recognized that they could choose from a range of voices, and they were adept at picking up the style appropriate for their writing task. Others wrote "English essays" no matter what the assignment called for, and you could tell from the first sentence that the writer was a student.

Awareness of rhetorical variation was not enough to ensure success in adapting to the demands of a new rhetorical context. Many students, like Pamela, wished to select, organize, and present their material to address a particular audience and purpose, but they did not know how to do it. As newcomers to the community organizations, they did not understand enough about the goals, values, and activities of the organizations to "talk the talk." But awareness was an important first step. Recognizing this, the CSW teacher I observed most closely changed her curriculum after the first semester to make rhetorical variation an object of study.

The distinction between *rhetorical awareness*—the understanding that discourse varies with its audience and purpose—and *rhetorical competence in a particular setting* is one that complicates the concepts of "transfer" and "situated learning." I would argue that both gaining an awareness of variation and gaining competence in a particular setting involve situated learning. Community Service Writing programs, like extracurricular writing opportunities, seem to be well suited as "situations" for gaining *rhetorical awareness* since they confront students with multiple rhetorical contexts and consequently with the fact of rhetorical variation. While the learning is situated, the knowledge that results from it is general: once students understand the degree to which discourse varies, once they have some practice analyzing "discourse communities" to see how language use reflects and perpetuates the goals of social groups, they are prepared to function as writers at other times, in other places. By contrast, gaining *rhetorical competence* at the Tenants' Council involves both situated learning—learning that really cannot happen unless you spend time at the Tenants' Council—and situated knowledge, knowledge about the ways of thinking and writing unique to that setting.

I think it makes sense to speak of rhetorical awareness as transferable; in fact, those students who had experience writing outside of classrooms seemed to transfer their awareness on the occasion of writing for the community, and it seems likely that students who participate in Community Service Writing will profit from their rhetorical awareness on future occasions. But the transfer of rhetorical awareness is just the first step: its effect is to set the writer on a learning path that leads toward a body of context-specific knowledge.

4. Motivation and Attitude Toward the Task

Students varied in their enthusiasm for the community-based writing assignment. Many, like Pamela, had chosen a CSW section specifically because they sought an opportunity to make a contribution to the community, and their motivation was heightened if they were interested in the organization's work and felt affinity with its goals and values. Often, these students organized their time throughout the semester so the community-based project could come first. Others signed up for the class because it met at a convenient time or because it fulfilled a graduation requirement. Some found that courses in their majors or events in their personal lives relegated Community Service Writing to the "back burner."

If we were to describe this variation in terms of transfer, students' motivation and attitudes might be characterized as factors that determine whether knowledge is operationalized. Since these factors had such a significant impact on students' performance, the affective dimension is itself worthy of investigation.

5. Social Relationships

As studies of nonacademic writing repeatedly stress, writing outside the classroom involves complex social relationships. Community Service Writing students got a taste of this reality as they collaborated with classmates, conducted interviews, and submitted their work to supervisors or editors at the community agencies. Their ability to establish relationships and assume appropriate social roles proved to be crucial to their success *as writers*.

The student-site supervisor relationships were especially instructive. It frequently happened that students expected their supervisors to act like teachers, while the supervisors expected student writers to act like professional free-lancers. Teachers design writing assignments with students in mind. They are aware of the extent and the limits of students' knowledge about the topic, they explain their expectations and criteria for evaluation, and they set deadlines consistent with the contours of an academic term. The supervisors at the community agencies, by contrast, designed writing assignments with their organizations' needs in mind, and, at least during their first experience with CSW, they seldom offered the explicit directions students expected. They often invited students to brainstorm with them about what direction a writing project might take, and they routinely expected documents to pass through three or four drafts.

Pamela's relationship with her supervisor was typical. Pamela and Jennifer liked each other, and Pamela was deeply impressed by Jennifer's commitment to the Tenants' Council. She was, however, frustrated when Jennifer's directions seemed unclear; she knew that she had questions ("I've never written a press packet before. I don't know what it is!"), but she hesitated to raise them because she didn't want to take up too much of Jennifer's time or to create a bad impression. And, while she appreciated Jennifer's patience, she was disconcerted by the assumption that a writing project could be transformed over time through rethinking and revising. It took several weeks for Pamela and Jennifer to understand their expectations of each other and to make appropriate accommodations in their roles.

When students were asked to reflect on Community Service Writing, they overwhelmingly discussed it as a social experience. The evaluative essays they wrote at semester's end barely touched upon the creation of texts: while a few commented briefly on having applied lessons about writing to a "real-world" task, not one wrote that he or she had learned how to produce a press release or newsletter article or brochure. Even when students were specifically asked to identify what they had learned *about writing*, they responded by discussing what they had learned about a community organization, its mission, the people there, their role as volunteer writers, or themselves as members of a larger community, connected with others and capable of making a contribution. Their responses reflect the fact that learning to write in a nonacademic setting is inseparable from learning to behave as a writer in relationship to others in that setting.

6. Learning Strategies

A writer's transition from school to nonschool contexts involves not just learning new genres but learning new ways of learning.[4] As the discussion above suggests, when students shifted from the role of "student" to that of "writer," they had to take an unaccustomed responsibility for defining and refining the assignment, for gathering information, and for familiarizing themselves with the discourse of the organization.

To know *what* to say, students needed to develop topic knowledge. They employed the familiar strategy of reading written materials, usually supplied by their site supervisors, and the less familiar steps of interviewing staff members and observing and/or interviewing the agency's clients. When Pamela was stuck, she decided to spend more time in the world of the Tenants' Council, so she went to observe a counseling session. While this may appear to be a common-sense strategy, it requires self-initiated action that students do not necessarily practice in school and that many students were not prepared to take.

To know *how* to present what they had learned to readers, students needed to develop discourse knowledge. The student writers who were most effective in producing texts whose organization and style were appropriate to the context engaged in some or all of these learning practices: drawing upon prior knowledge about relevant discursive conventions (e.g., using journalistic conventions in a newsletter article), studying models available at the agency, actively seeking and attending to specific directions from the site supervisor, and actively seeking and attending to the site supervisor's response to multiple drafts.

The process of developing topic and discourse knowledge was circular: as students learned more about the agency, they became more deeply involved in its work and more confident about taking initiative in that setting, and as their involvement and confidence grew, they were more effective in learning about the agency. Pamela was quite right to suggest that "you just have to get really involved with it." The learning strategies could not be simply imported; they depended upon conditions created jointly by the students and the people with whom they formed working relationships.

7. Identity as a Writer

When undergraduates write in response to school assignments, the purpose of the writing is to advance and to display their learning about some topic. Usually, the reader—the teacher—knows more about the topic than the writer, so her purpose for reading is primarily evaluative. The reader, then, has more power and authority than the writer. When people write in settings outside of school, this relationship is ordinarily reversed: the writer is the source of knowledge, and the reader turns to the text in order to learn what the writer has to say.

A crucial aspect of the transition students make when they move from classroom to community contexts for writing, then, is a shift in the authority granted to them as writers. For writers in a service-learning program, this shift is the more dramatic because, in addition to taking on the role of knower, they take on the role of community server. Students' reflective essays are full of comments like these:

> I gained the confidence to write a brochure thousands of people will read and was given the chance to volunteer my time for a worthy cause to better myself, but more importantly to better my community.

> I was part of a much larger purpose, a unit working for a common cause. The experience felt satisfying and meaningful throughout but especially when I faxed that final draft of my composition to the [agency]. I had completed an assignment not just for some professor to allot a grade, but for promoting a worthwhile organization that actively cares for the community.

Because they were writing for an audience beyond "some professor," most CSW students understood that there was more at stake than a grade. As writers, they represented the community agencies to anyone who might read their documents. The most conscientious students took this responsibility seriously; one pointed out to me that, since people often believe what they see in print, she felt an obligation to "use, not abuse" her power as a writer. Pamela, too, reported that her Community Service Writing experience made her aware of "the power of words:"

> . . . before this class I was convinced that the only way that I could make a difference in this world was if I studied Science and became a doctor. But with this experience I came to understand the utter importance of the ability to voice oneself through text and writing.

This kind of insight can, in part, be explained as a learning outcome of Community Service Writing. Given a new kind of writing experience, students expanded their theories of writing. But the data suggest that the shift was, for some students, not so much a lesson about writing as a transformation in their view of themselves. Having met the test of a "real-world" professional task, having made their mark in a public text, they could visualize themselves as having agency in the social world.

8. Identity as a Learner

Many students embraced the more active learning strategies and the more authoritative roles available to them in nonacademic settings. Pamela, for example, had long prided herself on her self-reliance, and she was in the habit of integrating her academic studies with analysis of her experience. Already an active, self-motivated learner, Pamela had no trouble positioning herself as a learner at the Tenants' Council.

At the other end of the spectrum were a small number of students who resisted learning at the community organizations. These students were committed to the idea that, before they went out into the world, someone at the university ought to tell them what they needed to know. They did not conceive of learning as an ongoing part of life outside of school, and they did not imagine themselves as having either the power or the responsibility to create knowledge.

Students coming to the Community Service Writing program varied, then, in terms of their identities as learners. The passive model of studenthood is, of course, pervasive in our culture: all of the students had extensive experience occupying the role of a student defined as someone who gets taught. But they were differentially invested in that role. Their degree of investment became yet another factor that determined the quality of their transition from school to nonschool writing.

CONCLUSION

In discussions of service-learning, we sometimes speak of our hopes for students in terms of several kinds of learning—academic learning plus moral learning, civic learning, development of social skills, and so on. Although my study began with a single focus on the academic component of Community Service Writing, expressed as a question about transfer, it soon became clear that the academic component was not an independent entity. Students' success *as writers* depended not so much upon mastery of the lessons typically covered in composition courses as upon affective and social aspects of the experience. The academic understandings they developed were shaped by prior and emerging knowledge about writing as well as by prior and emerging attitudes, social skills, and views of themselves as writers and learners.

Students who saw their own learning as a matter of acquiring knowledge in school, then applying it elsewhere, were ill equipped for their roles as volunteer writers. Those whose view of learning was more complex—involving more active personal engagement, a wider range of learning strategies, and more sensitivity to social relationships—were prepared for a smoother transition. Ideally, service-learning programs prompt students to question the passive model of studenthood, calling their attention to the way we participate, in the course of our everyday activities, in the construction of knowledge. Similarly, service-learning programs challenge us as researchers to develop sophisticated models of learning that can account not only for the particles of knowledge that may be deposited in learners' heads but for the active knowledge-building activities in which they engage.

NOTES

I thank Sarah Warshauer Freedman for her help at every stage of the study reported here. I am grateful to the people at San Francisco State who created the Community Service Writing program, particularly Jo Keroes and Susan Mallet.

1. For a fuller discussion of the relevance of situated learning theory to service-learning, see Wolfson & Willinsky (1998).

2. The study's methodology is explained in Bacon (1997).

3. "Pamela," "Jennifer," and "Tenants' Council" are pseudonyms.

4. Many researchers have observed the discomfort writers feel when they begin to write in settings outside the classroom (Anson & Forsberg, 1990; Doheny-Farina, 1989; MacKinnon, 1993; Trimmer, 1999). Aviva Freedman and Christine Adam (1996) attribute this discomfort to the fact that writers need to learn not only new genres but new ways of learning.

REFERENCES

Anson, C. M. & Forsberg, L. L. (1990). Moving beyond the academic community: Transitional stages in professional writing. *Written Communication, 7*, 200–231.

Bacon, N. (1997). *The transition from classroom to community contexts for writing.* Dissertation, University of California at Berkeley.

Bogdan, R. C. & Biklen, S. K. (1992). *Qualitative research for education.* Boston: Allyn and Bacon.

Doheny-Farina, S. (1989). A case study of one adult writing in academic and nonacademic discourse communities. In C. B. Matalene (Ed.), *Worlds of writing: Teaching and learning in discourse communities of work* (pp. 17–42). New York: Random House.

Ellis, H. C. (1965). *The transfer of learning.* New York: Macmillan.

Freedman, A. & Adam, C. (1996). Learning to write professionally: "Situated learning" and the transition from university to professional discourse. *Journal of Business and Technical Communication, 10*(4), 395–427.

Gick, M. L. & Holyoak, K. J. (1987). The cognitive basis of knowledge transfer. In S. M. Cormier & J. D. Hagman (Eds.), *Transfer of learning* (pp. 9–46). New York: Academic Press.

Joncich, G. M. (1962). Science: Touchstone for a new age in education. In G. M. Joncich (Ed.), *Psychology and the science of education: Selected writings of Edward L. Thorndike.* New York: Teachers College.

Lave, J. (1991). Situated learning in communities of practice. In L. Resnick, J. Levine, & S. Teasley (Eds.), *Perspectives on socially shared cognition* (pp. 63–82). Washington, DC: American Psychological Association.

Lave, J. & Wenger, E. (1991). *Situated learning: Legitimate peripheral participation.* Cambridge: Cambridge University Press.

MacKinnon, J. (1993). Becoming a rhetor: Developing writing ability in a mature, writing-intensive organization. In R. Spilka (Ed.), *Writing in the workplace: New research perspectives* (pp. 41–55). Carbondale: Southern Illinois UP.

Scardamalia, M. & Bereiter, C. (1986). Research on written composition. In M. Wittrock (Ed.), *Handbook of research on teaching* (pp. 778–803). Chicago: Rand McNally.

Smagorinsky, P. & Smith, M. W. (1992). The nature of knowledge in composition and literary understanding: The question of specificity. *Review of Educational Research 62,* 279–305.

Thorndike, E. L. & Woodworth, R. S. (1901). The influence of improvement in one mental function upon the efficiency of other functions. *Psychological Review 3,* 247–384.

Trimmer, J. (1999). Real world writing assignments. *JAC: A Journal of Composition Theory 19,* 35–49.

Wolfson, L. & Willinsky, J. (1998). What service-learning can learn from situated learning. *Michigan Journal of Community Service Learning 5,* 22–31.

32   Shifting Locations, Genres, and Motives: An Activity Theory Analysis of Service-Learning Writing Pedagogies

THOMAS DEANS

By extending the site for writing from classroom to local community, service-learning pedagogies change the location of composition: novice writers venture off campus to work with local citizens and organizations. Yet there is no normative model for community-based pedagogy. It comes in various shapes and sizes and enacts a diverse range of literacies, genres, and objectives. Some service-learning initiatives ask students to undertake client-based projects—Web site content, newsletter articles and profiles, research reports, press releases, and so on—that serve the workplace needs of local nonprofit organizations. Some initiatives invite students to compose personal and critical essays that reflect on their field experiences of tutoring youth, working at homeless shelters, and so on. Some initiatives structure direct partnerships with local citizens to facilitate collaborative writing ventures that provoke awareness, spark creative expression, or broker grassroots problem-solving. Many service-learning programs, even individual courses, mix and match these approaches.

We should note that most iterations of community-based writing instruction do not replace the classroom as a site for learning and doing; instead, they introduce additional sites in the local community. It is tempting to focus our analysis of service-learning on those locations for writing (college classrooms, local communities, nonprofit organizations) and especially on how each location shapes written discourse. Yet while place can be a promising locus of analysis, location runs up against its limits rather quickly because it is rooted in a spatial metaphor. In this essay I propose that we attend to location less in terms of *place* and more in terms of *activity*.

This leaves us with a guiding question: What happens when we imagine the locations for writing less as places and more as systems of activity? In pursuing it I rely on cultural-historical activity theory, and such an approach to service-learning writing pedagogy steers us away from thinking about how writing is relocated from classroom to community and toward thinking about

From *The Locations of Composition*, eds. Christopher J. Keller and Christian R. Weisser (Albany: State U of New York P, 2007), 289–306.

the interactions and contradictions between two activity systems (the university and the community partner organization) as they overlap in a third activity system: the service-learning classroom itself. I argue that activity theory reveals why some service-learning pedagogies thrive and others falter, suggest some concrete strategies that teachers can employ to help student writers effectively negotiate community-based writing projects, and offer a fruitful way to rethink how we do research on service-learning.

I limit the scope of my inquiry to what I have elsewhere called *writing for the community* and *writing with the community* versions of service-learning, each of which require students (even if as only one part of a course) to enter nonprofit organizations or local communities as novice writers, producing or coproducing documents in nonacademic genres that circulate beyond the classroom (Deans 2000). I set aside *writing about the community*, a popular mode of service-learning in which students perform direct service (such as tutoring youth or participating in an environmental cleanup), reflect upon it, and then fold that outreach experience into their academic writing (journals, personal essays, critical essays, research papers). I focus on *writing for* and *writing with* modes because those kinds of service-learning invite students to use writing itself as a tool to expand their involvement in activity and genre systems beyond college classrooms and academic disciplines.

DISCOURSE COMMUNITIES AND/OR ACTIVITY SYSTEMS

Scholarship on service-learning in composition started to gather momentum in the 1990s, in the wake of the social turn in composition, which so prominently featured the discourse community as a tool for understanding writing. Consequently, much research on service-learning and related phenomena such as school-to-work transitions relied heavily on the discourse community as a conceptual frame for analyzing writing across contexts.

More recently, some writing researchers have been building a case for using the activity system rather than the discourse community as the basic unit of analysis (Bazerman 2004; Bazerman and Russell 2002; Dias 2000; Dias et al. 1999; Prior 1998; Russell 1995; Russell 1997). It can be tempting to use the terms *discourse community* and *activity system* interchangeably. After all, both emphasize the social nature of writing; both help us imagine how individual writing practices are situated within and shaped by their institutional and cultural contexts; both upset the notion that writing is a discrete skill that can be readily transferred across contexts; and both help us explain how and why writers behave—even succeed or fail—in various situations. What, then, can approaches based on activity theory offer that those grounded in discourse community theory cannot?

While activity theory may have its roots in the Soviet psychology of L. S. Vygotsky and A. N. Leont'ev, I concentrate on how Yrjo Engeström has interpreted that tradition and on the ways that composition scholars such as Charles Bazerman, David Russell, and Paul Prior, among others, have used activity theory to help us understand the dynamics of writing in school and at work. Such proponents of activity theory tend to commend discourse community advocates for the ways that they affirm the social and context-driven nature of writing. Indeed, both movements emerged in large part as rejections of the tendency in Western cognitive psychology to view human behavior (including writing) apart from social context. But activity theorists point out that the discourse community is generally imagined as a static, uniform, ahistorical thing or place (Prior 1998). One *enters* a discourse community, almost as one would enter a building. The spatial metaphor suggests that individuals undergo enculturation into a location or apprenticeship to a community where shared rules and normative conventions prevail. Such a view calcifies the divide between outside and inside, between social context and individual behavior; it also assumes that context largely determines individual behavior. Using the discourse community as the main unit also masks the struggles and contradictions roiling within a community (Harris 1989). It steers our attention away from the dynamic interactions among various communities, it pays little attention to individual agency, and it offers no means for explaining how individuals or collectives change over time (Russell 1997).

In contrast, activity theory—also termed cultural-historical activity theory and sociohistorical theory—discourages us from seeing contexts as specific locations or as containers of behavior and encourages us to explore the dynamic relations between social contexts and the actions of individuals. Activity theory puts more emphasis on doing things than on being someplace (Prior 1998, xii). It also assumes that social systems are goal-driven rather than just there, examines tools as they are used to get things done in systems, and attends to the contradictions that emerge both within and between systems.

Activity theory posits the activity system as the basic unit of analysis. An activity system is any collective, ongoing, historically conditioned, tool-mediated human interaction (Russell 1997, 510). Some examples are a family, a religious organization, a nonprofit agency, a political movement, a college course, a school, an academic discipline, and a profession. An activity system can be large (such as a research university) or small (such as one course within that university) or smaller still (one's immediate family). And obviously we are all involved in several activity systems that overlap, interact, and even conflict. In this essay I consider universities and nonprofit organizations as separate activity systems but devote the bulk of discussion to how the service-learning classroom itself functions as an activity system deeply influenced by the other two.

The minimum elements of an activity system include the object, subject, mediating tools, rules, community, and division of labor (see Figure 32–1).

- The *subject* refers to the individual or subgroup that is chosen as the point of view in the analysis. For example, I will focus most on students as subjects, although teachers and community partners will also be considered.

- Activity theory assumes that human behavior is goal driven, something that tends to get washed out in discourse community theory, and *object* refers to

Figure 32–1   The Basic Structure of an Activity System, Featuring the Example
of a Typical First-Year Composition Course

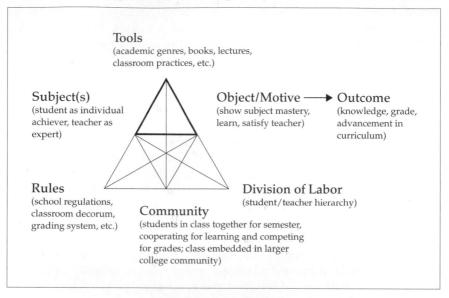

Tools
(academic genres, books, lectures,
classroom practices, etc.)

Subject(s)
(student as individual
achiever, teacher as
expert)

Object/Motive ⟶ **Outcome**
(show subject mastery,   (knowledge, grade,
learn, satisfy teacher)   advancement in
                           curriculum)

Rules
(school regulations,
classroom decorum,
grading system, etc.)

Community
(students in class together for semester,
cooperating for learning and competing
for grades; class embedded in larger
college community)

Division of Labor
(student/teacher hierarchy)

(Adapted from Engeström 1987 and Engeström 1996)

the intended purpose of the activity. Object is often conflated with *motive*, that
is, the motive or motives that inspire and propel the activity.

- *Tools* are the instruments—physical, linguistic, and otherwise—that help do
  the work of the system. To meet with sustained success in an activity system,
  individuals need to appropriate its tools, just as they must also, to some degree, adopt the objectives and motives of the system.

- The *community* comprises the individuals and/or subgroups that share the
  same general object/motive.

- The *division of labor* refers to both the horizontal division of tasks between the
  members of the community and to the vertical division of power and status.

- And *rules* refers to the explicit and implicit regulations and norms that constrain actions within the system. (Engeström 1987; Engeström 1996, 67)

These terms supply a vocabulary for analyzing individual behaviors in relation to social systems, and are represented visually in Figure 32–1. The heart
of the activity system is the trio at the top: subject, tools, and object/motive.
The rules, community, and division of labor form what Engeström calls its
"social basis" (1999).

All of the connecting lines run in both directions, and the components of
the system interact continually. The system involves what Paul Prior calls the
cogenesis of persons, practices, artifacts, tools, institutions, and communities
(1998, 32). Moreover, the whole activity system changes over time, often incrementally but sometimes through dramatic crises or upheavals.

By making a case for activity theory, I am not arguing that we abandon discourse community approaches entirely. In fact, in my own advanced service-learning courses I continue to introduce my students to discourse community theory to help them recognize the social and situated nature of composing. One of the weaknesses of the discourse community as a unit of analysis—that it tends to imagine community as static, unified, and ahistorical—can translate into a strength when one is teaching students to write across diverse contexts. Discourse communities sit still. We can pick them up and examine them. We can name discourse communities, define their boundaries, list their conventions, discuss the process of being socialized into them. Still, in this essay I push for an additional mode of analysis because activity theory directs our attention to several factors that are not sufficiently accounted for in discourse community approaches: *tools*, especially written genres as tools writers use; *motives*, both personal and institutional; and *contradictions*, both within systems and between systems. Service-learning, because it is a pressurized situation in which different activity systems are combined to form a new one, proves a revealing laboratory for activity theory.

Locating (and Teaching) Genres, Motives, and Contradictions

An activity theory analysis could begin with any one of the system's key elements—any of the nodes on the triangle in Figure 32–1. I begin with tools, especially written genres as tools, and then move on to motive/object. After considering each in brief, we will explore how contradictions are understood in activity theory and consider how these concepts pertain to service-learning writing pedagogies.

Genres

Perhaps no tool is more important to writers than is genre. Whereas discourse community approaches tend to emphasize the shared, seemingly fixed conventions of genres in a particular community—as well as the variation in those conventions across communities—activity theory sees genres as tools that writers use to get things done. They are "forms of life, ways of being, frames for social action" (Bazerman 1994, 1). Experienced writers use such tools routinely; newcomers must appropriate such tools if they have any hope of expanding their involvement with others in an activity system (Russell 1997, 521). But while genre theory—some of it informed by activity theory— has recently emerged as a vital strand of composition theory, few who study service-learning in composition have taken genre as a locus of analysis, which is curious, given the ways that many service-learning pedagogies invite a mix of academic and nonacademic genres.

David Jolliffe's work marks one exception. He has alerted us to how paying more attention to activity theory and genre theory can enrich our understanding of how community writing relates to school writing. He argues that we should pay more attention to how genres function as tools for writers and how the genres being employed in a classroom or in a service-learning project signal the writer's degree of participation in various activity systems. For example, while all service-learning courses describe themselves as engaged with the community, Jolliffe argues that only by examining whether and how students actually use written genres do we get a sense of their involvement *as writers* in activity systems beyond those of school. Do the students stick to the tools of school (essay, paper, journal)? Or do they pick up the tools—the civic and workplace genres—of community groups and nonprofits? In his call for attending more to genre, Jolliffe follows the lead of David Russell, who claims that by "tracing the relation of a disciplinary or professional genre system to an educational genre system, through the boundary of a classroom genre system, a researcher, reformer, or participant can construct a model of ways classroom writing is linked to writing in wider social practices" (Russell 1997, 546).[1]

More service-learning researchers need to do just that sort of tracing. Likewise, more service-learning teachers need to get students to reflect on how genres serve as active tools (rather than as passive formats), and on how learning particular genres can be a means of participating in new activity systems. When teaching students to write for nonprofits, many instructors approach the differences between academic and nonacademic contexts by inviting students to practice textual and audience analysis. And while those are fruitful strategies, I propose that we should devote just as much attention to genre analysis. Students should investigate not only *what* textual conventions prevail in a given community and *whom* their writing will address but also *how* particular tools (especially genres) are necessary for getting the work of writing done. Teachers should invite students to analyze the social action that genres perform: how they are tools-in-use rather than fixed formats (Miller 1984; Russell 1997, 511); how genres can be both stable and open to variation; and how single genres figure in larger genre sets and genre systems (Bazerman 1994).

In my own writing-for-the-community courses I have recently begun devoting more time to explicit reflection on genre. For example, I lecture on Carolyn Miller's notion of genre as social action and distill some key points from genre theory; I assign Anne Beaufort's *Writing in the Real World*, an ethnography of novice writers in a nonprofit agency, in which Beaufort concludes that writers need genre knowledge just as much as they need discourse community knowledge, rhetorical knowledge, subject matter knowledge, and process knowledge. After a student project team has held initial interviews of key contacts at their community partner organization and examined the texts that circulate within it, I require a genre analysis assignment. Each team must collect several examples of the genre that their project calls for (or the closest approximations of it that they can find), inventory the patterns of sameness and difference across the examples, reflect on how writers and readers use those genres in activity systems, and consider how the genre interacts with related genre sets, as well as if and how it has changed over time.[2]

Motives

Discourse community approaches privilege the *who, what* and *where* of writing over not only the *how* (tools) but also the *why* of the writing (its motive). Most tend to think of motivation as a psychological state located in the individual, but activity theory frames motivation as a social phenomenon. *Motive* is often conflated with *objective* or *goal*, and activity theory assumes that activities, including writing, are goal-directed. The motive signals "the overall direction of the activity" in the system (Russell 1997, 511). Activity systems have social motives, and individuals/subjects within those systems adopt, reject, or adapt those motives. Indeed, how one relates to a variety of social motives constitutes a significant part of one's identity. In this sense we move closer to Kenneth Burke's use of motive and can refine the term further by naming institutional or systemic objectives as *social motives* (Miller 1984; Dias et al. 1999, 20–21).

Some motives of activity systems, such as schools, are obvious (promoting learning, socializing youth) and some less so (reproducing cultural stratification, ranking students and sorting them into different fields). Likewise, a nonprofit agency may have obvious social motives (raising awareness on a particular issue, addressing a community need) and more opaque ones (perpetuating its own survival). Moreover, students arrive at college already deeply invested in other activity systems—those of family, friends, neighborhood, work, religion, and so on—and those life-world activity systems come with their own social motives (which often align powerfully with the "real world" or "doing good" traits associated with service-learning).[3] When the motives of all three activity systems (school, nonprofit, and life-world) complement one another, we find a powerful amalgam, one celebrated in the success stories of service-learning. When the social motives conflict too radically, we get trouble.

A key question for analysis then becomes *Which social motives are afoot in the service-learning writing classroom, and how do students navigate them?* Furthermore, *How do students align themselves with the social motives of the various activity systems in play (especially school and community organization), and how do they deal with the contradictions among them?* While I defer the discussion of contradictions to the next section, here I want to suggest that just as we can track if and how novices adopt, adapt, or reject the tools (genres) of disciplines and community organizations, we should attend to how they respond to the social motives of activity systems.

One pragmatic thing that teachers can do, as with genre, is to draw more deliberate attention to the social motives of all the stakeholders in a service-learning experience. For example, in anticipation of service-learning projects in my own classrooms I pose the most simple of questions: Why do we write in school? As students look at me with expressions that seem to say, "Come on, don't be an idiot," I nudge them to volunteer answers: "Because we have to." "To get a good grade." "Because teachers need a way to test whether we know the material." "To explore and share our ideas." We then push from these local responses to the deeper social motives, and I suggest those posited by Dias et al. in *Worlds Apart: Acting and Writing in Academic and Workplace Contexts*: students write to show what they know because schools use writing to promote and document learning (the epistemic motive); but writing also enables students to be "graded and slotted," which is another social motive of schools and universities: to sort and rank students (1999, 44).

And then I ask, Why do people write in workplaces such as nonprofit agencies? "To get their message out." "To get grant money." And so on. We find that in the workplace writers compose documents that contribute in pragmatic ways to shared organizational goals. Here people do not usually write to show what they know. (In fact, the carryover of that motive—usually manifest in showy overwriting—is one of the main frustrations that managers have with recruits fresh out of academia.) In class we put the social motives on the table and discuss how they might cooperate and conflict, and in these discussions the *why/social motive* of writing trumps the *where/location* of writing.[4]

Provoking in our students a meta-awareness of different social motives for writing can prove valuable in dispelling misunderstandings that surface as novices take on complex rhetorical projects in community settings. But awareness of social motives is not enough. To make service-learning projects work well, educators and community partners must to some degree *adopt* each other's social motives.

Teachers and community partners who opt into service-learning already share some common motives, such as a broad commitment to addressing social problems through service. But as an educator my priority is promoting individual student learning, while a manager in a nonprofit must be concerned with getting the work of the organization done, and done well. While I may be an educator, in a service-learning context I need to adopt some motives and practices of a manager, even when that seems to cut against my teaching instincts. And while my community partner may be a manager, he or she needs to adopt some of the motives and practices of a teacher, even when that puts a drag on efficiency. For example, in service-learning courses I implement several workplace-like practices that are absent from my other courses: I cancel classes to give students time for agency meetings; I replace whole classes with team work sessions; I cede much of my authority to judge what counts for quality writing—and even a fair amount of the authority to determine grades—to my community partner; I comment more assertively on drafts, giving up some of the let-students-muck-around-and-discover-their-own-mistakes learning motive for the get-it-done-right-for-the-organization motive. Likewise, my more effective community partners open spaces for learning and mentoring, even when doing so might prove time-consuming and inefficient. As experienced service-learning teachers know, some community partners work out much better than others, and the most helpful are the ones who see students as learners-in-development rather than as miniature professionals. Such community partners see themselves as not just project managers but also as educators, thereby adopting the epistemic motive of schooling. They stretch to appropriate some unfamiliar motives; I do the same.

Students, too, must to some degree adopt the motives of their community partner activity systems. When the teacher and community partner motives are reasonably well aligned (or at least understood), service-learning tends to go well. But trouble sets in when, for example, a student who holds fast to school motives, which keep the student focused on what he or she thinks the teacher wants rather than on what the community partner needs, on getting a good grade rather than on getting the job done well, and on individual learning rather than on the collective contribution to the community partner. More interesting and typical, though, are the cases where students genuinely struggle, as writers, with competing social motives. For example, when community partners ask my students to compose profiles of volunteers, clients, or events for use in their public relations materials, students usually embrace the project and do it well. However, often students feel caught in a double bind: they are under pressure to write public relations stories that celebrate the people and events, and from their genre analyses of similar profiles, they have learned that profiles put a positive spin on their subjects. But students often wince at having to portray people or events with too rosy a glow about them; rather they feel the pull of objectivity associated with academic and journalistic activity systems. By analyzing the social motives in play, students can negotiate the situation with more dexterity.

I have largely set aside consideration of the motives of the life-world activity systems that students bring to our courses, but ideally we should also account for those too, especially in service-learning. Career-minded students often find their motives reflected in the "real world" character of much community-based writing, but more powerful tend to be ways that the religious, ethical, and political sensibilities of our students converge with the social motives of organizations committed to social justice. One only need imagine what unfolds as a young man whose mother died of breast cancer takes on a writing project with a women's health advocacy organization. Likewise, one need only imagine the prickliness of projects that require students to work as writers in community organizations whose values and motives they reject.

Service-learning projects are at their most powerful when they create generative, complementary relationships among the school activity system, the community partner activity system, and the students' more personal identities as reflected in their life-world activity systems. In at least one of those systems—and more often in all three—students can discover compelling motives to write well. But they usually need to negotiate some tricky contradictions along the way, and activity theory can help us see those more clearly.

Contradictions

Those who adopt the discourse community model nearly always acknowledge that writers belong to several different communities at once, a phenomenon often represented visually by the overlapping circles of a Venn diagram. While such an approach affirms the complexity of a writer's context, it also tends to freeze time and divert our attention from the tensions and conflicts. In contrast, activity theory demands that we examine contradictions both within and between systems. In fact, contradictions are perhaps the most important locus of analysis—both the contradictions themselves and the ways that systems work through contradictions. Here I focus on the most salient contradictions that emerge as school and workplace/community systems intersect in the activity system of the community-based writing course.

Contradictions are natural to activity systems and should not necessarily be tagged as negative. As David Russell remarks, "An activity system constantly works through contradictions" (1997, 531). They surface within individual systems and when one activity system interacts with another. They present subjects (or indeed any node of the activity system triangle) with "double binds" that can sometimes be accommodated, sometimes prove disruptive or debilitating, and sometimes spark collective transformation or the creation of whole new activity systems (Engeström 1987).

Contradictions in the writing classroom are nothing new, of course. For example, teachers find themselves in the often contradictory roles of both advocate and judge (Elbow 1983), or trying to negotiate the double bind of both honoring process-oriented classroom practices and responding to institutional pressures to sort and rank students through grading systems (Agnew 1997). Nora Bacon has already recognized how service-learning occasions reflect one of the central contradictions of our profession: that composition theory affirms that acts of writing are tightly bound to their rhetorical contexts, the first-year composition requirement, and yet most teachers of writing, even as they make nods to rhetoric, still rely on assumptions about writing as a generalizable skill (2000, 1). As my discussion of motives suggests, writing-for-the-community and writing-with-the-community pedagogies stir up even more contradictions that tend to remain dormant in more typical composition classrooms.

Linda Flower and Virginia Chappell have been among the first to recognize how conceptualizing contradictions from an activity theory perspective can illuminate what happens with community-based writing initiatives. Yet they do so in different ways: Flower (2002) cites contradictions between academic and community cultural logics as a starting place for inquiry into local problems; Chappell (2005) argues that when teaching writing-for-the-community courses we should provoke student awareness of academic/nonprofit agency contradictions as part of a process of helping them navigate professional writing projects more critically and effectively. While my purposes run parallel with Chappell's, I rely more heavily on Engeström's detailed models of activity systems to reveal contradictions that emerge in the service-learning course activity system. Figures 32–2 and 32–3—one from a student point of view and the other from a teacher point of view—illustrate several of those contradictions.

These diagrams illustrate a variety of contradictions that are organic to service-learning, and as with my discussions of genre and motive, I suggest

FIGURE 32–2   Contradictions in the Service-Learning Classroom Activity
System from the *Student* Point of View

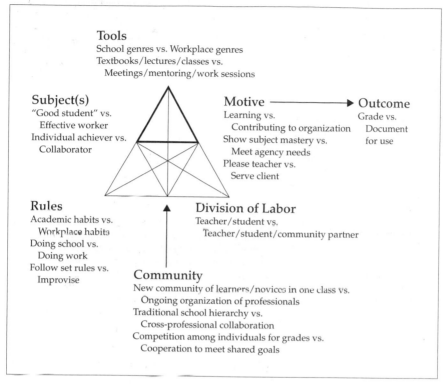

Tools
School genres vs. Workplace genres
Textbooks/lectures/classes vs.
    Meetings/mentoring/work sessions

Subject(s)
"Good student" vs.
    Effective worker
Individual achiever vs.
    Collaborator

Motive ———————→ **Outcome**
Learning vs.   Grade vs.
    Contributing to organization   Document
Show subject mastery vs.   for use
    Meet agency needs
Please teacher vs.
    Serve client

Rules
Academic habits vs.
    Workplace habits
Doing school vs.
    Doing work
Follow set rules vs.
    Improvise

Division of Labor
Teacher/student vs.
    Teacher/student/community partner

Community
New community of learners/novices in one class vs.
    Ongoing organization of professionals
Traditional school hierarchy vs.
    Cross-professional collaboration
Competition among individuals for grades vs.
    Cooperation to meet shared goals

(Adapted from Engeström 1996, 88)

that researchers look to contradictions as points for launching analyses and
that teachers make contradictions more visible to students. As we help students identify the double binds, we open contradictions to reflection.

I have already suggested how the social motives of schools and nonprofits can both contradict and cooperate. But I dodged some of the trickier
aspects of contradictions raised by university/community partnerships. What
happens, for example, if students and teachers eagerly adopt the social motives of their community partners? They focus all their energies on doing the
highest-quality collaborative writing in workplace and civic genres; they put
aside thoughts of grades; collaborative work—students with each other, student team with community partner, teacher with students—trumps creating
opportunities for individual learning. And the projects get done, and done
brilliantly, but no one person can claim ownership of the text, and individual
contributions are tough to decipher. When the school activity system makes
its demand for individual assessment, do all the students then get A's? If so,
at semester's end the teacher will no doubt encounter a double bind as a department chair or dean raises an eyebrow at the sight of such consistently
high marks and the implied lack of rigor. The sorting/ranking/gatekeeping

FIGURE 32–3   Contradictions in the Service-Learning Classroom Activity
System from the *Teacher and Institutional* Point of View

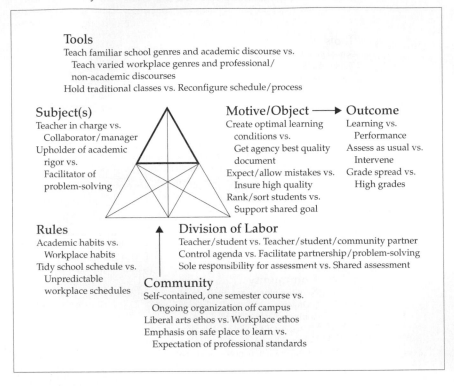

Tools
Teach familiar school genres and academic discourse vs.
   Teach varied workplace genres and professional/
   non-academic discourses
   Hold traditional classes vs. Reconfigure schedule/process

Subject(s)
Teacher in charge vs.
   Collaborator/manager
Upholder of academic
   rigor vs.
   Facilitator of
   problem-solving

Motive/Object ──► Outcome

Create optimal learning   Learning vs.
   conditions vs.   Performance
   Get agency best quality   Assess as usual vs.
   document   Intervene
Expect/allow mistakes vs.   Grade spread vs.
   Insure high quality   High grades
Rank/sort students vs.
   Support shared goal

Rules
Academic habits vs.
   Workplace habits
Tidy school schedule vs.
   Unpredictable
   workplace schedules

Division of Labor
Teacher/student vs. Teacher/student/community partner
Control agenda vs. Facilitate partnership/problem-solving
Sole responsibility for assessment vs. Shared assessment

Community
Self-contained, one semester course vs.
   Ongoing organization off campus
Liberal arts ethos vs. Workplace ethos
Emphasis on safe place to learn vs.
   Expectation of professional standards

(Adapted from Engeström 1996, 88)

social motive of schooling presses for stratification; the workplace motive presses for effective documents that serve the collective needs of the organization, even if at the expense of individual learning and assessment.[5] What kind of change, if any, this double bind will provoke is uncertain, but activity theory at least offers a way to put it on the table and analyze it. And as Figures 32–2 and 32–3 illustrate, service-learning invites a wide range of such contradictions, all potentially vexing and all potentially generative.

NOTES

    1. Service-learning researchers should account for both the *breadth* of the genres evident in a given activity system (that is, inventory how many different genres surface in a particular community-based writing course) and the *depth* of genre use (that is, assess how well students understand and practice the more specialized genres of particular academic disciplines and/or community groups). As David Russell remarks, "Genres embody expectations for the future, as well as linking us to past human activities. And learning to read or write a new genre can be— if one sees genre in its breadth and depth—a way of imaging different ways of being in the world, actually seeing one's self or one's student as potential participants [sic] in different worlds of human activity (activity systems) within the universe of discourse" (Russell 2002, 228).

    2. For details on the assignment see Deans 2006; for similar approaches, see Bazerman 2004 and Kain and Wardle 2005.

3. The term "life-world activity system" is borrowed from Russell 1997. Powerful personal motives can also emerge *during* college, as when students develop a new political awareness and align themselves with new (to them) social and ideological causes; personal motives can also emerge during service-learning projects themselves, usually as a result of interaction with community partners. Out of admiration for the work of the nonprofit organization and affection for its employees ("I don't want to let them down") students often discover the motivation to persist through multiple drafts.

4. One case that illustrates motive trumping location occurred several years ago when I taught a first-year writing course on a disability theme and as part of that course arranged service-learning projects (a research report on student attitudes toward disability, the revision of print materials to distribute to incoming students, and so on) with the disabilities services office on campus. Even though students never stepped off campus, they experienced whiplash as they shuttled between the social motives of school and workplace.

5. For an intriguing discussion of how this contradiction plays out in a client-based professional writing course, see Freedman and Adam 2000. Two other telling studies of students negotiating contradictions in activity systems are Ketter and Hunter 2002, and Lundell, Britt, and Beach 2002.

WORKS CITED

Agnew, Eleanor. 1997. "Cross Purposes: Grade Deflation, Classroom Practices." In *Grading in the Post-Process Classroom: From Theory to* Practice, ed. Libby Alison, Lizbeth Bryant, and Maureen Hourigan, 36–50. Portsmouth, NH: Boynton/Cook.

Bacon. Nora. 2000. "Building a Swan's Nest for Instruction in Rhetoric." *College Composition and Communication* 51, no. 4 (June): 589–609.

Bazerman, Charles. 1994. "Systems of Genres and the Enactment of Social Intentions." In *Genre and the New Rhetoric*, ed. Aviva Freedman and Peter Medway, 79–101. London: Taylor and Francis.

———. 2004. "Speech Acts, Genres and Activity Systems: How Texts Organize Activity and People." In *What Writing Does and How It Does It: An Introduction to Analyzing Texts and Textual Practices*, ed. Charles Bazerman and Paul Prior. Mahwah, NJ: Lawrence Erlbaum.

Bazerman, Charles, and David Russell, eds. 2002. *Writing Selves/Writing Societies: Research from Activity Perspectives*. Fort Collins, CO: WAC Clearinghouse and Mind, Culture, and Activity. Available at http://wac.colostate.edu/books/selves_societies/

Beaufort, Anne. 1999. *Writing in the Real World: Making the Transition from School to Work*. New York: Teachers College Press.

Chappell, Virginia. 2005. "Good Intentions Aren't Enough: Insights from Activity Theory for Linking Service and Learning." *Reflections* 4, no. 2 (winter): 34–53.

Deans, Thomas. 2000. *Writing Partnerships: Service-Learning in Composition*. Urbana, IL: NCTE.

———. 2006. "Genre Analysis and the Community Writing Course." *Reflections: A Journal of Writing, Service-Learning, and Community Literacy* 5, no. 1 and no. 2: 7–25.

Dias, Patrick. 2000. "Writing Classrooms as Activity Systems." In *Transitions: Writing in Academic and Workplace Settings*, 11–29. Cresskill, NJ: Hampton.

Dias, Patrick, Aviva Freedman, Peter Medway, and Anthony Pare. 1999. *Worlds Apart: Acting and Writing in Academic and Workplace Contexts*. Mahwah, NJ: Lawrence Erlbaum.

Elbow, Peter. 1983. "Embracing Contraries in the Teaching Process. *College English* 45 (April): 327–39.

Engeström, Yrjo. 1987. *Learning by Expanding: An Activity Theoretical Approach to Developmental Research*. Helsinki: Orienta-Konsultit Oy.

———. 1996. "Work as a Testbench for Activity Theory: The Case of Primary Care Medical Practice." In *Understanding Practice: Perspectives on Activity and Context*, ed. Seth Chaiklin and Jean Lave, 64–101. Cambridge: Cambridge University Press.

———. 1999. "Activity Theory and Individual and Social Transformation." In *Perspectives on Activity Theory*, ed. Yrjo Engeström, Reijo Mietinen, and Raija-Leena Punamaki, 19–38. Cambridge: Cambridge University Press.

Flower, Linda. 2002. "Intercultural Inquiry and the Transformation of Service." *College English* 65, no. 2 (November): 181–201.

Freedman, Aviva, and Christine Adam. 2000. "Write Where You Are: Situation Learning to Write in University and Workplace Settings." In *Transitions: Writing in Academic and Workplace Settings*, 31–60. Cresskill, NJ: Hampton.

Harris, Joseph. 1989. "The Idea of Community in the Study of Writing." *College Composition and Communication* 40 (February): 11–22.

Jolliffe, David A. 2001. "Writing Across the Curriculum and Service Learning: *Kairos*, Genre and Collaboration." In *WAC for the New Millennium*, ed. Susan McLeod, Eric Miraglia, Margot Soven, and Christopher Thaiss, 86–108. Urbana, IL: NCTE.

Kain, Donna, and Elizabeth Wardle. 2005. "Building Context: Using Activity Theory to Teach About Genre in Multi-Major Professional Communication Courses." *Technical Communication Quarterly* 14, no. 2: 113–39.

Ketter, Jean, and Judy Hunter. 2002. "Creating a Writer's Identity on the Boundaries of Two Communities of Practice." In Bazerman and Russell 2002, 307–29. Available at http://wac.colostate.edu/books/selves_societies/

Lundell, Dana Britt, and Richard Beach. 2002. "Dissertation Writers' Negotiations with Competing Activity Systems." In Bazerman and Russell 2002, 483–515. Available at http://wac.colostate.edu/books/selves_societies/

Miller, Carolyn. 1984. "Genre as Social Action." *Quarterly Journal of Speech* 70: 151–67.

Prior, Paul. 1998. *Writing/Disciplinarity: A Sociohistoric Account of Literate Activity in the Academy.* Mahwah, NJ: Lawrence Erlbaum.

Russell, David. 1995. "Activity Theory and Its Implications for Writing Instruction." In *Reconceiving Writing, Rethinking Writing Instruction*, ed. Joseph Petraglia, 51–77. Mahwah, NJ: Lawrence Erlbaum.

———. 1997. "Rethinking Genre in School and Society: An Activity Theory Analysis." *Written Communication* 14, no. 4: 504–54.

———. 2002. "The Kind-ness of Genre: An Activity Theory Analysis of High School Teachers' Perception of Genre in Portfolio Assessment Across the Curriculum." In *The Rhetoric and Ideology of Genre: Strategies for Stability and Change*, ed. Richard Coe, Lorelei Lingard, and Tatiana Teslenko, 225–42. Cresskill, NJ: Hampton.

33

Exploring Difference in the Service-Learning Classroom: Three Teachers Write about Anger, Sexuality, and Social Justice

ANGELIQUE DAVI
MICHELLE DUNLAP
ANN E. GREEN

> Creating community . . . involves this most difficult work of negotiating real divisions, of considering boundaries before we go crashing through, and of pondering our differences before we can ever agree on the terms of our sameness.
>
> –PATRICIA WILLIAMS

Community is often the site of tension in the service-learning paradigm. We are often, as Patricia Williams describes above, teaching students to negotiate real divisions between town and gown, between the service-learning classroom and the expectations of the site, and between one another. The three of us, all experienced service-learning scholars and teachers at predominantly white institutions, have also been thinking about the ideas of community and difference. To advance our understandings of service learning, writing, race, class, and gender, for this project we have come together to form our own small research community. While we are all teachers at predominantly white universities, our experiences differ according to our identities, the subject positions of our students, and the subject positions of the learners at the sites where our students serve. By working together as an intentional community of researchers located at different sites, we hope both to challenge one another to think more deeply about race, class, sexuality, and pedagogy, and to replicate the intensity of collaboration that is such an important aspect of the service-learning work that we ask students to do. What, we wonder, will we learn by attending to our differences of race, sexuality, and location and placing our stories about service learning in dialogue with each other?

Several perspectives serve as touchstones for our dialogue, primary among them Beverly Tatum's applications of Racial Identity Development Theory. Tatum considers Racial Identity Development in the context of the

From *Reflections* 6.1 (2007): 41–66.

classroom, illustrating that students arrive in our classrooms with different comfort levels concerning issues of race. Some students are still unaware that racism exists while others are both aware of racism and savvy about addressing issues of race and difference. Many students inhabit various stages along the continuum between these two extremes.

The variations that Tatum describes may be further intensified in a service-learning classroom, where each student is at a different stage of readiness to talk about race and other issues of similarity and difference as these issues relate both to the university and to community settings. Some students have lived with or talked about race—and racism—all of their lives, while others have not had to confront racial difference until they enter service-learning or other community engagement environments. Some students feel an initial alienation or division from the people they encounter and need support as they learn to navigate unfamiliar environments both within and beyond the university (Dunlap *Reaching*; Dunlap, Monroe, Green, and Davi).

Amy Winans also attends to students' willingness to engage in critical thinking about difference. In "Local Pedagogies and Race: Interrogating White Safety in the Rural College Classroom," she advocates crafting a local pedagogy based on location, demographics, and students' backgrounds to teach critical thinking and combat racism. As Winans writes, "Employing an effective local pedagogy in a predominantly white classroom entails taking students' ethical beliefs and goals seriously rather than seeing them as misguided assumptions to be worked through" (262). The two of us who teach in predominantly white classrooms must consider carefully the fears and "color blindness" expressed by white students in order to fashion a local pedagogy that works effectively to prepare students for encounters with differences at the service-learning site. Further, we must consider the ways in which students who encounter "difference" at the service site feel threatened. As Winans explains, "White students seek to remain safe from the threat of being perceived as racist," and so the service-learning paradigm which sends predominantly white students out to predominantly communities of color immediately threatens white students' notion of safety (257). We ask ourselves, How can we create a space for white students to feel "safe" enough to do the critical thinking that leads to change? How is this project different for people of color who teach service learning? And how is service learning different for students of color who are engaged in community settings? How does the idea of "safety" intertwine with the idea of social change?

If we engage with the idea of community seriously, then we must also consider how to negotiate divisions. In "Beyond Empathy: Developing Critical Consciousness through Service Learning," Cynthia Rosenberger argues that Freirean concepts of dialogue offer a critical frame for service-learning teachers. She writes, "Dialogue based on love, humility, and faith in people insists on the breaking down of traditional dichotomies of power. . . . If service learning is to be transformative, it must generate a thoughtful and critical consciousness in all stakeholders as they collaborate in creating a more just and humane society" (39). If we apply this Freirean lens to our thinking about race, sexuality, and difference, how can we think about the idea of "community"? Is it possible in the service-learning paradigm to build a community that acknowledges and appreciates differences?

We explore these questions from our three different physical locations—as well as our three different positions in the service-learning classroom. Ann Green is a white teacher of white students. Ann's white middle- and upper-class students choose to do service and are placed at non-profit agencies and schools that work with predominantly African American, Latino, and poor populations. Michelle Dunlap is an African American teacher, often the first professor of color that white students encounter. Her predominantly white students are also placed at service sites catering to predominantly people of color. The third member of our group, Angelique Davi, is a white teacher of predominantly African American and Latino students enrolled in a basic writing class. As a component of their required writing course, Angelique's students are required to do service at a predominantly white, middle-class elementary school.

Ann's Story

Preparing Students for Service Learning: Encountering Anger in the Classroom

In her 1981 keynote address to the National Women's Studies Association conference, Audre Lorde said:

> My response to racism is anger. I have lived with that anger, ignoring it, feeding upon it, learning to use it before it laid my visions to waste, for most of my life. . . . My fear of anger taught me nothing. Your fear of that anger will teach you nothing, also. ("Use of Anger" 124)

As a white teacher who embraces critical race theory and tries to incorporate it into the service-learning classroom, I mull over the connections between my pedagogy and Lorde's challenge to her mostly white, female audience. Is it the fear of Black anger that makes white students hesitant at service-learning sites? If fear, anger, and guilt are all possible emotions in the development of white racial identity, then how can we anticipate these feelings and assist service-learning students in working through them? Drawing on Winans's ideas of local pedagogy, I believe we should engage students in service-learning classrooms in talking about the relationships between race and power and exploring "how race and racial identity can change not only from minute to minute, but also historically across time" (264). But anger—more than fear or guilt—is the most difficult emotion for me to acknowledge in the classroom, and it poses a significant challenge to my efforts to craft a local pedagogy.

Teaching service-learning classes demands two distinct strategies in my predominantly white university. The first strategy involves building a community in the classroom by engaging students in a number of activities through which they begin to know each other as individuals in an intentional way and to come together as a community. As Elizabeth Ellsworth writes about her own creation of a classroom where racism can be discussed, "A safer space required high levels of trust and personal commitment to individuals in the class, gained in part by social interactions outside of class" (316). Although service-learning courses typically create better class interaction more quickly than traditional courses because of the time students spend together outside of class—particularly, as Eli Goldblatt shows, in traveling to and from the service sites—I also incorporate community building activities and reflection into the courses themselves.

The second strategy that I use involves addressing race and class directly throughout the course through the course materials I select, the reflections that students write, and the ways students are asked to link the course materials with their service-learning experiences. While these strategies are useful in creating a local pedagogy, they are not guarantees against anger, fear, or guilt. Or, or more precisely—since anger, guilt, and fear are expected responses from students at various stages of racial identity development—they are not necessarily guarantees that students can work through their anger, guilt, or fear in the limited time frame of a semester. Ultimately, my local pedagogy must be characterized by what Angelique Davi in the pages that follow calls "adaptability," and what Amy Rupiper Taggart and H. Brooke Hessler describe as "pedagogical change [in] ongoing response to the complex relationships and resources entailed in community-engaged learning" (154). By approaching race directly in my service-learning courses, I sometimes provoke the "heated exchange" that bell hooks finds makes some "students from upper- and middle-class backgrounds . . . disturbed." Like the teachers and students from working-class backgrounds whom hooks describes, I tend to feel that "discussion is deeper and richer if it arouses intense responses" (187). But while these "deeper and richer responses" intensify the learning for many students, they also disrupt the orderly, middle-class conventions of the classroom.

"Writing Fellows: Theory and Practice of Peer Tutoring," a credit-bearing service-learning course that trains students for work in our university Writing Center, provides the occasion to consider these tensions in one particular classroom setting. Writing Fellows includes a service-learning component through which students serve as writing tutors at local elementary and middle schools, adult literacy programs, and ESL programs. Students are provided with a variety of options for service, and over the semester are required to complete thirty hours of service in the community and in our school's Writing Center. Discussions of race, class, and language are prompted both by the readings—excerpts from Lisa Delpit's *Other People's Children* and bell hooks's *Teaching to Transgress*, June Jordan's "No Body Mean More To Me Than You and the Future Life of Willie Jordan," and additional articles on tutoring, teaching writing, and encounters with difference—and by the encounters the predominantly white tutors have with learners who are predominantly people of color. Conversations about race and class are also initiated by students in the class, depending on their personalities, learning styles, service sites, service partners, and their various stages of racial identity development. Given these differences, including texts by Carter, Tatum, and McIntosh, as Michelle Dunlap suggests below, might better help students recognize their own racial positioning. Nevertheless, recognizing one's own racial positioning and the anger or fear associated with it does not necessarily diminish the anger or fear. In other words, the emotions are real and not simply stages to be moved through. The emotions must be acknowledged.

One such angry conversation happened between Amanda and Lucy, a pair of service-learning "partners," one white and one Black, who tutored together at a site for adult English language learners. The women drove together to the service site, and accounts of their exchanges peppered their journals and in-class reflections. Amanda, a white student who had grown up in a state with a large Latino population, was struck by the lack of racial diversity among the other students at Saint Joseph's. She initially expressed a strong desire and motivation to connect with Lucy, one of the African American students in the class. In a journal entry reflecting on a class discussion, she described her respect for Lucy:

> When Lucy spoke during the second class period about how she felt through high school when teachers told her that she wasn't good enough to be in AP classes, I wanted to listen to her story. Later, she told us that she found herself in classes as the only black female. . . . I was very touched.

As the semester continued, however, Amanda's perception of Lucy changed, influenced both by their service experiences and by the anger that circulated in the class, a mood that varied according to students' stages of racial identity development, their encounters at the service site, their responses to the course readings, and their exchanges in the class itself.

Amanda describes her changing attitude in her journal as she reflects on a conversation with Lucy en route to their service site when she talked about her best friend from home:

> One day when we were going to service, I was talking about M. [my best friend] and mentioned that she was black. Lucy said, "That's great . . . you have a multicultural buddy. Good for you."

In her journal, Amanda describes feeling hurt and angered by Lucy's response.

Simultaneously, however, Lucy's own stage of racial identity development included anger at the predominantly white campus and the racism she encountered there. As was true for the students Angelique describes below, the service-learning course provided Lucy with an opportunity to recognize the regular, subtle acts of racism that so many students of color encounter on a predominantly white campus. Because the course work included writing by Audre Lorde, bell hooks, Gloria Anzuldúa, and others, Lucy's engagement in the course work—combined with her experiences tutoring ESL and her daily life on campus—created space for Lucy to recognize and articulate her anger.

While this was a necessary stage for Lucy in her own development of racial identity, it complicated her relationships with some of the other students in the class. Lucy reflects on this process in her final self-evaluation:

> I definitely think that my journal on "How to Tame a Wild Tongue" is one of my best. This piece really helped me to explore some aspects of my life and race in general that I have never explored before. . . . "How To Tame a Wild Tongue" was one of the most inspiring articles concerning race that I have read. The author openly identified the common shame and inferiority that some may have about their race and then turned the shame to pride. Kind of like a homosexual movement encouraging others to come out. Letting them know that they don't have to be ashamed, but instead can take pride in who they are. It's not that I didn't know the things that she was saying, it's that it has never been so concretely defined and confirmed for me. I was really moved.

In conversations with me about the course, Lucy talked about her distress at some of the white Writing Fellows' responses to her anger at racism on campus, her frustration with the slow pace of change, and the poetry she had written for her Black church. These moments of anger crystallized during a particular class discussion on race when Lucy posed a question to the class: "Do you see color? You say you don't, but I know you do."

In her journal, Amanda reflected:

> This was the single most frustrating moment for me this semester. When we were discussing race, Lucy posed a valuable question to the class; but before we were given the chance to answer, she both answered the question and blamed us for something she had no way of knowing. Yes. I see color. I know that Lucy is Black, just as I know that Sara has red hair. When Lucy said this, I felt that she was accusing the entire class of racism.

I excerpt these journals from Amanda and Lucy because I think that they raise important issues about how students at different moments of racial identity development may or may not respond well to readings about race, class, and writing. Moreover, because Amanda and Lucy tutored together, the tensions caused by their different stages of racial identity development trickled out to the service-learning site. It is important to recognize that anger, guilt, and fear cannot be avoided as possible responses from students, and it is also important to consider how a local pedagogy can adapt to the particular conditions that emerge from the particular class in front of us.

Interestingly, I think that one of the difficulties in Amanda and Lucy's relationship was that each had difficulty in interpreting the other's stage of racial identity development. On one hand, in conversations, Lucy often expressed relief at hearing comments from the white students who she perceived as being "more honest" about their feelings about race; from my point of view, "more honest" seemed to be "more racist." Often the remarks that Lucy expressed comfort with were the questions that white students asked her about Black stereotypes or the stories they told her about overt racism they had participated in or heard about. In my estimation, Amanda was further along in articulating a white anti-racist stance than many of the other white students in the class, but Lucy didn't trust Amanda's stance.

This may be true in part as a result of white privilege. Few models for white anti-racism are available; in fact, when we tried to name white people who had worked against racism, the class was surprised at how few people we could identify. Plus, the stance of a white anti-racist is quite possibly more difficult to interpret—for both white students and students of color—than the stance of the white racist. As Winans writes, "For many white students, race and racism are virtually interchangeable" (260). While Amanda may have had a more nuanced version of race and racism and did want to be identified as "color blind," Lucy's adopted a position in that particular class discussion that all of the white students in the room were embedded in a color blind stage of white racial identity development. At the service site this translated into Lucy perceiving the white nuns who ran the site as "racist."

As Michelle Dunlap writes below, we need to be aware that students can transfer some of their anger to us through their frustration with service learning, and we can—by sharing readings with them like those by Beverly Tatum and Peggy McIntosh—make them aware that guilt, anger, frustration, and fear are all expected components of the stages of racial identity development. Even so, crafting a local pedagogy is complex and depends on how students' conceptualizations of race and other factors—gender, class, etc.—evolve over time and can change from moment to moment. In thinking about the idea of a local pedagogy, we must consider the ways that different stages of racial identity development in a particular class affect the overall class dynamic. This dynamic is further complicated when we consider how white students' idea of "safety," rarely threatened in the predominantly white classrooms that students encounter in predominantly white institutions, is troubled by students' service-learning experience with people of color (Winans 254).

MICHELLE'S STORY

Close Encounters: Race and Sexual Orientation in the Service-Learning Process

I am a Black woman professor who grew up in somewhat economically challenged environments in Detroit in the 1960s and 70s. For the past thirteen years I have taught predominantly white students from relatively privileged environments at Connecticut College, a small, highly selective, liberal arts college in New London. As a Black woman—and as the person requiring my students to engage in racially diverse, economically-challenged environments—I could be an all too easy target for the discomfort and anxiety that often accompany first encounters in environments that are very different from the ones in which the majority of my students grew up. In the pages that follow, I share some of the local pedagogies I have developed.

The contexts in which my students engage in service-learning are located typically within a 1–3 mile radius of the college, sometimes even within walking distance. In these settings, they meet indicators of a world both similar to and different from the college and from the worlds with which they are familiar. According to city records from 1999, minorities make up about 44% of the city's population and 73% of the public school population; about 10% are immigrants. Reportedly nearly 22% of New London's 25-and-up adult population has not completed high school, 7.4% of its population is unemployed, and only 20% of residents have a college degree (New London School District). At the same time, New London is a close-knit community of great strength, accomplishment, and pride (Dunlap *Reaching*). Despite its many strengths, strides, and resources, the distance between the contexts from which my students tend to come and the contexts they encounter in the city often makes New London's urban challenges appear to them even more vivid and overwhelming.

Many students struggle when they first encounter economically, racially, and culturally diverse environments such as New London in significant or intimate ways, especially when they are away from the security of their caregivers and their home environments. For some students, service-learning experiences may provoke their first, emerging awareness of their own economic and racial privilege. Thanks to supportive colleagues, useful resources, and trial and error, I have begun to discover some of the many "triggers" of my students' anxiety and have developed responses for helping them to cope (Dunlap, Monroe, Green, and Davi). To illustrate some of my students' struggles with regard to place, race, class, gender, and sexual orientation, I turn now to passages from three different student journals and reflect on both my initial responses to what they shared and the sources of support we identified.

Student 1: *"What must we look like to these [minority] children?"*

> I am sure this is a typical thought, but the first thing that came into my mind was, "What must we look like to these children?" Here we are, a group of college girls, all white, all dressed up, there for only an hour in the day, ready to do art projects with them. Was it only in my head that I should feel ashamed, somewhat pathetic, useless, or did these kids have similar thoughts? *Who do these girls think they are?* Did the teachers think this of us? Perhaps it was only an insecurity of mine, a figment of my own imagination. Or perhaps those feelings arose from notions of what society has taught us to feel, how there are differences between people based on their gender, race, religion, etc. Perhaps they viewed us as nothing more, nothing less than people to play with them for an hour of their day. I guess I will never know. [Emphasis student's]

When I first began collecting and reading student journals, it was a challenge for me to understand the severity of students' struggle with feeling like an outsider. As an African American woman I am accustomed to initially feeling like an outsider when crossing gender, racial, cultural, or economic borders; as is true for many minorities, the duality or what Dubois called "double-consciousness" of my existence is something that I live with constantly. So it was difficult at first for me to understand why a short-term, relatively protected situation such as service-learning was so overwhelming to my students. I had to find a way to stop, listen to my students, and allow myself to fully perceive the unique struggle they were trying to articulate.

I have since learned firsthand that coming to terms with their own image or sense of themselves is one of the greatest struggles students experience as they come into contact with the poverty, socioeconomic challenges, and systems of racism made apparent in service-learning environments (Dunlap *Reaching*). Students may look at themselves differently and feel insecure about how they are being perceived by others who may not immediately trust them, finding their own more heroic self-conceptions challenged (Dunlap "The Role"). Ideally, this disruption will provide an appropriate opportunity to bring students to a new place in their intellectual development. Helping my students locate where they are in their familiarity and comfort with race and racial differences and similarities is one way of helping them to understand themselves within a larger framework or process of learning—a process that is not unique to them as individuals but is shared by many students.

Beverly Tatum's classic article on students' encounters with racial differences in the classroom, "Talking about Race," is a key support for my students. Normalizing their struggle helps students to feel less insecure, less self-conscious, and less defensive as they adjust and develop more realistic conceptions of their role within the service-learning environment (Dunlap *Reaching*). As they begin to better understand the emotional processes involved in learning about the environments that now surround them, they are better able to acknowledge their emotions and to grapple cognitively with and connect course content to the locales that surround them (Dunlap *Reaching*).

Student 2: *"I [had] never stopped to think about why our world is still so segregated."*

> I feel a huge amount of guilt after my first week of service-learning . . . because I never had to go to an after school program while my parents worked. I was fortunate enough to have an au pair to come and take care of my brother and me. When I think of the many opportunities these kids do not have I feel upset. . . . I do not know how long it will take for this feeling to go away but in class after our discussion about race and guilt I know I am not the only one experiencing this. The interesting part is that I have been doing community service for years and never had the same awareness of race. I mean, I am by no means colorblind and therefore have always recognized the minorities I have worked with. But I never stopped to think about why our world is still so segregated. After reading so much about race and discussing inequalities in class, I feel bad for my status as a white in today's society. I know I have no control over it

and am not to blame, but it is hard to face. I wonder what the kids I worked with this week thought of me. They may have preconceived notions of me as well. . . . I understand after reading Tatum's article that guilt is simply part of the process of learning about race.

Some courses and service-learning experiences provide students with the opportunity to consider and analyze the systemic causes and consequences of inequality for the first time. Resources such as Herbes-Sommers's documentary on the history of inequality in America and the many other texts mentioned throughout this article help to promote such analysis and to provide a context from which students may consider the systemic inequality they witness firsthand in their service-learning placements. As students become more aware of systemic inequalities they may respond in a number of ways. One common reaction is guilt. As they draw on helpful resources they may find productive ways to channel emotions such as guilt and may be less likely to fear the wariness, cautiousness, and sometimes anger of oppressed people that Ann and Angelique also discuss. As the above student passage suggests, having an opportunity to reflect on their own emotional process within service-learning, and being provided key resources such as Peggy McIntosh's classic work on male and white privilege and Tatum's works on racial identity development are crucial to student adjustment in the service-learning experience. These resources help students tie their observations in the local service-learning settings to larger, systemic trends that have historical and sociological bases that extend far beyond the one setting where they are placed. These resources also help prepare students and faculty for the reality that racial and inequity awareness is an emotional process, encouraging them to put their emotional energies to work for the cause of racial understanding, communication, and action as modeled for them through such materials.

Resources such as the work of Tatum, McIntosh, and Herbes-Sommers have provided immeasurable support to me, making me far less likely to be scape-goated by students as they grapple with their racial "stuff" or baggage, and far less likely to be seen as biased or as having a hidden agenda. My purpose and agenda for preparing them for the service-learning process and for a more diverse and ever-changing world becomes more obvious to them.

Student 3: *"I lied and said I had a boyfriend named C—, when the truth is that I have a girlfriend named C—."*

I am [working with] many seventh grade [girls], all who are students of color. There are more [college] mentors here than seventh graders, most of us are white. A few minutes into the session, I realized we were going to be dealing with the dating issue right off the bat. As a gay woman, this is an uncomfortable situation in surroundings where I am not sure how people will react to my sexuality. . . . One of the seventh graders went around and asked if we had a boyfriend and I found it strange that the facilitators didn't stop this. I wanted to scream out, tell them that I was uncomfortable, and that I had no desire to make others feel uncomfortable by me. When they got to me I froze, I lied and said I had a boyfriend named C—. The truth is I have been dating a woman named C— for almost a year now. [Then we all were asked] if we knew anyone who was Gay or Lesbian, this made me relax because it meant it was on people's radar and I felt more included. However, most of what people said was that gay men are really great, will always tell the truth, and are fun to shop with, whereas lesbians hit on you and it's weird. We talked about events we will have, one of which is a sleepover, and I do not feel comfortable with that. I am now really nervous about this volunteering opportunity because it feels like I have started it with a lie. I am very comfortable with my sexuality and telling people, however, this was a very different situation. . . . I am nervous about slipping up about being gay, but also about [being Caucasian]. I am working on how it feels to be in the minority in a racial sense because I already feel that within a heterosexist society.

In a society that is often racist, sexist, and heterosexist, many students struggle with self-disclosure. The above student is clearly wrestling with the decision and implications of whether or not to "pass." As I read her journal I was reminded of the many biracial African Americans who were faced with similar temptations and the devastating consequences of "passing" for individuals and families. Earlier in my career, heart-wrenching disclosures such as this student's would have overwhelmed me; I would not have felt that I could have credibility or legitimacy with lesbian, gay, and transgender students, when I myself am straight. Today, I respond much as I do when dealing cross-culturally with my students on whiteness issues: that is, to listen, learn, share, and locate and utilize resources and supports.

I should note that I often advise students that when they are not sure about what is appropriate in an environment to observe a supervisor or peer model as a guide. However, with disclosure of sexual orientation, a model may not be apparent or out in the open, even if they are present in the situation. And the lack of models may have the consequence of leaving the service-learner feeling even more vulnerable and isolated when trying to establish appropriate roles and disclosure boundaries within the service-learning environment. My written response to this student was: "This must have been a very difficult moment!" Later, where she said she would speak with her site supervisors, I responded with, "I hope you will share with me how it went." I felt a frustration about this situation and asked the student to see me personally so that we could process it together, and I could be sure that she was being appropriately supported. I encouraged her to: 1) speak to her site supervisors if she felt comfortable to do so in order to negotiate a process for handling such situations in the future; 2) utilize the on-campus supports for gay, lesbian, bisexual, and transgender students; and 3) continue to seek me out for support if I could be of further help. Such experiences help students to think in terms of how they—and thus others both alike and different from them—cope when they travel outside their own protective (or less protected) environments and move into other settings and systems.

Not every student journal comment or situation requires a response, resource, or intervention. Often things work themselves out on their own, especially if a good service-learning infrastructure is already in place (Campus Compact). There are, however, those occasions when a comment, redirection to resources, or full-blown intervention is required, and it may call for many different and simultaneous forms of support. Winans' concept of local pedagogies suggests that it is appropriate to consider a wide variety of experiential and contextual factors which, as Ann pointed out, are the very things that can influence the different ways that we hear, see, and perceive one another. Our role as facilitators requires our being ready to respond, support, and point our students to appropriate resources, while we ourselves remain open to constantly learning and evolving in the process.

ANGELIQUE'S STORY

Service-Learning and Community: Students of Color in "White Spaces"

For the past three fall semesters, I have included a service-learning component in my basic writing course that is made up of predominantly students of color recruited to Bentley via an intensive summer bridge program, called the Contractual Admissions Program (CAP). Many of the students enrolled in my fall section have taken the prerequisite writing course with me during the summer. Although a majority of service-learning programs place students in underserved communities, students in my course tutor students at a local elementary school in a predominantly white, middle-class suburb of Boston through a previously established program entitled "2+2=5: The Power of Teamwork" designed by a Bentley student. Each week, the service-learning student facilitators lead elementary school students through activities designed to develop their team-building skills.

Much service-learning scholarship examines the experiences of white students from privileged backgrounds who serve in communities different from their own. Here, however, I reflect on the experiences of students of color and the anxieties they express while participating in a service-learning program in a predominantly white environment. In addition, I want to think about the ways in which my own identity as a white woman from a middle-class background plays a role in the classroom.

For the students of color in my course, many of their initial journal responses emphasize a desire to give back to the community. One Latina writes, "It is important to do some sort of community service because every little bit helps for the better of our community." Students anticipate feeling good about doing something for others: "I can admit that I have done lots of community service, particularly because of the feeling that you get after you have helped someone in need." These responses reflect what Ann Green describes as "the familiar story of how service-learning feels good" ("Difficult Stories" 277).

Although faculty teaching white students may find themselves having to encourage students to push past these feel-good narratives to tell "the difficult story" (Green 277), many of the students of color in my courses come to the difficult stories and raise thorny issues more easily. One Latina writes:

> I am really excited to begin this new stage to our expos class!! This is time for me to heal my wounds by seeing what it is like for a teacher teaching little children. I'm really happy to be able to be nice and caring to these children. I can feel like I am making something RIGHT!

An African-American man writes, "I kinda hope that I find a kid kinda like I was at that age because I would have loved having someone like me to talk to." He adds, "I also hope that I make a difference in these kids' lives."

Both responses point to a recurring theme that emerges suggesting a different anxiety for some of the students of color in the course than the feelings expressed by most white students. Many students of color in my course perceive returning to the elementary classroom as an opportunity to rewrite some piece of their own past (Davi). The young woman sees her new classroom role as potentially offering her insights into her painful experiences as a child—painful enough for her to describe them as "wounds" that have yet to heal. The young man's observation suggests that something significant was missing from his own childhood.

While attention to race and class differences clearly occupies white students moving out of their comfort zones, anxiety around issues of race initially seems absent for students of color. Given the similar demographics of Bentley and the elementary school, students of color are unlikely to point to glaring distinctions of race, class, or gender between the university and the service-learning site. And many of them have spent their lives navigating cross-cultural differences between home and school. Indeed, students often remark after reading W. E. B. Dubois that his notion of double consciousness is all too familiar to them.

Instead, anxiety stems from "getting it right." Many of these students describe having felt marginalized in elementary school and high school. Some describe exchanges with teachers that made them feel insignificant and even unwelcome. As they now enter the elementary school classroom as the person in power, many put tremendous energy into creating conducive learning environments. One woman describes a class activity and uses it as a way to rethink her approach in future sessions:

> Now we are outside, it's time for us to see if what we talked about can be applied in this task. I believe that for the next meeting I am going to tell them before the activity or have them brainstorm the goal of this activity and how to go about it when they get outside.

She adds:

> Overall I was very happy with my group and I can't wait till next week when I see them again. I will use the new things that I noticed and the ideas that I have fostered from my previous visit.

In their on-line journal postings, they are thoughtful about what they said during tutorial sessions, how elementary students react to their words, and how they might approach a lesson differently in the future for better effect.

Despite the absence of anxieties stemming from issues of race at the start of the course, students of color struggled with racial incidents both at the service-learning site and on the Bentley campus. Coming into the course having already worked with these students in the summer program, I was already aware of their sensitivity toward and awareness of issues of difference. In fact, in creating the course syllabus, the first semester I used Mike Rose's *Lives on the Boundary*, hoping students would be able to use the stories of Rose's students as a jumping-off point for analysis of their own experiences. Winans describes this process of giving students the opportunity to analyze other people's stories about their lived experiences of race as one of the "most effective local strategies" in helping students develop a sense of their own understanding of race (263). Indeed, students were able to better understand and articulate the role of race in their own educational experiences with Rose's stories as context. One African American woman writes,

> I feel like my high school career was a life on the boundary. I went to a public school and did not receive the same high quality education as schools in the suburban area or private schools. This makes me feel as though they have a greater advantage in getting accepted into great colleges and succeeded in them better. Does anyone else agree with me?

A Latina student responds:

> I TOTALLY agree! My older sister went to the _____, she had just come from Puerto Rico and did not know the language or the culture. When she was accepted into college at Northeastern, she felt as though she was not prepared for the work in college. She did not know what a syllabus was or how to study. If she could only turn back time and use what she knows now then, she says her life would be much different and she would of been someone in her college. Do you believe that our leaders really don't know that this is happening? I believe that this is their strategy for them to stay in power and keep the people who would challenge their ideas and keep them at the bottom where they belong.

Another African American student writes,

> In the book it said: "You are finally sitting in the lecture hall you have been preparing to sit in for years. You have been the good student, perhaps even the star—you are to be the engineer, the lawyer, the doctor. Your parents have knocked themselves out for you. And you can't get what some man is saying in an introductory course" (p. 174). When I read this it immediately touched me because that's how I feel in some of my classes sometimes. In my biology class often times the information and the course material can be so confusing and overwhelming that it feels as though the teacher is talking a different language. It feels like I am disappointing the people who supported me when I can't even understand what the professor is saying in the lecture.

Herzberg describes the students in his service-learning Expository Writing course becoming "indignant" (312) after reading *Lives on the Boundary*. He writes, "The students are indeed distressed by systemic discrimination against poorer people and disenfranchised groups" (312). The students in my course express the same indignation, but for them, the stories in *Lives on the Boundary* resonate with *their own* experiences of discrimination. Unlike Herzberg's students who "do not seem to see this discrimination in the lives of their learners" (312), the students in my course have little difficulty seeing this discrimination everywhere.

In fact, the first time I taught the course, students' frustration stemming from issues of race escalated throughout the semester. By midterm, I found myself somewhat unprepared for the level of stress and anxiety my students expressed in response to racial issues both at the community service-learning site and on our college campus. There were very few, if any, explicit racist incidents reported on campus that semester. Nonetheless, a number of factors were coming together for my students. First, when they arrived on the Bentley campus for the CAP program, these students of color from working class backgrounds were in the majority. In the fall, though, the numbers change dramatically: 69% of the students in the incoming class of 2005 identified as white; 2% identified as African American. Second, CAP students who throughout their elementary and high school years described themselves as on the margins were now being asked to perform a central role in an academic setting; they were the teachers in the elementary school program. And finally in our classroom through readings and written assignments, students were allowed to question all aspects of the education system, including our own classroom space. In doing so, painful memories of racist incidents in elementary school and high school became "trigger events" for student anxieties (Dunlap et al.).

Given the sensitivity CAP students expressed towards issues of race throughout the summer and fall courses, I failed to keep in mind that each of them might be at a different stage of racial identity development. In fact, I watched as some students struggled through what Tatum describes as the preencounter stage where students of color have internalized "values of the dominant White culture" to the encounter stage, which is often triggered by an event that forces the individual to "acknowledge the impact of racism in one's life" (Tatum *Why* 10).

For example, during the beginning of that first fall semester, one Latina student would often open class discussions by recounting experiences she had on campus, in high school, or at the community site that she perceived as racially motivated. Initially, rather than discuss the complexity of these incidents, the other students in the course would dismiss her comments and describe the problem as her "seeing everything" as a racist incident. In one exchange, she described a comment made by one of the elementary school teachers that was evidence to her that teachers can reinforce racist attitudes. Students spent a significant amount of time debating whether or not the comment was racially motivated, most seeming reluctant to name it as such.

By the middle of the semester, though, something had shifted for many of the students. Students' energy level dropped. During class discussions, they seemed less patient with each other. Whereas students used to tease and laugh over their differing opinions, they now seemed lacking in humor and more invested in being correct. When I finally asked students about what I perceived as a change in attitude, even those few students who were initially resistant to naming things as racist were suddenly describing themselves as exhausted by the racism on campus. One woman said she was tired of the racism she was experiencing everywhere; she felt as though she couldn't get away from it.

After listening to students recount numerous incidents—both overt and subtle—I arranged for students to meet with the special assistant to the president who deals with cases of discrimination on campus. That afternoon in the administrator's office, it felt like most of the students of color had reached their breaking point. They described frustration with conversations in their dorms. They expressed disgust over seeing how service workers on campus were treated. Most significantly in terms of their racial identity development, they described feeling more aware of their race than they had ever been before.

Throughout the semester, I assigned readings designed to help students analyze the education system in the United States with attention to issues of race, class, and gender. Students read a piece by Fan Shen that exposes the classroom as a space that reinforces dominant ideologies. They applied Stuart Hall's notion of inferential racism to their experiences on campus at the community site. In reflecting on the course, I now realize both the students and I would have benefited from reading Tatum's piece on racial identity development. It may have helped students better understand their differing opinions, and I suspect my students would have been asking each other different questions and engaging in different debates had they been given these models of racial identity development.

In teaching the course for the third time, my local pedagogy continues to shift based on the needs and perspectives of the students. To help students further develop their analysis of the education system, I now also assign Jonathan Kozol's *Savage Inequalities*. The stories in Kozol's text serve as a point of comparison for the students as they find themselves in elementary classrooms. Kozol's text influences a Latino student to reflect in a journal posting on the physical classroom space. The student writes,

> Waltham Public Schools are in very good shape. The _____ School just underwent a major renovation. The school was in perfect condition. The halls were spotless. The equipment we used was in top notch shape. It was obvious the school had been recently built. Unlike inner city schools, the town of Waltham has the money to make sure that the children have the proper working conditions to succeed.

During a conference, yet another student admitted to not liking Rose's *Lives on the Boundary*. She said she didn't like reading other people's stories, and since his didn't resonate with her experiences at all, she found herself even less interested. Her reaction to Jonathan Kozol's *Savage Inequalities* started in a similar fashion. In one of her initial journal postings on *Savage Inequalities*, however, she begins to reveal the tension that it raises for her. The posting begins with the line "Every time I read *Savage Inequalities* I don't know what to think," and is followed by "I really like the book." But I'm most intrigued by her critique of it:

> After a while though I feel like Kozol's book is an attack on anyone who has gone to a suburban public school where upwards of $10,000 is spent on each student or a private school. Most of my life I attended schools much like Riverdale where there was something similar to the "well-tended park across the street, another larger park three blocks away. . . ." (92). I am not sure if there is anything that can be done by the person that lives in the suburbs besides realizing that the playing field for everyone is not level and the advantage happens to be in their favor. I wish there was something more that could be done because it only makes me feel guilt that I am a part of what seems to be the problem with the unequal distribution of money.

This response has less to do with race and much more to do with class, as this student of color struggles to confront her own socioeconomic privileges. She also uses Kozol's text to think through her own approach in the elementary school classroom. Later in the semester she wrote:

> The connection to service learning . . . is that I made a mistake that many teachers seem to make. I assumed that I might as well give up on the students when there was early disagreement on the team's name. I know that me giving up or leaping to conclusions about what the day was going to be like was a little mistake in comparison to teachers that are discussed in Kozol's book. Frequently those teachers consider their job as a joke and give up on the students over all.

Where she originally resisted the text, she comes to see useful applications of it in her own service experience.

Service-learning courses by their very nature seem to be less hierarchical spaces than traditional classrooms. Despite the planning that goes into any syllabus or course, I find service-learning courses demand greater flexibility and adaptability since each day's discussion and focus is determined in part by what students bring back to the classroom from the site and from their experiences. And as Ann points out, while we may anticipate certain responses to course readings, we can never predict how students will react. Despite having taught a particular text for several semesters, we find ourselves still surprised by the passages that catch our students' attention, challenged by students' questions, and invigorated by their passion. At times I have also felt frustrated and helpless.

Part of my local pedagogy has therefore been to share my process with my students. This past semester, for example, I used Jane Elliot's video *Eye of the Storm* to help students think about the ways in which young children grapple with discrimination. We eliminated some course readings and substituted others. We replaced discussions about writing with meetings with outside sources that might help them address their anxieties and frustrations. By asking students to become educators through a service-learning program and by allowing them to have a say in the direction of the course, I suspect they became more invested in their role as students on the college campus.

Both Ann and Michelle point to the unexpected and unpredictable in the service-learning classroom. Ann's experience highlights ways anger can be a very real and intense part of the service-learning classroom. Michelle's experience reminds me that all students, regardless of their background or experience, struggle as they cross borders. Both inside and outside the service-learning classroom, though, white students generally can choose to engage with or ignore the issues and feelings that stem from that border crossing. By contrast, most students of color cannot leave their pain and struggle behind until the next class meeting or service-learning session. Dealing with difference, prejudice, and oppression, for them, transcends the borders of the classroom.

Like Ann and Michelle, I, too, am required to assess the particulars of each situation, whether it is a classroom discussion or a student's journal entry, and to determine an approach that recognizes those particulars. As soon as I begin to think about the experiences of my students of color as uniform, I fail at my own local pedagogy. As a white faculty member, I must be sure to question my own assumptions every time I walk into that classroom space.

LOCAL PEDAGOGY AND THE SAFE ENOUGH CLASSROOM

In "Age, Race, Class, and Sex: Women Redefining Difference," Audre Lorde writes, "we have no patterns for relating across our human differences as equals" (15). As we craft our local pedagogies, each of us wrestles with this question of how to think about differences and the idea of community without, as Patricia Williams puts it, "crashing through." By addressing issues of difference directly via course readings, initiating conversations about race, racism, and white privilege, and providing opportunities for students to reflect in writing about their processes of racial identity development, we have worked to create spaces in our classrooms where students feel "safe."

But rather than idealizing safety as a permanent or transcendent state in our classrooms, we instead work to create classroom communities that are "safe enough"—safe enough that students, teachers, community members, and learners from the service sites might challenge each other—and be challenged—to think more deeply about issues of difference. As we work to define difference as more than a dichotomy between Black and White—as a category that also includes sexual preference, social class, and gender—we struggle with finding "patterns for relating across our human differences as equals." The complexity of the service-learning paradigm leads us to conclude that developing a local pedagogy means taking students' concerns seriously and working with issues that students generate from the service-learning site and in the classroom.

The service-learning classroom can be an emotional space where students grapple with complex issues around difference. Flexibility in creating assignments, assigning readings, and responding to writing is critical in the non-hierarchical spaces created by the service-learning experience. As Angelique notes above, having the opportunity to raise issues and shape their classroom experiences helps non-majority students to become more invested in their roles on college campuses. Creating spaces for affective responses and acknowledging one's own implications in systems of power are also important strategies for facilitating students' learning. As Michelle writes, not every journal entry needs to be acknowledged, but affirming students' right to response is important. Finally, attending to relationships in the classroom can also influence how students learn. As Ann muses, had she been better able to incorporate more community building work into the classroom, Lucy and Amanda might have been better able to find ways to learn across their differences. Relationships and trust were also key to Angelique and Michelle's interventions with students.

Service-learning pedagogy does not automatically bring issues of race, class, gender, or sexual orientation to the forefront, but in the safe enough classroom, engaging with communities gives the service-learning teacher rich opportunities not only to discuss "difference," but to complicate students' ideas of difference in ways that enhance their critical thinking, levels of engagement, and commitment to social justice.

WORKS CITED

Anzaldúa, Gloria. "How to Tame a Wild Tongue." *Teaching Developmental Writing: Background Readings*. Ed. Susan Naomi Bernstein. New York: Bedford/St. Martins, 2004. 301–10.

Carter, Robert T. "Is White a Race?: Expressions of White Racial Identity." *Off White: Readings on Race, Power, and Society*. Ed. Michelle Fine, Lois Weis, Linda C. Powell, L. Mung Wong. New York: Routledge, 1997. 198–209.

Delpit, Lisa. *Other People's Children*. New York: New Press, 1995.

Dubois, W. E. B. *The Souls of Black Folks*. Mineola, NY: Dover Publications, 1994.

Dunlap, Michelle. *Reaching Out to Children and Families: Students Model Effective Community Service*. Lanham, MD: Rowman & Littlefield, 2000.

———. "The Role of the Personal Fable in Adolescent Service Learning and Critical Reflection." *Michigan Journal of Community Service Learning* 4 (1997): 56–63.

Dunlap, Michelle, Jennifer Monroe, Patrick Green, and Angelique Davi. "'Trigger Events' and Privilege Awareness Among White Service-Learners Engaged in Homeless Shelters." *Michigan Journal of Community Service Learning*, in press.

Ellsworth, Elizabeth. "Why Doesn't This Feel Empowering?: Working Through the Myths of Critical Pedagogy." *The Education Feminism Reader*. Ed. Lynda Stone. New York: Routledge, 1994. 300–27.

Goldblatt, Eli. "Van Rides in the Dark: Literacy as Involvement in a College Literacy Practicum." *Journal of Peace and Justice Studies* 6.1 (1995): 77–94.

Green, Ann E. "'But You Aren't White': Racial Perceptions and Service Learning." *Michigan Journal of Community Service Learning* 8.1 (2001): 18–26.

———. "Difficult Stories: Service-Learning, Race, Class, and Whiteness." *College Composition and Communication* 55.2 (December 2003): 276–301.

———. "Literature and Service-Learning: Thinking through Subject Positions." *Reflections* 1.3 (2001): 14–16.

Hall, Stuart. "The Whites of Their Eyes: Racist Ideologies and the Media." *Gender, Race, and Class in Media*. Eds. Gail Dine and Jean M. Humez. Thousand Oaks, CA: Sage, 1995. 18–22.

Herbes-Sommers, Christine (director). *Race: The Power of an Illusion* [Documentary], California Newsreel, A. 2003.

Hertzberg, Bruce. "Community Service and Critical Teaching." *College Composition and Communication* 45 (1994): 307–19.

hooks, bell. *Teaching to Transgress*. New York: Routledge, 1994.

Jordan, June. "No Body Mean More To Me Than You, and the Future Life of Willie Jordan." *Some of Us Did Not Die: New and Selected Essays of June Jordan*. New York: Basic Books, 2002. 157–73.

Kozol, Jonathan. *Savage Inequalities: Children in America's Schools*. New York: Harper Perennials, 1991.

Lorde, Audre. "Age, Race, Class, and Sex: Women Redefining Difference." *Sister/Outsider: Essays and Speeches*. Freedom, CA: Crossing Press, 1984. 114–23.

———. "The Use of Anger: Women Responding to Racism." *Sister/Outsider: Essays and Speeches*. Freedom, CA: Crossing Press, 1984. 124–33.

McIntosh, Peggy. "White Privilege: Unpacking the Invisible Knapsack." *Independent School* 49(2) (1988): 31–39.

New London School District. *New London School District: Strategic School Profile 1998–1999*. New London, CT: Board of Education, 1999.

O'Grady, Carolyn. R. *Integrating Service Learning and Multicultural Education in Colleges and Universities*. Mahwah, NJ: Erlbaum, 2000.

Rose, Mike. *Lives on the Boundary: A Moving Account of the Struggles and Achievements of America's Educationally Underprepared*. New York: Penguin, 1989.

Rosenberger, Cynthia. "Beyond Empathy: Developing Critical Consciousness through Service Learning." *Integrating Service Learning and Multicultural Education in Colleges and Universities*. O'Grady. 23–44.

Shen, Fan. "The Classroom and the Wider Culture: Identity as a Key to Learning Writing in English." *College Composition and Communication* 40.4 (December 1989): 459–66.

Taggart, Amy Rupiper, and H. Brooke Hessler. "Stasis and the Reflective Practitioner: How Experienced Teacher-Scholars Sustain Community Pedagogy." *Reflections* 5.1 (2006): 153–72.

Tatum, Beverly Daniel. "Talking about Race: The Application of Racial Identity Development Theory in the Classroom." *Harvard Educational Review* 62.1 (1992): 1–24.

———. *"Why Are All The Black Kids Sitting Together in The Cafeteria?" And Other Conversations About Race*. New York: Basic Books, 1999.

Winans, Amy. "Local Pedagogies and Race: Interrogating White Safety in the Rural College Classroom." *College English* 67.3 (2005): 253–73.

34   *Slipping Pages through Razor Wire: Literacy Action Projects in Jail*

TOBI JACOBI

Razor wire. To many, razor wire represents security, safety, a boundary between the good and free and the deviant and dangerous. For writers and teachers who work within U.S. prisons and jails, razor wire symbolizes a series of challenges to the composing process. A sharpness that cuts the student-teacher relationship in often unfamiliar ways. A slicing of drafts that cuts certain topics, phrases, and confidentialities away without writers' consent. Historical and contemporary prison writing memoirs invoke an image of the solitary writer slipping pages through razor wire, and for some, this was and is reality. Yet, the jail where I facilitate writing programs isn't surrounded by the razor wire that is characteristic of so many institutions; this is not because it is a facility governed by progressive or alternative sentencing philosophies, but rather because the inmates simply never get out. Their "yards" are small walled and paved areas located deep within the building complex. And still razor wire has a significant cultural meaning that pervades even institutions without its physical presence.

To slip through the razor wire is to challenge the system. To slip through the razor wire is risky, whether you are trying to slip contraband in—or make it visible to the rest of the world. And to slip through, under, or around razor wire with language—written or verbal—I suggest, is the work of social justice and a growing number of scholars in composition and rhetoric who are motivated by such issues and the possibility of change. To complicate the possibility of change, this essay explores the intersection between writing studies and civic engagement through the action projects developed in a capstone English course focused on prison literature and writing. Such literacy activism creates immediate opportunities for advanced undergraduates to more fully understand the work of literacy in contested spaces like jails and extends a call to action for writing teachers to acknowledge the possibility of such writing collaborations.

From *Community Literacy Journal* 2.2 (2008): 67–86

CONFIGURING CHANGE IN COMMUNITY-BASED LITERACY
CLASSROOMS AND JAIL

> [I]t is when we open our classrooms to communication of all sorts not just to E. B. White (though he wrote beautifully) or to academic cultural critique (though much of it is timely and of great interest) and, especially, not just to *Time, Newsweek,* and *US News and World Report*—that we begin to understand the role communication plays in the lives of active participants in this democracy.
>
> —GEORGE 15–16

As Diana George and many community literacy scholars suggest, movement toward a more ethical and just world requires engagement beyond the traditional and canonical classroom.

To understand our world more fully than E. B. White's prose or handbook make possible requires critical attention to other contexts, processes, and relationships based in literate practice. Many recognize the need to locate and engage literacy beyond the conventional boundaries of school (Barton, Hamilton, and Ivanic; Gere; Heath; Higgins, Long, and Flower; Hull and Schultz). As Jeff Grabill argues, "If theorizing about literacy does not account for institutional systems in locating literacy, the possibilities for changes to the meaning and value of literacy are constrained. And this is the real problem" (44). Service learning and community-based research has often been correlated with social change (Cushman "Rhetorician"; Cushman "Public Intellectual"; Herzberg; Peck, Flower, and Higgins), and models for achieving change through reciprocity have been offered through curricula, assessments, and turns toward outside models for configuring community-university partnerships (Cushman "Sustainable"; Goldblatt; Mathieu; Carrick, Himley, and Jacobi).

In many service learning courses, however, change (for students) is projected as altered/expanded/exploded perception about a social issue, constituency group, or other aspect of their community experience. This itself does not constitute change in the minds of many community partners and activists. While the work accomplished may be good, useful, needed labor, change is more complex, and, as Gorzelsky, Goldblatt, and Mathieu suggest, there is a need to consider alternative models and purposes for engaging in community literacy work. In *The Language of Experience* Gwen Gorzelsky characterizes this initial labor as contact, suggesting that "when language practices support individual and communal change, they do so by expanding people's contact with unaware dimensions of their experience. This contact results from changed conditions of experience and in turn promotes change" (211).

Gorzelsky goes on to argue that such contact precedes the successful negotiation of difference and coalition-building and that learning experiences can be crafted to offer increased access to language experiences that will result in increased knowledge-making and negotiation in specific contexts (215–24). Eli Goldblatt argues that academics and teachers can engage more fully in community-based work by rethinking how and when contact occurs. He invokes Saul Alinsky's model of community organizing as a method of re-considering how community relationships can be forged and maintained beyond a semester-long course and situates collective social change through the contributions scholars and service learning practitioners can make as knowledge activists (defined as experience, resources offered "responsibly and cooperatively" through a non-interventionalist approach [292–93]). Such models of contact complicate the notion of *change-as-understanding* by requir-ing commitments that extend beyond the labor most service learning courses (and students) can offer. They complicate, but I don't believe they eliminate the possibility of engaging in meaningful work within the courses we teach.

How and to what end contact is negotiated and achieved is often framed in terms of a problem-solving model of community literacy or service learn-ing. In *Tactics of Hope: The Public Turn in English Composition*, Paula Mathieu argues that the difference between problem- and project-based approaches to community engagement is significant, that the project approach has the potential to avoid the "negative space" of the problem-solving approach that depends upon a solution (50). As Mathieu suggests, "a project orientation privileges creation and design" and responses to problems without being defined by an external measure (50). This is particularly notable when com-munity partnerships are forged within the correctional system. Community partners are often dually defined as the jail administrators and staff and the incarcerated learners and writers students work with. Both constituencies are driven by and impacted by external measures: the legal system, public as-sumptions and pressures, conflicted relationships with conventional social systems like school and more. Incarcerated participants are particularly vulnerable when "problems" are linked to their sense of self, a common re-habilitative measure that inspires feelings of shame, embarrassment, and "years of school failure, as well as an association of writing with constant cor-rections" (Boudin 143).

The use of a problem-based model also perpetuates the objectification that many inmates experience as institutions seek to prescribe generalist mod-els for individual rehabilitation. A ready example exists in the only required educational access many prisoners have: GED training. As Jeff Grabill and others have suggested, the GED curriculum does little to advance learners toward critical thinking and engagement.[1] On the other hand, carceral set-tings have a tremendous need for projects that privilege and promote "crea-tion and design" as a way of making space for reciprocities based in shared learning and diverse outcomes.

Literature on literacy work in carceral settings illustrates this tension and the complexity of negotiating change. Service learning experiences can afford students the opportunities to interact as mentors, but often such work is com-plicated by the challenge of context. Criminal justice students at the Univer-sity of West Florida mentored juveniles in adult jail and were confronted with the limitations of time, citing too much for one course, and too little to affect change (Swanson, King, and Wolbert 265). Lori Pompa's Philadelphia-based Inside-Out Prison Exchange Program moves "outside" students into prison as they join "inside" students for an engaging but similarly time bound Freirean reading of the justice world (26). Lisa Mastrangelo recounts the enthusiastic engagement of her first year composition students in a course focused on writing and women in prison. Unable to directly interact with women inside, students conducted research for an advocacy group interested in moving toward work with incarcerated women and sponsored a book drive for the Women's Book Project.

Though successful in these endeavors, both Mastrangelo and her students wonder about the possibility of reciprocity when constituency groups cannot come into contact (48), a concern echoed by students in my course. Tom Kerr's capstone writing seminar confronted this issue head on through a correspondence exchange with women in U.S. prisons that led to serious questions of power, ideology, and culturally-driven assumptions about our legal system. Ultimately, it was the women's responses to their queries rather than—or in addition to—the carefully scaffolded course texts that challenged students' notions about the rights and value of prisoners. One correspondent wrote: "I was a bit insulted and a lot of prisoners would be by questions that question my humanness" (69). Another addressed the issue of change: "You ask how you can help. One way you can help is to foster more dialogue between prisoners and society. You're a writer. The world changes through writing. You can help me by suggesting ways that I can more effectively communicate with America" (73). Direct correspondence such as this encourages students (including my own) to recognize and confront what it means to write inside—and the need for collaboration across razor wire. Each of the programs cited above presents a useful model for university-prison literacy projects that embody Freirean principles of problem-posing inquiry. Each demonstrates engaged dialogue on writing, justice, and life experiences by valuing incarcerated writers' voices and challenging university students to move beyond the analysis of a potentially static text.

Just as prisoners and students champion literate action as a powerful agent of change, so do many of the teachers working in (and in opposition to) the correctional system. Ann Folwell Stanford, workshop facilitator at Chicago's Cook County Jail and various correctional institutions throughout Illinois, argues that participation in a writing workshop is itself a radical move toward change. With participation comes the recognition of shared experience and the potential for a solidarity defined in opposition to institutional rehabilitative philosophies (291). Longtime prison teacher Irene Baird suggests that situating key writers (e.g., Angelou, Giovanni, Gaines) in the role of author mentor can inspire incarcerated learners to imagine themselves in the role of activist (6). Such rhetorics are well-entrenched in prison activist writing. In her 2003 *Are Prisons Obsolete?* Angela Davis outlines a continuum of alternatives to vengeful incarceration (105–15), possibilities that translate fears of lost reciprocity and institutional complicity into meaningful workshops based upon collective goals and classrooms engaged in dialogues about incarceration—and a world beyond the prison industrial complex. Programs like these inspire dynamic and thoughtful designs for prison-university collaborations by recognizing the inevitable complicities that accompany cross-institutional work while remaining committed to the possibility of change.

Along with many community literacy scholars and practitioners I recognize that change can be difficult to imagine and harder to sustain, that the material realities of post-incarceration—and even college—life make a writing workshop or capstone course seem rather insignificant. Yet, I also recognize these sites as spaces for collective and meaningful learning that can lead to social critique and public education. I offer the course description and literacy action projects, in many ways modeled on the programs cited above, that follow as examples of community-based writing collaborations that work toward negotiating these challenges and move toward new social realities.

THE COURSE: E465: PRISON LITERATURE AND WRITING

> This has been one of the best and most important classes I have taken at CSU. I hope you will be able to teach this class again.
> —COURSE EVALUATION

This capstone course worked to extend advanced undergraduate students' understandings of writing and genre through the examination of a range of prison literature and media. As cultural and rhetorical critics, students were trained to work in ways that will sound familiar to many readers—to study and critique issues of power, agency, and possibility in both canonical texts, Malcolm X's "Learning to Read," for example, and less conventional and undercirculated texts, such as those by nearly invisible groups of women writers. Our primary aim as a group of inquirers was to examine the production, consumption, and reception of communication practices demonstrated by writers located in prison globally and locally, and, not surprisingly, this was outside the experience of most of the students in the class.

Through exploration of canonical and undercirculated texts and media representations—film, photography, radio, online media—the following goals were pursued:

- To understand debates surrounding the nature of writing as well as the role of writing/language as cultural and social capital for incarcerated writers

- To consider the relationship between writing and the human experience by examining the will to compose by writers confined to small and/or highly structured spaces

- To consider the issues of identity and ethics that influence the composing processes of the twenty-first-century prison writer

- To apply course content and debate to lived experience through active engagement with the local justice system: a prison book drive, writing workshops, etc.

- Further the course aimed to complicate and extend disciplinary knowledge through connections between literature and the material world by considering how a diverse set of incarcerated writers approach writing as a meaning-making process

- Reading texts across gender, ethnicity, race, and time
- Tracing the circulation of those writings.

A primary goal, then, was to consider the role of language and literacy in constructing identities within discourse communities beyond the academy, recognizing, as Eli Goldblatt suggests, that students and faculty function "inside an institutional framework for literacy that is merely one among many" (293).

Course texts included historical and contemporary prison writings representing genres such as essays, poetry, drama, fiction, nonfiction, memoir, and documentary journalism, film, radio, and web materials. Course assignments included close readings of seven books and multiple critical essays, weekly online forum discussions, two reading response essays, a collaborative prison action project, and a final exam.[2] The collaborative action project component functioned to extend students' experience with incarceration and literacy practices by engaging them beyond the conventional boundaries of the classroom. Students developed and chose to participate in one of five community projects.

Choices impacted our local detention center and included the organization of an adult and children's book drive for their library, on-site GED tutoring, co-facilitation of an ongoing women's writing workshop called SpeakOut! a Writing Mentor Program distance exchange between prison and university writers, and work identifying and bringing a prison writer to campus. These service learning projects were designed to help students see the complexities of accessing and achieving dominant literacy education and of producing and circulating prison writings. Students collected over 700 books, mentored eighteen writers, led writing workshops, taught GED learners, and raised over $8,500 to bring renowned Latino poet Jimmy Santiago Baca to campus for a series of readings in classrooms and at the jail.

I'm going to highlight two of those action projects here as worthy of further consideration as literacy and writing scholars reconfigure and refine our understanding of what change, particularly social change, means and how it can be enacted. I also highlight them as models for projects that enact Goldblatt's call for more attention to the negotiation of university-community partnerships that precede and outlive individual students and semesters. The two projects are the Writing Mentor Program and the Speak Out! Women's Writing Workshop.

ACTION PROJECT #1: THE WRITING MENTOR PROGRAM AS STUDENT ENGAGEMENT

> My favorite part of the class was the action projects. Doing the GED tutoring . . . has opened my eyes to many issues I've never thought about.
> –STUDENT EVALUATION

The Writing Mentor Program paired fourteen university students with eighteen incarcerated writers at three adult and juvenile detention sites.[3] This program was inspired by and modeled after the national PEN American Center's prison writing mentorship program. Since that program required a commitment beyond one semester and wasn't open to undergraduate mentors, we developed a local program to foster working writing relationships between incarcerated writers and university mentors. The program's philosophy and goals emerged from a blend of pedagogical and social justice motives. These include the promotion of written literacy as a powerful form of self-expression, engagement in direct literacy training and advocacy, increased public awareness on issues of incarceration, and the increased and broadened circulation of writings by incarcerated writers.

Practically, students exchanged writing with an incarcerated teen or adult writer through an exchange of folders. Students were encouraged to develop the relationship by focusing on their shared interest in writing. In-class training included discussions on response style, available and appropriate pedagogical tools, and the ethics of publication as well as the importance of establishing clear boundaries (e.g., using our university address, exchanging first names only, sharing limited personal data). One issue that received much attention in the development of this program was the use of the labels "mentor" and "mentee." Even as I reflect, they seem imperfect terms, laden with implied power relations and conventional school strategies, an almost direct departure from the critical pedagogy that the program aimed to enact. Yet because inequity and power disparities were ever-present, "partners" wasn't an accurate descriptor. As Grabill has indicated, adult learners invest their time carefully and feel a sense of satisfaction when their concept of education has been fulfilled (43). Inmates needed the idea of a university "mentor" as motivation to join the program; similarly, when the program extended beyond the semester, university students were recruited with the promise of mentoring a prison writer. Our aim was to design the exchanges in ways that could allow the pair to become "partners"—through exchanged rather than only submitted/received writings, reciprocal talk about writing, etc.—if and when it felt right for both writers.[4]

Student mentors added their individual reflections to a collective blog site as a way of sharing individual experiences with "prison" writers as well as modeling and advising each other on effective—and floundering!—techniques for engaging with unseen writing partners. One mentor writes:

> My first response was kind of challenging. I am realizing that it is difficult to respond to writing without knowing what the writer is expecting/wanting you to look at. Plus, I had to respond to poetry—my first time ever! It was hard! I need some advice from some of you creative writers on effective ways of responding to poetry. I also hope that all of my comments were encouraging and not too harsh. Sometimes I feel like I get into teacher mode, which is what I *do not* want to do with these writers. Mostly, I am hoping to function as a person that my woman feels comfortable having correspondence with, and to encourage open writing. Improvement is obviously important, but more important for me is to keep the writer writing!

Issues of representation regularly surfaced for mentors. This student confronts her mentor identity in the opening lines, grappling with issues of audience, genre, and her own inexperience with poetry response. She also struggles with "teacher mode" and worries that her written notations will provoke associations with traditional schooling in ways that she is trying to avoid. Students regularly faced the question Flower so aptly articulates: "How do you support someone else's ideas and development when you are the one with all the technical knowledge and writing experience?" (251). Jail complicates this challenge further since the mentors didn't have access to their partners' educational or writing histories unless they were explicitly revealed.

Other mentors felt overwhelmed by the lack of context their writing exchanges made visible. This mentor expresses a clear desire for the "talk" that often accompanies peer review workshops or writing center tutorials:

> The biggest challenge I have seen confronted with as a mentor is that there is so little communication from the mentees along the lines of what they want to work on (at least I have not heard anything from mine). Mostly I just receive the piece and that is it, so sometimes I feel like I am repeating myself . . . trying to establish some kind of writing relationship. Often this seems very one sided, and I'm hoping to get more feedback from them for which to work on. It would be very helpful to have something to focus on, rather than just having the work to look at and mull over.

Although a feedback exchange form was offered with each exchange, the jail writers rarely completed them; more often writers submitted only writing, sometimes without even the folder. As this student muses, this became an ongoing frustration for mentors who were uncertain about how to frame responses and how to support the writers without threatening the growing relationship.

Other mentors pointed to the physical challenge of reading and responding to writing composed across time and with few material resources:

> I finally got a second piece of writing, though it is not from my first mentee, who, it appears, isn't going to be sending me any more stuff. This second piece is actually quite a challenge. Parts of it were written over a year ago and some just over a month ago. It looks like he just used any pieces of paper he could find and didn't just use them as a personal journal, but also for drawing. Visually it is hard to read, because the handwriting is small (trying to get the most out the space available) and sometimes a bit jumbled because of graphics that were on the page or that he drew.

Taken for granted on a college campus, paper can be a scarce resource in correctional settings. Here the materiality of jail collides with the mentor's expectations as the submission jumbles the notion of sequential drafting and organization with the necessity of using available space for multiple purposes. Another writer squeezed a lengthy microscopic narrative between the lines of a legal form, forcing the mentor to engage with an institutional document in a new way.

The missionary impulse is one the WMP actively worked to dismantle, though the desire for improvement and partnership was present for many mentors. One mentor writes:

> The second round of writings I received were better than the first, but the person I'm working with is still trying to write about too much in a single piece. In the first round of writings, I encouraged the person I'm working with to focus on one of the phrases she used in a poem to create a new, more focused poem. The result was awesome, so I encouraged her to do a bit more tweaking, and to consider the piece for publication. As far as the other two pieces I received this time, I suggested she take a single theme and focus her writing on that theme. Things are going well. My mentee and I have been corresponding through letters with every exchange, and I've even given her some of my own writing.

There are two observations worth noting in this excerpt. First, the progress narrative revealed in the opening lines of this blog entry represents the experience many students in mentor/tutorial roles assume: education and practice will result in improvement. Yet, as Flower notes, mentors may feel jarred when "they encounter the conflicts between community literacy and their own practices, standards, and assumptions about writing" (251). This mentor celebrates the shift she sees in her mentee's work from the first submission to the second. The implication is that if the mentee follows the advice that will follow for "tweaking," it will be ready for publication, an end product that indicates success for many writers. Second, the final line of the entry demonstrates a shift in the relationship through movement from a traditional mentor-mentee interaction to a relationship based in shared writing: correspondence and written work. It is also notable that the conditions of writing are not the focus of the mentor's reflection. This suggests either a conscious effort to understand this partner as a writer and base the relationship in literate activity—or it makes visible the ways that a distance writing exchange can mask the material realities of writing in prison.

The blog entries excerpted above are representative of the reflections shared by the students serving as mentors in the program, and while access to the written responses of the incarcerated mentees is confidential, I did observe the folders being received with great enthusiasm and being quickly returned to mentors with new writing and correspondence. The program is not without flaws, but as an action project intended to bring life to the conditions and challenges of accessing and engaging in literate activity in jail, it succeeded—and took up Mathieu's call for project-based community engagement that rethinks reciprocity. It engaged university students in an effort to challenge canonical constructions of the prison writing genre and took on the dual issues of low literacy levels among adult incarcerated populations and the invisibility of "low profile" inmate accounts of life in prison and beyond. A project such as this further takes up Mathieu's theorization of De Certeau to situate public writing as tactical, as capable of accomplishing context-driven, temporary, and often oppositional discourse as the writing mentors and mentees engaged in written exchanges.

Community literacy projects inevitably connect to the strength or weakness of community partnerships and (dis)satisfaction with the terms of engagement. As a teacher who works in university and jail settings, the Writing Mentor Program challenged me to rethink reciprocity. Reciprocity came to mean several things, as the blogs suggest. Students gained access to a new population of writers/students, a challenge to the often-insulated space of a university. They also gained access to a new audience for their ideas, one that did not function within semester time lines and evaluative expectations. Reciprocity for mentees might be configured as access to a tutoring relationship or an exchange of ideas between writers, or as access to individuals who are not employed by the correctional facility or members of a religiously sponsored recovery program, or simply as access to dialogic space with another student of writing. Such configurations allow us to imagine a prison writing partnership that enacts David Coogan's recent representation of civic dialogue as "a construction site for community, a functioning place with no real façade or formal entrance" (106). Although the Writing Mentor Program cannot free participants from the limitations of a semester-based project, the program does invite an engagement founded on the practice and collaborative interrogation of literacy rather than a model based in academic abstraction and grade point averages.

Action Project #2: SpeakOut! Women's Writing Workshops as Sustainability

> When we have established these relationships, we may be able to help the community partners identity problems and transform these problems into issues to act upon, only later considering how students in courses fit in and what university resources could be helpful in addressing the issues.
>
> —Goldblatt 283

The SpeakOut! Women's Writing Workshops at the Larimer County Detention Center (LCDC) began in 2005 and so preceded the class (highlighted here as a common way to engage in writing-based relationships in jail). The sessions provided a relatively safe and encouraging space for participants to express themselves through their writing and through dialogue within the workshop. In addition to refining writing skills, the workshops invited participants to foster space for creativity, evaluate past actions, envision life change, and promote community action and social change through writing and verbal storytelling. Facilitators design workshop curricula, attend weekly staff meetings, run weekly workshops, and respond to writing submissions. Workshops were cofacilitated by undergraduate and graduate students and a university professor at LCDC in Spring and Fall 2006 with over 90 women writers participating. Each workshop met for ninety minutes weekly and resulted in the publication of an issue of the *SpeakOut! Journal* and a "coffeehouse" reading at the jail for all female inmates to attend. In both Spring and Fall 2006, over 50% of all residents attended. The *SpeakOut! Journal* is published biannually and is circulated among writers, peers, and family, and within the community through a local bookstore.

As an action project for E465, this workshop impacted a relatively small number of students. Two to four students are handpicked annually to cofacilitate this project; it takes a mature student to work in a correctional setting without becoming overwhelmed or reproducing teaching and language practices that perpetuate rather than challenge patriarchal power relations. The students who have the most successful experiences are those who are motivated by more than a course requirement, often students with backgrounds in women's studies, critical literacy, or progressive pedagogy.

One outcome of the workshop is the development of community and a shared ownership of the workshop, work that offers an alternative to most of the time women spend in jail. Our community-based workshop is cultivated in several ways. The curriculum is largely organic and responsive. Each 90-minute session allows for activities ranging from invention and composing based on prompts to shared writings to informal oral response and debate on topics of interest to the group. Each facilitator contributes one prompt to the evening's lesson plan and shares in the administrative duties (e.g., typing and responding to submitted writings, opening the workshop and recording attendance, modeling writing techniques). Participants are invited to engage in every aspect of the workshop as well.

After the first meeting, facilitators invite returning writers to help orient newcomers by explaining, "what we do in the workshop" to encourage joint ownership. Workshop time focuses on process pedagogy inspired activities and relies upon collaborative and feminist methods. Group feedback follows each piece, and the workshop closes with the distribution of an "ideas for writing" handout. This resource includes two predetermined prompts for the women to work with during the week and the group collectively agrees on two more that are named and recorded in the moment. Such activities work to create an investment in the shared writing and storytelling—and ultimately the writing process. One facilitator notes a shift in the writers, a group that felt uncomfortable with labels such as "author" and "writer" only a few weeks earlier:

> The number of women who want to share increases with each session. I think this speaks to the sense of community we've created over the past few weeks.

While many have theorized "community," I raise it as a meaningful development here for several reasons. First, the student is naming the formation of community based in writing, and given the public perception of most prison writers composing in isolated cells, this seems significant to her learning and conception of how literacy can function in alternative spaces. Second, the formation of community is not purposefully cultivated in carceral settings. The institution aims to maintain control. Organizing is discouraged. Prisoners are often relocated without explanation. Since community is charged with implications not applicable in a "free" world, the workshop sometimes embodies what Anita Wilson calls "third space," the "space between inside and outside worlds where [prisoners] can 'occupy their minds'" (74). The workshop occupies a liminal space where, however temporary, *writer* becomes an identity the participants can claim. Finally, community serves as a useful way to configure the boundary crossing students (and faculty) do when engaging in action projects. David Coogan's metaphor of community as a "temporary tethering . . . across the racial and class boundaries that divide us" (107–8) creates space for considering the particular opportunities a semester project can offer. He suggests that academics can open inquiries because we are not "present bound" and I suggest that students engaged in action projects can actively join that inquiry as they correlate their observations and experiences with the study of literate practices—here organized around prison—across time and space.

As with the Writing Mentor Program, the SpeakOut! workshop forces participants to confront the complexities and complicities of context. I would argue, along with Stanford, that the conditions of incarceration make writing and writing spaces risky. Prisoners are not guaranteed "safe space" for the content or storage of their words. Cells are regularly ransacked, and writings of all kinds are often confiscated as evidence, contraband, or garbage. A writer's words (whether fictional or not) can be leveraged against her or her peers if deemed inflammatory, provocative, or violent. The SpeakOut! strategy has been to highlight such risks at the opening of each workshop series and to encourage writers to be intentional about the pieces they store, send out to friends and family, and/or publish in publicly circulating sources such as the *SpeakOut! Journal*.

The material realities of prison have implications for students as well. Facilitators were often frustrated by the shifting conditions of our work, as one student notes in her blog:

> One week we can't bring our pens in, but the next week we're allowed to bring in cookies? And then a lockdown? Maybe it's because I am new to the workshop, but I keep waiting to hit a "groove" where the workshop becomes more routine. However, with different circumstances each week, I don't think it's going to happen. I was pretty disappointed that we weren't able to facilitate the workshop, but considering the environment that the workshop takes place in, it seems inevitable that there will be obstacles such as lockdowns.

As this excerpt demonstrates, running a workshop inside prisons and jails creates a specific set of complications for community literacy projects. By nature jail is an unstable environment. Workshop participants move in and out of the institution at a moment's notice. Conditions range from easy access to the confiscation of facilitator tools to cancelled workshops—or suspended if a lockdown occurs during the workshop. The emotion economy in jail is unstable as well. Participants often have histories with each other that precede and influence workshop dynamics. Seemingly benign prompt choices elicit unexpected and sometimes painful associations: "Write about your favorite sound." "Mommy." Missed holidays and life events create heightened urgencies for affirmation when writers choose to share their narratives. While the workshop structure recognized and tries to support this risk-taking, there is always the possibility of provoking an emotional trajectory that cannot be supported by a weekly workshop or ill-funded justice system. University, jail, and other institutional constraints layer additional tensions into project design and function as power relations are navigated and challenged; program materials always have a dual administration/writer audience, for example. Finally, the notion of social justice that emerges strongly for some students must be tempered in recognition of the complicity the program experiences through its institutional sponsorship. The introduction of potentially revolutionary writings and ideas, critical literacy practices, and methods for promoting alternatives to socially constructed identity narratives of incarcerated writers must be navigated with care.

The SpeakOut! action project relies not only on engagement through weekly workshop sessions but also upon the publication and circulation of incarcerated women's writings, and the workshop disseminates writing farther than the other course-based projects. The anthologies travel to friends and family, administrators, to local coffee shops and to other prison writing programs and scholars around the country. Both facilitators and participants become invested in issues of representation as the final product is negotiated. One student facilitator mused:

> We had a few questions last night from new people about what the book will look like and we've been getting suggestions from the women about putting more pictures as well as page numbers in the book. [Co-facilitator] also suggested that as facilitators we should put in a few lines of our own reflections on our experiences in the workshop. I think we should let the women be as involved as possible in the creation of the book this time around. Maybe we could bring in sample covers and they could vote on which color or design they like best.

Though published in a basic and affordable form, the *SpeakOut! Journal* works to revise public perceptions of the writers' identities through what Brenton Faber calls "identity-stories," narratives that are not without risk, but that "act as protective counterweights to a daily barrage of messages, constructions and images" (171). Such work will not create earthquakes of change in a powerful system based in retribution, but we might locate small ruptures through moments of literate action as the workshop writings are produced and circulated, as student facilitators design and revise the space of the workshop, and importantly, as they move beyond the workshop into the other parts of their lives with new understandings of what and where writing occurs (also see Carter; Stino and Palmer). As Diana George suggests:

> [Community publications] do not exist in a vacuum. They reject the fragmentation many of us experience as or at least suspect is characteristic of life in the 21st century. Moreover, they actually do effect change, on the local level and beyond, in the lives of the people they work with and for. (8)

LITERACY ACTION AND SOCIAL CHANGE=COMPLEXITY AND POSSIBILITY

> Learning to take literate action is learning to live in a complicated world where theory is tested and ideas such as literacy take on a negotiated meaning.
>
> —FLOWER 255

Action projects like the SpeakOut! workshops and the Writing Mentor Program create what Powell and Takayoshi call "moments for reciprocity" by simultaneously engaging students in community-based action research and increasing inmates' access to functional and creative literacy programs. Further, these community-centered writing projects work to challenge the canon of "prison writing" by extending our disciplinary commitment to valuing and publishing the voices of historically un/derrepresented voices to include the words and experiences of prisoners. And that possibility inevitably leads me back to the question I continue to ask of each community-based course and project I design: what kind of change can such projects enable, represent, and enact? How can this contact result in responsible literacy activism?

This essay opened with the invocation of the image of razor wire and the possibility of slipping through political and personal acts of oppositional discourse without injury; yet it is also useful to refocus our gaze upon the spaces between the wire spirals instead of only noting sharp edges. The spaces between suggest room for the blending of sound waves and the transfer of sheets of paper marked by excitement, confusion, anger, questions, affirmation, and hope. In that world of possibility, this is how I imagine closing the story of this course and community partnership with the jail: university students participating in this course were deeply engaged in their action projects and moved on to brilliant careers armed with the tools to understand how to fight for what they believe in through literacy activism. Similarly, jail participants in our writing workshops, tutoring sessions, and mentoring partnerships gained experience interacting with university students and found ways to apply their new (or strengthened) literacy skills to the lives they imagined beyond jail. It isn't that easy, of course. If it were, university and correctional contexts wouldn't present such complex, interesting, frustrating, and rewarding work for composition and literacy specialists.

As I move between my role as university professor and community teacher, I find the issue of reciprocity central to the development of sustainability and, in turn, change. University-prison projects such as the Writing Mentor Program and the SpeakOut! Writing Workshop move toward sustainability by complicating factors such as economic and participant stability, cross-institutional collaboration, negotiated growth, and creative renewal:

Stability: Both the WMP and SpeakOut! projects challenge participants to rethink the concept of stability. Economic buoyancy depends largely on successful grant writing efforts, though in recent years we've been able to depend upon our community partners at the jail to provide significant support for the final celebrations we cohost. That said, stability goes far beyond economics in this context. Jails do not enable the participant stability of other settings (prison, for example); neither do semester-based coursework involvements provide the programmatic or mentor stability that many incarcerated writers need and desire to build meaningful and sustained relationships. What they can do is suggest the literate act as a process and tool that might contribute to individual and social stability.

Collaboration: A growing number of schools, non-profits, faith-based groups, and other community institutions have begun to develop strong and ongoing collaborations to meet the needs of women and men bound by the justice system (ranging from short-term counseling to program facilitation to post-prison services). Such collaboration across institutions indicates a growing recognition that the whole inmate must be acknowledged if former prisoners are to contribute meaningfully to a better world.[5] When colleges and universities join these partnerships different kinds of expertise can be contributed and challenged. The resources of higher education can often result in renewed public awareness; in the case of the SpeakOut! workshops our online presence and free publications attracted the attention of two teacher/performance artists who became guest facilitators and who may borrow our model to begin workshops in neighboring communities.

Growth: As Goldblatt argues, relationships and growth must be negotiated by forwarding clear and sustained commitments to community partners' needs. Many mentors and mentees expressed interest in continuing to grow their writing partnerships. The program ultimately extended a full year beyond the course. To compensate for the missing support of a bi-weekly class, with both its talk and required readings, materials such as a program philosophy and mentor training manual were developed. In Fall 2006, we trained fifteen new and returning student mentors and connected them with local and national incarcerated writers. An alternative way to imagine growth is to recognize the skills gained by student participants. Several former SpeakOut! co-facilitators have gone on to develop and/or participate in jail or at-risk writing programs in Arizona, California, and elsewhere in Colorado.

Renewal: There is a reciprocity that can take the form of a renewed interest in writing-as-change, both as a mode of communication with the outside world and a creative/learning process. University students often experience a creative renewal when participating in community-based work. Projects present opportunities for application and deepened understanding of theoretical training in a new context; similar opportunities are presented to our incarcerated partners as they experience a writing partnership, experiment with a process approach to composing, and explore multiple forms of writing to communicate effectively.

How do these movements inch toward sustainability and social change? Writing teachers and literacy workers have a responsibility to consider the potential needs and contributions of incarcerated writers—and the implications of not doing so. Partnerships built across institutions like prisons bring us one step closer to realizing an engaged democratic citizenry. I'm not advocating the romantic reconstruction of narratives that have been sliced and reordered by razors; rather this is a call for writing and literacy specialists to participate in language education as a medium for change, a way to claim space, to displace a fixed method of learning, and to imagine the larger cultural implications of locking up over two million people's words.

NOTES

1. Yet one of our action projects did pair university students with GED students at the jail in pursuit of this culturally sanctioned (if not required) achievement. Their experiences raised questions of purpose, consistency in teaching and learning given jail life, and relevance. Some students developed a relationship with one GED student over the semester; others experienced a new partner each week—and the frustration of "getting nowhere." See Paul Butler's work on teaching the GED in a jail context for an interesting discussion of gender performativity and transgender locality in one tutorial relationship.

2. A copy of the syllabus and course assignments can be found on the *Community Literacy Journal* website at communityliteracy.org/resources/authors/jacobi.

3. I would like to recognize the dedication of recent graduate student Aaron Leff for the development of the Writing Mentor Program. His interest—and ultimately thesis findings—made it possible for the program to move from a course action project to an independent community literacy program located in our Center for Community Literacy. Thanks to the CSU Student Leadership and Civic Engagement Office for their grant support in 2006–2007. Thanks also to the three *CLJ* reviewers who provided useful comments for revision.

4. Many literacy scholars have found Deborah Brandt's use of "sponsor" useful as a metaphor for describing the relationships learners have with teachers. There are several reasons why this is conflicted when applied to a carceral context. Most literally, the term "sponsor" invokes the model of mentorship advocated by Alcoholics Anonymous when used in prison. While this might seem irrelevant to a university teacher or researcher who can turn to other associations, the majority of programming inmates have access to are religiously affiliated and, well, sponsored. It is impossible to move outside this association within a correctional institution. Sponsorship also invokes a hierarchical relationship, one that traditionally invokes an expert/novice or teacher/student model for interaction. The sponsor will provide aid (intellectual, financial, emotional) and the sponsored will gain access to expertise, to opportunities for advancement, for growth. This suggests a progress narrative that might work in some contexts, but prison is seldom one of them.

5. I also recognize the value of peer tutoring programs such as Shannon Carter's HOPE program and the program Kathy Boudin helped to found at Bedford Hills Correctional Facility.

WORKS CITED

Baird, Irene. "The Evolution of Activists: Prison Women's Writing as Change Agent for Their Communities." Paper presented at the Adult Education Research Conference. 2001. 25 Jan 2008 <http://www.eric.ed.gov/ERICDocs/data/ericdocs2sql/content_storage_01/0000019b/80/1b/03/ae.pdf>.

Barton, David, Mary Hamilton, and Roz Ivanic. *Situated Literacies: Reading and Writing in Context.* New York: Routledge, 2000.

Boudin, Kathy. "Critical Thinking in a Basic Literacy Program: A Problem-Solving Model in Corrections Education." *Journal of Correctional Education* 46.4 (December 1995): 141–45.

Brandt, Deborah. *Literacy in American Lives.* New York: Cambridge UP, 2001.

Butler, Paul. "The GED as Transgender Literacy: Performing in the Learning/Acquisition Borderland." *Reflections* 6.1 (2007): 27–39.

Carrick, Tracy Hamler, Margaret Himley, and Tobi Jacobi. "Ruptura: Acknowledging the Lost Subjects of the Service Learning Story." *Language and Learning across the Disciplines* 4.3 (2000): 56–75.

Carter, Shannon. "HOPE, 'Repair,' and the Complexities of Reciprocity: Inmates Tutoring Inmates in a Total Institution." *Community Literacy Journal* 2.2 (Spring 2008): 87–112.

Coogan, David. "Community Literacy as Civic Dialogue." *Community Literacy Journal* 1.1 (2006): 95–108.

Cushman, Ellen. "Rhetorician as Agent of Social Change." *College Composition and Communication* 47.1 (1996): 1–28.

———. "The Public Intellectual, Activist Research, and Service Learning." *College English* 61.3 (1999): 328–36.

———. "Sustainable Service Learning Programs." *College Composition and Communication* 54.1 (2002): 40–65.

Davis, Angela. *Are Prisons Obsolete?* New York: Seven Stories Press, 2003.

De Certeau, Michel. *The Practice of Everyday Life*. Berkeley, CA: U of California P, 1984.

Faber, Brenton. *Community Action and Organizational Change: Image, Narrative, and Identity*. Carbondale: Southern Illinois UP, 2002.

Flower, Linda. "Literate Action." *Composition in the Twenty-First Century: Crisis and Change*. Ed. Lynn Z. Bloom, Donald A. Daiker, and Edward M. White. Carbondale: Southern Illinois UP, 1996. 249–60.

Freire, Paulo. *Pedagogy of the Oppressed*. Trans. Myra Bergman Ramos. New York: Seabury, 1968.

George, Diana. "The Word on the Street: Public Discourse in a Culture of Disconnect." *Reflections* 2.2 (2002): 5–18.

Gere, Anne Ruggles. "Kitchen Tables and Rented Rooms: The Extracurriculum of Composition." *College Composition and Communication* 45.1 (1994): 75–92.

Goldblatt, Eli. "Alinsky's Reveille: A Community-Organizing Model for Neighborhood-Based Literacy Projects." *College English* 67.3 (January 2005): 274–95.

Gorzelsky, Gwen. *The Language of Experience: Literate Practices and Social Change*. Pittsburgh: U of Pittsburgh P, 2005.

Grabill, Jeff. *Community Literacy Programs and the Politics of Change*. Albany: SUNY P, 2001.

Heath, Shirley Brice. *Ways with Words: Language, Life, and Work in Communities and Classrooms*. New York: Cambridge UP, 1983.

Herzberg, Bruce. "Community Service and Critical Teaching." *College English* 45.3 (1994): 307–19.

Higgins, Lorraine, Elenore Long, and Linda Flower. "Community Literacy: A Rhetorical Model for Personal and Public Inquiry." *Community Literacy Journal* 1.1 (2006): 9–43.

Hull, Glynda, and Katherine Schultz. *School's Out: Bridging Out-of-School Literacies with Classroom Practice*. New York: Teachers College P, 2002.

Kerr, Tom. "Between Ivy and Razor Wire: A Case of Correctional Correspondence." *Reflections* 4.1 (2004): 62–75.

Mastrangelo, Lisa. "First Year Composition and Women in Prison: Service-Based Writing and Community Action." *Reflections* 4.1 (2004): 43–50.

Mathieu, Paula. *Tactics of Hope: The Public Turn in English Composition*. Portsmouth: Boynton/Cook Heinemann, 2005.

Peck, Wayne, Linda Flower, and Lorraine Higgins. "Community Literacy." *College Composition and Communication* 46.2 (1995): 199–222.

Pompa, Lori. "Disturbing Where We Are Comfortable: Notes from Behind the Walls." *Reflections* 4.1 (2004): 24–34.

Powell, Katrina M., and Pamela Takayoshi. "Accepting Roles Created for Us: The Ethics of Reciprocity." *CCC* 54.3 (2003): 394–422.

Stanford, Ann Folwell. "More Than Just Words" Women's Poetry and Resistance at Cook County Jail." *Feminist Studies* 30.2 (2004): 277–301.

Stino, Zandra, and Barbara Palmer. "Motivating Women Offenders through Process-Based Writing in a Literacy Learning Circle." *Journal of Adolescent and Adult Literacy* 43.3 (1999): 282–91.

Swanson, Cheryl, Kate King, and Nicole Wolbert. "Mentoring Juveniles in Adult Jail: An Example of Service Learning." *Journal of Criminal Justice Education* 8.2 (1997): 263–71.

Wilson, Anita. "Four Days and a Breakfast: Time, Space and Literacy/ies in the Prison Community." *Spatializing Literacy Research and Practice*. Eds. Kevin Leander and Margaret Sheehy. New York: Peter Lang, 2004.

35

The Dinner Table III;
The Dinner Table IV

CAROL POLLARD

> With more than 2 million Americans currently incarcerated and
> funding for educational programming in correctional settings confined almost en-
> tirely to basic skills and GED preparation, numerous literacy projects have emerged
> to fill the gap and tap the power of writing to promote reflection, challenge assump-
> tions, overcome isolation, engage the imagination, and foster community. These ini-
> tiatives range from Lori Pompa's Inside-Out program, which brings university and
> incarcerated students together for semester-long courses ("Disturbing Where We Are
> Comfortable" on p. 509 in this volume), to distance letter exchanges, to the writing
> workshops and 'zines that Tobi Jacobi describes in "Slipping Pages through Razor
> Wire" (see p. 485). In the following two segments from a longer series, Carol Pollard,
> a participant in a writing workshop at Maryland's Correctional Institution for
> Women, writes multiple responses to a single prompt in order to reflect on her experi-
> ences at "the dinner table."

THE DINNER TABLE III (1995)

She glances at the clock on the microwave's control panel: 5:15. She hasn't
much time left. How had the day slipped away so quickly?

Pausing at the small oak table in the corner of the farmhouse's large
kitchen, she makes a last minute check. Two pink calico placemats she had
quilted and embroidered are placed at 3 and 6 o'clock on the round table. A
matching larger circular mat flanked by two pink candles in pewter holders
sits at the table's precise center, setting off the arrangement of flowers she'd
gathered earlier.

On each placemat are the Damask rose pattern china—salad plate, bread
plate, cup, saucer, and burgundy water glasses—all part of the trousseau she
had gathered decades ago for another marriage in another lifetime. Gold
plated flatware—salad fork, butter knife, dinner knife and fork, dessert and

---

From the *Collected Works of the Writing Workshop at the Maryland Correctional Institution
for Women*, Jessup, Maryland.

demitasse spoons—all bequeathed to her at her grandmother's funeral, lie precisely in their proper placements. Matching china butter dish and salt and pepper shakers sit on the table, while the empty china serving dishes and dinner plates sit warming in the oven.

Satisfied with the table's appearance, she glances again at the clock: 5:25. A rising nervousness flutters inside her, mounting into a gut-wrenching spasm as she hears the familiar tires crunching on the gravel driveway outside. Reaching, she opens a cabinet door and withdraws a large blue plastic bottle from behind the neat rows of alphabetized spice cans. Unscrewing its cap, she hastily swallows several mouthfuls of its thick chalky liquid, before thrusting it back into the cabinet's depths. Wiping the chalky remnants off her lips with her flowered apron, she hurries towards the door.

Summoning up a smile, she opens the door and beholds the heavy set muscular man in a blue suit waiting on the landing. Ice blue eyes survey her momentarily before the mustached lips give way to a smile.

Stepping inside the house, he pulls her roughly towards him in an embrace with one hand, while dropping his keys into her apron pocket with the other.

"Wha'cha been doing all day?"

"Oh, just the same ole stuff. Fed and watered the animals, gathered eggs, pulled some weeds, vacuumed and dusted. Same ole stuff."

Releasing her, he moves towards the small table next to her aquarium. The graceful, long-tailed goldfish lazily circle as they watch him deposit his wallet and badge into the small bowl and plug the walkie-talkie into the recharger. Taking the keys from her apron, she hangs them on the pegboard in the hallway between the dining room and kitchen.

With her boys gone to their father's, they wouldn't be needing the large dining room table tonight. She had chosen the smaller kitchen table for an intimate, romantic dinner for two.

Sounds of running water and splashing come from the washroom off the kitchen, as she fills the warmed serving bowls. Wrapping the freshly baked biscuits with an embroidered linen cloth, she gently places them in their wicker serving basket. As he emerges, changed into his favorite jeans and red plaid flannel shirt she'd hung on the back of the washroom door for him, she unties her apron and hangs it on a peg by the refrigerator.

They settle themselves into the heavy oak chairs, resting on the pillows she'd braided from the same pink calico material as the placemats.

"It smells good, Baby," he says, heaping baked chicken, mashed potatoes, peas, and onions onto his plate.

"Thank you," she replies, handing him the pickle dish filled with watermelon rinds and cucumber rounds.

In between mouthfuls of food, he entertains her with amusing anecdotes of his day at work. Beginning to relax, she starts to eat, too. While she laughs at the story, he reaches for the pepper and shakes it over his food. Nothing comes out, so he shakes it even more vigorously. Nothing. Angrily slamming it down on the table, he backhands her with enough force to topple both her and the chair over backwards.

As she slams into the linoleum floor, she sees a blinding flash of searing hot light. Then complete blackness, as she lies open eyed, like an astronaut ready for take-off, on the floor. Pin prick sparkles of light begin to dance before her eyes as he rages.

"What do you do all day, lazy bitch? Is it too much to fill a pepper shaker? Get up, bitch! Are you trying to ruin my meal, you stupid, incompetent bitch? I said, get up you lazy bitch!"

Slowly she rolls over and pushes herself up off the floor, clinging to the overturned chair for support. The dancing sparkles enlarge and merge until the whole room comes into a dizzy revolving focus. Righting the chair, she uses it to steady herself as she returns to her seat.

"What are you just sitting there for? Fill this up, you stupid bitch! Do I have to tell you everything?" and he shoves the pepper shaker within inches of her face. Trying not to flinch, she takes it from his hand and slowly and unsteadily makes her way to the pantry. With trembling hands, she fills the shaker.

"What are you doing there, Carol? What's taking you so long? Come on, hurry up, your dinner is getting cold, Baby."

Placing the pepper shaker before him, she smiles weakly at him and sits back in her place at the dinner table.

THE DINNER TABLE IV (1997)

Dusting the crumbs off a gray plastic chair, I gingerly sit down at the speckled beige plastic table. Before me is a beige plastic tray holding an assortment of five unidentifiable beige and gray clumps in its five sections. Bowing my head, I offer up a silent blessing for this meal.

"Bless us, O Lord, for these thy gifts, which we are about to receive, from thy bounty. . . ." The blessing, memorized many decades ago, weaves a quiet, sweet contra melody through the sounds blaring around me. "I'm grateful for this food before me: thankful that I didn't have to cook it, and thankful that I don't have to wash the dishes. Amen."

Lifting my head, I survey my dinner companions for tonight. To my left, my Wiccan roommate scowls at my performance of another "stupid Christian ritual." Across from me, a woman with a white state pillowcase wrapped around her head glares menacingly at me. She's mumbling something unrepeatable about having to eat with "blue eyed devils," so I'm glad I have brown eyes. To my right, a hefty barrel-shaped woman with a buzz haircut stares strangely at my shirt front. Self-consciously, I glance down to see if I have spilled a bit of the gray or beige on my shirt. Seeing none, I shrug and pick up my napkin. It's a quarter folded paper luncheon napkin, which I unfold and refold into a larger triangle. As I place it upon my lap, a voice behind me barks.

"Wha'd you put down there? Let me see it. Right now!"

"Just my napkin," I sheepishly reply, holding up the offending article.

"Why'd you do that?" the uniformed woman demands.

"Isn't that where you're supposed to place your napkin before beginning to eat?" I ask, bewildered by this conversation about table manners.

"Oh," she grunts and moves on to another row of tables.

"What's with her?" I ask my roommate.

"The bald headed bitch thinks you're stealing," she nonchalantly replies while stuffing her cheeks like a chipmunk preparing for hibernation.

"Stealing? Why would she think that? She's not bald, she has hair."

Pillowcase woman and Buzzcut woman are laughing at me. I don't know why, but my cheeks flush red hot all the same.

"Don't mind her. She's a newbee," my roommate says while reloading her jaw pouches.

"Oh? How long have you been here?" Buzzcut asks, mouth crammed full, gray and beige bits escaping in every direction.

"Four weeks."

We eat in silence for a few minutes. I am conscious of the continuing stares of Pillowcase and Buzzcut.

"Do you like women?" Buzzcut suddenly blurts out, bits of food spraying.

"Excuse . . . me?" I stammer.

"I bet you is real cute with them glasses off you. Do you like women?"

Realizing suddenly what she means, I again flush a deep hot-cheeked red.

"Not like that," I mumble, unable to look up.

"Well, if you ever change your mind, let me be your first."

"Thank you for the offer. I'm sure you mean it as a compliment. But . . . no thanks," I stammer, trying to placate without encouraging. The words stick, like the gray and beige clumps, in my mouth.

"This row! Time's up!" Uniform barks.

My roommate leans into me and whispers, "Don't let her take up your tray."

Snatching up the half eaten gray and beige slop, I maneuver through the herd of women, away from Buzzcut and the place that's not mine at the dinner table.

36 *O Tenacious Weed; Writing Inside*

KIMBERLY HRICKO

In prison writing workshops, as in many other community-based workshops that contribute to composition's "extracurriculum," facilitators often limit their roles to suggesting prompts or techniques, encouraging constructive feedback, cultivating leadership among the group, and providing outlets for publication. Participants typically find that craft provides the vehicle to sound emotional depths, connect across divides, and extract insight and hope from difficult terrain. In "O Tenacious Weed" and "Writing Inside," Kimberly Hricko, a participant in a workshop in a Maryland prison, experiments with formal poetic elements, generic conventions, and humor to share hard-won wisdom and affirm newfound resiliency.

O TENACIOUS WEED

O tenacious weed
You must serve a purpose
Determined as you are
To eke out life
On ground where
Self-respecting flowers
Refuse to squander their pedigree

O tenacious weed
You must serve a purpose
Your head high
And roots deep
Not simply leeching
What you won't be denied
But thriving

O tenacious weed
You must serve a purpose

From the *Collected Works of the Writing Workshop at the Maryland Correctional Institution for Women*, Jessup, Maryland.

Shouting to an audience
That fails to see beauty
In your lush green splendor
Blooming for a moment
Against looks of disdain

O tenacious weed
You must serve a purpose
So gifted at blending
That among haughty flora
A cursory glance
Would number you with them
The skilled mimic

O tenacious weed
You must serve a purpose
Destroying well laid plans
Of perfection and balance
Frustrating the gardener
Who arduously struggles
To yank your roots

I understand you
O tenacious weed.
I too am thorny
Taking life from inhospitable soil
Virtually impossible to exterminate
My existence an insult
As I hold my face to the sun.

WRITING INSIDE

In front of my typewriter, computer terminal or notebook, I am safe to strip away my armor. The layers of intellect, humor and aloofness that serve me all day long don't serve me when I write. The din of my noisy prison surroundings fades away. The hundreds of rules that dictate my behavior disappear. There is no razor wire. There is no life sentence. No line to wait in, no pass to show. Within this harsh environment I am alone to create my most private intimacy.

There is a great well of sadness within me. It is the anchor that holds me down, keeps me from floating out in the universe. The shape and the weight of this melancholy define me. When I write, I am able to touch this black mass. I can feel its edges and heft, put my cheek against its cold surface. In writing here where I am now confined, I do not write to exorcise this sadness, but rather to own it.

On paper my words can shock even me. It is as if my fingers on the keyboard know better how and what I feel than my brain ever can. They understand what my heart cannot bear. The paper does not judge me; the notebook calmly accepts my burdens without complaint.

When I write, I can allow myself freedom to remember things that would otherwise be too scary or painful. To someone who is locked up, there is often the sadness of loss attached to even the most celebratory of memories. Yet in this act of writing I can find wholeness. I can embrace the parts of my life that I keep most hidden and once they are set on paper I can find solace and peace in my own depths. Writing is my gift to myself. And if the sadness that I write from doesn't turn to happiness like Oprah or Dr. Phil say it should, that is okay too, because it is mine. Because I was brave enough to tell it.

37 Disturbing Where We Are Comfortable: Notes from Behind the Walls

LORI POMPA

ountless books have been written about "life on the inside," comprising quite a respectable body of prison literature. The idea of "prison literacies," however, transcends the act of reading about life behind the walls. To become truly "literate" about prisons, we need to move out of the safety that distance provides, and go there—in order to learn, to experience, to be disturbed, *to read the life itself*. It is the difference between "reading the word" and "reading the world" (Freire).

The "literacies" of prison life abound—layers of reality waiting to be "read" and understood by those on either side of the wall. The questions haunt: Who is incarcerated? Who is not? What variables (social, structural, systemic, economic, psychological, political, racial) led to the men and women on the inside being there? And what is life like on the inside? Is there any truth to the myths that we believe about prisons and the purposes they purport to serve? In the end, does anybody really care? Why should we?

These and many other questions bombarded me when I first set foot in prison nearly 20 years ago as a volunteer in the local jail system. On my first day, I went to Holmesburg Prison, a decrepit maximum security facility in Philadelphia, so unlivable that it was finally closed as it neared its hundredth year. I can remember that day as if it were yesterday—the smells, the sights, the sounds, the overall feeling of the place. It was a sensory cacophony of stale sweat, old sneakers, clanging bars, crumbling cement, deafening announcements over the P.A. system, and men . . . hundreds of men, who seemed to be locked in some bizarre dance, a listless fugue arrested in time. That was the sense I got that day—the feeling that, underneath the incessant noise and activity, lay silence and inertia. There were realities behind those walls that I wanted to understand, truths hidden beneath the surface that begged to be revealed.

Ironically, I began my involvement in prison as a "literacy" tutor, helping men behind the walls learn to read. Quickly realizing that my attempts at

From *Reflections* 4.1 (2004): 24–34.

tutoring left much to be desired, what happened instead is that I became literate—I learned, from some wonderful tutors over the years, how to "read" life as it is lived behind the walls. My sojourn has taken me inside prisons and jails thousands of times in varying capacities over the past two decades. During that time, the questions have not abated; in fact, they have grown only deeper, more disturbing, and consequently, more provocative.

Eleven years ago, when I began to teach criminal justice at Temple, I decided to give my students the gift of disturbance. What better way to examine the most central questions of crime and justice than to come face to face with the issues as experienced by the men and women caught up in the system? So far, more than 6,000 students have visited several correctional facilities in the area—county jails, state prisons, youth detention facilities, community correctional centers, and substance abuse treatment programs. These trips provide some of the most compelling experiences one could have—the kinds of experiences that are very hard to shake. And that is precisely why we do it. I don't want my students to be able to easily shake these encounters; in fact, I want the students to be shaken by them. Just as I have always been.

Sometime in the mid-90s, I took a class to meet with a group of life-sentenced men at a state prison three hours away from Temple's campus in Philadelphia. During the tour of this facility, the students began discussing with the "lifers" issues of economics, politics, race and class, and—related to it all—crime and how we respond to it. One of the prisoners remarked about how beneficial it would be to have an ongoing dialogue about these and other issues. Everyone agreed, while realizing that the distance was prohibitive.

However, the seed was sown, and within a few months, with the support of Temple and the Philadelphia Prison System, I created a course called "Inside-Out" (or, by its more formal title, "The Inside-Out Prison Exchange Program: Exploring Issues of Crime and Justice Behind the Walls"). Since 1997, Inside-Out has been conducted 13 times at the Philadelphia Industrial Correctional Center (PICC), part of a large urban jail system 25 minutes from campus, and twice at the State Correctional Institution at Graterford. To date, more than 500 students (from the "inside" and the "outside") have taken part.

A Literacy of Layers

Each semester, a group of 15–18 Temple students goes to prison to attend class. In the Fall, we have class with men in PICC; in the Spring, with women in PICC; and in the summer, with men in Graterford. We hold sessions once a week for 2½ hours and address a separate topic each time, including: what prisons are for; why people get involved in crime; the myths and realities of prison life; victims and victimization; and the distinction between punishment and rehabilitation. The entire course is conducted inside of prison, except for a briefing and debriefing—held separately with each group—at the beginning of the semester.[1]

College students and incarcerated students come together within the setting that serves as part of the context of the learning. The "outside" students and I are provided a unique window into the vicissitudes of the criminal justice system, and the more we go in and out each week, the deeper and more complex the questions become. It leads to a process of exploration, through which, together with the "inside" students, we come to "read" and interpret the manifold stories of life behind bars.

> Most college courses are lectures and readings which, later on, we are supposed to apply to real-life situations. This class was a real-life situation itself. The readings gave all of us facts, statistics, and the opinions of the "experts," but the class itself was what gave the course an additional meaning and another dimension. The students in the class gave it life— we taught each other more than can be read in a book. (Kerry, Temple participant)

This unique educational experience provides dimensions of learning that are difficult to achieve in a traditional classroom. At its most basic level, Inside-Out allows the "outside" students to take the theory they have learned and apply it in a real-world setting, while those living behind the walls are able to place their life experiences in a larger academic framework. However, much more occurs in the exchange—layers of understanding that defy prediction. In our discussions, myriad life lessons and realizations surface about how we as human beings operate in the world, beyond the myths and stereotypes that imprison us all.

As a class, we do quite a bit of reading—five or six books in all. The readings include both criminal justice texts and narratives by and about men and women who are incarcerated. In "reading the word" (the assigned texts), a more profound reading transpires: we enter into the process of what Paulo Freire calls "reading the world." Students from the outside not only read about issues of crime, justice, and incarceration, but also learn in a deeper way about these issues through the discussions, exchanges, and encounters that comprise the experience. The "inside" students offer a unique perspective on the various topics discussed, given their direct experience with criminal activity, the criminal justice system, and the daily realities of their life behind the walls.

At the same time, students from the inside have the opportunity to "read" their world in a different way. All too often, some of the incarcerated students will, with great poignancy, talk about seeing themselves on the pages of some of the books, especially in relation to statistics describing crime or incarceration rates. Though initially distressing, these revelations have proven to be both challenging and empowering to the "inside" students. For many, it is the first time that they have looked at their own issues in a larger framework, recognizing the text of their lives in relation to the context of the criminal justice system. It is a compelling example of "reading" one's life in an entirely new way.

> I am well aware that people feel disaffected, dehumanized, and at times downright angry at the system, as well they should be. Still, we need to be willing to not only take personal responsibility for our behavior, but also for allowing the system to function in its current condition. (Tom, Graterford participant)

The class also does a significant amount of writing throughout the semester: six or seven substantive reflection papers, as well as a more lengthy final integrative paper. These assignments afford both the "outside" and "inside" students the opportunity to make their own connections between the themes discussed in the prior class, the readings associated with that class session, and their own thinking about the particular topic.

Each reflection paper is divided into three sections: the first calls for students to make observations about and comment on the ongoing dynamics of the process; the second focuses on the topic of that week, requiring students to discuss pertinent issues, incorporating quotes and citations from readings; and the third asks the students to reflect briefly on their own reactions at that point in the semester—noting any internal shifts that may have occurred in response to what has been happening in the class meetings. The final paper is similar, though entailing more breadth and depth in its scope.

A LITERACY OF RECIPROCITY

As a particular model in the service learning genre, Inside-Out affords college students an experience of immersion, providing direct exposure to the exigencies of the particular context of prison, while engendering deep interaction and connection with the men and women incarcerated there. It is the ultimate border-crossing experience. When students attend class together as equals, borders disintegrate and barriers recede. What emerges is the possibility of considering the subject matter from a new context—that of those living within that context. The interplay of content and context provides a provocative juncture that takes the educational process to a deeper level.

The approach to service learning used in Inside-Out provides a reciprocal arrangement—everyone serves, everyone is served. The course is arranged in such a way that we all teach and we all learn together, in a true partnership. The service, therefore, is less a question of "doing for" than "being with," a mutual exchange. In this way, if anything is "done for" those on the inside, it is being afforded value as human beings with ideas and experiences to contribute, an opportunity that is extremely rare behind bars.

> From the first moment I came into contact with the students, it was an experience out of the ordinary. I felt like a saltwater fish moving into fresh water. Years of conditioning by brutality, anger, hatred, mistrust, and guarded emotions left me unprepared for the reception and humanness with which the Temple students greeted me. (Trevor, Graterford participant)

One of the strengths of this form of service learning lies in the dialogical interaction that takes place between and among those involved. This dialogue occurs on many levels and is multi-dimensional in character. We have come to call this process "interflecting," a practice of communal reflection on issues through a non-hierarchical, fully mutual exchange. Interflection takes the individual reflective process to a deeper level, as it calls for input from individuals to further advance the understanding of the group and, in so doing, enriches and enhances the insight of everyone involved. Participants share ideas, perceptions, perspectives, analyses, critiques—verbalizing realities with and for one another. Fundamentally, it fosters an atmosphere in which people feel increasingly free to "speak their lives," encouraged by the simple yet profound act of being together—an atmosphere characterized by reciprocity, dignity, and gradually developing trust.

> This class was not like anything I had experienced before. I did learn quite a bit, but it was the "interpersonal stuff" that I valued the most. I really feel like I connected with people, on a human level. What a change it is to be treated with kindness and respect. . . . My classmates not only wanted to hear what I had to say, but trusted me enough to share of themselves. (Tom, Graterford participant)

I see my role as facilitating a learning process, by creating an atmosphere in which those involved can experience, examine, and explore together. This perspective takes the focus off the instructor as receptacle and dispenser of knowledge, challenging learners to take responsibility for their own and each other's education. Through a participatory methodology, theoretical knowledge is enhanced in ways that are difficult to replicate through a solely didactic pedagogy. Since we don't live "from the eyebrows up," it may be time for us to reconsider our timeworn "eyebrows up" mode of education, recognizing the further dimensions of understanding that can be reached through a modality of total engagement. If we conceive of the process of education as "drawing forth," as its etymology suggests, we can then see these contextualized, engaged experiences as conduits through which newly integrated realizations can emerge.

> "Inside-Out" is the perfect name for this class for two main reasons. One reason is that the things we have learned on the inside, we can teach those individuals on the outside who might not understand what it is like to be in prison. The second reason is that over the course of the semester, everything that I have learned has changed my view of the criminal justice [system] and has in some ways changed me as a person. (Kim, Temple participant)

The heart of this methodology is in providing a framework within which the issues that we are studying can be examined in depth. This exploration is mediated through an ongoing group process, in which everyone is afforded the space to raise questions, challenge each other, offer diverse perspectives, and wrestle with the idiosyncratic nature of our system of crime and justice. My hope is that, by the end of the semester, each participant has developed more than merely the ability to take in information, but rather, the capacity to inquire, analyze, critique, challenge—or be challenged by—the information acquired. I want my students to know the issues thoroughly, especially as they impact their own lives and that of others, and to then take an active role in addressing issues of crime, justice, and incarceration as they are played out in the public arena. That, to me, is the essence of literacy.

A LITERACY OF CONTEXT

In shifting the focus from the passive acquisition of knowledge to a fully integrated, dynamic process of discovery, an essential ingredient is participatory dialogue. At the beginning of the semester, the class develops its own guidelines for dialogue, agreed to by everyone and adhered to throughout the semester. Defining and refining these guidelines is a fascinating process, calling for a relatively large group to negotiate consensus.

A subject that we explore during this guideline process is the idea of context—understanding that we each have one—and that our unique context, and all that has helped to form it, influences how we hear, speak, and take in our surroundings. Wrestling with complex issues, in which varying perspectives emerge, calls for participants to extend themselves and suspend their judgments to maximize the learning for the group as a whole.

> I learned to listen to others instead of talking. I learned there can be one issue with twelve different opinions on that issue. I learned people will always see a situation differently. (Sophia, Temple participant)

A fundamental issue that we discuss at this juncture is that each of us has a culture within which we were raised, comprised of our ethnicity, socio-economic status, religious beliefs, neighborhood, and many other factors. This culture heavily informs the lens through which we see, experience, and interpret the world. When we are "locked into" a particular cultural perspective—whether that is the culture of the prison, the culture of middle-class America, the culture of the streets, the culture of the "educated"—it becomes difficult to remain open to points of view that are divergent with that perspective. Often, these cultural influences are so deeply ingrained that we are unaware of the depth of their impact on us. By examining our cultural preconceptions, we realize that we overlay these perspectives on everything that we do and say, as well as on how we interact with the world.

> My worldviews and thought process have changed dramatically. I have thrown out the labels that are placed on people and have grown to understand that everyone comes from a different context and background. (Patrice, Temple participant)

A further dimension of context refers to the setting in which the learning takes place, and its effect on virtually every aspect of the experience. In prison, the environment has a significant impact on everyone involved and on everything we do. The simple act of getting into prison each week for class can, in and of itself, be an inordinately complex and frustrating task. What the college students glean from these experiences, however irksome, puts them directly in touch with the inherent frustrations of the context in which their incarcerated classmates reside. For those imprisoned in the facility, the setting from whence they come and to which they return each class day is authoritarian and oppressive. It is an environment that is antithetical to what is necessary for a productive, creative educational process.

The prison robs people not only of time on the outside, but it also robs them of time on the inside. When you stand inside the walls, it feels as though time is standing still. It feels as though you are not moving, not being productive, not being an active participant in the world, but rather a passive participant who has relinquished the right to control his or her own time. (Sarah S., Temple participant)

Attention and care are vital in fashioning a positive learning environment in which people feel safe to be themselves. In prison, where trust is elusive, creating this sort of setting calls for great awareness on the part of the instructor. Additionally, as issues that emerge can be difficult and sensitive, the group needs to feel that the experience is contained, on the one hand, and unrestricted, on the other. The instructor has to be alert to group dynamics at all times, developing a sense of how to balance the theoretical and the experiential, the personal and the generic, the individual and the collective. Fundamentally, the group needs the assurance that, no matter what happens— in the classroom interaction or in the prison setting itself—the instructor will be able to handle it.

Class sessions were not "classes" by the usual standard. They were safety nets, zones by which we could come together and discuss issues commonly significant to all of us, problems and solutions that we felt were important to consider and resolve. (Candy, Temple participant)

Developing an environment marked by trust and freedom of expression within the confines of a prison is a challenge, if not somewhat of a political act. In a place where human beings are confined to cages, and where security is the primary objective, bringing college students behind the walls to have class with men and women inside is a powerful statement. The fact that we are afforded the freedom to create a somewhat "normal" atmosphere in which to learn and discover is quite extraordinary.

Every time we go to [prison] and have class or even have "normal" interactions with the guys there, we are in fact engaged in an act of resistance. It is a space that humanizes the inmates and forces all of us to deeply question the utility of the existing system of punishment. (Diditi, Temple participant)

A LITERACY OF LIBERATION

Prisons come in different shapes and sizes. We all have them. There are things in each of our lives that constrain us, keeping us captive through subtle, often invisible, means. We allow our fears, anger, and despair to keep us locked in, locked up, locked out. Too often we are unaware of what keeps us imprisoned.

In light of this, there is a liberating quality to becoming literate. The inability to read—whether the writing in a book, or "the writing on the wall," or even the writing on our own hearts—can keep any one of us trapped in a narrow, limited world. Sometimes, I may allow myself to be confined by internal or external forces, unaware of the power that I have to "read" my reality differently. Personal "literacy," and consequently, some measure of liberation, may come from being able to "parse" the sentence that is my life, understanding the various parts that make up the whole and their relation to one another. It is fundamentally about self-knowledge—on the part of any one of us, no matter which side of the wall we are on—and the freedom that it bestows.

> Personally, I've never experienced the things which took place in this program from any other program. I went through countless emotional changes and learned things about myself I could never have learned from any other program. (Fox, Graterford participant)

To extend this analogy, as we each come to understand the components of our own individual "sentences," an appreciation for the larger story emerges—a story comprised of many sentences, all of which are synergistically connected. In the Inside-Out class, we develop and explore together our shared "story"—that of our class, our society, and our world. Through our ongoing dialogue, we come to understand the relationship between these individual "sentences" of ours and the larger "story," learning to "read" our personal and collective realities in new, creative, and critical ways.

> [This class] has acted as the catalyst in my passion for life and human rights, and was the pivotal point where I realigned my own path. . . . [T]his program has brought me to a new understanding of life, not just in prison, but in my own life. I have acquired the concrete knowledge of the true workings of the system, and at the same time come to realize my own captors in life. (Sarah C., Temple participant)

Yes, prisons come in different shapes and sizes. Fundamentally, we hold ourselves captive as we hold one another captive. But there is another choice. We can strive towards creating a society that includes rather than isolating, liberates rather than oppressing. The more that we each feel a sense of internal freedom—and encourage the same in others, the less anyone's freedom will need to be taken away through incarceration.

> Deep within the confines of the prison, there is a magnificent mural leading to a mosque. Access to the mosque is restricted; for whatever reason, the institution decided to lock the mural away—similar to the spirit of the prisoners. I would have never expected such beauty from a desolate place. There is a mural within every person. . . . During a class tour of [the prison], we saw how institutional life suppresses the human spirit and hides the true beauty in us all. Looking down the cellblock, one would never know that there were hundreds of people behind the locked doors. The beauty of the artwork at the mosque is kept locked away for no one to see. The beauty within the prisoners is kept locked away for no one to see. Inside-Out opens the door to that beauty. (David, Temple participant)

A LITERACY OF TRANSFORMATION

Over the years, I have watched as the same sights, sounds, and smells that invaded my senses and began my own prison sojourn years ago profoundly affect my students. The gate slams shut, the key turns in the lock, and suddenly, we are in a world that is no longer comfortable or predictable. But what we do have is our experience, and what we then come to understand through reflecting on it and studying it. This is the kind of learning that changes lives: it disturbs where we are comfortable, challenges what we thought we knew.

> Every week I get more frustrated. . . . I am ready to act. I tell as many people whose ear I can catch about the prison. . . . I expected to become frustrated and I actually looked forward to it. What I did not fully expect was how heightened my awareness would become. . . . I feel like everyone should be able to see what I see. I guess this increased sensitivity is the best thing that could have ever happened to me. (Sarah S., Temple participant)

What do we learn? We learn about crime and how it's addressed. But we go beyond the simple, if unassailable, reality that crime is a problem. We come to see crime as a symptom of a much deeper social illness—a societal dysfunction in which all of us, by omission or commission, play a part. This is what I want my students to understand. I want them to analyze what they see and question it all: who is locked up and why, how these decisions are made, what prisons are really about, and what each of us can do to change the situation.

The incarcerated students have the opportunity to place their particular experiences with the criminal justice system in a larger context. This leads to a fuller understanding of how society functions, how the system operates, and the effect of these forces on one's life and choices. Those who have been demonized, and consequently demoralized, by a fear-filled, retributive society, are—in this setting—treated with the respect and dignity they deserve as human beings. Based on both written and oral reactions to the experience, it is clear that this course is both empowering and healing for the classmates on the inside.

> Inside-Out has changed me so much; it showed me what life is about. In the eight years that I've been incarcerated, I've never felt so strong about wanting to make a change. (Maalik, Graterford participant)

After nearly two decades of going in and out of prison several times a week, I have become acutely aware of how information about crime and justice is gleaned from the media through biased and politicized reports. The complexity of policies cannot be accurately grasped through these sources; in fact, the faulty images of prisons and of the men and women locked inside have a devastating impact on the way our society understands crime and justice.

Inside-Out provides an opportunity to put a human face on a problem that can be kept simplified only if it remains faceless. The ability not only to look at issues in complex ways, but to recognize the complexity in ourselves and others, obviates our propensity for knee-jerk reactions. Stretching beyond our simplistic assumptions will, in time, produce a growing transformation in public thought. By exploring theoretical concepts inside the prison, theory is moved out of the purely mental sphere to a more powerful level—as the mind is engaged, so is the heart. If how we feel, to some extent, drives what we think, herein lies the crux of the transformative potential of this program.

Developing an appreciation for the gravity of what is at stake, those involved become inspired to learn as much as possible in order to make a difference in the injustices they see. The program motivates participants to generate new ideas and fresh solutions—all focused on making change, whether in individuals' lives or in the attitude of the public.

> This class is not just a course at Temple for simply three credits and a grade. This is my life and the lives of others. Inside-Out does not stop here. I am ready to forge onward, and make my contributions to the reform of the criminal justice system. (Eula, Temple participant)

The distinct form of literacy that ensues from a service learning experience--wherever it is practiced—has the power to turn things inside-out and upside-down for participants. It provokes one to think differently about the world, and consider one's relationship to the world in a new way. Service learning involves a critique of social systems, challenging participants to analyze what they observe, while inspiring them to take action and make change. Thus, service learning provides both an incubator for and impetus toward social change.

> We now carry the torch! We can provide a voice for those who can't speak, a battle for those unable to fight. (Abdul, Graterford participant)

Transformative experiences radically shift how we see things—the lens through which we previously had viewed reality is irrevocably altered. It is not just about looking at issues from another angle; often, an experience of this kind completely changes the perspective from which one now sees all of life.

So, we continue to go behind the walls—to become ever more literate about crime and justice from the inside, out. And as we do, the walls grow increasingly permeable. Thus, the silence and inertia—those hallmarks of life on the inside—give way to transformative power, hopefully turning our lives—as individuals and as a society—inside-out in the process.

Acknowledgments: I am grateful to the following people for their assistance with this article: Diana Blocker, Pat Finio, Anita Moran, R.V. Rikard, and Greg Zarro. I would also like to thank the Philadelphia Prison System and the State Correctional Institution at Graterford for welcoming and supporting this program, and the Department of Criminal Justice and the College of Liberal Arts Dean's Office at Temple for encouraging me to venture into this unique pedagogical territory. This article could not have been written without the input of the more than 500 "inside" and "outside" students who have taken part in 15 semesters of Inside-Out. This paper is a tribute to the courage it has taken for them to share their lives with one another and with me.

NOTE

1. Although in the past the incarcerated students have not received college credit for this linked course, for many, the course has served to reawaken an interest in continuing their education. We are in the process of developing a support system for those who wish to begin taking college classes upon their release. The incarcerated students are now given the option of being graded, and for those who opt to do so, we offer credit and a grade upon their matriculation at Temple.

WORK CITED

Freire, Paolo, and Macedo, Donaldo. *Literacy: Reading the Word and the World.* Westport, CT: Greenwood Publishing Group, 1989.

RECOMMENDED READING

Most of the books and articles listed here are from the field of rhetoric and composition, but works from the wider service-learning research community are also included. While gathered under the headings used to organize this book, many of the sources address issues that stretch across several categories.

Please note that the three journals listed first are rich, ongoing sources of scholarship. By browsing the online archives for each, one can find special issues on many topics, including prison writing, professional communication, Appalachian literacies, sustainability, and community-based research.

JOURNALS

Community Literacy Journal: http://www.communityliteracy.org/
Michigan Journal of Community Service Learning: http://www.umich.edu/~mjcsl/
Reflections: Studies in Writing, Service-Learning and Community Literacy: http://reflections.syr.edu/

WRITING IN COMMUNITIES

Beaufort, Anne. *Writing in the Real World: Making the Transition from School to Work.* New York: Teachers College P, 1999. Print.

Branch, Kirk. *Eyes on the Ought to Be: What We Teach When We Teach About Literacy.* Cresskill, NJ: Hampton, 2007. Print.

Comstock, Michelle R. "Writing Programs as Distributed Networks: A Materialist Approach to University-Community Digital Media Literacy." *Community Literacy Journal* 1.1 (Fall 2006): 44–66.

Cushman, Ellen. *The Struggle and the Tools: Oral and Literate Strategies in an Inner City Community.* Albany: SUNY P, 1998. Print.

Cushman, Ellen, Eugene R. Kingen, Barry Kroll, and Mike Rose. *Literacy: A Critical Sourcebook.* Boston: Bedford, 2001. Print.

Goldblatt, Eli. *Because We Live Here: Sponsoring Literacy Beyond the College Curriculum.* Cresskill, NJ: Hampton, 2007. Print.

Heath, Shirley Brice. *Ways with Words: Language, Life, and Work in Communities and Classrooms.* New York: Cambridge UP, 1983. Print.

Heath, Shirley Brice. "Work, Class, Categories: Dilemmas of Identity." *Composition in the Twenty-First Century: Crisis and Change.* Ed. Lynn Z. Bloom, Donald A. Daiker, and Edward M. White. Carbondale: Southern Illinois UP, 1996. 226–42. Print.

Howard, Ursula. "History of Writing in the Community." *Handbook of Research on Writing.* Ed. Charles Bazerman. New York: Erlbaum, 2008. 237–54. Print.

Hull, Glynda, and Katherine Schultz. *School's Out: Bridging Out-of-School Literacies with Classroom Practice.* New York: Teachers College P, 2002. Print.

Peck, Wayne Campbell, Linda Flower, and Lorraine Higgins. "Community Literacy." *College Composition and Communication* 46.2 (1995): 199–222. Print.

Sheridan-Rabideau, Mary P. *Girls, Feminism, and Grassroots Literacies: Activism in the Girlzone.* Albany: State U of NY P, 2008. Print.

Trimbur, John. "Composition and the Circulation of Writing." *College Composition and Communication* 52:2 (2000): 188–219. Print.

The Terms of Service-Learning

Adler-Kassner, Linda, Robert Crooks, and Ann Watters, eds. *Writing the Community: Concepts and Models for Service-Learning in Composition.* Washington, DC: American Association for Higher Education, 1997. Print.

Astin, Alexander W., Lori J. Vogelgesang, Elaine K. Ikeda, and Jennifer A. Yee. *How Service-Learning Affects Students.* Los Angeles: UCLA Higher Education Research Institute, 2000. Print.

Boyer, Earnest L. *Scholarship Reconsidered: Priorities of the Professoriate.* Princeton, NJ: Carnegie Foundation, 1990. Print.

Boyte, Harry C. "Community Service and Civic Education." *Phi Delta Kappan* 72 (1991): 765+. Print.

Butin, Dan W. *Service-Learning in Higher Education: Critical Issues and Directions.* New York: Palgrave Macmillan, 2005. Print.

Crews, Robin J. *Higher Education Service-Learning Sourcebook.* Westport, CT: Oryx, 2002. Print.

Cushman, Ellen. "The Public Intellectual, Service Learning, and Activist Research." *College English* 61 (1999): 328–36. Print.

Deans, Thomas. *Writing Partnerships: Service-Learning in Composition.* Urbana, IL: NCTE, 2000. Print.

Deans, Thomas. "Richard Rorty's Social Hope and Community Literacy." *Community Literacy Journal* 3.2 (2009): 3–18. Print.

Dewey, John. *Democracy and Education.* New York: Macmillan, 1916. Print.

Dewey, John. *Experience and Education.* New York: Macmillan, 1956. Print.

Eyler, Janet, and Dwight Giles. *Where's the Learning in Service-Learning?* San Francisco: Jossey-Bass, 1999. Print.

Eyler, Janet S., Dwight E. Giles, Christine M. Stenson, and Charlene J. Gray. "At a Glance: What We Know about the Effects of Service-Learning on College Students, Faculty, Institutions, and Communities, 1993–2000." Scotts Valley, CA: National Service-Learning Clearinghouse, 2001. Print.

Feldman, Ann. *Making Writing Matter: Composition in the Engaged University.* Albany, NY: SUNY P, 2009. Print.

Garbus, Julia. "Service-Learning, 1902." *College English* 64.5 (May 2002): 547–65. Print.

Gelmon, Sherril B., and Shelly H. Billig, eds. *From Passion to Objectivity: International and Cross-Disciplinary Perspectives on Service-Learning Research.* Advances in Service-Learning Research Series. Charlotte, NC: Information Age, 2007. Print.

Jacoby, Barbara, ed. *Service-Learning in Higher Education: Concepts and Practices.* San Francisco.: Jossey-Bass, 1996. Print.

Julier, Laura. "Community Service Pedagogy." *Composition Pedagogies: A Bibliographic Guide.* Ed. Gary Tate, Amy Rupiper, and Kurt Schick. Oxford: Oxford UP, 2000. Print.

Mathieu, Paula. *Tactics of Hope: The Public Turn in English Composition.* Portsmouth, NH: Boynton, 2005. Print.

Reardon, Kenneth M. "Participatory Action Research as Service Learning." *New Directions for Teaching and Learning* 73 (1998): 57–64. Print.

Rhoads, Robert A. *Community Service and Higher Learning: Explorations of the Caring Self.* Albany: State U of New York P, 1997. Print.

Roswell, Barbara. "Service-Learning and Composition: As Good as It Gets: An Interview with Edward Zlotkowski." *Reflections* 3 (Winter 2000/2001). Print.

Schutz, Aaron, and Ann Gere. "Service Learning and English Studies: Rethinking 'Public' Service." *College English* 60.2 (1998): 129–49. Print.

Stanton, Timothy, Dwight E. Giles, and Nadinne Cruz. *Service Learning: A Movement's Pioneers Reflect on Its Origins, Practice, and Future.* San Francisco: Jossey-Bass, 1999. Print.

Taylor, Joby. "Metaphors We Serve By: Investigating the Conceptual Metaphors Framing National Community Service and Service Learning." *Michigan Journal of Community Service Learning* 9:1 (Fall 2002): 45–57. Print.

Wurr, Adrian. J., and Josef Hellebrandt, eds. *Learning the Language of Global Citizenship: Service-Learning in Applied Linguistics* Bolton, MA: Anker, 2007. Print.

Rhetoric, Civic Writing, and the Public Sphere

Coogan, David. "Counter Publics in Public Housing: Reframing the Politics of Service Learning." *College English* 67 (2005): 461–82. Print.

Cooper, David, and Eric Fretz. "The Service-Learning Writing Project: Re-Writing the Humanities Through Service-Learning and Public Work." *Reflections* 5.1–2 (Spring 2006): 133–52. Print.

Crabtree, Robbin D., and David Alan Sapp. "A Laboratory in Citizenship: Service Learning in the Technical Communication Classroom. *Technical Communication Quarterly* 11 (2002): 411–31. Print.

Ervin, Elizabeth. "Encouraging Civic Participation among First-Year Writing Students; or, Why Composition Class Should Be More Like a Bowling Team." *Rhetoric Review* 15.2 (Spring 1997): 382–99. Print.

Fleming, David. "Subjects of the Inner City: Writing the People of Cabrini-Green." *Towards a Rhetoric of Everyday Life: New Directions in Research on Writing, Text, and Discourse.* Ed. Martin Nystrand and John Duffy. Madison, WI: University of Wisconsin Press, 2003. 207–244.

Flower, Linda, Elenore Long, and Lorraine Higgins. *Learning to Rival: A Literate Practice for Intercultural Inquiry.* Mahwah, NJ: Erlbaum, 2000. Print.

Flower, Linda. *Community Literacy and the Rhetoric of Public Engagement.* Carbondale: Southern Illinois UP, 2008. Print.

Flower, Linda. "Talking across Difference: Intercultural Rhetoric and the Search for Situated Knowledge." *College Composition and Communication* 55.1 (2003): 38. Print.

Halloran, S. Michael. "Rhetoric in the American College Curriculum: The Decline of Public Discourse." *Pre-Text* 3 (Fall 1982): 245–69. Print.

Herzberg, Bruce. "Service-Learning and Public Discourse." *JAC* 20.2 (2000): 391–405. Print.

Higgins, Lorraine D., and Lisa D. Brush. "Personal Experience Narrative and Public Debate: Writing the Wrongs of Welfare." *College Composition and Communication* 57.4 (2006): 694–729. Print.

Isaacs, Emily J., and Phoebe Jackson, eds. *Public Works: Student Writing as Public Text.* Portsmouth, NH: Boynton, 2001. Print.

Long, Elenore. *Community Literacy and the Rhetoric of Local Publics.* West Lafayette, IN: Parlor, 2008. Print.

Miller, Thomas P. "Treating Professional Writing as Social Praxis." *Journal of Advanced Composition* 11 (1991): 57–72. Print.

Mortensen, Peter. "Going Public." *College Composition and Communication* 5 (1998): 182–205. Print.

Simmons, W. Michele, and Jeffrey T. Grabill. "Toward a Civic Rhetoric for Technologically and Scientifically Complex Places: Invention, Performance, and Participation." *College Composition and Communication* 58.3 (2007): 419–48. Print.

Weisser, Christian R. *Moving Beyond Academic Discourse: Composition Studies and the Public Sphere.* Carbondale: Southern Illinois UP, 2002. Print.

Welch, Nancy. *Living Room: Teaching Public Writing in a Privatized World.* Portsmouth, NH: Boynton, 2008. Print.

The Ethics of Engagement

Bacon, Nora. "Differences in Faculty and Community Partners' Theories of Learning." *Michigan Journal of Community Service Learning* 9.1 (Fall 2002): 34–44. Print.

Ball, Kevin, and Amy Goodburn. "Composition Studies and Service Learning: Appealing to Communities?" *Composition Studies* 28.1 (Spring 2000): 79–94. Print.

Boyle-Baise, Marilynne. "Learning Service: Reading Service as Text." *Reflections* 6.1 (Spring 2007): 67–86. Print.

Chappell, Virginia "Good Intentions Aren't Enough." *Reflections* 4.2 (Winter 2005): 34–53. Print.

Cruz, Nadinne L., and Dwight E. Giles, Jr. "Where's the Community in Service-Learning Research?" *Michigan Journal of Community Service Learning* 7 (2000): 28–34. Print.

Freire, Paulo. *Pedagogy of the Oppressed*. Trans. Myra Bergman Ramos. New York: Continuum, 2000. Print.

Gabor, Catherine. "Ethics and Expectations: Developing a Workable Balance between Academic Goals and Ethical Behavior." *Reflections* 5.1–2 (2006): 27–48. Print.

Gelmon, Sherril B. "How Do We Know That Our Work Makes a Difference? Assessment Strategies for Service-Learning and Civic Engagement." *Metropolitan Universities: An International Forum* 11.2 (2000): 28–39. Print.

Graves, Richard. "Responses to Student Writing from Service Learning Clients." *Business Communication Quarterly* 64 (2001): 55–62. Print.

Himley, Margaret. "Facing (up to) 'the Stranger' in Community Service Learning." *College Composition and Communication* 55 (2004): 416–38. Print.

McKnight, John. *The Careless Society: Community and Its Counterfeits*. New York: Basic, 1995. Print.

Palmer, Parker. *The Courage to Teach: Exploring the Inner Landscape of a Teacher's Life*. San Francisco: Jossey-Bass, 1998. Print.

Stoecker, Randy, Elizabeth A. Tryon, and Amy Hilgendor, eds. *The Unheard Voices: Community Organizations and Service Learning*. Philadelphia: Temple UP, 2009. Print.

Welch, Nancy. "'And Now That I Know Them': Composing Mutuality in a Service Learning Course." *College Composition and Communication* 54.2 (2002): 243. Print.

Zimmer, Steve. "The Art of Knowing Your Place: White Service Learning Leaders and Urban Community Organizations." *Reflections* 6.1 (Spring 2007): 7–26. Print.

WRITING PROGRAMS AS COMMUNITY ENGAGEMENT

Amare, Nicole, and Teresa Grettano. "Writing Outreach as Community Engagement." *Writing Program Administration* 30 (2007): 57–74. Print.

Barton, Ellen, and Laurie Evans. "A Case of Multiple Professionalisms: Service Learning and Control of Communication About Organ Donation." *Journal of Business and Technical Communication* 17 (2003): 413–38. Print.

Cushman, Ellen. "Sustainable Service Learning Programs." *College Composition and Communication* 64.1 (2002). 40–65. Print.

Grabill, Jeffrey. *Community Literacy Programs and the Politics of Change*. Albany: State U of NY P, 2001. Print.

Grabill, Jeffrey. "Technical Writing, Service Learning, and a Rearticulation of Research, Teaching, and Service." *Innovative Approaches to Teaching Technical Communication*. Ed. Tracy Bridgeford, Karla Saari Kitalong, and Dickie Selfe. Logan: Utah State UP, 2004. 81–92. Print.

Jolliffe, David A. "Writing Across the Curriculum and Service Learning: *Kairos*, Genre, and Collaboration." *WAC for the New Millennium: Strategies for Continuing Writing-Across-the-Curriculum-Programs*. Ed. Susan H. McLeod et al. Urbana, IL: NCTE, 2001. 86–108. Print.

McComiskey, Bruce, and Cynthia Ryan, eds. *City Comp: Identities, Spaces, Practices*. Albany: SUNY P, 2003. Print.

Owens, Derek. *Composition and Sustainability: Teaching for a Threatened Generation*. Urbana, IL: NCTE, 2001. Print.

Porter, James E., et al. "Institutional Critique: A Rhetorical Methodology for Change." *College Composition and Communication* 51 (2001): 610–42. Print.

Spigelman, Candace. "Politics, Rhetoric, and Service-Learning." *WPA: Writing Program Administration* 28.1/2 (Fall 2004): 95–113. Print.

PEDAGOGIES IN ACTION

Adler-Kassner, Linda. "Digging a Groundwork for Writing: Underprepared Students and Community Service Courses." *College Composition and Communication* 46.4 (1995): 552–55. Print.

Bacon, Nora. "Building a Swan's Nest for Instruction in Rhetoric." *College Composition and Communication* 51:4 (June 2000): 589–609. Print.

Cleary, Michelle Navarre. "Keep It Real: A Maxim for Service-Learning in Community Colleges." *Reflections* 3.2 (2003): 56–64. Print.

Crabtree, Robin, and David Sapp. "Technical Communication, Participatory Action Research, and Global Civic Engagement." *Reflections* 4.2 (Winter 2005): 8–33. Print.

Davi, Angelique. "In the Service of Writing and Race." *Journal of Basic Writing* 25:1 (2006): 73–95. Print.

Deans, Thomas. "Genre Analysis and the Community Writing Course." *Reflections* 5.1–2 (Spring 2006): 7–26. Print.

Eyler, Janet, Dwight Giles, and Angela Schmiede. *A Practitioner's Guide to Reflection in Service-Learning: Student Voices and Reflections.* Nashville, TN: Vanderbilt UP, 1996. Print.

Feldman, Ann M., et al. "The Impact of Partnership-Centered, Community-Based Learning on First-Year Students' Academic Research Papers." *Michigan Journal of Community Service Learning* 13.1 (2006): 16–29. Print.

Green, Ann E. "Difficult Stories: Service-Learning, Race, Class, and Whiteness." *College Composition and Communication* 55.2 (2003): 276–301. Print.

Heffernan, Kerrissa. *Fundamentals of Service-Learning Course Construction.* Providence, RI: Campus Compact, 2001. Print.

Henson, Leigh, and Kristene Sutliff. "A Service Learning Approach to Business and Technical Writing Instruction." *Journal of Technical Writing and Communication* 28 (1998): 189–205. Print.

Howard, Jeffery, ed. *Service-Learning Course Design Workbook.* Ann Arbor, MI: OCSL, 2001. Print.

Jacobi, Tobi. "Writing Workshops as Alternative Literacy Education for Incarcerated Women." *Corrections Today* 1 (February 2009): 52–57. Print.

McEachern, Robert W. "Problems in Service Learning and Technical/Professional Writing: Incorporating the Perspective of Nonprofit Management." *Technical Communication Quarterly* 10 (Spring 2001): 211–24. Print.

Taggart, Amy Rupiper, and H. Brooke Hessler. "Stasis and the Reflective Practitioner." *Reflections* 5.1–2 (Spring 2006): 153–72. Print.

Winter, Dave, and Sarah Robbins. *Writing Our Communities: Local Learning and Public Culture.* Urbana, IL: NCTE, 2005. Print.

TEXTBOOKS THAT SUPPORT COMMUNITY-ENGAGED TEACHING

Bowdon, Melody, and J. Scott Blake. *Service-Learning in Technical and Professional Communication.* Allyn and Bacon Series in Technical Communication. New York: Longman, 2003. Print.

Columbo, Gary, Robert Cullen, and Bonnie Lisle. *Rereading America: Cultural Contexts for Critical Thinking and Writing,* 8th Ed. Boston: Bedford, 2010. Print.

Deans, Thomas. *Writing and Community Action: A Service-Learning Rhetoric with Readings.* New York: Longman, 2003. Print.

Dunlap, Louise. *Undoing the Silence: Six Tools for Social Change Writing.* Oakland, CA: New Village, 2007. Print.

Flower, Linda. *Problem-Solving Strategies for Writers in College and Community.* Fort Worth, TX: Harcourt, 1998. Print.

Ford, Marjorie, and Elizabeth Schave Sills. *Community Matters: A Reader for Writers.* New York: Longman, 2004. Print.

Lazare, Donald. *Reading and Writing for Civic Literacy: The Critical Citizen's Guide to Argumentative Rhetoric.* Boulder, CO: Paradigm, 2009. Print.

Odell, Lee, and Susan M. Katz. *Writing Now: Shaping Words and Images.* Boston: Bedford, 2010. Print.

Ross, Carolyn, and Ardel Thomas. *Writing for Real: A Handbook for Writers in Community Service.* New York: Longman, 2003. Print.

Sunstein, Bonnie S., and Elizabeth Chiseri-Strater. *FieldWorking: Reading and Writing Research* (3rd ed.). Boston: Bedford, 2007. Print.

ABOUT THE EDITORS

Thomas Deans teaches at the University of Connecticut, where he also directs the writing center and the writing across the disciplines program. His teaching and research interests include composition theory, service-learning, rhetoric, writing across the curriculum, prose style, writing in workplace and civic settings, pragmatist philosophy, Shakespeare, and the relationship between literature and composition. He is the author of *Writing Partnerships: Service-Learning in Composition* and *Writing and Community Action*.

Barbara Roswell teaches at Goucher College, where she has also directed the Writing Program, WAC, and the First Year Colloquium. The founding editor of *Reflections* and co-author of *Reading, Writing, and Gender*, her scholarship has appeared in *Assessing Writing, Educational Assessment, Writing Center Journal*, and the *Community Arts Network*. She has been instrumental in developing the Baltimore Read A Story — Write A Story afterschool program and the college degree program at the Maryland Correctional Institution for Women.

Adrian J. Wurr is Assistant Director for Service-Learning and Internships and adjunct professor of Curriculum and Instruction at the University of Idaho. A Fulbright Scholar in spring of 2007, he has published numerous scholarly articles in the United States and abroad on literacy, assessment, service-learning, and TESOL. He serves on the editorial boards of *The Reading Matrix* and *Reflections: A Journal of Writing, Service-learning, and Community Literacy* and is co-editor of *Learning the Language of Global Citizenship: Service-Learning in Applied Linguistics* (Wiley, 2007).

ACKNOWLEDGMENTS *(continued from page iv)*

Nora Bacon, "The Trouble with Transfer: Lessons from a Study of Community Service Writing." From *Michigan Journal of Community Service Learning*, 6 (1999): 53–62. Reprinted with permission of the Center for Community Service and Learning, University of Michigan.

Heather Bargeron, "Finding a Home for Rick." Originally published in *Hospitality*, newspaper of the Open Door Community, 910 Ponce de Leon Ave, NE, Atlanta, CA 30306-4212 www.opendoorcommunity.org. Reprinted with the permission of The Open Door Community.

Deborah Brandt, "Sponsors of Literacy." From *College Composition and Communication*, CCC/49.2 (May 1998), 165–85. Copyright © 1998 by the National Council of Teachers of English. All rights reserved. Reprinted with permission.

Tracy Hamler Carrick, Margaret Himley, and Tobi Jacobi, "Ruptura: Acknowledging the Lost Subjects of the Service Learning Story." From *Language and Learning Across the Disciplines* 4.3 (2000): 56–74. Reprinted with permission of Across the Disciplines, Georgia Southern University.

Chi-an Chang, "Grandma Dearest." Originally published in *Journal of Ordinary Thought*, Spring 2009. Reprinted with permission of *Journal of Ordinary Thought* and the Neighborhood Writing Alliance.

David Coogan, "Service Learning and Social Change: The Case for Materialist Rhetoric." From *College Composition and Communication*, CCC/57.4 (June 2006), 667–91. Copyright © 2006 by the National Council of Teachers of English. All rights reserved. Reprinted with permission.

Ellen Cushman, "The Rhetorician as an Agent of Social Change." From *College Composition and Communication*, CCC/47.1 (Feb. 1996): 7–28. Copyright © 1996 by the National Council of Teachers of English. All rights reserved. Reprinted with permission.

Angelique Davi, Michelle Dunlap, and Ann E. Green, "Exploring Difference in the Service-Learning Classroom: Three Teachers Write about Anger, Sexuality, and Social Justice." From *Reflections* 6.1 (2007): 41–66. Reprinted with the permission of Reflections: reflections.syr.edu.

Thomas Deans, "English Studies and Public Service." From *Writing Partnerships: Service-Learning in Composition*. Copyright © 2000 by the National Council of Teachers of English. All rights reserved. Reprinted with permission.

Thomas Deans, "Shifting Locations, Genres, and Motives: An Activity Theory Analysis of Service-Learning Writing Pedagogies." From *The Language of Composition*, by Christopher Keller and Christopher Weisser. (Albany: SUNY Press, 2007): 280–306. Reprinted by permission from The Locations of Composition edited by Christopher Keller and Christian Weisser, the State University of New York Press © 2007, State University of New York. All rights reserved.

James M. Dubinsky, "Service-Learning as a Path to Virtue: The Ideal Orator in Professional Communication." From *Michigan Journal of Community Service-Learning*, 8 (2002): 64–75. Reprinted with the permission of the Michigan Journal of Community Service and Learning, University of Michigan.

Cheryl Hofstetter Duffy, "Tapping the Potential of Service-Learning: Guiding Principles for Redesigning Our Composition Courses." From *Reflections* 3.1 (2004): 1–14. Reprinted with the permissions of Reflections: reflections.syr.edu.

Linda Flowers, Excerpts from *Naming the LD Difference: Dilemmas in Dealing with Learning Disabilities* (Fall 2003): iv, 3–6, from The Carnegie Mellon Community Think Tank. Used with permission of the Pittsburgh Community Literacy Center. www.cmu.edu/outreach/thinktank.

Sandra Gildersleeve Freeman, "Don't You Know Everybody Got Issues?" Originally published in *Journal of Ordinary Thought* (Winter 2009). Reprinted with the permission of the *Journal of Ordinary Thought* and the Neighborhood Writing Alliance.

Jakk G. III, "A Tattoo's Story." From *Soul Talk: Urban Youth Poetry*. Published by Syracuse University Press, 2008. Reprinted with the permission of New City Community Press, newcitypress.org.

Diana George, "The Word on the Street: Public Discourse in a Culture of Disconnect." From *Reflections*, Volume II, Number 2 (Spring 2002): 5–18. Reprinted with the permissions of Reflections: reflections.syr.edu.

Anne Ruggles Gere, "Kitchen Tables and Rented Rooms: The Extracurriculum of Composition." From *College Composition and Communication*, CCC/45.1 (Feb. 1994): 75–92. Copyright © 1994 by the National Council of Teachers of English. All rights reserved. Reprinted with permission.

Eli Goldblatt, "Alinsky's Reveille: A Community-Organizing Model for Neighborhood-Based Literacy Projects." From *College English* 67:3 (Jan. 2005): 274–95. Copyright © 2005 by the National Council of Teachers of English. All rights reserved. Reprinted with permission.

Brock Haussamen, "Service-Learning and First-Year Composition." From *Teaching English in the Two-Year College*, 24:3 (Oct. 1997) 192–98. Copyright © 1997 by the National Council of Teachers of English. All rights reserved. Reprinted with permission.

Bruce Herzberg, "Community Service and Critical Teaching." From *College Composition and Communication* CCC/45.3 (October 1994): 307–19. Copyright © 1994 by the National Council of Teachers of English. All rights reserved. Reprinted with permission.

Lorraine Higgins, Elenore Long, and Linda Flower, "A Rhetorical Model for Personal and Public Inquiry." From *Community Literacy Journal* 1.1 (Fall 2006): 9–43. Reprinted with permission.

Kim Hricko, "O Tenacious Weed; Writing Inside." From *The Collected Works of the Writing Workshop at the Maryland Correctional Institution for Women* in Jessup, Maryland.

Mark Howard, "Maybe the Reason Why." Excerpts from *Street Life* (Fall 1993).

Glynda A. Hull and Michael Angelo James, "Geographies of Hope: A Study of Urban Landscapes, Digital Media, and Children's Representations of Place." From *Blurring Boundaries: Developing Writers, Researchers, and Teachers: A Tribute to William L. Smith*, edited by Peggy O'Neill. Reprinted with permission of Hampton Press, Inc.

Tobi Jacobi, "Slipping Pages through Razor Wire: Literacy Action Projects in Jail." From *Community Literacy Journal* 2.2 (Spring 2008): 67–86. Reprinted with permission.

Michelle Hall Kells, "Writing Across Communities: Diversity, Deliberation, and the Discursive Possibilities of WAC." From *Reflections* 11.1 (Spring 2007): 87–108. Reprinted with permission of Reflections: reflections.syr.edu.

Jesús Villicana Lopez, "My Decision." From *Espejos y Ventanas/Mirrors and Windows*. Reprinted with the permission of New Community Press, newcitypress.org.

Paula Mathieu, "Students in the Streets." From *Tactics of Hope: The Public Turn in English Composition* by Paula Mathieu. Published by Boynton/Cook, Portsmouth, NH. All rights reserved. Reprinted with permission.

Keith Morton, "The Irony of Service: Charity, Project, and Social Change in Service-Learning." From *Michigan Journal of Community Service Learning* 2 (Fall 1995): 19–32. Reprinted with permission of the Center for Community Service and Learning, University of Michigan.

Steve Parks and Eli Goldblatt, "Writing beyond the Curriculum: Fostering New Collaborations in Literacy." From *College English* 62 (2000): 584–606. Copyright © 2000 by the National Council of Teachers of English. All rights reserved. Reprinted with permission.

Carol Pollard, "The Dinner Table III; The Dinner Table IV." From *The Collected Works of the Writing Workshop*, at the Maryland Correctional Institution for Women in Jessup, Maryland.

Lori Pompa, "Disturbing Where We Are Comfortable: Notes from Behind the Walls." From *Reflections* 4.1 (Winter 2004): 24–34. Reprinted by permission Reflections: reflections.syr.edu.

Ellis Roberts, "The Death Penalty: Deterrent or Legalized Murder?" Originally published in *Hospitality*, newspaper of the Open Door Community, 910 Ponce de Leon Ave, NE Atlanta, GA 30306-4212 www.opendoorcommunity.org. Reprinted with permission of The Open Door Community.

Tiffany Rousculp, "When the Community Writes: Re-Envisioning the SLCC DiverseCity Writing Series." From *Reflections* 5.1–2 (Spring 2006): 67–88. Reprinted with permission of Reflections: reflections.syr.edu.

Susan Wells, "Rogue Cops and Health Care: What Do We Want from Public Writing?" From *College Composition and Communication*, CCC/47.3 (Oct. 1996): 325–41. Copyright © 1996 by the National Council of Teachers of English. All rights reserved. Reprinted with permission.

Adrian Wurr, "Text-Based Measures of Service-Learning Writing Quality." From *Reflections* 2.2 (2003): 40–55. Reprinted with the permission of Reflections: reflections.syr.edu.

Table 30.4, "Rhetorical Appeals Scale." From "Cross-Cultural Variation in Persuasive Student Writing" by Ulla Connor and Janice Lauer, in *Writing Across Languages and Cultures*, edited by Alan C. Purves, Newbury Park, CA: Sage 1988, p. 138. Copyright © 1988 Sage Publications. Reproduced with permission of Sage in the format Textbook via Copyright Clearance Center.

Table 30.5, "Criteria for Judging the Quality of Claim, Data, and Warrant." From "Cross-Cultural Variation in Persuasive Student Writing" by Ulla Connor and Janice Lauer, in *Writing Across Languages and Cultures*, edited by Alan C. Purves, Newbury Park, CA: Sage, 1988, 138. Copyright © 1988 Sage Publications. Reproduced with permission of Sage in the format Textbook via Copyright Clearance Center.

Table 30.6, "Bamberg's Four Point Holistic Coherence Rubric." From "Understanding Persuasive Essay Writing: Linguistic/Rhetorical Approach," by Ulla Connor and Janice Lauer, in *Text* 5.4 (1985): 311. Copyright © Mouton Publishers. Reprinted with permission. Interdisciplinary Journal for the Study of Discourse. Band 5, Heft 4, Seiten 309–326, ISSN (Online) 1613-4117, ISSN (Print) 0165-4888, DOI: 10.1515/text.1.1985.5.4.309, //1985 De Gruyter, Berlin/New York.

INDEX